ShaderX³

Advanced Rendering with DirectX and OpenGL

ShaderX³

Advanced Rendering with DirectX and OpenGL

Edited by Wolfgang Engel

CHARLES RIVER MEDIA, INC.

Hingham, Massachusetts

Publisher: Jenifer Niles
Cover Design: The Printed Image
Cover Images: Far Cry © 2004 Crytek. All rights reserved.

CHARLES RIVER MEDIA, INC.
10 Downer Avenue
Hingham, Massachusetts 02043
781-740-0400
781-740-8816 (FAX)
info@charlesriver.com
www.charlesriver.com

This book is printed on acid-free paper.

Wolfgang Engel. *ShaderX³: Advanced Rendering with DirectX and OpenGL.*
ISBN: 1-58450-357-2

All brand names and product names mentioned in this book are trademarks or service marks of their respective companies. Any omission or misuse (of any kind) of service marks or trademarks should not be regarded as intent to infringe on the property of others. The publisher recognizes and respects all marks used by companies, manufacturers, and developers as a means to distinguish their products.

Library of Congress Cataloging-in-Publication Data
ShaderX³ : advanced rendering with DirectX and OpenGL / Wolfgang Engel, editor.-- 1st ed.
   p. cm.
 Includes bibliographical references.
 ISBN 1-58450-357-2 (hc with CD ROM : alk. paper)
 1. Computer games--Programming. 2. Three-dimensional display systems. 3. Computer graphics.
4. DirectX. 5. OpenGL. I. Engel, Wolfgang F.
 QA76.76.C672S49 2005
 794.8'1526--dc22
                                     2004023069

Printed in the United States of America
04 7 6 5 4 3 2 First Edition

Contents

About the Editors

Dean Calver

Dean started his professional game career on a war game, then did 3 years of racing games followed by an X-COM style game, then arcade classic updates, and is currently doing a 3D graphic adventure. He studies various subjects including optics, mathematics and other geeky things for fun. This preoccupation with learning means that he has been taking exams every year for over half of his life, and is well prepared to write the first game for a quantum computer.

Willem H. de Boer

Willem is a software engineer at Playlogic Game Factory, where he works on graphics technology. His current work centers around real-time simulation of subsurface scattering, and other aspects that have to do with the interaction of light and matter. He also enjoys dabbling in mathematics. He contributed to several books, including *Graphics Programming Methods*, and he also has a couple of journal articles pending, which he hopes will be published in the not too distant future. His homepage can be found at *http://www.whdeboer.com*.

Wolfgang Engel

Wolfgang is a Senior Special FX Engineer at Wings Simulations. He is the editor of the ShaderX book series and the author of *Programming Vertex and Pixel Shaders*. Wolfgang is a frequent speaker on conferences world-wide and publishes articles on several websites. As a contractor he also worked on the DirectX 8 shaders of *Medal of Honor: Pacific Assault*.

Tom Forsyth

Tom Forsyth has been obsessed by 3D graphics since seeing Elite on his ZX Spectrum. Tom has written triangle-drawing routines on the Spectrum, Sinclair QL, Atari ST, Sega 32X, Saturn, Dreamcast, PC, GamePark32 and XBox, and he's getting quite good at them now. Tom's coding past includes writing curved-surface stuff for Sega and graphics drivers for 3Dlabs. Currently he works in Guildford at Muckyfoot Productions, where past projects are *Urban Chaos, StarTopia,* and *Blade II.*

Eric Haines

Eric Haines, a graduate of the Cornell Program of Computer Graphics, is currently a lead software engineer at Autodesk, Inc. He coauthored the book *Real-Time Rendering,* now in its second edition. He is also a member of the editorial board for the *journal of graphics tools,* the archivist for the *Graphics Gems* repository, and the webmaster for *ACM Transactions on Graphics.* He is currently addicted to the game *Battlefield 1942* . His homepage is *http://www.erichaines.com.*

Dean Macri

Dean is a software engineer with Intel Corporation where he works with software developers in optimizing the processor-specific aspects of their titles. He wrote his first graphics application, a line and circle drawing program in TMS9900 assembly language, in 1984 on a Texas Instrument's 99/4A. Since then he's been hooked on graphics and programming, majoring in computer science as an undergraduate student and graduate student. Starting in 1992, he spent five years developing high-speed assembly routines for 2D graphics transition effects at a multimedia kiosk development company. Then in 1998 he joined Intel where he continues to evangelize the benefits of new processors and technologies to software developers and provide their feedback to the processor architects.

Jason L. Mitchell

Jason is the team leader of the 3D Application Research Group at ATI Research, makers of the RADEON family of graphics processors. Working on the Microsoft campus in Redmond, Jason has worked with Microsoft for several years to define key new Direct3D features. Prior to working at ATI, Jason did work in human eye tracking for human interface applications at the University of Cincinnati, where he received his Master's degree in Electrical Engineering in 1996. He received a B.S. in Computer Engineering from Case Western Reserve University in 1994. In addition to this book's chapters on HLSL Programming, Advanced Image Processing, and Procedural Shading, Jason has written for the *Game Programming Gems* books, *Game Developer Magazine,* Gamasutra.com and academic publications on graphics and image processing. He regularly presents at graphics and game development conferences around the world. His homepage can be found at *http://www.pixelmaven.com/jason/.*

Nicolas Thibieroz

Like many kids of the same generation, Nicolas Thibieroz discovered video games on the Atari VCS 2600. He quickly became fascinated by the mechanics behind those games, and started programming on C64 and Amstrad CPC before moving on to the PC world. Nicolas realised the potential of real-time 3D graphics while playing *Ultima Underworld*. This game inspired him in such a way that both his school placement and final year project were based on 3D computer graphics. After obtaining a BEng of Electronic Engineering in 1996 he joined PowerVR Technologies where he is now responsible for Developer Relations. His duties include supporting game developers, the writing of test programs or demos, and generally keeping up to date with the latest 3D technology.

About the Contributors

Brief biographies are included here for those contributors who submitted them.

Homam Bahnassi

hbahnassi@inframez.com

Homam holds a bachelor's degree in engineering management. During his study, he focused on 3D graphics creation with 3D games being a special case. He has been in the graphics industry for over four years, working on 3D modeling and animation applications. During the time, he worked as a director for several 3D real-time projects at different companies. Now he works as a 3D supervisor at In|Framez, researching the art pipeline for DirectSkeleton, the company's flagship 3D engine. He enjoys developing both real-time and MentalRay shaders.

Wessam Bahnassi

wbahnassi@inframez.com

Games are one thing in life that interest Wessam the most. Actually, he is interested in everything, ranging from electronics to music to architecture (his current study) to novelty, and ultimately to programming and shaders. Being an experienced C++ programmer for over six years, Wessam has done many real-time 3D projects based on Direct3D, and was rewarded as a Most Valuable Professional (MVP) in DirectX by Microsoft. Currently, he is a lead programmer at In|Framez, where he is employing his experience in designing and programming the DirectSkeleton 3D engine.

Ron Barbosa

Since the days of the Atari 2600 Ron Barbosa has been an avid fan of gaming and game technology. Since 1993 he has worked as a professional network/software engineer for many companies producing Internet technologies including the former Compaq Computer Corporation and Lucent Technologies, Inc. Throughout his adult years and his professional career, his passion has always been for gaming, and therefore he co-founded Exibeo Corporation (*http://www.exibeo.net/*), a young startup company focused on the development of gaming technologies. He is presently studying graphics and game development at GameInstitute.com where he serves as a Teaching Assistant for their Game Mathematics and Graphics Programming with DirectX 9 courses.

Florian Born

After his studies of mathematics and physics, Florian worked as a teacher before he started at Vulpine in 2000. In 2003 he and some colleagues from Vulpine founded Trinigy, a German middleware provider for the Vision game engine. Like many others, Florian started his career in computer programming 20 years ago on a C64. Later, on a PC, he was especially fascinated by 3D graphics and the technology behind it.

Clint S. Brewer

Clint currently works with NVIDIA's Technical Developer Relations group helping game developers make their engines run smoothly on current hardware, writing demos, tools, and speaking at GDC. Before that he spent five years working at Haptek creating interactive character software used by NASA, Sony, and Stan Lee Media. Clint has a BS in Computer Science from the University of California, Santa Cruz and still loves coding and gaming in his spare time. His main game programming interests are in rendering large-scale natural environments, World Building, and Artificial Intelligence.

Ronny Burkersroda

Ronny wrote his first computer game at the age of ten in a computer club. His first commercial game, for which he did everything but music and sound, was published in 2000. After that he wrote the 3D engine for "BomberFUN" (*www.bomberfun. com*) and is currently developing games and the "TigerHeart" engine, which used by LightBrain (*www.lightbrain.de*) and Media Seasons (*www.mediaseasons.com*), where Ronny is the Development Director of a small team.

Nicolas Capens

Nicolas is a masters student in Civil Engineering in Computer Science at Ghent University, Belgium. For the last four years he has focussed on software optimization related to 3D graphics rendering. With the use of dynamic code generation and shader technology he is reaching unlimited possibilities. His current goal is to provide a DirectX compatible software rendering standard that runs on every system at performance far beyond that of the reference rasterizer.

Kwok-Hung Choy

Kwok-Hung Choy received his BEng degree in Electronic Engineering from City University of Hong Kong in 2002. He is currently working toward the Master of Philosophy degree at the same university. His research interest is image compression.

Joachim Diepstraten

diepstraten@vis.uni-stuttgart.de

Joachim is a Ph.D. Student at the Visualization and Interactive Systems Group in Computer Science at the German University, Stuttgart. He became interested in real-time Computer Graphics at the age of 15 by starting to write his own EGA and VGA graphics and rasterization routines, first in PASCAL and later with C/ASM under the DOS operating system. He moved on to Sun's Java, to program a realtime software 3D engine and a simple realtime raytracer, but soon realized that hardware graphics accelerators are the key to maximum interactive performance. Joachim is currently doing research on finding solutions for interactive mobile graphics, squeezing the latest out of the programmable features of graphics hardware, non-photorealstic-rendering, and rendering everyday, natural objects using graphics hardware for achieving real-time performance. His personal slogan is: If it can not be done in real-time, it is impractical!

Mike Eißele

mike@eissele.net

After graduating in computer science, Mike joined the Visualization and Interactive Systems Group as a Ph.D. student at the University of Stuttgart. He started programming on the C64 where he coded real-time graphic demos. For hardware accelerated graphics programming, he started with OpenGL but switched to DirectX since the introduction of the Vertex- and PixelShader paradigms.

Dag Frommhold

Dag started programming in the mid-to-late eighties on the ZX81 and the MSX. From the beginning, he has always had a weakness for computer games and the technologies driving them. After working in the games industry as a freelancer for several years (while getting a university diploma in psychology), Dag founded the German middleware developers Vulpine and, later on, Trinigy, whose Vision game engine forms the basis for a number of commercial game titles on PC and Xbox.

David R. Gosselin

Dave is currently the lead for the demo team in the 3D Application Research Group at ATI Research, where he has been working on the launch demos for the past couple generations of ATI cards. In addition to the demos, he also wrote the NormalMapper tool for generating bump/normal maps from high resolution models. He has published articles in *ShaderX* and *Game Programming Gems 3* and spoken at Meltdown 2003 and

GDCE 2003. Previously he worked at several companies, including Oracle, Spacetec IMC, Xyplex, and MIT Lincoln Laboratory, on varied projects from low level networking and web technologies to image processing and 3D input devices. Dave graduated with an MS in Computer Science from Worcester Polytechnic Institute.

Shawn Hargreaves

Shawn is mostly a graphics programmer, despite the occasional diversion, such as taking a degree in music, or writing the network code for Climax's *MotoGP* bike racing game. He started out coding 2D graphics in DOS, where he created the popular Allegro library (*www.talula.demon.co.uk/allegro*), and has since written rendering engines for N64, PS2, Xbox, and DX9 class hardware. He thinks HLSL is one of the coolest things ever, but wishes it had a more easily pronounceable name!

O'dell Hicks

O'dell has been a professional game programmer since 1998, working on a number of projects on the PC and Xbox. Recently, he has returned to school fulltime, while running a small software company on the side. His website can be found at: *http://tephragames.com/*

Kent F. Knox

Kent graduated from the University of Texas at Austin in 1999 with a BS degree in Computer Science. After graduation he accepted a job at Advanced Micro Devices with their DirectX team, which is responsible for optimizing the vertex processing pipeline for AMD processors. He began his work with the fixed function pipeline in DirectX 7, and then transitioned to the Just-In-Time compiling virtual machine for vertex shaders introduced in DirectX 8. This work continues on through DirectX 9. Kent is concurrently working and attending the Software Engineering Master's program at UT Austin.

Jesse Laeuchli

Jesse is a self-taught programmer who is currently pursuing a degree at the University of Notre Dame. As a child of a Foreign Service officer, he has lived in foreign countries such as China, Taiwan, Africa, Saudi Arabia, and Hungary. He has written articles on graphics programming for several computer books and Web sites, including *Game Programming Gems 2, Graphics Programming Methods,* and *ShaderX².* He is also an avid epée fencer.

Stefano Lanza

Stefano Lanza is a student in Telecommunications Engineering at Politecnico in Milan, currently working on his master thesis. His main interest has always been computer graphics. His first 3D engine was a software *Quake* viewer for DOS (*www. gameprog.it/twister*). In the last years his interest focused on the simulation and rendering of natural scenes and gave life to the Typhoon engine (*www.gameprog.it/typhoon*). The engine is also the framework on which Stefano researches and tests new rendering techniques. Once he receives his degree, he intends to work as a professional graphic coder for videogames.

Lutz Latta

Lutz Latta has worked as a software developer in the games industry since 2002. He was lead programmer for the DirectX 9 benchmark AquaMark3 at Massive Development in Mannheim, Germany. Previously he worked there on the action game *Aquanox2: Revelation,* both on the PC and video game consoles. In 2001 he finished his studies at the University of Applied Sciences Wedel, Germany and at the University of the West of England, Bristol. His dissertation on realistic real-time rendering was published in the papers program at Siggraph 2002. He also spoke at the Game Developers Conference 2004 about hardware-accelerated particle simulation.

Chi-Sing Leung

Chi-Sing Leung received a Ph.D. degree in computer science from the Chinese University of Hong Kong. He is currently an Associate Professor in the Department of Electronic Engineering, City University of Hong Kong. His research interests include neural computing, communications, and computer graphics. He has published over 40 journal papers, and from 1995 to 1997, he worked on the bidirectional associative memory model. He proved that the recalling processing of higher order BAM is unstable and proposed a statistical method to analyze the behavior of higher order BAM. In 1997, he proposed a neural-based data protection method for vector quantization data over noisy channels. From 1998 to 2002, he worked on the property of extended Kalman filtering learning in neural networks. From 2001, he has been working on several projects related to compressing image-based rendering data. He proposed a two-level compression method for handling image-based rendering data. In 2001 and 2004, he provided consultancy service for DBS bank (Hong Kong) Limited.

Jörn Loviscach

Jörn Loviscach published many articles in popular computing magazines about programming and electronic music, before receiving his doctorate degree in mathematical physics in 1993. He later worked at sever computer magazines, becoming deputy editor-in-chief of the German computer magazine *c't*. He remained in this position for three years before accepting a professorship at Hochschule Bremen (University of Applied Sciences) in 2000, where he now teaches and researches in the field of computer graphics.

Khanh Phong Ly

Khanh published his first game on the Atari ST and graduated from Cambridge University with a bachelors degree in physics in 1995. He then did a masters in computer science at Manchester University. He worked in the games industry for 6+ years, including at SCEE (Sony) and has several released titles to his credit.

Jason L. Mitchell

Jason is the team leader of the 3D Application Research Group at ATI Research, makers of the RADEON family of graphics processors. Working on the Microsoft campus in Redmond, Jason has worked with Microsoft for several years to define key new Direct3D features. Prior to working at ATI, Jason did work in human eye tracking for human interface applications at the University of Cincinnati, where he received his Master's degree in Electrical Engineering in 1996. He received a B.S. in Computer Engineering from Case Western Reserve University in 1994. In addition to this book's chapters on HLSL Programming, Advanced Image Processing, and Procedural Shading, Jason has written for the *Game Programming Gems* books, *Game Developer Magazine,* Gamasutra.com and academic publications on graphics and image processing. He regularly presents at graphics and game development conferences around the world. His homepage can be found at *http://www.pixelmaven.com/jason/*.

Henning Mortveit

Henning Mortveit has an extensive background in mathematics, physics, and programming. His current work in graphics and visualization includes incorporation of natural phenomena and global illumination in real-time/interactive applications.

Markus Nuebel

Markus holds a Master of Computer Science and has been programming professionally for over 8 years. Some years ago, he discovered his passion for graphics and game programming. He has been interested in shader programming since NVIDIA launched CG, and is spending every free minute to enlarge his knowledge of interesting graphic programming algorithms.

Chris Oat

Chris Oat is a software engineer in the 3D Application Research Group at ATI where he explores novel rendering techniques for real-time 3D graphics applications. As a member of ATI's Demo Team, his focus is on shader development for current and future graphics platforms. He has published several articles in the *ShaderX* and *Game Programming Gems* series and has presented his research at GDC and GDC Europe.

Magnus Österlind

Magnus works as lead Xbox programmer at Warthog Sweden, where he is busy finishing off *Richard Burns Rally*. In-between hands of poker, and watching pay-per-view wrestling, he is also trying to complete his Master's Thesis in Computer Science.

Aras Pranckevičius

The same day he got his first ZX Spectrum, Aras wrote some mosaic-drawing programs. Apparently, that left him impressed and since then he's been doing graphics demos, small games and similar stuff for ZX, Atari, and PC. After school he went to university, has worked in a "real" software development company, and is now developing real-time motion recognition technology and in-house graphics/game engine for Interamotion LLC. In his spare time he's contributing to the Lithuanian demo- and game-scene, and playing classical guitar.

Thorsten Scheuermann

Thorsten is a software engineer in ATI's 3D Application Research Group where he works on graphics demos and novel rendering techniques as part of ATI's Demo Team. Prior to working at ATI, he was a member of the Effective Virtual Environments research group at the University of North Carolina at Chapel Hill, which gave him the opportunity to play with all sorts of expensive VR toys and to create sickness-inducing immersive games. Thorsten received a Master's degree in Computer Science from UNC and previously studied at the University of Karlsruhe in Germany.

Tiago Sousa

Tiago Sousa is a self-taught game and graphics programmer, who has worked as a programmer at Crytek for two years. Before joining Crytek, he co-founded a pioneer game development team in Portugal and studied Computer Science at a local University. Tiago is addicted to shader programming, does research on real-time and non-real-time graphics, jogs and works out at the gym.

Marco Spörl

As with many others, Marco started programming way back on a C64. After buying a PC (actually just because of his affection for chainsaw-wielding space marines) he became interested in and learned computer graphics. After receiving his diploma in computer science, he worked at Codecult Software, contributing to the Codecreatues Engine and the Codecreatures-Benchmark-Pro. After a short walk on the wild side as a freelance software developer, he currently earns his keep working on driving simulators for training on trains, trucks, cars, and tanks, and is seriously thinking about opening his own game studio.

Vlad Stamate

Vlad became passionate about computer games when he discovered them on a Spectrum Sinclair 128+. These games were his road to learning computer programming. After studying in a Computer Science High School, he graduated with a BS degree in Graphic Design from Richmond College. After graduation he started working in the R&D department of PowerVR technologies as a Design Engineer. Currently Vlad works for Sony Computer Entertainment Europe as part of their Technology Group, and is involved in software development for Sony game related products.

Natalya Tatarchuk

Natasha Tatarchuk is a software engineer working in the 3D Application Research Group at ATI Research, Inc., where she is the programming lead for the RenderMonkey™ IDE project. She has been in the graphics industry for over 6 years, working on 3D modeling applications and scientific visualization, prior to her employment at ATI. Natasha graduated from Boston University with a BS in Computer Science, a BS in Mathematics, and a minor in Visual Arts.

Michal Valient

Michal is a Ph.D. student at the Faculty of Mathematics, Physics and Informatics, Comenius University, Slovakia and works for Caligari corporation as project leader and Direct3D programmer. He is interested in shadow algorithms and various light transfer techniques and implementations on current and future graphics hardware. His home page can be found at *http://www.dimension3.sk*.

Terry Welsh

With bachelor's degrees in Physics and Art, and a master's degree in Computer Engineering, Terry brings a unique combination of practical engineering and creativity to the field of computer graphics. His work and interests include programming for complex synthetic environments, real-time rendering techniques, physical simulations such as flight dynamics models, and creating stunning visual effects. Terry has worked as an Applied Engineer at Silicon Graphics and as a flight simulation programmer at NASA Ames Research Center. He is currently VP of Technology at Infiscape, a company which he co-founded. For fun, he enjoys making real-time artwork, such as screen savers, and experimenting with various rendering techniques.

Matthias Wloka

Matthias Wloka works in the technical developer relations group at NVIDIA, where he gets to collaborate with game-developers on performance-optimizing their game, among other things. He is always tinkering with the latest graphics hardware to explore the limits of interactive real-time rendering. Before joining NVIDIA, Matthias was a game developer himself, working for GameFX/THQ Inc. He received his MS in Computer Science from Brown University in 1990, and his BS from Christian Albrechts University in Kiel, Germany in 1987.

Tien-Tsin Wong

Tien-Tsin Wong is an associate professor in the Department of Computer Science & Engineering in the Chinese University of Hong Kong (CUHK). He is head of the committee advisory board of the Computer Game Technology Centre in the department. He has been programming for the last 16 years, including writing publicly available codes/libraries/demos/toolkit (check his homepage) and codes for all his graphics research. His research interest includes GPU techniques, rendering, image-based relighting, natural phenomenon modeling, and multimedia data compression. He proposed a method to simulate dust accumulation and other surface imperfections in 1995 (IEEE CGA). He also proposed, the apparent BRDF of pixel, one of the earliest techniques for relighting in 1997. Besides academic papers, he has written game development related articles in *Graphics Gems V, Graphics Programming Methods,* and *ShaderX³*. Recently, he has been working on projects for general purpose usage of GPU, such as discrete wavelet transform on GPU. *http://www.cse.cuhk. edu.hk/~ttwong*

INTRODUCTION AND GEOMETRY MANIPULATION TRICKS

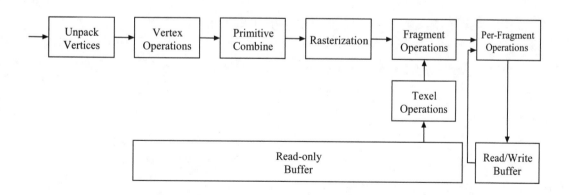

Introduction

Dean Calver

Most of this book is concerned with the far end of the rendering pipeline—the pixel shaders. This section is devoted to earlier parts of the pipeline: from an introduction and the latest shader language, to redefining the geometry representation of a model itself. An often forgotten part of rendering, geometry manipulation is fundamental. The ability to morph between two meshes, remove polygons from an area of a mesh, or even bend and deform a mesh, are tricks the movie world has long since integrated into its work flow. Now it's the real-time world's turn.

"Accessing and Modifying Topology on the GPU," by Calver demonstrates how vertex shader 3.0 texturing can allow shaders to modify the topology of a mesh. By using the concepts of vertex maps and topology maps, it shows face and vertex normal generation on the GPU, removing polygons from a mesh, and a completely GPU rendered height field via "render-to-vertex" techniques.

"Rendering of Complex Formulas," by Kleinhuis, builds a GPU explorer of the complex number plane (fractals). Demonstrating how to beat pixel shader length limitations of unextended pixel shader 2.0, it also shows how complex patterns can be produced from repeating relatively simple bits of code.

In another article, "Deforming of Mesh Objects Using HLSL," Kleinhuis applies procedural mesh modifiers to objects. Tapering along an axis, twisting, and spherication of meshes are presented in a position and normal interpolation framework.

"Morphing between Two Different Objects," by Burkersroda implements a geometrical morphing system. Similar to effects used in many movies, this technique allows you to blend one object into another easily over time.

"Silhouette Geometry Shaders," by Loviscach, calculates silhouettes in a vertex shader in a manner useful for both NPR and shadow techniques. Loviscach demonstrates a geometry-based haloing technique with curved nonpolygonal edges.

"GLSL Real-Time Shader Development," by Tatarchuk and Licea-Kane introduces OpenGL high-level shader language GLSL, recently ratified into the core with OpenGL 2.0. This article covers all the information you need to write shaders that for the first time, are open, cross-platform, and vendor natural, in order to push current and future graphics development forward.

1.1

Accessing and Modifying Topology on the GPU

Dean Calver

A vertex shader can only access a single vertex at a time; the hardware has a fixed function indexed triangle model that doesn't allow a vertex shader to manually do a vertex indirection. This seems to limit the extent that topology can be accessed and modified on the GPU. This article introduces several techniques that essentially bypass this limitation, allowing complex operations that involve accessing, and in some cases modifying, topology on the GPU.

The two major techniques are the related ideas of topology and vertex maps: texture maps that hold the mesh itself. The ability of vertex shaders to access video memory surfaces (textures) is the heart of the system and limits this technique to vertex shader 3.0 or higher. The article also discusses using the render to vertex map approaches to optimize many operations by caching data across shader executions. In some cases the vertex maps themselves are created on the GPU just prior to being used to generate the visuals.

Overview

Vertex shader 3.0 introduced vertex texturing—the ability of a vertex shader to access a texture for data. The canonical use is for displacement mapping, but the ability to use a texture as a 2D array allows for more exotic uses. Using this capability we can treat textures as a large, but slow memory pool, giving us the possibility of topology and vertex maps—texture maps that encode the actual physical mesh.

This article will discuss using this to construct shader programs to look at and modify the mesh topology at each vertex. Topology access requires the mesh structure to be uploaded into memory accessible at each vertex or pixel. This is either constant RAM or texture RAM. Constant RAM is fast but extremely limited in size. Texture RAM can be much larger, but has high latency in a vertex shader. However it's much cheaper in a pixel shader.

One of the more confusing aspects is that many of the standard names that D3D/OpenGL use for various parts of the pipeline are re-used for different usage's, i.e., vertex streams might hold indices and textures holding vertex data. To ease this it's sometimes helpful to drop the traditional view of the graphics pipeline and see it as a stream processor with different types of memory. Doing this and setting some standard sizes we can expect for vertex shader 3.0 hardware, we can see the real power of modern GPUs more clearly (see Figure 1.1.1).

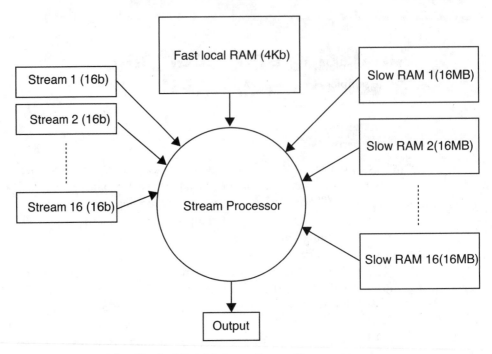

FIGURE 1.1.1   *Vertex Shader Model 3.0 as a Stream Processor.*

 The estimated RAM sizes in Figure 1.1.1 are common memory configurations based on 256 vertex constants, 1024×1024 4-tuple float textures and 4-tuple float vertex streams.

The streams undergo a massive redeployment of function. They become your counters, primitives, or index data—in fact they become just about anything that can vary across the mesh. The RAM pools usually hold all of your vertex data and topology maps. This allows them to be read by both vertex and pixel shaders, and to be written to, by the rasteriser.

Implementation

Recreating What We Already Have

Before we can start doing complex operations we have to be able to handle the simple topology that standard meshes are made of.

An Indexed Triangle Mesh

First we need to encode the vertex data itself as vertex maps. Each texture can only hold a 4-tuple of data, and with current vertex shader 3.0, we only have 4 vertex texture samplers. But by treating textures as linear arrays we can encode more data at the expense of more texture look-ups and a complicated topology map.

Vertex Data As Vertex Maps

A simple vertex format might be position, normal and uv, represented as:

```
struct Vertex
{
        Vector3 position;
        Vector3 normal;
    Vector2 uv;
};
```

Without packing, this can be represented as three vertex maps each having a 4-tuples element. For high precision, the vertex map format is D3DFMT_A32R32G32B32F. The vertex maps are texture maps that hold the data accessed via vertex streams, but as textures they can be rendered to and even accessed in a pixel shader.

Vertex streams are 1D while textures are 2D or 3D. This requires us to rearrange our data. By using D3DTADDRESS_WRAP in the U dimension on the texture (which will effectively perform the modulus operation for free) we can do this function on the GPU as:

```
float2 GPUConvert1DAddressTo2D( float OneD )
{
    oneD = oneD * (1.f / TextureWidth);
    return( float2(OneD, OneD  * (1.f / TextureHeight) ) );
}
```

The texture width and height may be different for each vertex or topology map, so the actual function will probably take a float2 constant per texture. It can also be optimized into a single multiple, so it's very cheap in practice.

Generally you want to use point sampling, so you get the exact vertex you're indexing, but you may be able to do some limited vertex tweening by using linear filtering.

Index Data As Vertex Streams

For an indexed triangle mesh, we have three indirections that point to the vertices this triangle is made of. Here we store this index data in a stream, but we could equally have placed it in a texture itself. We will discuss this use later when we encounter topology maps.

Depending on the number of vertices we need to index we can pick a variety of stream formats. But to replace the standard 16-bit index we can use D3DDECLTYPE_SHORT4.

Along with the per-primitive data, we need an indicator for the vertex we are currently working on. In this case this is a simple repeating 0, 1, 2 per triangle. As this data is repeating we can use the new vertex frequency functionality of vertex shader version 3.0 in order not to have a physical copy of this data for every primitive[1].

If the topology is continuous then vertices can be shared; however, if the topology (or the modifications) involves a discontinuous change then vertices will have to be duplicated. In other words, if the values calculated are the same for each vertex sharing a primitive regardless of the primitive it was calculated on, then you can share data. Otherwise you will need to have a unique vertex for each primitive.

For the simple case of replicating a standard indexed triangle mesh, the rules are exactly the same. Wherever the model is continuous in nD space (8D for the standard x, y, z, nx, ny, nz, u, v case) you can share data. It is worth noting that when we start modifying topology, sharing has to be considered post-modification. So for example, if you want to arbitrarily remove triangles you won't be able to share any vertex data.

One important thing to note is that in many cases you are dealing with floats pretending to be integers. In most cases this doesn't make much difference, but you have to alter all comparisons to accommodate. In the HLSL below we never use an equality ($==$) operator; instead we use $<$ to achieve the same results.

Vertex Shader Primitive Assembly

The vertex shader retrieves the primitive data and vertex index from the stream. This is used to select the vertex data from the vertex maps, which is then processed as normal.

```
struct Vertex{
float3 position;
float3 normal;
float2 uv;
};

Vertex GetVertex( float3 primitiveData, float vertexIndicator )
{
   Vertex Data;

   float address1D = 0;
   // pick which of the 3 vertices of this triangle we are currently
processing
   if( vertexIndicator < 0.5 ) // vertexIndicator == 0
```

---

[1]At this writing the vertex frequency API is new and has a few "gotchas." Depending on what you want to do, you may have to expand the data fully, repeating the same data over and over, as there are some fairly simple things the current API doesn't allow.

```
    {
            address1D  = primitiveData.x;
    } else if( vertexIndicator < 1.5 )   // vertexIndicator == 1
    {
            address1D = primitiveData.y;
    } else if( vertexIndicator  < 2.5 )   // vertexIndicator == 2
    {
            address1D = primitiveData.z;
    }

    // convert vertex indice to texture UV
    // tex2Dlod takes a float4 with the w being the mip map, which is
always 0 for this article
    float4 texAddr = float4( GPUConvert1DAddressTo2D ( address1D ),
0, 0 );

    // grab the data from the vertex maps
    Data.position = tex2Dlod( posSampler,  texAddr ).xyz;
    Data.normal = tex2Dlod( normSampler,  texAddr ).xyz;
    Data.uv = tex2Dlod( uvSampler, texAddr ).xy;

    return Data;
}
```

Extending Things

By implementing indexed triangle mesh via this method, all we managed to do is to slow our rendering down. But now with this basic framework we can start accessing topology.

Topology Maps

We are used to thinking about texture maps holding color values, but as graphics hardware has advanced they are being used to hold arbitrary data. The leap to holding vertex data itself isn't that great, but the leap to storing the structure of the mesh itself requires closer scrutiny.

In a topology map, we use the texture to store indices and pointers to various parts of the mesh. A simple case is storing the standard triangle indices in a texture; a more complicated example is holding indices to the faces that surround each vertex.

By using textures to hold the mesh structure itself, we can perform operations on the GPU that usually would have to be done with a CPU. Any structure can be represented, but some (like linked lists) are very inefficient and should be avoided. Generally, we use arrays of indices. While this sometimes feels a bit alien to a generation brought up with C/C++ and its complex pointer types, this basic idea has been in use since the birth of high-level languages and it poses no real limitations. The only major problem is having to decide on a maximum array size for all data. If this poses a problem, an indexed-linked list can be constructed.

To demonstrate topology maps, we will calculate normals in the shader itself. Face normals are fairly trivial but smooth vertex normals are more complex as they require not only data on the vertex and face we are currently rendering but also on the surrounding ones.

Calculating Face Normals in a Vertex Shader

Calculating face normals requires access to the vertices of the polygon being rendered. A vertex map will hold the vertex positions and a topology map will hold the structure of the mesh itself (we only need a fairly simple mesh structure for this function).

A triangle structure that can be used for face normal generation is:

```
struct TriangleFace
{
    int vertexIndex[3];
};
```

We simply store the vertex indices for this triangle in a texture. Then in the stream we store the triangle index of the triangle and the vertex indicator.

```
struct StreamElement
{
    int triangleIndex;      // 1D address of triangle face
    int vertexIndicator;    // 0,1,2
};
```

The triangle face topology map is looked up per vertex and then the vertex map is referenced to calculate the plane equation. The position is calculated in the same manner as before, but uses the triangle face indirection to obtain the vertex index instead of looking it up in the stream.

```
float3 CalcFaceNormal( float triangleIndex )
{
    float2 triIndex2D = GPUConvert1DAddressTo2D ( triangleIndex );
    // get vertex indices that make up this triangle
    float3 vertexIndices = tex2Dlod( TriangleFaceSampler, triIndex2D,
0 ).xyz;
    // convert indices in UV form
    float2 i0 = GPUConvert1DAddressTo2D(vertexIndices.x);
    float2 i1 = GPUConvert1DAddressTo2D(vertexIndices.y);
    float2 i2 = GPUConvert1DAddressTo2D(vertexIndices.z);

    // get the vertex position of all 3 vertices
    float3 v0 = tex2Dlod( PositionSampler, float4(i0,0,0) ).xyz;
    float3 v1 = tex2Dlod( PositionSampler, float4(i1,0,0) ).xyz;
    float3 v2 = tex2Dlod( PositionSampler, float4(i2,0,0) ).xyz;

    // calculate plane equation to get normal from
    return CalcPlaneEquationOf( v0, v1, v2 );
}
```

In practice, the types we can use hardware vertex texturing with are extremely limited on some hardware and you may have to use D3DFMT_A32B32G32R32F for all your data. In the future, this hardware limitation is likely to become more relaxed, to the point that any texture you can use in the pixel shader can be used in the vertex shader.

Calculating Vertex Normals in a Vertex Shader

To generate smooth vertex normals we need the surrounding faces and vertices. In this case, accessing this data requires us to examine the vertex valency to see how much space we will need to allocate.

There is no actual limit to the vertex valency (each vertex can potentially have an unlimited number of faces attached), and while a linked list is possible in theory, a fixed-sized array is preferable. In practice, restricting the number of surrounding faces doesn't alter the visual result that much, as each face influences the normal, less than the greater, vertex valency. So, in this example, we limit the maximum vertex valency to 7, greatly simplifying the code.

The triangle face topology map is the same as for generating face normals, but now we add an extra topology map which has a list of the surrounding faces at each vertex in the model. There is a one-to-one mapping between the vertex map and vertex valency topology map, so we simply use the vertex indices to look up the vertex valency topology map.

```
#define MAX_VERTEX_VALANCY 7
struct vertexValency
{
    int valenceNum;
    int faceIndex[ MAX_VERTEX_VALANCY ];
};

#define SizeOfVertexValencyStructIn4Tuples 2

float3 CalcVertexNormal( float triangleIndex, float vertexIndicator )
{
    float2 triIndex2D = GPUConvert1DAddressTo2D ( triangleIndex );
    float3 vertexIndices = tex2Dlod( TriangleFaceSampler, triIndex2D,
0 ).xyz;

    float vertValencyAddr1D = 0;
    if( vertexIndicator < 0.5 )
    {
        vertValencyAddr1D  = vertexIndices.x;
    } else if( vertexIndicator < 1.5 )
    {
        vertValencyAddr1D  = vertexIndices.y;
    } else if( vertexIndicator  < 2.5 )
    {
        vertValencyAddr1D  = vertexIndices.z;
    }

    float2 index = GPUConvert1DAddressTo2D( vertValencyAddr1D );
    index = index *  SizeOfVertexValencyStructIn4Tuples;
```

```
        // get faces indices that surround this vertex
        vertexValency VVStruct;
        float4 tmp0 = tex2Dlod( VertexValencySampler, float4( index, 0,
0) ).xyzw;
        float4 tmp1 = tex2Dlod( VertexValencySampler, float4( index +
float2(1,0), 0, 0) ).xyzw;
        // copy indices into area accessable form
        VVStruct.valenceNum = tmp0.x;
        VVStruct.faceIndex[0] = tmp0.y;
        VVStruct.faceIndex[1] = tmp0.z;
        VVStruct.faceIndex[2] = tmp0.w;
        VVStruct.faceIndex[3] = tmp1.x;
        VVStruct.faceIndex[4] = tmp1.y;
        VVStruct.faceIndex[5] = tmp1.z;
        VVStruct.faceIndex[6] = tmp1.w;

        // accumulate face normals
        float3 vertexNorm(0,0,0);
        int curFaceIndex = 0;
        while( curFaceIndex < VVStruct.valenceNum )
        {
                vertexNorm += CalcFaceNormal( VVStruct.faceIndex[curFaceIn-
dex] );
                curFaceIndex++;
        };

        return Normalize( vertexNorm );
}
```

As you will notice, this is very expensive, but there are optimizations that can speed it up. The most important uses the fact that the vertex maps are just textures and can be generated on the fly by the GPU. But before we get to optimizations lets explore some other examples of uses for these techniques.

Removing Triangles

Removing a triangle using a topology map is trivial. The only caveat is that you can't share vertices between triangles, because to remove a triangle each of its vertices must be placed into a position the clipper will reject. This requires no sharing with a triangle that is visible. The `triangle kill` command just places a clip space vertex position that definitely will be clipped (for example, w = −1) for each vertex in the triangle and the triangle will be removed.

This can be used to easily remove groups of polygons (i.e., arms, heads, etc.). We give each primitive a group id, and then a constant list of whether or not each group is processed.

```
struct TriangleFace
```

```
{
    int vertexIndex[3];
    int groupID;
};
```

In the stream we store the triangle index of the triangle and the vertex indicator:

```
struct StreamElement
{
    int triangleIndex;      // 1D address of triangle face
    int vertexIndicator;    // 0,1,2
};
```

and then a quick check and dynamic branch will avoid processing too much code for removed triangles.

```
float TriangleGroups[ MAX_GROUPS ]; // bool as float
(false = 0.f, true = 1.f)

Output TriKiller( float vertexIndicator )
{
    float2 triIndex2D = GPUConvert1DAddressTo2D ( triangleIndex );
    float4 triangleFace = tex2Dlod( TriangleFaceSampler, float4( tri-
Index2D, 0 ,0) ).xyzw;
    if( TriangleGroups[ triangleFace.w ] > 0.5 ) // true
    {
        // process vertex as normal
    } else
    {
        // group is invisible kill the vertex
        // set the output to somewhere the clipper considers off
screen
        Output.position = float4(-1,-1,-1,-1);
    }
}
```

Sprite-Based Quads

You want to render a crazy particle system (or old school 2D shooter), that is limited by the speed you can get the data from CPU to GPU. Point sprites aren't good enough because the no-rotation limitation doesn't work in your situation. Is there a way to reduce bandwidth requirements to the GPU by using topology maps?

For this we use the stream input as a primitive stream not a vertex stream—the user supplies no data per vertex, just the sprite data itself. Also we use the fast local memory (constant) to reduce bandwidth into the vertex shader to an absolute minimum.

The only per-vertex information is the vertex indicator field (which, because we are using quads, now has values of 0, 1, 2, and 3). The vertex frequency API allows us to repeat this data for every primitive, reducing the actual external GPU bandwidth to zero per vertex (the stream is so small it will easily fit into pre-vertex shader cache on the GPU).

We set up a sprite structure (this is obviously application specific, the one described here is the one used in the sample code on the disk).

```
struct SpritePrim
{
    float16 Position[2];        // 16 bit float is enough range for
                                // this sprite system
    byte        SpriteNum;      // Index to look-up size and texture data
    byte        Rotation;       // byte encoded rotation parameter
    byte        ScaleHi;        // scale is encoded as 8.8 fixed point
                                // number integer byte
    byte        ScaleLo;        // fraction byte
};
```

This is placed in stream 0, and stream 1 simply consists of the numbers 0, 1, 2, and 3. The vertex frequency system is then programmed to stream 0 only every fourth vertex and stream 1 to update every vertex but repeat after every fourth. We do this by using each primitive as an instance. But instancing changes the way we count, so the number of sprites we want to render is passed to SetStreamSourceFreq for the instanced parameter.

For DirectX 9.0c this is enabled via:

```
D3DDevice->SetStreamSourceFreq( 0, numSprites | D3DSTREAMSOURCE_
INDEXEDDATA );
// update the data updated every vertex repeated numSprites times
D3DDevice->SetStreamSourceFreq(1, 1 | D3DSTREAMSOURCE_INSTANCEDATA );
// update stream 1 per instance (2 triangles in this case)
```

then we just call DrawPrimitive with the number of triangles of 2 (2 triangles per quad).

In the actual vertex shader, instead of placing the sprite size and texture data in a texture, we place it in constant memory. This saves us bandwidth because constant memory is much faster to access.

Render to Vertex Map

Having the mesh as a texture allows us to use "render-to-vertex" techniques. These techniques use the rasteriser itself to modify mesh data. This allows caching of complex operations across multiple invocation of the complex operations.

Speeding Up Vertex Normal Generation

Previously, when calculating the vertex normal we had to call GetFaceNormal() multiple times per vertex, recalculating the face normal for every surrounding face. Using render to vertex we can do a single pass over the faces calculating the face normals, which can then be quickly accessed per vertex.

We need an intermediate face normal surface that we will calculate when the face normal changes. As this is normal data we can probably use an 8-bit integer format. Of course, if the precision isn't enough for your application, you can use a higher precision format.

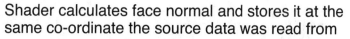

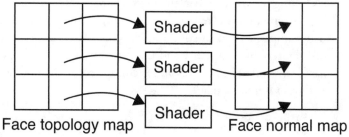

FIGURE 1.1.2   *Positioning in the face normal map.*

We render quads that cover each face in the triangle face topology map, rendering one-to-one with the face normal map. The shader accesses each face one by one, calculates the face normal, and then outputs it into the same position in the face normal map (see Figure 1.1.2).

But why stop at just the face normals? If the reason we are calculating vertex normals is something that can be cached, we can continue with this technique until the actual object renderer is fairly conventional (and fast). Just perform the complex topology operations when the cache becomes invalid. This approach is especially relevant where normals change infrequently. The actual cost is mainly contained in the update functions when the vertex used is low.

To do this we add another pass where every vertex is mapped one-to-one with a vertex normal texture. A quad is rendered that takes the vertex input, calculates the vertex normal, and outputs it into the vertex normal texture. Using the massively parallel pixel shader to process multiple vertex normals we can perform the job significantly faster than with most other approaches to the problem.

Putting It All Together for a Simple Terrain Renderer

To demonstrate the various techniques we use a completely GPU-modifiable terrain system, with datalike normals being calculated when the mesh changes. The terrain position itself is represented by a displacement map (note: the method of rendering displacement maps isn't discussed here; see [Calver02] and [Calver03] for details) but it can easily be a full 3D world position (it's a displacement map more for the terrain modification algorithm than anything). This doesn't take advantage of any inherent topology from the displacement map, but it is advisable in real code (in a real displacement map renderer you can calculate the face indices directly).

The rendering is split into two portions, one is called when the mesh topology changes (i.e., the terrain is damaged), the other is called to actually render the terrain itself. We set up the data so that the terrain render is fairly fast with the expensive work taking place only when the mesh changes.

The actual terrain render is fairly simple: the vertex data is split between static and dynamic. Static data comes in via a standard vertex stream; in the example this is just the terrain texture u,v and the vertex index. The dynamic data is the dynamic vertex maps stored in textures and is computed by the update code.

Terrain Render Code:

```
SetRenderTarget( BackBuffer );
SetTexture( 0, VertexPositionSurface );
SetTexture( 1, VertexNormalSurface );
SetPixelShader( TerrainRenderVS );
RenderMesh();

// HLSL Shader vs_3_0
Struct RenderVSInput
{
    float2    texUV : TEXCOORD0;
    float     vertexIndex : TEXCOORD1;
};
struct RenderVSOutput
{
    float4 HclipPos : POSITION;   // position for the rasterisor
    float2 texUV : TEXCOORD0;     // pass the old fashioned texture
                                  // coordinate
    float3 normal : TEXCOORD0;    // pass the world space normal
                                  // through to the pixel shader
};
sampler2D sampPositionVec;
sampler2D sampNormalVec;
void TerrainRenderVS( in RenderVSInput inp,
        out RenderVSOutput outp )
{
    float4 vertUV =  float4( GPUConvert1DAddressTo2D( inp.vertexIn-
dex), 0, 0 );
    float3 position = tex2Dlod( sampPositionVec,  vertUV ).xyz;
    float3 normal = tex2Dlod( sampNormalVec,  vertUV ).xyz;
    outp.HclipPos = mul( float4(position,1), transformMatrix );
    outp.normal = normal;
    outp.texUv = inp.texUV;
}
```

The real work occurs in the update pass where we create two render-targets textures for position and normal maps. We also need the displacement map (also a render-target so we can modify it via the GPU) and a couple of topology maps hooking everything together. We also need a temporary render-target to hold the face normals (this isn't currently used outside the update cycle but potentially it could be used to optimize terrain damage).

The topology maps are basically the same as we previously used, one face to vertex map and the other encoding surrounding faces per vertex. For the displacement map grid we use a fixed vertex valancy of 6, as in the majority of cases this will be true (only edges of the map have a vertex valency not equal to 6).

```
// face to vertex map
struct TriangleFace
{
    int vertexIndex[3];
};

// vertex to surrounding faces
struct vertexValancy
{
    int faceIndex[ 8 ];
};
```

When the displacement maps are altered we need to update the vertex maps for the renderer. This is done in three passes: the first calculates the vertex positions from the displacement map, the second calculates face normals, and the third finally calculates the vertex normals.

First Pass: Vertex Positions

This is an easy one: we simply read each displacement value and output the world space position.

```
SetRenderTarget( VertexPositionSurface );
SetTexture( 0, DisplacementMap );
SetPixelShader( VertexPositionGenerator );
RenderFullSurfaceQuad();

// HLSL Shader ps_3_0
sampler2D sampDisplacementMap;
float4 VertexPositionGenarator( in float2 uv ) : COLOR0
{
    float displacement = tex2D( sampDisplacementMap, uv ).xyz;
    return WorldPositionFromDisplacement( displacement );
}
```

Second Pass: Face Normals

The face normal generator takes each `TriangleFace` structure and outputs the face normal. The vertex stream contains a *u,v* coordinate matching the source and destination pixels.

```
SetRenderTarget( FaceNormalMap );
SetTexture( 0, TriangleFaceTopoMap );
SetTexture( 1, VertexPositionSurface );
SetPixelShader( FaceNormalGenerator );
RenderFullSurfaceQuad();

// HLSL Shader ps_3_0
sampler2D sampTriangleFace;
sampler2D sampVertexPosition;
float4 FaceNormalGenerator( in float2 uv ) : COLOR0
{
    float3 vertexIndices = tex2D( sampTriangleFace, uv ).xyz;
    float2 i0 = GPUConvert1DAddressTo2D(vertexIndices.x);
    float2 i1 = GPUConvert1DAddressTo2D(vertexIndices.y);
    float2 i2 = GPUConvert1DAddressTo2D(vertexIndices.z);

    float3 v0 = tex2D( sampVertexPosition, i0 ).xyz;
    float3 v1 = tex2D( sampVertexPosition, i1 ).xyz;
    float3 v2 = tex2D( sampVertexPosition, i2 ).xyz;

    return Normalise( CalcPlaneEquationOf( v0, v1, v2 ) );
}
```

Third Pass: Vertex Normals

The vertex normal generators take each vertex and sum the surrounding faces (the edge cases can be handled in various ways and will be ignored here for clarity) before normalizing the normal. The use of a fixed vertex valency with a pixel shader process greatly simplifies the code. One extra complication over the last few passes is that the vertex valency structure takes two texture look-ups, so the UVs have to be adjusted.

```
SetRenderTarget( VertexNormalSurface );
SetTexture( 0, VertexValencyTopoMap );
SetTexture( 1, FaceNormalMap );
SetPixelShader( VertexNormalGenerator );
RenderFullSurfaceQuad();

// HLSL Shader ps_3_0
sampler2D sampFaceNormal
sampler2D sampVertexValency;
float4 VertexNormalGenerator( in float2 uv ) : COLOR0
{
    float4 vv0 = tex2D( VertexValancySampler, expUV ).xyzw;
    float4 vv1 = tex2D( VertexValancySampler, expUV +
float2(OneTexel,0) ).xyzw;
    float3 vertexNorm;
```

```
        vertexNorm = tex2D( sampFaceNormal, GPUConvert1DAddressTo2D(
    vv0.x ) );
        vertexNorm += tex2D( sampFaceNormal, GPUConvert1DAddressTo2D(
    vv0.y ) );
        vertexNorm += tex2D( sampFaceNormal, GPUConvert1DAddressTo2D(
    vv0.z ) );
        vertexNorm += tex2D( sampFaceNormal, GPUConvert1DAddressTo2D(
    vv0.w ) );
        vertexNorm += tex2D( sampFaceNormal, GPUConvert1DAddressTo2D(
    vv1.x ) );
        vertexNorm += tex2D( sampFaceNormal, GPUConvert1DAddressTo2D(
    vv1.y ) );

        return normalise( vertexNorm );
    }
```

Conclusion

The technique shows that Pixel Shader 3.0 is almost a complete graphics pipeline capable of techniques well beyond the classic vertex- and pixel-level effects. By using Topology Maps and Vertex Maps, we have fundamentally changed the classic idea of how meshes are rendered and processed by GPUs. The use of the pixel shader hardware as a method for mesh manipulation is something that will be used a lot in the future as we move to treating the GPU as another general purpose processor.

The examples presented here are mainly illustrative, and in many cases (like the terrain renderer) they can be mixed with more conventional rendering techniques for faster throughput. In practice, losing the cost of vertex texture fetches isn't easy but real rendering generally has more optimization potential than the simple example code here. In the terrain example, the UV coordinates could have had a texture matrix applied while waiting for one of the fetches to finish.

The techniques demonstrated here are merely the tip of the iceberg. Some obvious future techniques that could benefit from these techniques are caching of skinning data, advanced animation techniques, and subdivision surfaces. There are probably many other systems, that with future development, will benefit from the unification of topology, vertex, and pixel data.

References

[Calver02] D. Calver, "Vertex Decompression Using Vertex Shaders" in *ShaderX*, Engel, Wolfgang, ed., Wordware, May 2002.
[Calver03] D. Calver, "Vertex Decompression Using Vertex Shaders Part 2" in *ShaderX²*, Engel, Wolfgang, ed., Wordware, August 2003.

Rendering of Complex Formulas

Christian Kleinhuis

This is an approach to render as many complex formulas as you want on a pixel shader, serving this time as a formula parser within MS HLSL shader language. As an example, we introduce the rendering of fractals with an arbitrary amount of iteration steps. One usage for rendering abstract images on a GFX card could be the fast rendering of tileable image sets. Another usage may be the visualization of a complex formula in a 2D matrix.

Prerequisites

What Is a Complex Number?

A complex number[1] is a two-component number denoted in the form:

$$x + yi \tag{1.2.1}$$

where x and y are real numbers, i is the imaginary number equal to the square root of -1, $\sqrt{1}$, which is some kind of virtual because this root is never used directly.

A single letter can be used as a variable to contain this two-component number.

$$z = x + yi \tag{1.2.2}$$

In HLSL we use `float2` data type to hold the real and imaginary parts of a complex number.

A set of functions is needed to work with this data type: addition and subtraction are the same as vector addition and subtraction, but multiplying and dividing need to be especially defined. Additionally, Complex Sine and Cosine will be defined to have a suitable amount of function ready for use.

Complex Multiplication

Complex multiplication in parametric form looks like:

```
Z=c*d ->
  real      = c.real * c.real - d.real*d.real
  imaginary = c.real * d.imaginary + c.imaginary*d.real
```

It can be seen that raising Z to a power of 2 simplifies to:

```
Z=c^2 ->
  real      = c.real * c.real - c.imaginary * c.imaginary
  imaginary =  2 * c.real * c.imaginary
```

For multiplying, the function in HLSL has to look:

```
inline complex m_c_mul(complex x,complex y)
{
    complex temp;
    complex t=x*y;
      temp.x=t.x-t.y;
      temp.y=x.x*y.y+x.y*y.x;
      return temp;
}
```

The other functions will just be described in parametric form; it should be easy to convert them to HLSL syntax.

Complex Absolute

Complex Absolute is the same as calculating the length of a 2D vector, thus returning a real number:

```
Abs(z) = sqrt(z.real*z.real+z.imaginary*z.imaginary)
```

Complex Modulus

Complex Modulus returns a real number also:

```
Modulus(z)=  (z.real*z.real+z.imaginary*z.imaginary)
```

Complex Division

Complex Division in parametric form is defined:

```
Z=c/d -> \
  real      = (c.real* d.real + c.imaginary * d.imaginary ) / modu-
lus(d)
  imaginary = (c.imaginary * d.real  - c.real * d.imaginary ) / modu-
lus(d)
```

Complex Sine

The sine function in complex space is defined:

```
Sin(z) -> real = sin(z.real) * cosh(z.imaginary)
      Imaginary = cos(z.real) * sinh(z.imaginary)
```

where cosh is the hyperbolic Sine/Cosine.

Complex Cosine

Complex Cosine in complex space is defined:

```
Cos(z) -> real      = sin(z.real)*cosh(z.imaginary)
          Imaginary = cos(z.real)*sinh(z.imaginary)
```

Conjugate

The conjugate is like negating a value; in complex number space negating the imaginary value:

```
Conjugate(z)-> z.real=z.real
               z.imaginary=-z.imaginary
```

completing the set of functions to be used with the HLSL Compiler.

A framework capable of interpreting various complex formulas is needed, which will then be included into the HLSL Pixel Shader Script, leaving all the work to be done to the HLSL Compiler. These complex formulas are defined like usual HLSL Functions; they all get an identifier in front of them, likely m_sin(float) instead of sin(float) and m_sin(complex), as an overloaded function in complex number space. Using this naming standard we can safely access built-in functions of HLSL.

```
m_c_mul -> complex multiplication
m_c_div -> complex division
m_c_add -> complex add, same like vector add
m_c_sub -> complex sub, same like vector sub
m_c_sin -> Complex Sine
m_c_cos -> Complex Cosine
m_c_conj-> Complex Conjugate ( Negate )
m_c_mod -> Complex Modulus
```

Texture Formats

A commonly used texture format is A8R8G8B8 using 8-bits for each color channel. Since DX9, numerous different formats have been introduced, the format used here is a signed floating point format. There are 16-bit floating point formats and 32-bit floating point formats. The 16-bit format is saved in the form s10e5 meaning:

```
Purpose S EEEEE FFFFFFFFFF
Bit  ID 0 1   5 6        15
```

using 1 bit as Sign bit S, 5 bits for the Exponent E, and 10 bits for the Fraction F.

The 32 bit is commonly known as Single Precision Floating Point Format s23e8:

```
Purpose S EEEEEEEE FFFFFFFFFFFFFFFFFFFFFFF
Bit    0 1      7 8                     31
```

Calculation precision differs much from card to card, some cards internally use only 24 precision bits internally even if a 32-bit format is chosen.

The Action

An HLSL Effect Technique with three passes will be defined with the following purpose for the different passes:

- 1st Pass Initialization
- 2nd Pass Iteration
- 3rd Pass Finalization

To achieve a high amount of iterations we need to use some kind of in-between memory, due to the fact that more complex formulas cannot be compiled under Pixel Shader 2.0 configuration. For this purpose we use two textures which serve as this memory: the D3DFORMAT D3DFMT_G16R16F or D3DFMT_G32R32F which are Signed Floating Point 16/32-Bit Texture formats. We are using a Pixel Shader Output structure to save these values, they don't have to be in the range of 0–1. because we are using a signed floating point format.

These two textures are swapped during the rendering process, although this is the bottleneck of the method, saving the whole in-between results in a raster as big as the current texture size. It allows us to either run many iterations on it, or divide a very long and complex formula into different parts fitting to the 64 PS Command limit. It is obvious how time expensive this method is, perhaps it could be used as some kind of memory-throughput benchmark. Some cards support many more than 64 commands as a limit, some even support real looping; in this case it is not necessary to use a second texture as in-between memory. Instead everything can be done within a single pass.

However, the three effect passes are now used as follows:

- 1st pass initialization is where we initialize a complex variable z with start value, and write it into the r and g output structure namely into the first texture memory.
- 2nd pass is then used in a loop (the number of iterations). Every iteration the render target and the source texture are swapped, so that it's always reading the last result of the iteration out of the texture.
- 3rd pass then reads the result of the last iteration step. Transforming the current result into a color can be done in many ways: one is to use the x/y values as r/g colors. Another way may be the use of these x/y values as a texture address to a gradient texture.

To ensure that every Texture Reads will obtain the same data we use untransformed Coordinates; no Vertex Shader is needed.

Hints and Improvements

Coloring can be improved when not using D3DFMT_G16R16F as in-between memory. D3DFMT_A16R16G16R16F may be chosen to save the iteration depth of each pixel; this iteration depth is then taken as another index to a gradient table. As stated before, on GFX cards with a higher instruction set all of the calculation can be done in a single step, resulting in an immense calculation speed bonus. As defined by [2] you can alternate the seed values *each* iteration step, resulting in an arbitrary fractal with many more parameters. Besides that, you can try to change even the fractal formula *each* iteration step, resulting in completely new fractal types.

Examples

See Figures 1.2.1 through 1.2.7 for pictures of these formulas. Examples are in HLSL format:

Mandelbrot^2

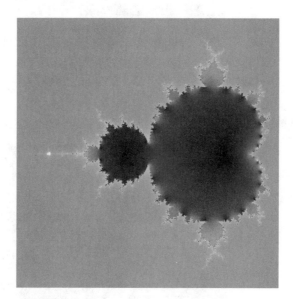

FIGURE 1.2.1   z= m_c_power2(z)+c

Mandelbrot^4

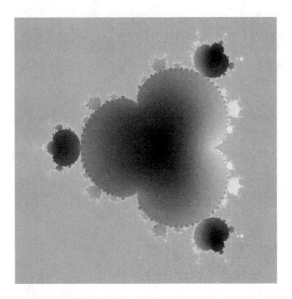

FIGURE 1.2.2   z= m_c_power2(m_c_power2(z))+z

Sine Mandelbrot

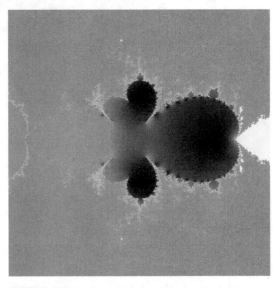

FIGURE 1.2.3   z=m_c_power2(m_c_sin(z))+z

Magnet 1

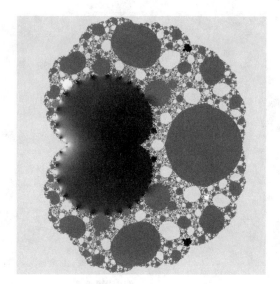

FIGURE 1.2.4   `z = m_c_power2(m_c_div(m_c_power2(z) +`
`Seed - float2(1,0) ,    2*z + Seed - float2(2,0)))`

Barnsley 1

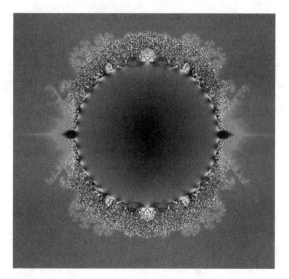

FIGURE 1.2.5   `If(z.x>=0){`
`        z = m_c_mul((z — float2(1,0)) , Seed)`
`}else{`
`        z = m_c_mul((z + float2(1,0)) , Seed)`
`}`

Barnsley 2

 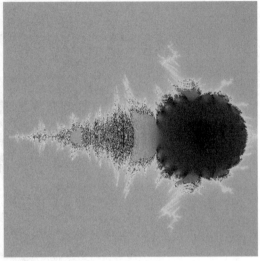

FIGURE 1.2.6

```
if(z.x*Seed.y+Seed.x*z.y>=0){
        z=m_c_mul(z-float2(1,0),Seed)
}else{
        z=m_c_mul(z+float2(1,0),Seed)
}
```

FIGURE 1.2.7

```
if(z.x > 0){
  z=m_c_power2(z)-float2(1,0)
}else{
  z=m_c_power2(z)-float2(1,0)+Seed*z.x
}
```

References

[1] *http://mathworld.wolfram.com/ComplexNumber.html*
[2] *http://fractalmovies.com/alternating_fractals/*

1.3

Deforming of Mesh Objects Using HLSL

Christian Kleinhuis

This article is about standard deformation of mesh objects using Vertex Shader. *Deforming* is applying a function to a vertex, transforming it to a new position (see Figures 1.3.1 through 1.3.8).

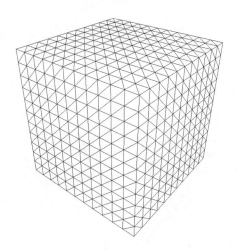

FIGURE 1.3.1 *Normal*

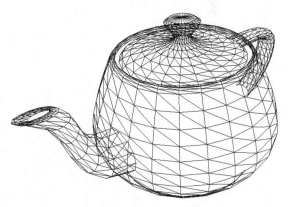

FIGURE 1.3.2 *Normal*

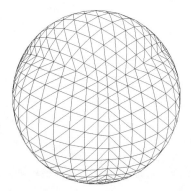

FIGURE 1.3.3 *Spherify*

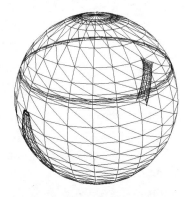

FIGURE 1.3.4 *Spherify*

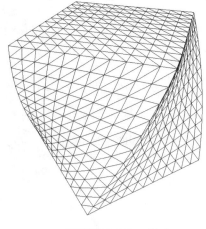

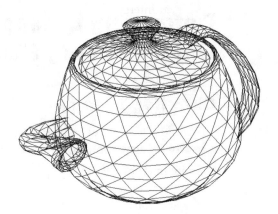

FIGURE 1.3.5   *Twist*

FIGURE 1.3.6   *Twist*

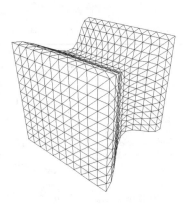

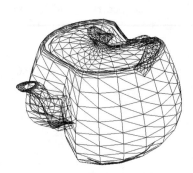

FIGURE 1.3.7   *Tape*

FIGURE 1.3.8   *Tape*

Prerequisites

Interpolation

Interpolation appears when two values are given (e.g., for animation) and a smooth transition between these values is needed. Interpolation is described here for one dimension only, extending it to more than one dimension is simple, because each axis needs to be interpolated the same way.

Linear Interpolation

Linear interpolation is the easiest interpolation:

$$Nx = x2^*t+x1^*(1-t)$$

(1.3.1)

where:
   x1 = Start value
   x2 = End value
   t = In-between value ranging from 0 to 1

Hermite Interpolation

Hermite interpolation allows us to add a tangent to each value, so that the interpolation appears to be smoother. A tangent value of 0 means that interpolation starts slowly and ends slowly. Linear interpolation is a sub-form of Hermite Interpolation with corresponding values. The math behind Hermite Interpolation is a polynomal of fourth degree:

$$F(x) = ax^4 + bx^3 + cx^2 + dx$$

(1.3.2)

The factors a, b, c, and d are calculated as follows:

$$a = 2 * y1 - 2 * y2 + k1 + k2$$
$$b = -3 * y1 + 3 * y2 - 2 * k1 - k2$$
$$c = k1$$
$$d = y1$$

(1.3.3)

where:

y1 and y2 are the values between where the interpolation appears.
K1 and k2 are the tangents at y1 and y2 respectively and a, b, c, and d are the factors.

The outcoming values are simply set into the above polynomal, where *x* ranges from 0 to 1. One of the most exciting features of hermite interpolation is when using more than two values that need to be interpolated. Each value is interpolated with its direct neighbor.

Taping

Taping is an easy deformation of a Mesh Object. Considered scaling, it is achieved through multiplying each axis with a constant factor:

$$v^*f = v(x^*f,y^*f,z^*f)$$

(1.3.4)

where f is the scaling factor, tapering is achieved when not transforming one certain axis:

Tapering along **Z** axis:

$$v*f = v(x*f, y*f, z)$$ (1.3.5)

Tapering along **Y** axis:

$$v*f = v(x*f, y, z*f)$$ (1.3.6)

Tapering along **X** axis:

$$v*f = v(x, y*f, z*f)$$ (1.3.7)

where $f = \texttt{mapFunc(z)}$.

When implementing this within a Vertex Shader on a GFX Card, using Microsoft's Directx9 HLSL Shader Language, one mapping function is needed to transform the Axis Position into a Factor, which can be taken as the scaling factor at this axis position. It makes sense, defining a Range and a Center Position on a certain axis, thus:

Mapper Function for Taper:

```
mapFunc(f) =   {   Interpolate( cs,1,abs(c-z))   if abs(c-z)<r
                          1                       if abs(c-z)>r }
```

where:

   c = center position
   z = axis position
   cs = scaling factor used at the center position
   r = interpolating range

Interpolate (x, y, z) = An interpolating function, where x is the start value, y the end value, and $0 <= z <= 1$. One of the pictures shown is a Hermite interpolation, for getting smooth transitions, but if you need some more GPU Power, try to use a linear interpolation here.

In HLSL Code it looks like this:

```
float taperf(float x){
float t=(tcenter-x)/trange;
if(abs(t)>1){
        return 1;
}else{
      return Hermite(1-g_fact,1,0,0,abs(t));
}
}
```

this result then can be taken as the scaling factor of the remaining axis coordinates, in HLSL:

```
float4 VS_DoTaperZ(float4 vPos,float t){
float4 vNewPos;
vNewPos.x=vPos.x*t;
vNewPos.y=vPos.y*t;
vNewPos.z=vPos.z;
vNewPos.w=vPos.w;
return vNewPos;
}
```

Because homogenous coordinates are used, the w position remains untouched. t is the result of the taper function described above. Note that the scaling factor is applied only to two axes: the x and the y axes. The z and w coordinates remain untouched.

A Word about Normals

Transforming the normals for this transformation is quite complicated, if not impossible.

Twist

Twisting, compared to tapering, is rotating a certain vertex around one axis, instead of scaling it; resulting in a rotation of a point in just two dimensions, for example:

$$nx = x^*\cos(\text{delta}) - y^*\sin(\text{delta})$$
$$ny = x^*\sin(\text{delta}) + y^*\cos(\text{delta}) \tag{1.3.8}$$

where delta is the rotation angle and x and y are the coordinates.

Where nx and ny are the rotated coordinates, the remaining third coordinate stays like before:

$$nz = z \tag{1.3.9}$$

as with tapering, a function that returns a useful delta value is needed:

$$\text{delta} = \texttt{mapFunc(z)} \tag{1.3.10}$$

One possible mapping function looks like this.

The mapping function for the twist needs to return a value that determines the rotation angle at this axis position. This will be achieved by multiplying the axis position with a factor:

```
float twistf(float x){
return (x+1000)*g_fact;
}
```

with $-1000 < x < 00$, $0 < $ `g_fact` $ < 1$.

Adding 1000 to the z coordinate gives us just positive axis positions. The HLSL function for applying the twist looks like this:

```
float4 DoTwistZ(float4 vPos,float t){
float st=sin(t);
float ct=cos(t);
float4 vNewPos;s
vNewPos.x=vPos.x*ct-vPos.y*st;
vNewPos.y=vPos.x*st+vPos.y*ct;
vNewPos.z=vPos.z;
vNewPos.w=vPos.w;
return vNewPos;
}
```

This function rotates the points around the z axis; the z coordinate remains the same.

A Word about Normals

The normal is transformed by applying the twisting function to the normal of the vertex. Due to rotating just around one axis, transforming the normal is the same as rotating the vertex:

```
newNormal= doTwistZ(Normal,twistf(Position.z))
```

Spherification

Spherification is mapping the vertex data of a mesh object to form a sphere. This is determined through a center c which is a 3D vertex, a radius r, and a spherification factor f with $0 < f < 1$.

To transform a specific vertex v on to this cube a ray is traced from the center of the sphere to that point. This ray intersects the sphere at the desired point. The last step is to procentual interpolate between these two points.

A Word about Normals

The normal is rotated to the sphere normal at the end point. The sphere normal is the normalized sphere position.

The start normal is crossed with the end normal:

$$N = S \times E \qquad (1.3.11)$$

S is the starting normal
E is the normal on the sphere for that point
N is the axis that will then be used as rotation axis

The rotation amount is determined through:

$$\text{Angle} = \text{acos}(S \circ E)*f \qquad (1.3.12)$$

E is rotated around N to determine the current normal.

Implementation

To realize this within a vertex shader, it is desirable to have each vertex data in normalized form, (e.g., −1 to 1 for x/y/z coordinates). Besides that, a normal is needed for correct lighting calculations. The way we implement it within the vertex shader is to define a function for each deformation we have in the form:

```
functionName(inout float4 vertexData,
              inout float4 NormalData,
        [Parameters])
```

The `inout` identifier stands for a variable which gets changed by the function.

Having defined all our deformations this way, we can easily pass each vertex of format `float4` and normal of format `float3`, to a deformation function described above. This new coordinate can then be sent again to another deformation function or finally be transformed and projected.

1.4

Morphing Between Two Different Objects

Ronny Burkersroda

Theory

In the early 1990s a movie impressed the audience by showing computer generated effects, which had never been seen before. *Terminator 2* and *Judgment Day* can be called the beginning of photo-realistic computer graphics in movies. The most significant effects were the various transformations of the T-1000—an enemy machine in the story. Those transformations were made by a technique called "morphing." This is done in image space, where one two-dimensional image or video source is transformed into another. For *Terminator 2* it was done three-dimensional, which means that one 3D mesh was transformed into another. Both versions are not meant to be used in real time, but it is possible with today's graphics hardware. We will only look at an implementation of the 3D version.

Vertex tweening is an easy way to move a vertex of a mesh independently from others. Here every vertex has got a relative or absolute destination position vector beside the source one. With a dynamic blending factor, which is equal for all vertices at a time, you can interpolate between source and destination position. The formula looks like this for a relative destination:

$$\mathbf{Position}_{Output} = \mathbf{Position}_{Source} + \mathbf{Position}_{Destination} \cdot Factor \qquad (1.4.1)$$

And with an absolute destination position we need to calculate the relative:

$$\mathbf{Position}_{Output} = \mathbf{Position}_{Source} + \left(\mathbf{Position}_{Destination} - \mathbf{Position}_{Source} \right) \cdot Factor \qquad (1.4.2)$$

The positions are 3D vectors with x, y and z components and the blending factor is a scalar value. For the article we will use only relative destination vectors, because it saves rendering time and code as you can see by comparing the two formulas above.

Using only this technique results in a lot of limits, because start and target mesh are the same as the vertex positions. That means there is no difference in the number of vertices and the faces and attributes are the same. Start and target mesh have got equal materials, textures, shaders, and further states. So vertex tweening is only useful to animate objects in a way, where mesh skinning fails.

To morph between two different objects we can use vertex tweening, but we will transform and render both meshes at once. Beforehand, the destination positions of the mesh vertices have to be calculated. This can be done by projecting the vertices of the first mesh to the second one and vice versa. We use the vertex position as the origin for a ray-mesh-intersection test, which is a function that checks if and where a ray intersects at least one face of a mesh. If there are multiple intersections, the nearest is a good vector to use as a destination position. No intersection source should be used as destination. In this case the relative destination is the zero vector.

For the intersection ray we also need a direction vector beside the origin. This can be the normal of a vertex or we calculate a vector from the origin to the mesh or a user-defined center. We also should invert the direction vector to get all possible intersections. This is not needed if an origin is situated out of both meshes since we do not have to use the vertex position as origin. For example, it is possible to use the bounding sphere of a mesh:

$$\textbf{Direction} = \textbf{Center} - \textbf{Position}$$

$$\textbf{Origin} = -\textbf{Direction} \cdot Radius + \textbf{Center} \qquad (1.4.3)$$

This is very useful if you have got complex objects like helicopters with cockpit interiors. Using the bounding sphere projects every vertex of one mesh to the hull of the other one. Otherwise it could be possible that some hull vertices are projected to faces of the interior. Choosing the best values always depends on the kind of mesh design. After the destination vector is computed we store it into the vertex data.

Now we know where a vertex has to be moved to get an object that has structures like another one. It is possible to tessellate objects to increase the accuracy of those structures, but you do not have to, because we want to use the good performance of optimized low-polygon objects. Other tricks to improve quality are described later in this article.

After the preprocessing is done we are able to render the objects with the morphing effect. This can be done by the application but we are concentrating on vertex shader, because this improves performance on DirectX-8-compatible graphics cards and works in software mode for older hardware.

We have to set the current interpolation factor as shader constant to render a morphing mesh. For the target, one factor has to be inverted by subtracting it from one. In this way both meshes are always at the same state. Now we use the factor to interpolate between source and destination position. Other vertex processing like lighting and texture coordinate transformation can be done normally. It is possible to render both objects per frame, or only render the start mesh to the half and then the target one. This can look strange or ugly but there are optimizations, which can be done (see Optimization section).

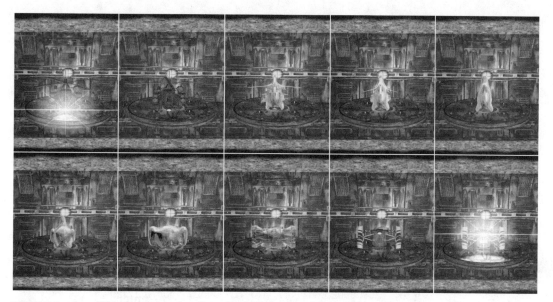

FIGURE 1.4.1 *This is a screenshot from LightBrain's game prototype "Rise of the Hero" implementing the morphing effect, which was originally created for that project.* ©*2004 LightBrain GmbH, Hamburg, Germany.*

Implementation

We are using DirectX 9 to show an implementation of the morphing algorithm. DirectX extensions will help us save time, so the basic functions of 3D graphics programming will not be implemented here. For experienced OpenGL programmers it should be no problem to convert it or write their own program on the base of the algorithm.

For the objects we are able to use extension meshes, whose objects are accessed over the `ID3DXMesh` interface. A mesh is storing vertices, an index list of triangle faces between them, and a table of attributes for the triangles. The attributes are identification numbers, which divide the mesh into different subsets that can be rendered with various states like materials or textures.

It is possible to load a mesh over the `D3DXLoad[…]MeshX[…]` functions or to define your own mesh by locking vertex, index, and attribute buffer and setting the data. For now we are going the first way and are loading the meshes from common DirectX files, which other programs are able to read and write. Beside the meshes we are getting an array of materials including texture file names for all subsets. A subset is rendered by setting material and textures first and then calling `ID3DXMesh::DrawSubset(nSubset)`, where `nSubset` is the number of the subset.

To preprocess the meshes we have to enhance the vertex data first, so the relative destination position can be stored. There are two formats in Direct3D to define the structure of a vertex: flexible vertex formats are the ones to use for fixed function pipeline processing, which transform the vertex data with a set of functions. The parameters of those functions can be set over Direct3D. Because the possibilities of the functions were limited, vertex shaders, in which the processing can be programmed, had been introduced. For vertex shaders there is a much more flexible format: the vertex declaration allows everybody to include all data, which is needed. We are using vertex shaders so we will also use such declarations. First they seem to be more complicated but they enable us to be more compatible to other effects.

A common 3D vertex includes position and normal vector and one 2D texture coordinate. The vertex declaration for such a vertex looks like this:

```
D3DVERTEXELEMENT9 pStandardMeshDeclaration[] =
{
    { 0,  0, D3DDECLTYPE_FLOAT3, D3DDECLMETHOD_DEFAULT,
        D3DDECLUSAGE_POSITION, 0 },
    { 0, 12, D3DDECLTYPE_FLOAT3, D3DDECLMETHOD_DEFAULT,
        D3DDECLUSAGE_NORMAL,   0 },
    { 0, 24, D3DDECLTYPE_FLOAT2, D3DDECLMETHOD_DEFAULT,
        D3DDECLUSAGE_TEXCOORD, 0 },
    D3DDECL_END()
};
```

Now we add a second position vector, which must have an increased usage index over the standard one. The following line must be placed before `D3DDECL_END()`:

```
    { 0, 32, D3DDECLTYPE_FLOAT3, D3DDECLMETHOD_DEFAULT,
        D3DDECLUSAGE_POSITION, 1 },
```

The whole enhancement can be done automatically with the following steps.

We use `D3DXGetDeclVertexSize()` to retrieve the vertex size of the original declaration and we are going through the declaration to store the highest usage index of a position element. Next, the destination position element for morphing can be set to the `D3DDECL_END()` entry. `D3DXGetDeclLength()` returns the number of this entry increased by one. As usage index we take the highest index and add one to it. The last thing is to write the `D3DDECL_END()` at the end. If `pStandardMeshDeclaration` was the original declaration, it has been enhanced to `pMorphingMeshDeclaration`. You can see the routine in Listing 1.4.1.

Listing 1.4.1 Enhancing the Vertex Declaration for a Morphing Mesh

```
D3DVERTEXELEMENT9 pMeshDeclaration[ MAX_FVF_DECL_SIZE ];
DWORD             nPosition                            = 0;
DWORD             nUsageIndex                          = 0;
DWORD             nOffset;
```

```
    ...

    // process all declaration elements until end is reached
    while( pMeshDeclaration[ nPosition ].Stream != 0xFF )
    {
        // check for higher index of a position usage
        if(
            ( pMeshDeclaration[ nPosition ].Usage
                == D3DDECLUSAGE_POSITION )
            && ( pMeshDeclaration[ nPosition ].UsageIndex
                >= nUsageIndex )
        )
            nUsageIndex = pMeshDeclaration[ nPosition ].UsageIndex + 1;

        // increase position in declaration array
        ++nPosition;
    }

    // get element number for new entry
    nPosition = D3DXGetDeclLength( pMeshDeclaration ) - 1;
    nOffset   = D3DXGetDeclVertexSize( pMeshDeclaration, 0 );

    // move end element
    memmove( &pMeshDeclaration[ nPosition + 1 ] ,
        &pMeshDeclaration[ nPosition ], sizeof( D3DVERTEXELEMENT9 ) );

    // add new position element
    pMeshDeclaration[ nPosition ].Stream     = 0;
    pMeshDeclaration[ nPosition ].Offset     = nOffset;
    pMeshDeclaration[ nPosition ].Type       = D3DDECLTYPE_FLOAT3;
    pMeshDeclaration[ nPosition ].Method     = D3DDECLMETHOD_DEFAULT;
    pMeshDeclaration[ nPosition ].Usage      = D3DDECLUSAGE_POSITION;
    pMeshDeclaration[ nPosition ].UsageIndex = nUsageIndex;
```

The next step is to clone the start mesh using the new declaration as a parameter. ID3DXMesh::Clone() creates a new mesh object with the same data as the original one but includes space for the destination position. If you do not want to use the original mesh any longer (e.g., for rendering it without morphing), it can be released.

The vertex buffer of the cloned mesh must be locked now, so we can calculate its destination positions. Every vertex has to be projected to the target mesh. To do this there is an extension function of Direct3D: D3DXIntersect() checks where a ray intersects an extension mesh. We can use the ray origin and direction we want and will get all possible projection points. As I mentioned it is most useful to take the nearest one. The source position has to be subtracted to get the relative destination vector, which can be stored to the vertex data (see Listing 1.4.2). Fortunately reading and writing vertex data is not as hard as it seems. Vertex declarations make it easy to get the offset of a specific vertex element. To retrieve the source position we should look for an element of type D3DDECLTYPE_FLOAT3, usage D3DDECLUSAGE_POSITION, and index 0. And to get the normal the usage has to be D3DDECLUSAGE_NORMAL. Then we take the offset to read the 3D vector from the vertex data. Accessing a specific vertex is possible by doing the following:

```
VOID* pVertex = (BYTE*) pData + nVertexSize * nVertex;
```

pData is the start address of the vertex buffer data, nVertexSize is the size of one vertex, which can be calculated by calling D3DXGetDeclVertexSize(), and nVertex is the number of the vertex that should be accessed. pVertex stores the address of this vertex and can be used to read and write the vectors:

```
D3DXVECTOR3 vct3SourcePosition
    = *(D3DXVECTOR3*)( (BYTE*) pVertex + nOffsetSourcePosition );

...

*(D3DXVECTOR3*)( (BYTE*) pVertex + nOffsetDestinationPosition )
    = vct3DestinationPosition;
```

The offsets, which we got from vertex declaration, are stored in nOffsetSource-Position for source and nOffsetDestinationPosition for destination position.

Listing 1.4.2   Calculating the Destination Position for a Vertex

```
ID3DXMesh* pmshDestination; // pointer to destination mesh interface
D3DVECTOR3 vct3Source;      // source position (vertex input)
D3DVECTOR3 vct3Destination; // destination position (vertex output)
D3DVECTOR3 vct3Direction;   // ray direction vector
D3DVECTOR3 vct3Center;      // bounding sphere center (parameter)
FLOAT      fRadius;         // bounding sphere radius (parameter)
FLOAT      fDistance;       // distance from sphere to mesh
BOOL       bIntersection;   // intersection flag

...

// calculate direction from sphere center to vertex position
D3DXVec3Normalize( &vct3Direction,
    &D3DXVECTOR3( vct3Center - vct3Source ) );

// compute intersection with destination mesh from outstanding point
    on the bounding sphere in direction to the center
D3DXIntersect( pmshDestination,
    &D3DXVECTOR3( vct3Center - vct3Direction * fRadius ),
    &vct3Direction, &bIntersection, NULL, NULL, NULL, &fDistance,
    NULL, NULL );

// check for intersection
if( bIntersection )
{
    // calculate projected vector and subtract source position
    vct3Destination = vct3Center + vct3Direction *
        ( fDistance - fRadius ) - vct3Source;
```

```
}
else
{
    // set relative destination position to zero
    vct3Destination = D3DXVECTOR3( 0.0f, 0.0f, 0.0f );
}
```

After storing the destination position vector of each vertex to the buffer of the start mesh, the same has to be done with the target mesh, which is being projected to the start one. Then the preprocessing is finished.

Now we need the vertex shader, which can transform a vertex of a morphing mesh between source and destination position. At the beginning of the shader we declare the version and inputs, which are loaded from the data of the vertex using its declaration:

```
; declaration of required vertex shader version
vs_1_1          .

; declaration of the input registers
dcl_position0   v0        ; source position
dcl_position1   v1        ; destination position

...
```

At this point we are able to calculate all output values but oPos in any way we want. The position output is an interpolated vector between source and destination position. If the blend factor is stored in the shader constant c0, then the code can look like this:

```
...

; transform and project vertex to screen
mul     r0.xyz, v1.xyz, c0.x      ; blend destination vector
add     r0.xyz, r0.xyz, v0.xyz    ; add source position
mov     r0.w,   v0.w              ; copy w component

...
```

First the relative destination vector is multiplied with the interpolation factor. Next the source vector is added to the result. After that r0.xyz includes a vector, which lies between source and destination position, if c0.x is a value between 0 and 1. At last we have to copy the unchanged w component of the source position. Normally the value is 1.0f.

Now r0 can be processed as if it would include the unprocessed vertex position (e.g., transformation from object to screen space).

The rendering code of your application has to set the constant of the blend factor, which is c0.x in the shader above. This can be done with the following call:

```
IDirect3DDevice9::SetVertexShaderConstantF( 0,
    &D3DXVECTOR4( fBlendFactor, 0.0f, 0.0f, 0.0f ), 1 );
```

Remember that you have to invert the blend factor for the target mesh by calculating 1.0f − fBlendFactor. Now you are able to render the meshes the way you want: Up to the half blend factor you can draw the start one and then the target, or you can render both at the same time with activated z-buffering. For the second type you should draw the target mesh first and then the source one up to the half blend value and afterwards reversed, if your objects have semi-transparent faces or texels. Each alone will not produce successful results for most kinds of objects.

Optimizations

To get the best looking morphing effect there are a lot of things we can do. We will explain some here.

Blending the Alpha Value

The most powerful extension is easy to enable, but difficult to make good. We interpolate the alpha value of the object materials, too. For that, both objects have to be rendered at the same time. Instead of using the same blend factor as for morphing, now we let the alpha blend value of one mesh to be 1. Otherwise both objects would become a little transparent while they are morphing. When we start morphing the start mesh stays opaque until the half, while the target is fading in. At the half the blend value of both objects is one and next the start mesh fades out. The mesh, which has got the blend value of 1, has to be rendered first, so the semi-transparent pixels or second one are mixed with the opaque of the first.

Because of the possibility of intersecting triangles, which can be semi-transparent, there are some cases, in which the morphing will still look bad. This can happen, if the start and target mesh have got semi-transparent materials originally. One way to make it better is to blend the semi-transparent materials away, which is good in combination with reflection mapping. Here we have to blend the transparencies of the start mesh away, then fade in the target, next fade the start one out, and at last blend the transparencies of the target mesh in. Then there are overlapping semi-transparent pixels between the source and target mesh.

If you do not want to let semi-transparent materials become opaque you can use the second method. There we use two render-target textures with alpha channel for rendering each object to one without alpha fading. Before that we have to set the alpha values of the textures to 0. Then the two textures are rendered on quad to the screen blending between both, using the morphing blend factor. Here you should pay attention that the texels of the textures are correctly mapped to the pixels of the screen. If you also need the z-values of the morphing meshes (e.g., when rendering other objects) the application can write those to the z-buffer while rendering to the textures. To do that we have to use textures, which have got at least the dimensions of the back buffer. But we do not need to use a quad as large as the screen. Transforming the bounding boxes of the meshes to screen space will help us get the rectangle we need to render. For that we also have to calculate the correct texture coordinates.

For applications that can enable anti-aliasing we cannot render directly to the textures, because those are not supporting multi-sampling. Since DirectX 9b it is possible to render to a multi-sampled surface like the back buffer and then copy it to a render-target texture.

Using Step Objects

When you are morphing between objects with hard edges the effect may seem very squared, too. If you want a softer or more complex morphing step, objects can be used. Instead of direct interpolation between source and target mesh we are morphing multiple times in a line. With two-step objects it looks like:

Start Object ⇔ First Step

First Step ⇔ Second Step

Second Step ⇔ Target Object

These are the objects that we have to morph between and which we project to.

If you want a softer effect the step meshes should be modeled with a round shape. Maybe you or the artist creates the same sphere for both steps and edits them to shapes similar to the source and target object, only softer.

Tessellating Source and Target Mesh

To improve the accuracy of the mesh projection we can tessellate the source and target morphing meshes before they are projected. Unfortunately this results in many more vertices, but if vertex processing is not the bottleneck, you are able to do it. This is good for objects that have got relatively large faces, which are projected to different faces of the other mesh. For the step object we do not need it because these should already be optimized for their task. But source and target mesh are often optimized for rendering them separately at best quality-performance relation, and not for morphing.

Mapping Effect Textures

In the mind of a viewer our two morphing objects become one unit. To amplify this feeling we can give the morphing objects a single texture or the same set of textures, which are mapped the same way. It seems the materials of the start object are melting to become the new ones, so they are also one unit.

We have to blend the effect textures at the beginning in and at the ending out. A possibility to get the look of T-1000 from *Terminator 2* is to use an environmental cube map, which is reflected by the objects. In the first quarter the original materials of the start mesh are faded out, so we see the half effect along only the reflections and in the last quarter the target materials are faded in.

Another way is to use one or more "lightning" textures, which are mapped spherical and animated or rotated by time to get an electricity effect. This could also be improved by a particle effect.

FIGURE 1.4.2   *Morphing effect extended by two-step objects, alpha blending, reflection cube mapping, and blooming.*

Using Particle Systems

If you want morphing for a fantasy styled game, in which you do not want to use technical-looking effects like reflections, then particles are suitable to create a more magical effect. You can move some stars or flares around the objects. Or a demon, which rises from the ground, could be surrounded by fire. There are a lot of particle effects to imagine and a lot of them can enhance the morphing of two objects.

A benefit of particles is that they are able to cover possible artifacts of a morphing effect.

Blooming the Scene

Overexposure and blooming make the lighting of objects more realistic and help to cover artifacts, too. You can use them to let an object become hot while morphing or to increase the specular highlights of reflecting surfaces.

Interpolating Other Data

Beside the position vectors we are able to blend other vertex data like normal or tangent vectors, too. This is important if you want to change the lighting or reflect more correctly while morphing. Be patient with such direction vectors. Because of the interpolation they lose their length of one. If you need them for calculation (e.g., lighting, reflection, or transformation to tangent space) you have to normalize these vectors after interpolation.

Loading Pre-processed Objects

The pre-processing of the objects costs so much time that it cannot be done between the renderings of two frames. For objects with thousands of faces it also increases the waiting time noticeably. So it is a good idea to pre-process an object combination once and then to store it to file. Then the morphing objects can be loaded from it by the application that wants to morph these. As with many other things, this saves a lot of time, which seems for players to be the time of loading a level.

Conclusion

If you need to transform an object to another this morphing algorithm is nice eye-candy to achieve that. Unfortunately, there are also some disadvantages:

Table 1.4.1 Advantages and Disadvantages of Morphing Algorithm

Pros	Cons
• Real time rendering. • 3D meshes do not have to be changed. • Objects can have completely different attributes. • A lot of tricks to make the effect better.	• Pre-processing takes some time, but can be removed from the final application, if source and target mesh combination is known before. • Vertex projection has to be optimized manually for the best possible result. • Not flexible enough to work with any kind of object animation. (Skinned meshes should be a much lower problem than objects, whose subsets are transformed completely independent.)

You can look at the CD-ROM to find the complete implementation of a demo that presents the morphing effect. There is also a library, which can easily be included into any Direct3D 9 project, to pre-process meshes.

ON THE CD To learn more about LightBrain or "Rise of the Hero," visit the Web site *www.lightbrain.de.*

1.5

Silhouette Geometry Shaders

Jörn Loviscach

Introduction

Silhouettes suffer much from a coarse tessellation of 3D objects. We propose two different methods to improve their look: first, a method to render semi-transparent halos with sub-polygon accuracy, see Figure 1.5.1, second, a method to fake curved silhouettes for convex parts of 3D meshes, see Figure 1.5.2. In spirit, the latter method resembles the CPU-based "Silhouette Clipping" [Sander00]. Both presented approaches employ special pseudo-geometry besides the original mesh. A vertex shader detects the silhouette and extrudes quadrangles from the pseudo-geometry along it. For the halo, we use one quadrangle per triangle of the original mesh; we extrude quadrangles from its edges, however, to smooth the silhouette visually.

FIGURE 1.5.1 *A soft shining halo can be implemented by extruding quadrangles from the silhouette.*

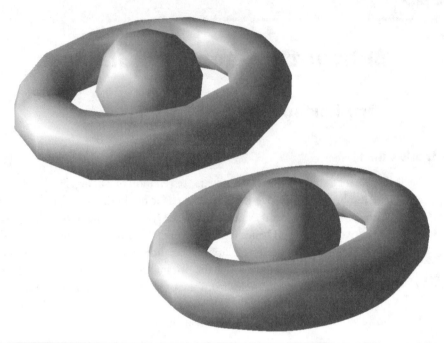

FIGURE 1.5.2   *To hide the angular look of a coarse mesh (left) we add curved fins to its silhouette (right).*

The extrusion of the edges of a mesh via a vertex shader has already been used for cartoon effects [Card02, McGuire04, Loviscach04] and for the computation of soft shadows [Arvo04]. In a straightforward manner [McGuire04] it can be applied to generate shadow volumes. Because this effect has not been used much, we elected to also include a shadow volume computation in the demo code for the present chapter. The silhouette extraction via a vertex shader is the same for the shadow volumes as for the curved silhouettes.

Sub-Polygon Accuracy Halos

The typical way to extract silhouettes from a mesh is to find edges that are adjacent to both a forward-facing and a backward-facing polygon. While this criterion is geometrically precise, it introduces complex zigzag structures [Isenberg02], which may not be favorable for many applications.

The demo code shows a simple example of such an application: the silhouette edges are extruded into a halo, which is perpendicular to the local viewing direction. They are painted with an alpha gradient in order to simulate a smooth glow. The glow is rendered using additive alpha blending. Here, zigzag layers of the halo become immediately visible. The resulting artifacts may be diminished by using alpha blending with the maximum operation. However, this workaround introduces strange shapes where the halos of glowing objects intersect in screen space.

Sub-polygon accuracy silhouettes [Hertzmann99, see also Appendix A of McGuire04] come to the rescue. They do not run along the edges of the original mesh but across its faces, see Figure 1.5.3. For each vertex the dot product of the vertex normal **n** and a unit vector **v** to the viewing position is formed. If the result is positive for three vertices of a triangle, it is considered as facing forward; if the result is negative for all, it is considered as facing backward. In both cases it is discarded as not containing part of the silhouette. All other triangles contain two edges that intersect the silhouette, see Figure 1.5.4.

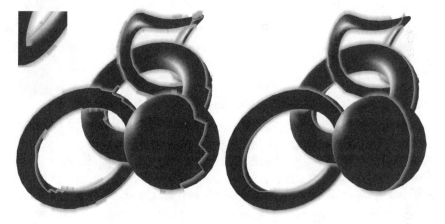

FIGURE 1.5.3 *While edge-based silhouettes (left: seen from a different view point) display strong zigzag structures resulting in artifacts (inset upper left), sub-polygon accuracy silhouettes (right) are virtually clean.*

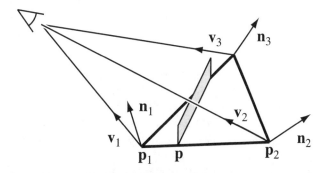

FIGURE 1.5.4 *The silhouette line is computed through linear interpolation and extruded into a quadrangle.*

There is a silhouette between the vertices 1 and 2 if $\mathbf{n}_1 \cdot \mathbf{v}_1$ and $\mathbf{n}_2 \cdot \mathbf{v}_2$ have different signs, where $\mathbf{v}_1$, $\mathbf{v}_2$ denote the local directions to the viewing position. Thus, it suffices to check whether $(\mathbf{n}_1 \cdot \mathbf{v}_1) \cdot (\mathbf{n}_2 \cdot \mathbf{v}_2) < 0$. The actual intersection point $\mathbf{p}$ on the edge 1-2 can be estimated through linear interpolation: $\mathbf{p} = ((\mathbf{n}_1 \cdot \mathbf{v}_1)\mathbf{p}_2 - (\mathbf{n}_2 \cdot \mathbf{v}_2)\mathbf{p}_1)/(\mathbf{n}_1 \cdot \mathbf{v}_1 - \mathbf{n}_2 \cdot \mathbf{v}_2)$, where $\mathbf{n}_1$, $\mathbf{n}_2$, $\mathbf{v}_1$, $\mathbf{v}_2$ are the vertex normals and the unit vectors to the viewing position at the edge's end points. To generate a halo, the line across the triangle from one intersection with an edge to the other has to be extruded.

To implement this through a vertex shader, we generate a vertex buffer containing four vertices per face of the original mesh and an index buffer connecting them to two triangles forming a quadrangle. The shader determines unit vectors from all three points to the viewing position and computes the dot products with the corresponding vertex normals. Thus, all of this data has to be present within every vertex. We use four vertices per triangle with the following attributes:

$$\mathbf{p}_1, \mathbf{n}_1, \mathbf{p}_3, \mathbf{n}_3, \mathbf{p}_2, \mathbf{n}_2, u = 1, v = 0 \tag{1.5.1}$$

$$\mathbf{p}_1, \mathbf{n}_1, \mathbf{p}_2, \mathbf{n}_2, \mathbf{p}_3, \mathbf{n}_3, u = 0, v = 0 \tag{1.5.2}$$

$$\mathbf{p}_1, \mathbf{n}_1, \mathbf{p}_3, \mathbf{n}_3, \mathbf{p}_2, \mathbf{n}_2, u = 1, v = 1 \tag{1.5.3}$$

$$\mathbf{p}_1, \mathbf{n}_1, \mathbf{p}_2, \mathbf{n}_2, \mathbf{p}_3, \mathbf{n}_3, u = 0, v = 1 \tag{1.5.4}$$

Two vertices contain the points in the order 1-2-3, the other two use the order 1-3-2. This change in arrangement allows simplifying the logic of the shader: We do not need to test all three, but only two edges per vertex for an intersection with the silhouette. If there is a silhouette between the first two points, the shader sets the resulting position to the linear interpolation of them. If there is not, the shader tests if there is a silhouette between the last two points and sets the resulting position correspondingly. If either test fails, there is no silhouette at all on the triangle, and the position is set to a fixed far position. The latter will happen to all four vertices so that the triangle is not only reduced to zero area but will also be clipped away. As an example, consider a triangle where the silhouette intersects the edges 2-3 and 1-3. The position of the first and the fourth vertex will be set to the intersection on the edge 2-3; the second and the third vertex will be positioned on the edge 1-3.

The v coordinate of the vertices is used to control the extrusion: The 3D point determined as described beforehand is offset by v times a vector pointing outside the mesh. Here, we employ the interpolated normal vector $\mathbf{n} = ((\mathbf{n}_1 \cdot \mathbf{v}_1)\mathbf{n}_2 - (\mathbf{n}_2 \cdot \mathbf{v}_2)\mathbf{n}_1)/(\mathbf{n}_1 \cdot \mathbf{v}_1 - \mathbf{n}_2 \cdot \mathbf{v}_2)$, which is in good approximation perpendicular to the local viewing direction. The u coordinate is only used for illustration.

The resulting kind of halo rendering works fine for convex objects. Concave objects may show isolated bursts of light on their faces. This effect, however, is much more intense with a silhouette generated from the edges of the mesh instead of the proposed method.

Thanks to their smoothness, sub-polygon accuracy silhouettes may also prove helpful in the generation of soft shadows through quadrangles appended to the silhouette in a shadow map rendering [Arvo04]. Somewhat surprisingly, sub-polygon accuracy silhouettes do not prove very useful to render shadow volumes: the relationship between the vertex normals and the actual geometry of the mesh is quite complex; in principle, the vertex normals may even be chosen freely. This leads to situations where back-facing parts of a shadow volume lie outside of the corresponding front-facing part. Such geometry causes a bright area in the shadow, as can be seen with complex meshes in the demo code. Note that to get useful shadow volumes at all, the silhouettes have to be oriented correctly. As it turns out, all that is needed in the vertex shader is an inversion according to the sign of $\mathbf{n}_1 \cdot \mathbf{v}_1$.

Sub-polygon accuracy silhouettes offer the advantage that the corresponding vertex and index buffers can easily be built from the data of the original mesh. There is no need to collect the edges of the mesh. The data needed amounts to *six* vectors plus one float per vertex with four vertices per *triangle*. An edge-based halo (see next section) needs *four* vectors plus one float per vertex with four vertices per *edge*. On a closed mesh, there are three half edges for every triangle, so that in total the sub-polygon accuracy method uses a little less data.

Curved Silhouettes

The convex parts of polygonal silhouettes can be smoothed by appending curved fins to them. We use a pixel shader to cut these fins from quadrangles that are perpendicular to the silhouette, see Figure 1.5.5. The quadrangles themselves are extruded from pseudo-geometry based on the edges of the original mesh.

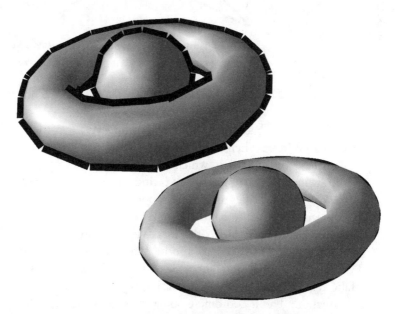

FIGURE 1.5.5   *Quadrangles that extend perpendicularly from the silhouette (left) are trimmed to only display the curved fins (right).*

The vertex buffer of this pseudo-geometry contains four vertices per edge of the original mesh; again, an index buffer is used to connect those four vertices to two triangles forming a quadrangle. The attributes of the four vertices are selected as follows:

$$\mathbf{p}_1, \mathbf{n}_1, \mathbf{p}_2, \mathbf{n}_1, \mathbf{n}_{11}, u = 0, v = 0 \tag{1.5.5}$$

$$\mathbf{p}_2, \mathbf{n}_2, \mathbf{p}_1, \mathbf{n}_1, \mathbf{n}_{11}, u = 1, v = 0 \tag{1.5.6}$$

$$\mathbf{p}_2, \mathbf{n}_2, \mathbf{p}_1, \mathbf{n}_1, \mathbf{n}_{11}, u = 1, v = 1 \tag{1.5.7}$$

$$\mathbf{p}_1, \mathbf{n}_1, \mathbf{p}_2, \mathbf{n}_1, \mathbf{n}_{11}, u = 0, v = 1 \tag{1.5.8}$$

Here, $\mathbf{n}_1, \mathbf{n}_2, \mathbf{p}_1, \mathbf{p}_2$ are the positions and normals of the edge's end points, $\mathbf{n}_1$ and $\mathbf{n}_{11}$ are the face normals of the adjacent triangles, see Figure 1.5.6.

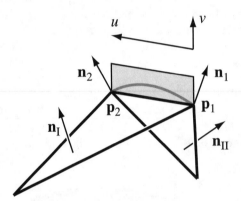

FIGURE 1.5.6   *The face normals are used to decide if an edge is to be extruded. The vertex normals, however, control the form of the curved fin.*

The vertex shader uses the first position vector to determine a vector v to the viewing position. Then it checks if $(\mathbf{v} \cdot \mathbf{n}_1) \cdot (\mathbf{v} \cdot \mathbf{n}_{11}) < 0$ which means that $\mathbf{v} \cdot \mathbf{n}_1$ and $\mathbf{v} \cdot \mathbf{n}_{11}$ have different sign, which in turn means that one of the adjacent triangles is front-facing and the other is back-facing: We have a silhouette edge. If that is not the case, the position is set to a fixed far point.

Again, v is used to control the extrusion of the edge. Using the vertex normal $\mathbf{n}_1$ projected perpendicular to the local viewing direction, the silhouette edge can be extruded into a halo. It may also be extruded along the light ray to form a shadow volume. Both uses are demonstrated in the accompanying code. Again we have to take care that the polygons bounding the shadow volumes are drawn with correct orientation. The u coordinate and the position of the other point of the edge are needed neither for halos nor for shadow volumes. Note a difference between point and directional light sources. The shadow volumes for a directional light source located behind the viewer converge at the vanishing point of the light's direction. Thus, they can be drawn extruding only a single triangle from each silhouette edge.

For curved silhouettes, we extrude the silhouette edge perpendicular to itself and perpendicular to the local viewing direction. To this end we form the cross product of the local viewing direction and the vector along the edge. The latter vector is computed using the position of both end points of the edge. It could also be computed using the normals of the two adjacent edges, but that would be computationally more intensive. Anyway, we need both end positions of the edge as attributes of every single vertex for a different reason.

The extrusion leads to quadrangles along the silhouette that appear to the viewer almost perfectly as rectangles. This simplifies the computation of texture coordinates. Furthermore, the interpolation of texture coordinates would incur a shearing effect along the diagonal of a non-rectangular quadrangle. That the extruded quadrangles do not close to a continuous silhouette does not bother us, because we will trim away from the left, upper, and right side in the pixel shader.

Using the vertex normal, the vertex shader computes the illumination at the original position of every vertex. This is automatically linearly interpolated on the way to the pixel shader so that the color gradient on the fin exactly matches that of the adjacent triangle.

We trim away the unwanted pixels of the extruded quadrangle using the HLSL instruction clip in the pixel shader. The uv coordinates are handed to the pixel shader so that every extruded quadrangle carries interpolated values of u ranging from 0 to 1 along the edge of the mesh and v from 0 to 1 approximately perpendicular to that. We build a cubic function $u \cdot (1 - u) \cdot ((1 - u)\mathbf{a} + u\mathbf{b})$ for certain $\mathbf{a}$, $\mathbf{b}$ and check if v (apart from a scaling) is above that value. If so, the pixel is clipped; otherwise it is painted. $\mathbf{a}$ and $\mathbf{b}$ are determined from the vertex normals in such a way that the resulting curve runs perpendicular to the projection of the vertex normal onto the screen. This is the part of the computation, where we need the other point of the edge: to compute the vector from one point of the edge to the other.

The cubic method ensures that curves on two quadrangles that meet at a single vertex have the same tangent: no crease will appear between them. While the cubic expression may read complex, it can be reduced: we write $\mathbf{a}$ at one vertex of the edge, $\mathbf{b}$ at the other, and the automatic linear interpolation happening between vertex shader and pixel shader will yield $(1 - u)\mathbf{a} + u\mathbf{b}$, the last factor of the cubic expression.

In this method, we do not care about perfectly accurate computation of screen-oriented rectangles. This may be done at the cost of working in screen coordinates, which means that the vertex shader has to do perspective division. Given the approximating nature of the method we elected to stick with less accuracy but also less overhead.

Conclusion and Outlook

The proposed methods can be used in many different ways to improve the look of silhouettes for intermediate levels of tessellation. On very coarse meshes they have severe difficulties in estimating the original form. In the demo code we use the mesh simplification of DirectX in order to show the behavior at different levels of tessellation.

The relatively high number of vertex attributes still poses a high load on the memory interface. This is aggravated by the circumstance that the vertices cannot be reused: while a vertex in a regular mesh may be shared by all adjacent polygons, the vertices of the pseudo-geometries introduced here depend too much on their geometric context. Using quadrangles generated through "instancing" under Shader Model 3.0 may offer improvements here. Furthermore, this shader model may offer a drastic speedup of both presented methods, because it allows an "early out" in the shader and will let it finish quickly if there is no silhouette. However, first experiments show that current hardware profits from this only if the number of code lines that are branched over is much larger than used here for silhouette geometry.

References

[Arvo04] Arvo, Jukka, and Westerholm, Jan, "Hardware Accelerated Soft Shadows Using Penumbra Quads," *Journal of WSCG,* Vol. 12 (2004), No. 1, pp. 11–18.

[Card02] Card, Drew, and Mitchell, Jason L., "Non-Photorealistic Rendering with Pixel and Vertex Shaders," *ShaderX: Vertex and Pixel Shaders Tips and Tricks,* ed. Wolfgang Engel, Wordware, 2002, pp. 319–333.

[Hertzmann99] Hertzmann, Aaron, "Introduction to 3D Non-Photorealistic Rendering: Silhouettes and Outlines," SIGGRAPH Course Notes, 1999.

[Isenberg02] Isenberg, Tobias, Halper, Nick, and Strothotte, Thomas, "Stylizing Silhouettes at Interactive Rates: From Silhouette Edges to Silhouette Strokes," *Computer Graphics Forum* (EUROGRAPHICS 2002), Vol. 21 (2002), No. 3, pp. 249–258.

[Loviscach04] Loviscach, Jörn, "Stylized Haloed Outlines on the GPU," SIGGRAPH 2004 Poster.

[McGuire04] McGuire, Morgan, and Hughes, John F., "Hardware-Determined Feature Edges," Proc. NPAR 2004, pp. 135–145.

[Sander04] Sander, Pedro V., Gu, Xiafeng, Gortler, Steven, Hoppe, Hugues, and Snyder, John, "Silhouette Clipping," Proc. SIGGRAPH 2000, pp. 327–334.

1.6

GLSL Real-Time Shader Development

Natalya Tatarchuk and Bill Licea-Kane

Introduction

In this article we present the foundations of the OpenGL shading language—a new standard for cross-platform portability of real-time shader-based visual effects. GLSL has a familiar C-like syntax with expressive power to code an almost unlimited variety of graphical effects, including vision and image processing algorithms which can be directly executed in graphics hardware—providing enormous opportunities for optimization. The OpenGL shading language is a cross-vendor extension to the OpenGL 1.5 specification and will serve as a foundation for the OpenGL 2.0 specification for an open, non-proprietary standard.

The article describes the semantics of the new high-level shading language in great detail, focusing on the particulars of the language syntax and various optimization techniques for writing high-level shaders in OpenGL shading language. We present the structure of OpenGL objects relevant for real-time shader programming, such as shader and program objects—understanding the object organization aids in better optimization of real-time effects. We will describe a shader development environment IDE for artists and effect programmers called RenderMonkey and explain how OpenGL shading language has been integrated into this IDE to facilitate OpenGL shader effect creation.

Brief OpenGL and Shading History

Interestingly enough, programmable graphics pipeline is not new to OpenGL. Before we start in 1992 with OpenGL history, let's go back to the prehistoric days. Early commercial graphics systems in the 1960s, such as DEC systems, spanned architectures from a dumb attached display system (which could display a single point) to programmable attached display processors (including conditional subroutines and stacks). This variety of programmable systems in commercial and research systems led to the coining of the term "the wheel of reincarnation" for hardware evolution [Myer86]. A DEC Type 30 with a dumb attached display system would be at the start of the wheel of reincarnation.

In the 1980s, several Application Programmer Interfaces (APIs) for abstracting interactive graphics emerged, trading some programmability for portability on a class of systems. Proprietary graphics APIs such as IRIS GL (SGI), Starbase (HP), and XGL (Sun) allowed an application to be easily ported to new members of a workstation family. Early standardization efforts of GKS, PHIGS, X, and PEX allowed graphics applications to be easily ported to hardware supplied by different vendors. The proliferation of UNIX workstations also dramatically broadened the use of the C programming language. The burden of programming the underlying hardware was lifted from the application writer and placed on the providers of the graphics library and C compiler. A DEC station PXG (a MIPS R3000 CPU with an attached graphics subsystem containing and i860 CPU with pixel stamping special purpose hardware) would be 1 1/2 turns around the wheel of reincarnation.

During this same period, an explosion of research and commercialization was driven by offline graphics. Major breakthroughs in lighting models led to the rejection of the simple and fast but rigid Phong Lighting/Gouraud Shading model. Shading languages were invented [Cook84], [Perlin85]. This led quickly to the development of a formal shading language, RenderMan [Hanrahan90], based on a subset of C but specialized for shading. While there was a brief attempt at hardware for shading, shading systems evolved rapidly into farms of general purpose CPUs. The "offline" shading systems are at the start of the wheel of reincarnation.

In 1987, PIXAR and SGI briefly considered, but rejected, joint development on a new API [Akeley01]. By the late 1980s, one of the goals of IRIS GL, portability, was less than completely successful. Each implementation of IRIS GL proved to be slightly different. Performance differences were to be expected, but even coverage and semantics differed slightly. Application programmers had long ago learned to live with the death by a thousand cuts while porting floating point algorithms between platforms. But these very small differences in IRIS GL implementations could lead to death by a million (pixel) cuts. Most of the time ports between IRIS GL implementations were nearly trivial, but sometimes not.

An effort to more formally specify GL, "GL 5.0" began in 1989, and morphed into collaboration with Microsoft and others to specify a cross-platform API. On September 17, 1991, SGI announced this effort [SGI91], and the Architecture Review Board (ARB) was soon formed. The ARB's founding members were Digital Equipment, IBM, Intel and Microsoft, and SGI. The ARB controlled the final editing and evolution of the API. Nine months later, on June 10, 1992, the OpenGL 1.0 specification was published [Segal92].

The OpenGL specification left it as an exercise to the reader to discover that it was a proudly fixed function. A white paper stated it simply: Because programmability would conflict with keeping the API close to the hardware and reduce optimum performance, OpenGL does not provide a programming language [Segal94]. In 1993 the first OpenGL implementations shipped [Dennis93], and nearly immediately, William C. Archibald asked if OpenGL could do programmable shaders. The answer came back quickly: The response was that this was not possible with the current API [Akeley93]. By the end of the year, Digital Equipment, SGI, and IBM were all shipping OpenGL systems.

OpenGL later also shipped on Windows/NT 3.51, and then came to Windows 95 and its descendants. A game developer in Texas made a wonderful decision to use OpenGL. Perhaps most significantly, OpenGL, which was designed to be extended, was indeed extended—hundreds of times. Some of these extensions were trivial. Others were for research. The PixelFlow [Olano98] project at UNC extended OpenGL [Leech98] for programmable shading.

The wheel of reincarnation began turning again with the introduction of programmable vertex and fragment processors to the pipeline. Initial OpenGL extensions exposed this programmability with device specific assembly language programs. The ARB approved `ARB_vertex_program` and `ARB_fragment_program`, which attempted to provide device independent "assembly language" programs. But nearly as soon as they were approved discussions started on extending these "assembly language" extensions. Perhaps these extensions provided device independence only to a single generation of implementations?

According to [Segal94], it's possible that a "high-level" shading language is the lowest possible that will still provide device independence. The first public call for a "high-level" shading language came from 3Dlabs at the SIGGRAPH 2001 OpenGL BOF [Trevett01]. By September, an ambitious proposal for future directions of OpenGL included the Shading Language for vertex, fragment, unpack processors, time control, memory management, and data buffers. And in June 2003, the OpenGL Shading Language and the associated extensions were approved by the ARB.

OpenGL Shading Language Overview

How We Replaced Fixed Function

Before we look at programmable pipeline, let's take a brief look at existing fixed function. Here, we will look at the geometry path (Figure 1.6.1). (The image path is analogous.)

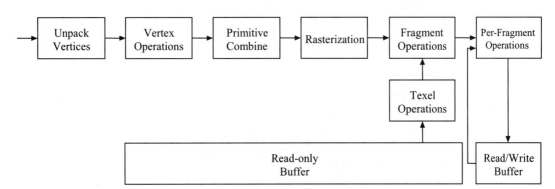

FIGURE 1.6.1 *Fixed Function Pipeline—geometry transformation and rasterization.*

First, each vertex is specified and unpacked. Then vertex operations transform each vertex and its associated data (such as texture coordinates) and light the vertex, creating the final color(s) of each vertex. Next, the vertices are combined to form primitives and clipped. The primitives, which are points, lines, or polygons, are then rasterized. The associated data is interpolated during rasterization, creating resulting fragments. Each fragment's color can be modified by texture application; it is then fogged and the primary and secondary colors are summed. Finally, each fragment is subject to per-fragment operations of pixel ownership, alpha test, depth test, stencil test, and blending.

With OpenGL Shading Language, most of the fixed function pipeline remains untouched. We simply insert two processors into the OpenGL pipeline (see Figure 1.6.2), each of which will subsume a small portion of the fixed function [Kessenich03].

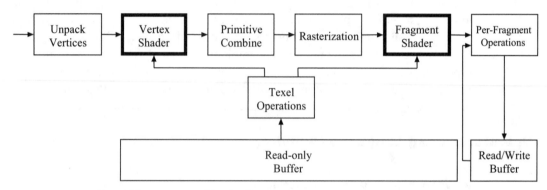

FIGURE 1.6.2   *OpenGL programmable pipeline.*

Vertex shader unit replaces the following vertex operations:

- Vertex Transformation
- Normal Transformation and normalization and rescaling
- Texture coordinate generation
- Texture coordinate transformation
- Color material application
- Lighting

And the fragment shader replaces the following fragment operations:

- Operations on interpolated values
- Texture access and application
- Fog
- Color sum

In addition, texel operations, which in fixed function OpenGL are available only in fragment operations, may be consumed by both the vertex shader and fragment shader. Just like the earlier extensions `ARB_vertex_program` and `ARB_fragment_program`, both the vertex processor and the fragment processor are stream processors. Each takes as input one vertex or fragment and outputs one transformed vertex or fragment.

OpenGL Shading Language API

Before we describe OpenGL Shading Language constructs in details, let us first introduce the API for creating and managing shaders in the OpenGL programmable pipeline. Additional entry points have been added to the OpenGL API to facilitate shader creation, loading, compilation, and linking of shader objects. Another set of additional API entry points has been added to allow programmer passing of vertex attribute and uniform variables to shaders.

We can think of the program that will run on the GPU programmable units in the same manner as a regular executable running on the CPU (for example, a C++ application). The shader objects that will be used by the programmable stages of OpenGL are collected together to form a "program object" [ARB03]. The programs that are executed by these programmable stages are called "executables." All of the information needed for a particular program execution is encapsulated in a program object. There can be one or more source files, each of which can be thought of by OpenGL as a shader object. Each shader object (source file) needs to be first created, and then compiled. Finally in order to use a shader object by the executable, it must be attached to a program object.

Once all shader objects are compiled successfully, we must link a program object in order to produce an executable to run on the programmable unit. This executable then can be loaded to make it part of the current OpenGL state.

During compilation and linking phases of creation of the program object, a text string is generated (the info log) that can be queried to get more information about the results of each operation. Thus a programmer can determine if there were any compile errors during the compilation stage, link errors when trying to link shader objects into a single program object, any optimization hints, etc. Finally, once a program object is set to be part of the OpenGL current state, values for shader parameters (uniforms, see discussion below) declared in the shader can be set by the application and used to control the shader's behavior at runtime. Note that since multiple shader objects can be linked into a single program object, these shader objects in fact share a single namespace. Therefore, any variables that were declared as global in one of the shaders will be visible to the other shaders in the linked program object. The reader must differentiate, however, between the concept of a shader parameter that is common among multiple program objects and what is described above. The shader parameter can be shared only between shader objects that are linked into a single executable, but not among multiple program objects.

Stages of shader programming in OpenGL:

1. Create shader object
2. Provide shader source code
3. Compile shader code
4. Create a program object
5. Attach shader objects to the program object
6. Link the program object
7. Install the executable program as part of OpenGL's current state
8. Set shader parameter values
9. Set vertex shader attributes

Shader Object Creation

Before we can create and use a shader in a program, we need to create an empty shader object by using `glCreateShaderObjectARB` API entry point (for a detailed specification for this and other methods we refer the reader to the OpenGL Extention Registry [ARB03]):

```
GLhandleARB glCreateShaderObjectARB(GLenum shaderType)
```

Setting Shader Source Code

We need to provide a source for the shader. In order to do that, we must define a function that will be the body of the shader (see Figure 1.6.3 for a simple shader example).

```
void main(void)
{
gl_Position = ftransform();
}
```

FIGURE 1.6.3   *A trivial vertex shader example outputting transformed vertices.*

Shaders are passed to OpenGL as strings. Note that these strings do not have to be null-terminated (however, they can be) since it isn't required by OpenGL. This was added to facilitate development of shaders from files directly. To provide the source code, we can call `glShaderSourceARB` API entry point:

```
void glShaderSourceARB(GLhandleARB shaderObj,
                       GLsizei count,
                  const GLcharARB **string,
                       const GLint *length)
```

Shader Compilation

The source code loaded into a shader object is expected to form a valid shader as defined by the OpenGL Shading Language Specification. Now that we have loaded the source code, the next step is to compile the shader code by using the `glCompile-ShaderARB` method.

```
void glCompileShaderARB(GLhandleARB shaderObj)
```

This function will compile a given shader object `shaderObj`. Note that each shader object has an associated Boolean status `OBJECT_COMPILE_STATUS_ARB` that is modified as a result of compilation.

This status can be queried with `glGetObjectParameter{fi}vARB` ([ARB03]). This status will be set to `TRUE` if the given shader object was compiled without errors and is ready for use; and `FALSE` otherwise.

Note that shader compilation can fail for a variety of reasons. If current compilation failed, any information about a previous compilation is lost and not restored. Therefore, the old state of the input shader object isn't restored after an unsuccessful compilation. Also note, that if shader object instance wasn't compiled successfully and therefore will not reference a valid shader object, the error `INVALID_OPERATION` is generated. Each shader object has an information log (the *info Log*) which is modified as a result of compilation and other operations. To retrieve information about the compilation attempt, `glGetInfoLogARB` entry point can be used.

Working with Program Objects

Once we have one or more successfully compiled shaders (for example, a vertex and a fragment shader pair), we can create a program object that will use them. First we must create the actual program object that will store these shaders. We can use the following command:

```
GLhandleARB glCreateProgramObjectARB(void)
```

Note that at the point of creation, the program objects are empty. If the program object is successfully created, a non-zero handle will be returned and its attribute `OBJECT_TYPE_ARB` is set to `PROGRAM_OBJECT_ARB`. A zero object handle will be returned if the program object's creation has failed.

One can think of a program object as a container object. Each program object can store one or more multiple shader objects, which need to be attached to the program object with the `glAttachObjectARB` command.

```
void glAttachObjectARB(GLhandleARB containerObj,
                       GLhandleARB obj)
```

Shader objects can be attached to a program object even before source code is loaded into any shader objects, or before a shader object is compiled. Multiple shader objects of the same type can be attached to a single program object; however, they must have a single entry point (main function). One can also reuse existing shader objects and attach them to multiple program objects as necessary. This allows shader programmers an efficient API for shader library creation, where each executable can be a permutation of existing shader objects.

Once we have a program object with attached shader objects, we must link the executable from objects. We can use this API entry point:

```
void glLinkProgramARB (GLhandleARB programObj)
```

The result of linking operations can be checked by looking at the program object's OBJECT_LINK_STATUS_ARB flag which can be queried with glGetObjectParameter {fi}vARB (which will be set to TRUE in the case of successfully linked program object and FALSE in case of any errors that occurred). Linking can fail if one of the shader objects attached to this program object is not compiled successfully, or if the program attempts to use more active uniform or sampler variables that are allowed in a particular implementation. One can also query the info log for more information about the linking operation.

If, during linking operation, one of the shader objects from the vertex/fragment pair isn't present in the program object, the linking will not automatically fail. It isn't required in OpenGL to supply both shader types (vertex and fragment) as a pair in a program object. If one is missing, OpenGL will substitute the standard OpenGL 1.4 fixed function pipeline for the one not present.

Finally, once we have a valid executable, we can use it to set it as part of OpenGL's current rendering state. To install an executable to run, use this API method:

```
void glUseProgramObjectARB(GLhandleARB programObj)
```

Note that if this method is called with a zero handle, this is equivalent to installing the fixed function pipeline and removing any programmable stages execution. While the application is using a particular program object executable, it can modify attached shader objects, compile them, and attach and detach additional shader objects to the program object. None of these operations will affect the executable that is being run in the system. The executable code is *only* affected when the program object is re-linked, at which point the glLinkProgramARB will install the generated code as a part of the GL current rendering state if the program object being linked is already in use.

We will discuss the details of setting shader parameter values and vertex attributes in the language section devoted to a discussion of uniforms and attributes.

OpenGL Shading Language Structure

The OpenGL Shading Language is a high-level language, similar to C and C++ in language constructs. Unlike ARB_vertex_program and ARB_fragment_program, the shading language is based on a subset of C/C++ but extended and customized for lighting and shading calculations (similar to RenderMan) [Hanrahan90]. Unlike RenderMan, it is not nearly exclusively float, but is a float-centric language. It also differs by having hardware-centric vector types, rather than the functional-centric float, color, point, types of RenderMan.

In this article we will not describe the exact language syntax for OpenGL Shading Language. Interested readers can refer to [Kessenich03] for an in-depth discussion of GLSL specifications.

Let's begin by looking at some details of the language, starting with the types.

Types

OpenGL Shading language supports the C/C++ types float, int, and bool which are also extended for a small vector processor. Since many shader operations can be vectorized to take most advantage of the graphics hardware, each of the basic types float, int, and bool have a vector form of two components, three components, or four components. In addition, GLSL supports square float matrices of size 2×2, 3×3, and 4×4. Note that OpenGL shading language does not support strings or pointer types.

Supported basic types:

```
void
float   vec2   vec3   vec4
        mat2   mat3   mat4
int     ivec2  ivec3  ivec4
bool    bvec2  bvec3  bvec4
```

OpenGL Shading Language reserves three additional floating point types. OpenGL requires floating point operations to be accurate to about 1 part in 10^5 and represent a magnitude of at least 2^{32}. The type double is reserved for a floating type with higher precision, half for a floating point type with lower precision, and fixed for a floating type with lower precision and substantially reduced range.

Reserved basic types:

```
double dvec2 dvec3 dvec4 // reserved
half   hvec2 hvec3 hvec4 // reserved
fixed  fvec2 fvec3 fvec4 // reserved
```

Additionally, types specific to texturing are added; namely *samplers*. One can think of samplers as special shader parameters (also referred to as *uniforms*) used to identify the texture objects used for each texture lookup. The value of a sampler indicates the texture image unit being accessed with each instruction. The type of the sampler identifies the target on the texture image unit where the texture object bound to that texture image unit's target is used for the texture lookup. Essentially, samplers are opaque handles to textures that can be used by the built-in texture functions (which is similar to RenderMan's constant strings as opaque handles to textures).

Supported sampler types:

```
sampler1D sampler2D    sampler3D        samplerCube
sampler1DShadow        sampler2DShadow
```

Recently a few reserved sampler types were reserved in anticipation of approval of `ARB_texture_rectangle`. These types will become supported sampler types when and if that extension is promoted to core OpenGL.

Reserved sampler types:

```
sampler1DRect          sampler2DRect     // reserved
sampler1DrectShadow    sampler2DRectShadow // reserved
```

Users can define their own data structures with the use of the `struct` keyword. Although they are similar to C/C++, several minor restrictions are imposed, such as no qualifiers, no bit fields, no forward references, and no in-place definitions. One may also not use anonymous structures in OpenGL.

Shader programmers can also define arrays in OpenGL shading language, with minor restrictions. The dimensions must be specified with a constant integer for size, and the arrays can only be one dimensional. A more serious restriction is the fact that arrays in GLSL cannot be initialized at declaration.

Note that since shader parameters used in vertex and fragment shaders share scope in a single program object, shared global parameters must be of the same type and size in all shaders that refer to them. This is the only exception for the scope of types, which otherwise follows expected C rules.

Type Qualifiers

Any variable or parameter in the OpenGL Shading Language shader must have a type qualifier that explains the purpose of this parameter. The OpenGL Shading Language has several new type qualifiers. If there is no qualifier (the default qualifier), the type is qualified as a local read-write variable, or an input parameter to a function. `const` is a compile-time constant, or a read-only function parameter.

Declaring variables a constant allows more descriptive and robust shaders that simply use predefined numerical constants in the code. This qualifier can be used with any of the basic data types but not with structure fields. Note that any constant variable must be initialized at declaration time, for example:

```
const vec4 vLightPosition = vec4(100.0, 200.0, 150.0, 0.0);
```

`atttribute` qualifier is used to specify variables that are passed to a vertex shader from OpenGL on a per-vertex basis. Declaring any variable as `attribute` in any shader but the vertex shader generates an error. Attribute variables are always read-only in the shader. The values for attribute variables are passed to a vertex shader through the OpenGL vertex API or as a part of a vertex array or vertex buffer. Note that the attribute qualifier can be used only with the data types `float`, `vec2`, `vec3`, `vec4`, `mat2`, `mat3`, and `mat4`.

Example declarations:

```
attribute vec4 position;
attribute vec3 normal;
attribute vec2 texCoord;
```

Standard OpenGL vertex attributes have built-in variable names to allow convenient access and easy integration between user programs and OpenGL vertex functions. However, users can bind user-specified attributes to vertex attributes by using `glBindAttribLocationARB` API entry point. The index of the generic vertex attribute to be used can be assigned by calling this method. Note that this method must be called prior to linking. OpenGL can also assign vertex attribute index automatically during linking, and the user can query the index for a particular attribute by calling `glGetAttribLocationARB` or by using `glGetVertexAttribPointerARB` and `glEnableVertexArrayPointer` methods with the standard OpenGL vertex API. For example, RenderMonkey IDE uses the second approach to automatically bind tangent and binormal vertex data to known attribute types. It declares its custom attribute slots for tangent data as `rm_Tangent` and binormal data as `rm_Binormal` and then calls `glGetAttribLocationARB` method during the linking stage to determine the location for binding these attribute arrays.

Note that each particular OpenGL implementation sets a specific limit on the number of attribute variables that can be used by a given vertex shader. If this number is exceeded, it will cause a link error. Note that only attributes that are actually used in the vertex shader count toward that limit. Attribute variables are required to have global scope and must be declared outside of function bodies, before their first use.

`uniform` qualifier is used to specify global variables which are the same across the entire primitive being processed. These variables are read-only in the shaders and can be initialized directly by the application via API commands or indirectly by OpenGL (if it is one of the built-in variables).

Example declaration:

```
uniform vec4 lightPosition;
```

This qualifier can be used with any of the basic data types, with variables with structure type, or an array of basic data types. Note that there is an implementation dependent limit on the amount of storage for uniforms and if it is exceeded it will cause a compile- or link-time error. Only uniforms that are used in the shader ("active" uniforms) count toward that limit. Note that if the shader uses built-in uniforms, they count toward the implementation-dependent uniform limit. If multiple shaders are linked in a single program object, they share a single uniform name space, and therefore types of uniforms with the same names must match across all shaders linked into a single executable.

Uniforms are program object specific state. Note that once loaded, they retain their state, and their values are restored whenever a program object is used, as long as the program object has not been re-linked. By default, after a successful link, all active uniforms belonging to the program object are initialized to zero. A successful link will also generate a location for each active uniform. In order to change values for active uniforms, this location must be used in conjunction with the appropriate `glUniform*ARB` command.

```
int glGetUniformLocationARB(GLhandleARB programObj,
                            const charARB *name)
```

Note that all locations are invalidated and reassigned after each successful re-link. We refer the reader to [ARB03] for a more in-depth discussion of OpenGL API entry points for determining uniform locations and setting their values.

`varying` qualifier provides the interface for specifying the values passed between the vertex shader, the fragment shader, and the fixed functionality between them. The vertex shader computes these values per vertex (such as color, texture coordinates, and so on). It will write them to the variables declared with `varying` qualifier. These values are read-write access for the vertex shader; however, it can only read these values after they are written to.

The varying values are then interpolated in a perspective-correct manner over the primitive being rendered. In single sampling, the values are interpolated at the pixel-center. In multi-sampling, the interpolated values can be anywhere within the pixel, including the center, any of the samples, or the centroid. (See example in Figure 1.6.4.)

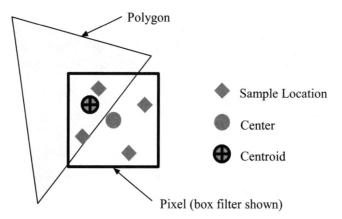

FIGURE 1.6.4   *Varying interpolation locations (example with four samples).*

A fragment shader may read from varying variables and the value read will be the interpolated value, as a function of this fragment's position within the primitive. Note that varying parameters are read-only for the fragment shader. The type of varying variables of the same name must match in both vertex and fragment shaders; otherwise the linking of the program object will not be successful.

Example:

```
varying vec3 normal;
```

Note that the `varying` qualifier can be used only with data types `float`, `vec2`, `vec3`, `vec4`, `mat2`, `mat3`, and `mat4`, or arrays of these. No other data types are allowed for varying variables.

The OpenGL fixed functionality pipeline will compute values for the built-in varying variables if no vertex shader is active, as is necessary for the pixel shader. If no fragment shader is active, the vertex shader is responsible for computing and writing necessary varying variables values' for OpenGL's fixed functionality fragment pipeline.

Note that varying variables must be declared in the global scope before their first use. `in out inout` qualifies function parameters as input, output, or both.

Operators and Expressions

Now let's look at how we extend operators, expressions, and functions and flow control for a hardware-centric small vector language. There are several differences from C/C++. Most importantly, there are no casts supported in OpenGL Shading Language. That means that there aren't any implicit or explicit casts, only explicit constructors.

Three vector sets of swizzles and masks are added:

```
.x  .y  .z  .w
.r  .g  .b  .a
.s  .t  .p  .q
```

One can also access each component of a vector with array syntax:

```
[0] [1] [2] [3]
```

Arithmetic operations are vectorized, and generally operate per component. Exception: vector*matrix, matrix*vector, and matrix*matrix perform the linear algebraic multiply.

All bitwise operations are reserved. OpenGL Shading Language is a float-centric language, and there are integers, but bit operators are reserved. In this way, integers in the language can be implemented as floating point numbers.

Functions and Flow Control

Function names can be overloaded. Because there is no casting (implicit or explict), and only explicit constructors, the overloaded function is located by exact matching rules. User-defined functions match before built-in functions.

Note that in OpenGL Shading Language flow control is scalar only. `if`, `for`, `while`, and `do` take scalar conditional expressions. This means that the flow control for a `for` loop would not be able to loop the x component of the counter 5 times, the y component of the counter 17 times (independently of the x component), and so on. This model is different from the DirectX HLSL.

In addition to basic extensions to the programming language, we also extend the language to embed it into the OpenGL pipeline. We do this by providing built-in and user-defined variables.

Built-In Variables

Because the vertex processor and fragment processor subsume a small part of fixed function, shaders can interface with the fixed functionality of OpenGL through built-in variables available to each type of shaders. Some built-in variables are only available in the vertex shader language and some are available only in the pixel shader language.

Vertex Shader Special Variables

These built-in variables are available in the vertex shader language:

```
vec4  gl_Position;          // must be written
vec4  gl_ClipPosition;      // may be written
float gl_PointSize;         // may be written
```

The variable `gl_Position` is dedicated for writing the homogenous vertex position. All vertex shader executions must write a value into this variable. This value will be used by primitive assembly, clipping, culling, and other fixed function operations that operate on primitives after vertex processing has occurred.

Optional vertex shader built-in output variables are `gl_ClipPosition` and `gl_PointSize`. The second variable is intended for a vertex shader to output the size of the point being rasterized, measured in pixels. The first, `gl_ClipPosition`, is intended to write the coordinate to be used with the user clipping planes. The user must ensure the clip vertex and user clip planes are defined the same coordinate space.

OpenGL provides a list of built-in vertex attributes that can be used to access vertex data provided via the OpenGL vertex API:

```
attribute vec4 gl_Color;            // per-vertex color
attribute vec4 gl_SecondaryColor;   // per-vertex
attribute vec3 gl_Normal;           // vertex normal
attribute vec4 gl_Vertex;           // vertex position
attribute vec4 gl_MultiTexCoord0;   // vertex texture
                                    //       coords
attribute vec4 gl_MultiTexCoord1;   // 0..7
attribute vec4 gl_MultiTexCoord2;
attribute vec4 gl_MultiTexCoord3;
attribute vec4 gl_MultiTexCoord4;
attribute vec4 gl_MultiTexCoord5;
attribute vec4 gl_MultiTexCoord6;
attribute vec4 gl_MultiTexCoord7;
attribute float gl_FogCoord;        // Per vertex fog
```

Fragment Shader Special Variables

These built-in fragment output variables are available in the fragment language:

```
bool  gl_FrontFacing;      // may be read
vec4  gl_FragCoord;        // may be read
vec4  gl_FragColor;        // may be read/written
vec4  gl_FragData[n];      // may be read/written
float gl_FragDepth;        // may be read/written
```

Fragment shaders can interface with the back end of the OpenGL pipeline by either outputting values to gl_FragColor and gl_FragDepth or by executing the dis-card command which signifies to stop processing a given fragment. The last value written to these variables will be used in the subsequent fixed function pipeline. Writing to gl_FragColor variable provides the fragment color for all subsequent operations. Writing to gl_FragDepth specifies the depth value for the fragment being processed. The fixed function pipeline computes depth value, which can be accessed by reading gl_FragDepth.z and can be used by subsequent operations. Note that if a shader statically writes a value into this variable, it is responsible for always writing it.

OpenGL provides a list of built-in varying attributes that can be used to access interpolated values from the fragment shader:

```
varying   vec4  gl_FrontColor;      // vertex
varying   vec4  gl_BackColor;       // vertex
varying   vec4  gl_FrontSecColor;   // vertex
varying   vec4  gl_BackSecColor;    // vertex
varying   vec4  gl_Color;           // fragment
varying   vec4  gl_SecondaryColor;  // fragment
varying   vec4  gl_TexCoord[];      // both
varying   float gl_FogFragCoord;    // both
```

User-Defined Attribute and Varying Variables

In addition to or instead of using built-in attribute and varying variables, a shader writer may choose to define its own attribute and varying variables (as described in an earlier RenderMonkey example). For example:

```
attribute vec3  myTangent;
attribute vec3  myBinormal;
varying   vec3  myNormalPrime;
varying   vec3  myTangentPrime;
varying   vec3  myBinormalPrime;
```

Built-In Uniform Variables

OpenGL Shading Language provides a set of convenient variables for querying all of the current rendering state during the program execution from within a shader. See [Kessenich03] for a complete list. For example:

```
uniform    mat4    gl_ModelViewProjectionMatrix;
uniform    mat4    gl_ModelViewMatrixInverseTranspose;
```

Built-In Functions

OpenGL Shading Language provides a list of convenient built-in functions (see Table 1.6.1) which, with rare exceptions, are overloaded and generalized for vectors. See [Kessenich03] for complete detailed descriptions of each available function. Note that they return a genType which may be one of float, vec2, vec3, or vec4. Some of these functions provide access to hardware functions.

Table 1.6.1   Built-In Functions of OpenGL Shading Language

Angles and trigonometry:

radians	sin	asin
degrees	cos	acos
	tan	atan

Exponential:

pow	log2	inversesqrt
exp2	sqrt	

Common:

abs	mod	clamp
sign	mod	clamp
floor	min	fract
ceil	max	

Interpolations:

mix	step	smoothstep
mix		

Geometric:

length	dot	faceforward
distance	cross	reflect
	normalize	refract

Vector relational:

lessThan	greaterThanEqual	any
lessThanEqual	equal	all
greaterThan	notEqual	

Texture:

texture1D	texture1DProj	texture1DProj
texture2D	texture2DProj	texture2DProj
texture3D	texture3DProj	texture2DRect
textureCube	textureCubeProj	texture2DRectProjEXT
		texture2DRectProj

Shadow:

shadow2D	shadow2DProj	shadow2DRectProj
shadow1DProj	shadow2DRect	

Noise:

noise1	noise3	noise4
noise2		

Vertex-only:

ftransform

Fragment-only:

dFdx	dFdy	fwidth

Before we go further, let's briefly discuss a couple of the vertex-only and fragment-only functions. First, `ftransform(void)` provides a function that transforms a vertex in a manner that is invariant with fixed function. This function is quite useful with multipass algorithms.

The fragment-only functions `dFdx`, `dFdy`, and `fwidth` provide approximate derivatives of the neighborhood around the fragment being shaded. This is similar to, but different from, equivalent RenderMan functions. The micro-polygons shaded by RenderMan are tiny bicubic patches. In OpenGL, they are planar patches. RenderMan shades along the u-v directions of the bicubic patches. OpenGL rasterizes along X-Y directions of the screen. Since the neighborhood in OpenGL is a planar patch, the second derivatives in OpenGL may be undefined.

The algorithms to estimate the derivatives are allowed to assume they are estimating a derivative of a piece-wise continuous function. So beware of `dFdx`, `dFdy`, and `fwidth` inside of varying conditionals. Varying conditionals can introduce discontinuities. (And for that matter, take care with texture functions inside of conditionals, since they too require derivatives to calculate lambda in trilinear mipmapping.) The values returned by `dFdx`, `dFdy`, and `fwidth`, or the mipmap levels selected for filtering in a texture function, are undefined in such a case (see Figure 1.6.5).

So, we've looked at how C/C++ was subsetted and extended for the OpenGL Shading Language. The language was designed to be easy to use, although it assumes familiarity with OpenGL and perhaps even with `ARB_vertex_program` and `ARB_fragment_program`. Some familiarity with RenderMan may be useful as well.

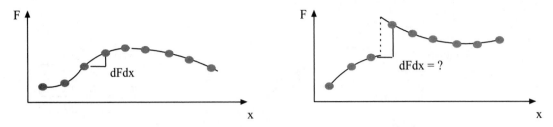

FIGURE 1.6.5   *dFdx of continuous (left) and discontinuous (right) functions.*

But even though the language is easy to use, let's take a look at a few common "gotchas."

OpenGL Shading Language "Gotchas"

First, we'll start with some common errors that are hard to spot initially. Shader writers often bring expectations from either C/C++ or other shading environments to OpenGL Shading Language. Some early beta implementations of the Shading Language were not as pedantic about reporting these errors.

No Casts

Remember that in OpenGL Shading Language there are no casts, implicit or explicit, in the shading language. Use a constructor or a swizzle instead.

```
float Function( vec4  p ) // C assumptions
{
   float f;
   f = (float)p;          // WRONG no casts
   f = float( p );        // OK constructor
   f = p.x;               // OK swizzle
   return f;
}
vec4  Function( vec4  p ) // C or RenderMan assumptions
{
   vec4  f;
   f = 2 * p;             // WRONG no implicit casts
                          // 2 is an int
   f = 2.0 * p;           // OK float * vec4
   f = float( 2 ) * p;    // OK float * vec4
   return f;
}
```

No vec4 Centricism

With some "assembly language" extensions, the abstract instruction set architecture was vec4-centric, assuming all implementations would be a SIMD vec4 processor.

The OpenGL Shading Language makes no such assumptions. Each individual implementation can select the set of rules to follow: it can be implemented on a pure scalar machine, or on a SIMD processor capable of co-issuing multiple instructions, or even a MIMD array.

```
vec4  Function( float p ) // ARB_*_program assumptions

{
    vec4 f;
    f = p.xxxx;      // WRONG invalid swizzle, p is a float
    f = p.x;         // WRONG lvalue - rvalue mismatch
    f = vec4( p.x ); // OK explicit constructor
    return f;
}
```

Must Declare before First Use

The OpenGL Shading Language allows C++ style declare before first use, rather than the C style declare before executable instruction. However, because of the vector extensions and masks, what might "look" like a declare before use is actually a declare after use. Examples should help clarify:

```
vec4  Function( vec3  p ) // Shading Language assumptions
{
    vec4  f.a = 1.0;       // Wrong declared after use
    f.rgb = p;
    vec4  g[3] = 1.0;      // Wrong declared after use
    g.rgb = p;
    vec4  h;               // OK declared before use
    h.rgb = p;
    h.a = 1.0;

    vec4  i = vec4( p, 1 );// OK declared before use
    return f;
}
```

No Vector Scalar Assignment

The type of the l-value and r-value must match with OpenGL Shading Language. So you cannot, unlike some other shading languages, assign a scalar to a vector. However, you can accumulate a scalar into a vector, since the vec4 * float is overloaded to each component of the vec4 by a float, resulting in a vec4.

```
vec4  Function( vec4  p ) // HLSL assumptions
                          // ARB_*_program assumptions
{
    vec4 f = 0.0;         // WRONG lvalue rvalue mismatch
    f = vec4( 0.0 );      // OK constructor
    f += p.x;             // OK vec4 = vec4+float;
    return f;
}
```

Transpose (and Inverse) of Built-In Matrices

The only derived matrix state available in the first versions of OpenGL Shading Language were the gl_NormalMatrix and gl_NormalScale. After many complaints from many developers porting ARB_*_program to OpenGL Shading Language, the current version of the OpenGL Shading Language includes transpose, inverse, and inverse-transpose built-in uniforms as well. However, note that using the built-in transpose or transposing the multiple will almost certainly not be invariant, and therefore must be used with caution.

```
vec4  Function( vec4  p ) // ARB_*_program
                          // assumptions
{
   vec4 f;
   f = gl_ModelViewMatrix.transpose * p; // WRONG
   f = gl_ModelViewMatrixTranspose  * p; // NEW
   f = p * gl_ModelViewMatrix;           // OK
   f = gl_ModelViewMatrixTranspose  * p  // f != vec4(0)
       - p * gl_ModelViewMatrix;         // NOT INVARIANT
   return f;
}
```

Extending the Shading Language

How will the shading language be extended? After frank and open discussions, extensions to the shading language will need to be enabled within the shader. Use of an extension without an enable will result in an error. Extension built-in functions will be decorated with a Vendor, EXT, or ARB suffix. For example:

```
#extension GL_EXT_cool_extension : enable // or require
                                          // or warn
                                          // or disable
#ifndef GL_EXT_cool_extension
#error "GL_EXT_cool_extension required"
#endif
vec4  Function( vec4  p )
{
   vec4 color;
   color = coolFunctionEXT( p );
   color.rgb *= color.a;
   return color;
}
```

OpenGL Shading Language Performance Hints and Kinks

Several implementations of the OpenGL Shading Language and related extensions are available today. Some general advice is already available for performance hints and kinks.

Physical Limits

We'll start with the most obvious. The OpenGL Shading Language virtualizes the number of temporary variables a shader may consume and the number of instructions a shader may execute. Other resources such as gl_MaxVaryingFloats have hard limits. This is no different from core OpenGL. The number of texture units is fixed (GL_MAX_TEXTURE_UNITS) but the number of texture objects that can be created and the resources they consume is virtual. Obviously, exceeding the physical texture resources of an implementation could cause texture thrashing, an unpleasant performance wall to hit. All of this is true with OpenGL Shading Language. These are physical processors with physical memory for temporaries and instructions. Exceeding those physical resources will have consequences. But the good news is: these physical resources are currently growing at remarkable rates.

Early OpenGL Shading Language Compilers

A rich shading language has been developed where shader writers can efficiently express their algorithms with float, vec2, vec3, and vec4 types. The reader should take advantage of them and write vector-efficient code. It's perfectly acceptable to write scalar code to get something working. However, remember that current hardware performs more efficiently on vector quantities—look for vectorizing opportunities and use them!

For example:

```
float Function( vec4  p ) // VECTORIZE
{
    float f;
    f = p.x*px+p.y*p.y+p.z*p.z+p.w*pw;  // scalar!
    f = dot ( p ,p );                   // vector! More efficient
    return f;
}
```

Scalarize Early, Don't Procrastinate

Just because there are computing resources available, one shouldn't feel compelled to use them. Even early implementations of OpenGL Shading Language Compilers are quite good at optimizing *and* rescheduling resources. Simple examples:

```
float Function( vec4  p ) // THIS NEEDS TO BE SCALARIZED
{
    vec4 v;
    float f;
    v = texture2D( baseTexure, p.st ) * 2.0 - 1.0;
    v *= noise4( p * vec4( 1.0, 1.0, 0.0, 0.0) );
    f = float( v );
    return f;
```

```
      }
      float Function( vec2 p ) // THIS HAS BEEN SCALARIZED
      {
         float f;
         f = texture2D( baseTexure, p ).x * 2.0 - 1.0;
         f *= noise1( p );
         return f;
      }
```

Read the Release Notes

There is good information in release notes. For example: one early implementation fails to compile any shader with any built-in noise function. One early implementation compiles a shader with a built-in noise function, but always returns 0.0—not very noisy noise. Another implementation faithfully executes noise—but slowly, *very* slowly. Two are non-conformant, one is conformant. But do we want any of the above? Or should a user-defined function be provided overriding the built-in noise function for now?

GLSL Shader Development in RenderMonkey

Real-time high-performance shaders are at the heart of all new visual effects and they will continue to be the foundation of the amazing graphical experience for the future. Although real-time shaders have been available for a few years, their adoption into existing projects has been slow due to a lack of convenient tools. The RenderMonkey IDE has been created to fill the need for shader content creation in a coherent environment—flexible and powerful for programmers, yet familiar and intuitive for artists. With the introduction of the DirectX and OpenGL high-level shading languages, the complexity of real-time shaders has increased. With the rapid improvement in shading capabilities of current graphics hardware, the amount of shader content necessary for real-time graphics projects has exploded, fueling the need for a powerful real-time shader IDE. The RenderMonkey environment not only allows easy shader prototyping and development, but also provides a mechanism for managing the shaders and all of the associated visual resources in a single environment.

RenderMonkey has been designed with the needs of programmers and artists in mind, allowing both to collaborate on shader effects. Separate interfaces exist in RenderMonkey for setting up familiar controls for technical shader developers as well as for purely visual modification by non-technical artists. RenderMonkey allows anyone interested in creating shaders to bypass the tedious setup steps and dive straight into the shader creation process. The program allows visualization of a visual effect's inputs and assets in a tree structure as well as the visualization of the body of the shader itself. Users can view the gradual build up of an effect by examining individual rendering passes in the application's rendering windows or by dynamically examining the contents of all renderable textures. RenderMonkey enables quick debugging of shaders via interactive output of intermediate results computed by the shader. We have found this to be particularly useful in the environments where visualizing an intermediate result is fundamental to understanding. RenderMonkey has been chosen by several universities to teach shader technology in their graphics curriculum.

The application includes a variety of convenient features enabling programmers control over their development environment (see Figure 1.6.6 for an image of the user interface). To enable development of fast, efficient shaders, RenderMonkey provides developers with optimization hints for high-level shader development for better analysis of shader performance in real time. Both artists and programmers can use intuitive GUI widgets for interactively editing visual parameters for shaders—to modify a color or the dissipation parameter for fluid flow and see the results instantly in the rendering window.

FIGURE 1.6.6   *RenderMonkey user interface displaying a glass refraction effect.*

Integrating into Existing Production Pipelines

Another key feature of RenderMonkey is its flexible, extensible framework that supports easy integration of custom components. RenderMonkey can be easily customized and integrated into any developer's regular workflow by using its standard SDK for component development. The application ships with a set of plug-in examples and a plug-in wizard, enabling easy creation of custom components and thus allowing fast integration into an existing production workflow. The SDK gives developers full access to the entire runtime database of shader data. The SDK is written in standard C++ with all of the necessary components for plug-in development. It also provides libraries for user interface widget creation to allow developers to maintain the look and feel of the application without investing significant effort into UI development. A variety of game companies are integrating RenderMonkey into their shader production pipelines for the upcoming projects.

RenderMonkey is designed to make adoption of shader technology easier for both developers and artists, providing easy integration into existing workflows and the ability to customize desired components to suit the needs for any production. The interactivity of the program provides the advantage of reducing time for shader content development, enabling quicker iteration on each design, and thus improving the final look of the product for any production.

ON THE CD

In the *ShaderX²* article "Shader Development Using RenderMonkey" [Tatarchuk03] we have introduced the shader development process for DirectX shaders. In this article we demonstrate how to create GLSL-based effects successfully using this powerful IDE. The application can be found on the CD-ROM or downloaded from *www.rendermonkey.net*. The installer for the program comes with an excellent set of detailed documentation describing the application user interface in great depth. This article assumes the reader's familiarity with the main interface of RenderMonkey and focuses on how GLSL is integrated into the program.

GLSL Integration in RenderMonkey

RenderMonkey supports OpenGL Shading Language by allowing the user to create effects using that API. Note that DirectX and OpenGL effects are created separately and cannot intermix. RenderMonkey also doesn't support `ARB_fragment_program` and `ARB_vertex_program` for shader creation using OpenGL API. Each OpenGL effect in RenderMonkey can have multiple draw calls (passes) where each may contain a pair of vertex or fragment shader objects (created and maintained individually). Note that if either of these shader objects is missing, RenderMonkey will notify the user; however, it will revert to fixed function pipeline functionality for rendering. At present time, only a pair of shaders (a vertex and a fragment shader each) is assembled into a single program object used to render each draw pass. However, the settings of OpenGL shader/program objects are maintained for the shader objects in RenderMonkey—a pair of vertex and fragment shader objects that is used to render a particular draw call shares a name space. RenderMonkey allows draw calls to inherit common shaders between passes and even provides a special location to store common shaders—a default effect. If it cannot find an inherited shader, it will revert to fixed function pipeline.

In order to define which vertex attributes for the vertex data, users need to create stream mapping nodes in their effects and create a pair of stream map and geometry object references in each draw call. This notifies RenderMonkey which of the vertex attributes it needs to set up and send by using the OpenGL vertex API. If Render-Monkey does not find a particular data channel in the selected geometry object for a draw call, it will notify the user about the lack of data.

In order to define interpolated data, the user should simply follow the OpenGL Shading Language convention by declaring *varying* parameters in both vertex and fragment shaders.

To set up shader parameters such as uniforms and samplers, the user must first create objects whose values will be mapped to individual variables. In case of uniforms, RenderMonkey provides a variety of native data types, such as `float`, `vec4`, `bool`, `int`, `mat4`, etc. in full support of the OpenGL basic data types for use in shaders. Once a variable node of desired type is created, RenderMonkey will allow users to modify its value by providing a convenient UI widget associated with variable data type. The shader writer can then simply drop a variable onto the shader node to create a declaration for that uniform parameter and use it in their shader. RenderMonkey will take care of setting up the uniform location and value automatically for each active uniform used in the shader and created in the effect database as a variable node.

To set up samplers, a user has to first create texture variable nodes—these are used to store texture data directly from associated file or procedurally created texture. Then in order to setup a texture stage, the developer can create a RenderMonkey texture object in the draw call that will use it. Note that indexing for texture stages is implicit in RenderMonkey by the order of texture objects in the pass tree. The users can drag and drop texture object nodes to modify texture stage indices for each object. Each texture object must reference a valid texture variable, which can include a renderable texture object. The user can then simply drag and drop a texture object onto a fragment shader node to create a declaration for that sampler variable and go on using it in their shaders.

To make shader development more convenient, RenderMonkey will take care of all grunt work associated with texture and model loading and setting up of vertex attributes to allow shader writers to focus solely on their shaders. RenderMonkey will automatically calculate tangent space basis vectors (tangent and binormal) for each vertex for each model loaded into a RenderMonkey geometry object. In order to use that data as a vertex attribute, one just has to add this declaration to their shaders:

```
attribute vec3 rm_Tangent;
attribute vec3 rm_Binormal;
```

RenderMonkey will automatically create attribute data for tangent and binormal vertex data and bind it correctly to the attribute location once it is used in a shader.

Most of the GLSL built-in constructs are available to shader writers in Render-Monkey (such as `glModelViewProjectionMatrix`, `glNormal`, `glVertex`, etc.). However, there is a part of the OpenGL rendering state that at present time cannot be explicitly modified by users in the RenderMonkey environment, such as lighting and material parameters, texture matrices, and so on. This will be added in future versions of the application.

Aside from the standard built-in state provided by OpenGL, RenderMonkey provides a variety of application-specific built-in states for common quantities frequently used in shaders. This is provided by *predefined* variables, which can be created through the *Add Variable* menu, and treated as any variables in RenderMonkey with the exception that their values cannot be modified directly by the user. RenderMonkey provides shader writers the access to various time-related counters, frame rate data, viewport dimensions and inverse of those, randomly calculated parameters, mouse button states and coordinates, and a set of utility matrices among many predefined values (see Figure 1.6.7).

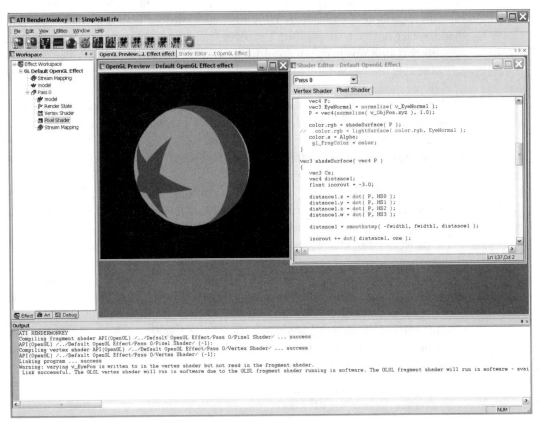

FIGURE 1.6.7   *A classic RenderMan shader implemented in GLSL in RenderMonkey development environment.*

Conclusion

We hope that this article showed the reader the power and flexibility of the programmable pipeline in OpenGL using the shading language and the new OpenGL shader API. The chapter also described an innovative, intuitive shader development environment—the RenderMonkey IDE—created to improve shader prototyping and development for both artists and developers.

Acknowledgments

The authors would like to thank Ben Mistal and Toshiaki Tsuji for their steadfast creative hard work on the RenderMonkey IDE as well as the 3D Application Research Group for various ideas and general inspiration in creation of this product—without the wonderful environment that this group provides it simply would not be possible.

References

[Akeley93] comp.graphics.opengl posting, available online at *http://groups.google.com/ groups?selm=29h8kt$af6@fido.asd.sgi.com*, October 13, 1993.

[Akeley01] Kurt Akeley and Pat Hanrahan, "*Real-Time Graphics Architectures Fall 2001,*" available online at: *http://graphics.stanford.edu/courses/cs448a-01-fall/ lectures/lecture15/opengl.2up.pdf,* 2001.

[ARB03] OpenGL Architecture Review Board, ARB_Shader_Objects Extension Specification, OpenGL Extension Registry: *http://oss.sgi.com/projects/ogl-sample/ registry.*

[Cook84] Robert L. Cook, "Shade Trees," *Computer Graphics,* Vol. 18, no. 3 (SIGGRAPH 1984): pp. 223–231.

[Dennis93] comp.graphics.opengl posting, available online at: *http://groups.google. com/groups?selm=1993Aug19.151033.22061@peavax.mlo.dec.com,* August 19, 1993.

[Hanrahan90] Pat Hanrahan and Jim Lawson, "A Language for Shading and Lighting Calculations," *Computer Graphics,* Vol. 24, no. 4 1990 (SIGGRAPH 1990): pp. 289–298.

[Kessenich03] John Kessenich, Dave Baldwin, Randi Rost, "The OpenGL Shading Language Version 1.051", available online at:*http://www.opengl.org/documentation/ oglsl/ShaderSpecV1.051.pdf ,* February 28, 2003.

[Leech98] Jon Leech, OpenGL Extensions and Restrictions for PixelFlow, *UNC CS Technical report TR98-019,* available online at: *http://www.csee.umbc.edu/ ~olano/s2000c27/,* April 20, 1998.

[Myer86] T. H. Myer and I.E. Sutherland, "On the Design of Display Processors," *Communications of the ACM,* Vol. 11 no. 6, June, 1968.

[Olano98] Marc Olano, "A Shadling Langauge on Graphics Hardware: The PixelFlow Shading System," *Computer Graphics,* Vol. 32, no. 3 1998 (SIGGRAPH 1998): pp. 159–168.

[Perlin85] Ken Perlin, "An Image Synthesizer," *Computer Graphics,* Vol. 19, no. 3 (SIGGRAPH 1985): pp. 287–296.

[Segal92] *The OpenGL Graphics System: A Specification,* (V1.0) June 30, 1992.

[Segal94] Mark Segal and Kurt Akeley, "*The Design of the OpenGL Graphics Interface,*" 1994.

[SGI91] "*Silicon Graphics Opens IRIS Graphics Library for General Licensing,*" available online at: *http://groups.google.com/groups?selm=9109182229.AA06185@forest.asd.sgi.com*, September 17, 1991.

[Tatarchuk03] Natalya Tatarchuk, "*Shader Development Using RenderMonkey*™, *ShaderX²: Introductions & Tutorials with DirectX 9,*" pp. 279–338, Wordware, 2003.

[Trevett01] Neil Trevett, "*OpenGL BOF - Shading Language,*" August 15, 2001.

RENDERING TECHNIQUES

Introduction

Nicolas Thibieroz

Since the introduction of the programmable vertex and pixel pipelines in 3D graphic hardware, a huge number of visual effects have been implemented and used in real-time rendering applications like games. While some of these effects are based on existing shaders already used in the Computer Graphics Imaging industry, the availability and affordability of shader-enabled 3D graphic hardware gave the development community—professionals and enthusiasts alike—the complete flexibility and creativity they needed to invent new visual effects through the writing of shader-assisted rendering techniques. This section comprises a range of articles describing various rendering techniques utilizing either the DirectX or OpenGL shader models.

An advanced bump mapping technique known as parallax bump mapping has recently seen a resurgence on a number of graphic-oriented forums; as a result, games are already adding this technique to their rendering paths. Terry Welsh's "Parallax Mapping" article explains the theory behind parallax mapping and why it is best used in conjunction with bump mapping to achieve outstanding visual results.

Dean Calver's "Deferred Lighting on PS 3.0 with High-Dynamic Range," takes advantage of the pixel shader 3.0 model to perform high-dynamic range tone mapping in a deferred lighting context—although the main algorithm described in his article can also be applied to conventional rendering.

"Reflections from Bumpy Surfaces," by Henning Mortveit offers a solution to the delicate issue of obtaining accurate reflections from bump-mapped textures when the environment to reflect is close to the reflector.

Particle effects form an important part of any game: explosions, projectiles, flow, etc. are often modelled with particles. As graphic hardware becomes more powerful the number of particles that can be handled concurrently increases, allowing more realistic effects to be implemented. Lutz Latta's "Massively Parallel Particle Systems on the GPU" presents a GPU-based implementation of a particle system capable of handling a huge amount of particles without requiring extensive resources from the CPU.

Natalya Tatarchuk and Zoe Brawley's "Parallax Occlusion Mapping: Self-Shadowing, Perspective-Correct Bump Mapping Using Reverse Height Map Tracing" pushes the concept of parallax bump mapping further by using a back-tracing operation into a height map to determine accurate parallax and self-shadowing effects for the pixels to render. The visual results are outstanding.

One of the most common reasons for switching render states between each geometry submission is changing the texture surface. By combining multiple textures into one large texture "atlas" Matthias Wloka's "Improved Batching via Texture Atlases" teaches the reader how to optimize the rendering of multiple objects and offers solutions to the issues sometimes associated with this technique.

O'dell Hicks describes a pair of efficient vertex and pixel shaders for simulating thermal imaging in his article "A Simulation of Thermal Imaging."

"Real-Time Texture-Space Skin Rendering" by David Gosselin, Pedro V. Sander, and Jason L. Mitchell describes how a real-time render-to-texture operation can be used to render realistic and self-shadowed skin materials onto a character's face. In order to speed up the technique a number of optimizations are also discussed.

Ron Barbosa's "Dot3 Cel Shading" exploits the geometrical properties of view and normal vectors to present a high-quality method for rendering cel-shaded scenes.

Markus Neubel's "Hardware Accelerated Charcoal Rendering" presents an engine that uses shaders to render a model with a grainy, hand-drawn feel.

Aliasing artifacts are a common problem in real-time computer graphics. Temporal aliasing will occur whenever the frame rate cannot keep up with the speed at which high-frequency details evolve, causing undesirable visual artifacts in the process. Shawn Hargreaves' "Detail Texture Motion Blur" implements various blur techniques to represent fast anti-aliased movements in flat geometry.

"Animation and Display of Water," by Stefano Lanza is an article about modelling the physics of water waves and rendering realistic-looking water effects at interactive frame rates.

Chris Oat describes a technique to simulate the various depths of multi-layer surfaces in his article "Rendering Semitransparent Layered Media."

Thorsten Scheuermann's "Hair Rendering and Shading" presents a polygon-based, performance-optimized method to model realistic-looking hair for real-time character rendering.

"Reduction of Lighting Calculations using Spherical Harmonics," by Vlad Stamate explains the basics behind Spherical Harmonics, and how they can be used to model a lighting environment in game scenes.

2.1

Parallax Mapping

Terry Welsh

Introduction

Parallax is exhibited when areas of a surface appear to move relative to one another as the view position changes. This can be observed on any surface that is not flat, such as tree bark, wavy beach sand, or rock walls. Parallax can be simulated well in computer graphics by constructing a complete geometric model of a surface, but it can be computationally expensive to draw all the necessary polygons. The method presented here requires no extra polygons and approximates surface parallax using surface height data. Parallax Mapping [Kaneko01] is a method for approximating the correct appearance of uneven surfaces by modifying the texture coordinate for each pixel.

Figure 2.1.1 shows a textured polygon that is accurately lit with Bump Mapping [Blinn78]. Because the rock wall being simulated has many hills and valleys, the polygon looks unnaturally flat. Using Parallax Mapping, the rendering in Figure 2.1.2 more accurately simulates the irregular shape of the rock wall.

FIGURE 2.1.1 *A surface rendered with Bump Mapping.*

FIGURE 2.1.2   *A surface rendered with Bump Mapping and Parallax Mapping.*

Description

Concept

Compare a real surface and a texture-mapped polygon that simulates that surface as in Figure 2.1.3. If the surface has variations in height, it will exhibit parallax effects. However, when simulated by a simple flat polygon, those parallax effects disappear. Point A on the real surface corresponds to texel T_A on the polygon, and point B corresponds to texel T_B.

Imagine viewing a point on the surface from a position indicated by the eye vector in Figure 2.1.3. With ordinary texture mapping, the eye would perceive point A because the eye vector intersects texel T_A. However, the eye vector also intersects point B on the real surface. Point B is what would be seen if observing the actual surface instead of a texture-mapped polygon. In order to see point B, an offset must be added to T_A to produce T_B. If this process is performed for every pixel in the polygon, a parallax effect is achieved.

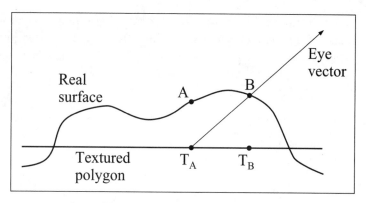

FIGURE 2.1.3   *The observed texel does not correspond to the point on the real surface that should be seen.*

Required Information

A surface is usually described with at least a diffuse color map, and sometimes other maps, such as normal maps and gloss maps for lighting effects. In order to compute a texture coordinate offset at each pixel, information about the surface's height values is required. This information is stored in an additional texture map called a height map.

A vector pointing to the eye is also required at each pixel. Since the final value being computed is a modified texture coordinate, the calculation will be performed in tangent space. The eye vector can easily be computed in world space, but it will need to be translated into tangent space. Therefore, a world to tangent space transformation matrix is required at each vertex. With this information, the tangent space eye vector is computed at each vertex, and the tangent space eye vector for each pixel is found by interpolation across the polygon.

The Math

In the case of ordinary texture mapping, each vertex on the textured polygon has a texture coordinate associated with it. When the polygon is rendered, the vertices' texture coordinates are interpolated across the polygon to give a specific texture coordinate at each pixel. This coordinate is used to index the polygon's texture maps. To perform Parallax Mapping, this texture coordinate is used to index a value in the height map and then modified before being used to index the remaining texture maps.

A texture coordinate offset is found, as in Figure 2.1.4, by tracing a ray from point A (at the height of the real surface) parallel to the polygon until it intersects the eye vector. The point where the ray intersects the eye vector does not necessarily lie on the real surface. This is why Parallax Mapping is only an approximation and not an exact simulation of parallax. Finding an exact offset—or just achieving a better approximation—requires a more complicated solution, perhaps involving multiple height samples and surface curvature data.

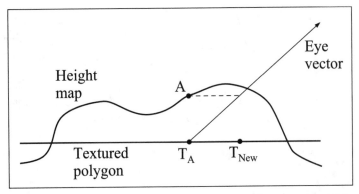

FIGURE 2.1.4   *A ray is traced from point A to the eye vector. This ray is the texture coordinate offset.*

To find this offset, the tangent space eye vector must first be normalized. Since this vector is in tangent space, it has components *x* and *y*, which lie in the plane of the surface, and a *z* component, which is perpendicular to the surface. These are represented in Equation 2.1.2 as $V_{\{x,y\}}$ and $V_{\{z\}}$, respectively.

Next, the values from the height map must be scaled and biased. A height value from a height map lies in the range {0.0, 1.0}, but it needs to be remapped to a range more appropriate to the surface being simulated as in Equation 2.1.1. For example, a brick wall texture might cover a 2 × 2 meter area. Also imagine the surface of the bricks and the recessed grout give the surface a thickness of 0.02m. The correct scale factor for this material would be 0.02 / 2 = 0.01. A bias of 0.0 would give the appearance that the grout lies in the plane of the polygon, while a bias of −0.01 would give the appearance that the surface of the bricks lies in the plane of the polygon and the grout sinks below it. A height *h* is modified by a scale *s* and bias *b* to produce a remapped height h_{sb}.

$$h_{sb} = (h \cdot s) + b \qquad (2.1.1)$$

Finally, the modified texture coordinate, T_{New} from Figure 2.1.4, can be calculated as:

$$\vec{T}_{New} = \vec{T}_A + \frac{\vec{V}_{\{x,y\}} \cdot h_{sb}}{V_{\{z\}}} \qquad (2.1.2)$$

Equation 2.1.2 is sensible, but it has problems artistically. As the angle between the eye vector and the polygon approaches zero, $V_{\{z\}}$ also approaches zero. This creates very large texture coordinate offsets, and the Parallax Mapping approximation falls apart. Visually, textures on the polygon become a splotchy mess.

To avoid this problem, simply drop the $V_{\{z\}}$ term as in Equation 2.1.3. This modification limits the texture coordinate offset so that is can grow no larger than h_{sb}. It causes little difference in the result when the eye vector makes a steep angle to the polygon. And when the angle is shallow, the quality of the original texture is preserved.

$$\vec{T}_{New} = \vec{T}_A + \left(\vec{V}_{\{x,y\}} \cdot h_{sb} \right) \tag{2.1.3}$$

Implementation

Since vector data can be interpolated between connected vertices by graphics hardware, a vertex program is responsible for computing non-normalized tangent space eye vectors. In the language of ARB_vertex_program, these vectors can be calculated with the following code.

```
# input data
PARAM mvit[4] = {state.matrix.modelview.invtrans};
ATTRIB tangent = vertex.texcoord[1];
ATTRIB binormal = vertex.texcoord[2];
ATTRIB normal = vertex.normal;
# vector pointing to eye
SUB eyevec, mvit[3], vertex.position;
# transform eye vector into tangent space (DO NOT NORMALIZE)
DP3 result.texcoord[3].x, eyevec, tangent;
DP3 result.texcoord[3].y, eyevec, binormal;
DP3 result.texcoord[3].z, eyevec, normal;
MOV result.texcoord[3].w, 1.0;
```

The tangent, binormal, and normal attributes represent the coordinate axes of the tangent space surrounding each vertex. The eye vector is stored in texcoord[3], which is a parameter that will be interpolated across the surface so that each pixel drawn will receive a unique eye vector.

The remainder of the computation is performed on a per-pixel basis in a fragment program. Scale and bias values are supplied as local parameters so that they can be specific to the simulated material. Remember, normalize the eye vector in the fragment program, not in the vertex program. Normalizing it in the vertex program will result in an incorrect eye vector, which can be a decent approximation if the polygon is sufficiently small, but it is not a good general solution. The following code fragment uses the language of ARB_fragment_program.

```
PARAM scale_bias = program.local[0];
TEMP height, eyevects, newtexcoord, temp;
# normalize tangent space eye vector
DP3 temp, fragment.texcoord[3], fragment.texcoord[3];
RSQ temp, temp.x;
```

```
MUL eyevects, fragment.texcoord[3], temp;
# calculate offset and new texture coordinate
TEX height, fragment.texcoord[0], texture[2], 2D;
MAD height, height, scale_bias.x, scale_bias.y; # scale and bias
MAD newtexcoord, height, eyevects, fragment.texcoord[0];
```

The variable `newtexcoord` stores the shifted texture coordinate, which is used to index other texture maps.

Analysis

Advantages

The main advantage to Parallax Mapping is that it is computationally inexpensive. There are more complicated image-based techniques for achieving a parallax effect, such as Relief Texture Mapping [Oliveira00] and View Dependent Displacement Mapping [Wang03], but they require a great deal more computation or intermediate steps.

Displacement Mapping [Cook84] will simulate a surface accurately, but it requires many more polygons than Parallax Mapping. Parallax Mapping can often produce adequate results with very simple geometric models.

Disadvantages

Parallax Mapping makes the false assumption that the points A and B in Figure 2.1.3 are the same distance from the polygon. This assumption results in artifacts that are apparent near steep height changes on the surface. A high-frequency height map will make these artifacts apparent across a rendered polygon. It is best to use a low-frequency height map for the parallax effect and to rely on plain texturing, detail mapping, or Bump Mapping to supply the high-frequency details or lighting for a surface.

An extreme case would be when part of a surface becomes vertical in tangent space. This would cause the worst artifacts with Parallax Mapping. Besides, no texture map would contain information for these vertical parts of the surface. A surface like this would need to be simulated by a more complicated image-based solution or by a complete geometric model. Parallax Mapping works best for surfaces with slopes that are less than one.

Parallax Mapping does not simulate self-occlusions. Self-occlusions occur when one part of a surface blocks another part from view. Since Parallax Mapping performs no actual ray intersections with a surface model, occlusions will never look right. This is usually only a problem when using a height map that has steep value changes.

Complex silhouettes should be observed around the edges of objects with surfaces that vary in height. Parallax Mapping does not affect the alpha value of pixels, and it does not deform surfaces as with Displacement Mapping. Polygon edges will always appear perfectly straight with Parallax Mapping, so silhouettes are not simulated.

Demo

ON THE CD The demo on the CD-ROM compares the standard texture mapping, Bump Mapping, Parallax Mapping, and Parallax Mapping combined with Bump Mapping. Several materials are simulated to give the user ideas of situations where Parallax Mapping might be applied. The demo is written in OpenGL. It requires The OpenGL Utility Toolkit (GLUT) dynamic library and the extensions `ARB_multitexture`, `ARB_vertex_program`, and `ARB_fragment_program`.

Conclusion

Parallax Mapping offers a computationally inexpensive solution to simulating many surfaces that are not flat. Surfaces that are simulated with regular texturing and Bump Mapping may have very detailed shading, but they will often still appear flat. Parallax Mapping will produce no shading or lighting effects on its own, and, because it is an approximation, can produce some distracting artifacts. It is best to use Parallax Mapping together with Bump Mapping. The effects enhance one another and Bump Mapping helps to hide the artifacts produced by Parallax Mapping.

References

[Blinn78] Blinn, James F., "Simulation of Wrinkled Surfaces," *Computer Graphics,* Vol. 12 (SIGGRAPH 1978): pp. 286–292.

[Cook84] Cook, Robert, "Shade trees," *Computer Graphics,* Vol. 13, no. 3 (SIGGRAPH 1984): pp. 223–231.

[Oliveira00] Oliveira, M., et al., "Relief Texture Mapping," *Computer Graphics* (SIGGRAPH 2000): pp. 359–368.

2.2

Deferred Lighting on PS 3.0 with High Dynamic Range

Dean Calver

Introduction

Deferred lighting is a technique increasingly being used for real-time rendering. With the new capabilities of PS 3.0 and high-precision blending we can easily move to high-dynamic range. This article also covers high dynamic range tone-mapping for PS 3.0 in detail, using a GPU-efficient method. The technique is independent of the method of creating the buffer that needs to be tone-mapped, and therefore can also be used with conventional rendering techniques.

Overview

The use of geometry buffers (G-Buffers) to store the lighting parameters for post-processing lighting in real-time has been used in PC hardware since the introduction of PS 1.1. Although the fixed point precision and short pixel shaders meant that only the simplest lighting models could be used, the constant cost for lighting was already attractive enough to be used in several games (particularly on the Xbox where the lower-level access to the GPU allowed more functionality to be extracted from the relatively limited hardware). PS 2.0, floating-point render targets, and greater internal pixel shader precision considerably increased the usefulness of the technique but the lack of dynamic branching and the inability to use alpha blending meant there was still some way to go.

The introduction of graphic hardware with PS 3.0 support and blending to float surfaces has opened up new ways of working with deferred lighting, including HDR.

Implementation

This article assumes you have a working PS 2.0 deferred lighting system, as the article is built upon an existing article published on the Internet [Calver02]. Another good article that covers the general implementation of deferred shading and lighting in detail is "Deferred Shading with Multiple Render Targets" [Thibieroz02].

To recap, a deferred lighting system breaks the render pipeline into three major phases:

1. Geometry phase
2. Lighting phase
3. Post-processing phase

The geometry phase deals with filling the G-Buffer with parameters and except for the ability to support multiple light models, is largely the same as before. The lighting phase changes significantly in order to accommodate multiple lighting models and output results into a much higher precision buffer. Finally, the post-processing phase has the responsibility of tone mapping the high dynamic range into a low fixed range capable of being displayed on a monitor.

Multiple Light Models

With the length of PS 3.0 shaders and dynamic branching we can now allow multiple light models in the lights shaders. This dramatically increases the variety of surfaces through the high number of different code paths possible. However there are a number of caveats that make this simple process more involved due to the differences in how a GPU handles dynamic branching.

A GPU is designed to work in parallel and for pixel shaders the basic unit of operation is usually a quad of 2×2 pixels running in lock step with each other. The main reason for this structure is to allow the computation of gradients of any variable in a pixel shader by just taking the difference between the value of its neighbors at any point.

Since any pixel in a 2×2 quad can take different branches, dynamic branching breaks lock stepping and therefore breaks the method used to calculate gradients. As such, any operation that requires gradient calculation cannot work inside a dynamic branch. Not only does this affect obvious gradient instructions like DDX and DDY, but also it affects all texture loads since gradients are used internally for determining which MIP map level to use. Therefore to make texture loads useable inside a dynamic branch this value must be passed explicitly. A new HLSL instruction called tex2Dlod achieves this purpose.

As we generally won't be using MIP maps in light shaders, this limitation does not prove to be much of a difficulty as we can simply pass 0 as the LOD parameter to the function to retrieve data from the top level.

The basic approach consists of storing a light model ID in a channel of the geometry buffer that selects the light model to use for this pixel. Then each light retrieves this value and uses a switch/case statement to execute the desired code for this shader.

Unfortunately PS 3.0 does not support enough functionality to allow fast switch/case statements. So we have to use a series of "if" statements to select the correct light model, which unfortunately means we have to be frugal with the number of different light models supported. Ideally we would use a jump table but this isn't yet possible (if future architecture allows indexed jumps then this should be used). Care should be taken as all compares are floating point and therefore exact equality isn't guaranteed. One possibility is to store the light models IDs exactly in the floating point mantissa; these will then compare exactly, with the only restriction being the limited number of models supported. As float16 has ten bits for the mantissa (giving

1024 IDs) this is unlikely to be a problem in this context. The approach used here is a simple epsilon on compares for simplicity.

```
const float FloatLMEpsilon   = 1e-5f;
const float SpecialLightModel = 1.0f;
const float ExtraLightModel   = 2.0f;

PixelShader( ... )
{
    float lmID = GetLightModelIDFromGBuffer();

    if( lmID < (SpecialLightModel — FloatLMEpsilon) )
    {
        // lmID is between 0 and (1-epsilon)
        // we have to use tex2Dlod in the if statement
        float4 param = tex2Dlod( texture, uv, 0 );
    } else if( lmID < (ExtraLightModel - FloatLMEpsilon) )
    {
        // lmID is between (1-epsilon) and (2-epsilon)
        // we have to use tex2Dlod in the if statement
        float4 param = tex2Dlod( texture2, uv, 0 );
    } else
    {
        // lmID is above  (2-epsilon)
        // we have to use tex2Dlod in the if statement
        float4 param = tex2Dlod( texture3, uv, 0 );
    }
}
```

HDR

High dynamic range rendering pioneered by Debevec [Debevec97] has quickly become the de facto standard for both offline and cutting edge real-time systems. The principle is simple: all rendering should be performed at a high range and only at the end of the graphics pipeline should this be reduced into a range that fits the output gamut. This last stage is known as tone-mapping and usually takes the form of an approximation of the eyes' response to light.

The principal problem with supporting HDR in real-time graphics hardware has been the lack of render targets with enough precision. With the support of float render targets brought in by the PS 2.0 generation of cards (NVIDIA, GeforceFX, and ATI 9500+) it looked like this problem was solved, but quickly another problem emerged: cards of this generation are unable to blend to these high-precision targets, and without alpha blending the only legal option is ping-ponging between render-targets.

 It is possible to set a texture as both an input texture and a render-target at the same time but many graphics cards do not have a way of synchronizing the texture and render-target caches and visual anomalies can result. As such this is defined as an illegal set-up under Direct3D and OpenGL.

Ping-ponging consists of setting two render textures; one as input and one as output, and manually performing the blend inside the shader by reading one texture and writing out the result of the blend to the other. After every alpha blend the input and output are swapped and the process is repeated. While this works, the amount of copying and number of render state changes can cause a considerable impact on performance (the NVIDIA NV40 chip is the first to support full alpha blending to a `float16` buffer, eliminating the expensive ping-pong process completely).

The following code is used to check whether the graphic hardware supports a `D3DFMT_A16B16G16R16F` texture as a render target *and* has support for post pixel shader blending with this format.

The DirectX 9 API call

```
D3D->CheckDeviceFormat( D3DADAPTER_DEFAULT, D3DDEVTYPE_HAL,
                        DisplayFormat,
                        D3DUSAGE_QUERY_POSTPIXELSHADER_BLENDING |
                        D3DUSAGE_RENDERTARGET,
                        D3DRTYPE_TEXTURE,
                        D3DFMT_A16B16G16R16F );
```

will return `D3D_OK` if the card has the necessary support.

If both capabilities are supported we create a `D3DFMT_A16B16G16R16F` render target and let every light accumulate into it using standard additive blending. Using a `float16` buffer allows us to have a large range of lights, from incredible dark spaces (which the tone-mapping will brighten) to lights (like the sun) thousands of times brighter than normal, without worrying about over/under flow.

When the lighting phase has finished, the HDR destination lighting buffer has to be post-processed via tone-mapping.

Tone-Mapping

Tone-mapping is required to work around the low dynamic range nature of the display unit. Normally the human visual system adapts to the high dynamic range in the real world via a method known as visual adaptation [Durand02]. Because the monitor itself is unable to produce high enough dynamic range to trigger this visual adaptation we must do it ourselves before outputting the image to the display unit.

There are a number of separate processes we can simulate to implement tone-mapping, including dark adaptation, light adaptation, and chromatic adaptation. The model we choose to implement here is a simple model of light adaptation. Light adaptation is the fast change that happens when going from a lit environment to a dark one.

The method used here is basically the operator presented in "Photographic Tone Reproduction for Digital Images" [Reinhard02] but missing the dodging and burning feature. This method is easy to implement in real-time but further research in this field might have already been conducted by the time you read this. This technique only models luminance changes so the color of the scene is converted into luminance before use.

The key to this algorithm is to calculate the average luminance of the scene at full dynamic range and then use it and the white point to scale the pixel value. The white point is by default the maximum luminance in the scene.

Calculating $\bar{L}_w$

Equation (2.2.1) calculates the average luminance in world luminance (high dynamic range).

$$\bar{L}_w = \exp\left(\frac{1}{N}\sum_{x,y}\log(\delta + L_w(x,y))\right) \qquad (2.2.1)$$

Where N is the number of pixels, x,y are the 2D coordinates of each pixel, δ is a small constant number and L_w is the luminance function.

This equation doesn't translate easily to GPU operations as it needs to read every pixel in the frame buffer, and even current Pixel Shader 3.0 hardware doesn't allow us to implement this in a single pass. It does however allow us to reduce it to only two passes in many cases. Potentially future Pixel Shader 3.0 hardware will support more instructions which could reduce this even further to a single pass. The single pass version is an easy modification from the version provided here and source is provided in the sample program running on the reference driver.

δ *is a tiny epsilon to stop log(0) being introduced at black pixels.*

In the first pass we create a small destination render target and draw a quad covering the entire render target. At each pixel on the destination surface the pixel shader sums a vast number of luminance values from the sources and stores the result. The second pass then sums this much smaller buffer and runs the final part of the calculation producing a texture containing $\bar{L}_w$.

Pixel Shader 3.0 guarantees 512 actual instructions, but the total number of instructions executed is variable; current hardware allows loops up to 65,535 instructions to be executed in a single shader. The number of instructions we have to execute per pixel read wholly decides how many passes we have to perform.

We drop back to pixel shader assembler for this shader, as this is such an expensive operation that we want total control and an exact count of instructions used.

To get a single log luminance sample we need to execute $logL_w = \log(\delta + L_w(x,y))$, using Equation 2.2.2 to convert RGB to luminance:

$$L = 0.27R + 0.67G + 0.06B \qquad (2.2.2)$$

The pixel shader 3.0 assembler code for the summation with x = i1, y = i2 is then:

```
// v0.xy = start uv co-ordinate for this block        Instruction count
// c0.z = 0
// c1.xyzw = xy = delta uv for each pixel, z = 0, w = 1
// s0 = frame buffer sampler
// c3 = 0.27, 0.67, 0.06, sqrt(delta)
mov r0.xy, v0.xy // set uv to start of this block               1
mov r0.zw, c0.z  // clear accumulator                           1
mov r1.w, c3.w   // set w = sqrt(delta) so r1.w * r1.w = delta  1
mov r2.w, c1.x   // optimise the inner loop                     1

rep i2              // loop across y                            3
  rep i1            // loop across x                            3
      texld r1.xyz, r0, s0  // get the pixel from the framebuffer 1
      dp4 r2.x, r1.xyzw, c3.xyzw  // delta + L(x,y)             1
      log r2.x, r2.x        // log(x)                           1
      add r0.xw, r0.xwww, r2.wxxx // Inc u and sum log-luminance 1
  endrep            // end x loop                               2
  mad r0.xy, r0.xy, c1.zw, c1.zy  // increment v and set u to 0 1
endrep              // end y loop                               2
mov oC0.xyzw, r0.wwww           // output accumulator           1
```

giving us nine cycles per x pixel with another six cycles to increment a y line.

If we calculate luminance in blocks of 128×56 pixels by setting i1 = 128 and i2 = 56 this code consumes 64,853 cycles. For a 1280×1024 frame buffer, we would need to sample into 10×19 destination textures which then would be read by the next pass of the algorithm.

We can optimize this further by noticing that the loops themselves are the most expensive part. By unrolling the x loop as much as memory allows and removing the x loop we can greatly speed this code up. In theory the shader compilers inside the driver should do this automatically where appropriate, but here we do it manually just in case it's missed.

By removing the x loop the code for each log luminance sample goes from nine cycles to four cycles. We can repeat it 125 times and still fit in instruction limits. Unfortunately the pixel shader assembler doesn't have a repeat block macro, so you will have to do it manually using cut and paste or using your own code creator.

```
// v0.xy = start uv co-ordinate for this block        Instruction count
// c0.z = 0
// c1.xyzw = xy = delta uv for each pixel, z = 0, w = 1
// s0 = frame buffer sampler
// c3 = 0.27, 0.67, 0.06, sqrt(delta)
mov r0.xy, v0.xy  // set uv to start of this block              1
mov r0.zw, c0.z   // clear accumulator                          1

mov r1.w, c3.w    // set w = sqrt(delta) so r1.w * r1.w = delta 1
mov r2.w, c1.x    // optimise the inner loop                    1
```

```
rep i2              // loop across y                              3
    BEGIN_REPEAT_BLOCK(125) // imaginary macro to physically repeat
                            // the code 125 times
        texld r1.xyz, r0, s0        // get the pixel from the frame buffer1
        dp4 r2.x, r1.xyzw, c3.xyzw// delta + L(x,y)                1
        log r2.x, r2.x              // log(x)                      1
        add r0.xw, r0.xwww, r2.wxxx    // Inc u and sum log-luminance  1
    END_REPEAT_BLOCK                   // total cost of block 500
        mad r0.xy, r0.xy, c1.zw, c1.zy // increment v and set u to 0   1
endrep              // end y loop                                  2
mov oC0.xyzw, r0.wwww       // output accumulator                  1
```

Each y loop takes 506 instructions so we can work on 125×128 pixel block taking 64,773 cycles in total, writing into an 11×8 render target. Loop unrolling will cause problems at the right edge of the texture; one possible solution is to have a non-unrolled version for the last column, but another is to use BORDER mode texture addressing to return a luminance of 0. This will introduce a tiny error (0 actually equals delta) but it shouldn't be visible in practice.

This optimization is largely theoretical at this stage. While it is more efficient in terms of cycles, the actual gains will be graphic chipset-specific as this stresses the texture fetch units and pixel threading system which can vary greatly across different implementations (it may be more efficient for a specific chip to use different numbers and methods).

The second pass takes this smaller texture and sums each pixel, then completes the calculation. N is set to the number of samples from the original destination light buffer. This pass is so small compared to the last pass, that for most frame buffer sizes this can be completely unrolled and still fit within 512 instructions.

This second pass doesn't perform the dot product or the logarithm operations as they have already been done on the previous pass.

```
// c0.x = 1/N
// c0.z = 0
// c1.xyzw = xy = delta uv for each pixel, z = 0, w = 1
// s0 = frame buffer sampler
mov r0.xy, v0.xy      // set uv to start of this block
mov r0.zw, c0.z       // clear accumulator
mov r2.w, c1.x        // u delta
BEGIN_REPEAT_BLOCK(ysize)              // ysize = 8 in the example above
    BEGIN_REPEAT_BLOCK(xsize)          // xsize = 11 in the example above
        texld r2.x, r0, s0             // get the pixel from the last pass
        add r0.xw, r0.xwww, r2.wxxx    // Sum log-luminance and inc u
    END_REPEAT_BLOCK                   // end x loop
        mad r0.xy, r0.xy, c1.zw, c1.zy // increment v and set u to 0
END_REPEAT_BLOCK        // end y loop
mul r0.x, r0.w, c0.x // multiple by 1/N
exp r0.x, r0.x       // and convert back into a luminance value
mov oC0.xyzw, r0.xxxx
```

Using $\bar{L}_w$

The equation suggested in [Reinhard02] is used:

$$L_d(x,y) = \frac{L(x,y)\left(1+\dfrac{L(x,y)}{L_{white}^2}\right)}{1+L(x,y)} \tag{2.2.3}$$

Where $L_d(x, y)$ is the tone mapped pixel and L_{white} is the white point, which is the HDR value that causes complete white out. L_{white} can be set to infinity (or a very large value) to bring all luminance values produced into a displayed value. $L(x,y)$ is produced via Equation 2.2.3:

$$L(x,y) = \frac{a}{\bar{L}_w} L_w(x,y) \tag{2.2.4}$$

with a being the Key Value (basically a tuneable magic number between 0 and 1, the default suggested in the paper is 0.18) and L_w and $\bar{L}_w$ being the same as the previous operations.

Equation 2.2.2 calculates the new monochromic luminance value for a pixel. To color it, we implement a simple scale of the original pixel color into the new scale.

The following HLSL shader is used:

```
Sampler TexToToneMap;
sampler BarLwTexture;
float4 main( in float2 uv : TEXCOORD0,
        uniform in float RecipA,
        uniform in float RecipLwhiteSqrd )
{
    // get average Lw from the texture we calculated previously
    float BarLw = tex2D( BarLw, float2(0,0) );
    float aOverBarLw = KeyA * (1.f/BarLw);

    // calc L(x,y) by getting the Luminance of this pixel and
    // scaling by a/BarLw
    float4 hdrPixel = tex2D( TexToToneMap, uv );
    float lumi = dot( hdrPixel, float3( 0.27, 0.67, 0.06 ) );
    float Lxy = aOverBarLw * lumi;

    // now calculate Ld
    float numer = (1 + (Lxy * RecipLwhiteSqrd)) * Lxy;
    float denum = 1 + Lxy;
    float Ld = numer / denum;

    // we now have to convert the original  color into this range.
    float3 ldrPixel = (hdrPixel / lumi) * Ld;

    // currently don't process hdr alpha just saturate on the output
to LDR
    return float4(ldrPixel, hdrPixel.a);
}
```

The render target this shader outputs into is a low dynamic range surface capable of being output to the display unit.

Conclusion

Pixel Shader version 3.0 enables us to reduce the number of render target switches to implement tone-mapping and float16 blending provides us the ability to use HDR without restriction or limitation. Adding these capabilities to a deferred lighting renderer allows us to get even closer to off-line renderer quality.

References

[Calver02] D. Calver, "Photorealistic Deferred Lighting," available online at *http://www.beyond3d.com/articles/deflight/*

[Thibieroz02] "Deferred Shading with Multiple Render Targets," *ShaderX² Tips and Tricks,* Wordware Publishing 2002.

[Debevec97] P. Debevec, "*Recovering High Dynamic Range Radiance Maps From Photographs,*" Proceedings of SIGGRAPH 97, available online at *http://www.debevec.org/Research/HDR/debevec-siggraph97.pdf.*

[Durand02] F. Durand et al., "*Interactive Tone Mapping,*" Proceeding of the Eurographics Workshop on Rendering 2002, available online at *http://graphics.csail.mit.edu/~fredo/PUBLI/EGWR2000/durandInteractiveTM.pdf.*

[Reinhard02] E. Reinhard et al., "*Photographic Tone Reproduction for Digital Images,*" ACM, available online at *http://www.cs.utah.edu/~reinhard/cdrom/tonemap.pdf.*

2.3

Reflections from Bumpy Surfaces

Henning Mortveit

Introduction

Reflections are a great way to add realism to rendered scenes. There is a whole range of techniques available for implementing reflections. On one side of the spectrum there are techniques like *ray-tracing* which can produce stunning results. The downside is that they generally come with hefty rendering times. On the other side of the spectrum there are fast techniques like the standard "render-scene-reflected-through-mirror." This approach, as least in its most basic version, assumes a perfectly smooth reflector, and as a result, the generated images tend to look unrealistically perfect.

The reflection seen at a given point x of a perfectly reflective object depends on the viewpoint, the point x, and the object normal at x. Environment mapping (EM) is an approximate technique commonly used to handle this. In EM it is assumed that the reflected environment is infinitely far away from the reflective object. With this assumption it is clear the reflection at the point x only depends on x through the reflected view vector. Cube maps are a natural tool for this setup.

For many scenes the EM assumption works out all right, as for example when rendering sky reflections on a water surface. However, when the items in the environment get close to the reflector artifacts can arise. A typical example of such artifacts is discussed in the following and illustrated in Figure 2.3.1. Almost planar surfaces are standard objects where this becomes particularly noticeable. One way to improve on this is described in [Apodaca99]. They assume that the (finite) environment map exists on the interior of a sphere with a known, finite radius and center. Let V_r denote the view vector reflected about the point normal at x as in Figure 2.3.1. Using a regular cube map produces the point P_{EM} on the sphere interior. They obtain the point P from the intersection point between the line $x + V_r \cdot t$ and the sphere, and use the vector $V_{mod} = P - O$ to index a cube map based at O.

This works fine in an offline setting like the one targeted in [Apodaca99]. However, we want to apply this to interactive applications with dynamic environments like games, and there are performance limitations with this approach. It uses a cube map, and dynamic cube maps are expensive. Moreover, solving for the intersection point P involves a second order equation. Finally, handling this in a robust way on a per-fragment basis is also expensive.

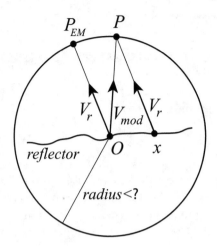

FIGURE 2.3.1   *Cube map lookup mod-ification for a finite environment as in [Apodaca99].*

The technique described in this article is based on an idea similar to the one just outlined, but it *only involves a regular 2D texture map.* It mainly applies to near-planar surfaces (see the rotating platform in the "ATI Car Demo" [ATI] for an example of such a surface).

The technique in this article is based on the following setup and approximation:

- The reflective surface is planar and its ruggedness is represented as a normal map.
- Similar to [Apodaca99] it assumes that the objects that will be reflected are at a distance h from the reflective surface.

This article presents the math behind this technique along with a GLSL shader implementation. Shaders using `GL_ARB_vertex/fragment_program` can be found on the CD-ROM.

ON THE CD

Overview of Technique and Article Outline

The reflection technique in this article uses two rendering passes. In the first pass the reflection image is rendered to a texture. In this pass the viewpoint or camera position used is the reflection of the original viewpoint about the reflector plane. The rationale for this is explained in the next section.

In the second pass the reflective surface is shaded using the reflection texture from the first pass. If the reflector was perfectly flat one would base the shading of the incoming fragment directly on the fragment's world coordinates. However, since the reflector is no longer flat but has per-fragment normals derived from a normal-map this approach no longer produces a realistic-looking result. The texture coordinates used to index the reflection texture will be based on an offset of the fragment's world coordinates. This article shows how to derive this offset with the setup and assumption stated in the introduction.

In the remainder of the article the following topics are explained:

- How to render reflections to a texture (first render pass) and the matrix math needed for the texture lookups that are done in the fragment shader (second render pass) when the reflector is rendered.
- A derivation of the formulas needed to compute the offset that is used for the texture lookups.
- Simplifications that can be done when the distance between environment/objects and the reflector is very large. This simplification roughly corresponds to the normal cube map lookups that are only based on direction.
- Implementation notes and a description of the GLSL shaders and their parameters.
- A discussion of normal maps. Using only 8 bits per component in the normal maps is often insufficient for this and related techniques. Normal maps with 16 bits per components and floating point normal maps are discussed.
- A summary and comparison of this effect with other approaches to reflections, and suggestions on how this technique can be used for similar effects like refractions.

Rendering Reflections to Texture

One could use the standard approach in [Kilgard98] for example, to draw objects that should be reflected. In this case the scene is rendered reflected through the mirror plane. A clipping plane makes sure that only objects that are on the same side of the reflector as the viewpoint are included. In this case special care is required for scene lighting: when the reflection or scaling transformation is applied one must make sure that the light directions and positions in the reflected scene are all consistent with the lighting in the original scene. Another issue is that the transformation changes the handedness of the underlying coordinate system, which results in issues with front and back faces when culling is used.

A better approach is to reflect the current viewpoint about the reflector plane and then render the relevant parts of the scene from this point. Actually, reflecting the viewpoint is only half of the story. The other half is the camera orientation. We can reflect the whole viewpoint reference frame which includes the viewpoint, *and* the forward, right, and up vectors. This, however, also changes the handedness of the coordinate system and we get the same culling issues as before. We can avoid changing the handedness of the coordinate system, by flipping the reflected up vector. See Figure 2.3.2

Assume the reflective surface is contained in the plane a. If the viewpoint/camera position is E and the forward, right, and up vectors are F, R, and U, then:

$$E_r = reflect_a(E), \ F_r = reflect_a(F), \ R_r = reflect_a(R) \text{ and } U_r = -reflect_a(U)$$

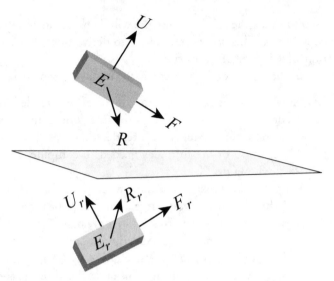

FIGURE 2.3.2   *Reflecting the camera position and orientation.*

By transforming the viewpoint reference frame we effectively go from the original view matrix V to the reflected view matrix V_r. The model matrices and the projection matrix P all stay the same. A clipping plane is still needed so that only the correct objects cast reflections.

Reflection Texture Lookup

Having generated the reflection texture we now turn to the texture lookup math required for rendering the reflector. Here is a description of how to do this for a perfect reflector. It will be a breeze to handle the bumpy reflector after this.

Assume we are rendering the reflector and that there is an incoming fragment with world coordinate *Fpos*. To find the reflection at this point simply follow the transformation pathway used in the render-to-texture pass that was just finished: first multiply *Fpos* by V_r to get to eye space. Next multiply by the projection matrix P to get to post-projective space (also called homogenous clipping space). Finally, multiply by a standard scale-translate matrix S to get all coordinates from $[-1,1]$ to $[0,1]$. The x and y coordinates of the result is exactly what is needed for the 2D texture lookup. That is, we would use the expression $(S \cdot P \cdot V_r \cdot Fpos)xy$ for the texture lookup. Note that this is the same thinking and math that lies behind texture projection techniques like shadow maps. From an implementation point of view we would naturally compute the transformation matrix $S \cdot P \cdot V_r$ on the CPU and pass it in as a constant/uniform variable to the fragment shader.

This covers the perfect reflector case. To get to the bumpy reflector we will compute an offset for the coordinate *Fpos*. Adding this offset to *Fpos* gives the modified world coordinate *Fpos*₁. We use this new coordinate instead of *Fpos* for the texture lookup. A procedure for calculating the offset is given in the next section.

Formula Derivations

The setup and assumption for the technique are displayed in Figure 2.3.3 along with the variables needed for the derivation of the offset. This offset is used in the shading of the reflector during the second rendering pass.

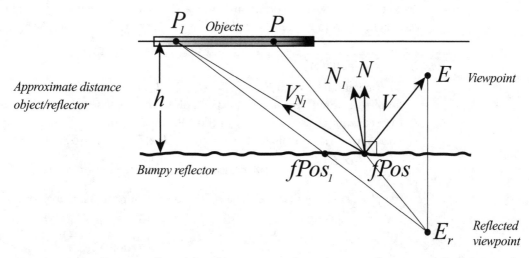

FIGURE 2.3.3 *(Bumpy reflector) Rendering a near-planar bumpy reflective surface: the reflector is represented as a planar surface with normal vectors derived from a normal map. The normal vector for the planar surface is* N, *the viewpoint is* E, *and the reflected viewpoint is* E$_r$. *A fragment on the reflector with world coordinates* x *and fragment normal* N$_1$ *is shown. The view vector* V *reflected about* N$_1$ *is* V$_{N1}$, *and therefore the reflection image at the point* x *comes from the point* P$_1$—*it would come from* P *for a perfect reflector. The intersection point* x$_1$ *of the line through* E$_r$ *and* P$_1$ *is required for the reflection texture lookup.*

 Please refer to Figure 2.3.3 for the setup used and an explanation of the notation used.

The view vector at the point x is $V = E - x$, and the fragment normal at x is N_1. With the assumption that the environment/objects are at an approximate distance h from the reflector it is clear that the reflection of the point P_1 is observed at x. In contrast, if the reflector was perfectly flat the reflection of the point P would be seen at x. With the render-to-texture setup x is used in the texture lookup for the perfect reflector—the reflection of P_1 is obtained by replacing x with x_1 in the texture lookup (the offset mentioned earlier is $x_1 - x$).

Let x_0 be a point in the reflector plane α. The equation of α can then be written $(N, \xi - x_0) = 0$. The intersection point x_1 of the line through the reflected viewpoint E_r and the point P_1 can be computed using these steps:

1. Compute the reflected viewpoint as $E_r = E - 2\,\mathrm{dot}(V,N)N$. Note that this is a constant in the rendering pass and that it was already obtained in the render-to-texture pass.

2. Compute the reflection of the view vector V about the fragment normal N_1 as $V_{N_1} = 2\,\mathrm{dot}(V,N_1)N_1 - V$. It is clear that this quantity must be computed per fragment.

3. The point P_1 is the point on the line $l_1 : x + t \cdot V_{N_1}$ that is at a signed distance h from the reflector plane. This happens for $t = h\,/\,\mathrm{dot}(N,V_{N_1})$ so

$$P_1 = x + \frac{h}{\mathrm{dot}(N,V_{N_1})}V_{N_1}.$$

4. The line through P_1 and E_r is $l_2 : E_r + t \cdot (P_1 - E_r)$. Inserting this in the equation for α to determine the intersection point gives (after some small manipulations) the equation $\mathrm{dot}(N,E_r - x_0) + (\mathrm{dot}(N,P_1 - x_0) - \mathrm{dot}(N,E_r - x_0)) \cdot t_1 = 0$ for t. Since N is normalized this is simply $-d(\alpha,E) + (h + d(\alpha,E)) \cdot t_1 = 0$ or $t_1 = \dfrac{d(\alpha,E)}{h + d(\alpha,E)}$. Here $d(\alpha, E)$ denotes the distance from the viewpoint E to the plane α. Note that the value t_1 is a constant for the rendering pass. The

$$x_1 = E_r + t_1 \cdot (P_1 - E_r) = (1 - t_1) \cdot E_r + t_1 \cdot \left(x + \frac{h}{\mathrm{dot}(N,V_{N_1})}V_{N_1} \right) \quad (2.3.1)$$

It is clear from Equation 2.3.1 that x_1 depends on the fragment world coordinate, the distance h and the reflected view vector V_{N_1}. From a computational point of view Equation (2.3.1) is quite tractable (a constant LRP of a constant and a MAD expression in GL_ARB_fragment_program lingo). The following alternative equation for (2.3.1) may shed some more light on what is happening:

$$x_1 = x + \left[(1 - t_1) \cdot (E_r - x) + t_1 \cdot \frac{h}{\mathrm{dot}(N,V_{N_1})}V_{N_1} \right] \quad (2.3.2)$$

The vector in the square brackets of Equation 2.3.2 expresses the x-offset vector as a function of fragment position, viewpoint, distance to environment, and the reflected view vector. It is easy to check that the offset vector is indeed normal to N.

If h is very large compared to the other quantities involved then Equation 2.3.2 can be simplified somewhat. Taking the limit $h \to \infty$ in Equation 2.3.2 leads to

$$x_{1,\infty} = E_r + \frac{d(\alpha,E)}{\mathrm{dot}(N,V_{N_1})}V_{N_1} \quad (2.3.3)$$

Whether the use of $x_{1,\infty}$ gives satisfactory rendering results or not depends on many factors and case-by-case testing is probably required. Note that this equation is analogous to the case of a suitably aligned cube map located at E_r. In Equation 2.3.3 V_{N_1} is used for the lookup.

Implementation

OpenGL was used as graphics API. What is described above is essentially API independent, and the GLSL shader given below should be easy to implement using DirectX HLSL. The effect was also implemented using a combination of GL_ARB_ fragment_program and GL_ARB_vertex_program. These are not presented here, but can be found on the CD-ROM.

ON THE CD

Since we have assumed that the reflective surface is planar we will also assume that the tangent space basis (tangent T, binormal B, normal N) is constant on the reflector. This information is passed to the fragment shader as a uniform/constant matrix $[T\,|\,B\,|\,N]$. Here $[T\,|\,B\,|\,N]$ denotes the 3×3 matrix where the first column is R, the second column is U and the third column is T.

The GLSL shader for bumpy reflections is given below. The $h \to \infty$ case is easily adapted from this general case.

Listing 2.3.1 GLSL: Bumpy Reflections

```
{GLSL Vertex Shader}

varying vec4 pos; // World position
varying vec2 tex; // texture coord. for base map and normal map

void main()
{
  gl_Position = gl_ModelViewProjectionMatrix * gl_Vertex;
  pos = gl_Vertex;
  tex = gl_MultiTexCoord0.xy;
}

{GLSL Fragment Shader}

uniform float h;      // average distance object-reflector
uniform mat4 Te;      // texture matrix S.P.Vr
uniform float ratio;// the ratio t1 = d(alpha,E)/(h+d(alpha,E))
uniform mat3 M;       // tangent space basis [T|B|N]
uniform vec3 E;       // viewpoint
uniform vec3 Er;      // reflected viewpoint
uniform vec3 N;       // reflector normal

uniform sampler2D baseTexture;
uniform sampler2D normalMap;
uniform sampler2D reflectionTexture;
```

```
varying vec4 pos;  // Fragment position
varying vec2 tex;  // Shared texture coordinate for
                   // base texture and normalmap

void main()
{
  // Base texture
vec4 colorBase = texture2D(baseTexture, tex);

  // fragment normal in tangent space
vec3 n1 = 2.0*((texture2D(normalMap, tex)).xyz) - 1.0;

  // world-aligned fragment normal
  vec3 N1 = M*n1;

  // normalized fragment position
  vec3 Fpos = pos.xyz/pos.w;

  // view vector
  vec3 V = E - Fpos.xyz;

  // reflected view vector
  vec3 VN1 = -reflect(V, N1);

  // reflection image point
  vec3 P1 = Fpos + (h/dot(VN1, N)) * VN1;

  // modified fragment position
  vec4 Fpos1 = vec4( mix(Er, P1, ratio), 1.0);

  vec4 colorRefl = texture2DProj(reflectionTexture, Te*Fpos1);

  // Use an infinite lightsource with direction lDir
  const vec3 lDir = vec3(0.57735, 0.57735, 0.57735);

  // Blend between base texture and reflection.
  gl_FragColor = dot(N1, lDir) * mix(colorRefl, colorBase, 0.30);
}
```

The following numbers were obtained using a scene with one bumpy reflection plane, two animated objects, both with a triangle count around 1500, and a skybox. The application was run in 1024×768 windowed mode on a Pentium IV 1.6GHz with a Radeon 9800Pro. Using a pair of ARB_vertex_program/ARB_fragment_program assembly shaders the frame rate stayed at about 100 fps in the case where the reflective plane covered the entire viewport. The GLSL shader pair consistently performed at about 90% of this. We did not try to optimize the GLSL shaders too much. This and the fact that GLSL driver support is in its early stages can probably explain the difference in performance between GLSL and assembly shaders.

Images

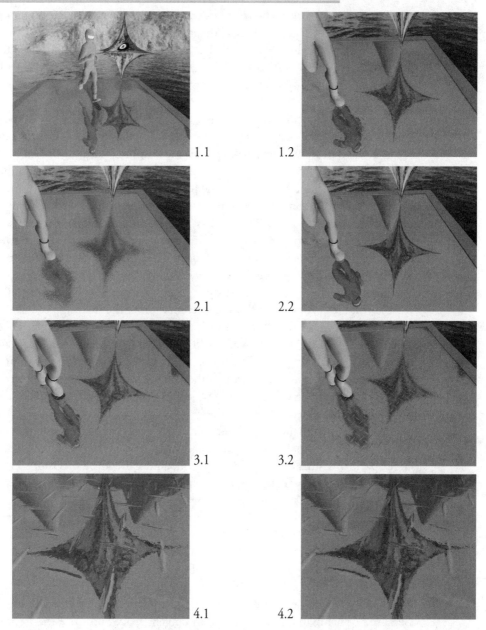

FIGURE 2.3.4   *Image 1.1 shows the scene. Images 1.2 and 2.1 show the scene rendered using a 16-bit and an 8-bit normal map, respectively. Image 2.2 shows the scene with "plain" reflections. Images 3.1 and 3.2 contrast the regular bumpy reflection shader (left) and the shader for the infinity case (right). Smearing is clearly visible. Finally, the last row contrasts the effects of using a 16-bit integer based normal map (left) and a 32-bit floating point normal map (right). Pixelation caused by lack of filtering can be seen.*

Normal Maps

For many purposes it is sufficient to use normal maps with 8 bits per component. The three components (RGB) represent the x, y, and z-coordinates of the normal vectors. Each component is in the range [–1.0, 1.0]. There are $2^8 = 256$ discrete levels to represent this range of width 2.0, so there is a gap of $\Delta_8 = 2/(2^8 - 1) > 0.007$ between "neighbor" values. Whether this is tolerable or not depends on the particular application.

For the technique described in this article and the type of reflective surfaces considered, it is likely to cause problems. In the demo program on the CD-ROM the normal maps are derived from height fields where the minimum and maximum height values differ by at most 0.15. Filtering in the generation of the normal map and the fact that values tend to vary gradually within the height field should make it clear that we easily get close to the Δ_8 threshold. The reflection equation $V_{N_1} = 2\,\text{dot}(V, N_1)N_1 - V$ tends to propagate significant numerical errors when the input normal vector is not encoded with sufficient precision; this will result in even greater inaccuracies in the reflected vector resulting from this equation. The other mathematical operations performed in the shaders may affect the propagated error even more.

For near-planar surfaces where the normal vectors are very close to (0.0, 0.0, 1.0) we also run into problems with the representation of the floating point 0.0. It should ideally be right in the middle of 0 and 255 which is 127.5. The 0.5 difference between 127 and 127.5 as well as 127.5 and 128 corresponds to a difference $\Delta_8/2 > 0.0039$ in the components of the normal vector. If the conversion from floating point to integer in the normal map encoding discards the fractional part then normal vectors will tilt slightly—the component values will be slightly smaller. For the effect discussed here this can be noticeable.

One could probably do certain tricks to work around these problems. If you know that your normal map has the x and y components in the range [–0.1, 0.1] you could pack this smaller range into 256 bits and gain some precision. However, for integration and maintenance, this trick and similar ones seem like a bad idea for any project larger than a 200-line demo program.

The demo program uses 16-bit normal maps. With the same reasoning as above we see that $\Delta_{16} = 2/(2^{16} - 1) > 0.00003$. This increase in precision is sufficient for the demo program setup.

One may incur a penalty in terms of rendering speed when passing from 8-bit to 16-bit normal maps, at least if all three components are represented. Using all three components in the normal map means that there will be $3 \cdot 16 = 48$ bits per pixel. Because normal maps are represented in tangent space and since the z component is usually positive, one can get away with storing only the x and y components in the normal map and later derive the z component as $z = \sqrt{1 - x^2 - y^2}$. This way we again have images with 32 bits per pixel. However, we might have to work around speed and precision issues with math functions in the fragment shader. Also, note that filtering a normal map that only encodes the x and y components of a normalized vector can produce inaccuracies on sharp normal transitions.

The demo program on the CD-ROM allows you to switch between 8-bit and 16-bit normal maps. The two maps are the same resolution and they were generated in identical ways with the same type of filtering. You should notice a slight jump of the reflection as you switch from a 16-bit to an 8-bit normal map, at least if your graphics card and drivers respect the 16-bit normal maps you pass them. The jump is the result of the problems around the representation of 0.0 which was discussed above. If your API and video driver support a floating point texture format it may sound tempting to take advantage of this and encode your normal maps using for example the OpenEXR image format [OpenEXR], or some float format of your own. Unfortunately, support for floating point textures varies from one vendor implementation to another, and currently most implementations exposing those formats have the added drawback that filtering is not supported on them, which would cause aliasing artifacts at close range. For those reasons, encoding normal maps in float textures may not currently be considered an attractive solution.

Extensions of Technique

The technique described here can also be used for other effects. One prime example is refractions: if the underwater parts of the scene are roughly at a distance h below the water surface the same reasoning as above could be used. One could even combine reflection and refraction and take advantage of the fact that both effects use the same fragment normal vector and the same reflected view vector. An additional rendering pass for the underwater parts of the scene is required though. The reflection and refraction terms should be combined using a Fresnel term.

Summary and Discussion

The article has shown a method analogous to the cube-map-based technique in [Apodaca99] for rendering realistic reflections from bumpy surfaces. The technique here only requires a single 2D texture map which allows for significant speedups compared to an equivalent dynamic cube map technique which can require up to six render passes of the full scene per frame.

How about implementing this effect in a larger framework? It would be natural to do so using an LOD-like scheme. If the viewer is far away from the bumpy reflector simply use regular reflections. As the viewer gets close to the surface simply switch to the shader pair presented here.

An obvious question is the following: does the effect stand out from "quick and dirty" bumpy reflections? There are probably smart choices of fixed offset maps, special setups, and so on for which a simpler approach could give nice results. However, the advantage of the effect explained here is that it is based on the underlying physics and thus looks visually convincing to the human eye. Whether this implementation or a cheaper approach is used depends on the usual trade-off between visual quality and the level of performance available on the target system.

On the CD-ROM

ON THE CD

The CD-ROM contains high-resolution screen shots of the effect. A demo program is included. It allows you to compare bumpy reflection and regular reflections. You can also compare 8-bit and 16-bit normal maps and switch between GLSL shaders and `ARB_vertex_program`/`ARB_fragment_program` shaders provided that your graphics card supports these features. The shaders and normal maps are all on the CD-ROM. If your graphics card/driver supports the extension `GL_ATI_texture_float` the demo will also allow you to use a floating point normal map (32 bits per component). The lack of filtering in this case becomes evident at close range. Please refer to the README.TXT file for details and additional options.

Acknowledgments

Thanks to the section editor Nick Thibieroz for the helpful advice provided during the writing of this article.

References

[Apodaca99] Apodaca, Anthony A. and Gritz, Larry, *Advanced RenderMan,* Morgan Kaufmann Publishers, 1999.

[ATI] The ATI Car Demo. ATI. Online at *http://www.ati.com/developer/demos/r9700.html,* 2004.

[Kilgard98] Kilgard, Mark J., "Improving Shadows and Reflections via the Stencil Buffer," NVIDIA Corporation, Online at *http://developer.nvidia.com/attach/1591,* 2004.

[OpenEXR04] The OpenEXR image file format. Industrial Light and Magic. Online at *www.openexr.com,* 2004.

2.4

Massively Parallel Particle Systems on the GPU

Lutz Latta

Introduction

Reality is full of motion, full of chaos, and full of fuzzy objects. Physically correct particle systems (PS) are designed to add these essential properties to the virtual world. Over the last decades they have been established as a valuable technique for a variety of volumetric effects, both in real-time applications and in pre-rendered visual effects of motion pictures and commercials.

Particle systems have a long history in video games and computer graphics. Very early video games in the 1960s already used 2D pixel clouds to simulate explosions. The first publication about the use of dynamic PS in computer graphics was written after the completion of the visual effects for the motion picture *Star Trek II* at Lucasfilm [Reeves83]. Reeves describes basic motion operations and basic data representing a particle—both have not been altered much since. An implementation on parallel processors of a super computer has been done by [Sims90]. He and [McAllister00] also describe many of the velocity and position operations of the motion simulation that are used below. The latest description of CPU-based PS for use in video games has been done by [Burg00].

Real-time PS are often limited by the fill rate or the CPU-to-graphics hardware (GPU) communication. The fill rate, the number of pixels the GPU can draw for each frame, is often a limiting factor when there is a high overdraw, i.e., single particles are relatively large and a lot of them overlap each other. Since the realism of a particle system simulation increases when smaller particles are used, the fill rate limitation loses importance. The second limitation, the transfer bandwidth of particle data from the simulation on the CPU to the rendering on the GPU, now dominates the system. Sharing the graphics bus with many other rendering tasks allows CPU-based PS to achieve only up to 10,000 particles per frame in typical game applications. Therefore, it is desirable to minimize the amount of communication of particle data. This can be achieved by integrating both parts—simulation and rendering—of this visualization problem on the GPU.

To simulate particles on a GPU you can use stateless or state-preserving PS. Stateless PS require a particle's data to be computed from its birth to its death by a closed form function which is defined only by a set of start values and the current time. State-preserving PS allows using numerical, iterative integration methods to compute the particle data from previous values and a changing environmental description (e.g., moving collider objects). Both simulation methods have their areas of applications and should be chosen based on the requirements of the desired effect.

Stateless PS have been introduced on the first generation of programmable PC GPUs [NVIDIA01]) and are described in the next section. The state-preserving simulation has recently become possible on floating-point graphics hardware and is described in the following sections. This particle physics simulation on a GPU can be a flexible combination of a multitude of motion and position operations, e.g., gravity, local forces, and collision with primitive geometry shapes or texture-based height fields. Additionally, a parallel sorting algorithm can be used to perform a distance-based sorting of the particles for correct alpha-blended rendering (see page 127).

Stateless Particle Systems

Some PS have been implemented with vertex shaders (also called vertex programs) on programmable GPUs [NVIDIA2001]. These PS are, however, stateless, i.e., they do not store the current positions and other attributes of the particles. To determine a particle's position you need to find a closed form function for computing the current position only from initial values and the current time. As a consequence, such PS can hardly react to a dynamic environment.

Particles that are not meant to collide with the environment and that are only influenced by a global gravity acceleration $\mathbf{g}$ can be simulated quite easily with a simple function:

$$\mathbf{p} = \mathbf{p}_0 + \mathbf{v}_0 t + \tfrac{1}{2}\mathbf{g}t^2 \qquad\qquad (2.4.1)$$

where $\mathbf{p}$ is the computed particle position, $\mathbf{p}_0$ the initial position, $\mathbf{v}_0$ the initial velocity, and t the current time. Adding simple collisions or forces with local influence, however, lead to much more complex functions.

Particle attributes besides velocity and position (e.g., the particle's orientation, size, and texture coordinates) have generally much simpler computation rules than the position. It is often sufficient to calculate them from a start value and a constant factor of change over time, which makes them ideal for a stateless simulation. This holds true even if the position is determined with the state-preserving simulation in the next section.

The strengths of the stateless PS make it ideal for simulating small and simple effects without influence from the local environment. In action video games these might be a weapon impact, splash, or the sparks of a collision. Larger effects that require interaction with the environment are less suitable for the technique.

Particle Simulation on Graphics Hardware

The following sections describe the algorithm of a state-preserving particle system on a GPU in detail. After a brief overview of the algorithm, the storage, and then the processing of particles is described.

Algorithm Overview

The state-preserving particle system stores the velocities and positions of all particles in textures. These textures are also render targets. In one rendering pass the texture with particle velocities is updated using the previous velocities as input. The update performs a one-time step of an iterative integration which applies acceleration forces and collision reactions. Another rendering pass updates the position textures in a similar way, using the just computed velocities for the position integration. Depending on the integration method, it is possible to skip the velocity update pass, and directly integrate the position from accelerations.

Optionally, the particle positions can be sorted depending on the viewer distance to avoid rendering artifacts later on. The sorting performs several additional rendering passes on textures that contain the particle distance and a reference to the particle itself.

Then the particle positions are transferred from the position texture to a vertex buffer. Finally this geometry data is rendered to the screen in a traditional way—as point sprites, primitive triangles, or quads.

These six basic steps of the algorithm are described in the following sections:

1. Process birth and death
2. Update velocities
3. Update positions
4. Sort for alpha blending (optional)
5. Transfer texture data to vertex data
6. Render particles

Particle Data Storage

The most important attributes of a particle are its position and velocity. The positions of all active particles are stored in a floating point texture with three color components that will be treated as x, y, and z coordinates. Each texture is conceptually treated as a one-dimensional array; texture coordinates representing the array index. The actual textures however, need to be two-dimensional due to the size restrictions of current hardware. The texture itself is also a render target, so it can be updated with the computed positions. By drawing a full-screen rectangle, the GPU is instructed to call a pixel shader once for each pixel in the render target. The pixel shader also needs to read the previous position values from the texture. As a texture cannot be used for reading and rendering at the same time, we use a pair of these textures and a double buffering technique to compute new data from the previous values (see Figure 2.4.1).

A pair of velocity textures can be created in the same way as the position textures. Due to their reduced precision requirements it is usually sufficient to store the velocity coordinates in a 16-bit floating point format. Depending on the integration algorithm there is no need to store the velocity explicitly (see page 126). If the velocity is not stored in textures, you need a third position texture, which basically forms a triple buffer.

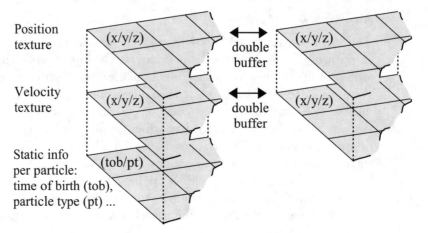

FIGURE 2.4.1   *Particle data storage in multiple textures.*

If other particle attributes (like orientation, size, color, and opacity) were to be simulated with the iterative integration method, they would need double buffer textures as well. However, since these attributes typically follow simple computation rules or are even static, we can take a simpler approach. An algorithm similar to the stateless particle system (see page 120) can be used to compute these values only from the relative age of the particle and a function description, e.g., initial and differential values or a set of keyframes. To be able to evaluate this function, we need to store two static values for each particle: its time of birth and a reference to a set of attribute parameters for its particle type. They are stored in a further texture, but the double buffer approach is not necessary.

We assume that the particles can be grouped by a particle type in order to minimize the amount of static attribute parameters that need to be uploaded during the final rendering of the particles. This particle type can either be directly coupled in a one-to-one relationship to the particle emitter or a group of emitters emits all particles of the same type.

The mass of a particle needs to be known to calculate accelerations from forces. Possible approaches are: treating all particles as having equal mass, uploading a mass value or function as particle-type parameters, or storing the mass of each particle in the static data texture described above.

To sum up: a single particle consists of data values spread between several textures, but placed at equal texture coordinates in all those textures. According to demand, particle-type parameters also allow the computation of further particle values.

Process Birth and Death

The particles in a system can either exist permanently or only for a limited time. A static number of permanently existing particles represents the simplest case for the

simulation, as it only requires uploading all initial particle data to the particle attributes textures once. As this case is rather rare, we assume a varying number of short-
living particles for the rest of the discussion. The particle system must then process the
birth of a new particle, i.e., its allocation and the death of a particle—its deallocation.

The birth of a particle requires associating new data with an available index in the
attribute textures. Since allocation problems are serial by nature, this cannot be done
efficiently with a data-parallel algorithm on the GPU. Therefore an available index is
determined on the CPU via traditional fast-allocation schemes. The simplest allocation method uses a stack filled with all available indices. A more complex allocator
uses a heap data structure that is optimized to always return the smallest available
index. Its advantage is that if a particle system has a highly varying number of particles, the particles remain packed in the first portion of the system. Thus the following
simulation and rendering steps only need to update that portion of data. After the
index has been determined, the new particle's data is rendered as single pixel into the
attribute textures. This initial particle data is determined on the CPU and can use
complex algorithms, e.g., various probability distributions for initial starting positions
and directions etc. (see [McAllister00]).

A particle's death is processed independently on the CPU and GPU. The CPU
registers the death of a particle and adds the freed index to the allocator. The GPU
does an extra pass over the particle data: the death of a particle is determined by the
time of birth and the computed age. The dead particle's position is simply moved to
invisible areas, e.g., infinity. As particles at the end of their lifetime usually fade out or
fall out of visible areas anyway, the extra pass rarely really needs to be done. It is basically a clean-up step to increase rendering efficiency.

Update Velocities

The first part of the simulation updates the particles' velocity. The actual program
code for the velocity simulation is a pixel shader which is executed for each pixel of
the render target by rendering a screen-sized quad. The current render target is set to
one of the double buffer velocity textures. The other texture of the double buffer is
read by the pixel shader and contains the velocities from the previous time step. Other
particle data, either from inside the attribute textures or as general constants, is set
before the shader is executed.

There are several velocity operations that can be combined as desired (see
[Sims90] and [McAllister00]): global forces (e.g., gravity, wind), local forces (attrac-
tion, repulsion), velocity dampening, and collision responses. For our GPU-based
particle system these operations need to be parameterized via pixel shader constants.
Their dynamic combination is a typical problem of real-time graphics. It is comparable to the problem of light sources and material combinations and can be solved in
similar ways. Typical operation combinations are to be prepared in several variations
beforehand. Other operations can be applied in separate passes, as all operations are
completely independent.

Global forces, e.g., gravity, influence particles regardless of their position with a constant acceleration in a specific direction. The influence of local forces however depends on the particle's position which is read from the position texture. A magnet attracting or repelling a particle has a local acceleration toward a point. This force can fall off with the inverse square of the distance or it can stay constant up to a maximum distance (see [McAllister00]). A particle can also be accelerated toward its closest point on a line, leading to a vortexlike streaming.

A more complex local force can be extracted from a flow field texture. Since texture look-ups are very cheap on the GPU, it is quite efficient to map the particle position into a 2D or 3D texture containing flow velocity vectors. This sampled flow vector $\mathbf{v}_{fl}$ can be used with Stoke's law of a drag force $\mathbf{F}_d$ on a sphere:

$$\mathbf{F_d} = \underbrace{6\pi\,\eta\,r}_{c}\left(\bar{\mathbf{v}} - \mathbf{v_{fl}}\right) \tag{2.4.2}$$

where η is the flow viscosity, r the radius of the sphere (in our case the particle) and $\bar{\mathbf{v}}$ the particle's velocity. The constants can all be combined to a single constant c, for efficient computation and for simpler manual adjustment.

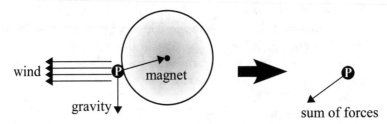

FIGURE 2.4.2   *Adding various forces to one force vector.*

Global and local forces are accumulated into a single force vector, as in the example in Figure 2.4.2. The acceleration can then be calculated with Newtonian physics:

$$\mathbf{a} = \frac{\mathbf{F}}{m} \tag{2.4.3}$$

where $\mathbf{a}$ is the acceleration vector, $\mathbf{F}$ the accumulated force and m the particle's mass. If all particles have unit mass, forces have the same value as accelerations and can be used without further computation.

The velocity is then updated from the acceleration with a simple Euler integration in the form:

$$\mathbf{v} = \bar{\mathbf{v}} + \mathbf{a}\cdot\Delta t \tag{2.4.4}$$

where $\mathbf{v}$ is the current velocity, $\bar{\mathbf{v}}$ the previous velocity and Δt the time step.

Another simple velocity operation is dampening, i.e., a scaling of the velocity vector, which imitates viscous materials or air resistance. This is basically a special case of equation 2.4.2 with a flow velocity of zero. The reverse operation, an un-dampening, can be used to imitate self-propelled objects, e.g., a bee swarm.

A more important operation is collision. Collisions with a plane or bounding spheres are simple and rather cheap. The real strength of collision on the GPU, however, is collision against texture-based height fields that are typically used to model terrain. By sampling the height field three times a normal can be computed which is then used for calculating the reflection vector. The normal can also be stored in the height field, basically making it a scaled normal map. Note that the height field can also be computed dynamically, by rendering the depth values of an object into a texture, similar to shadow mapping algorithms. With this approach it is also possible to perform collisions with complex geometries, that can be approximated with one or more height fields. This technique is described in detail in [Kolb04].

If a collision has been detected, the collision reaction, i.e., the velocity after the collision, has to be computed (see [Sims1990]). First the current velocity has to be split into a normal and a tangential component. If $\mathbf{n}$ is the normal of the collider at the collision point, these can be computed as:

$$\mathbf{v_n} = \left(\mathbf{v_{bc}} \cdot \mathbf{n} \right) \mathbf{v_{bc}}$$
$$\mathbf{v_t} = \mathbf{v_{bc}} - \mathbf{v_n} \tag{2.4.5}$$

where $\mathbf{v_{bc}}$ is the velocity computed so far, i.e., before the collision occurs, $\mathbf{v_n}$ is the normal component of the velocity, and $\mathbf{v_t}$ the tangential one. The velocity after the collision can now be computed with two further parameters describing material properties. Dynamic friction μ reduces the tangential component, and resilience ε scales the reflected normal component. The new velocity is computed as:

$$\mathbf{v} = \left(1 - \mu \right) \mathbf{v_t} - \varepsilon \mathbf{v_n} \tag{2.4.6}$$

This default handling of the collision however has two problems which cause visual artifacts. The slow-down effect of the dynamic friction will lead to situations where the velocity is (very close to) zero. Since in our case the collision is processed after acceleration forces like gravity, this might lead to particles hanging in the air. They virtually seem to be attached to the side of a collider, e.g., at the equator of a sphere collider with respect to the global gravity. Therefore the friction slow-down should not be applied if the overall velocity is smaller than a given threshold.

The second problem is caused by particles getting caught inside a collider. A collider with sharp edges, e.g., a height field, or two colliders close to each other might push particles into a collider. This can be avoided by trying to push a caught particle out of the collider. Normally, the collision detection is done with the expected next particle position to avoid the particle from entering an object for the time of one integration step (see Figure 2.4.3a). The expected particle position $\mathbf{p_{bc}}$ is computed as:

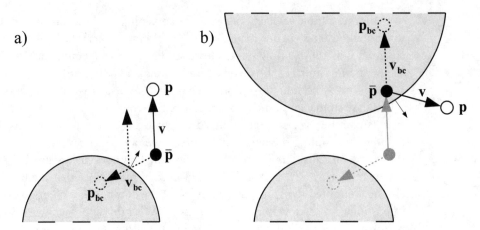

FIGURE 2.4.3   *Particle collision: a) Normal collision reaction before penetration b) Double collision with danger of the particle getting caught inside a collider.*

$$\mathbf{p}_{bc} = \overline{\mathbf{p}} + \mathbf{v}_{bc} \cdot \Delta t \qquad (2.4.7)$$

where $\overline{\mathbf{p}}$ is the previous position. Doing the collision detection twice, once with the previous and once with the expected position, allows differentiating between particles that are about to collide and those having already penetrated (see Figure 2.4.3b). The latter can then be pushed out of the collider, either immediately or by applying the collision velocity without any slow-down. The direction of the shortest way out of the collider can be guessed from the normal component of the velocity:

$$\mathbf{v} = \begin{cases} \mathbf{v}_{bc} & \mathbf{v}_{bc} \cdot \mathbf{n} \geq 0 \\ \mathbf{v}_t - \mathbf{v}_n & \mathbf{v}_{bc} \cdot \mathbf{n} < 0 \end{cases} \qquad (2.4.8)$$

Update Positions

The second part of the particle system simulation updates the position of all particles. Here we are going to discuss the possible integration methods in detail that have been mentioned earlier (see page 121). For the integration of large data sets on the GPU in real-time only simple integration algorithms can be used. Two good candidates for particle simulation are Euler and Verlet integration.

Euler integration has already been used in the previous section to integrate the velocity by using the acceleration. The computed velocity can be applied to all particles in just the same way. This leads to:

$$\mathbf{p} = \overline{\mathbf{p}} + \mathbf{v} \cdot \Delta t \qquad (2.4.9)$$

where $\mathbf{p}$ is the current position and $\overline{\mathbf{p}}$ the previous position.

In some ways even simpler than Euler integration is Verlet integration (see [Verlet67]). Verlet integration for a particle system (see [Jakobsen01]) does not store the velocity explicitly. Instead, the velocity is implicitly deduced by comparing the previous position to the one before. The great advantage of this handling for the particle simulation is that it reduces memory consumption and removes the velocity update rendering pass.

If we assume the time step is constant, the combination of the velocity and position update rules from the Euler integration can be combined to a position update rule based only on the acceleration:

$$\mathbf{p} = 2\bar{\mathbf{p}} - \bar{\bar{\mathbf{p}}} + \mathbf{a} \cdot \Delta t^2 \qquad (2.4.10)$$

where $\bar{\bar{\mathbf{p}}}$ is the position two time steps ago. Verlet integration handles simple (global or local) acceleration forces quite efficiently. However, complex velocity operations, like the collision reaction discussed above, require position manipulations to implicitly change the velocity in the following frames. Alternatively, collision can be handled more efficiently with position constraints that simply move the position out of the collider. Due to the deduction of velocity based on this constraint movement, an implicit reflection velocity is set. Other constraints can be used to limit the distance between a pair or group of particles, which is useful for particle simulation of cloth or hair (see [Jakobsen01] for more details).

Sort for Alpha Blending

If particles are alpha blended, a distance-based sorting should be applied or else particles in the front will not be blended correctly with particles behind them. This error might be intolerable depending on the size and amount of the partially transparent pixels of each particle. Due to the cost of sorting, first examine whether these particles can instead be rendered with a commutative blending function, e.g., additive or multiplicative.

A particle system on the GPU can be sorted quite efficiently with the parallel sorting algorithm "odd-even merge sort" [Batcher68]. It is independent of the data's sortedness, i.e., it always has a constant number of iterations for a data set of a given size. This is important as the parallel hardware execution makes it inefficient to check whether all data is already in sequence. This algorithm also guarantees that with each iteration the sortedness never decreases. If you assume a high frame-to-frame coherence of the sort order, this property allows you to distribute the whole sorting sequence over 20–50 frames. This will of course lead to some visual errors, especially when newly added particles need to be moved to their correct location in the sort order. However, these errors are usually hard to notice except when two particles with very different appearance swap their order. Game applications often know the maximum velocity with which the viewer and the particle objects can move, so assumptions about an acceptable number of frames to distribute the sorting over can be made.

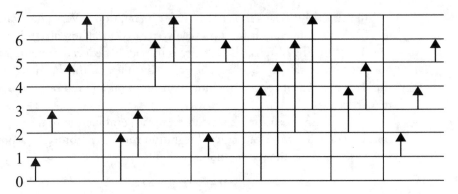

FIGURE 2.4.4 *Odd-even merge sorting network for eight values. y-axis: elements to sort, x-axis: sorting steps.*

The basic principle of odd-even merge sort is to divide the data into two halves, to sort these, and then to merge the two halves (for further details see [Lang03]). The algorithm is commonly written recursively and in a serial way, but a closer look at the resulting sorting network shows its parallel nature. Figure 2.4.4 shows the sorting network for eight values, an arrow marking a comparison pair. The first arrow indicates that element 0 is compared to element 1 and possibly swapped in case the order is not fulfilled. You can see that several consecutive comparisons are independent of each other. They can be grouped for parallel execution, which is indicated here by the vertical lines.

The Cg (see [Mark03]) code for odd-even merge sorting a one-dimensional texture contains two entry points:

```
float4 mergeSort1DEnd(float _Current : TEXCOORD0,
    uniform int _Step) : COLOR
{
  float currentSample = (float)texRECT(_SortData, (float2)_Current);
  float direction = (fmod(_Current / _Step, 2.0) < 1.0 ? 1.0 : -1.0);
  float otherSample = (float)texRECT(_SortData,
    (float2)(_Current + direction * _Step));
  if (direction >= 0)
    return max(currentSample, otherSample);
  else
    return min(currentSample, otherSample);
}

float4 mergeSort1DRecursion(float _Current : TEXCOORD0,
    uniform int _Step, uniform int _Count) : COLOR
{
  float currentSample = (float)texRECT(_SortData, (float2)_Current);
  int modulus = fmod(_Current / _Step, (float)_Count);
  if (modulus >= 1 && modulus < _Count - 1)
  {
```

```
        if (fmod((float)modulus, 2.0) > 1.0)
          return max(currentSample,
            (float)texRECT(_SortData, (float2)(_Current + _Step)));
        else
          return min(currentSample,
            (float)texRECT(_SortData, (float2)(_Current - _Step)));
      }
      else
        return currentSample;
    }
```

This Cg code can be ported to Microsoft HLSL (see [Microsoft02]) by simply mapping the texRECT instruction onto a tex2D instruction. The code is slightly simplified for readability and sorts only a one dimensional texture. To enhance the shader for sorting two dimensional textures the texel index needs to be split into u and v coordinates before look-up. The sorting has two alternative sort shaders, a "recursion" and an "end" step. The pseudo code to trigger the sort passes on the CPU is shown here:

```
MergeSort(int _Count) :
  if (_Count > 1)
    MergeSort(_Count / 2)
    Merge(_Count, 1)

Merge(int _Count, int _Step) :
  if (_Count > 2)
    Merge(_Count / 2, _Step * 2)
    Render with mergeSortRecursion shader
  else
    Render with mergeSortEnd shader
```

The sorting requires $\frac{1}{2}\log_2^2 n + \frac{1}{2}\log_2 n$ passes, where n is the number of elements to sort. For a 1024×1024 texture this leads to 210 rendering passes. Just like in the particle simulation, they always render the full texture into a render target using a double buffer. As mentioned earlier, running all 210 passes each frame is far too expensive on current hardware, but spreading the whole sorting sequence over 50 frames, i.e., 1–2 seconds, reduces the workload to only four passes each frame, which results in acceptable performance.

This general sorting algorithm is applied to the particle simulation in the following way: the sorting data textures contain the particle-viewer distance and the index of the particle. The distance in this texture is updated after the position simulation. After sorting, the rendering step (see the next two sections) looks up the particle attributes via the index in this texture. Note that this indirection will cause a rather random access to the texture and can therefore be quite cache unfriendly.

Transfer Texture Data to Vertex Data

The copying of position data from a texture to vertex data is a hardware feature that is only just coming up in PC GPUs. Currently there are two approaches to this problem:

DirectX and OpenGL offer vertex textures with the vertex shader (VS) version 3.0 model (see [Microsoft02]) and the `ARB_vertex_shader` extension (see [OpenGL03]). To render the particles with vertex textures, one large static vertex buffer is necessary, that is, filled with texture coordinates of all pixels in the particle position texture. When this buffer is rendered the vertex shader uses these texture coordinates to read the particle position from the texture (see Figure 2.4.5). Currently reading from a vertex texture has quite a high latency, i.e., the time between sending of a texture read command in the shader until that data is available is rather high. Fortunately the shader can process other arithmetic operations that do not depend on the texture read while waiting for its result. The particle system vertex shader contains many operations independent of the particle position (see page 131), and is able to hide the latency of the texture read.

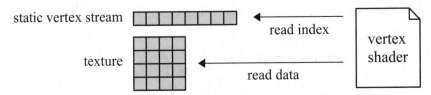

FIGURE 2.4.5   *Accessing a texture from the vertex shader to render particles.*

The alternative solution to vertex textures are "über-buffers" (also called super buffers; see [Mace04]) which basically are a data-agnostic storage of vertex or pixel data in a buffer. This concept is available in hardware since the first generation of floating-point GPUs, but up to now, it is only supported by the OpenGL API. The current implementation uses OpenGL with the `EXT_pixel_buffer_object` extension (see [NVIDIA04]), which offers accelerated asynchronous copying of data inside the GPU memory. Since the data can be copied from pixel to vertex memory (as illustrated in Figure 2.4.6), this is a basic implementation of the über-buffer concept.

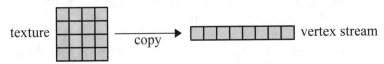

FIGURE 2.4.6   *Transferring pixel to vertex data with the über-buffer concept.*

The particles can be rendered as point sprites, triangles, or quads (see page 131). If vertex textures are used for the data transfer, it does not matter which type of base geometry is used. If multiple vertices per particle are needed, the static vertex buffer can simply contain the texture coordinates replicated three or four times for each particle. Alternatively, the so-called "vertex stream frequency" is introduced on hardware supporting the VS3.0 version. This feature allows reducing the update frequency of vertex input data to a vertex shader. Basically, one entry in a vertex stream can be used for a range of several consecutive vertices, whereas other vertex streams change at a different rate. So, for the particle data, the vertex buffer does not need to contain replicated data, and instead uses an update frequency of three to render triangles or four to render quads.

On hardware that does not support vertex textures or the vertex stream frequency feature, using the über-buffer concept for data transferal requires manual replication of the particle position before rendering. In a further rendering step, the positions need to be rendered three or four times into pixels lying next to each other in a texture. To avoid this overhead, the current implementation uses point sprites which need only one vertex per particle.

Render Particles

Finally, the transferred vertex positions are used to render primitives to the frame buffer in a traditional way. For the reasons mentioned in the previous section and in order to reduce the workload of the vertex unit, particles are currently rendered as point sprites. Compared to rendering single triangles or quads this reduces the number of vertices to a third or a quarter. The disadvantage though is that particles are always axis-aligned and do not have a 2D rotation about the screen space z axis. To overcome this limitation, a 2D rotation is applied to the texture coordinates inside the pixel shader. The decision about using point sprites or generating triangle/quad geometry is made depending on the distribution of workload between vertex and pixel units of a particular application.

During the rendering, other attributes (e.g., color and size) are computed inside the vertex shader from the particle-type parameters (see page 121). Some of them take into account the relative age of the particle or a pseudorandom function.

The current implementation uses the following computation rules for these particle attributes: the size of a particle is random within a range that is defined by the particle type. The initial orientation and a rotation velocity (2D in screen space) are also determined randomly within a defined type-based range.

Based on the relative age of the particle the color and opacity are interpolated from four keyframes. These keyframes are defined for each particle type and need not be equidistant. They define three linear function segments that are first converted into a form for efficient GPU evaluation and then uploaded with the particle type data.

It is not possible to switch textures on a per-particle basis while rendering. Thus it is necessary to combine different textures into tiles of a larger 2D texture. Each particle then modifies the texture coordinates appropriately. If point sprites are used, the texture coordinates will be generated automatically by the rasterizer in the range [0–1] × [0–1]. The sub-texture selection then needs to be done in the pixel shader. Fortunately, the texture coordinate transformation for the 2D rotation we described above will do the sub-texture selection basically for free, as a transformation by a 2×2 or by a 3×2 matrix both need two vector instructions.

Conclusion

Of course processors are never fast enough, so the implementation on the recent generation of GPUs simulates and renders a 1024×1024 texture of particles in real-time only with few effects and without sorting. Sharing the GPU with other techniques and using the full feature set currently allows up to 512×512 particles. The performance is expected to improve significantly with the next generation of PC graphics hardware.

This article has shown how to design and implement a state-preserving physical particle simulation on current programmable graphics hardware. The simulation can use either Euler or Verlet integration to update the particle positions. Other particle attributes are simulated with less complex algorithms. Without permanent storage they are always evaluated on demand. Additionally, an efficient parallel sorting algorithm for particles has been described.

The main strength of GPU-based particle systems is the low cost of individual operations on the data set. Once a basic algorithm is implemented, endless ideas for manipulating velocity and position come up and are easily implemented in higher level shading languages.

How applicable to upcoming video game console hardware the introduced state-preserving particle simulation is, remains to be seen. But the trend toward increased multi-processing hardware is a good indication that the parallel computation of particle systems will grow in importance.

Acknowledgments

Thanks to Wolfgang Engel, Nicolas Thibieroz, my colleagues at Massive Development, especially Ingo Frick, Dr. Christoph Luerig, and Mark Novozhilov, and Prof. Andreas Kolb from the University of Siegen for the fruitful discussions and support in writing this article. Also thanks very much to Sieggi Fleder for never giving up on my Germanic English. Furthermore, much appreciation is owed to Matthias Wloka and his colleagues at NVIDIA, who helped the demo implementation to stay *on* the cutting edge of technology.

References

[Batcher68] Batcher, Kenneth E., "Sorting Networks and their Applications," Spring Joint Computer Conference, AFIPS Proceedings 1968.

[Burg00] van der Burg, John, "Building an Advanced Particle System," *Game Developer Magazine* (03/2000).

[Jakobsen01] Jakobsen, Thomas, "Advanced Character Physics," GDC Proceedings 2001.

[Kolb04] Kolb, Andreas; Latta, Lutz; Rezk-Salama, Christof, "Hardware-based Simulation and Collision Detection for Large Particle Systems," Graphics Hardware Proceedings 2004.

[Lang03] Lang, Hans W., "Odd-Even Merge Sort," available online at *http://www.iti.fh-flensburg.de/lang/algorithmen/sortieren/oemen.htm*, 2003.

[Mace04] Mace, Rob, "OpenGL ARB Superbuffers," available online at *http://www.ati.com/developer/gdc/SuperBuffers.pdf*, 2004.

[Mark03] Mark, William R.; Glanville, R. Steven; Akeley, Kurt; Kilgard, Mark J., "Cg: A System for Programming Graphics Hardware in a C-like Language," SIGGRAPH Proceedings 2003.

[McAllister00] McAllister, David K., "The Design of an API for Particle Systems," Technical Report, Department of Computer Science, University of North Carolina at Chapel Hill, 2000.

[Microsoft02] Microsoft Corporation, "DirectX9 SDK," available online at *http://msdn.microsoft.com/directx/*, 2002–2004.

[NVIDIA01] NVIDIA Corporation, "NVIDIA SDK," available online at *http://developer.nvidia.com/*, 2001–2004.

[NVIDIA04] NVIDIA Corporation, "OpenGL Extension `EXT_pixel_buffer_object`," available online at *http://www.nvidia.com/dev_content/nvopenglspecs/GL_EXT_pixel_buffer_object.txt*, 2004.

[OpenGL03] OpenGL ARB, "OpenGL Extension `ARB_vertex_shader`," available online at *http://oss.sgi.com/projects/ogl-sample/registry/ARB/vertex_shader.txt*, 2003.

[Reeves83] Reeves, William T., "Particle Systems—Technique for Modeling a Class of Fuzzy Objects," SIGGRAPH Proceedings 1983.

[Sims90] Sims, Karl, "Particle Animation and Rendering Using Data Parallel Computation," SIGGRAPH Proceedings 1990.

[Verlet67] Verlet, Loup, "Computer Experiments on Classical Fluids. I. Thermodynamical Properties of Lennard-Jones Molecules," *Physical Review* (159/1967).

2.5

Parallax Occlusion Mapping: Self-Shadowing, Perspective-Correct Bump Mapping Using Reverse Height Map Tracing

Zoe Brawley and Natalya Tatarchuk

Introduction

Throughout history artists specialized in creating the illusion of detail and depth without actually building a concrete model of reality on the canvas. Similarly, in computer graphics we frequently want to create a compelling impression of the scene without the full cost of highly detailed geometry. To avoid creating extremely high-polygon count models, bump mapping was introduced in early computer graphics days in [Blinn78]. Bump mapping is a technique for making surfaces appear detailed and uneven in some pre-determined manner by perturbing the surface normal using a texture. This approach creates the visual illusion of surface detail that would otherwise eat up most of the project's polygonal budgets such as fissures and cracks in terrain and rocks, textured bark on trees, clothes, wrinkles, etc. Since then there have been many extensions to the basic bump mapping technique including emboss bump mapping, environment map bump mapping, and the highly popular dot product bump mapping (normal mapping). For a more detailed description of these techniques look in [Möller02].

Bump mapping doesn't take into account the geometric depth of the surface and therefore does not exhibit parallax. Since this technique displays various visual artifacts (described in detail in the next section), several approaches were introduced to simulate the parallax effect for bump mapped geometry. However, existing parallax techniques cannot account for self-occluding geometry or add shadowing effects. Indeed, shadows provide a very important visual cue for surface detail. The main contribution of this article is an advanced technique for simulating the illusion of depth on uneven surfaces without increasing the geometric complexity of rendered objects. This is accomplished by computing a perspective-correct bump map preserving parallax effect using a novel reverse height map tracing technique. We also describe a method for computing self-shadowing effects for self-occluding objects. The resulting approach allows us to simulate pseudo-geometry displacement in the pixel shader instead of modeling geometric details polygonally. This allows us to render surface detail providing a convincing visual impression of depth from varying viewpoints, utilizing the per-pixel capabilities of the latest generation of graphics hardware.

Common Bump Mapping Artifacts

When standard bump mapping techniques are applied per-pixel, the appearance of surface detail is marginally believable. Although they offer a relatively inexpensive way to add surface detail, there are several downsides to these techniques. Common bump mapping techniques lack the ability to represent view-dependent unevenness of detailed surfaces, and therefore fail to represent the motion parallax effect—the apparent displacement of the object due to viewpoint change. In recent years, new approaches for simulating displacement on surfaces have been introduced. [Kaneko01] and [Welsh03] described an approach for parallax mapping for representing surface detail using normal maps, [Wang03] introduced a technique for view-dependent displacement mapping which improved displaying surface and silhouette detail.

Another limitation of bump mapping techniques is the inability to properly model self-shadowing of the bump mapped surface, adding an unrealistic effect to the final look. [Sloan00] described a horizon mapping technique, first introduced in [Max88]. With this approach the height of the shadowing horizon at each point on the bump map for eight cardinal directions is encoded in a series of textures which are used to determine the amount of self-shadowing for a given light position during rendering. A variety of other techniques were introduced for this purpose. Again, the reader may refer to an excellent survey in [Möller02].

A further drawback is the smooth silhouettes of bump mapped objects, not displaying the surface detail on the boundaries (since during bump mapping only the normal used in the lighting equation is perturbed, not the actual geometric surface normal). The approach described in this article does not address this concern; however, several approaches have been implemented to resolve this issue. Displacement mapping is an excellent solution for this problem. It is a technique for tessellating the original surface into a large number of small triangles, vertices of which are displaced by using a supplied height function. However a major disadvantage of this approach is the fact that it isn't available in most consumer hardware at the present time and that displacement mapping requires fairly highly tessellated models in order to achieve satisfactory results, thus negating the polygon-saving effect of bump mapping.

[Wang03] describes a per-pixel technique for self-shadowing view-dependent rendering capable of handling occlusions and correct display of silhouette detail. The precomputed surface description is stored in multiple texture maps (the data is precomputed from a supplied height map). The view-dependent displacement mapping textures approach displays convincing parallax effect by storing the texel relationship from several viewing directions. However, the cost of storing multiple additional texture maps for surface description is prohibitive for most real-time applications; despite the fact that this technique does produce very realistic images at high frame rates.

Parallax Occlusion Mapping

Parallax mapping approximates the correct appearance and lighting of uneven surfaces by modifying the texture coordinate for each pixel [Kaneko01]. The effect of parallax is seen by the viewer when portions of a surface appear to move relative to one another due to a change in the view position. Thus parallax is a very important visual cue for viewing non-flat surfaces. However, creating a complex geometric object to simulate the details of the surface is computationally expensive and thus prohibitive to real-time rendering practices. Instead surface height data can be used for approximating surface appearance using techniques described in this chapter.

The effect of motion parallax for a surface can be computed by applying a height map with additional surface details and offsetting each pixel in the height map using the geometry normal and the eye vector. As you move the geometry away from their original positions using that vector, the parallax is obtained by the fact that the highest points on the height map would move the farthest along that vector and the lower extremes would appear not to be moving at all. To obtain satisfactory results for true perspective simulation, one would need to displace every pixel in the height map using the eye vector and the geometry normal. However, that approach can be fill-limiting and computationally expensive for large height maps in real-time scenarios, although it yields excellent results simulating the parallax effect for the entire surface.

Tangent Space

Before we can introduce a detailed explanation of real-time computation of parallax effect, we must clarify the concept of tangent space since our technique relies on this understanding. Bump mapping works by perturbing the geometric normal or replacing it altogether with a normal vector stored in a texture map. The normal vectors are computed in the tangent space for each vertex. Tangent space is used for orientation of the texture map at each vertex. Since texture coordinates basis vectors $\bar{u}$ and $\bar{v}$ can be oriented arbitrarily at each vertex, a question arises in regard to the correct orientation for applying texture maps. We can use the tangent space basis vectors $\bar{T}$ and $\bar{B}$ to orient $\bar{u}$ and $\bar{v}$ respectively.

From a mathematical standpoint, if we view a polygonal vertex as a point on a differentiable manifold, this vertex has a real vector space that contains all possible directions for passing through the given point tangent to the surface. Although we are operating on 3D objects, the actual surfaces that we are computing lighting equations for are in fact 2D manifolds. For 2D surfaces, the tangent space is planar (generally speaking, tangent space has the same dimensions as the manifold's dimensions). It can be pictured as follows: if the given surface is a sphere, the tangent space at each sphere's vertex is the plane that touches the sphere at that point and is perpendicular to the sphere's normal through that point.

Figure 2.5.1 displaces tangent space basis vectors on a sphere and a torus, where vector T is the tangent vector, $\bar{B}$ is the binormal vector, and $\bar{N}$ is the normal vector for each vertex.

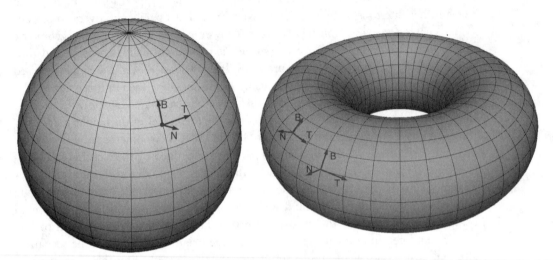

FIGURE 2.5.1   *Tangent space basis vectors on sphere and torus manifolds.*

Given a normal in tangent space, in order to correctly compute the result of the lighting equation for any point on the surface, we need to transform the light vector into tangent space. That's done via a simple matrix multiplication by a tangent space transformation matrix formed by unit tangent, binormal, and normal vectors as follows:

$$\begin{pmatrix} t_x & t_y & t_y & 0 \\ b_x & b_y & b_z & 0 \\ n_x & n_y & n_z & 0 \\ 0 & 0 & 0 & 1 \end{pmatrix}$$

where $(b_x, b_y, b_z$ is the binormal vector, computed by simply taking the cross product $\bar{B} = \bar{N} \times \bar{T}$. Typically the tangent basis vectors are precomputed at preprocessing time. Note that the light vector must be transformed into tangent space separately for each vertex, since for non-planar objects, tangent basis vectors will vary for each vertex.

Basic Parallax Mapping

In order to understand how parallax mapping works, we first visualize a height map representing the geometry of a simple pyramid, mapped onto a flat plane (Figure

2.5.2). If we display this object with plain texture mapping without shifting texture coordinates, the geometry will appear flattened because we are not fully taking the height map into account. If we were to view the actual geometry for the pyramid, the elevated points on the pyramid would correctly move away from the viewer and the points in valleys would move toward the eye. This aids the perspective perception of the geometry in space. In order to achieve this effect, we must displace the texture coordinates for sampling the height map in texture space according to the apparent screen space distortion. Therefore the viewed objects will appear to shift in perspective thus simulating their actual geometric properties.

FIGURE 2.5.2 *A height map representing a pyramid.*

Figure 2.5.3 shows how the texture map for this pyramid would distort in texture space in order to appear as if it is shifting in perspective when mapped onto a flat surface.

FIGURE 2.5.3 *Perspective distortion for a pyramid when mapped onto a plane.*

One way to create texture distortion to simulate parallax is to use the view vector to shift samples from a height map. This approach samples the height map per-pixel at the original texture coordinates, scales and biases it, and then uses the view vector at that point to shift the texture coordinates. This is described in more detail in [Welsh04]. The vector used to offset the texture coordinates in the direction of the view vector is called the parallax vector. Figure 2.5.4 shows the vectors in tangent space, where $\bar{N}$ is the normal vector at the sampled point, $\bar{T}$ is the tangent vector, $\bar{B}$ is the binormal vector, $\bar{E}$ is the eye (view) vector, and $\bar{P}$ is the desired parallax vector.

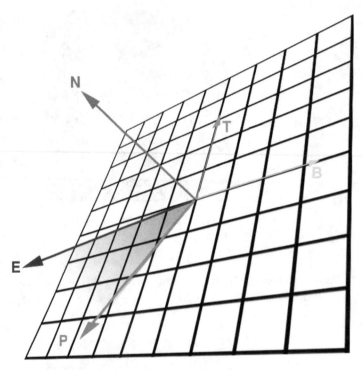

FIGURE 2.5.4 *Tangent space vectors.*

The length of this parallax vector represents the distance that the highest points in the height map for the original sample would displace in texture space. The pixel is then displaced in the height map along the parallax vector by a distance that is a percentage of the parallax vector's length based on the height map values at the starting sample point. In order to get satisfactory results we would need to set appropriate scale and bias based on the actual represented height values in the height map. The resulting shifted texture coordinate can be used to sample the height map approximating the same sample point that we would have if we had actual geometric object representation.

One serious visual artifact with this simple approach is the resulting shimmering of textured pixels when viewed at grazing angles when the view vector is nearly perpendicular to the surface normal. This happens because at these viewing angles, texture coordinate displacement values tend to be large, and for objects with varying per-pixel heights, this results in low coherency for height map samples, thus producing a strong shimmering effect. In order to reduce this shimmering, [Welsh04] introduces an offset limiting concept, whereby we would limit the parallax displacement for each pixel so that it doesn't exceed the original height sampled from the height map at the starting texture coordinate. Although this technique reduces shimmering, since it's simply a heuristic, it doesn't perform in a reasonable fashion for many complicated height maps.

Parallax Occlusion Mapping

In order to improve the approach for computing parallax, we describe a novel technique using the reverse of the above process to efficiently achieve parallax. The core idea is to trace the pixel being currently rendered back in the height map to determine which texel in the height map would yield the rendered pixel location if in fact we would have been using actual displaced geometry.

To determine a new location for the perspective-correct pixel, we use the parallax vector. In order to compute the parallax vector, we construct a plane between the view vector and the geometric normal from the normal map of the surface. The parallax vector lies on the intersection of this plane with the tangent plane at the sample point. To determine the length of the parallax vector we can use the world space apparent height for the displaced geometry and the angle between the view vector and the parallax vector. The desired displaced pixel will lie along the profile of the parallax vector. We will next sample the height map along the direction of the reversed parallax vector. The accuracy of this technique depends on the number of samples that we will take from the supplied height map. By plotting the resulting samples we construct a profile of the displaced geometry along the parallax vector. We create a line by tracing from the maximum displacement at the end of the reversed parallax vector to the original starting point. The intersection point of that line will yield the perspective-correct displacement location that we set out to find.

This technique also allows for the simulation of geometric occlusion and self-shadowing effects. By using the light vector instead of the view vector in the above algorithm we can create proper self-shadowing effect for perspective-shifted bump maps to further increase the illusion of depth and surface detail.

For this method to work properly, it would require moving every pixel in the texture map [and filling in gaps between them], and the result would have to be completely recalculated for every pixel on the screen. To apply this in any useable application the solution is to instead back trace on the reversed parallax vector, sampling as many points as possible, and solve for the point which should displace forward to the point we started from.

Determining Perspective-Correct Parallax Displacement Offset

Determining an accurate parallax displacement vector is at the heart of this approach. Although we are going to be computing this displacement value per-pixel, we can improve the efficiency of the algorithm by computing the initial parallax displacement vector in the vertex shader, and then by simply using hardware interpolators to yield the resulting per-pixel starting parallax displacement vector. In order to compute this displacement vector, we need to first calculate the view, tangent, binormal and normal vector for the point. Since we are computing an offset vector for sampling the height map in tangent space, all of these vectors must first be transformed into tangent space and then normalized.

To simulate a height map for convex surfaces extending outward from the flat geometry, we compute the parallax displacement vector using dot products of the view, tangent, and binormal vectors. Figure 2.5.5 shows the vectors where $\overline{N}$ is the surface normal, $\overline{T}$ is the tangent vector, $\overline{B}$ is the binormal, $\overline{E}$ is the view (eye) vector, and $\overline{P}$ is the reversed parallax displacement vector.

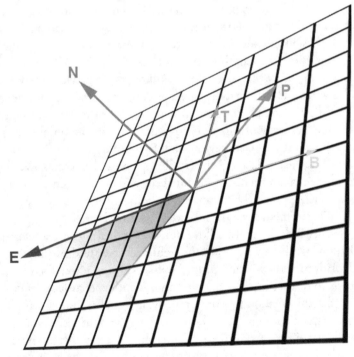

FIGURE 2.5.5   *Tangent space reversed parallax vector.*

To determine the direction of the parallax vector for texture displacement, we compute it as:

$$P_x = \bar{E} \cdot \bar{T}$$
$$P_y = \bar{E} \cdot \bar{B} \qquad (2.5.1)$$

This will give us the correct direction for the parallax vector. However, if we simply use the length of this vector as the actual displacement amount, we would achieve incorrect results. Although this parallax vector would display proper direction for shifting of the texture coordinate, it would miscalculate the displacement amount, resulting in an excessive parallax shift when the surface is angled towards the camera, and lack of parallax shift as the surface approaches angles perpendicular to the camera plane.

Therefore we must compute a more accurate parallax vector. In order to do that, we introduce a parallax binormal vector, $\bar{P}_b$, which is the cross product between the normal vector and the view vector (see Figure 2.5.6 for visualization of these vectors in tangent space for the sample point, where $\bar{N}$ is the surface normal, $\bar{T}$ is the tangent vector, $\bar{B}$ is the binormal, $\bar{E}$ is the eye (view) vector, $\bar{P}_b$ is the parallax binormal vector, and $\bar{P}$ is the parallax displacement vector):

$$\bar{P}_b = \bar{N} \times \bar{E} \qquad (2.5.2)$$

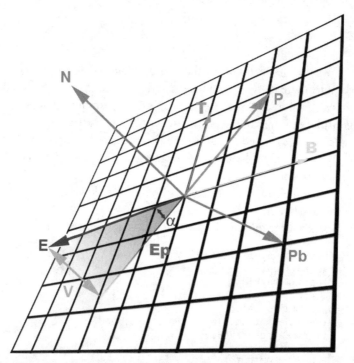

FIGURE 2.5.6 *Vectors used for parallax displacement amount computation.*

Then, using this parallax binormal vector, we compute the new parallax displacement vector as follows:

$$\vec{P} = \vec{N} \times \vec{P_b} \qquad (2.5.3)$$

Next, we need to determine the length of the parallax displacement vector. This is crucial for the correct approximation of the desired displaced height for the sample pixel since the displacement amount will determine the apparent height for the given point and thus will be the controlling factor for a good parallax effect. If we were to use the input height map to actually displace geometry, the amount of height displacement would be equal to the quantity V that we see in Figure 2.5.6, which is the apparent vertical scale for parallax. Notice that this value is highly dependent on the content created by the artist. To solve for the amount of parallax displacement, i.e., parallax vector length, we should look at the right angle triangle formed by vectors $\vec{V}$, $\vec{E}$, and $\vec{E}_p$ (the view vector projected onto the tangent plane). The length of the parallax displacement amount will be equal to the length of $\vec{E}_p$. The angle between $\vec{E}$ and $\vec{E}_p$, α, can be computed as follows:

$$\alpha = \text{acos}\,(\vec{E} \cdot \vec{P}) \qquad (2.5.4)$$

where $\vec{P}$ is the parallax displacement vector computed in Equation 2.5.4. Note that $\vec{P}$ should be normalized prior to computing (Equation 2.5.4).

Then using the result obtained from Equation 2.5.4, we can compute the length of the parallax displacement as:

$$l_p = \frac{1}{\tan(\alpha)} * |\vec{V}| \qquad (2.5.5)$$

Create a 2D vector from the x and y displacement values, normalize its length, and multiply that by the parallax length and we now have correct x and y displacement values in texture space. Our goal is to determine which points in the height map will displace to the sample point currently being rendered. In order to calculate these sample points, we need to sample the height map in the reverse direction of the apparent parallax vector. Therefore we negate the computed parallax displacement vector for resulting computations.

After some simplifications, we obtain the following vertex shader for computing parallax displacement direction and amount:

Vertex shader for computing parallax displacement vector (vs_2_0):

```
float4x4 matViewInverse;
float4x4 matViewProjection;
float4x4 matView;

float fBaseScale;
float fHeightScale;
float fPerspectiveBias;

struct VS_OUTPUT
{
```

```
      float4 Position    : POSITION;    // Transformed position
      float2 TexCoord    : TEXCOORD0;   // Initial texture coordinate
      float2 vParallaxXY : TEXCOORD1;   // Parallax displacement vector
};

VS_OUTPUT vs_main(
   float4 inPosition: POSITION,
   float2 inTexCoord: TEXCOORD0,
   float3 inNormal  : NORMAL,
   float3 inBinormal: BINORMAL,
   float3 inTangent : TANGENT)
{
   VS_OUTPUT Out = (VS_OUTPUT) 0;

   // Transform and output vertex position:
   Out.Position = mul( matViewProjection, inPosition );

   // Propagate texture coordinates:
   Out.TexCoord = inTexCoord;

   // Compute view vector (in view space):
   float3 vView = -mul( matView, inPosition );

   // Compute tangent space basis vector (in view space):
   float3 vTangent  =  mul( matView, inTangent  );
   float3 vBinormal =  mul( matView, inBinormal );
   float3 vNormal   =  mul( matView, inNormal   );

   // Normalize the view vector in tangent space:
   float3 vViewTS = mul( float3x3( vTangent, vBinormal, vNormal),
                         normalize( vView ) );

   // Compute initial parallax displacement direction:
   float2 vParallaxDirection = normalize( vViewTS.xy );

   // Compute the length of parallax displacement vector
   // i.e. the amount of parallax displacement.
   float fParallaxLength= -sqrt(1 - vViewTS.z * vViewTS.z ) /
vViewTS.z;

   // Compute parallax bias parameter which allows
   // the artists control over the parallax perspective
   // bias via an artist editable parameter 'fPerspectiveBias'
   // Use view vector length in tangent space as an offset
   // limiting technique as well:
   float fParallaxBias = fPerspectiveBias + (1 - fPerspectiveBias) *
                         (2 * vViewTS.z - 1 );

   // Compute the actual reverse parallax displacement vector:
   Out.vParallaxXY = -vParallaxDirection * fParallaxLength *
                      fParallaxBias * fHeightScale;

   return Out;
}
```

Reverse Height Map Tracing

In order to understand the process for reverse height map tracing, let's first imagine that we are trying to determine parallax displacement for the original sample point P_s in Figure 2.5.7. The green curve in this figure represents the actual profile of the input height map. Note that if we were to directly sample the height map at P_s, we would see the height profile for point 0 along the green line. This point represents our original, non-displaced texture coordinate for a given pixel. However, for a given viewing direction, when simulating accurate parallax, the viewer actually should be seeing point P_d instead. How do we arrive at this point P_d given a reversed parallax vector $\bar{P}$?

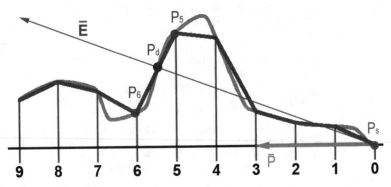

FIGURE 2.5.7   *The process for reverse height map tracing.*

If we were to trace along the reversed parallax vector $\bar{P}$ and discretely sample the height map along the intervals 0–9, the resulting discrete height map samples will yield a profile drawn as a thick blue line over the green profile of actual continuous height map values.

In order to compute the location of point P_d, we should start at interval 9 and trace along the parallax vector toward the starting point, computing the height map sample profile. The first intersection between the sampled height map profile and the view vector will yield the desired height value that the viewer would see if the height map was actually used to displace the geometry.

In order to compute the intersection point P_d, we test each sample height value for each interval to see if it's above the height value of the view vector at that point. The first time when the sampled height value is higher than the view vector height (as projected onto the tangent plane) will determine the segment of the height profile that will contain the desired displacement height. The intersection point P_d will be located between the found sample point and its previous interval. To yield the actual value, we solve the line-line intersection equation between the view vector $\bar{E}$ and the height sample profile between the points that contain P_d. In the example shown in

Figure 2.5.7, the desired intersection point P_d falls in the interval between samples 5 and 6. The line formed by the sampled height map values P_5 and P_6 is intersected with the view vector to yield the actual value for P_d.

Pixel shader for computing parallax displaced coordinate (ps_2_0):

```
sampler tNormalMap;

float4 ps_main( float2 inTexCoord: TEXCOORD0,
                float2 vParallax : TEXCOORD1 ): COLOR0
{
    // Compute height map profile for 8 samples:
    // Note that the height map is contained in the alpha channel
    // of the input normal map:
    float h0 = tex2D( tNormalMap, inTexCoord - vParallax * 1.000 ).w;
    float h1 = tex2D( tNormalMap, inTexCoord - vParallax * 0.875 ).w;
    float h2 = tex2D( tNormalMap, inTexCoord - vParallax * 0.750 ).w;
    float h3 = tex2D( tNormalMap, inTexCoord - vParallax * 0.625 ).w;
    float h4 = tex2D( tNormalMap, inTexCoord - vParallax * 0.500 ).w;
    float h5 = tex2D( tNormalMap, inTexCoord - vParallax * 0.375 ).w;
    float h6 = tex2D( tNormalMap, inTexCoord - vParallax * 0.250 ).w;
    float h7 = tex2D( tNormalMap, inTexCoord - vParallax * 0.125 ).w;

    // Determine the section in the height profile that contains
    // a sample that is higher than the view vector. This determines
    // the correct displacement point:
    float x,  y;
    float xh, yh;

    if        ( h7 > 0.875 ) { x = 0.875; y = 1.000; xh = h7; yh = h7; }
    else if ( h6 > 0.750 ) { x = 0.750; y = 0.875; xh = h6; yh = h7; }
    else if ( h5 > 0.625 ) { x = 0.625; y = 0.750; xh = h5; yh = h6; }
    else if ( h4 > 0.500 ) { x = 0.500; y = 0.625; xh = h4; yh = h5; }
    else if ( h3 > 0.375 ) { x = 0.375; y = 0.500; xh = h3; yh = h4; }
    else if ( h2 > 0.250 ) { x = 0.250; y = 0.375; xh = h2; yh = h3; }
    else if ( h1 > 0.125 ) { x = 0.125; y = 0.250; xh = h1; yh = h2; }
    else                   { x = 0.000; y = 0.125; xh = h0; yh = h1; }

    // Compute the intersection between the view vector and the high-
est
    // sample point in the height profile:
    float fParallaxEffect = ( x * (y - yh) - y * (x - xh) ) /
                            (( y - yh ) - ( x - xh ) );

    return float4( vParallax * (1 - fParallaxEffect), 0.0, 1.0 );
}
```

Note that the accuracy of this calculation depends on the number of samples taken for the height map profile. In reality this factor is gated by the number of available pixel shader texture fetches. If one desires to improve the accuracy of resulting parallax occlusion mapping computation, separate sections of height profiles can be computed with greater accuracy in individual passes and composited together in the final pass, thus resulting in a multipass approach. Another way to improve the accuracy is to use more advanced shader models available on the latest graphics hardware, for example, pixel shaders ps_2_b, which contain a greater number of ALU instructions and texture fetches. The desired accuracy depends greatly on the quality and intent of the art content developed for this effect.

Lighting for Pseudo-Displacement Mapping Effect

The height value of the intersection point P_d is assumed to be a value in the 0 to 1 range. Using this value and the original parallax displacement direction and amount, we can generate a more correct perspective displacement value, d_{offset}. Using the original texture coordinates for a given pixel and displacing them by the new d_{offset} amount, we compute an accurate position in texture space for representing true parallax shift of the apparent texture by the height map as seen by the viewer. We can use the new displaced texture coordinate for all subsequent queries for applied texture maps, such as a normal map, diffuse, specular, detail maps, etc. This results in the surface of the object having the distinct appearance of displacement mapping using the input height map (see Figure 2.5.8). Thus we've effectively achieved geometric pseudo-displacement at the pixel shader level.

FIGURE 2.5.8   *Result of applying lighting with parallax occlusion mapping.*

Since reverse height map tracing in the pixel shader 2.0 model typically consumes all available texture fetch instructions, we compute the lighting effects for the surface in a subsequent pass. However, in pixel shader 2.b we can compute both parallax displacement and the lighting for the surface in the same pixel shader, which performs very efficiently on the latest generation of graphics hardware. The vertex shader and the pixel shader for the lighting pass can be found in the RenderMonkey parallax occlusion workspace on the CD-ROM accompanying this book.

ON THE CD

Self-Occlusion and Shadowing Computation

An additional advantage of the parallax occlusion mapping technique lies in the fact that it can be used to simulate self-occlusion and shadowing effects. The height map can in fact cast shadows on itself. This is accomplished by substituting the light vector for the view vector when computing the intersection of the height profile to determine the correct displaced texel position during the reverse height mapping step. We can re-use the parallax displacement vector computed in an earlier pass. We do not solve for the first intersection between the light vector and the height profile. Instead we simply test whether any point in the sampled height profile is above the light vector for the sample point. If that is the case, we then know that the height map geometry for the sampled profile is in fact blocking the light source for the sample point, and therefore it will be in shadow. Figure 2.5.9 shows shadows computed as a result of this test.

FIGURE 2.5.9 *Self-Occlusion shadowing effects with parallax occlusion mapping.*

Notice that the shadows are correctly aligned with the occluded displaced texture. In order to achieve this effect, the height map values used to create the sampled height map profile for this test must use the displaced texture coordinates computed during the parallax occlusion part of the algorithm. This way the self-occlusion shadows correctly line up with pseudo-displaced geometry. If we were to use the original input texture coordinate during computations of the shadows, they would appear floating on the surface of the object (as shown in Figure 2.5.10) since they would actually be computed for initial sample points, rather than for displaced texture coordinates.

FIGURE 2.5.10   *Incorrect shadow resulting due to non-shifted texture sample point.*

Computing shadows with parallax occlusion mapping is a straightforward technique to implement and yields very convincing self-shadowing effects that can be otherwise very expensive to compute. This technique also doesn't require much additional memory cost, since for multipass approaches we can output the shadow map in the alpha channel of the parallax occlusion map computed during the parallax displacement part of the algorithm. If we are operating in shader model 2.b then we can simply use longer shaders to compute a shadowing term before calculating the lighting equation result.

Limitations of the Parallax Occlusion Mapping Technique

Although parallax occlusion mapping is a very powerful and flexible technique for computing real-time lighting in detailed objects, we must make the readers aware of its limitations. One of the key limitations of this technique is that any peak in the height map profile which falls between the height map sample points will be missed. If we look at Figure 2.5.11, we will see that peaks in sample regions 9–8, 8–7, 7–6, 4–3, and 3–2 will be missed by the sampled height map profile due to insufficient sampling frequency.

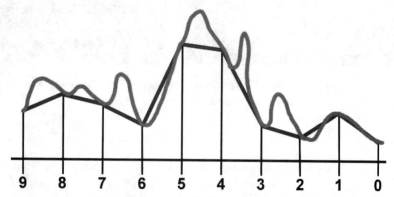

FIGURE 2.5.11 *Missed height details resulting due to very high-frequency height map profile.*

Another obvious downside of this approach is the fact that it will not create apparent object detail along the boundaries of the displayed objects (unlike displacement mapping technique, which exhibits correct object silhouettes since it actually modifies geometry). This limitation is common to all bump mapping techniques since they rely on perturbed surface normal used for lighting computations, not by modifying geometry directly.

When parallax-mapped objects are viewed at angles nearly perpendicular to the surface normal, the parallax displacement amount approaches infinity. Therefore entire features in the height map may be missed completely. This results in severely flattened objects when viewed at grazing angles. This is particularly visible when displacing planar objects. Figure 2.5.12(a) shows a nearly planar disc with parallax—all of the bumps display correct profile along the surface of the disc. However, if we were to rotate this disc so that the view vector is nearly perpendicular to the surface normal, we would see that most of the height details have disappeared from the surface (Figure 2.5.12(b)) and the height map would appear distorted and flat.

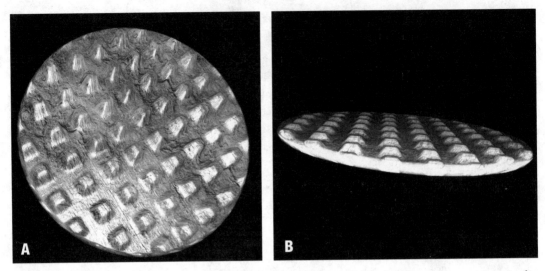

FIGURE 2.5.12   *Steep viewing angles of artifacts of parallax mapping. (a) Correct perspective parallax display (b) Flattened height map due to grazing view angles.*

This artifact is common to all parallax approaches. One solution to this problem is to introduce an additional parameter during the computation of the parallax displacement amount in the vertex shader. The parameter can reduce the displacement amount when the angle between the view vector and the surface normal approaches 90°. This is similar to the offset limiting approach described in [Welsh04]. However, we use a more accurate observation to constraint the parallax distortion amount as a function of the dot product between the surface normal and the view vector. To allow the artist a level of control for finer parallax effect, we can also further constraint the parallax displacement amount by raising the above dot product to the power of some value n, where n is the artist-controlled parameter for visually adjusting the optimal balance for oblique angle distortion due to separation between nearby parallax levels in texture space.

Non-planar objects do not exhibit this artifact as strongly, so another solution can be to simply use slightly convex geometry instead of flat surfaces (see Figure 2.5.13).

Art Content Suggestions for Parallax Occlusion Mapping

Parallax occlusion mapping technique is a very efficient and compelling technique for simulating surface details. However, as with many other bump mapping techniques, its quality depends strongly on the quality of its art content. Empirically, we found that low-frequency height map textures yield much more coherent parallax due to the limitations described in an earlier section of this chapter. Certain types of high-

FIGURE 2.5.13   *Non-planar geometry with parallax occlusion mapping.*

frequency height maps do perform adequately, such as, for example, a pyramid height map with straight edges (see Figure 2.5.2). Generally speaking, however, we recommend avoiding noisy or extremely detailed height maps since that will likely result in shimmering pixels. High-frequency changes, such as very tall thin spikes in the height map, present the biggest problem during parallax simulation using this technique.

For underlying geometry we recommend using planar, spherical, or cylindrical geometry since its smooth rate of change along the surface ensures a high level of coherency for parallax displacement computation. Complex concave geometry yields very poor results and in particular will display visually distracting artifacts in the valleys. Of course if one already has complex concave geometry, this approach simply may not be as necessary. Note that also, if the base texture map has baked-in lighting information, then if there is a need to save pixel shader instructions or avoid the multipass approach, we can just compute the parallax displacement offset and use it to offset the base texture map for a simple, yet convincing effect without additional lighting or shadowing computations. This particular case is very useful for highly-detailed base maps used with simple geometry and low-frequency height maps.

Sample Effect

ON THE CD   We have provided a RenderMonkey workspace named "Parallax Occlusion Mapping.rfx" demonstrating our technique on the CD-ROM accompanying this book. This requires RenderMonkey 1.5 or higher.

Conclusion

Parallax occlusion mapping can be used effectively to generate an illusion of very detailed geometry exhibiting correct motion parallax as well as producing very convincing self-shadowing effects. It takes advantage of the per-pixel capabilities of the latest graphics hardware to compute all necessary quantities using the programmable pipeline. We hope to see more games implementing compelling scenes using this technique.

References

[Blinn78] Blinn, James F., "Simulation of Wrinkled Surfaces," *Computer Graphics (Siggraph '78 Proceedings)*, August 1978.

[Möller02] Akenine-Möller,T., Haines, E., "Real-Time Rendering," 2nd Edition, *A.K. Peters*, July 2002.

[Kaneko01] Kaneko, T., Takahei, T., Inami, M., Kawakami, N., Yanagida, Y., Maeda, T., Tachi, S., "Detailed Shape Representation with Parallax Mapping," *ICAT*, 2001.

[Sloan00] Sloan, P-P. J., Cohen, M. F, "Interactive Horizon Mapping," *11th Eurographics Workshop on Rendering*, June 2000.

[Max88] Max, N. L., "Horizon Mapping: Shadows for Bump-mapped Surfaces," *The Visual Computer 4*, 2 (July 1988).

[Heidrich00] Heidrich, W., Daubert, K., Kautz, J., Seidel, H-P., "Illuminating Micro Geometry Based on Precomputed Visibility," *ACM Transactions on Graphics (Siggraph 2000 Proceedings)*, July 2000.

[Welsh04] T. Welsh, "Parallax Mapping with Offset Limiting: A Per Pixel Approximation of Uneven Surfaces," 2004.

2.6

Improved Batching via Texture Atlases

Matthias Wloka

Introduction

Batching, or rather, the lack of batching, is a common problem for game developers. A batch consists of a number of render-state changes followed by a draw-call. Submitting hundreds or worse, thousands of batches per frame inevitably makes an application CPU-limited due to inherent driver overhead. See [Wloka03] for a detailed characterization of this problem.

While game developers are aware of and understand this problem, it is nonetheless difficult to avoid: most games require many objects of different characteristics to be displayed, thus they typically require a significant number of render-state changes. Therefore, game developers require practical techniques that allow them to eliminate state-changes and merge batches.

An internal survey of a few recent DirectX 9 titles reveals that the following render-state changes occur most frequently: `SetTexture()`, `SetVertexShaderConstantF()`, `SetPixelShader()`, `SetStreamSource()`, `SetVertexDeclaration()`, and `SetIndices()`.

`SetTexture()` is one of the most common batch-breakers. This article describes a technique for reducing batches caused by having to repeatedly bind different textures, i.e., repeated calls to DirectX 9's `SetTexture()`.

The technique copies multiple textures into one larger texture: we call this larger texture an atlas (sometimes also called a texture page). Models using these packed atlases need to remap their texture coordinates to access the relevant sub-rectangles out of the texture atlas.

We describe this technique in practical detail in "How Batching via Texture Atlases Works". "Using Atlases in Everyday Life" explains why atlas techniques work, despite common misconceptions. Finally, the section "Conclusion" sums up our findings.

How Batching via Texture Atlases Works

The most straightforward way to render, say, two textured quads is to bind the texture of the first quad (i.e., call `SetTexture()`), draw the first quad (i.e., call `DrawPrimitive()`), then bind the texture for the second quad, and finally draw the second quad:

```
SetTexture();
DrawPrimitive();
SetTexture();
DrawPrimitive();
```

This rendering technique requires two batches. If we combine the two textures into a texture atlas, as shown in Figure 2.6.1, we no longer need to call `SetTexture()` between drawing the two quads, and thus are able to combine the two `DrawPrimitive()` calls into one. In other words, we reduce batch-count from two to one:

```
SetTexture();
DrawPrimitive();
```

To access the same texels out of an atlas instead of the original texture, however, one has to modify the texture coordinates of the models referring to that texture. For example, a quad displaying an entire texture uses texture coordinates (0, 0), (0, 1), (1, 0), and (1, 1). In contrast, a quad wanting to show the same texels, but accessed out of an atlas, refers to the atlas's sub-rectangle containing that texture. Figure 2.6.1 shows the texture coordinates for the corner texels of textures A and B, as well as the texture coordinates required to access the same information out of their common atlas.

The following sequence of steps thus enables improved batching via texture atlases:

1. Select a collection of textures that are responsible for breaking batches.
2. Pack this texture collection into one or more texture atlases.
3. Update the texture coordinates of all models using any of the textures in that collection to access the appropriate sub-rectangles of an atlas instead.
4. Ensure that sequential `DrawPrimitive()` calls that are uninterrupted by state-changes issue as a single `DrawPrimitive()` call.

Ideally, steps 1–3 integrate into an existing tool chain, and step 4 is part of the rendering engine.

Selecting a suitable collection of textures for step 1 could be as easy as grouping all textures of the same format into an atlas. To help with steps 2 and 3 NVIDIA provides free tools that are also included on the CD-ROM of this book:

ON THE CD

- The Atlas Creation Tool [AtlasCreation04] is a command-line tool that accepts a collection of textures and packs them into atlases. It also generates a file describing how textures and texture coordinates map from the original texture to a texture atlas. The accompanying user's guide describes its options.
- The Atlas Comparison Viewer [AtlasViewer04] reads and interprets these mapping-files so as to correctly display textures out of atlases. The Atlas Comparison Viewer also demonstrates the feasibility of texture atlases: it provides a pixel-by-pixel comparison of the results of texturing out of textures versus atlases.

A tool to re-map texture coordinates of general models, i.e., a solution to Step 3 above, is not provided: game developers use a variety of model formats and their toolchains differ, so creating such a general tool is ambitious. But since the Atlas Compar-

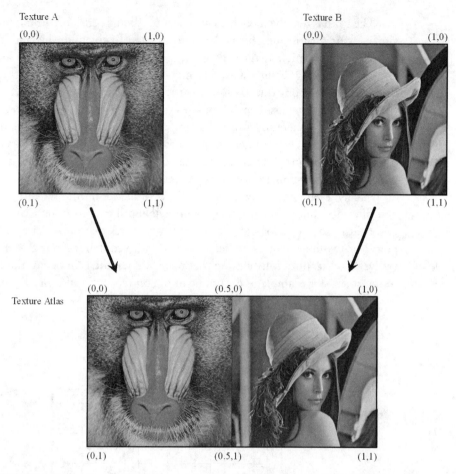

FIGURE 2.6.1 *Combining two textures into an atlas. The texture coordinates for accessing data out of an atlas are adjusted according to where the original texture is in the atlas.*

ison Viewer performs a similar task (re-mapping of texture coordinates for quads), and since its source code is included, we hope that game developers are able to use the provided source as blueprints for their internal tools.

Using Atlases in Everyday Life

Using Mipmaps with Atlases

Mipmapped textures are essential for achieving rendering performance. Packing mipmapped textures into an atlas, however, seems to imply that the mipmaps of these packed textures combine, until eventually the lowest mip-level of 1×1 resolution smears all textures of an atlas into a single texel. It thus seems that using an atlas with mipmaps creates undesirable image-artifacts.

The truth is that the tool-chain generates (or should generate) the mipmaps for individual textures before these are packed into an atlas. To obtain the highest fidelity results a special-purpose mipmap filter should be used (see for example, [TextureTools00]).

When packing textures and their mip-chains into an atlas, the textures as well as their mip-chains copy directly into their respective mipmap levels. Because we never combine texels—we just copy them—no smearing or cross-pollution occurs.

Even when generating a complete mipmap chain for an atlas on the fly, polluting mipmaps with texels from neighboring textures is avoidable: the filter generating the mipmaps should properly clamp at a texture's borders, a requirement also common when generating mipmaps for non-atlas textures.

Finally, even generating mipmap chains of atlases on the fly with a two-by-two box-filter does not pollute mipmaps with neighboring texels if the atlas is a power-of-two texture and contains only power-of-two textures that do not unnecessarily cross power-of-two lines. For example, a 16×16 atlas containing one 8×8 texture and twelve 4×4 textures must ensure that the 8×8 texture is in one of the four corners of the atlas—for example, it cannot be in the center of the atlas (see Figure 2.6.2).

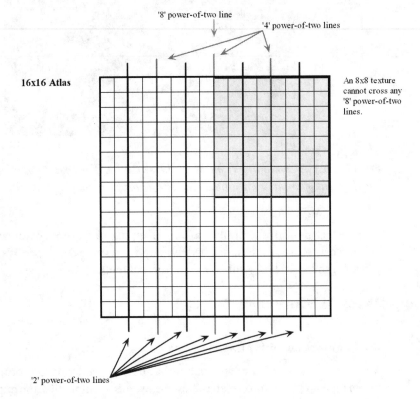

FIGURE 2.6.2   *The '8,' '4,' and '2' power-of-two lines for a 16×16 atlas (note that only vertical power-of-two lines are shown). A sub-texture of dimensions $W \times H$ cannot cross 'W' power-of-two lines horizontally nor can it cross 'H' power-of-two lines vertically.*

As we generate the various mip-levels for such an atlas, texels of separate textures do not combine until the 2×2 level. In the 4×4 atlas-level, the 8×8 texture corresponds to a 2×2 texel block and the 4×4 textures reduce to single texels each. To be able to represent the 8×8 texture with a single texel, we also need to generate the 2×2 level of the atlas. And thus the 2×2 level contains one texel representing the 8×8 texture and three texels representing the combination of four 4×4 textures each: pollution occurs (see Figure 2.6.3).

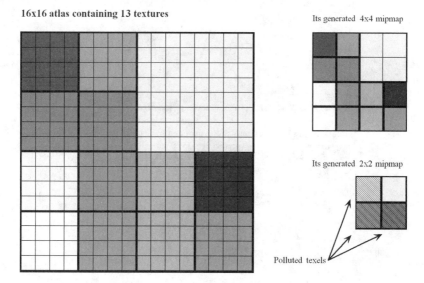

FIGURE 2.6.3   *Texture pollution at the 2×2 mip-level for an atlas containing 8×8 and 4×4 textures.*

Even when copying mip-chains into an atlas a similar problem occurs: because textures can differ in size and large textures have longer mip-chains than smaller textures, the largest texture packed into an atlas determines the minimum number of mipmap levels in that atlas. The smaller textures thus have effectively longer than necessary mip-chains whose bottom-most levels are uninitialized (see Figure 2.6.4).

Solution approaches might be to abridge an atlas's mip-chain to the length of the mip-chain of the smallest texture contained in the atlas—at the expense of performance and image quality. Another approach is to limit only same or similar size textures to pack into the same atlas. Luckily, these measures are uncalled for.

Because models using texture atlases use modified texture coordinates (see above section "How Batching via Texture Atlases Works"), a triangle's texture coordinates never span across multiple atlas sub-rectangles containing separate textures. Thus, even when a single triangle spans an entire sub-texture in an atlas, and even if that triangle maps to a single pixel on screen, then only the one-texel representation of that

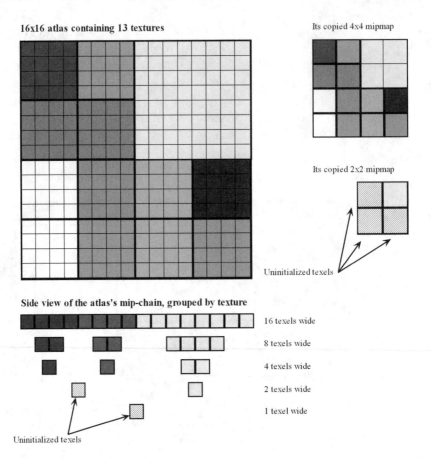

FIGURE 2.6.4   *Uninitialized texels at the 2 × 2 and 1 × 1 mipmaps for an atlas containing 8 × 8 and 4 × 4 textures.*

texture is accessed. This one-texel representation is filled with valid non-polluted data (see Figure 2.6.5). In other words, in order to be able to access the bottom-most, uninitialized, or polluted mip-levels, a sub-texture spanning triangle would have to be smaller than half a pixel. DirectX's rasterization rules make it unlikely that such a triangle generates any pixels. Thus, corruption due to accessing these bottom-most mip-levels does not occur. Using a positive mipmap LOD-bias to artificially blur textures, however, forces access to these bottom-most mip-levels and should be avoided.

To save video-memory, it is nonetheless good practice to avoid storing completely uninitialized mip-levels. For example, a 1k × 1k atlas containing 16 256 × 256 textures should only store eight mip-levels: the 2 × 2 and 1 × 1 levels do not contain relevant data and are superfluous.

The Atlas Creation Tool [AtlasCreation04] follows these principles and copies a texture's mip-chain into the generated atlas. For textures without complete mip-chains

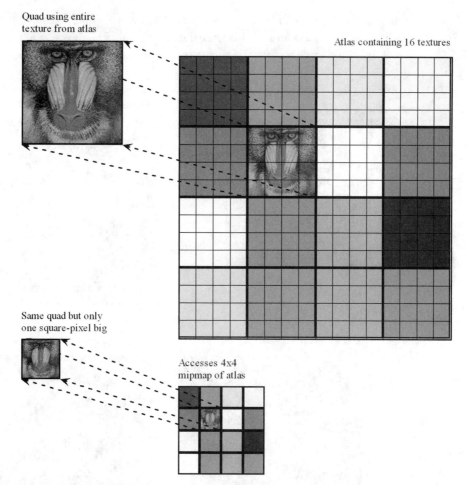

Quad using entire
texture from atlas

Atlas containing 16 textures

Same quad but only
one square-pixel big

Accesses 4x4
mipmap of atlas

FIGURE 2.6.5 *Because all models have remapped texture coordinates to only access an atlas's sub-texture, even single-pixel quads that access an entire sub-texture only access valid, initialized, and non-polluted texels.*

it first generates the complete mip-chain and then copies the data. The uninitialized texels of an atlas contain black. The Atlas Comparison Viewer [AtlasViewer04] shows no visible artifacts even at extreme viewing angles that force access to the lowest mipmaps.

Using Clamp, Wrap, or Mirror Modes with Atlases

GPUs provide different address modes for when texture coordinates are outside the zero to one range. In clamp mode, coordinates outside the [0, 1] interval clamp to either zero or one. The visual effect of this mode is that a texture's border texels repeat indefinitely. Wrap mode discards the integer part of a texture coordinate and just relies on the fractional part to address a texture. Mirror mode repeatedly mirrors the texture image for texture coordinates outside the [0, 1] interval. Figure 2.6.6 illustrates these different texture addressing modes.

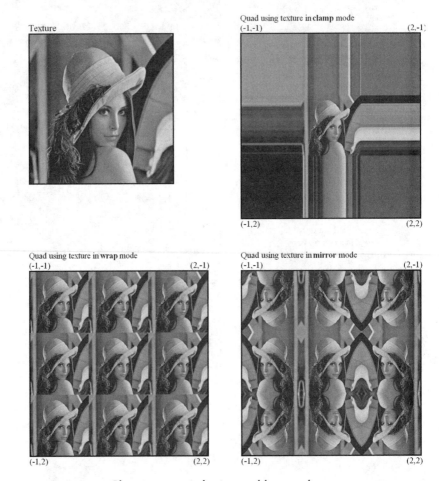

FIGURE 2.6.6   *Clamp, wrap, and mirror address modes.*

To access a texture packed into the center of an atlas one uses texture coordinates that are a strict subset of [0, 1], thus a GPU's address modes never apply. Worse, remapping texture coordinates outside of the [0, 1] range, i.e., texture coordinates making use of address modes, results in atlas coordinates that access neighboring textures in the atlas (see Figure 2.6.7).

A possible workaround is to replicate the same texture multiple times into an atlas. For example, if a texture wraps up to five times, then this texture copies five

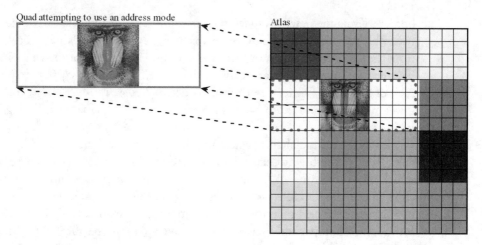

FIGURE 2.6.7 *Original texture coordinates outside the [0, 1] range, i.e., coordinates indicating the use of an address mode, map to atlas coordinates that access texels outside the intended sub-texture.*

times into an atlas. This technique wastes large amounts of texture memory, especially when address modes in the u- and v-dimensions are used simultaneously. It also complicates the atlas-packing algorithm, as it now requires usage information about the textures: what address modes are particular textures using and what are their minimum and maximum texture coordinates in use?

Fortunately, replicating textures multiple times into an atlas is unnecessary. The preferred solution is to tessellate models so that their texture coordinates are always in the [0, 1] range. These resulting additional vertices typically do not incur a performance penalty as modern GPUs are rarely vertex-processing bound.

Another solution is to emulate these address modes with a pixel shader; the next section provides the details.

Emulating Clamp, Wrap, and Mirror Addressing with Pixel Shaders

The Atlas Comparison Viewer [AtlasViewer04] implements clamp, wrap, and mirror addressing for textures that are part of an atlas. It uses pixel shaders to emulate these addressing modes.

For example, to implement clamping, a shader modifies the texture coordinates used to access an atlas. Instead of using the incoming texture coordinates directly to access the atlas, the shader first clamps these coordinates to the maximum and minimum values allowed for the given sub-rectangle that contains the relevant texture in the atlas.

For wrapping and mirroring, shaders similarly transform the incoming texture coordinates to emulate the respective address modes. In particular for wrapping, care has to be taken to avoid skewing which mip-level is used for pixels at the wrap borders. Using the newly wrapped texture coordinates directly via HLSL's tex2D(s, t) (assembly's tex1d) call is inadvisable: tex2D(s, t) computes which mip-level to use from the supplied texture coordinates. Pixels displaying texels at the wrapping borders have texture coordinates that are discontinues, i.e., jump from say 0.99 to 0.0 over the span of one pixel. The texture-coordinate derivatives are thus very large, forcing use of lower mip-levels, and thus producing wrong results (see the Section "Using Mipmaps with Atlases").

Instead, we avoid altering which mip-level is accessed. The HLSL call tex2D(s, t, ddx, ddy) (assembly tex1dd) instructs GPUs to use particular derivatives to decide which mip-level to use. We thus compute the arguments ddx and ddy in the shader from the original texture coordinates using HLSL's ddx() and ddy() (assembly dsx, dsy) instructions and then use the results to access the atlas. See also the source code for the Atlas Comparison Viewer [AtlasViewer04], more specifically the Wrap.ps pixel shader for how this technique works.

Emulating address modes in the pixel shader as described has drawbacks compared to tessellating models to enforce texture coordinates in the [0, 1] range (see the Section "Using Clamp, Wrap, or Mirror Modes with Atlases" above). First, emulation requires use of the pixel-shader assembly instructions dsx, dsy, which are only supported by pixel shader profiles ps_2_a and later. Thus, it excludes GPUs that only support ps_2_0 or ps_2_b profiles. Second, selecting which sub-rectangle of an atlas to clamp, wrap, or mirror to has to be encoded in the vertex stream and passed to the pixel-shader. Simply changing a pixel-shader constant as demonstrated in the Atlas Comparison Viewer [AtlasViewer04] is unacceptable as it would break the batch. Thus, additional software work is required to integrate this feature into an existing engine. Third and finally, modifying texture coordinates in the pixel shader costs pixel shader performance: a concern since today's games are more likely pixel shader bound than vertex shader bound.

Using Coordinates in the Zero to One Range

DirectX defines texture coordinates zero and one to coincide, i.e., a vertex with texture coordinates (0, 0) and a vertex with texture coordinates (1, 1) both access the identical texel (irrespective of filtering mode) when using the wrap texture addressing mode. To access all texels of a texture of dimensions width by height once and only once, models need to reduce the addressable range of the texture by using u-coordinates in the range:

$$\left[\frac{1}{2\,width}, 1 - \frac{1}{2\,width} \right] \tag{2.6.1}$$

and v-coordinates in the range:

$$\left[\frac{1}{2\,height}, 1 - \frac{1}{2\,height} \right] \tag{2.6.2}$$

Most applications, however, use texture coordinates ranging from zero to one inclusive, nonetheless. While such coordinates actually invoke wrap, clamp, or mirror address modes, the benefit of being texture-dimension independent outweighs the slight image-quality reduction.

Because texture coordinates in the inclusive [0, 1] interval thus address an area larger than the actual texture, directly re-mapping these coordinates to atlas coordinates also accesses an area larger than the texture's assigned sub-rectangle. The Atlas Creation Tool [CreationTool04] offers several solutions to this problem.

The first option is to use the Atlas Creation Tool's default setting. In that case, the Atlas Creation Tool maps the coordinates directly. If the original texture coordinates are in the range specified by Equations 2.6.1 and 2.6.2, then the atlas coordinates correctly access only texels of the original texture. The Atlas Comparison Viewer's [ComparisonViewer04] display mode 'Original Adjusted, Atlas Adjusted' demonstrates the resulting image quality.

If the original texture coordinates, however, range from zero to one inclusive, then, yes, the atlas coordinates do access texels of neighboring textures. The resulting image artifacts are, however, minimal as the Atlas Comparison Viewer demonstrates via its 'Original NOT adjusted, atlas NOT adjusted' display mode.

A better solution is to specify the Atlas Creation Tool's '-halftexel' option. It instructs the tool to rescale all texture coordinates to fit into the range specified by Equations 2.6.1 and 2.6.2. The corresponding Atlas Comparison Viewer's display mode 'Original NOT adjusted, atlas adjusted' thus shows this scaling in the difference view. If the intent of specifying zero to one inclusive coordinates is to refer to an entire texture and no more, while maintaining texture-dimension independence, then integrating the Atlas Creation Tool into the tool-chain realizes both intents.

Applying the previous section's pixel-shader to fix the one-texel wrapping, clamping, or mirroring is another possible solution. This solution, however, is heavy-weight and unnecessary as the Atlas Comparison Viewer's display mode 'Original NOT adjusted, atlas NOT adjusted' demonstrates.

Applying Texture Filtering to Atlases

Specifying coordinates in the range of Equations 2.6.1 and 2.6.2 (see previous section) samples texels at their exact center. Sampling a texel at its center means that only that texel contributes to the filtered output, even when bilinear filtering is enabled. Conversely, sampling a texel off-center and bilinearly filtering it, results in adjacent texels to contribute. This behavior, however, is to be avoided for texels lining the border of sub-textures in an atlas, as they are in danger of pulling in texels from unrelated textures (an effect also known as "color bleeding").

While bilinear filtering of the highest resolution mip-level is thus safe, anisotropic filtering of the same mip-level does potentially access unrelated neighboring texels. Worse, bilinear or anisotropic filtering of all lower mip-maps also access unrelated neighboring texels, as Figure 2.6.8 demonstrates.

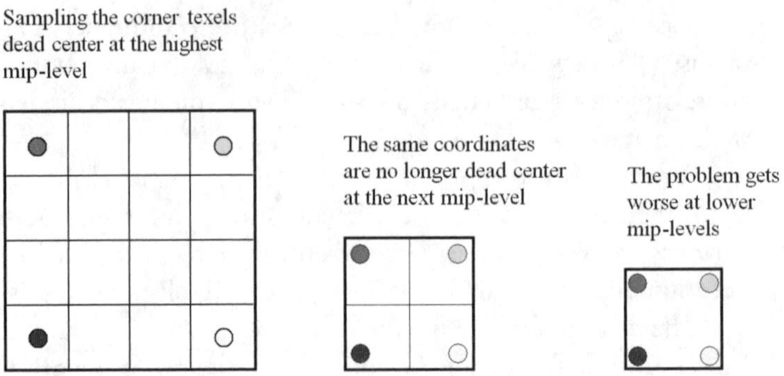

Sampling the corner texels
dead center at the highest
mip-level

The same coordinates
are no longer dead center
at the next mip-level

The problem gets
worse at lower
mip-levels

FIGURE 2.6.8   *Bilinear filtering of lower mip-levels accesses texels from unrelated neighboring textures.*

Unfortunately, these artifacts are not easily overcome. While their overall effect on image quality is small, they are nonetheless noticeable (see Atlas Comparison Viewer [ComparisonViewer04]). Experimentation with the Atlas Comparison Viewer shows that enabling anisotropic filtering actually minimizes these errors. That behavior seems counter-intuitive since an anisotropic filter penetrates deeper into a bordering texture than a bilinear filter. Anisotropic filters, however, have by definition narrower footprints than bilinear filters, and thus fewer unrelated texels enter the equation.

Adding border texels to a texture is a possible solution for reducing artifacts due to texture filtering. For example, to add an n-pixel border to a width × height texture, one would rescale the original texture to dimensions width-2n × height-2n, place this rescaled texture at the center of the new texture, and extend the scaled texture's border texels to the borders of the new texture. Rescaling textures is necessary to maintain, for example, power-of-two restrictions on a texture's dimensions.

Placing textures with similar hues, similar border texels, or similar mipmaps into a common atlas is another way to minimize texture-filtering artifacts.

Using Volume Textures as Atlases

Volume textures are seemingly perfect for storing multiple textures: each slice of a volume texture stores exactly one original texture. To access different textures one only varies the third, i.e., w, texture-coordinate.

Clamp, wrap, or mirror address modes work correctly for the u- and v-dimensions of each slice of the volume texture even without pixel-shader emulation, as long as all textures stored in slices are of the same dimensions. If a texture is smaller than the dimension of a slice, then texture memory is wasted and clamp, wrap, or mirror only work correctly if the slice's empty space duplicates texel data according to the desired address mode.

Unfortunately, mipmaps of volume textures reduce in size in all dimensions, e.g., a $4 \times 4 \times 4$ volume texture has mipmaps of dimension $2 \times 2 \times 2$ and $1 \times 1 \times 1$. Thus, storing mipmapped textures in a volume texture proves impossible, as there is not enough space available in a volume texture's mip-chain.

Volume textures are nonetheless useful as texture atlases for textures guaranteed to not need mipmaps, such as 2D user-interface textures. 2D user-interface textures are always screen-aligned and maintain the same distance from the camera, i.e., they do not minify. Thus, if they have a mip-chain, a GPU never accesses it; storing a mip-chain for these textures is superfluous. These textures are therefore ideal for storing into a non-mipmapped volume texture for batching purposes. To avoid accessing data from neighboring volume slices, care has to be taken to only sample at the center of w-slices when bilinear filtering is on. The Atlas Creation Tool [AtlasCreation2004] supports volume textures via the '-volume' option.

Conclusion

Texture atlases are not a new technique; many games use them for specialized situations, e.g., rendering text or sprite animations. Some games even use them as described here.

As GPUs continue to follow Moore's Law squared [Wloka03] and GPUs thus become comparatively faster than CPUs, it is important for game developers to aggressively reduce batches. For a CPU-limited game fewer batches means higher frame-rates or more eye-candy, physics, and AI CPU-computations.

The texture atlases technique is one tool that can reduce batch-counts. While texture atlases have the stigma of producing lower image quality, the Atlas Comparison Viewer [AtlasViewer04] demonstrates this to be largely a misconception. This article explains how to use texture atlases and how to avoid common pitfalls. Where appropriate we point out potential performance, visual quality, and programming costs associated with atlases. Since the Atlas Comparison Viewer [AtlasViewer04] and the Atlas Creation Tool [AtlasCreation04] are enclosed with source code, we hope game developers take a second look at texture atlases as a technique to be integrated into their tool chains.

References

[AtlasCreation04] "Atlas Creation Tool User Guide," NVSDK 7.0, March '04 and enclosed on the ShaderX3 CD.

[AtlasViewer04] "Atlas Comparison Viewer User Guide," NVSDK 7.0, March '04 and enclosed on the ShaderX3 CD.

[TextureTools00] "Texture Tools User Guide," NVSDK 7.0, March '04.

[Wloka03] "Batch, Batch, Batch: What Does It Really Mean," Matthias Wloka, GDC 2003, San Jose, CA. *http://developer.nvidia.com/docs/IO/8230/BatchBatch-Batch.ppt.*

2.7

A Simulation of Thermal Imaging

O'dell Hicks

Introduction

As forms of non-realistic rendering are becoming popular in graphics, so are simulations of technology-aided imaging, particularly in spy/military video games. Though the resulting images are aesthetically inferior to realistic rendering styles, such techniques can immerse players into the role of the spy they are controlling. This article presents a technique for a visual interpretation of temperature.

A Form of Lighting

While temperature is what is gauged, the reality is that objects with temperature emit infrared radiation (even ice cubes!), and they act as a kind of point light, emitting invisible light from everywhere on the surface. With a simple lighting algorithm, a heat reference for the object surface, and a color lookup texture, we can easily fake thermal imaging.

The Technique

The most time-consuming part of this technique is the surface temperature source. It could be done on a per-vertex basis, but that won't give much temperature detail unless the mesh is heavily tessellated. A better way is to take the base texture(s) and produce a grayscale temperature map, where pure black is the coldest and pure white is the hottest. Temperatures for non-living objects are pretty straightforward. For humans, exposed skin is generally the hottest area. Thin t-shirts should be cooler, and thicker clothing should be even cooler than that. If you desire, you may wish to blur out all distinguishable detail from the temperature map (such as facial features). In real life, imaging hardware does a variety of things, from featureless temperature gauging, to more detailed compositions.

The vertex shader first calculates the intensity of the infrared radiation reaching the eye/camera. This is the dot product between the eye's forward vector and the normal of the emitting object. In this sample, it's done on a per-vertex basis, but you may use normal maps to get a more detailed sampling. As the normal deviates from the direction of the eye, just like regular light, the infrared radiation is attenuated, resulting in a "cold" outline along the object edges. The shader passes this value (ranging from 0 to 1) as a texture coordinate. The following snippet is the vertex shader for the technique:

```
vs_1_1
dcl_position  v0  ; vertex position
dcl_normal0   v1  ; vertex normal
dcl_texcoord0 v2  ; texture coordinate
m4x4 oPos, v0, c0 ; transform pos to homogenous clip space
m4x4 r0, v1, c4   ; Transform normal to world space
; Normalize the normal
dp3 r0.w, r0, r0
rsq r0.w, r0.w
mul r0, r0, r0.w
dp3 r1, c8, r0 ; Intensity of infrared emittance relative to the eye
 ; Texture coordinates
mov oT0.xy, v2 ; thermal map
mov oT1, r1    ; generated color lookup
```

This technique can be done with pixel shader version 1.4 and up; the sample provided uses version 1.4. In phase one of the pixel shader, we multiply the sampled temperature map (0 to 1, coldest to hottest) with the texture coordinate generated in the vertex shader (0 to 1, based on the intensity of the infrared radiation reaching the eye). The product of these values can be thought of as an overall temperature, and it coincides with the range in the thermal lookup texture. This texture is a gradient of colors, ranging from "coldest" to "warmest." In phase 2, we sample the thermal lookup texture with this coordinate. The following snippet is the pixel shader for the technique:

```
ps_1_4
texld r0, t0        ; thermal map
texcrd r1.rgb, t1   ; generated texture coordinate
mul r1.xyz, r0, r1  ; scale the thermal coordinate
phase
texld r1, r1        ; sample the color lookup with the coordinate in
r1
mov r0, r1          ; output the pixel
```

Conclusion

This article presents a simple way to produce the technique often referred to as "heat vision." As in real life, this technique can be modified to produce the green-hued "night vision." Using a different thermal color lookup and modulating it with the object's base texture would produce this effect. Finally, it is common to render a bit of noise or "snow" over the scene to further simulate imperfections in thermal imaging hardware. In this sample, the noise is achieved by drawing two triangles over the entire screen, with the texture coordinates randomly sampling an area of a static noise texture. The random change in texture coordinates gives the appearance of the noise being animated.

2.8

Real-Time Texture-Space Skin Rendering

David R. Gosselin, Pedro V. Sander, and Jason L. Mitchell

Introduction

Rendering of human skin is an important research problem in Computer Graphics. Obtaining realistic results can be very challenging, especially when it has to be accomplished in real time. We present an overview of methods used to simulate the appearance of skin, and describe their implications to real-time rendering. Finally, we describe a real-time algorithm that approximates the appearance of subsurface scattering by performing a blur operation in texture-space using graphics hardware. The advantages of this approach are its simplicity and efficiency, while still achieving a realistic result. We also present additional post-processing techniques to prevent texture seams from being generated by the blur operation, as well as methods to efficiently compute soft shadows using this framework.

Skin Rendering in Real Time

Historically, skin has been shaded much like other materials in real-time games due to a lack of sophistication in hardware shading models. Developers rendering real-time skin have traditionally used tweaked Phong and environment map-based shading models with rim lighting to try to approximate the look of skin [Beeson04]. Most games today don't even go that far, resulting in a very plastic and unrealistic look. Even offline rendering techniques used in films such as *Final Fantasy: The Spirits Within* use Phong models with fairly arbitrary tweaks to select between different textures based upon viewing angle [Bjorke01]. While this gives a decent look and has the advantage of being artist-driven, even this technique does not explicitly attempt to simulate subsurface scattering. A more recent offline rendering technique, used in *The Matrix Reloaded*, simulated subsurface scattering with texture-space lighting and blurring steps [Borshukov03]. In this technique, the illumination of the skin is rendered to a texture map and then blurred to simulate the effect of subsurface scattering. As it turns out, this technique can be implemented using graphics hardware and is the basis for the approach to skin rendering discussed in this article.

Texture-Space Skin Rendering Overview

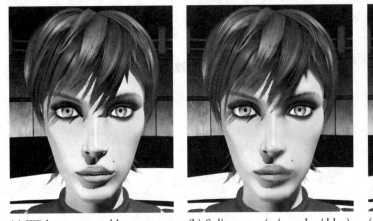

(a) Without texture blur   (b) Split screen (w/o and w/ blur)   (c) With texture blur

FIGURE 2.8.1   *Comparison of skin rendering with and without the texture-space blur operation.*
Images from ATI's demo Ruby: The Double Cross. © *ATI Technologies 2004.*

The basic idea of the texture-space skin rendering algorithm is to render the diffuse illumination to a light map, blur this light map (see Figure 2.8.2b) in order to approximate subsurface scattering, and finally use the blurred light map to render the final image [Borshukov03]. The specular illumination does not use the light map and thus is not blurred. In addition, prior to rendering the light map, we create a shadow map which is then used to attenuate shadowed regions when rendering the diffuse illumination to the light map.

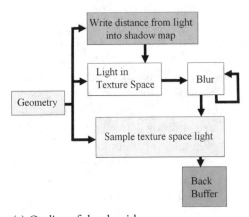

(a) Outline of the algorithm   (b) Rendered light map

FIGURE 2.8.2   *The structure of the texture-space algorithm (left), and the texture-space lightmap used to render Figure 2.8.1 (right).*

In summary, the algorithm proceeds as follows:

1. Create shadow map from the point of view of the key light.
2. Render diffuse illumination to a 2D light map (z test against shadow map).
3. Dilate the boundaries and blur the light map.
4. Render final mesh (use the blurred light map for diffuse illumination).

Next we describe each of the above steps in detail. Then we describe some additional acceleration techniques.

Create Shadow Map

Using this texture-space skin rendering technique, the computation of soft shadows is relatively inexpensive. A shadow map algorithm is used to determine visibility from the light and attenuate the samples when rendering to the light map. The blur operation performed in Step 3 will not only create the appearance of subsurface scattering, but it will also provide soft shadows at no additional cost. The blur pass also significantly reduces aliasing, making it practical to use the shadow map algorithm.

First, for each frame, we need to compute the view-projection matrix in order to render the scene from the point of view of the light. To make the best use of the samples in the shadow map, we use a frustum that tightly bounds the bounding sphere of the geometry (see Figure 2.8.3). This is standard practice when creating shadow maps and can be accomplished with a call to D3DXMatrixLookAtLH() to compute the view matrix, and a call to D3DXMatrixPerspectiveLH() to compute the projection matrix.

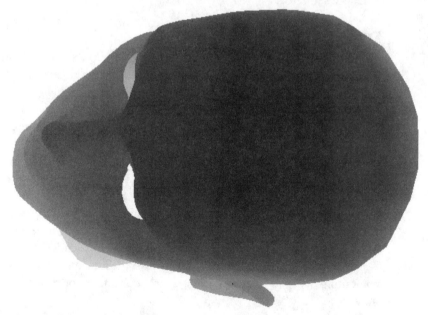

FIGURE 2.8.3 *Shadow map.*

When rendering into the shadow map, we use a shader that stores the depth on the alpha component of an RGBA texture. Figure 2.8.3 shows the depth stored on the alpha channel.

The vertex shader simply has to pass a float containing the depth to the pixel shader in one of the color interpolators:

```
VsOutput vsmain (VsInput i)
{
    VsOutput o;

    //multiply position by light matrix
    o.pos = mul (i.pos, mSiLightAgent);

    //pass depth to pixel shader
    o.depth = o.pos.z/o.pos.w;

    return o;
}
```

And the pixel shader just outputs the interpolated depth:

```
float4 psmain (PsInput i) : COLOR
{
    //output the interpolated depth
    return i.depth;
}
```

Note that since we only write to the alpha channel, the RGB channels should remain set to zero.

Translucent Shadows

Translucent shadows can be computed using a hybrid shadow algorithm. The basic idea is to first render the opaque geometry as described above, and then, on a second pass, render the translucent objects (e.g., the glass lens on Figure 2.8.4) with z testing turned on and z writing turned off. On the second pass, we accumulate the opacity of the samples on the RGB channels of the shadow map texture using additive blending. Then, when computing the shadows from the shadow map, if the sample is not shadowed by an opaque object, its diffuse contribution is attenuated by the value in the alpha channel. As a result, the opaque geometry shadows itself, and the translucent geometry shadows the opaque geometry. The alpha channel, which stores the depth for the opaque geometry should not be changed in the translucent geometry pass. To ensure this, we only enable writing to RGB. Note that translucent objects that are behind the opaque geometry are z culled and thus not rendered.

The vertex shader is similar to the one for the previous pass, except that instead of computing depth, it just passes the texture coordinates for the opacity map lookup to

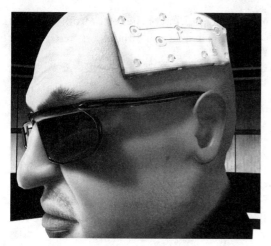
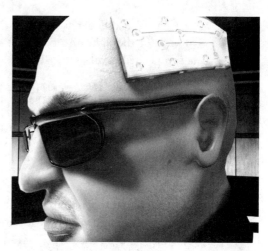

(a) Without transparency   (b) With transparency

FIGURE 2.8.4   *Comparison of rendering the glass lens with and without translucent shadows. Images from ATI's demo* Ruby: The Double Cross. *© ATI Technologies 2004.*

the pixel shader in one of the interpolators. The pixel shader returns the result of the texture lookup:

```
return tex2D(tOpacity, i.texCoord);
```

Note that the opacity map is an RGB texture in order to allow for colored translucent materials, such as purple shades casting a purple shadow (Figure 2.8.4(b)). To use a single-channel opacity map, just output the red channel of the opacity map:

```
return tex2D(tOpacity, i.texCoord).rrrr;
```

Remember that the alpha channel, which contains the depth values for the opaque geometry is not touched during this pass.

Render Diffuse Illumination to Light Map

The next step of the algorithm is to render the diffuse illumination of the opaque geometry to the light map. The vertex shader sets the output positions to be the texture coordinates of the vertices, thus rendering to a 2D texture map, which consistently samples the entire surface, independent of the camera position. This is accomplished by the following vertex shader code fragment, which maps the texture coordinates to positions in the [−1, 1] range:

```
o.pos.xy = i.texCoord*2.0-1.0;
o.pos.z = 0.0;
o.pos.w = 1.0;
```

The vertex shader also needs to compute the position of the vertex from the point of view of the light and pass that in to the pixel shader for the depth test. This is accomplished as follows:

```
o.posLight = mul(pos, mSiLightAgent);
o.posLight /= o.posLight.w;
o.posLight.xy = (o.posLight.xy + 1.0f)/2.0f;
o.posLight.y = 1.0f-o.posLight.y;
o.posLight.z -= 0.01f;
```

The above code computes the vertex position from the point of view of the light, and puts it on the [0, 1] range, in order to do the lookup on the shadow map. The z value is slightly biased to prevent z fighting when the z value in the shadow map is equal to the current z value. If that is the case, the shadow test should determine that the pixel is not in shadow.

The pixel shader does the diffuse light computation for all of the scene lights. We only do shadow computation for one light (the key light, which provides most of the lighting contribution for our scene). However, the algorithm can be easily adapted to handle shadows for multiple source lights by using multiple shadow maps. One may be able reuse the same shadow map when rendering a shadow map for a second light, since this algorithm only makes use of two out of the four channels of the RGBA texture when using a single-channel opacity map. Here is the code to compute the diffuse contribution of the light that is attenuated by the shadow:

```
//diffuse lighting computation
float NdotL = dot(vNormal, vLight);

//read from shadow map
float4 t = tex2D(tShadowMap, i.posLight.xy);

//set shadow factor to the value it should attenuate light
//if it is in shadow (e.g., 0.0)
float3 vShadowFac = fOccluded;

//if light is NOT in shadow
if(i.posLight.z < t.a && NdotL > 0)
{
    //compute translucency.
    //Large values of transShadowAlpha make shadow darker
    float3 alpha = pow(t.rgb, transShadowAlpha);

    //set shadow factor to be a lerp between
    //shadowed color and white
    vShadowFac = lerp(fOccluded.xxx, float3(1.,1.,1.), alpha);
}

//attenuate light by the shadow factor
float3 diffuse = vShadowFac * saturate (NdotL * vLightColor);
```

Now, the light map contains the diffuse contribution of all lights and is ready to be blurred. During this pass, we also render the blur kernel size to the alpha component of the light map. Therefore, only one texture needs to be accessed during the texture blur pass.

The Texture Blur

The next step in the process is to blur the 2D light map texture. This operation is performed in hardware by using a pixel shader. A number of filter kernels were examined to determine which gave acceptable results: Box, Gaussian, Poisson, and Kwasi. The Poisson disc filter was chosen because it gave good results for a reasonable cost and also allows a variable kernel size to be specified. The reason why this is important is described below.

The vertex shader for blurring is just a simple pass through; the pixel shader is where the main work is accomplished. The first part of the pixel shader is just filter kernel setup. In this case the filter kernel is composed of twelve samples generated via the Poisson distribution and the center sample.

```
float2 poisson[12] = {float2(-0.326212f, -0.40581f),
                      float2(-0.840144f, -0.07358f),
                      float2(-0.695914f, 0.457137f),
                      float2(-0.203345f, 0.620716f),
                      float2(0.96234f, -0.194983f),
                      float2(0.473434f, -0.480026f),
                      float2(0.519456f, 0.767022f),
                      float2(0.185461f, -0.893124f),
                      float2(0.507431f, 0.064425f),
                      float2(0.89642f, 0.412458f),
                      float2(-0.32194f, -0.932615f),
                      float2(-0.791559f, -0.59771f)};
```

The next part of the pixel shader reads from the center sample as well as the artist generated blur kernel size, which is stored in the alpha component of the light map. The other samples will be scaled by this kernel size in order to grow or shrink the blur kernel per texel. The vPixelSize variable represents the reciprocal of the width and height of the off-screen texture. The vBlurScale variable represents the scale and bias for the blur kernel texture.

```
float2 vPixelSize (0.001953125, 0.001953125);
float2 vBlurScale (3, 2);
float4 ss = tex2D (tRenderedScenePong, i.texCoord);
float2 pixelRadius = vPixelSize *
(ss.a*vBlurScale.x+vBlurScale.y);
```

The final part of the shader sums up the samples and divides by the number of samples, in this case thirteen. In addition, the pixel shader outputs the blur kernel size read from the center sample. This allows for further blurring passes if desired.

```
float3 cOut = ss.rgb;
for (int tap = 0; tap < 12; tap++)
{
```

```
            float4 s = tex2D (tRenderedScenePong, i.texCoord +
                              (poisson[tap] * pixelRadius));
            cOut += s.rgb;
    }
    return float4(cOut / 13.0f, ss.a);
```

By using two temporary buffers, we are able to perform several blurring passes on the diffuse illumination in order to achieve a soft, realistic look.

Variable Kernel Size

Borshukov and Lewis [Borshukov03] addressed translucency on the model's ears by ray-tracing. Unfortunately, in real time this is not currently an option. This visual cue is still important for achieving realistic-looking skin. When looking at a person who is backlit, typically you will see a lot of light passing through areas like the ears. In order to try to address this issue, our technique uses a blur kernel size texture that is artist generated. While it is theoretically possible to rearrange the texture coordinates to achieve a similar effect, this would require quite a bit of either artist or programmer time. The kernel scalar texture which was artist generated was a more time efficient approach. A blur kernel texture is shown in Figure 2.8.5.

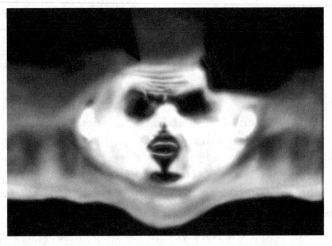

FIGURE 2.8.5   *The blur kernel for the model in Figures 2.8.4, 2.8.6, and 2.8.7.*

Texture Boundary Dilation

In order to prevent boundary artifacts when fetching from the light map, the texture needs to be dilated prior to blurring. We needed an efficient real-time solution to this problem. We accomplished this by modifying the Poisson disc filter shader to check whether a given sample is just outside the boundary of useful data, and if so, copy from an interior neighboring sample instead. We only need to use this modified, more expensive filter in the first blurring pass.

The pixel shader modifications to the blur shader needed to accomplish this dilation are relatively small. The first step is to determine if a particular texel in the off-screen light map has been written. Since the alpha of the off-screen light map is cleared to 1.0 before any processing and the light map rendering pass writes the blur kernel size into the alpha channel, as long as the blur kernel texture is never 1.0, we can use the alpha channel to determine which texels were written. The first step in the actual blur shader is to store off the center pixel alpha value (which represents blur kernel size). This happens before the main filter loop.

```
float flag = ss.a;
```

Within the filter loop this flag is updated by taking the maximum value of the current sample and the current flag. Additionally, the variable `ss` is updated if the current filter sample has a lower alpha value.

```
flag = max(s.a, flag);
if (s.a < ss.a)
{
    ss = s;
}
```

Finally, after the filter loop is finished, the flag is checked, and if a texel was found which was not written by the lighting shader, the sample with the lowest alpha (blur kernel size) is used instead. This gives the desired dilation effect (Figure 2.8.6).

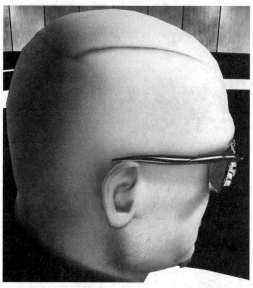
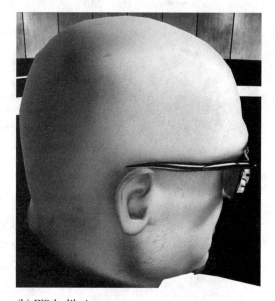

(a) Without dilation   (b) With dilation

FIGURE 2.8.6   *Renderings with and without texture dilation. Images from ATI's demo* Ruby: The Double Cross. © *ATI Technologies 2004.*

```
    if (flag == 1.0f)
        return float4(ss.rgb, 1.0f);
    else
        return float4(cOut / 13.0f, ss.a);
```

It is possible to consider more complicated schemes for doing the dilation. For example, only samples that were written could be included in the filter average. In our case, however, this proved to be unnecessary to achieve the results desired.

Render Final Mesh

After the light map has been blurred, we are ready to render the object. In this final rendering pass, we render the model with diffuse and specular lighting. When computing the diffuse illumination, we simply set it to be the value stored in the light map multiplied by the value in the color map for that surface point:

```
float4 cBase = tex2D (tBase, i.texCoord.xy);
float4 cLightMap = tex2D (tLightMap, i.texCoord);
float3 diffuse = cLightMap*cBase;
```

Specular Lighting with Shadows

Since it can be expensive to perform a separate blur pass for the shadow component, we cannot directly apply shadows to the specular illumination. We have found, however, that the luminance of the blurred light map can be used to attenuate the specular term of the shadow casting light to obtain a natural look. In Figure 2.8.7, note the

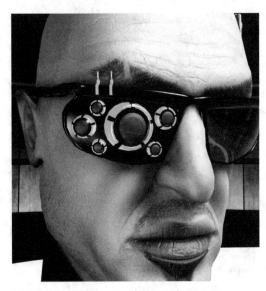

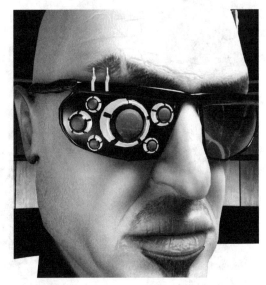

(a) Without shadowing the specular term   (b) Shadowing the specular term

FIGURE 2.8.7   *Renderings with and without shadowing the specular term. Images from ATI's demo* Ruby: The Double Cross. © *ATI Technologies 2004.*

improvement on the shadows above the mouth of the model. In order to do this, the specular component is computed as follows:

```
//compute luminance of light map sample
float lum = dot(float3(0.2125, 0.7154, 0.0721), cLightMap.rgb);

//possibly scale and bias lum here depending on the light setup

//multiply specular by lum
specular *= lum;
```

Acceleration Techniques

In order to further optimize this technique, we employ hardware early-z culling to avoid processing regions of our light map that are outside of the view frustum, facing away from the viewer, or simply too far away to need updating. These optimizations significantly improve performance, since many or all pixels in the light map rendering and blurring passes can be skipped. We perform three inexpensive "z pre-passes" in texture space in order to set pixels in the texture-space z buffer to zero or one. These zeroes and ones in the z buffer don't represent distances but, rather, a logical value that indicates whether the pixel needs to be processed on subsequent passes. On those subsequent passes, these z values will drive the early-z culling hardware in order to avoid processing certain pixels [Krüger03].

Frustum Culling

Before rendering to the light map, we clear the z buffer to 1 and perform a very simple and cheap texture space rendering pass in which we just set the z value to 0 for all rendered samples. If the bounding box of the model's head lies outside the view frustum and is culled by the graphics engine, the z value is not modified. On all further texture-space passes, we set the z value to 0 in the vertex shader and the z test to "equal". This ensures that if the model lies outside the view frustum, hardware early-z culling will prevent all pixels from being processed.

Backface Culling

Similarly, in yet another cheap rendering pass, backface culling can be performed by setting the z value accordingly. This time, a dot product of the view vector and normal is computed in the vertex shader and passed on to the pixel shader. If the sample is frontfacing, a 0 is written to the z buffer, otherwise the pixel is clipped, leaving the z buffer untouched. We bias the result of the dot product by 0.3 so that samples that are "slightly" backfacing are not culled. This is because some of these samples may be within the blur radius of frontfacing samples. Figure 2.8.8 shows a texture with backface culled regions rendered in black. Here is the vertex shader code for the backface culling pre-pass:

```
//compute+bias the dot product of the view vector and the normal
//output result to a color interpolator
float3 viewVec = normalize ((float3)(worldCamPos-pos));
viewVec = normalize(viewVec);
o.dotp = dot(viewVec, i.normal);
o.dotp += 0.3;
```

and the pixel shader code for the z pre-pass:

```
float4 main (PsInput i) : COLOR
{
    //clip backfacing regions, otherwise return background color
    clip(i.dotp);
    return cBackColor;
}
```

We noticed that if we do backface culling on the ears of the model, sometimes a culled sample bleeds into a visible sample after blurring. That is because of the curvature on the ear is significantly higher than in other regions of the face. To address this problem, we added a texture coordinate check on the vertex shader which prevents culling the region around the ears.

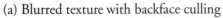

(a) Blurred texture with backface culling   (b) Rendered model

FIGURE 2.8.8   *The texture space computation is culled on backfacing regions. Images from ATI's demo* Ruby: The Double Cross. © *ATI Technologies 2004.*

Distance Culling

If the model lies very far from the camera, the z value is set to 1, and the light map from the previously rendered frame is used (the light map buffer never needs to be cleared). We only use this optimization in instances where it does not affect the quality of the result. Note that the specular illumination is still computed, so the "shiny spots" will be rendered correctly.

The vertex shader code below simply checks whether the vertex position is too far from the camera (in this case, 1500 units away), and if so, sets the z to 1, which will cause all triangles adjacent to that vertex to be clipped. This could potentially cause problems if different vertices of a triangle fell on opposite sides of this distance. In practice, however, as long as this distance is carefully chosen for the application, the triangles will be small enough that no visual artifacts will result.

```
if(length((float3)(pos - worldCamPos)) > 1500.f)
{
    o.pos.z = 1.0;
}
```

All of the rendering optimizations described above can actually be performed using a single Z pre-pass. In this way, the expensive pixel lighting passes will only be applied to the pixels/texels that are actually needed to render on screen geometry or texels needed for blurring.

Conclusion

This article presents a real-time algorithm for skin rendering. The algorithm approximates the appearance of subsurface scattering by performing a blur operation in texture space using graphics hardware. The algorithm is simple, efficient, and yields realistic results.

Acknowledgments

We would like to thank Chris Brennan from ATI Research for suggesting using a three-channel RGB opacity map, thus allowing for colored translucent materials. We also thank Eli Turner from ATI Research for his help with the artwork.

References

[Beeson04] Curtis Beeson and Kevin Bjorke, "Skin in the 'Dawn' Demo," *GPU Gems*, ed. Randima Fernando, Addison-Wesley, 2004.

[Bjorke01] Kevin Bjorke, "Using Maya with RenderMan on *Final Fantasy: The Spirits Within*," *SIGGRAPH 2001*—Course 48, Chapter 6.

[Borshukov03] George Borshukov and J. P. Lewis, "Realistic Human Face Rendering for *The Matrix Reloaded*," *SIGGRAPH 2003*—Technical Sketches.

[Krüger03] Jens Krüger and Rüdiger Westermann, "Acceleration Techniques for GPU-based Volume Rendering," IEEE Visualization 2003.

2.9

Dot3 Cel Shading

Ron Barbosa

Introduction

The goal of this tutorial is to present a simplified process of rendering cel shaded graphics without sacrificing image quality. To accomplish this task, the methods presented here will serve to eliminate the need to use a texture map to produce the hard edge, or silhouette, that has become the trademark of cel shaded graphics. This simplified process is GPU efficient, relying mostly on the dot product operation for three-dimensional vectors, and, as such, has been dubbed *Dot3 Cel Shading*.

In the first book of this series, *Direct3D ShaderX: Vertex and Pixel Shader Tips and Tricks*, Drew Card and Jason L. Mitchell [Card00] provide a generous treatment to Non-Photorealistic Rendering techniques. They include details of several effects including cel shading. The vertex shader presented by Card and Mitchell involved preprocessing the geometry into quad-fins and it made use of z-buffering to produce the silhouette. And, while many cel shading methods index into a texture map for shading, the process outlined in [Card00], as well as the method employed in this tutorial, will calculate the color analytically in the pixel shader.

Dot3 Cel Shading will seek to simplify many of the processes associated with cel shading. It does not require any preprocessing of geometry, and, in fact, has a modest vertex shader, which simply transforms the geometry through the rendering pipeline and calculates the dot product of the viewing vector with the vertex normal for passage to the pixel shader. The methods presented here use the camera position as a light source, but the code can easily be modified to include positions of real light sources.

The goal of the techniques presented here is to simplify the process of cel shading. It certainly does not seek to replace any existing methods in use today, but only provides the user with an additional option. In the end, experimentation with the myriad of methods available will most likely provide users with the results they seek.

Regardless of the methods employed by the developer, the goal of any cel shading technique is to render a model or mesh in such a way that it appears as though it was hand drawn by an artist.

With this common goal in mind, the purpose of most cel shading code is to accomplish two things: create a hard edge to highlight the most outstanding features of the model and reduce the visible color set to a create the ink and paint effect evident in hand drawn animation cels. We will add a third requirement to the Dot3 Cel Shading process that should be evident in all programmable effects: the flexibility to allow the user to adjust a great deal of options to govern the final output of the shader.

Implementation

Figure 2.9.1 shows a top-down projection of a cylinder and several surface normal vectors that give an approximation of the orientation of the faces that make up the model.

FIGURE 2.9.1   *A top-down view of a cylinder with several surface normal vectors. The vector* vLos *represents the line of sight vector from the view position to the model.*

If you look carefully at the diagram in Figure 2.9.1, you can see that, as the viewer looks at the model, the vLos vector is most closely aligned with the front facing surface normal vector. But, as the diagram shows, the polygons around the *edges* of the cylinder have surface normals that are perpendicular, or nearly perpendicular to the *vLos* vector.

We can use the dot product of each vertex normal and the inverse of the vLos vector to determine the cosine of the angle between them. The cosine can then be used to determine whether or not a particular vertex or pixel qualifies as being *on the edge* of the model, taking the view position into consideration. The HLSL pseudocode might look something like this:

```
float fCos = dot(vNormal, -vLos);

if(fCos == 0.0f)
{
    // This is a silhouette pixel on the edges of the model
}
else
{
    // This pixel is not part of the silhouette
}
```

While that might be a good way to start, it certainly doesn't give us the flexibility we will need. It will likely generate a very thin outline since it only colors pixels as part of the silhouette if they are perfectly perpendicular to the inverse of the viewing vector, vLos. A better solution would likely include a user definable variable that will represent some threshold value. The pixels of faces with normals that have cosines less than this threshold would be colored as part of the hard edge.

```
float fCos = dot(vNormal, -vLos);

if(fCos <= fThreshold)
{
    // This is a silhouette pixel on the edges of the model
}
else
{
    // This pixel is not part of the silhouette
}
```

While this will allow the user some more control over the width of the hard edge, it is still a very rigid method, and will likely not suit the needs of a wide range of users. Once we begin adding color to the model, this method might also appear unnatural.

Our implementation will require a color banding mechanism that goes from full intensity color to hard edge color in a way that makes the user believe that they are watching a cartoon. To accomplish this, we will add a color scaling process based on the cosine of the angle between the vertex normal and the normalized vector from the vertex to the view position (the inverse of the vLos vector). Using the cosine as a scale will result in full color intensity for those surfaces most closely aligned with the viewing vector, while gradually darkening the color as it renders the surfaces along the edges of the model.

The only problem with this approach is that Cel Shaded graphics do not typically present a gradual color darkening. The colors are typically banded and not blended, as shown in Figure 2.9.2.

FIGURE 2.9.2 *A side-by-side comparison of a Dot3 Cel Shaded teapot with a Gouraud Shaded teapot. Notice the color banding evident in the cel shaded model.*

To address this problem, the Dot3 Cel Shading method includes an estimating process to group surfaces that share similar alignment to the viewing vector together and render them all with the same color. Surfaces that fall outside the range will belong to the neighboring color groups and will be rendered with a brighter intensity (for surfaces more closely facing the viewer) or a lesser intensity (for surfaces closer to the edge). The estimation mechanism will also ensure that the group of surfaces closest to the outskirts is rendered as part of the silhouette.

Listing 2.9.1 shows the entire vertex shader code and the accompanying pixel shader code written in the High-Level Shader Language. This code is intended for vertex and pixel shader 2.0 targets.

Listing 2.9.1   The Vertex Shader for Dot3 Cel Shading

```
// Vertex shader input structure
struct VS_INPUT
{
    float4    Pos:        POSITION;
    float3    vNorm:      NORMAL;
};

// Vertex shader output structure
struct VS_OUTPUT
{
    float4    Pos:        POSITION;
    float     Scale:      TEXCOORD;
};

// Constant registers
float4x4    view_proj_matrix: register(c0); // View/Proj matrix
float4      view_position:    register(c4); // In world space
float4x4    world_matrix:     register(c5); // Object world matrix

// Vertex Shader entry point
VS_OUTPUT vs_main(VS_INPUT inData)
{
    // Declare output structure
    VS_OUTPUT Out;

    // Transform the input data into world space
    inData.Pos  = mul(world_matrix, inData.Pos);
    inData.vNorm = mul((float3x3)world_matrix, inData.vNorm);

    // Calculate and normalize the eye vector.  The dot product of the
    // eye and normal vectors will be used to scale the render color.
    float3 vEye = normalize(view_position - inData.Pos);

    // Store the color scale in the output structure.
    Out.Scale = dot(inData.vNorm, vEye);
```

```
// Transform the vertex into clip space
Out.Pos = mul(view_proj_matrix, inData.Pos);

return Out;
}
```

The first few blocks of code define the input and output structures for the vertex shader, as well as the standard matrices required to transform the geometry from object space to world space and then into homogenous clip space. The view_position constant represents the world space camera position, and is used to calculate the eye vector.

Next comes the main body of the vertex shader. The vs_main function serves as the vertex shader entry point. vs_main accepts a VS_INPUT structure as input and returns a VS_OUTPUT structure, which is declared in the first block of code of the vs_main function.

The next block of code simply transforms the vertex position and vertex normal into world space.

With the vertex data transformed into world space, the next code block declares and calculates the inverse line of sight vector, vEye. This vector is analogous to inverting the vLos vector from the diagram and pseudocode examples.

The dot product is used in the following code section to determine the cosine of the angle between the vertex normal and the eye vector. The cosine will be used by the pixel shader as a scaling factor for determining the final color of the pixel, so it must be passed to the pixel shader.

Lastly, the remaining two blocks of code simply transform the vertex data into clip space and return the fully populated VS_OUTPUT structure (see Listing 2.9.2).

Listing 2.9.2 The Pixel Shader Code for Dot3 Cel Shading

```
// Pixel Shader input structure
struct PS_INPUT
{
    float       Scale:  TEXCOORD;
};

// Constant registers
float    shades:              register(c0);  // Number of color shades
float    excluded_shades:     register(c1);  // Number of hard edge
shades
float4   render_color:        register(c2);  // Base rendering color
float4   edge_color:          register(c3);  // Silhouette color

// Pixel shader entry point
float4 ps_main(PS_INPUT inData) : COLOR0
{
    // Output color
    float4 color;
```

```
// This truncation mechanism is used to create the color banding.
int scalefactor = floor(inData.Scale * shades);
inData.Scale    = scalefactor / shades;

// Determine if the scale creates a color that is excluded.
if(inData.Scale < excluded_shades / shades)
{
    // This color is excluded and is part of the hard edge.
    color = edge_color;
}
else
{
    // This is not an edge pixel.  Scale it and add a bias of 1
shade.
    color = (render_color * inData.Scale) + (render_color /
shades);
}

return color;
}
```

The pixel shader code begins by defining a structure for input data. The only input parameter required is the color scaling factor, which is stored as a texture coordinate.

The next section declares a series of constant values. These constant variables must be assigned values by your application as follows:

- The shades constant is used to determine the total number of color shades to be returned by the pixel shader. Increasing this value will create more color bands in the render.
- The excluded_shades constant tells the pixel shader how many color shades should be excluded from the normal rendering process and, instead, rendered as part of the hard edge. Increasing this value thickens the hard edge around the model's details.
- The render_color constant determines the base rendering color of the model. This can be thought of as the material diffuse color.
- The edge_color constant sets the color of the hard edge.

The function that follows is the entry point for the pixel shader. The ps_main function accepts a PS_INPUT structure as its sole argument, and it returns a float4 RGBA color. The first line of this function declares a float4 output variable called color.

The code block that follows is one of the core components of the Dot3 Cel Shading technique. This code represents an estimating mechanism that can be used to effectively reduce the resolution of the color scaling factor that was passed in to the pixel shader in the PS_INPUT structure. This reduction in resolution will create the color banding that will be needed to emulate the ink and paint effect that we're looking for.

Since inData.Scale is the result of a dot product operation with unit length vectors, it will always be in the range from 0.0 to 1.0 for the visible pixels of front-facing polygons. Therefore, multiplying this value by the number of desired shades, stored in the shades variable, will yield a value between 0.0 and shades. Using the floor() intrinsic HLSL function will truncate the decimal portion of the value, leaving us with an integer value between 0 and shades. Dividing the resulting integer value by shades returns the value to the 0.0 to 1.0 range, however, since the truncation of the decimal portion was achieved using the floor() intrinsic, we are now left with an estimated color in the 0.0 to 1.0 range, with a resolution of 1/shades. Take some time to digest this paragraph, as understanding it is key to the shader's tuneability. Use the example below to see this code in action. Assume the user is requesting 10 color shades, and the inData.Scale value at a given pixel is equal to 0.78:

Example:

```
int scalefactor = floor(inData.Scale * shades);
inData.Scale    = scalefactor / shades;
```

The parenthetical expression in the first line of code will evaluate to 0.78 * 10 or 7.8. Using the floor() intrinsic will drop the decimal portion, assigning a value of 7 to the integer variable scalefactor.

The second line of code will assign a value of 7 / 10 or 0.7 into the inData.Scale variable.

The next block of code determines whether or not the truncated result should be rendered as part of the silhouette of the model. The shades constant determines the total number of shades that can be represented by the truncated scaling factor, but it does not necessarily indicate the number of visible shades in the final rendered model. The excluded_shades constant is used to determine how many of the darkest color shades (which will be closest to the model's edges) will be eliminated and drawn using the edge_color constant. This is accomplished by comparing the truncated inData.Scale value to the value represented by excluded_shades / shades. This may seem a bit confusing at first, so let's return to our previous example. Let us also further assume the user is requesting that 3 shades be excluded from rendering and drawn as the hard edge:

Example:

```
if(inData.Scale < excluded_shades / shades)
```

The conditional statement above attempts to determine if the truncated color scaling factor is less than excluded_shades / shades or 3 / 10, for our example. Since 0.7 is greater than 0.3, this expression evaluates to false. This particular pixel is not part of the hard edge and will be rendered using a properly scaled shade of the requested render color. The else clause multiplies the requested rendering color stored in the render_color constant by the truncated scaling factor and adds a bias of

1 color shade. This additional bias is required because the truncating mechanism used to produce the color banding always rounds down to the nearest integer. Adding a bias of 1 color shade, or `render_color / 10` for our example, will keep the image from becoming too dark.

In order to see what happens when the scaling factor represents an excluded color shade, let's consider a new example. Assume the user is requesting 5 color shades, 2 excluded shades, and the truncated scale factor of the current pixel is 0.2:

Example:

```
if(inData.Scale < excluded_shades / shades)
```

The conditional statement would now equate to `true`, since 0.2 is less than 2 / 5. In this case, the color is simply set to the value stored in `edge_color`.

The behavior of this conditional statement allows the user to vary the thickness of the model's silhouette by modifying the `excluded_shades` constant. Larger values for this constant will result in thicker lines around the model's hard details. Smaller values will make the hard edge thinner. A value of 0 will allow the user to make use of the color banding effects without rendering a silhouette.

Variations of Dot3 Cel Shading

The HLSL code shown in Listings 2.9.1 and 2.9.2 results in only 16 per-vertex operations, including all vertex transformations, and a mere 10 per-pixel operations. Since we have some processing power to spare, we'll conclude this tutorial on Dot3 Cel Shading by exploring a variant of the shader, which includes reflection mapping. Listings 2.9.3 and 2.9.4 show a variation of the Dot3 Cel Shading method that includes spherical environment mapping. This effect can be used to render highly polished surfaces in a cel shaded environment. We'll only list the code changes below. The entire shader, and other variants, can be found on the CD-ROM that accompanies this book.

ON THE CD

Listing 2.9.3 The Vertex Shader Code Changes for Reflective Dot3 Cel Shading

```
// The new vertex shader output structure now passes the interpolated
// vertex normal transformed into camera space.
struct VS_OUTPUT
{
    float4    Pos:              POSITION;
    float     Scale: TEXCOORD0;
    float3    vCSNorm:          TEXCOORD1;
};

// The view_matrix constant will be used to transform the
// vertex normals into camera space.
float4x4 view_matrix: register(c9);
```

```
// Transform the vertex normal from world space into view space
Out.vCSNorm = mul(view_matrix, inData.vNorm);
```

The only changes to the vertex shader are the inclusion of the view_matrix constant and the transformation of the vertex normal from world space to view space. The view space normal is required by the pixel shader for sampling from the environment map texture.

Listing 2.9.4   The Pixel Shader Code Changes for Reflective Dot3 Cel Shading

```
// The pixel shader input structure now accepts the camera space
// vertex normal in addition to the color scaling factor.
struct PS_INPUT
{
    float       Scale: TEXCOORD0;
    float3      vCSNorm:        TEXCOORD1;
};

// The intensity_adjustment constant is used to ensure that the
// blending of the environment_map colors do not over burn the image.
float           intensity_adjustment: register(c4);
sampler environment_sampler:    register(s0);

// Sample environment map.  Calculate the UV coordinates with the
// standard sphere map equations; U = Nx / 2 + 0.5 & V = -Ny / 2 + 0.5.
float2 UV = float2(inData.vCSNorm[0]  / 2.0f + 0.5f,
                   -inData.vCSNorm[1] / 2.0f + 0.5f);
float4 environment_color = tex2D(environment_sampler, UV);

// The intensity_adjustment constant allows for a final adjustment of
// the color after blending, similar to an "Add Signed" texture blend.
return(color + environment_color + intensity_adjustment);
```

FIGURE 2.9.3   *The image was rendered using Reflective Dot3 Cel Shading.*

Reference

[Card00] Drew Card and Jason L. Mitchell, "Non-Photorealistic Rendering with Pixel and Vertex Shaders," *Direct3D ShaderX: Vertex and Pixel Shader Tips and Tricks*, Wordware Publishing, 2002, pages 319–333.

2.10

Hardware Accelerated Charcoal Rendering

Markus Nuebel

Introduction

With the arrival of programmable pipelines, the variety of visual effects used in modern computer games has increased dramatically. Although it has taken some time for shader hardware to become widespread in the consumer market, we have now reached a point where some games no longer support older hardware, and rely more and more on shader technology. While developers have ventured deeply into improving photorealistic rendering using shaders, many have also started to explore non-photorealistic rendering techniques and improvements. In a market where visual brilliance is taken as being "matter of fact," non-photorealistic rendering is increasingly interesting, as it allows the creation of unique effects that have not been available before.

In this article, we describe a non-photorealistic rendering technique based on [Majumder02]. It produces results similar to classic charcoal drawings, i.e., those created by artists drawing on paper using charcoal sticks. We will discuss how to simulate smooth tonal variation and grainy strokes, which are typical for charcoal paintings, as well as the closure effect used to achieve soft silhouettes.

Overview

Below is a short overview of the steps involved in hardware accelerated charcoal rendering. Each step will then be discussed in greater detail.

1. **Grayscale Diffuse Lighting:** Start by calculating the brightness of each vertex according to the Lambert diffuse lighting model.
2. **Illumination Contrast Enhancement:** A modified brightness value is calculated by applying a contrast enhancement operator to the value calculated in step 1.
3. **Contrast-Enhanced Noise Texture Generation:** The same contrast enhancement operator used in step 2 is applied to a grayscale noise texture. This produces a contrast-enhanced texture that is used in the following steps.
4. **Model Texturing:** For each pixel, the contrast-enhanced brightness is used as one component of a 2D texture coordinate. The other component is generated randomly, and the model is textured using the contrast enhanced noise texture created in step 3.

5. **Color Blending:** The color from the contrast enhanced noise texture is modulated by the brightness from step 2.
6. **Background Paper Blending:** 2D clip space coordinates are calculated and look up a color from a background paper texture, and are then blended with the result from the previous step. The technique is implemented using exactly one vertex (vs_1_1) and one pixel shader (ps_1_4).

Details Description

Grayscale Diffuse Lighting

In the vertex shader, we transform the surface normal to world-space, and then calculate the Lambert diffuse lighting term for use in shading.

Optionally we can oversaturate the intensity to more emphasis the closure effect, described later on.

```
// Calculate light intensity
float3 vecNormal = mul(Input.Normal, matWorld);
float fIntensity = saturate(dot(vecLight1, vecNormal));
float fLambertIntensity = saturate(fAmbientIntensity + fIntensity);
// Optionally oversaturate, to increase the closure effect
fLambertIntensity = saturate(fLambertIntensity * 1.5);
```

Figure 2.10.1 shows the model of a chameleon, lit with the above shader. (Note that the bumpmap and light vectors are not yet used in the pixel shader, only LambertIntensity is used for this figure.)

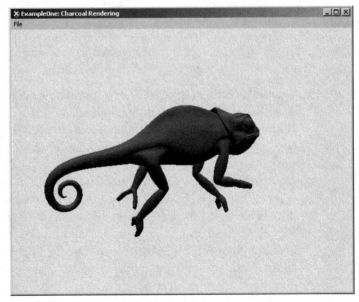

FIGURE 2.10.1   *Grayscale diffuse-lit model.*

Illumination Contrast Enhancement

A contrast enhancement operator OP is a function that maps a coordinate x, $x \in [0, 1]$ to a value y, $y \in [0, 1]$. For our purposes, we will use an exponential function $y = x^{\alpha}$ with $\alpha > 0$.

By applying OP to the calculated brightness, we get a new contrast-enhanced brightness value for every vertex. The nature of the exponential function results in more noticeable shadows in areas that are not directly lit, and produces a sharper rendering result.

The following code snippet shows the application of OP to the previously calculated brightness value.

```
// Applying a contrast enhancement operator.
// y = x^exponent
float fEnhIntensity = pow(fIntensity, fContrastExponent);
Out.Diffuse = fEnhIntensity.xxxx;
```

The result is stored in an output variable to be used in the pixel shader.

FIGURE 2.10.2 *Intensity-enhanced shaded model.*

Finally, the vertex shader is used to pass 2D clip-space coordinates for each vertex to the pixel shader, for use as paper-texture coordinates in Step 6.

```
// Calculate the clip space position
Out.Position    = mul(Input.Position, matWorldViewProj);
// Calculate 2D clip coords
Out.CoordPaper  = (Out.Position / Out.Position.w) * 0.5f + 0.5f;
```

Contrast-Enhanced Noise Texture Generation

In a pre-processing step we calculate a contrast-enhanced grayscale noise texture. This texture is static and used by the pixel shader to obtain grayscale noise.

We start with a simple noise texture that is generated by randomly distributing black spots on a white background. See Figure 2.10.3 for this intermediate step.

FIGURE 2.10.3   *Simple grayscale noise texture.*

By applying the exponential contrast enhancement operator *OP* to the y-coordinate of all the plotted pixels of the generated noise texture, we achieve a polarized distribution with more white areas at one end and more black areas at the other end.

See Figure 2.10.4 for some contrast-enhanced noise textures. Notice that using $\alpha < 1.0$ produces a noise texture with a white area at the top while using $\alpha > 1.0$ results in a white area at the bottom.

FIGURE 2.10.4   *Contrast-enhanced grayscale noise textures using exponents:* $\alpha = 0.5$, $\alpha = 1.5$, $\alpha = 4.5$.

Texturing the Model Using the Enhanced Grayscale Noise Texture

The next step is to texture the model with the enhanced noise texture using the contrast-enhanced intensity value calculated in step 2 as a texture coordinate. This in fact, results in applying the enhancement operator twice.

Normally, the u/v texture coordinates are interpolated across each triangle, and are used in the pixel shader to sample the texture. In our case, the artist-assigned texture coordinates of the model are not used directly. Instead they are used in the following way:

- The artist-assigned coordinates index into a random noise texture, effectively generating random values.
- The u coordinate is set to one of the random values from the random noise texture.
- The v coordinate is set to the contrast enhanced intensity value of the vertex, plus a different random value from the noise texture.

By using the contrast-enhanced intensity value as the v coordinate we are in fact applying the contrast enhancement operator OP to texture the model. The reason we use random values in the u and v coordinates is to prevent the structure of the noise texture showing up in the final output. Imagine areas where the influence of lighting does not change much between vertices. These vertices will produce similar contrast-enhanced intensity values and therefore similar v texture coordinates, increasing the possibility of the noise map showing up. In addition, adding a random value to the v coordinate reduces banding artifacts caused by mipmapping.

To generate a random value in the pixel shader, we use a static noise texture that is also generated during pre-processing. This texture is constructed by calculating a random color for each pixel in the texture.

In the pixel shader we use the artist-assigned texture coordinate to sample the random noise texture.

```
// Retrieve random value (from random noise texture)
float4 colRandom = tex2D(texRandomNoise, Input.CoordRandom);
```

These values are simply noise in all four channels of the texture (the different channels contain different noise—it is colored noise not grayscale noise). Now we just have to fill the two components of a `float2` variable with a combination of the random value and the intensity value already computed in the vertex shader.

```
float2 vecCoordLookup;
vecCoordLookup.x  = colRandom.x * 0.05f;
vecCoordLookup.y  = Input.CoordContrast.y + colRandom.y * 0.05f;
```

Finally we sample the contrast-enhanced grayscale noise texture with the computed texture coordinate.

```
// Sample the contrast enhanced grayscale noise texture with
// the above calculated texture coordinate
float4 colEnhanced = tex2D(texContrastEnhancedNoise,
                           vecCoordLookup);
```

The scaling by 0.05 stops the texture accesses from being too far apart. If this happens, the mipmap hardware selects very high mipmap levels, and thus a very small texture, and banding becomes obvious. Using a small variance in the u coordinate prevents this. Perturbing the v coordinate also helps prevent banding.

Figure 2.10.5 shows an example of the textured model. Referring back to Figure 2.10.4, look at the two noise textures with $\alpha > 1.0$. Notice that the noise pattern is much more visible in the darker areas at the top, while it is not so noticeable at the bottom, where the texture appears much lighter.

Figure 2.10.5 shows that the noise pattern is more intensive in darker regions of the model, while there is hardly any pattern in the very bright locations. This is the result of using an indirect texture read instead of a calculated gradient, and creates the grainy stroke effect that is typical in charcoal drawing.

FIGURE 2.10.5   *Model index-textured with contrast-enhanced grayscale noise texture.*

The contrast enhancement done in step 3 helps achieve an effect known as "closure." Closure is used when artists do not explicitly draw parts of an object's silhouette, leaving the closure of the object to the interpretation of the viewer.

Figure 2.10.6 shows the sample model rotated at a slightly different angle compared to the previous screenshots. The closure effect at the top of the chameleon's head and tail is more noticeable in this perspective.

It is also used where you would normally expect a specular highlight caused by a bright light. Modifying the oversaturation factor in the vertex shader controls the visibility of this effect.

FIGURE 2.10.6 *Final output with closure effect visible at head and tail of the chameleon.*

Blending the Textured Model with the Enhanced Model

In this step we blend the colors looked up from the contrast enhanced texture with those calculated earlier using the diffuse reflection model.

```
// Retrieve the blend ratio from a pixel shader constant
float fRatio = vParams.x;
// Blend the color from the texture with the enhanced diffuse color
float4 colSmudged = lerp (Input.Diffuse.xxxx, colEnhanced, fRatio);
```

The value of the blend ratio is passed to the shader by the application in a pixel shader constant register. This blending operation controls the sharpness of the final output. By blending toward the noise texture components (colEnhanced), the image is more blurred, while blending in more of the intensity-enhanced pixel color (stored in `Input.Diffuse`) results in a sharper and brighter output.

Figure 2.10.7 shows the sample model blended with two different ratios. There is no "rule of thumb" that defines how to choose the blend ratio for special kinds of materials. Depending on your application, you might want to have the same model shown sharper in one place, while it may be displayed more smudged in other places.

FIGURE 2.10.7   *Result of blending: smudged model. The left image uses a ratio of 60/40, the right one a ratio of 40/60.*

Blending the Final Result with a Background Paper Texture

The last step is optional and is only needed to exactly simulate the effect of artistic charcoal drawings.

The 2D clip coordinates calculated in the vertex shader at the end of step 2 are used in the pixel shader to sample the paper texture. The scene background is this same paper texture.

The texture is used to bump map the model by multiplying the color value calculated so far with the dot product of the normal extracted from the paper texture and the interpolated light vector passed in from the vertex shader.

This happens in the pixel shader.

```
// Bumpmap with paper texture
float4 vecBump  = tex2D(texPaper, Input.CoordPaper) *2.0f - 1.0f;
float3 vecLight = Input.Light*2.0f - 1.0f;
float colPaper    = saturate(dot(vecLight.xyz, vecBump));

// Multiply with previously calculated pixel color
float4 colFinal   = colPaper * colSmudged;
```

Note here that we are not transferring the light normal into tangent space. Instead, we use the 2D clip space coordinates to look up a normal for the paper texture and calculate the dot product with the worldspace light direction. This bump maps the model in a 2D way that achieves the effect of the model drawn on paper.

Doing tangent space bump mapping here would produce the effect of a paper-skinned model which would destroy the impression of a charcoal drawing, because it would result in "breaks" in the surface paper structure near the model boundaries.

The contrast enhancement results in bright areas being shaded with white colors. Doing the final multiplicative blend with the background paper texture makes the background structure more dominant in areas where the model is brightly lit.

This is the reason that color enhancement also helps to simulate the "closure effect," since multiplication with values around 1.0 makes the background more visible.

Figure 2.10.8 (along with Figure 2.10.9) shows the final result, where our index-textured and lighting-enhanced model is blended with a bumpy paper texture.

FIGURE 2.10.8 AND FIGURE 2.10.9 *The final result.*

Applications

Due to the non-photorealistic nature of the presented charcoal rendering technique, it can be used to implement a wide variety of real and unreal effects, such as flashback scenes or dream sequences, as well as old-fashioned black and white TV displays, or unnatural and maybe confusing environment lighting. As always in the field of computer graphics, there are nearly no limits for the application of such effects, just the limits to our imagination.

Sample Code

All of the code discussed above is on the book's CD-ROM. This article has talked about most of the shader code, but it may also be interesting to look at other parts we have not discussed, such as the generation of the random noise texture and the contrast enhanced grayscale noise texture as well as all the general shader management code.

Reference

[Majumder02] A. Majumder and M. Gopi, "Hardware Accelerated Real-Time Charcoal Rendering," NPAR 2002: Symposium on Non-photorealistic Animation and Rendering, 2002.

2.11

Detail Texture Motion Blur

Shawn Hargreaves

Introduction

Outside the Climax Brighton office, there is a road. This road consists of pieces of gravel embedded in tar. The size and spacing of the gravel is variable, but for the sake of argument, let's say it is on average about 2 centimeters from one lump to the next.

To represent this road surface in a texture, we will need at least 8 texels per pebble to maintain any degree of clarity. This means a detail texture sized 512 by 512 will cover 128 centimeters of unique real world surface, and will tile approximately once per meter.

Now let's suppose we have a game, running at 60 frames per second, in which a car is driving down this road at 100 kilometers per hour: a fairly typical game scenario. 100 kph is 27.7 meters per second, which is 0.46 meters per frame, or approximately half the distance covered by each tiling of our detail texture.

Whenever the frequency at which you are sampling some data reaches half the repeat rate of that data, you have a problem. This is a magical value called the Nyquist frequency, and when you hit it, things start to go wrong. In the case of moving too quickly over a repeating ground texture, the symptom of the problem is an optical illusion where the texture will appear to stop moving, then gradually start to slide in the opposite direction. This is the same thing that makes wagon wheels spin the wrong way in old cowboy movies, and can be immensely distracting!

An easy workaround would be simply not to put such high-frequency detail in your texture, but that is rather a cop-out. Even using a larger and hence less tiled texture isn't enough to properly fix the problem, because as well as the one meter texture tiling frequency, individual pieces of gravel are repeating far more often, with a Nyquist velocity as little as 2 kilometers per hour! One piece of gravel will never be an exact copy of the next, so this is unlikely to cause the "scrolling backwards" illusion, but they are certainly similar enough to produce a chaotic and noisy visual effect, rather than the intended sense of a fast, smooth forward motion.

The rest of this article discusses the background issues of motion aliasing in more detail, and then presents a specific solution for the problem of tiled ground textures in the context of a racing game.

Standard Antialiasing Techniques

Computers deal in digital approximations, and whenever you take a digital sampling of a continuous function, aliasing occurs. Much of the science of computer graphics is devoted to minimizing the effects of such problems, but relatively little of this deals with the time domain.

The ideal way to sample any continuous value is by integrating it over the range in question, but a fully correct mathematical integration is rarely practical in real time. Common real-world approaches work either by sampling the input data at a higher frequency and then scaling down to the output resolution, or by precalculating various blurred versions of the input data and then selecting between them based on the sampling frequency.

For instance, multisampling hardware addresses the problem of position aliasing for polygon edges by sampling their positions at a higher resolution than the final output.

Mipmapping deals with texture aliasing by choosing the most suitable from a set of pre-blurred copies of the texture, but this approach has a serious flaw. Mipmaps are generated entirely as a texture space operation, but their selection depends on the screen space projection of that texture. This is fine as long as the mapping from texture space to screen space is simple and undistorted, but in situations with extreme perspective, such as looking sideways along the length of a wall, the texture sampling frequency will be different along each axis, so there can be no single correct mip level.

This demonstrates a very important point. Because mipmapping uses precalculated data, it is extremely efficient, but because it operates in the wrong coordinate system, it can only ever be a rough approximation, no matter how useful it may turn out to be in practice.

Anisotropic filtering, on the other hand, tackles the same problem as mipmapping, but in the correct coordinate system. It works by transforming the screen space extents of each pixel back into the texture space where the filtering is being carried out, and then taking multiple samples spread over this area. This cannot be precalculated, but gives higher quality results at a correspondingly greater runtime cost.

Temporal Antialiasing

Movies run at 24 frames per second, and television at 25 or 30 fps depending on your choice of continent. I've yet to hear anyone mention this as a problem, but if an action game dropped to such low frame rates, gamers would be up in arms!

Partly this is because games are interactive, so fast updates are more important than for read-only media, but it is also because film and TV have good temporal antialiasing, while games generally do not. A physical camera naturally provides high quality motion blur, accumulating all the light it receives over the duration of the exposure time. Every now and then a director will play around with this for artistic effect, for instance Spielberg using a very short exposure to give a deliberately aliased, gritty feeling to parts of *Saving Private Ryan*, but in general, the interaction between light and film automatically does the right thing to produce a nice smooth result.

We programmers are not so lucky. If we want motion blur, we have to program it ourselves. The ultimate solution is to supersample in the time domain. If your final game is running at 60 fps, you could render intermediate frames at 120 or 240 fps, and blend these together before presenting the results. This might actually be a sensible way of spending the extra horsepower if you ever find yourself running on hardware more capable than your original target spec, but few of us can generally afford the cycles to render our entire scene multiple times.

Lacking a practical fullscreen motion blur capability (other than the crude "blend in some amount of the previous frame" trick, which can be useful as a special effect but doesn't actually address the underlying aliasing), we have to concentrate on just the few places where temporal aliasing is causing the most objectionable artifacts, and find one-off solutions for each of these specific problems. When a character swings a sword, draw an alpha blended polygon to simulate a motion trail. If an object is travelling unusually quickly, render it a second time with a shader that displaces vertices along the axis of motion. If one particular texture is strobing too badly, change it to make the problem go away.

Detail Texture Blurring

The easiest way of dealing with a problematic texture is simply to fade it out as the speed of motion increases, in a kind of temporal equivalent of mipmapping. This is trivial to do using the D3DSAMP_MIPMAPLODBIAS renderstate, but the results don't look so great: although it does fix the strobing, we also lose all the detail from our texture. It would be better to do something more like anisotropic filtering along the time axis, rather than this simplistic global blur.

The ability to precalculate is crucial, however. Anisotropic filtering hardware is not programmable, and even if it were, high-end cards typically only provide something like 16 tap anisotropic filters, while our camera is moving a lot faster than 16 texels per frame! This would be prohibitively expensive to emulate in a pixel shader.

Motion happens in world space, but a precalculated solution would be easiest in texture space. A direct mapping between these two spaces only exists if the following conditions are met:

- The texture in question is uniformly mapped across the landscape.
- The ground is entirely flat.
- The camera is using an orthographic projection, or looking straight down from above, and is not rotating.

The first condition can be trivially enforced: use a planar mapping to generate the detail texture UV coordinates and tell your artists never to manually edit these.

The second condition is unlikely to be true, but probably close enough that you can get away with ignoring the minor inaccuracy.

The third condition is almost certainly not true, but we will just ignore this, pretend it doesn't matter, and do our best not to feel guilty about it.

So now the rendering process is:

1. Create a `rendertarget` texture the same size as your original detail texture, using the `D3DUSAGE_AUTOGENMIPMAP` flag.
2. Transform the direction and speed of motion from world space into texture space. This is an inherently approximate operation because of the camera restrictions mentioned above, so some heuristics may be needed. A chase view should probably just use the camera velocity, ignoring rotation, while a distant, heavily zoomed replay camera might look better if it tracked the position of its target object, thus including an approximation of any camera rotation.
3. Draw the original detail texture onto the `rendertarget` texture, using a shader that blurs it along the texture space direction of motion.
4. Render the scene, using the generated `rendertarget` texture in place of the original.

The nice thing about this approach is that it is entirely a preprocess. Once a blurred version of the texture has been created, any kind of subsequent rendering can continue as normal, substituting this modified texture into the existing pipeline. Figures 2.11.1 and 2.11.2 are taken from the accompanying sample program.

FIGURES 2.11.1 AND 2.11.2 *The technique in action with a particularly difficult texture, both still and at high speed. The inset in the top left corner shows the contents of the generated* `rendertarget` *texture.*

Precalculation

Pixel shader 2.0 is good at image processing, but it would be nice if we could use this technique on older hardware; even on the latest and greatest cards, applying large blur kernels to large textures is still expensive.

Our input is a 2D texture. The blur is controlled by a pair of direction and amount parameters, so in total this is a four dimensional problem. But there is no such thing as a 4D texture, besides, precalculating so much data would take up a ridiculous amount of space.

Ignoring the blur amount for a while, we could just precalculate images for a number of different blur directions. Because a directional blur is symmetrical between forwards or backwards motions, we only need to bother with half of the circle, so 64 different images allows one for every 2.8 degree change in direction. By lerping between the two closest rotations as the angle changes, this is easily enough to create smooth changes of blur direction: in fact, as few as 32 rotations can be acceptable.

64 rotated copies of a 512 by 512 texture adds up to 8 megabytes even in DXT1 format, but this can be dramatically reduced. Having blurred the image along one axis, we can then scale it down along this same axis without losing any significant detail, as shown by Figures 2.11.3 through 2.11.5:

FIGURE 2.11.3 *Original blurred texture.*

FIGURE 2.11.4
Shrunk to 1/8 size.

FIGURE 2.11.5   *Bilinear filtered back up to the original resolution.*

This obviously only works when the blur direction is along the horizontal or vertical axis, so we need to make sure that will always be the case. This means rotating each image by the opposite of the blur angle, then blurring it horizontally and shrinking horizontally. At runtime, modify the texture coordinates so as to rotate it back in the opposite direction.

When you rotate a square image, the resulting shape can go outside the bounds of the original, but will always lie inside the circle with radius sqrt(2) larger than the texture width as shown in Figure 2.11.6.

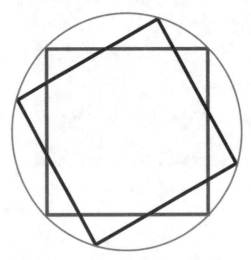

FIGURE 2.11.6   *Rotate square image.*

To avoid cropping the corners, before rotating you must shrink around the center by a factor of sqrt(2), filling the borders with a repeating tile of the original data. The file blurdetailtexture.cpp from the sample program shows one implementation of this, and the lerpDetailBlur() function from detail_demo.cpp shows how to rotate it back to the original location at runtime.

The blurred image width can be dropped to 32 pixels with negligible quality loss, and often as low as 16 or even 8, taking the total data size down to as little 128 or 256 k.

Variable Blur Amounts

With just a single precalculated image for each blur direction, we have no way to smoothly vary the amount of blur, although we can do a simple crossfade to the original non-blurred texture (as shown in the sample program if you set the blurring technique to "full color, single channel").

Ideally we would like to store an image for every possible combination of blur amount and direction, but that would explode the size of the dataset. In the particular case of a monochrome texture, however (which is often the case for detail maps), we have a spare data axis across the three color channels. We can encode three different blur levels into the red, green, and blue components of a single DXT1 texture for no extra storage cost as shown in Figure 2.11.7 through 2.11.11:

FIGURE 2.11.7 *Source texture.*

FIGURE 2.11.8 *Blur level 1.*

FIGURE 2.11.9   *Blur level 2.*

FIGURE 2.11.10   *Blur level 3.*

FIGURE 2.11.11   *Combined blurs in R, G, and B.*

Due to the nature of the DXT encoding scheme, this sort of data packing can increase the compression lossyness, but the results are still acceptable.

The runtime texture blurring shader now reads from three sources: the original non-blurred, non-rotated image, and the two packed rotation textures closest to the desired angle. It also takes three constant inputs:

- rot_lerp—how far are we between the two rotated images.
- rot_dot—a float3 indicating how much of each color channel to include.
- base_amount—how much of the original, non-rotated image to include.

The caller should ensure that (rot_dot.r + rot_dot.g + rot_dot.b + base_ amount) is normalized to one. Gradually decreasing one of these values and increasing another can smoothly fade between a total of four distinct blur amounts.

The final shader is:

```
float3 base = tex2D(base_texture, base_uv);
float3 rot1 = tex2D(rot1_texture, rot1_uv);
float3 rot2 = tex2D(rot2_texture, rot2_uv);

float3 rot = lerp(rot1, rot2, rot_lerp);

return dot(rot, rot_dot) + (base * base_amount);
```

Not only does this work with pixel shader 1.1, but it can even be implemented on fixed function DX7 hardware if you are willing to split it over a couple of passes.

Shader 2.0 Enhancements

So far we have developed a temporal equivalent of anisotropic filtering, implemented as a texture space preprocess using precalculated data. This is highly efficient, but depends on the direction of motion being transformed from world space into texture space. The technique works well for a vehicle driving over a flattish, planar mapped surface, but it cannot deal with arbitrary texture mapping or geometry, and there is a fundamental approximation in the way it handles camera rotation and perspective.

With a shader 2.0 card, it is possible to fix all these problems. Precalculate and pack multiple rotated images as described above, but leave out the render-to-texture stage. Instead, make all the rotated images available to the main scene shader by stacking them in a volume texture. Per-pixel, this shader can then evaluate a localized direction of motion, use a set of tangent space vectors to transform it into texture space, make a local selection between the various rotated and blurred images, and then lerp between them as described above.

This would be an extremely expensive shader, however, and the low-tech approximation produces good results when used within the right constraints. Is a more robust implementation really the most worthwhile use of shader cycles? We suspect not.

A more practical use of newer hardware is to perform the render-to-texture blur in real time, rather than using precalculated data. This can give smoother transitions between different blur amounts and directions, at the cost of fillrate.

Sample Program

The sample program on the accompanying CD-ROM lets you compare the precalcu-
ON THE CD lated technique with a real-time render-to-texture blur, or using mipbias to fade out

the detail texture, or no blurring at all. Click on the main 3D scene to focus it, then use the arrow keys to move around. Use the attributes pane on the right to try out different textures, change the precalculated image size and number of rotations, and choose between a monochrome image holding three different blur levels or a full color image with only a single amount of blur.

Further Reading

Temporal Antialiasing in Computer Generated Animation, Jonathan Korein, Norman Badler: *http://portal.acm.org/citation.cfm?id=801168&jmp=citings&dl= GUIDE&dl=ACM.*

A Human's Eye View: Motion Blur and Frameless Rendering, Ellen J. Scher Zagier: *http://www.acm.org/crossroads/xrds3-4/ellen.html.*

Using vertex displacement to simulate per-object motion blur: *http://developer.nvidia. com/object/motion_blur.html.*

The DX9 PixelMotionBlur sample program applies motion blur in 2D image space, having stored the velocity of each pixel during scene rendering.

Explanation of conventional anisotropic filtering for 2D textures: *http://developer. nvidia.com/object/Anisotropic_Filtering_OpenGL.html.*

MotoGP 2 (Xbox and PC), developed by Climax and published by THQ, uses the precalculated detail texture blurring technique described in this article: *MotoGP 1* used mipbias to fade out the detail texture as speed increased.

2.12

Animation and Display of Water

Stefano Lanza

Introduction

This article presents techniques designed to animate and display an unbounded water surface at high rendering quality and interactive rates on DirectX 9 graphic hardware.

Water is animated using a statistical wave model evaluated with Fast Fourier Transform (FFT). The water surface itself is organized as a quadtree on top of which two level-of-detail algorithms are run: the first algorithm simplifies geometry to an appropriate detail while the latter is a novel approach to map normals on water geometry designed for high quality lighting. A technique to simulate reflections and refractions is then shown. Finally, vertex and pixel shaders written in HLSL are used to render water and simulate the main optical effects that affect its appearance.

Quadtree Organization

The water surface is organized as a quadtree where a node stands for a square chunk of water. At the extremes the root represents the whole ocean while leaf nodes correspond to the minimum chunks of water handled by the rendering system. The levels of the quadtree are enumerated in descending order. The terms "node" and "chunk" will represent the same concept from now on.

Animation

Mathematical Model

Several models have been developed in literature to animate water waves. The first category of models studies the appearance of water at the air-water interface through equations like the Navier-Stokes Equations (NSE). However, these models are, in general, too computationally demanding for games.

The second group of models corresponds to spectral approaches. The basic idea is to produce a wave field having the same spectrum as the ocean and then transform it to spatial domain by an inverse Fourier transform. The water surface is thus expressed as the linear sum of many sinusoidal waves generated by wind:

$$\eta(\vec{X},t) = \sum_{\vec{K}} \hat{\eta}(\vec{K},t)e^{+i\vec{K}\cdot\vec{X}} \qquad (2.12.1)$$

In this equation η is the height of water at position $\vec{X}$ on the grid at time t, $\vec{K}$ is the wave vector and $\hat{\eta}$ has the form:

$$\hat{\eta}(\vec{K},t) = \hat{\eta}_0(\vec{K})e^{iw(K)t} + \hat{\eta}_0^*(-\vec{K})e^{-iw(K)} \qquad (2.12.2)$$

The spatial spectrum $\hat{\eta}_0$ is built by filtering complex white noise:

$$\hat{\eta}_0(\vec{K}) = \frac{1}{\sqrt{2}}(\varepsilon_r(\vec{K}) + i\varepsilon_i(\vec{K}))\sqrt{P_h(\vec{K})} \qquad (2.12.3)$$

where ε_r and ε_i are the values of the noise image seeded by a Gaussian random number generator (mean 0 and standard deviation 1) and $P_h(\vec{K})$ is the Phillips spectrum ([Tessendorf2001]) calculated at the wave vector $\vec{K}$:

$$P_h(\vec{K}) = a\frac{1}{k^4}e^{-1/(kL)^2}\left|\vec{K}\cdot\vec{W}\right|^2 \qquad (2.12.4)$$

where $\vec{W}$ is the wind vector, k is the module of $\vec{K}$, a is a constant that scales the waves amplitude and $L = \left\|\vec{W}\right\|^2 / g$ is the largest possible wave arising from continuous wind.

To animate waves the dispersion relation between the module of $\vec{K}$ and the frequencies states that:

$$w^2(k) = gk \qquad (2.12.5)$$

where g is the gravitational acceleration at the sea level.

The spectrums $\Delta\hat{x}$, $\Delta\hat{y}$ of the two gradient components of the wave height field turn out to be:

$$\Re e(\Delta\hat{x}) = -K_x * \Im m(\hat{\eta}(\vec{K})) \qquad (2.12.6)$$

$$\Im m(\Delta\hat{x}) = K_x * \Re e(\hat{\eta}(\vec{K}))$$

$$\Re e(\Delta\hat{y}) = -K_y * \Im m(\hat{\eta}(\vec{K})) \qquad (2.12.7)$$

$$\Im m(\Delta\hat{y}) = K_y * \Re e(\hat{\eta}(\vec{K}))$$

FFT

The FFT is the mathematical tool to fast evaluate sum (1). The sum is done over a finite number of wave vectors expressed as:

$$\vec{K}_{x,y} = (2\pi x / w, 2\pi y / w) \qquad (2.12.8)$$

where x, y are two indices in the range $-n/2 <= x, y < n/2$, n is the size of the grid and w is the dimension of the grid in world units.

The term $\hat{\eta}_0(\vec{K})$ is time-independent and hence can be pre-calculated; we break it into the three components $S(\vec{K}) = \frac{1}{\sqrt{2}}\sqrt{P_h(\vec{K})}, \varepsilon_r, \varepsilon_i$ that we store in tables of $n*n$ values for each possible $\vec{K}$. These components will be used at each frame to evaluate Equation 2.12.2.

Note that each spectrum is Hermitian (i.e., $\hat{\eta}(\vec{K},t) = \hat{\eta}^*(-\vec{K},t)$ because it represents a real (in the mathematical sense) surface. As a consequence we can specify only half of the spectrum (for example, only the positive x frequencies) and use an optimized transformation from complex to real domain that takes into account this property.

We create a 64×64 height map using the FFT. The 2D gradient of the water surface is calculated as well with two additional FFTs (finite differencing can be used instead for efficiency) using formulas (2.12.6) and (2.12.7). Normals are then extracted from the gradient map, with a normalized cross-product of the two gradient vectors, and stored in a normal map. The gradient of the surface along the x direction is stored as well in a texture, called a tangent map, which will be used by a bump mapping technique in a pixel shader.

Mesh Extraction

The next step is the creation of a set of meshes that we will use to render chunks of water at different levels of detail. All these meshes have the same number of triangles but different geometrical resolutions because they cover different areas. For instance the most detailed meshes will be associated with the leaf nodes of the quadtree, while larger and less detailed meshes with nodes higher in the quadtree will be used to render distant water.

We will build a set of meshes of 17×17 points sampling the 64×64 height map. We start extracting 16 highly detailed meshes from the height map as shown in Figure 2.12.1, left. The meshes of the next level of detail cover four times the area than the previous ones and are obtained by down-sampling the height map by a factor of 2; there are four such meshes (Figure 2.12.1, middle). Next we can build only one mesh with a 1:4 down-sampling.

The next mesh is obtained by tiling the height map two times in order to form a group of 2×2 height maps, and then down-sampling this group by a factor of 8. The process goes on until a terminal level of detail is reached.

Note that since geometrical detail is lost for larger and larger meshes it is possible to avoid a per-frame update of the full set of meshes. Only the detailed meshes belonging to the first levels need to be dynamic and updated each frame. Less detailed meshes can instead be pre-calculated and stored as static vertex buffers for efficiency but they will still look animated because they will be rendered with the animated normal map applied to them.

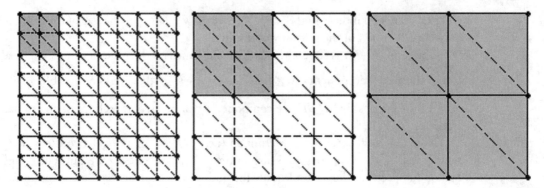

FIGURE 2.12.1   *Meshes (in black) of levels 0, 1, and 2 of detail.*

Visible gaps may appear between adjacent meshes displayed at different resolutions. An easy solution to this problem that really works well is to simply fill in the gaps with a vertical quadrilateral at each edge of a mesh.

Geometrical Simplification

An unbounded water surface like an ocean features waves at any scale that extend up to the horizon. The equivalent polygon count of this scenario is virtually infinite, thus a scheme to drastically reduce it is necessary to achieve interactive rendering frame rates.

Quadtree Traversal

The simplification mechanism works hand in hand with the quadtree organization of water. The quadtree is traversed in both directions in search of a proper level of detail, moving from lower to higher nodes (merging) when the level of detail is excessive and toward lower nodes to gain geometrical detail (splitting) according to the viewer position.

The traversal of the quadtree starts from the node containing the viewer and then visits all its ascendants till the root in a bottom-up fashion. At each level the geometrical resolution of the node is evaluated. Valid nodes are inserted into a list and all their ascendants forced to split. Nodes lacking geometrical detail are instead recursively split. Frustum culling is performed as well during the process as shown in Figure 2.12.2.

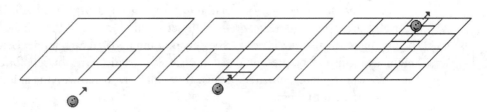

FIGURE 2.12.2   *Selection of level of detail based on viewer position.*

When the quadtree traversal is complete we have a list of visible water nodes with the appropriate geometrical level of detail. Before rendering we must assign the correct mesh to each node according to its level in the quadtree: leaf nodes will be rendered with the most detailed meshes (level 0), higher nodes with coarser meshes.

Evaluation

The following idea is employed to evaluate the validity of a certain representation: the minimum bounding box of a node is extended by a certain amount, equal in the x and z directions, lower in the y direction because water geometry loses detail faster as the viewer moves upwards.

The extended box of the parent node is calculated as well. The two boxes define three regions called A, B, and C in Figure 2.12.3.

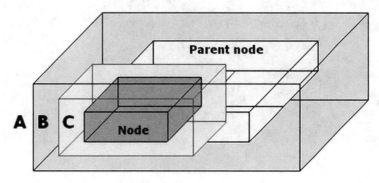

FIGURE 2.12.3 *Regions of evaluation.*

When the viewer is in region A, its distance to the node is far enough to switch to a coarser representation thus a "merge" request is returned. When the viewer instead enters region C the current representation lacks detail and a "split" request is returned. In between (region B) the current representation is valid.

Normal Mapping

The appearance of water is determined to a great extent by the optical effects that take place at its surface like reflections, refractions, and sun highlights. When modelling these effects the normal vector plays a fundamental role because it intervenes in almost all related calculations.

The proposed scheme introduces a continuous mapping of normals on water geometry free from aliasing and repetitiveness. A continuous representation is necessary because the human eye easily perceives abrupt variations in lighting conditions determined by sudden changes of texture maps.

Frequency Selection

This algorithm works again on top of a quadtree data structure: each node produced by the geometrical simplification mechanism undergoes a process of frequency selection that affects the quality of the mapping. The process evaluates the current mapping and moves to a higher or lower frequency accordingly; these two operations are called "splitting" and "merging."

Each node is initially mapped with the full normal map covering it. The splitting operation consists in recursively breaking the node into its four children and applying the full normal map to them to obtain a mapping with higher detail (see Figure 2.12.4). In this case the geometry of the mesh that represents the node is split as well.

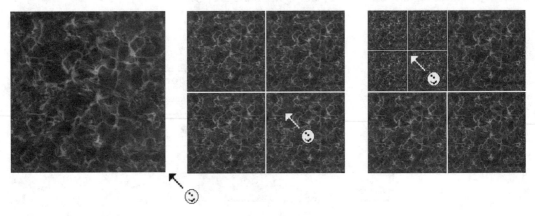

FIGURE 2.12.4   *Splitting.*

The merging operation consists in recursively mapping only a portion of the normal map to the node in order to obtain a lower frequency mapping (Figure 2.12.5).

The code actually calculates the parent node to which the full mapping is applied and then exploits the spatial relationship between the node and this parent to properly scale and offset the texture coordinates of the normal map in a vertex shader. This is done for both the valid and the coarser representation. In two fields mapping, and mapping2 we store in the x and z components the coordinates of the top-left corner of the node to which the full mapping applies and in the w component the inverse of the width of this node.

Evaluation

The idea behind the evaluation of a mapping is exactly the same used by the geometrical simplification scheme. In addition the evaluation returns an interpolation value that represents a blending factor between the valid representation and the coarser one.

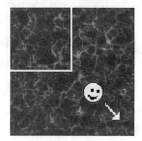
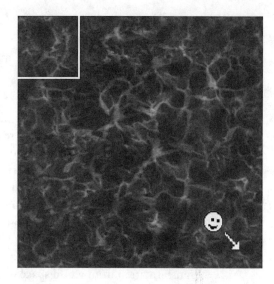

FIGURE 2.12.5 *Merging.*

This value "alpha" is used by pixel shaders to gradually interpolate two normals for a smooth display of water lighting as the viewer moves. With reference to Figure 2.12.3, it is calculated as:

```
alpha = max(0, 1 - dist/delta)
```

where `delta` is the minimum distance between region A and C and `dist` is the minimum distance between the viewer and region C.

Reflections and Refractions

The reflections and refractions made by water are simulated using two target textures that show the reflected and the refracted scene respectively. These textures are rendered with two additional passes treating water as a planar surface. They are then mapped onto the water geometry through projective texture mapping [Everitt] with perturbed coordinates to account for the non-planar nature of water. The two textures are finally blended according to a `Fresnel` term computed per pixel.

In order to render the reflected scene we first set a texture as the current render target. Ideally the texture should match the size of the frame-buffer but to limit bandwidth usage you can use a lower size (say 512×512). The perturbations used when fetching the texture data will mask this lower resolution well. Then we create a clipping plane to clip the objects below the air-water interface because they cannot be physically reflected. Objects completely below water can instead be rejected immediately. Next we mirror the geometry in world space with respect to the water plane using the following mirroring matrix:

$$\text{Mirroring matrix} = \begin{bmatrix} 1 & 0 & 0 & 0 \\ 0 & -1 & 0 & 2h \\ 0 & 0 & 1 & 0 \\ 0 & 0 & 0 & 1 \end{bmatrix}$$

where h is the height of the water plane. In the end we render the scene to a texture. Both reflection and refraction are rendered from the same camera position and orientation that were used to render the standard scene.

The texture that shows the refracted scene is rendered in a similar way but this time we render only the objects that are inside water, clipping those that are partially above it. Special shaders are employed to render the refracted scene simulating underwater scattering and caustics. Those are discussed in the final part of the article.

We must create a proper matrix for projective texture mapping: the textures are projected from the camera position in the direction the camera is looking at so the transformation from world space to clip space is nearly the same used when rendering the scene. A minor difference concerns the transformation from view to clip space; since real water reflects slightly more than a flat plane, we use a larger field of view (around 10% more). A last matrix then converts texture coordinates from clip space to texture space. In the end the projective matrix is:

$$\text{Projective matrix} = \begin{bmatrix} 0.5 & 0 & 0 & 0.5 \\ 0 & -0.5 & 0 & 0.5 \\ 0 & 0 & 0.5 & 0.5 \\ 0 & 0 & 0 & 1 \end{bmatrix} * \text{world to clip matrix}$$

Water Rendering

The final rendering of water is done by vertex and pixels shaders 2.0 written in HLSL.

Vertex Shader

The vertex shader uses these constants:

```
float4x4 viewProjMatrix;        // world to clip space matrix
float4x4 projTexMatrix;         // projective texturing matrix
float3   nodeOrigin;            // world space origin of node
float4   mapping, mapping2;     // see chapter on normal mapping
float3   viewer;                // viewer in world space
```

The constants `nodeOrigin`, `mapping` and `mapping2` are passed to the shader for each different water node before rendering. The following vertex structures are used in input and output:

```
struct VS_INPUT {
    float4 pos      : POSITION;   // position in object space
};

struct VS_OUTPUT {
    float4 pos      : POSITION;    // position in world space
    float4 uv       : TEXCOORD0;   // two sets of tex. coordinates
    float4 projUv   : TEXCOORD1;   // projective  tex. coordinates
    float3 view     : TEXCOORD2;   // view vector in world space
    float2 perturb  : TEXCOORD3;   // perturbations
};
```

The vertex shader performs the following operations: first of all it transforms the vertex position taken in input from object space to world space:

```
VS_OUTPUT main(const VS_INPUT In) {
    VS_OUTPUT Out;

    float4 worldPos = float4(In.pos+nodeOrigin, 1);
```

Then it transforms this position to clip space:

```
Out.pos = mul (viewProjMatrix, worldPos);
```

The shader then generates two sets of texture coordinates used by the pixel shader to fetch the normal of the valid and coarser mapping:

```
Out.uv.x = (worldPos.x - mapping.x)  * mapping.w;
Out.uv.y = (mapping.z  - worldPos.z) * mapping.w;
Out.uv.z = (worldPos.x - mapping2.x) * mapping2.w;
Out.uv.w = (mapping2.z - worldPos.z) * mapping2.w;
```

We calculate a set of 4D texture coordinates for projective texture mapping:

```
Out.projUv = mul(projTexMatrix, worldPos);
```

Then the shader calculates the normalized view vector in world space:

```
float3 viewVector = viewer − worldPos;
float  viewDist = length(viewVector);
Out.viewVector = viewVector / viewDist; // normalize
```

We use the distance from the vertex to the viewer to exponentially decrease how much the waves distort the reflections and refractions:

```
float p = exp(-A*viewDist);
Out.perturb = float2(B*p, C*p);

return Out;
}
```

A, B, and C are small positive constants that we can tweak to get the best visual results.

Pixel Shader

The pixel shader uses three textures: the normal map, the reflection, and the refraction texture:

```
sampler normalMap, reflectionTex, refractionTex;
```

The constants are:

```
float3 sunColor;        // color of sun
float3 sunDirection;    // direction of sunlight
float  alpha;           // alpha value to blend two normals
```

The output of the vertex shader is taken as input. The shader first fetches the normal map using the first two sets of texture coordinates, linearly interpolating the samples with the `alpha` value. The x and z coordinates of the normal are then expanded from the range $[0, 1]$ to the range $[-1, +1]$:

```
float4 main(VS_OUTPUT v) : COLOR {

    float3 normal = lerp(tex2D(normalMap, v.uv.zw),
                         tex2D(normalMap, v.uv.xy),
                         alpha
                         );
    normal.xz = 2*(normal.xz-0.5);
```

We then calculate the texture coordinates used to fetch the reflection and refraction textures, first projecting the coordinates (projective texture mapping), then adding some perturbations. The perturbations must be higher for tall waves characterized by a large projection of their normal on the 2D plane.

```
float2 projUv = v.projUv.xy / v.projUv.w;
float2 reflUv = projUv + v.perturb.x*normal.xz;
float2 refrUv = projUv + v.perturb.y*normal.zx;
```

The reflectance and transmittance of water are modulated by a `Fresnel` term:

```
float  Fresnel = fastFresnel(v.viewVector, normal, 0.0204, 5);
```

Next we fetch the reflection and refraction textures:

```
float3 reflection = tex2D(reflectionTex, reflUv);
float3 refraction = tex2D(refractionTex, refrUv);
```

The two textures are blended according to the `Fresnel` term calculated above:

```
float3 color = lerp(refraction, reflection, Fresnel);
```

We now calculate the specular highlights of sun shining on water using the Phong illumination model and taking into account the `Fresnel` term:

```
float3 R = reflect(-v.viewVector, normal);
float  specular = max(0, dot(R, -sunDirection) );
float3 specularColor = Fresnel*sunColor*pow(specular, 512);
```

The specular contribution is added to the water color to obtain the final color:

```
    return float4(color + specularColor, 1);
}
```

The `Fresnel` term is approximated by the following function, as explained in [Wloka02]:

```
float fastFresnel(float3 I, float3 N, float R0, float power) {
    return R0 + (1-R0)*pow(1.0 - dot(I, N), power);
}
```

where I is the incident ray, N is the normal, and R0 and power are two constants (0.0204 and 5 for water).

Bump mapping

The nearest water surface is rendered with an alternative pixel shader that incorporates a form of bump mapping to give the illusion of finer lighting effects. In comparison to the previous shader it also uses a tangent map where tangent vectors are stored.

First of all the tangent vector is extracted from the tangent map using the first set of texture coordinates:

```
float3 tangent = tex2D(tangentMap, v.uv.xy);
tangent.xyz = 2*(tangent.xyz-0.5);           // expand tangent
```

A high-frequency normal vector is then fetched from the normal map:

```
float3 bumpNormal;
bumpNormal = tex2D(normalMap, v.uv.xy * 8);
// expand x, z components to the range [-1, 1]:
bumpNormal.xz = 2*(bumpNormal.xz-0.5);
```

The effects of bump mapping must disappear as the viewer looks further, to prevent aliasing, and before switching to a coarser representation of water that is rendered by the previous pixel shader. When the vector `bumpNormal` equals (0, 1, 0) this shader is functionally equivalent to the previous one so the following line of code suits our needs:

```
bumpNormal = lerp(float3(0,1,0), bumpNormal, v.perturb.x*alpha);
```

The following code is standard among bump mapping techniques [Kilgard00]; we first set up a transformation from object space to tangent space:

```
float3 binormal = cross(normal, tangent);
float3x3 obj2tanSpace = { tangent, normal, binormal };
```

Now we transform the view vector, calculated in the vertex shader, and the sun direction from object space to tangent space (actually these two vectors are the same in world and object space):

```
float3 tanV = mul(obj2tanSpace, v.viewVector);
float3 tanL = mul(obj2tanSpace, sunDirection);
```

To perturb the texture coordinates we use the bump normal back-transformed from tangent to world space (we need only the x, z coordinates):

```
float2 Nxz;
Nxz[0] = tangent.x*bumpNormal.x + normal.x*bumpNormal.y +
         binormal.x*bumpNormal.z;
Nxz[1] = tangent.z*bumpNormal.x + normal.z*bumpNormal.y +
         binormal.z*bumpNormal.z;
float2 projUv = v.projUv.xy / v.projUv.w;
float2 reflUv = projUv + v.perturb.x*Nxz.xy;
float2 refrUv = projUv + v.perturb.y*Nxz.yx;
```

The Fresnel term is calculated now in tangent space as:

```
float  Fresnel = fastFresnel(tanV, bumpNormal, 0.0204, 5);
```

The specular factor is calculated as:

```
float3 tanR = reflect(tanV, bumpNormal);
float  specular = max(0, dot(tanR, tanL) );
```

Water Optics

Light penetrating the water surface is absorbed and scattered by water molecules and by suspended and dissolved particles. Water turbidity, due to sediments or coastal runoff, can also significantly an increase in both absorption and scattering. Usually blue light is attenuated the least while orange and red light are attenuated the most, which gives the familiar blue color of water.

A simplified model of water absorption and scattering is now introduced. The model is applied to the underwater environment when rendered on the refraction texture.

Light is exponentially attenuated as it travels through water because of absorption and out-scattering; the resulting effect is called *extinction* and is simulated assuming that lights travels two times (gone and away) the distance under water between the camera and the point to be lit.

```
float  viewDist = length(viewer - worldPos);
float  depth = max( waterHeight – worldPos.y,  0 );
float  L = viewDist* depth / (viewer.y – worldPos.y);
float3 extinction = exp(-attenuation*2*L);
```

In-scattering refers to light that is scattered by molecules in the direction of the viewer and it is calculated as:

```
float3 inScattering = diffuseRadiance*(1 - extinction*exp(-depth*kd))
```

The derivation of these formulas and of the `attenuation`, `diffuseRadiance` and kd constants can be found in [Premoze01].

The above code can be computed per vertex or per pixel according to the desired rendering quality; usually for coarse meshes it is better to run it in a pixel shader since the results of exponentiations may vary considerably over a triangle. The scattering terms so calculated are applied to the color of the underwater object as:

```
float3 color = color*extinction + inScattering
```

Caustics are the well known patterns of sunlight caused by the refraction of light beams at the water surface and are generated in real time using the procedure described in [Jensen01]. The caustics texture is then projected and added on objects under water just before applying scattering.

Conclusion

The article presented techniques for the real-time animation and rendering of water, developed for DirectX 9 compliant graphic cards.

The CPU is loaded with the task of animating water and running level-of-detail algorithms that simplify geometry and select appropriate normal mappings. Two textures that show the reflected and refracted scene are then rendered. The dataset so prepared is passed to the GPU for rendering using shaders of version 2.0 that simulate the main optical factors that affect the appearance of water. The result is the display of realistic water on current graphic hardware at interactive frame rates.

Future extensions include the simulation of underwater scenario and improvements in the appearance of water under both the geometrical and the lighting aspect.

CD-ROM Contents

ON THE CD

The companion CD contains a demo of the Typhoon engine (*www.gameprog.it/typhoon*) that shows water animated and rendered with the techniques described in this article. The source code of the HLSL shaders is included as well.

References

[Tessendorf01] Tessendorf, J. "Simulating Ocean Water," SIGGRAPH 2001 Course notes. *http://home1.gte.net/tssndrf/index.html.*

[Jensen01] Jensen, L. "Deep-Water Animation and Rendering," Gamasutra, September 26, 2001. *http://www.gamasutra.com/gdce/jensen/jensen_01.htm.*

[Everitt] C. Everitt. "Projective Texture Mapping," available online at *http://developer.nvidia.com/object/Projective_Texture_Mapping.html.*

[Wloka02] M. Wloka. "Fresnel Reflection Technical Report," available online at *http://developer.nvidia.com/object/fresnel_wp.html.*

[Kilgard00] M. J. Kilgard. "A Practical and Robust Bump-mapping Technique for Today's GPUs," GDC 2000, July 5, 2000.

[Premoze01] Simon Premoze and Michael Ashikhmin. "Rendering Natural Waters," *Computer Graphics Forum,* 2001.

2.13

Rendering Semitransparent Layered Media

Chris Oat

Introduction

This article presents a technique for rendering semitransparent, layered media. Modern graphics hardware provides the capability to apply many texture layers onto a single surface. However, simply alpha blending many textures onto a surface does not give the appearance of surface depth that one would expect from semitransparent surface layers. Normal mapping, transparency masking, offset mapping, and image filtering are combined here to produce realistic looking layered surfaces. This technique may be used to render multi-layer surfaces with interesting layer interactions.

Background

Many real world surfaces, particularly biological tissues, get their unique appearance from the complex light interactions that occur between surface layers. Figure 2.13.1 illustrates the difference in lighting complexity between a simple, single layer surface and a semitransparent, multi-layered surface. The deeper a given light ray travels into a surface the more opportunities there are for scattering; this results in subsurface layers appearing blurry relative to the top most surface layer.

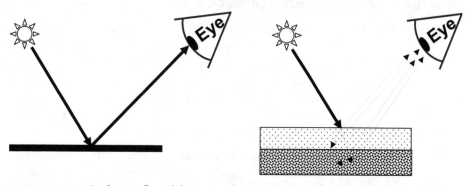

FIGURE 2.13.1 *Light is reflected from a surface. (Left) Light is reflected from a simple single layer surface, this is the lighting model used in most games today. (Right) Light enters and scatters, reflecting off many surface layers before reaching the viewer.*

In addition to appearing blurry, subsurface layers should exhibit parallax. Parallax is the apparent shift in position due to a change in the viewer's line of sight. Figure 2.13.2 illustrates two different viewpoints of the same surface. If simple, multi-texture blending was used to render this surface, as the viewpoint changed the under layer would remain fixed relative to the top layer and this would result in the various surface layers appearing flat or squashed. By exploiting the effects of parallax in our shader we can add a sense of depth to the surface layers; this proves to be a very important visual cue that will allow us to render more realistic looking layered surfaces.

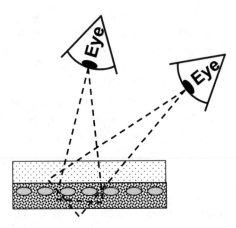

FIGURE 2.13.2 *As the view changes, the under layer will appear to move relative to the top layer.*

Semitransparent Layered Surfaces

The techniques presented in this article have been used to successfully render a realistic human heart as shown in Figure 2.13.3. This heart model uses two layers to represent the outer most surface and some internal subsurface structure (such as veins and other bits of tissue). A single pass pixel shader is used to compute and blend each layer's contribution to the final heart surface.

Outer Surface Layer

The outer most surface layer is composed of a base map, a normal map, and a transparency map as shown in Figure 2.13.4. This layer uses well known rendering techniques to achieve a bumpy, glossy surface. A per-pixel surface normal is sampled from the normal map and used to calculate the diffuse and specular lighting (specular contribution is sampled from a cubic environment map). A transparency map is also used

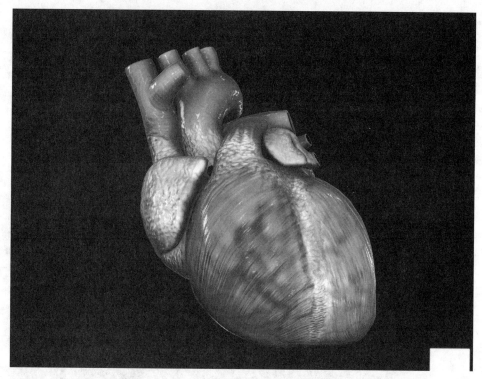

FIGURE 2.13.3   *A realistic human heart rendered using multiple semitransparent layers.*

to provide per-pixel transparency values which will be used later to blend the outer and inner layers.

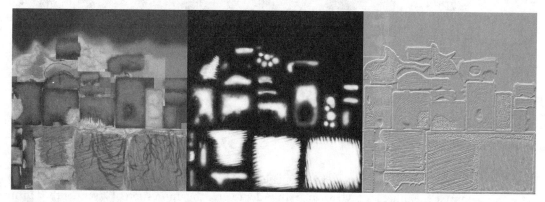

FIGURE 2.13.4   *Three textures are used to create the outer most layer of the heart: (Left) Base map, (Center) Transparency map, (Right) Normal map.*

Inner Surface Layer

The inner layer of the heart is far more interesting than the outer surface layer. This layer only uses a single texture (a base map) as shown in Figure 2.13.5 but requires slightly more complex pixel shader code to achieve the blurring and parallax effects we desire.

FIGURE 2.13.5   *The base map for the heart's inner layer.*

Our first challenge is to calculate the correct texture coordinate from which to sample the inner layer's base map. In order to give the impression of layer depth, a form of parallax mapping is used to offset the outer layer's texture coordinates [Kaneko01] [Welsh04]. These offset coordinates are then used to sample the inner texture layer.

In order to calculate the offset texture coordinate we must first calculate a transmission vector. The transmission vector points from the outer surface layer's sample point to the inner surface layer's sample point as shown in Figure 2.13.6. The offset texture coordinate is determined by finding the intersection of the transmission vector with the inner layer.

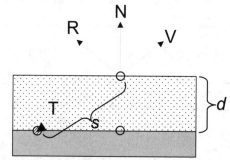

○ = Base coordinate: <u,v>
◉ = Offset coordinate: <u',v'>

FIGURE 2.13.6 *The outer layer's texture coordinate is offset before using it to sample the inner layer's texture.*

We use a very simple approximation to calculate the transmission vector; the tangent space view vector is reflected about the per-pixel normal (from our normal map) to find a reflection vector. The reflection vector is then reflected about the surface plane such that it points into the surface. Because these vectors are in tangent space, reflecting the reflection vector about the surface plane is simply a matter of negating its z component. Equations in (2.13.1) are used to calculate the offset texture coordinate that will be used to sample the inner layer. Unit length vectors are assumed and the distance value should be in "texel units" (<1/texture width, 1/texture height>).

$$\vec{R} = -\vec{V} - 2 * dot(-\vec{V}, \vec{N}) * \vec{N}$$
$$\vec{T} = \langle R_x, R_y, -R_z \rangle$$
$$s = d / |T_z|$$
$$\langle u', v' \rangle = \langle u, v \rangle + s \langle T_x, T_y \rangle \tag{2.13.1}$$

We now have an offset texture coordinate that may be used to sample the inner layer's texture map. The next step is to blur the inner layer based on the distance along the transmission vector between the inner and outer sample points. The deeper we see through the top layer, the blurrier the inner layer should appear. In order to achieve the correct amount of blurring, a variable-sized filter kernel is used to sample the inner layer's texture map.

Our filter kernel takes 13 samples, the first sample is centered at the offset texture coordinate position and the remaining 12 samples are taken from nearby texels. Our filter uses stochastic sampling, following a Poisson disc distribution, to determine the 12 "nearby" sample positions. This filter is well suited for our needs because its kernel size can be configured on a per-pixel basis, thus allowing us to scale the per-pixel blurriness of the inner layer based on its distance along the view vector from the top layer. HLSL shader code is included below for implementing this filter.

```
//====================================================================
===
// Growable Poisson Disc Filter (13 tap)
//
// sampler tSource = source texture being filtered.
// float2 texCoord = texture coordinate for destination texel.
// float2 pixelSize = size of a texel in the source and destination
//                    image. usually this will be a vector like:
//                    <1/width, 1/height>
//
// float radius =     size of kernel in texels (0 will only sample
from
//                    texel at texCoordDest, 1.0 will sample from at
//                    most a texel away, etc).
//====================================================================
===
float3 GrowableFilterRGB (sampler tSource, float2 texCoord,
                          float2 pixelSize, float radius)
{
    float3 cOut;
    float2 poisson[12] = {float2(-0.326212f, -0.40581f),
                          float2(-0.840144f, -0.07358f),
                          float2(-0.695914f, 0.457137f),
                          float2(-0.203345f, 0.620716f),
                          float2(0.96234f, -0.194983f),
                          float2(0.473434f, -0.480026f),
                          float2(0.519456f, 0.767022f),
                          float2(0.185461f, -0.893124f),
                          float2(0.507431f, 0.064425f),
                          float2(0.89642f, 0.412458f),
                          float2(-0.32194f, -0.932615f),
                          float2(-0.791559f, -0.59771f)};

    // center tap
    cOut = tex2D (tSource, texCoord);


    for (int tap = 0; tap < 12; tap++)
    {
        float2 coord = texCoord.xy + (pixelSize * poisson[tap] * ra-
dius);

        // Sample pixel
        cOut += tex2D (tSource, coord);
    }
```

```
      return (cOut / 13.0f);
   }
```

We now have a bumpy, glossy outer layer color and a blurry, offset inner layer color. The layers may now be blended using a weighted average based on the per-pixel transparency value and the dot product of the view vector with the surface normal. By adding a view dependant term (N.V) to the weighted average we bias the average toward the outer layer's color at glancing angles where the viewer expects to see more reflection than subsurface diffusion. This also prevents artifacts from cropping up as our texture coordinate offset calculation nears a divide by zero (the z component of the transmission vector approaches zero as the view vector becomes perpendicular to the surface normal).

Pixel Shader

Using these techniques, semitransparent, layered surfaces can be rendered on consumer-level programmable graphics hardware. The HLSL code provided below was used to render the multi-layered heart shown in Figure 2.13.1 and uses the concepts described above. Since the shader code is rather lengthy and all of the interesting math happens at the pixel level, the vertex shader code has not been included here. The vertex shader only computes view and light vectors in tangent space and passes these vectors to the pixel shader.

```
sampler tBaseOuter;  // outer layer base map (transparency in alpha)
sampler tBaseInner;  // inner layer base map
sampler tBump;       // normal map
sampler tEnv;        // cubic env map

float4  fLayerDepth; // animated layer depth for pulsing heart


struct PsInput
{
   float2 vTexCoord    : TEXCOORD0; // base tex coords
   float3 vInvNormal   : TEXCOORD1; // inverse tangent space matrix
   float3 vInvTangent  : TEXCOORD2;
   float3 vInvBinormal : TEXCOORD3;
   float3 vViewTS      : TEXCOORD4; // tangent space view vec
   float3 vLightTS     : TEXCOORD5; // tangent space light vec
};

float4 main (PsInput i) : COLOR
{

   // Sample outer base, transparency, and normal maps
   float4 cBaseOuter = tex2D(tBaseOuter, i.vTexCoord);
   float3 cNormal = tex2D(tBump, i.vTexCoord);
   float fTransparency = cBase.a;  // transparency in alpha of base
```

```
// Scale and bias normal to convert from [0,1] to [-1,1]
float3 vNormal = normalize((cNormal * 2.0) - 1.0);

// Renormalize interpolated vectors
float3 vLightTS = normalize(i.vLightTS);
float3 vViewTS = normalize(i.vViewTS);

// Recreate the inverse tangent space rotation matrix
float3x3 mInvTangent = {i.vInvTangent, i.vInvBinormal, i.vInvNor-
mal};

// Compute tangent space reflection vector then covert to world
space
// for cubemap lookup
float3 vReflectionTS = reflect(-vViewTS, vNormal);
float3 vReflectionWS = mul(mInvTangent, vReflectionTS);

// N.V
float fNV = saturate(dot(vNormal, vViewTS));

// Compute diffuse illumination
float3 cDiffuse = saturate(dot(vNormal, vLightTS));

// Compute specular illumination (sampled from cubemap)
float3 cSpecular = texCUBE(tEnv, vReflectionWS);

// Compute transmission vector
float3 vTrans = float3(vReflectionTS.xy, -vReflectionTS.z);

// Distance along transmission vector to intersect inner layer
// fLayerDepth : distance between layers as heart beats (calcu-
lated
//              on the CPU as sin(time)*4 and in the range [0,4])
float fTransDistance = fLayerDepth / abs(vTrans.z);

// Find offset tex coords (inner base map is 512x512)
float2 vTexelSize = float2(1.0/512.0, 1.0/512.0);
float2 vOffsetTexCoord = vTexelSize * (fTransDistance *
vTrans.xy);
vOffsetTexCoord = i.vTexCoord + vOffsetTexCoord;

// Sample inner surface layer with variable size blur filter
float3 cInnerLayer = GrowableFilterRGB(tBaseInner, vOffsetTexCo-
ord,
                                        vTexelSize,
fTransDistance);

// Final base color is lerp of inner and outer weighted by
// transparency mask and (N.V)^2
float3 cBase = lerp(cBaseOuter.rgb, cInnerLayer.rgb,
                    fTransparency * fNV * fNV);
```

```
// Compute final lighting
float4 o;
o.rgb = cBase.rgb * cDiffuse;
o.rgb += cSpecular;
o.a = 1.0f;

return o;
}
```

Results and Conclusion

This article presented several tricks for rendering realistic, semitransparent, multi-layered surfaces (see Figure 2.13.7). Well-known rendering techniques such as normal mapping, transparency mapping, and environment mapping were combined with a parallax-offset mapping and a variable-size blur filter to render a throbbing human heart with outer and inner surface layers. There are many ways in which the techniques shown here could be extended; notably, relative computational simplicity could be sacrificed to implement more physically correct scattering and reflectance models such as those described in [Pharr02].

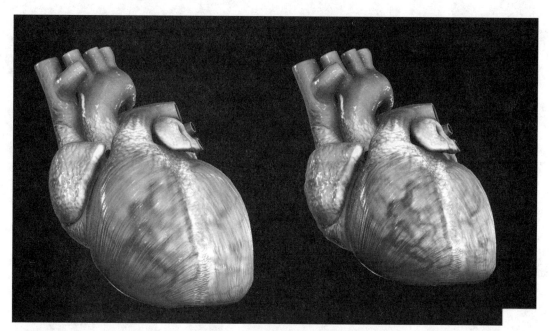

FIGURE 2.13.7 *A realistic looking human heart, rendered using the techniques discussed in this article. Two frames of animation are shown here, as the heart contracts, the distance between surface layers is reduced and the subsurface structure becomes more visible.*

References

[Kaneko01] Tomomichi Kaneko, et al. "Detailed Shape Representation with Parallax Mapping," ICAT, 2001.

[Pharr02] Matt Phar. "Layered Media for Subsurface Shaders," Advanced Render-Man, SIGGRAPH 2002 Course Notes.

[Welsh04] Terry Welsh. "Parallax Mapping with Offset Limiting: A Per-Pixel Approximation of Uneven Surfaces," 2004.

2.14

Hair Rendering and Shading

Thorsten Scheuermann

Introduction and Overview

Rendering hair is an important part of rendering virtual human characters. However, hair rendering is a challenging problem for several reasons. First, there simply is a lot of it: an average human head is covered by 100,000–150,000 individual hair strands. Another factor is that human hair comes in many different styles (long, short, curly, straight, frizzy, etc.), some of which can be hard to reproduce convincingly. Finally, hair has complex light scattering properties, and self-shadowing is an important aspect of the way hair looks.

Unfortunately, rendering hair using a large number of line primitives is not practical in the context of current games because of insufficient performance in typical game environments with several characters visible at once.

FIGURE 2.14.1   *A screenshot of ATI's demo "Ruby: The Double Cross" showing off the hair shader.* © *ATI Technologies 2004.*

The hair rendering technique described in this article is used in ATI's demo "Ruby: The Double Cross" (see Figure 2.14.1). The main character's hair is rendered using a polygon model, with realistic hair shading computed in the pixel shader. The hair shader combines ideas from both Kajiya and Kay's classic hair shading model [Kajiya89] and from a recent paper on hair shading by Marschner et al. [Marschner03]. This article also presents a simple technique for rendering the semi-transparent hair in an approximate back-to-front order, which is necessary for correct alpha blending.

Hair Model and Textures

A hair model suitable for our rendering technique should be built using layers of 2D patches, as the example in Figure 2.14.2(a) shows. Filling up the volume occupied by hair with layers gives the hair a fuller look when rendering.

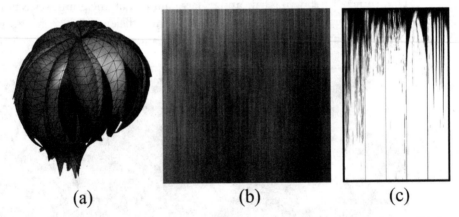

(a)   (b)   (c)

FIGURE 2.14.2   *(a) shows the hair model, colored to reveal the different layers. (b) shows the grayscale base texture and (c) the alpha texture for the hair.*

To give the individual 2D patches the appearance of a hair bundle, we apply two textures. The grayscale base texture provides the fine structure of individual hair strands. The texture used in the examples (see Figure 2.14.2(b) was created in Photoshop by first rendering noise and then scaling it in one direction. The hair color is set using a shader constant, but it would be possible to use a colored base texture instead if more variation in the hair color is desired.

The alpha texture is used to give the patches a less uniform shape and fringed appearance at the hair tips. In our case it contains a set of different maps, which are applied to different patches of the model (see Figure 2.14.2(c).

Hair Shading

Kajiya-Kay Model

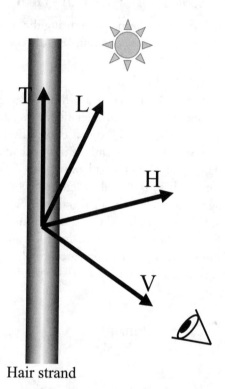

Hair strand

FIGURE 2.14.3 *The vectors used in the Kajiya-Kay lighting calculations: hair tangent (T), view vector (V), light vector (L), and half-angle vector (H).*

A commonly used hair shading model is the anisotropic strand lighting model by Kajiya and Kay [Kajiya89]. In this model, a hair strand is modeled as an infinitely thin cylinder and standard Phong lighting computations are adapted to use the hair tangent instead of a surface normal. As seen in Figure 2.14.3, the parameters used in the shading model are the hair tangent (T), the view vector (V), the light vector (L), the half-angle vector (H), and the exponent s which specifies the sharpness of the highlight. In the equations below, sin(X, Y) and cos(X, Y) denotes the sine and cosine of the angle between vectors X and Y.

The diffuse and specular terms are computed as follows:

$$diffuse = \sin(\mathbf{T},\mathbf{L}) = \sqrt{1-\cos(\mathbf{T},\mathbf{L})^2} = \sqrt{1-(\mathbf{T}\cdot\mathbf{L})^2}$$

$$specular = \sin(\mathbf{T},\mathbf{H})^s = \sqrt{1-(\mathbf{T}\cdot\mathbf{H})^2}^s \qquad (2.13.1)$$

The trick is to transform the sin using the equality $\sin^2 x + \cos^2 x = 1$ and realizing that the cosine between two unit-length vectors is equal to their dot product.

Marschner's Model

In a recent paper Marschner et al. [Marschner03] reported measurements of light scattering properties of human hair fibers and derived an improved shading model from the results. They made several observations about the appearance of specular highlights on hair that we will model in our shader.

The main observation is that hair has two distinguishable specular highlights. The first specular highlight is caused by light reflecting off the hair surface. The secondary specular highlight is caused by light transmitted through the hair surface, reflected off the other side in the hair interior and transmitted back out toward the viewer, as illustrated in Figure 2.14.4. Because the light for the secondary highlight travels through the hair interior, its color is modulated by the hair's pigment color. The secondary highlight was also found to have a view-dependent sparkling appearance.

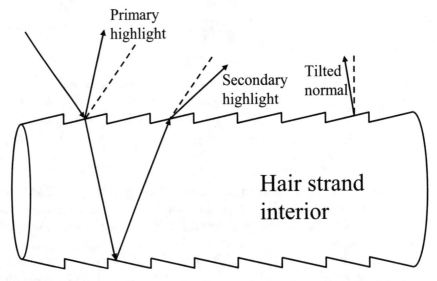

FIGURE 2.14.4   *The hair strand surface structure is the reason behind the two distinguishable highlights. This diagram illustrates the path light travels for the primary and secondary highlight.*

The reason the two highlights are distinguishable lies in the surface structure of a hair fiber: it is composed of overlapping scales whose surface normals are tilted toward the hair tip by about 3 degrees. As illustrated in Figure 2.14.4 the tilt of the scales cause the first and second highlights to spread in opposite directions, making them distinguishable. For the viewer, the first highlight appears shifted toward the tip of the hair strand while the secondary highlight is shifted toward the hair root.

Vertex Shader

None of the actual shading is computed in the hair vertex shader. Apart from applying the standard view and projection transform, it passes the texture coordinates, the view and light vector, the geometric normal of the hair model, and the hair tangent direction down to the pixel shader. If the hair model is set up for it, the vertex shader can also perform skinning.

The per-vertex hair tangent is just one of the pre-computed tangent space vectors that are also used for effects like tangent space bump mapping. By using one tangent space basis vector for the hair tangent direction, we can control the layout of the hair strands through the texture coordinate mapping.

Pixel Shader

In our hair shader we combine three lighting terms: diffuse, specular, and ambient occlusion. The ambient occlusion term [Landis02] is pre-computed per vertex and used to darken the inner hair layers, which is a simple and cheap approximation of hair self-shadowing. During pre-processing the ambient occlusion is computed as if the hair model was semi-transparent, so that the inner hair layers do not get too dark when they are covered by other layers.

If we computed the diffuse term according to the Kajiya-Kay model, the hair would look too bright, because we are not taking real self-shadowing or shadowing of the head on the hair into account. On the other hand, using the geometric normal of the hair model and computing standard $N \cdot L$ diffuse lighting would make the hair look too much like a solid body and too dark in the areas facing away from the light. A good compromise that models the fact that hair—especially light-colored hair— also exhibits strong forward scattering is to use a tweaked $N \cdot L$ term that brightens up areas facing away from the light. Scaling and biasing the $N \cdot L$ term as discussed in [Vlachos04] can be applied here to obtain the desired effect using the following HLSL function:

```
float HairDiffuseTerm(float3 N, float3 L)
{
    return saturate(0.75 * dot(N, L) + 0.25);
}
```

To compute the specular term using the specular highlight properties discussed above, we sum the contribution of two separate specular terms per light. Each term has different specular colors, different exponents, and is shifted in different directions along the hair strands. Here is the HLSL function for computing a single specular highlight term:

```
float HairSingleSpecularTerm(float3 T, float3 H, float exponent)
{
    float dotTH = dot(T, H);
    float sinTH = sqrt(1.0 - dotTH*dotTH);
    return pow(sinTH, exponent);
}
```

For a simple approximation of the sparkling appearance of the secondary highlight, we modulate its term with a noise texture. As for the diffuse term, the lack of real self-shadowing will cause the specular highlights to be too bright on the hair facing away from the light. To fade out the specular highlights on the shadowed side of the hair, we multiply the specular term with an attenuation term that is similar to the diffuse term.

As explained, the specular highlights are shifted because the scales on the surface of a hair strand have tilted normals. To shift the highlights in the shader, instead of tilting normals—which are not used in the Kajiya-Kay equations—we tilt the tangent used for computing the specular terms. Ideally, we would tilt the tangent in the direction of the viewer by adding a vector that is orthogonal to the original tangent and lies in the plane spanned by the **T** and **V** vectors. In practice it is easier and sufficient to tilt in the direction of the geometric normal. The length of the added vector determines how far the highlight is displaced. Here is the HLSL function used to shift a tangent:

```
float3 ShiftTangent(float3 T, float3 N, float shiftAmount)
{
    return normalize(T + shiftAmount * N);
}
```

To make the specular highlights look less uniform, the tangent can be shifted differently for each pixel using a shift amount looked up in a texture. Figure 2.14.5 shows the change in appearance when using a specular shift texture. The shift texture (shown in Figure 2.14.5(c)) was created using procedural noise.

To combine the different lighting terms for the final pixel shader output we add the diffuse and specular terms and modulate the sum by both the ambient occlusion term and the base texture. Modulating the specular term with the base texture gives the specular term a more interesting look, which can be made more visible by increasing the base texture's contrast in the shader before multiplying it with the specular term.

The alpha value of the final output is read directly from the transparency texture. Here is the final HLSL function for lighting hair with one light source:

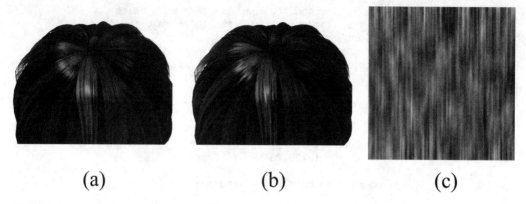

(a)   (b)   (c)

FIGURE 2.14.5 *Per-pixel tangent shifting increases visual complexity. (a) uses no per-pixel shifting, while (b) uses the specular shift map shown in (c).*

```
float4 ComputeHairLighting(float3 T,            // hair tangent
                           float3 N,            // hair normal
                           float3 V,            // view vector
                           float3 L,            // light vector
                           float3 diffuseLightColor,
                           float3 specularLightColor,
                           float2 texCoord,
                           float  ambientOcc,
                           float3 hairBaseColor,
                           float3 specularColor[2], // one for each
                           float  specularExp[2],   // specular term
                           float  specularShift[2],
                           sampler tBase,
                           sampler tAlpha,
                           sampler tSpecularShift,
                           sampler tSpecularMask)
{
    // shift tangents
    float shiftTex = tex2D(tSpecularShift, texCoord) - 0.5;

    float3 T1 = ShiftTangent(T, N, specularShift[0] + shiftTex);
    float3 T2 = ShiftTangent(T, N, specularShift[1] + shiftTex);

    // diffuse term
    float3 diffuse = hairBaseColor * diffuseLightColor *
                HairDiffuseTerm(N, L);

    // specular term
    float3 H = normalize(L + V);
    float3 specular = specularColor[0] *
                HairSingleSpecularTerm(T1, H, specularExp[0]);

    float3 specular2 = specularColor[1] *
                HairSingleSpecularTerm(T2, H, specularExp[1]);
```

```
// modulate secondary specular term with noise
float specularMask = tex2D(tSpecularMask, texCoord);
specular2 *= specularMask;

// specular attenuation for hair facing away from light
float specularAttenuation = saturate(1.75 * dot(N, L) + 0.25);

specular = (specular + specular2) * specularLightColor *
           specularAttenuation;

// read base texture
float base = tex2D(tBase, texCoord);

// combine terms for final output
float4 o;

o.rgb = (diffuse + specular) * base * ambientOcc;
o.a = tex2D (tAlpha, texCoord);    // read alpha texture

return o;
}
```

Rendering

The semitransparent regions of the hair model require the use of alpha blending for rendering, which means the hair model must be rendered in back-to-front order. The general approach is to sort the hair geometry by camera distance on the CPU each time the orientation of the hair relative to the camera changes beyond a certain threshold. Here we will explore a simpler alternative approach to drawing hair in an approximately correct order that is applicable to hair on a human head.

As illustrated in Figure 2.14.6 drawing hair in back-to-front order is very similar to an ordering by distance to the head. Using this inside-to-outside ordering only produces an incorrect draw order at grazing angles. It is straightforward to compute the view-independent inside-to-outside ordering of the hair patches at pre-processing time by computing the average distance to a reference head model. The sort order can be converted into an index buffer that draws the hair patches in this order. However, because of the ordering problem at grazing angles we cannot just use the pre-sorted index buffer to draw. Instead, using the pre-sorted index buffer we render the model in three passes: one for the opaque regions of the hair and two for the transparent parts.

Pass 1: Render opaque hair regions:

- Enable alpha test to discard all fragments with an alpha value less than 1
- Disable backface culling
- Set Z test to less
- Enable writing to Z buffer
- Render hair model with hair pixel and vertex shader

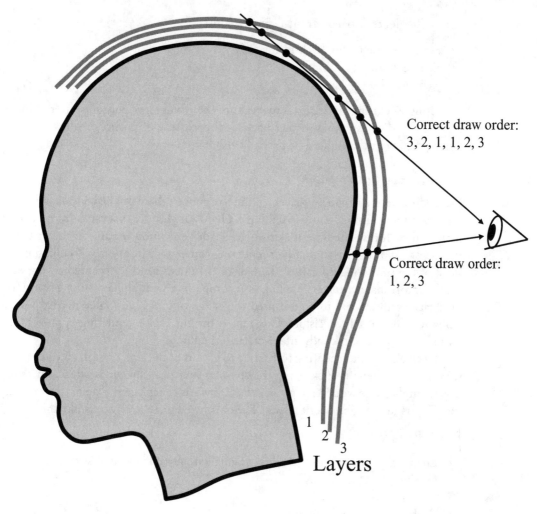

Correct draw order:
3, 2, 1, 1, 2, 3

Correct draw order:
1, 2, 3

1
2
3
Layers

FIGURE 2.14.6   *Hair Sorting: for most regions rendering from the inside out is the correct draw order; however, at grazing angles this ordering is not valid.*

Pass 2: Render transparent parts of the hair that are facing away from the viewer:

- Set alpha test to discard all fragments with an alpha value of 1
- Set cull mode to cull front-facing polygons
- Enable alpha blending
- Disable writing to Z buffer
- Render

Not writing Z values in this pass causes the blending order to be generally incorrect, but this is not really a problem because the third pass will cover these artifacts. The purpose of this second pass is to add some depth to the hair.

Pass 3: Render transparent front-facing regions:

- Set cull mode to cull back-facing polygons
- Enable writing to Z buffer
- Render

Using Z writing in this pass makes sure the front-most polygons are not incorrectly covered by anything further back, at the expense of possibly culling polygons during the Z test that should be partially visible.

Performance Optimization

Depending on the number of layers in the hair model, there can be considerable overdraw when rendering it. Early-Z culling is a hardware feature that can improve performance in such cases because it skips pixel shader execution for any fragment failing the Z test. Another reason that hair rendering can benefit from early-Z culling is that most of the time roughly half of the hair on a human head is occluded by the head itself. Unfortunately, early-Z culling is incompatible with alpha testing because the pixel shader always has to be executed to get the output alpha value needed for the alpha test to make its decision. This means the three-pass rendering approach presented above cannot take advantage of early-Z culling.

By changing the rendering technique to get rid of the alpha test in all three passes we can get the benefit of skipping the complex hair pixel shader as often as possible. To accomplish this we add a new pass that allows us to replace the alpha test with regular Z tests in the subsequent passes. The optimized technique works like this:

Pass 1: Prime Z buffer:

- Enable alpha test to discard all fragments with an alpha value less than 1
- Disable backface culling
- Set Z test to Less
- Enable writing to Z buffer
- Disable writing to color buffer
- Render hair model with hair vertex shader and a very simple pixel shader that only returns the alpha channel

The first pass still uses alpha test to pass only opaque fragments and will prime the Z buffer for opaque hair regions. This pass will not benefit from early-Z, but its shader is much simpler so that adding this additional pass still yields an overall performance increase.

Pass 2: Render opaque hair regions:

- Disable alpha test
- Set Z test to equal
- Disable writing to Z buffer

- Enable writing to color buffer
- Render hair model with hair pixel and vertex shader

With these render state settings only opaque fragments will pass the Z test, because the Z values will only match where they were written in the previous pass.

Pass 3: Render transparent parts of the hair that are facing away from the viewer:

- Set cull mode to cull front-facing polygons
- Enable alpha blending
- Set Z test to less
- Disable writing to Z buffer
- Render

With the Z comparison function set to less, the Z test will pass transparent fragments and discard opaque fragments.

Pass 4: Render transparent front-facing regions:

- Set cull mode to cull back-facing polygons
- Enable writing to Z buffer
- Render

The benefit of the optimized rendering technique over the original version depends on how extensive the opaque hair regions are. With few opaque regions early-Z culling cannot discard as many fragments. In our example using the acceleration technique yielded a considerable performance improvement: We measured frame rate improvements between 10% and 60% depending on the size of the hair model on the screen.

Tradeoffs

As mentioned in the introduction, the main advantage of rendering hair with a polygon model over line rendering is better performance, at the expense of possibly lower visual fidelity. Additionally, using a polygon model for a virtual character's hair has the benefit that it can take advantage of the art pipeline for polygon models that is typically already in place for any game project. Using lines as hair rendering primitives might necessitate additional work on export plugins for 3D modeling packages.

The multi-pass hair rendering technique presented here is very simple to implement because no sorting has to be performed at runtime. However, by using the static pre-sorted index buffer this technique is based on the implicit assumption that the hair model does not animate too much. The individual hair patches in particular cannot move too much relative to each other, otherwise artifacts due to the incorrect rendering order will become increasingly visible. Another limitation is that for hairstyles like pony tails, sorting geometry by distance from the head will not give the desired mostly view-independent sort order. In these cases, runtime sorting on the CPU can be used to avoid artifacts.

Conclusion

This article presented a method for rendering hair based on a polygon model. A pixel shader was employed to provide the necessary visual detail like realistic specular highlights and self-shadowing using ambient occlusion. It also discussed a simple rendering technique to render the hair model in approximate back-to-front order, and how to optimize it by taking advantage of early-Z culling hardware.

References

[Kajiya89] Kajiya, J. and Kay, T. 1989. "Rendering Fur With Three Dimensional Textures," In *Computer Graphics (Proceedings of ACM SIGGRAPH 89)*, 23, 3, ACM, 271–280.

[Landis02] Landis, H. "Production-Ready Global Illumination," Siggraph 2002 Course Notes, Course 16: Renderman in Production, pp. 87–102.

[Marschner03] Marschner, S. R., Jensen, H. W., Cammarano, M., Worley, S., and Hanrahan, P. 2003. "Light Scattering from Human Hair Fibers," *ACM Transactions on Graphics*, 22, 3, 780–791.

[Vlachos04] Vlachos, A. and Oat, C. "Adjusting Real-Time Lighting for Shadow Volumes and Optimized Meshes," *Game Programming Gems 4*, Charles River Media, 2004.

2.15

Reduction of Lighting Calculations Using Spherical Harmonics

Vlad Stamate

Introduction

In today's real time applications, whether it's games or other types, we often find scenes where light is emitted from a large variety of sources. Those light sources must be modeled accurately in order to render the scene realistically. For example, if the Phong lighting model is used (Equation 2.15.1) would have to be resolved for all light emitters at the pixel level in order to achieve convincing lighting:

$$L = Ambient + Attenuation * (Diffuse + Specular) \qquad (2.15.1)$$

where each member is in turn a complex equation.

This is too time-consuming to be done in situations where there are many light sources and the amount of geometry in the scene is considerable. What we propose is a method to identify a small number of important lights and only calculate the full lighting equation for those. The remaining lights would only have their diffuse contribution added to the scene through simpler calculations.

Choosing which lights are important can be tricky and depends very much on the rendered scene. But generally high-intensity lights, lights with a biased color component (high chromacity), or lights that are generally very close to most of the geometry can be chosen. For those lights we apply the full lighting equation.

The remaining lights are projected onto an environment map (be it cubemap or sphere map) and the first nine coefficients of the second order Spherical Harmonics (SH) are then extracted out of the environment map[1]. The process of calculating the SH coefficients is done only once for all the lights and by integrating across the environment map. At the lighting calculation stage we will perform the full lighting calculation for the "important" lights and then apply diffuse lighting based on the Spherical Harmonics coefficients and the surface normals.

---

[1]As explained later in the article, we can sometimes get away without actually doing any projection by going directly from light source information to Spherical Harmonics coefficients.

Spherical Harmonics Based Lighting

Spherical Harmonics (SH) have recently seen a resurgence in the field of computer graphics. The interest in them has been boosted by the latest generations of graphic hardware which can execute complex fragment and vertex programs on the GPU, as well as the capability of reading and writing to floating point texture formats. One common problem sometimes associated with the use of SH is the complexity of the math involved. The aim of this article is not to give a full mathematical demonstration of the theory but rather to provide a "hands-on" view of the technique. However, some background is useful.

Irradiance, which is the amount of light incident onto a point, can be expressed in terms of the lighting environment as the following integral:

$$E(n) = \int (n \bullet w) L(w) dw \qquad (2.15.2)$$

In layman terms this integral means that the irradiance E is a function of the normal (of the surface we try to light). The irradiance is computed by integrating (summing) the incoming light, scaled by the dot product of the normal of the surface n and the incoming light direction w, across the whole environment map $L(w)$. We consider w and n to be normalized vectors as shown in Figure 2.15.1.

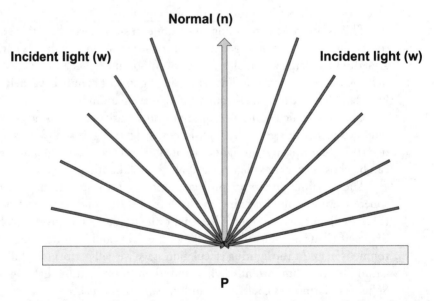

FIGURE 2.15.1   *The total irradiance at a point is a function of all incident light vectors, and the normal at that point.*

Because this integral is expensive to compute in real time, what we can do is express E and L in terms of Spherical Harmonics. Spherical Harmonics are a set of orthonormal basis functions over the sphere.

Spherical Harmonics are a mathematical tool used to approximate an arbitrary spherical representation by decomposing it into a set of finite elements, similar to the way Taylor series operate. For more information about the full formula of Spherical Harmonics please refer to [Sloan03] and [Green03].

Coming back to Equation 2.15.2, we can express (project) the E and L in terms of Spherical Harmonics:

$$\vec{L} = \sum_{lm} L_{lm} Y_{lr} \tag{2.15.3}$$

$$\vec{E} = \sum_{lm} E_{lm} Y_{lm} \tag{2.15.4}$$

where l and m define the degree of the Spherical Harmonic.

The full representation of Spherical Harmonics (as detailed in Equations 2.15.6 and 2.15.8 later on in this article) includes an infinite number of coefficients Y_{lm}. The first few of them are exemplified in Equation 2.15.5 (in polynomial form):

$$Y_{0,0} = c_1$$

$$Y_{1,-1} = c_2 y$$

$$Y_{1,0} = c_2 z$$

$$Y_{1,1} = c_2 x$$

$$Y_{2,-2} = c_3 xy$$

$$Y_{2,-1} = c_3 yz$$

$$Y_{2,1} = c_3 xz$$

$$Y_{2,0} = c_4 \left(3z^2 - 1 \right)$$

$$Y_{2,2} = c_5 \left(x^2 - y^2 \right) \tag{2.15.5}$$

where x, y, and z are the 3D Cartesian coordinates of the incident vector.

As can be seen, those coefficients are a function of direction. The constants c1, c2, etc. are derived from the convolution properties of Spherical Harmonics. The values of the constants are:

$$c_1 = \frac{1}{2\sqrt{\pi}} = 0.282095$$

$$c_2 = \frac{\sqrt{3}}{2\sqrt{\pi}} = 0.488603$$

$$c_3 = \frac{\sqrt{15}}{2\sqrt{\pi}} = 1.092548$$

$$c_4 = \frac{\sqrt{5}}{4\sqrt{\pi}} = 0.315392$$

$$c_5 = \frac{\sqrt{15}}{4\sqrt{\pi}} = 0.546274 \qquad (2.15.6)$$

As [Ramamoorthi01] demonstrates we can now express E as a function of L, but expressed in terms of Spherical Harmonics coefficients:

$$E(\theta,\phi) = \sum_{lm}^{\infty} AL_{lm} Y_{lm}(\theta,\phi) \qquad (2.15.7)$$

where θ and ϕ are spherical coordinates, and A is a term which is dependent on n and w. The conversion from polar to Cartesian coordinates is obtained using the parameterization of the unit sphere:

$$(x,y,z) = (\sin\theta\cos\phi, \sin\theta\sin\phi, \cos\theta) \qquad (2.15.8)$$

where x, y, and z are 3D Cartesian coordinates.

Based on the range of l and m we can control the error generated by the approximation. Obviously the more components in our sum, the better the approximation. In Equation 2.15.9, the term α represents the error term, and p and q represent the number of terms.

$$E(\theta,\phi) = \sum_{l,m}^{p,q} AL_{lm} Y_{lm}(\theta,\phi) + \alpha \qquad (2.15.9)$$

To determine this light contribution to the lighting environment we only need to calculate a finite number of coefficients of the Spherical Harmonics function. [Ramamoorthi01] has shown that using only the first nine coefficients of the Spherical Harmonics is enough to produce high accuracy. [Ramamoorthi01] mentions that for any pixel the average error obtained is around 9% (as a fraction of the total intensity of the illumination). However, high-frequency lighting information is lost. Because of this mainly diffuse, low-frequency lighting can be modeled accurately by an SH representation containing a limited number of terms.

The coefficients are mathematically symbolized by the term Y_{lm} where

$$l \geq 0$$

and

$$-l \leq m \leq l$$

l defines the degree of the terms and to obtain the needed nine terms we need $l = 0$, 1, and 2 that gives us constant terms, linear terms and quadratic terms. Those coefficients are listed in Equation 2.15.5.

This is where the game code breaks in two. First we need to encode the lighting environment in Spherical Harmonics terms. In a game this usually represents all the light sources in a scene, plus any environment lighting (sky, distant Sun, etc.). For static lighting environments we can do all the calculations offline. Note that "static" does not mean the lighting environment cannot be rotated: one property of SH is that they are rotationally invariant; thus models can still be lit properly by aligning them with the original "placement" of the light environment using the inverse of the transformation matrix that was used to rotate it.

However, for dynamic light sources situations (e.g., sky going from bright to overcast) we need to do this encoding in real time. This actually means calculating the L_{lm} terms.

The second part is calculating the actual irradiance, E. This depends on θ and ϕ (spherical coordinates), as well as the surface normal. Therefore this needs to be done at the geometry rendering stage when either the vertex or fragment normal is available.

The Two Methods

There are two ways we can use Spherical Harmonics Irradiance-based lighting and which one we choose depends on what we intend to do (or the type of data produced by artists).

If our lighting data contains only analytical lights (spot light, point light, etc.) defined from a set number of properties then we can jump straight from that data to SH coefficients.

On the other hand, lighting data may contain arbitrary configurations of light emitters, which is a possibility in applications that know the details of the light sources (for example: how big the bulb, how long and thick the neon light). Also some applications may use pre-rendered images representing a given lighting environment (an overcast sky as mentioned earlier). In those cases, SH coefficients will have to be calculated by integrating across the environment maps involved.

This part of the article explains both methods.

Analytical Lights

This is the simplest and most straightforward way of using Spherical Harmonics Irradiance lighting. We presume all lights' position to be at infinity. However, we are still looking at the lighting environment as a whole. Consider the example model shown in Figure 2.15.2 with two lights.

We build a sphere of radius 1 on which we project each light. This way the points on the sphere are actually the normalized light directions.

If we consider the sphere as our environment lighting then in the case of Figure 2.15.1 the only light contribution comes from the projection of the two lights on the sphere surface. Hence doing an integral is not actually needed. So instead of summing over the whole map we just add the lights positions that we know about. In this case the x, y, and z terms in the Equation 2.15.5 are the normalized light direction.

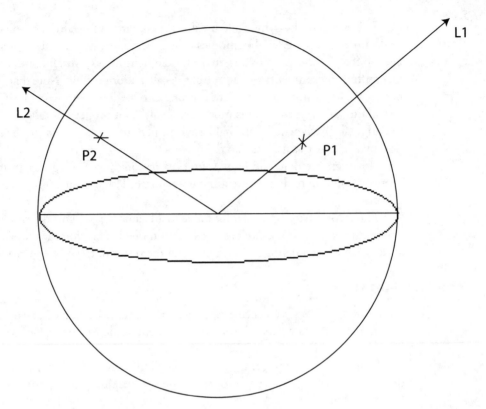

FIGURE 2.15.2   *Two lights' projection on the unit sphere.*

Since Spherical Harmonics are basis functions over a sphere we can add several lights together by adding their Spherical Harmonics coefficients. This is possible since light is additive both in spatial domain and in frequency domain. This property is very useful when calculating coefficients for multiple lights: just project each light and then add the coefficients, thus making it easy for an application to pick at run time which light sources to project onto SH and which not.

Surface Lights

Surface light sources are useful for games because they can be used to represent real light environments more accurately (e.g., sky, pre-rendered environment maps or even real-time rendered HDR or non-HDR maps). However, they are not frequently used in real-time applications due to the complexity of their implementation. This is where Spherical Harmonics can come in handy. At the beginning of this article we mentioned that Equation 2.15.2 represented the incident light at any point covered by a given lighting environment. After projecting Equation 2.15.2 onto SH we ended up with Equation 2.15.6. Because we are dealing with discrete sets of data we can effectively replace the integral in Equation 2.15.6 with a sum. What Equation 2.15.6

actually represents is a sum of all the points in the environment map (L_{lm}) weighted by the Spherical Harmonics coefficients (Y_{lm}).

Since we have decided to calculate up to nine coefficients, we need to calculate nine sums, one for every Y_{lm} with:

$$l = (0, 1, 2) \text{ and } m = (-2, -1, 0, 1, 2)$$

The nine sums will represent (to a certain degree of approximation) the whole of the environment map.

What we have done is compress the whole of the environment map (which can be a large texture or a set of textures) to nine single values. "Compress" is the word because the technique has similarities to the way DCT compression based algorithms work (e.g., JPEG): by projecting the data into frequency space and then applying a filter on this data before projecting it back into the original domain. Here we are using Spherical Harmonics transforms to perform the projection to frequency space.

When rendering we will use these nine values together with the surface normals to compute the radiance (the amount of light leaving each point). To do this we plug in the normals into Spherical Harmonics Equation 2.15.6. This operation is necessary since we are decoding back the information from frequency domain to spatial (image) domain. This can be compared to a cube map look up into lighting data encoded as Spherical Harmonics.

Per Frame or Offline Calculation

When doing all those calculations to "compress" the environment map we have two choices: either we do it offline or at runtime, in a per-frame fashion. If we intend to use this technique as a light reduction technique then we can use it per frame to reduce the number of lights for which we compute full light calculations. This way we can do a runtime decision of which lights to keep (the "important" lights) and which lights to project onto Spherical Harmonics.

Offline calculations can be done in cases when we have a pre-rendered environment map (Sun and sky, ground, or more complex lighting environments which will be hard to express using analytical lighting techniques).

Determining the Lights' Contribution to the Scene

This step is important because it determines both the look and the speed of our algorithm. What is explained here is not totally related to Spherical Harmonics and can be used anytime when we try to coalesce our lights. The main point of this section is to explain how to determine which lights will have the full lighting calculations applied to them and which lights will benefit from SH lighting calculations instead.

There are many methods to do this and the one to choose depends on each particular application. In the demo accompanying the article we use the following algorithm.

There are three important factors: the intensity of the light, the chromacity of the light, and the distance of the light to our geometry. We have to sort our lights by a function of the three factors above. What function to use is usually a case of trial and error.

Chromacity represents the bias in color of a certain light. A light with high chromacity will be further away from grey. For example if we have three lights with an RGB of (100, 100, 100), (125, 125, 125) and (255, 0, 0) and we eliminate the last one our scene will turn from "reddish" to grey which is wrong. The red light is the light with the highest chromacity among the lights above.

How do we quantify all this into an algorithm? We compute three values:

$$D_{RG} = |R - G|$$

$$D_{GB} = |G - B|$$

$$D_{RB} = |R - B| \qquad (2.15.10)$$

The chromacity factor is:

$$C_f = \max(D_{RG}, D_{GB}, D_{RB}) \qquad (2.15.11)$$

The intensity factor is:

$$I_f = R + G + B \qquad (2.15.12)$$

The light factor will be:

$$L_f = c_1 C_f + c_2 I_f \qquad (2.15.13)$$

ON THE CD

where c_1 and c_2 are arbitrary percentage/weights factors. In the demo application provided on the accompanying CD-ROM the following two values are used:

$$c_1 = 0.7$$

$$c_2 = 0.3$$

We now calculate an L_f for every light and then sort all the lights according to L_f. For the top number of lights we compute the full Phong lighting equation—the rest are dealt with using SH.

Putting It All Together—Code Explanation

Spherical Harmonics are used to assist us in lighting calculations and they require work to be done both on the host (CPU) and on the graphic device (GPU). Where the partition of the work lies depends mainly on the capabilities of the GPU. For each of the cases discussed, the next section describes the tasks that need to be carried out for both the CPU and GPU.

Surface Lights

The algorithm is the same regardless of how the environment map is obtained. Environment maps usually represent 360° of data and there are different ways to store them. Let's take the example of environment maps stored in 2D textures. To compute the Spherical Harmonics' coefficients we need to sum all the pixels in the texture (which represents lighting information) and weigh them by the coefficients Y_{lm}. The algorithm for doing this is:

```
For every l and m (degree of the SH)
    For every x,y of pixels in the texture
        Calculate theta and phi, spherical coordinates out of 2D
          coordinates
        Calculate x,y,z, 3D coordinates out of spherical
          coordinates
        /* x, y, and z now represent a direction in the unit
          sphere which corresponds to the x and y coordinates of
          the pixel in the texture */
        Depending on l and m compute Ylm following the formula in
          Equation (5)
        integral += Sample(x, y, EnvMap) * Ylm;
```

Because there are nine combinations of l and m, we will end up with nine `integral` values. Those are our nine coefficients.

However, our lighting environment might not always come from a spherical environment projected onto a plane but also from a cube map. In this case the calculations required to obtain the Spherical Harmonics coefficients are a bit different. The two diagrams shown in Figure 2.15.3 show the steps necessary when having either plane or cube map representations.

Analytical Lights

The code to turn analytical lights into SH is shown here:

```
for(i=0; i<ui32NumberOfLights; i++)
{
    sSHCoeff[0] += Light.color * fConst1;
    sSHCoeff[1] += Light.color * fConst2 * Light.x;
    sSHCoeff[2] += Light.color * fConst2 * Light.y;
    sSHCoeff[3] += Light.color * fConst2 * Light.z;
    sSHCoeff[4] += Light.color * fConst3 * (Light.x * Light.z);
    sSHCoeff[5] += Light.color * fConst3 * (Light.z * Light.y);
    sSHCoeff[6] += Light.color * fConst3 * (Light.y * Light.x);
    sSHCoeff[7] += Light.color * fConst4 * (3.0f * Light.z *
Light.z - 1.0f);
    sSHCoeff[8] += Light.color * fConst5 * (Light.x * Light.x -
Light.y * Light.y);
}
```

Depending on which level we want to calculate the actual lighting (vertex or fragment) the same code can be used for both.

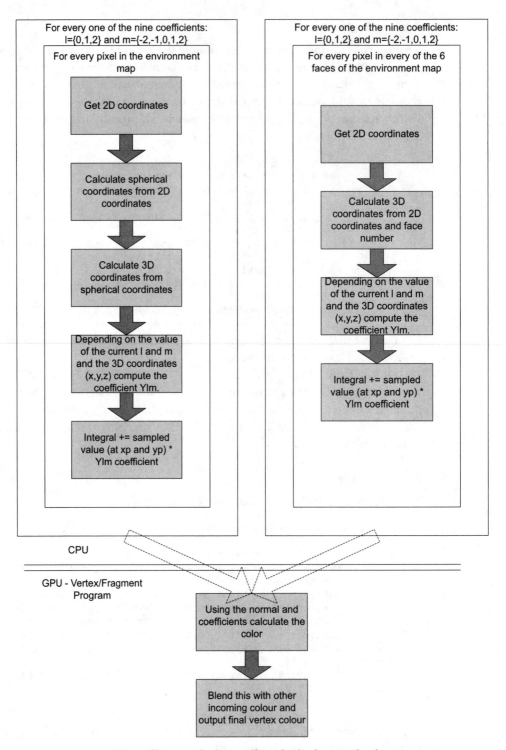

FIGURE 2.15.3 *SH coefficient calculations from both plane and cube map environment maps.*

Vertex Program Work

- Advantages: faster than fragment program solution
- Disadvantages: image quality poor in low tessellated geometry

Fragment Program Work

- Advantages: looks good, giving us diffuse lighting per pixel
- Disadvantages: quite slow since there is a big program that needs to be executed for every fragment

Pros and Cons of Spherical Harmonics

There is no such thing as a perfect technique. This part of the article sums up the advantages and disadvantages of this specific one.

Pros

- When using analytical light sources it does not matter how many light sources we add since the SH lighting can be done in one pass; therefore, rendering performance will not be affected.
- In the case of analytical light sources the algorithm is simple enough to allow calculations to be performed at runtime.
- Possibility of expressing a whole lighting environment using only nine values.

Cons

- Some lighting effects cannot be modeled using Spherical Harmonics (e.g., shadows, radiance transfer, Phong light effects, etc.). There are, however, techniques (not described in this article) which extend the basic Spherical Harmonics algorithm to achieve more complex effects. One of these techniques is called *Precomputed Radiance Transfer* (or PRT) [Green03], which requires more data besides lighting information to be available (visibility information for example).
- When using arbitrary light environments, the process of projecting onto Spherical Harmonics is quite costly (an integration across the whole environment map is needed). Therefore, it's not always doable at runtime.

CD-ROM Demo

ON THE CD

The demo included in the companion CD-ROM provides an example implementation of the Spherical Harmonics lighting calculations. The demo requires hardware support for vertex and fragment program, accessible through the OpenGL API. For the host part of the calculations the relevant files are sh_env.cpp and sh_analytical. cpp. The part of the Spherical Harmonics algorithm that needs to be done on the GPU has been implemented using both OpenGL Shading Language and the assembly shading language extensions. Have a look at sh_lighting.vs for an implementation using the former and sh_lighting.vp using the latter.

Conclusion

This article describes the basics of Spherical Harmonics and how they can be used to represent a lighting environment either composed of analytical light sources or arbitrary lighting data. Techniques for compressing a given lighting environment to just nine RGB values have been shown. Two gamelike scenarios have been presented: one using analytical lights and one using surface (environment map) type lights. This article is by no means a comprehensive Spherical Harmonics theory but it introduces the reader to their world and opens the road to more advanced techniques, e.g., Precomputed Radiance Transfer or visibility/depth compressing methods.

References

[Forsyth03] Forsyth, Tom, "Spherical Harmonics in actual games," available online at: *http://www.tomforsyth.pwp.blueyonder.co.uk/papers.html.*

[Green03] Green, Robin, "Spherical Harmonics Lighting: The Gritty Details," January 16, 2003.

[Ramamoorthi01] Ramamoorthi, Ravi et al., "An Efficient Representation for Irradiance Environment Maps," [SIGGRAPH 2001]. Code to show technique used in the paper can be found online at: *http://graphics.stanford.edu/papers/envmap/ prefilter.c.*

[Sloan03] Pike-Sloan, Peter, "Efficient Evaluation of Irradiance Environment Maps," *Shader X² —Shader Programming Tips and Tricks,* Wordware Publishing, 2003.

SOFTWARE SHADERS AND SHADER PROGRAMMING TIPS

1.18	2.27	3.20	11.35	10.24	9.07
1.32	0	100.3			7.96
1.18	2.23	3.09	Mountains		6.85
1.12	1.16	100.1	3.68	4.67	5.95
1.16	0	1.16	2.59	3.75	4.94
1.12	1.16	1.12	2.20	3.33	4.48

Introduction

Dean Macri

Shader programming has arisen primarily as a result of the proliferation of graphics cards with programmable shader hardware. Yet situations exist where appropriate hardware is unavailable or unusable due to a lack of shader support or the need for the output of the shading by the CPU. In these cases, software solutions that run entirely on the CPU must be used. Additionally, there are non-graphics related uses for shader hardware and developing complex shaders can be made simpler with appropriate tools. This section consists of four articles that address these needs.

In the article, "Optimizing DX9 Vertex Shaders for Software Vertex Processing," Knox describes the behind-the-scenes implementation of the processor-specific graphics pipeline (PSGP) and discusses ways to optimize vertex shaders for high-performance on the CPU. Using software vertex processing addresses the first two needs outlined above and Knox makes clear the tuning tips necessary to get the best performance.

In the article, "Software Shaders and DirectX DLL Implementation," Capens describes in detail the implementation of a software rendering pipeline that can be wrapped with DirectX interfaces. Such a configuration can enable applications to run advanced 3D rendering without a graphics hardware solution. The technique is useful in a variety of situations including support for systems without 3D graphics hardware and for consistency across platforms.

The article, "Tactical Path-Finding Using Stochastic Maps on the GPU," by Khanh Phong Ly shows how to implement pathfinding with a stochastic map with two pixel shaders on the GPU.

Finally, Maughan and Horowitz describe the extensibility details of a shader design tool in "FX Composer 1.5—Standardization." Focusing on the design decisions made to enable developers to maximize the use of the tool through COM support and scripting, Maughan and Horowitz detail ways in which FX Composer can be incorporated into development tool chains and achieve a long-term lifespan as an efficient tool for building .fx files.

3.1

Optimizing Dx9 Vertex Shaders for Software Vertex Processing

Kent F. Knox

Introduction

Microsoft® DirectX 8 introduced a new method of programming real-time graphics with the concept of shaders. Shaders were certainly not new to the world of graphics, but they had never really been applied to the world of real-time rendering before. DirectX 9 continues and expands on this concept by introducing three new shader models: 2.0, 2.x, and 3.0. Typically, when a user plays a game written with shaders, the shaders are tweaked and massaged by the video drivers and downloaded to the video card to be executed natively by the host processor. That is the core benefit of shaders; they allow the programmable GPU on the video card to execute a customized, optimized instruction stream. Systems with shader-compatible hardware will have significant performance advantages. However, DirectX provides a fallback mechanism for optimized execution of vertex shaders in software rather than hardware. This only applies to vertex shaders; pixel shaders are always computed in hardware and are excluded from software optimizations. This is accomplished through a Just-In-Time (JIT) compiling vertex shader virtual machine built into the Microsoft DirectX libraries. AMD and Intel each provide Microsoft with a virtual machine that optimizes specifically for their respective architecture. DirectX detects which platform it is running on and makes sure that the appropriate virtual machine gets instantiated.

In the previous volume of this series, *ShaderX²*, Dean Macri from Intel wrote an excellent and highly recommended article entitled "Software Vertex Shader Processing." The scope of this article is to expand upon and to complement his work, but it will also stand on its own.

This article will most directly benefit developers who are concerned about the performance of their DirectX vertex shaders in software. The performance optimizations enumerated in this article are all focused at the shader assembly level. Although some developers may constrain themselves to coding entirely with HLSL, it is critical to know exactly what the compiler is doing and producing. Always pay attention to the output of the compiler because it may be necessary to rewrite some code to produce optimal assembly. After all, it is the shader assembly that is ultimately executed, not the high-level code. Knowledge of shaders and DirectX is assumed.

The Benefits of Software Vertex Processing

AMD has been helping Microsoft optimize their Software Transform & Lighting (ST&L) code since DirectX 6. At that time this meant optimizing the fixed-function pipeline with 3DNow!™ optimizations before the time of hardware Transform & Lighting engines. Much of the same work was applied to the software technology in DirectX 7, and it was around this time-frame that fixed-function hardware T&L was introduced. With the introduction of vertex shaders in DirectX 8, things really got interesting. The only way to produce optimal software emulation for vertex shader execution was to introduce a JIT compiler that would translate shader assembly into SSE/SSE2 instructions to run under a software virtual machine, effectively emulating the video card hardware. One of the great advantages of this virtual machine is that it is effectively transparent to the developer and the user. For the most part, the application code does not change from HT&L to ST&L; different flags need to be passed to the `CreateDevice` API call and careful attention needs to be paid to ensure that game resources are created in system memory, not video memory.

There are several situations under which a vertex shader may benefit from running in software:

- The user's video card does not support native execution of shaders.
- The developer chooses to run the shader in software rather than hardware for algorithms or game feature reasons.
- Prototyping of future/experimental shaders.
- vs_*_sw (e.g., v2_sw) shaders; software shaders that surpass hardware limits.

An elaboration for each of the bullets mentioned above is provided here:

No Hardware Shader Support

Events like the Game Developer's Conference have provided the opportunity to talk to real developers on some of the issues that they have had to deal with. A lot of developers still need to support DirectX 7 class hardware for their gaming titles. This may be a diminishing concern in the future, but for now there is concern. Many Massively Multiplayer Online Role Playing Games (MMORPGs) like to have as wide of an audience as possible. DirectX 7 class hardware does not support vertex shaders, so typically a developer had to write fixed-function DirectX code to run on the hardware. However, in order to create a game that competes in today's marketplace, games need to support the latest and greatest video cards with engines capable of rendering shaders. In the end, most developers end up supporting and maintaining two (or more) separate rendering paths. Most of the time, this can not be avoided if support for legacy hardware is needed. However, if vertex shaders for the advanced cards need to be written, why not try running the shaders in software on the legacy hardware devices? This is possible, and it is easy to do. Simply create a software device with `CreateDevice`, and set up the vertex shader with `CreateVertexShader` and

SetVertexShader. Do not forget to set up the fixed-function pixel pipeline with SetTexture, SetTextureStageState and so on. Now, a device that crunches vertex data in a software shader and pixel data in fixed-function hardware is created, even for DirectX 7 devices. This will help keep the advantages that vertex shaders provide the developer over the fixed-function (a customizable, handwritten T&L engine), and could hopefully simplify the development process. Of course, there are a couple of caveats. This suggestion assumes that the processor in the system is comparable to DirectX 7 class hardware, which is feasible with 3DNow! and SSE enhanced processors. Also, remember that pixel shaders will not run fast in software, as they are not optimized (as of today) and only run under the reference rasterizer.

It is worth noting that UMA (unified memory architecture) systems with an integrated video card using system memory may be more widespread in the future. Sometimes, to cut costs and to save on precious die area, hardware manufactures will elect not to implement HT&L on die and will instead use software to do the job. Take the popular GeForce4 MX card for example, it does not implement HT&L on die and it is integrated into most nForce2 brand motherboards. In the future, such systems may become even more prevalent, as the popularity of the small form factor Shuttle XPC systems clearly indicates.

Developer Runs Shader in Software

A developer may elect to run a vertex shader in software rather than hardware. There are three good ways to ensure that a shader will run in software. One is to create a software device through the CreateDevice API. Simply pass the D3DCREATE_SOFT-WARE_VERTEXPROCESSING flag through the parameter list and a device will be created where all shaders will run through software vertex processing. The second way is to create a mixed device with the D3DCREATE_MIXED_VERTEXPROCESSING flag and switch the device to software processing with the SetSoftwareVertexProcessing API. Last is the ProcessVertices API call, which is only available on software or mixed devices; it is not available on hardware devices. It takes the previously set input streams and generates a stream of vertex data to an output vertex buffer provided as a parameter argument. This function can be really useful to the developer because it allows output vertices to be stored in projection space and this output could be sent as a second pass to hardware for further processing.

In addition, ProcessVertices can be advantageous to developers who want to do collision/occlusion tests. For instance, suppose a developer is writing a game where they have a character walking around, and they need to pick up equipment dropped from a corpse after slaying the monster. There is a nice, shiny sword lying on the ground, and the game user clicks with the mouse over the sword. The sword has been transformed into world space and sent to the video card to be drawn, so essentially those vertices are gone. However, the game now needs to determine what the user has just clicked on, to take the appropriate action. A ray is cast from the mouse click to the post-transformed objects to see if anything intersects. This is a perfect use for `ProcessVertices` and bounding volumes. Create a bounding box around the sword and transform that using `ProcessVertices`, which will keep the Post-T&L vertices in system memory. Something like this would be suboptimal for hardware, because the post-transformed vertices need to be read back causing a considerable bottleneck for hardware. The AGP bus is asymmetric; it has fast download bandwidth but a much slower/limited upload bandwidth. Using `ProcessVertices` automatically uses efficient software vertex processing with optimized JIT SSE SIMD code and would be a great way of accessing post-transformed vertices.

Prototyping

Whenever Microsoft releases new vertex shader models, through some new release of DirectX, an optimal software vertex machine is provided. AMD and Intel work closely with Microsoft to make sure that vertex shaders run as fast as possible given the time allowed to optimize. Take DirectX 9 for instance, vertex shader model 3.0 was introduced in December of 2002, and software provides for very reasonable performance on these shaders. In 2004, the first video card that supports shader model 3.0 was announced. It is not likely that a game would launch with only software support of v3.0 (hardware support is faster), but the games could be prototyped and developed in software while the software vendor waits for hardware to catch up.

Software Shaders: vs_3_0

On a related note to prototyping, DirectX provides what is known as software shaders. These shaders are written specifically with software processing in mind, to take advantage of the fact that there are no hardware limits in software. This gives the opportunity for the developer to really cut loose and see what his imagination can create. Many of the restrictions with shaders are relaxed; here is a list of what a developer can expect:

- An unlimited number of shader instructions
- Up to 8192 floating point constants
- Up to 2048 integer and boolean constants
- An unlimited number of flow control instructions
- 16 output registers (O-regs, normal is 12) in v3.0
- No read port limits

The benefits of software shaders are clear when applied to prototyping; one may create shaders that hardware will probably support in the future. Software shaders may also prove useful during debugging. A developer may be able to isolate a problem by removing a hardware restriction while debugging. They may also be able to rewrite an algorithm with fewer restrictions to test if the algorithm is buggy.

Software Shader Optimizations

For the most part, optimizations that work for hardware tend to work for software. For example, it makes sense that the shorter the shader is (less instructions), the faster that the shader will run. However, software does have a few special cases that are different than hardware, which are illustrated below. Please refer to *ShaderX²* for even more software optimization hints.

Send Data Down in Large Batches

This is a page torn from the hardware optimization cookbook, but it applies equally well to software performance. The DirectX API has a fixed overhead associated with each call to the API, and it is best if that cost is mitigated as much as possible by sending as much work down the pipeline as possible. Take a look at Figure 3.1.1 to get an idea. No numbers are given on the y-axis because those numbers change with frequency, features, and brand. However, plotting Vertices per Second / Vertex Batch size gives a measure of pipeline efficiency. Notice how low batch sizes corresponds to low pipeline efficiency. As the batch size increases, efficiency continues to grow until it flattens out around 800 vertices in a batch. The drop in efficiency at the tail end of the graph is where the vertex batch size gets so big that it blows cache and vertices start trampling each other. Thanks to judicious use of prefetches, the drop off is not so bad and it is still several orders of magnitude better than small batches.

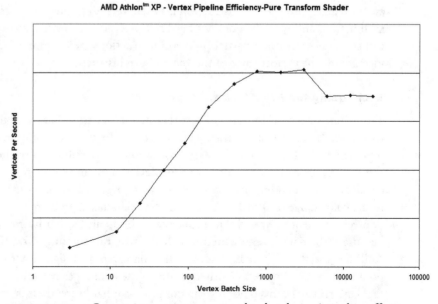

FIGURE 3.1.1 *Comparing vertices per second to batch size / pipeline efficiency.*

DirectX 9: The First Multi-Processor Aware API

Starting with DirectX 9, DirectX checks for multiple processors in the system, both for AMD and for Intel systems. The developer does not have to do anything to enable support for multi-processor systems; if more than one processor is detected, they are automatically used. What the runtime will do is try and split batches that are sent down the pipeline evenly among all the processors, sharing the load. However, multi-processor support is not free; there is some overhead for synchronization issues and batch-splitting costs. If a batch is not big enough, the cost of splitting the batches and using the other processors may exceed the benefit of the parallel computation. In those cases, multi-processing is aborted and the entire batch is loaded on a single processor. The exact size of the batch that needs to be sent down the graphics pipeline to enable multi-processor support will vary among platform, pipeline conditions, and vertex size, but this is another good example of why it is important to batch your vertices in large buffers. Using large batches increases the likelihood that all processors will be used.

Use Partial-Precision Instructions

Since v1.1, there have been instructions that provide for a reduced amount of precision when dealing with shader arithmetic. These instructions are logp, expp, and lit. The DirectX specification says that logp and expp only need to have 10 bits of precision, whereas the full-precision varieties need 21 bits of precision. These lower bits of precision mean that fewer iterations of an algorithm need to be executed, leading to faster processing time. The lit instruction also has lower precision requirements than the pow instruction, so the lit instruction is faster. Vertex lighting uses these transcendental functions and typically does not need full-precision arithmetic, so often a developer can get away with using partial-precision instructions. See Figure 3.1.2 to get a good idea of how the performance of the log and exp instructions relate to each other.

Avoid Using the Float16 Data Type

This is one of the optimization hints that may differ from hardware to software. For hardware, Float16 data types are advantageous. The trend in computer graphics is to represent data as floating point types for as long as possible, up to the instant when the data needs to be sent to the output device. Floating point representations help eliminate color banding artifacts and enable representing values outside of the traditional color range of 0 to 1. However, not all data needs to be represented by 32 bits of precision, hence DirectX 9 introduces a 16-bit float. For hardware, this is beneficial because if the data is represented in half the size, the amount of traffic sent over the AGP bus is reduced in half. Also, graphics hardware is designed with 16-bit floating point in mind and can efficiently operate on the data types natively.

Unfortunately, this is not the case for processor hardware; there is no native support for 16-bit floating point numbers. The software virtual machine has to "up-cast" the

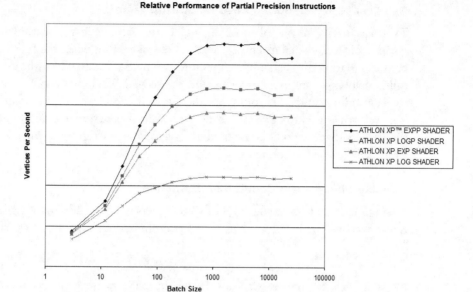

FIGURE 3.1.2   *Relative performance of partial-versus full-precision instructions.*

16-bit floats to 32-bit floats before the virtual machine can process the data, and this "up-cast" is not a trivial operation. What could end up happening is that a developer has native 32-bit vertex stream data and then decides to "down-cast" (or compress) it to 16-bit data before sending it off to the device, thinking that he is optimizing runtime. Then, the software device receives the 16-bit data, and "up-casts" it to 32-bit data again, completing a cycle. This is bad because it is a useless cycle; no work was done on the data while it was 16-bit.

The lesson here is that if a developer has a software device, or is about to call `ProcessVertices`, keep the data 32-bit. If the developer knows he is using a hardware device, it may be worth the time to compress the data before sending the data off to the card. D3DX 9 provides convenient functions to help developers convert floats from 32-bit to 16-bit, and vice versa.

The `TEXLDL` Instruction Is Not Optimized

V3.0 shaders include an instruction to be able to read a texture inside of a vertex shader. At the time of this writing, `TEXLDL` is not optimized inside any vertex shader virtual machine, and a callback is called to reference code to properly execute. The good news is that everything will look correct on a shader with `TEXLDL`, the bad news is that frame rates will be suboptimal. For the most part, this instruction will only prove useful for prototyping purposes.

Call `CreateShader` during Load Or Startup Time

This may seem like one of those obvious optimization hints, but it's worth stating. For the software virtual machine, the `CreateShader` API is when the JIT compile happens, translating the shader bytecodes into x86 bytecodes. In effect, the `CreateShader` call is invoking a mini-compiler behind the scenes. While the compile time is measured in milliseconds, depending on the size and complexity of the shader, these are not cycles that need to be spent during game time. Make sure to compile and cache all the shaders that are going to be used at level load or startup time, when the user will least likely notice the compiles.

Benchmark Dynamic Conditional Branches

One of the main feature additions of v2.0 shaders was the addition of static branches. Static branches are branches that remain constant throughout the batch, such as:

```
if b0 endif
```

B0 is a register that is set outside of the shader, through a `SetVertexShader ConstantB` call. With respect to features, static branches allow shaders to perform multiple tasks: variable lighting, different number of blend weights, variations that previously had to be written as separate shaders in vs_1_1. With respect to performance, static branches are nice because the virtual machine can know which way all the vertices in a batch are going to go, and generate optimal code for that.

vs_2_x and vs_3_0 introduce what is termed "dynamic branching," which changes the playing field a bit. `Ifc`, `ifp`, `breakc` and `breakp` are instances of dynamic branches. These are branches that are not set at the API layer, they are determined at runtime. It is a condition that can change for each vertex through the shader. Due to the nature of the virtual machine inside of DirectX, which tries to maximize the performance of the extended multimedia sets (SSE/SSE2), the virtual machine is actually processing four vertices at the same time thanks to the fact that the SSE registers are SIMD 4-wide. With static branches, the virtual machine is assured that when it hits that conditional, all four vertices will travel the same path; all the vertices behave the same. With dynamic branches, no such assurance exists. When shader execution hits a dynamic branch, some of the four vertices might take the branch, some might fall through and the four vertices that are bundled together may need to execute different codepaths. The virtual machine has to execute both halves of the branch, remember the results, and at the end of the dynamic branch generate a lot of extra housekeeping code to merge the separate results together again to form the correct result. This extra housekeeping code can add significant overhead to the code.

So, what does this all mean to the developer? Despite appearances, dynamic conditional branching may not save the developer any cycles. Now, the next logical question to ask is: "How do I know when it is beneficial to use dynamic branches"? Ultimately, the answer is *Benchmark it*! See if your algorithm improves any; but there are some basic heuristics that one can apply to get a 1st order estimate if dynamic branches are going to help.

If the body of the conditional code is simplistic and small, it may not be worth inserting a dynamic branch around the code, it may be faster to execute the code. If the body of the conditional code is long, or contains macro instructions such as `m4x4`, `lit`, `sincos`, `pow`, or any of the others, it is probably beneficial to wrap that code in a dynamic branch. The trick is that the speedup gained from skipping the conditionally executing code needs to outweigh the cost of the housekeeping code.

Here are some code snippets from some example shaders, to illustrate the points. Below is a code snippet one might find in a shader for a partial calculation for diffuse lighting:

```
if_gt  r0.x, c[9].x            ; skip if negative
mul    r1.xyz, r0.x, c[aL+5]   ; scale diffuse color
add    r1.xyz, r1, c[aL+5]     ; add ambient
mad    r10.xyz, r1, r2.x, r10  ; attenuate color and add
endif                          ; if_gt
```

The inside of this conditional branch is the equivalent of two multiplies and two adds. This is simple code and the overhead of the conditional branch may overcome the savings of skipping these instructions. In the very least, as illustrated in "Software Vertex Shader Processing," this code could be predicated to eliminate the branch altogether and achieve the same effect. Predication is fast because it is atomic to the instruction that it operates on and no branch is generated. However, predication does not stop execution of the instruction that is predicated, it only masks the output. So, predicating a complicated instruction such as `sincos` does not stop execution of `sincos`, it only prevents the output from being written.

The next shader is an example of a complicated dynamic branch. This code snippet is calculating a more complicated specular component to lighting:

```
if_gt  r0.x, c[9].x           ; skip if negative
add r3.xyz, c[8], -v0         ; vector from vertex to eye
nrm r4, r3                    ; normalize
add r1.xyz, r1, r4            ; r1 = half vector
nrm r4, r1                    ; normalize
dp3 r0.y, v1, r4              ; dot normal with half vector
mov r0.w, c[7].x              ; get specular power
lit r3, r0                    ; calculate lighting
mul r1.xyz, r3.y, c[aL+5]     ; scale light diffuse color
add r1.xyz, r1, c[aL+5]       ; add ambient
mad r10.xyz, r1, r2.x, r10    ; attenuate diffuse color
mul r1.xyz, r3.z, c[aL+5]     ; scale light specular color
mad r11.xyz, r1, r2.x, r11    ; specular colors
endif                         ; if_gt  r0.x, c[9].x
```

There are two details to notice here: the conditional code is much bigger, plus the addition of complicated instructions like `lit` and several `nrm`'s. The `lit` instruction itself calculates a power and is very complicated (much bigger than the visible code), so any opportunity to skip that computation is worthwhile. Predication will not be as effective here because it does not stop the execution of the individual instructions. In a case like this, it should be better to use dynamic branching.

To reiterate, it is hard to determine ahead of time whether an optimization is going to be effective or not. *Benchmark it* and find out for sure.

64-Bit DirectX

The new Microsoft Windows Server 2003 SP1 is planned to include support for AMD64 systems. This necessitated a port of DirectX 9 for 64-bit systems. Of course, the API for DirectX 9 did not change at all, or that would cause unnecessary compatibility issues. Instead, some mechanics underneath the hood changed related to the fixed-function pipeline when software vertex processing is selected. The fixed-function pipeline for 32-bit systems is a complicated separate codepath of flags and states, and has been deprecated by Microsoft. On the transition to 64 bit, they took the extra effort to implement the fixed-function pipeline in terms of individual vertex shaders. DirectX keeps a cache of such fixed-function shaders around, which are compiled on the fly as the fixed-function pipeline state changes. There is a cost associated with this compilation process, so it is desirable for performance reasons for newly developed games to use shaders natively. The transition of the fixed-function pipeline to vertex shaders is advantageous because it leverages all of the compiler technology built into the JIT virtual machine to optimize the fixed-function shader as much as possible. Again, this process only happens with software vertex processing, not hardware vertex processing. As we improve the virtual machine over time by adding smarter optimizations, the performance of the old fixed-function pipeline should similarly increase.

D3DX Optimizations

D3DX deserves a section of its own. D3DX was introduced in DirectX 8 and is Microsoft's attempt to provide a library of commonly used code to developers so that they do not have to invent the wheel over and over again. It started out mostly as math routines, but recently Microsoft has been adding more and more functionality, such as mesh routines and precomputed radiance transfer functions.

AMD and Intel have worked with Microsoft to optimize many of the math routines included in D3DX. These routines are fast. D3DX detects the processor features present in the system and utilizes any extended multimedia instruction sets, such as 3DNow! and SSE/SSE2. These routines are highly optimized for their target processors. This is not a guarantee that a faster way to do a matrix multiply can not be found, but the effort is better spent elsewhere. Use D3DX to your advantage!

D3DX 9 introduced *Array (e.g., `D3DXVec4TransformArray` or `D3DXVec3TransformNormalArray`) versions of many common vector and matrix operations. These functions are especially suited to the SIMD nature of the extended multimedia register sets, and are faster than their scalar versions on sets of data. Use them when work needs to be performed on a batch of data, such as when a batch of normal vectors needs to be transformed to point in a new direction. If only one scalar entity needs to be worked on, such as one normal vector, it is more efficient to just go ahead and call the scalar routine.

Conclusion

Software vertex processing is fast, reliable, and available on all modern processors that support 3DNow! and/or SSE. It is highly easy to use and in many cases does not differ significantly from programming for hardware vertex shaders. There are certain scenarios where using software vertex shaders will be beneficial to the games developer, such as when the developer needs to have access to Post-T&L vertices for further processing. When software vertex shaders are being used, a four-wide optimizing JIT SSE virtual machine runs behind the scenes that processes vertices four at a time through the T&L pipeline. Armed with this knowledge, a developer should be able to create a shader that really blazes through software!

Acknowledgments

Special thanks to the other individuals on the AMD DirectX team: Jim Conyngham, Mark Santaniello, and our co-op, Navreet Gill. Everybody works equally hard on the DirectX project; DirectX is a group effort they taught me so much from everybody. Special thanks goes to Brent Hollingsworth for providing some polish to this article. Also, thanks to Iouri Tarassov, my Microsoft contact, for providing technical feedback and corrections on my article.

3.2

Software Shaders and DirectX DLL Implementation

Nicolas Capens

Introduction

Shaders are software. For this reason it makes sense to discuss software rendering in a book about hardware rendering. Graphics hardware is becoming increasingly more programmable and it is inevitable that professional graphics programmers need to have the same deep knowledge about 3D graphics theory and mathematics that is required for rendering everything in software.

Of course the discussion would end here if there wasn't also a practical use of software rendering. To make it look good, we'll start with the disadvantages and end with the many advantages compared to hardware rendering. Actually there's only one disadvantage: performance, and improving it is what the biggest part of this article is about. We'll present many new techniques to maximize performance and even totally eliminate some problems experienced with a naive implementation. The advantages of software rendering are many, but can also be summarized in one word: programmability. Not just the shaders, but every single aspect of the rendering pipeline is programmable with software rendering. Any and all problems experienced with hardware rendering, except performance, can be solved completely with software rendering.

When using hardware rendering, the result on screen depends on four things: the application, the API, the driver, and the hardware. Of these four things you are only in control of the implementation of the application. All the rest is variable on different systems. This means there is always a risk that the things you intend to render, do not show up consistently on every system. Or it might not run at all, due to unsupported hardware features. It might even crash, due to driver bugs. It might show visible flaws, due to incorrect driver or hardware implementations. Last but not least, there might not exist hardware that does what you want to do. Either way, what you see, isn't always what you get. Software rendering can solve all of this, by putting you in control of the API, the driver, and the hardware as well. An important side effect is that you have total freedom to implement new ideas. Even rapid prototyping an architecture that is eventually meant for hardware implementation is possible. So, if at any moment this article looks overcomplicated, becomes boring, or seems pointless, remember that the future of programmable hardware will look quite similar.

Throughout this article, we'll work toward a full implementation of DirectX 9 functionality, and finally also use the DirectX 9 interface. Here are the titles of the sections and a brief explanation:

Soft-Wiring Technology: introduces you to the key technology to efficient software rendering.

Fixed-Function Pipeline: implements the DirectX 9 fixed-function pixel pipeline, using soft-wiring technology.

Programmable Pipeline: starts with a straightforward v2.0 implementation, then compares some architectures for pixel processing. And with an advanced architecture we'll implement ps 3.0 shaders.

Optimization and High-Level Implementation: analyzes and solves some small performance issues encountered in previous sections; also shows some techniques that make soft-wiring technology more elegant to use.

Clipper and Rasterizer Implementation: illustrates using the new techniques for the clipper and rasterizer, solving each situation optimally.

Caching and Batching: departs from a straightforward implementation; focuses on the limitations of the DirectX 9 interface and how we can work around them. We'll also closely compare the CPU to the GPU.

Overdraw Reduction: finds ways to reduce software rendering, theoretically and practically, as it suffers a lot from overdraw.

DirectX Library: discusses turning DirectX 9 functionality into a d3d9.dll. All the pieces are brought together to run your favorite software application!

Ideas and Closing: looks back at the goals reached and discusses their actual usefulness; and some inspiring thoughts for the future of this rapidly evolving technology.

So let's first see what revolutionary technology drives efficient software rendering.

Soft-Wiring Technology

Straightforward software rendering is often very slow. There are two main reasons for this. First of all rendering is a very arithmetic intensive task. So to get maximum performance we have to make use of all the CPU has to offer. This can be done by using the MMX and SSE assembly instructions. Both are SIMD instruction sets, which stands for Single Instruction Multiple Data. They process respectively four integer and four floating-point numbers in parallel. This offers a much higher performance than any high-level programming can offer, because SIMD instructions are hardly used by any compiler, let alone optimally. So we're going to have to write a lot of assembly code. A good knowledge of x86 assembly will make some parts of this article easier to understand, but don't worry if you have little experience with it. The SIMD instruction sets are quite structured. We'll show you that there's hardly ever a need to write much complicated x86 code at all. For those really unfamiliar with SIMD, [Tommesani.com] provides a gentle introduction.

But even when using SIMD, we still haven't got a software renderer that is guaranteed to be efficient. It's easy to write one optimized function for one specific task, but we might have millions of valid render states! So it seems the only solution is to use lots of state checks and jumps. Unfortunately, this way we end up with spending more time comparing and jumping than actually executing the arithmetic operations. Even worse, modern CPUs with long pipelines have big penalties for mispredicted jumps. If only we had a way to eliminate those compare and jump operations.

We can! We'll just select exactly those instructions which are required to perform the render operations, place them in a buffer, and make a function call to that buffer. This is the core idea of the soft-wiring technology. As its name implies, it's nearly like wiring your processor to do exactly and only the requested operations. Depending on how you look at it, this sounds either too simple, or completely infeasible. It's somewhere in between. What we'll need is a code generator, a kind of assembly compiler, which can produce the binary code for the instructions we require, at runtime. Because no such project already existed, we created one.

SoftWire is the name of our runtime code generator. It's available as an opensource project at [SourceForge.net] It's released under the LGPL license, so it isn't very restrictive. Although it is intended to be usable in a wide range of applications, it serves extremely well for soft-wiring render functions. SoftWire can generate code in two ways: assembled from a file, or used with runtime intrinsics. Assembling from a file already opens many possibilities, especially when using conditional compilation, but it's not that easy to work with, and it is increasingly complex to add new features. In this article, we'll focus on runtime intrinsics. They are regular C++ functions, with the name of an assembly instruction, that place the corresponding binary code in a buffer. To alleviate confusion, here's an example:

```
add(eax, ebx);
```

This is just a C++ function, defined in one of SoftWire's classes. It makes SoftWire generate the corresponding code, and places it in an internal buffer. When calling a whole series of runtime intrinsics that form a function, the buffer can be retrieved from SoftWire, and it can be called as a function, just like that. Here's a slightly more advanced example:

```
static char data[16];
mov(byte_ptr [&data+4*edx], cl);
```

Note that since runtime intrinsics are just C++ code, we can easily use data we defined in C++, in the callable assembly function. The above code takes the address of the data variable, and uses it as a constant. C++ operator overloading makes sure SoftWire interprets this code as a write to memory operation. Note the underscore in byte_ptr that was required to make use of the [] operator.

All runtime intrinsics are defined in the SoftWire::CodeGenerator class. The easiest way to work with runtime intrinsics is to derive from that class, so no namespaces or class names have to be prepended to the functions (add, mov, ...) and variables (eax, byte_ptr, ...). Retrieving the generated code can be done with the CodeGenerator::callable method. The returned type is a function pointer, which you can call by just adding (). Following is a complete working example:

```
#include "CodeGenerator.hpp"
#include <stdio.h>

class Script : public SoftWire::CodeGenerator
{
public:
void compileHello()
{
static char *string = "Hello world!";

push((int)string);
call((int)printf);
add(esp, 4);
ret();
}
};

int main()
{
Script script;
script.compileHello();
script.callable()();
}
```

There are lots of new things in this code, but you should be able to roughly understand what's being done. There's more information in the [online tutorial], and the best way to learn things is by doing them. The rest of the article contains plenty of soft-wired code so just read on and it will quickly make sense. The similarity between soft-wired code and shaders will also become very clear.

So what we have here is a tool that can help us add new functions to our application at runtime. Not just "adding" like from a dynamically linked library (.dll); we actually generate them. The biggest flexibility of being able to generate functions is that it's easy to make small variants by conditionally calling different sequences of runtime intrinsics. This is exactly what we need for efficient software rendering; selecting only those instructions that perform the rendering operations. One example is only reading the depth buffer value when the depth buffer is active (it is enabled and its compare mode is not set to 'always' or 'never'). It could look like this:

```
if(isDepthBufferActive())
{
        // Read depth value into xmm0
        movss(xmm0, dword_ptr [esi+4*eax]);
}
```

Without soft-wiring, it would have looked like this:

```
if(isDepthBufferActive())
{
        // Read depth value into z
        z = depthBuffer[x];
}
```

This can be a little confusing. It might seem that this code is entirely equivalent. But remember, the first code is for constructing the render function, the second is the render function. The conditional code and the call to `isDepthBufferActive()` is only executed once for the first code, but it's executed for every pixel in the second. It's clear that this will win us some performance. And this is only a small example, as there are dozens of render states to be checked, and most of them can have several values. That's hundreds of checks, and most of them are for features that are rarely used anyway. Furthermore, we can place the above soft-wiring code in a handy function so we can implement it once and forget about it. No more assembly to look at, and it's nicely structured.

But you might also have spotted a problem. We automatically assumed the depth buffer address was in `esi`, the pixel position was in `eax`, and the depth value had to be read into `xmm0`. That's hard to work with, because we would constantly have to check what registers are used in what part of the pipeline, and for what variable. One solution would be to write several of these functions, that check what registers are already in use, and marks what SSE register will be used for the depth value. This is a lot of work and also problematic to handle. But this is C++, and anything is possible! What if we wrote functions that return the registers we need to use? So instead of writing `esi`, `eax`, and `xmm0`, we call those functions. It could look like this:

```
if(isDepthBufferActive())
{
        // Read depth value into regZ()
        movss(regZ(), dword_ptr [regDepthBuffer()+4*regX()]);
}
```

But now the functions `regZ`, `regDepthBuffer`, and `regX` would contain the same functionality; allocating and managing registers. We can just as well write general functions for register allocation. What we would have to pass into these functions would be a unique identification of the variable. How about a reference to a static variable that we give a logical name? This would be unique and easy to use. This method for register allocation is build into SoftWire, and it looks like this:

```
static float z;
static float *depthBuffer;
static int x;
// ...
if(isDepthBufferActive())
{
        // Read depth value into z
        movss(rSS(&z), dword_ptr [r32(&depthBuffer)+4*r32(&x)]);
}
```

It's not that elegant, but before we delve into the details, look what we've gained. This can be put into one function, which handles loading the depth value. And we hardly ever have to look at it again, since the registers that are being used are abstracted with variables.

There is another reason why the register allocator needs references to variables other than their uniqueness. The number of x86 registers is quite limited, while there are dozens of registers needed for interpolants, indices, pointers, and temporary variables. So the register allocator has to do more than just assigning free registers to variables. When there are no more available registers, it has to free some by writing back their value(s) to memory. This is called register spilling. SoftWire can only do this when it knows where the registers can be written to. That's the double usage of the memory reference that we use. When a register is spilled it is effectively written back to the memory location it is associated to. Generally, SoftWire spills registers that have not been used frequently and recently, to keep the currently used variables in registers for best performance.

There are several functions in SoftWire that control register allocation. The most important are r32, r64, r128, and rSS. They associate a register with a memory reference, and load that register with the value stored at that memory location when it wasn't allocated before. r32 is for general-purpose 32-bit registers, r64 is for MMX registers, r128 is for SSE registers, and rSS is for single-component SSE registers. This last one can be tricky so it needs some more explanation. To work with single floating-point variables using SSE, SoftWire has to know that the memory reference you use is a single floating-point variable. This is because when the associated register has to be spilled, it shouldn't write all four components of the register to memory. Other important functions are m32, m64, m128, and mSS. In general they just return the memory reference, but when the associated variable is already allocated in a register, that register is returned. So these functions never perform an allocation themselves. This is very useful when a variable is used only once, because then we don't have to first load it into a register. We never have to use dword_ptr [] again (except for instructions that accept only a memory operand). An example of their usage follows.

Besides allocation functions, there are also functions to control the lifetime of variables. They are often not required, because SoftWire will spill registers automatically, but for optimal performance they are crucial. The simplest function is spill(). It takes a memory reference as argument and writes the associated register back to memory. The register is then free to be used by other variables. This is a fool-proof function; you can call it as often as you like, but of course for best performance you want to keep as many variables in registers as possible. There are three cases where it is very useful. First of all, if you know a variable won't be used for a long time, it is best to free its register so more important variables can use it. Secondly, at the end of the function you often will want to write back all registers to memory, otherwise their value will be lost. To simplify this, there's also a function spillAll(). Last but not least, we have to spill all registers when using a jump. SoftWire generates our code sequentially, but the code is not always executed sequentially. So there is no way to automatically know what registers are associated to what variables after a jump. Therefore, before every jump, and before every target label, all registers need to be spilled. This requires some illustration:

```
comiss(rSS(&z), mSS(r32(&depthBuffer)+4*r32(&x)));
spillAll();

switch(depthCompareMode)
{
case DEPTH_LESS:                    jnb("zFail");  break;
case DEPTH_GREATEREQUAL:       jnae("zFail"); break;
// ...
}

// Rest of pixel pipeline
// ...

spillAll();
label("zFail");
```

Here we compare the interpolated z value to the depth buffer value. Note the use of mSS instead of dword_ptr []. This code is also another example of conditional compilation. But what we actually want to show is the use of spillAll(). The idea is that before and after the jump, the state of the register allocator is the same: empty. Therefore, if the conditional jump is taken, or it is not, the registers have to be allocated again. This is a small trade-off for all the flexibility we get from runtime compilation. The section about Optimization and High-Level Implementation shows how to avoid unnecessary spills.

Spilling means writing back registers to memory. Sometimes however, this is not required. For example when we use a variable only as a temporary, we are not interested in its value after it has been used. So spilling it does make the register directly available again, but it also writes it to memory, which isn't necessary. Therefore Soft-Wire also has a free() function. It takes a reference argument, and tells SoftWire to make the associated register available again, without writing its value back to the reference's memory location. So this function can be used for lifetime control. Use it as much as possible, but with caution. If the variable is used after its register has been freed, the original value that was stored in memory will be used.

Again in the Optimization and High-Level Implementation section we will see new powerful ways of working with runtime intrinsics. But for now you know plenty to implement a complete fixed-function rendering pipeline.

Fixed-Function Pipeline

This section looks at practical aspects, using SoftWire as a tool.

Rendering triangles can be split into two main tasks: rasterization and pixel processing. Rasterization identifies the pixels that are covered by the triangle, and provides the pixels with their input parameters by interpolating vertex components. Pixel processing is what this section is mainly about. So for the rasterization part we refer to Chris Hecker's [Perspective Texture Mapping] articles. Unlike what you might expect from the title, it really focuses on rasterization, and it's a must read for flawless rendering. In the Clipper and Rasterizer Implementation section, we'll take a closer look at implementation and optimization details.

There are many stages to the overall structure of a pixel processing pipeline. To limit the length of this article, we'll only focus on the most important ones. Once you fully understand those, the rest are easy to add. Note that we don't have to follow this order strictly. What is optimal for hardware, often isn't optimal for software. And don't forget, there are no restrictions on what you do and how you do it when working in software! So always stay critical about what is considered to be the most optimal.

But for now we'll just try to mimic hardware functionality. The staged design suggests that we can implement them individually and independently. By using one function per stage we'll indeed get manageable code. And SoftWire's register allocation capabilities make them independent. We can put it all in one class, `PixelPipeline`:

```
class PixelPipeline : public SoftWire::CodeGenerator
{
public:
        PixelPipeline();

        virtual ~PixelPipeline();

        void execute();

private:
        void depthTest();
        void sampleTexture(int stage);
        void blendUnit(int stage);
        void addSpecular();
        void writePixel();
};
```

Several stages are not shown in the above diagram. It only shows the operations that are being done for one isolated pixel. But for software rendering we have little other choice than to work per scanline (one line of pixels in a triangle). So we'll also need a function to setup all variables that are interpolated over the scanline, and a function that does the actual interpolation.

There are dozens of variables needed for this pixel pipeline. Storing them in the `PixelPipeline` class is, however, not optimal. These variables will be accessed frequently, and the setup variables have to be rapidly accessible from outside the class. Also, to avoid unnecessary copying some of them even should be shared with other classes. So it is best to put them all in one central place. Inspired by hardware rendering, I'll store these variables in a `Context` class. Don't confuse it with a hardware rendering context though. We'll store render states in it as well, but all of the variables will be made static for fast access and easy sharing. So this class only stores data about the active rendering context. Only one variable really belongs to `PixelPipeline` and that's the pointer to the binary code of the generated scanline function. So let's take one more high-level view at our pixel pipeline again:

```
class PixelPipeline : public Context, public SoftWire::CodeGenerator
{
public:
        PixelPipeline();

        virtual ~PixelPipeline();

        void execute();

private:
        void setup();
        void depthTest();
        void sampleTexture(int stage);
        void blendUnit(int stage);
        void addSpecular();
        void writePixel();
        void interpolate();

        void (*binaryCode)();   // This isn't a function... yet
}
```

Let's start implementing! The constructor is responsible for the scanline loop and linking all stages together:

```
PixelPipeline::PixelPipeline()
{
        push(edi);
        push(esi);
        push(ebx);
        freeAll();   // From here we'll start using register allocation

        mov(r32(&x), m32(&lx));   // Left scanline limit
        setup();

        spillAll();
        label("scanlineLoop");
        {
                depthTest();
                {
                        for(int i = 0; i < 8; i++)
                        {
                                sampleTexture(i);
                                blendUnit(i);
                        }

diffusePixel();
                        specularPixel();

                        writePixel();
                }
                spillAll();
                label("zFail");

                interpolate();
        }
```

```
        inc(r32(&x));
        cmp(r32(&x), m32(&rx));    // Right scanline limit
        spillAll();
        jnge("scanlineLoop");

        emms();

        freeAll();
        pop(ebx);
        pop(esi);
        pop(edi);

        ret();
    }
```

For this fixed-function pipeline we'll mainly use MMX for color values, because then we can have 16-bit integer values per component, in a 4.12 fixed-point format. For texture coordinates we can use SSE. All the setup() function has to do is take the rasterizer's interpolated values, which are stored in the Context, and copy them into MMX and SSE registers appropriately. With automatic register allocation, naturally. This function is quite trivial so we won't spend more time on it. We also already implemented depthTest() in the previous section!

The sampleTexture() function is the hardest to implement. It has to do three things: perspective correction, mipmap level determination, and filtering. For the latter two operations there is no general method, so it's not useful to discuss it further. Perspective correction deserves some attention though, since it's quite a slow operation but can be solved efficiently. The trick is to use the SSE rcpss instruction which provides a reciprocal approximation, and to refine it using Newton's algorithm. Here's the resulting code:

```
    static float tmp;

    movss(xSS(&tmp), dword_ptr [&RHW]);
    rcpss(rSS(&W), rSS(&tmp));
    mulss(rSS(&tmp), rSS(&W));
    mulss(rSS(&tmp), rSS(&W));
    addss(rSS(&W), rSS(&W));
    subss(rSS(&W), rSS(&tmp));
```

These are six fast instructions, and it is generally not worth it to optimize it further by using linear interpolation and such. However, it is possible to use just the rcpss instruction, when texel density is low, in other words when using a low detail mipmap level. For every polygon, a simple test can determine if the mipmap level at every vertex is lower than some threshold. Depending on this test the appropriate pipeline is selected. Note once more that thanks to soft-wiring there is no per-pixel cost to do the test or conditional execution. This technique has been used in the [Real Virtuality] demo, where it makes some scenes over 20% faster without any noticeable quality loss.

The blend units give the pipeline its real flexibility. It makes thousands of combinations of render operations possible. Before showing how to implement this, let's address a few questions first. How do we manage all these pipelines and render states? Do we generate a pipeline for every possible combination? Or do we regenerate a pipeline every time the render state changes? The solution has to be somewhere in between because generating every combination takes too much memory, and regenerating takes too much time. What we need is a cache where we store the last few pipelines which have been used. This works very well because most applications use only a handful of render states. Every frame, the same objects are rendered with the same render state. So now that we don't have to worry about that any more, we can safely implement every blend operation:

```
void PixelPipeline::blendUnit(int stage)
{
        word4 *arg1;    // typedef short word4[4];
        word4 *arg2;
        word4 *res;

        static word4 diffuse;
        static word4 specular;

        // Select first argument
        switch(sampler[stage].firstArgument)
        {
        case Sampler::SOURCE_TEXTURE:
           arg1 = &texture; break;
        case Sampler::SOURCE_CURRENT:
           arg1 = &current; break;
        case Sampler::SOURCE_DIFFUSE:
                movq(r64(&diffuse), m64(&v[0]));
                psrlw(r64(&diffuse), 4);    // From 0.16 to 4.12 format
                arg1 = &diffuse; break;
        case Sampler::SOURCE_SPECULAR:
                movq(r64(&specular), m64(&v[1]));
                psrlw(r64(&specular), 4);    // From 0.16 to 4.12 format
                arg1 = &specular; break;
        case Sampler::SOURCE_TEMP:
           arg1 = &temp; break;
        }

        // Select second argument
        switch(sampler[stage].secondArgument)
        {
        case Sampler::SOURCE_TEXTURE:
           arg2 = …
        }

        // Select destination argument
        switch(sampler[stage].destinationArgument)
        {
        case Sampler::DESTINATION_CURRENT:
           res = &current; break;
```

```
case Sampler::DESTINATION_TEMP:
   res = &temp; break;
}

// 0.5 in 4.12 fixed-point format
static const word4 half = {0x0800, 0x0800, 0x0800, 0x0800};
static const word4 neg = {-1, -1, -1, -1};

// Perform operation
switch(sampler[stage].stageOperation)
{
case Sampler::STAGE_SELECTARG1:          // Arg1
      movq(r64(res), m64(arg1)); break;
case Sampler::STAGE_SELECTARG2:          // Arg2
      movq(r64(res), m64(arg2)); break;
case Sampler::STAGE_MODULATE:            // Arg1 * Arg2
      movq(r64(res), m64(arg1));
      pmulhw(r64(res), m64(arg2));
      psllw(r64(res), 4); break;
case Sampler::STAGE_ADD:                 // Arg1 + Arg2
      movq(r64(res), m64(arg1));
      paddw(r64(res), m64(arg2)); break;
case Sampler::STAGE_ADDSIGNED:           // Arg1 + Arg2 - 0.5
      movq(r64&res), m64(arg1));
      paddw(r64(res), m64(arg2));
      psubw(r64(res), qword_ptr [&half]); break;
case Sampler::STAGE_SUBTRACT:
      ...

   }
}
```

The texture, current, temp, and v[] variables are all stored in the Context class, with texture being the sampled color from sampleTexture(). Note that this is just one page of code, and it already implements several hundred combinations of render states! With eight stages and more blend operations the possibilities are gigantic. Imagine how much work it would have been to manually write the assembly code for just a few simple situations!

But we still have to remain careful. The observant reader might have noticed some flaws in the above code. Imagine that we perform a modulate operation, with the diffuse color as the first argument, the current color as the second argument, and the current color as the destination operand. This would copy the diffuse color to the current color, then multiply with the current color. But the old current color is already overwritten with the diffuse color! So the result is that we've squared the diffuse color and stored that in the destination operand. What we have to prevent is that we overwrite any useful values in the destination operand. This can be done by making it a separate temporary variable, which is later written to the destination operand, or by reversing the order of operations when the second argument is equal to the destination operand. The former method needs a redundant copy operation, so we'll have to use the second method for efficiency. In the Optimization and High-Level Implementation section we'll present ways to solve this more elegantly.

The `addSpecular()`, `writePixel()`, and `interpolate()` functions are all very straightforward and need no in-depth explanation. So this is it! It's hard to believe that writing a blazing fast and flexible pixel pipeline is this easy, isn't it? The MMX assembly code can sometimes be hard to understand, but using a reference like [Tommesani.com] is a great help. Of course this pipeline can be extended in many ways, with extra render states and many texture sampling techniques. If you want to have a look at a complete implementation, check out [swShader]. An early version (0.3.0) is freely available on *SourceForge.net* and implements nearly full DirectX 9 functionality.

The fixed-function vertex pipeline can be implemented quite similarly, but instead of mainly using integer MMX, we'd use floating-point SSE instructions. However, there is little use having a fixed-function vertex pipeline if we have a programmable pipeline. There is nearly no performance advantage and the fixed-function pipeline can be implemented using the programmable pipeline.

Programmable Pipeline

In case you forgot: shaders are software. Executing them on a CPU is not that much different from executing them on a GPU. All it needs is binary code that is specific for the processor. So what we'll do is compile the shader code to SSE assembly instructions. Compilation is done in two main steps: parsing and code generation. For the parsing part, refer to specialized books like [*The Dragon Book*]. The parser generator used for swShader is [CppCC], which is very easy to use and the generated parser class integrated nicely with the swShader classes.

So let's focus on the code generation. There are only two things that separate shader code from SSE code. First of all, shaders can use dozens of registers, while SSE has only eight. Secondly, shader instructions are often more complex operations than SSE instructions. Both problems can be solved very elegantly using SoftWire. Its automated register allocation makes it easy to dynamically map shader registers to SSE registers. Here's how it's done in swShader:

```
void *VS_2_0Assembler::reference(const Operand &reg)
{
        switch(reg.type)
        {
        case Operand::ADDRESS_REGISTER:
                return &vs.a0;
        case Operand::INPUT_REGISTER:
                return &vs.v[reg.index];
        case Operand::CONSTANT_FLOAT_REGISTER:
                return &vs.c[reg.index];
        case Operand::CONSTANT_INTEGER_REGISTER:
                return &vs.i[reg.index];
        case Operand::CONSTANT_BOOLEAN_REGISTER:
                return &vs.b[reg.index];
```

```
case Operand::TEXTURE_COORDINATE_REGISTER:
        return &vs.oT[reg.index];
case Operand::LOOP_COUNTER_REGISTER:
        return &vs.aL;
case Operand::TEMPORARY_REGISTER:
        return &vs.r[reg.index];
case Operand::DIFFUSE_SPECULAR_REGISTER:
        return &vs.oD[reg.index];
case Operand::POSITION_REGISTER:
        return &vs.oPos;
case Operand::POINT_SIZE_REGISTER:
        return &vs.oPts;
case Operand::FOG_REGISTER:
        return &vs.oFog;
}
}
```

This function simply returns the address of a memory location associated with a shader register, described by the Operand class. Once again, these variables are stored in the Context class as static data for easy and fast access. The vs structure is used only to keep them separate from pixel shader registers. When using this function together with SoftWire's r128() function we can work with SSE as if it has as many registers as there are shader registers. The syntax would be r128(reference(op)) but this can be simplified to r128(op) using overloading. One more thing is needed though: since shader instructions can be more complex than SSE instructions, we'll need internal registers for temporary results. These are best to be used as Operands as well, so we need to define one more register type. In swShader these registers are tmp0, tmp1, etc.

Mapping shader instructions to SSE instructions is fun. Here is the simplest example:

```
void VS_2_0Assembler::ADD(const Operand &dst, const Operand &src0,
const Operand &src1)
{
        movaps(tmp0, src0);
        movaps(tmp1, src1);

        addps(r128(tmp0), m128(tmp1));

        movaps(dst, tmp0);
}
```

You can clearly see that even this simple example can be broken up into: reading input registers, performing calculations, and writing the result. Every shader instruction can use source swizzling and destination masking though. So instead of just using movaps we'll use more generalized operations:

```
void VS_2_0Assembler::ADD(const Operand &dst, const Operand &src0,
const Operand &src1)
{
```

```
                    NEG_SWIZZLE(tmp0, src0);
                    NEG_SWIZZLE(tmp1, src1);

                    addps(r128(tmp0), m128(tmp1));

                    SAT_MASK(dst, tmp0);
}

void VS_2_0Assembler::NEG_SWIZZLE(const Operand &tmp, const Operand
&src)
{
static const int4 SIGN_MASK = {0x80000000, 0x80000000, 0x80000000,
0x80000000};

                    movaps(r128(tmp), m128(src));

                    if(src.mod == Operand::NEGATE)
                    {
                            xorps(r128(tmp), xmmword_ptr [SIGN_MASK]);
                    }

                    shufps(r128(tmp), r128(tmp), src.swizzle());
}

void VS_2_0Assembler::SAT_MASK(const Operand &dst, const Operand
&tmp)
{
                    if(instruction->modifier == Instruction::_SAT)
                    {
                            static const float4 ZERO = {0, 0, 0, 0};
                            static const float4 ONE = {1, 1, 1, 1};

                            maxps(r128(tmp), xmmword_ptr [ZERO]);
                            minps(r128(tmp), xmmword_ptr [ONE]);
                    }

                    if(dst.sel == xMask)
                    {
                            movss(xSS(dst), mSS(tmp));
                    }
                    else if(dst.sel == xyzwMask)
                    {
                            movaps(r128(dst), m128(tmp));
                    }
                    else
                    {
                            static const int4 MASK[] = {{-1,  0,  0,  0},  // x
                                                        { 0, -1,  0,  0},  // y
                                                        { 0,  0, -1,  0},  // z
                                                        { 0,  0,  0, -1},  // w
                                                        {-1, -1,  0,  0},  // xy
                                                        {-1,  0, -1,  0},  // xz
```

```
                                  {-1,  0,  0, -1},   // xw
                                  { 0, -1, -1,  0},   // yz
                                  { 0, -1,  0, -1},   // yw
                                  { 0,  0, -1, -1},   // zw
                                  {-1, -1, -1,  0},   // xyz
                                  {-1, -1,  0, -1},   // xyw
                                  {-1,  0, -1, -1},   // xzw
                                  { 0, -1, -1, -1},   // yzw
                                  {-1, -1, -1, -1}};  // xyzw

        int m = 0;
        if(dst.sel == xMask) m = 0;
        if(dst.sel == yMask) m = 1;
        if(dst.sel == zMask) m = 2;
        if(dst.sel == wMask) m = 3;
        if(dst.sel == xyMask) m = 4;
        if(dst.sel == xzMask) m = 5;
        if(dst.sel == xwMask) m = 6;
        if(dst.sel == yzMask) m = 7;
        if(dst.sel == ywMask) m = 8;
        if(dst.sel == zwMask) m = 9;
        if(dst.sel == xyzMask) m = 10;
        if(dst.sel == xywMask) m = 11;
        if(dst.sel == xzwMask) m = 12;
        if(dst.sel == yzwMask) m = 13;
        if(dst.sel == xyzwMask) m = 14;

        subps(r128(tmp), m128(dst));
        andps(r128(tmp), xmmword_ptr [&MASK[m]]);
        addps(r128(dst), m128(tmp));
    }
  }
```

The NEG_SWIZZLE and SAT_MASK functions, or macro instructions, can be reused for every instruction. So simple instructions like ADD, SUB, MUL, MAD, MIN, MAX, SLT, SGE, and ABS only need a couple of SSE instructions. The real fun starts with the less straightforward instructions like DP3, CRS, M3X3, SINCOS, LOG, EXP, etc. There's more freedom here to search for the shortest possible way to compute something. Also, some of these shader instructions need an approximation that stays within precision specifications, which is also challenging to get the fastest implementation. Please note that the publicly available version of swShader is not very optimal, and some instructions are not implemented fully correctly. So there's some fun left for you.

To complete the vertex shader implementation, all that is needed is a big switch statement to call the correct function to generate the code for every shader instruction, and the code to read vertex stream elements into the input registers. This can get a bit complicated, but it's still quite straightforward and just a matter of sticking close to DirectX 9 specifications.

The overall approach we've used is relatively simple and besides being runtime compiled, we haven't done any special effort to optimize it further. For the vertex pipeline, this works okay, since it doesn't need ultimate performance. The pixel pipeline of a software renderer is stressed a lot harder since there are many more pixels than vertices. So every small optimization will immediately result in an overall performance improvement. Therefore, we should look for a new approach for pixel shaders.

What is the main problem? Let's have a look at the pixel shader DP3 implementation from the publicly available swShader code, which is entirely the same as the implementation for DP3 in the vertex shader:

```
void PS_2_0Assembler::DP3(const Operand &dst, const Operand &src0,
const Operand &src1)
{
        NEG_SWIZZLE(tmp0, src0);
        NEG_SWIZZLE(tmp1, src1);

        mulps(r128(tmp0), m128(tmp1));
        movhlps(r128(tmp1), r128(tmp0));
        addss(rSS(tmp1), mSS(tmp0));
        shufps(r128(tmp0), m128(tmp0), 0x01);
        addss(rSS(tmp0), mSS(tmp1));
        shufps(r128(tmp0), r128(tmp0), 0x00);

        SAT_MASK(dst, tmp0);
}
```

This is six SSE instructions for essentially only three multiplications and two additions! The mulps instruction does four multiplications, while only three are really needed. The movhlps and shufps instructions are essentially only used to rearrange components, and they also do more than really needed. The two addps instructions do exactly what we need, but unfortunately they are not four times faster than the vector operations.

SSE clearly wasn't designed to be used this way. To use it optimally, we should process four individual scalar values at a time that need the same operation. That's what SIMD really stands for. For the DP3 shader instruction this means we should compute four dot products in parallel. This can be done by storing four x components in one register, four y components in another register, etc. This way, we need only three mulps and two addps instructions for four dot products where we used to need six inefficient instructions for one individually computed dot product! Dependencies between registers in one case and pipelining in the other makes the difference even bigger.

It's not a panacea though. The first difficulty is that four pixels have to be processed in parallel. An obvious way to do this is to process polygons in blocks of

2 × 2 pixels, also called a quad. This requires more advanced rasterization than using a scanline-based approach. Then we have to split up every input register and interpolant into its components and store it in four registers. Since we only have eight registers, this also implies that a lot less data can stay in registers so more memory read and write operations will have to be used. Also, not all shader instructions have an implementation as inefficient as DP3. Finally, for quads at the edge of the polygon we might be shading pixels that are not visible, and this visibility has to be determined per quad before the color register(s) can be unpacked and written to the frame buffer.

So is it still worth it? Definitely. Not only the arithmetic shader instructions benefit from it, but also the texture sampling code can be parallelized using MMX instructions. There are also other possibilities to improve performance. For example, the mipmap level can now be computed efficiently per quad instead of per pixel. It even makes the implementation of the DSX and DSY instructions trivial. Also, perspective correction can be parallelized or done only once per quad. The z-buffer can be reordered so that z-values of one quad are stored sequentially so that visibility determination per quad can be done in a minimum of instructions. The end result is still twice as fast as the straightforward implementation, and it becomes even better for long shaders.

To implement it, we need to fourfold the register space, using one 4D vector per component. Arithmetic shader operations are easier to implement since it's like working with scalar values. Shuffle instructions are only required for unpacking and packing the quad's pixel fragments, not in the actual shader instructions. For example, the CRS instruction will look like this:

```
void VS_2_0Assembler::CRS(const Operand &dst, const Operand &src0,
const Operand &src1)
{
        // dst.x = src0.y * src1.z - src0.z * src1.y;
        // dst.y = src0.z * src1.x - src0.x * src1.z;
        // dst.z = src0.x * src1.y - src0.y * src1.x;

        NEG_SWIZZLE(tmp0, src0);    // Modified implementation!
        NEG_SWIZZLE(tmp1, src1);

        movaps(r128(dst.x), m128(tmp0.y));
        mulps(r128(dst.x), m128(tmp1.z));
        mulps(r128(tmp0.z), m128(tmp1.y));
        subps(r128(dst.x), m128(tmp0.z));

        movaps(r128(dst.y), m128(tmp0.z));
        mulps(r128(dst.y), m128(tmp1.x));
        mulps(r128(tmp0.x), m128(tmp1.z));
        subps(r128(dst.y), m128(tmp0.x));

        movaps(r128(dst.z), m128(tmp0.x));
        mulps(r128(dst.z), m128(tmp1.y));
        mulps(r128(tmp0.y), m128(tmp1.x));
        subps(r128(dst.z), m128(tmp0.y));

        SAT_MASK(dst, tmp1);
}
```

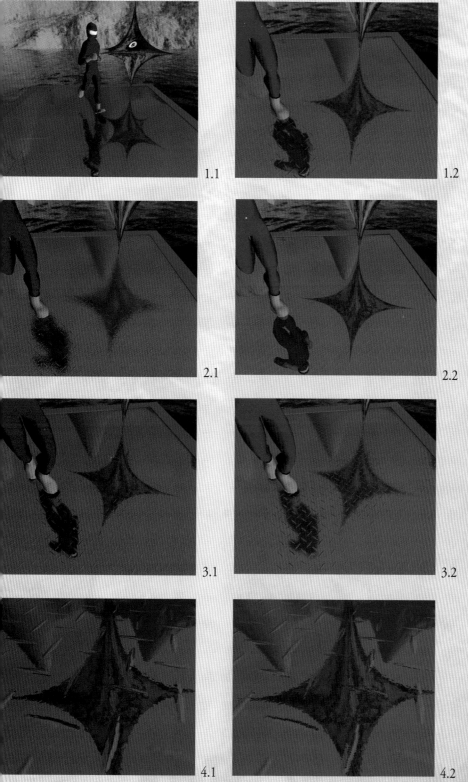

1.1

1.2

2.1

2.2

3.1

3.2

4.1

4.2

Color Plate 1 Image 1.1 shows the scene. The images 1.2 and 2.1 show the scene rendered using a 16-bit and an 8-bit normal map, respectively. Image 2.2 shows the scene with plain reflections. Images 3.1 and 3.2 contrast the regular bumpy reflection shader (left) and the shader for the infinity case (right). Smearing is clearly visible. Finally, the last row (4.1 and 4.2) contrasts the effects of using a 16-bit integer-based normal map (left) and a 32-bit floating-point normal map (right). Pixelation caused by lack of filtering can be seen. This is described in the article "Reflections from Bumpy Surfaces" (page 107) by Henning Mortveit.

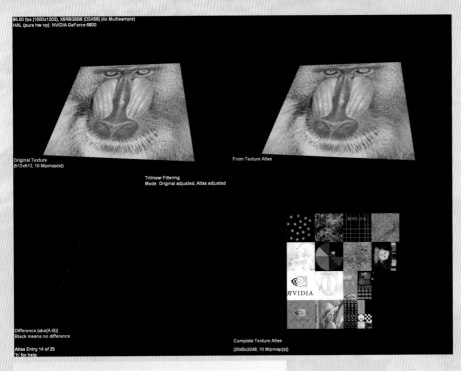

Color Plate 2 Texture Atlas as described in "Improved Batching Via Texture Atlases" (page 155) by Matthias Wloka.

Color Plate 4 Rendering hair as described in the article "Hair Rendering and Shading" (page 239) by Thorsten Scheuermann.
© ATI Technologies, 2004.

Color Plate 3 Water as described in the article "Animation and Display of Water" (page 215) by Stefano Lanza.

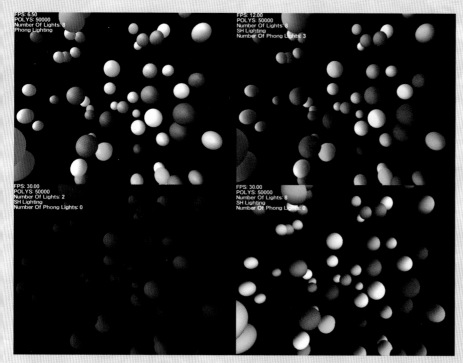

Color Plate 5 Applying Spherical Harmonics algorithms to lighting calculation as described in the article "Reduction of Lighting Calculations Using Spherical Harmonics" (page 251) by Vlad Stamate. **(Top left)** Lighting performed using per vertex Phong calculations. **(Top right)** Three lights out of eight use Phong lighting and the rest are projected onto Spherical Harmonics. **(Bottom left)** Two lights projected onto Spherical Harmonics. **(Bottom right)** Eight lights projected onto Spherical Harmonics. Notice how the rendering speed does not change between using two and eight lights.

Color Plate 6 Glare effects in Cryteks, CryEngine and in the game *Far Cry* (as described in the article "Adaptive Glare" (page 349) by Tiago Sousa. CryENGINE © 2004 Crytek. All rights reserved. *Far Cry* © 2004 Crytek. All Rights Reserved. Published by UbiSoft Entertainment. Trademarks belong to their respective owners.

Color Plate 8 Real-time soft shadows on ps_2_0 hardware. The shadow map resolution is 256×256. Shown in the article "Fractional-Disk Soft Shadows" (page 411) by Michael Valient and Willem de Boer. Courtesy of Playlogic Game Factory BV, 2004.

Color Plate 7 Non-photorealistic rendering as described in the article "Shaderey—NPR Style Rendering" (page 393) by Aras Pranckevičius.

Color Plate 9 Fake soft shadows in static scenes using precomputed visibility distance functions as described in the article "Fake Soft Shadows Using Precomputed Visibility Distance Functions" (page 425) by Aras Pranckevičius.

Color Plate 10 Instanced geometry and instanced shadows as described in the article "Drawing a Crowd" (page 505) by David R. Gosselin, Pedro V. Sander and Jason L. Mitchell. © ATI Technologies, 2004.

Color Plate 11 Rendering volumetric light shafts as described in the article "Light Shaft Rendering" (page 573) by Jason L. Mitchell. © ATI Technologies, 2004.

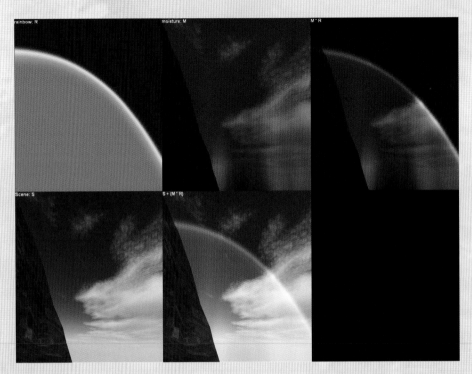

Color Plate 12   Render of photo-realistic rainbows in real time as described in the article "Rendering Rainbows" (page 589) by Clint S. Brewer.

Color Plate 13   Plausible rendered sky and physically correct attenuation of distant objects as described in the article "A Practical Analytic Model for Daylight with Shaders" (page 597) by Marco Spörl.

Note that this is three instructions per cross product, while the naive implementation in swShader 0.3.0 required eleven vector instructions. Luckily the register usage is also limited to six. Also, look how strikingly similar the C++ code in the comment is compared to the SSE code. Can't we just automate this? Of course we can! Using C++ operator overloading we'll just let SoftWire generate the corresponding code for every operation. This way very complex formulas can be written and C++ will automatically call the right runtime intrinsics to generate the assembly code. Exciting, isn't it? But before we delve into that, we have to solve some low-level optimization problems we encountered.

Optimization and High-Level Implementation

There were some problems in the previous sections related to optimization. We ignored them because it would have complicated the explanation of the soft-wiring technique and its usage, and because premature optimization is not good. But now we're ready to address some of these issues.

The first optimization problem is the use of SoftWire's r32(), r64(), and r128() functions. If we use them with the corresponding mov instructions, we can get redundant code. This is because when they allocate a register, they also load it with the corresponding value, but when used as the mov's destination operand this value immediately gets overwritten (often even copying the same value)! To fix this situation, it was easy to add new functions to SoftWire, x32(), x64(), and x128(), which also do register allocation, but don't pre-load the register with its value. This works correctly, but should strictly only be used for instructions that overwrite their destination register. Failing this can cause nasty bugs that only pop up in some situations. Although SoftWire still has these functions, and they are still used in swShader 0.3.0, there's a more elegant and less error-prone method. Inside SoftWire, every register (or rather, the structure that describes it), is given a pointer to the mov instruction that last used it as a destination operand (the load instruction). When this register is overwritten before any other instruction uses it, its previous load instruction is eliminated. This effectively solves all problems with x32(), x64(), and x128(), and even optimized other situations.

Remember that there was a problem with the PixelPipeline::blendUnit() function when the second argument was equal to the destination operand? Using a temporary register for the result would have been inefficient because it required a copy operation that in most cases is redundant. It is redundant because it just "copy propagates" a value from one register to the next, while we could have continued to work the first register. This problem also occurs in the programmable shader implementation for the NEG_SWIZZLE and SAT_MASK functions because often there are no register modifiers. Luckily it can again be solved as a low-level optimization. The trick is to detect when a register is copied, but the original is never used again. Then the copy can be eliminated and we keep working with the original. Unfortunately there is no way in SoftWire to look ahead to what will happen to registers. Run-time intrinsics are called one by one and SoftWire immediately produces the binary code. Linking operations are done in a very fast second pass, but it's practically impossible to rewrite the instructions at this point. But there's still a way to perform copy propagation, which is appropriately called [linear-scan copy propagation]. In short: it always assumes copy propagation for mov instructions. It eliminates the instruction and keeps working with the original register, which is now associated with the variable that was used as the destination operand. But when the variable of the source operand is used, the eliminated instruction is restored and both variables just swap place. They are copies anyway!

Jump operations require that you spill all registers. Really, all of them? No. Writing them all back to memory is conservative and always works, but it's not the most efficient. A complex scanline loop might use nearly all general-purpose, MMX, and SSE registers. But when the same register is used for the same variable at the start and the end of a loop, it doesn't need spilling! The solution is to take a 'snapshot' of the register allocation state. It's just a simple table that stores the address of each register's associated variable. Such AllocationTable can be retrieved from SoftWire with the getAllocationState function. Then before or after a jump, this state is "restored" with a minimal number of spilling and allocation operations. Note that a forward jump only requires spilling and a backward jump also requires reallocations. This is implemented in SoftWire using the restoreForward() and restoreBackward() functions. This optimization can be very effective, but it comes at a price. It's not foolproof and requires a thorough understanding of the involved operations so use it with care.

Let's revisit SoftWire's free() function as well. To prevent the register allocator from writing back registers to memory that are no longer used, we have to use it as often as possible. But once again it is error-prone because it can easily be used in the wrong place. Here we can get a little help from C++ again. By using a class specifically for temporary variables, we can control its lifespan automatically with the constructor and destructor. We can immediately solve two other annoyances: the wasted memory with static variables, and constantly having to write r128(&tmp). By allocating memory on the stack, these temporaries can re-use memory efficiently. And by having a cast operator that calls r128() for us, we simplify the syntax further. Here's what the usage looks like for the (parallelized) perspective correction code:

```
{
Float4 tmp;

movps(tmp, dword_ptr [&RHW]);
rcpps(r128(&W), tmp);
mulps(tmp, m128(&W));
mulps(tmp, m128(&W));
addps(r128(&W), m128(&W));
subps(r128(&W), tmp);
}
```

The Float4 class is defined in SoftWire's CodeGenerator class. But there's also a Float, Dword, Word2, Byte4, Qword, Dword2, Word4, and Byte8 class with the corresponding behavior. There's a small disadvantage to use them though: the casting operator that calls r128() cannot be overloaded to call m128(). In other words, it always forces the use of a register, even when a memory operand would have been more appropriate. However, for temporaries this isn't bad at all, because we only need them a few times and rather keep them in a register. Note that in the above example, the code is enclosed in curly brackets. This limits the lifetime of tmp so that its associated register is freed when we don't need it any more. C++ doesn't allow us to use tmp outside the brackets so we automatically detect when we try to use an already freed variable. Last but not least, note that we can't use a temporary variable for W. In particular, it would cause problems if we don't spill all registers in a scanline loop. This is because temporaries get allocated on the stack, and this memory location is also used to identify them. So when SoftWire analyzes what registers it has to spill before a jump, it can mistakenly decide not to spill a register if they have the same stack address, even though they are in fact different variables. This problem, together with the casting operator that uses m128(), will be addressed in future versions of SoftWire. For now, only use temporaries for temporaries.

Now the step from temporaries to classes that generate code automatically is really small. Remember the CRS shader instruction we wanted to implement? Because of the source and destination register modifiers, this code only works with temporaries anyway. So we can just write the formulas in C++, and overload the assignment operator and arithmetic operators for Float4 to create the corresponding code! This can use some illustration:

```
void VS_2_0Assembler::CRS(const Operand &dst, const Operand &src0,
const Operand &src1)
{
        Float4 tmp0;    // src0
        Float4 tmp1;    // src1
        Float4 tmp2;    // dst

        NEG_SWIZZLE(tmp0, src0);
        NEG_SWIZZLE(tmp1, src1);

        tmp2.x = tmp0.y * tmp1.z - tmp0.z * tmp1.y;
        tmp2.y = tmp0.z * tmp1.x - tmp0.x * tmp1.z;
        tmp2.z = tmp0.x * tmp1.y - tmp0.y * tmp1.x;

        SAT_MASK(dst, tmp2);
}
```

There's not a single line of assembly (actually runtime intrinsics) needed here! The Float4's overloaded operator* generates a mulps, the overloaded operator- generates a subps and the overloaded operator= generates a movps. Partial results will introduce new temporaries, but thanks to copy propagation optimizations it will get optimized to produce exactly the same code we first wrote manually!

Last but not least let's talk about emulation and portability. That seems crazy because we're already emulating things on a system that misses hardware features. But we've always assumed that we're working on an x86 platform and SSE is available. Fortunately, porting to another processor family is not an impossible task. All that needs to be done is to rewrite the platform-dependent parts of SoftWire. Thanks to abstractions like the `Float4` class's overloaded operators, there isn't too much work to rewrite the shader compilation. For full portability we could even write a toolset with a common interface for "intermediate instructions" for every platform. Also, on the same platform we can work this way. Most notably, SSE isn't available on every processor of the target audience. There are still a lot of Pentium II and classic Athlon systems that lack it. For this reason we overloaded all SSE runtime intrinsics and gave them an alternative implementation using only the FPU, when SSE support is not detected. It is much slower though, since we didn't take the effort to make optimal use of the FPU stack. But rest assured, it's still faster than the DirectX reference rasterizer and time-critical software rendering will be done on newer systems with SSE support anyway, where also the full power of all optimizations is enabled.

But to conclude this section; let's not get over-excited. Most encountered problems have been addressed but optimizations always introduce restrictions that create new ones. You shouldn't blindly rely on SoftWire that it generates the code you intended to create. It has proven to be very stable but sometimes you really have to think twice what will happen behind the scenes. That's why we first didn't make any mention at all about these features. That being said, the introduced optimizations are very effective and free us from constantly checking for situations where some instructions can be eliminated. Let's now apply this to something we haven't optimized yet.

Clipper and Rasterizer Implementation

Until now we've considered the clipper and rasterizer to be implemented the "classical" way, totally unrelated to shaders or soft-wired code. But if we analyze closely what kind of operations they perform, we see there's a lot of opportunity for optimization. After all, now that the pixel and vertex pipeline are highly optimized, these two components have become new bottlenecks.

The clipper uses the [Sutherland-Hodgman] algorithm. It mainly does two things: it tests what edges have to be clipped and calculates the intersections. The tests are very simple but the intersections are a lot of operations. Furthermore, it depends on the vertex format what components are used. Classically, we would just test what vertex components are used, to calculate the intersection vertex. But this situation just screams for runtime code generation, since we're wasting time with checking the vertex format for every vertex, even though many applications only use a few vertex formats. So we'll generate a "shader" specialized at computing the intersection point for one type of vertex. We could again use a cache to store them and re-use them, but it's really not worth it. We can just regenerate the shader every time the vertex format is changed. It doesn't happen very often anyway, and the generating function is very fast.

It also needs attention that visible vertices should not be copied completely. Copying big vertices takes a lot of time so we really want to avoid it. This is possible by implementing the [Sutherland-Hodgman] algorithm with a list of polygons containing pointers to vertices, and a static table of real vertices having all components, one row per polygon. When a vertex only needs copying, we only copy its pointer. When an edge has to be clipped, we create the new vertex in the static table, and reference it in the pointer table. This ensures that a minimal of operations is needed to send a completely visible polygon through all clipper stages (one per clipping plane). It's not even worth it to check in advance if the polygon is fully visible. That would be double work. The resulting polygon (pointers to vertices having all components) can then be passed to the rasterizer.

These "full" vertices are easier to process by the rasterizer since every component is stored at a fixed position. If we had used a variable vertex format in the clipper we would constantly have to check the vertex format again to calculate where a component is stored in the vertex. But that doesn't solve all performance problems of the rasterizer. It is responsible for interpolating the components of the vertices, and we should also only interpolate the components that are really present in the vertex format. We also only want to calculate the gradients and compute prestepping for used components. So this calls for soft-wiring again. It's a really big task though. Rasterization is already very complicated, and writing it all in assembly makes it even worse. Luckily the Float4 class and its friends come to rescue! We're not concerned about the tiny bit of performance loss that this higher-level code generation causes. We can just translate a full C++ version of the rasterizer to an almost identical looking soft-wired version without much effort. And really critical code can still be optimized further with specific runtime intrinsics. Caching the generated code is also very useful this time, because it's long and complex.

That concludes this section. We could throw in whole listings of clipper and rasterizer implementations, but that would bring us off focus. These optimizations really aren't that crucial, and it's important not to optimize prematurely.

Caching and Batching

We have now completely discussed how to use the soft-wiring technique to perform rendering operations efficiently. But that's only the low-level part of the full renderer. The introduction promised to work toward a full DirectX 9 compatible implementation, and so this section and the next will discuss the issues with the high-level functionality. But we won't jump into the straight jacket of DirectX yet. Software rendering has a lot more freedom to offer and also shouldn't be restricted to one interface. We'll give a lot of attention to work around the limitations a hardware rendering API brings. We do this by closely comparing the GPU and the CPU.

The first big difference is that a GPU is a very efficient state machine, while the CPU requires explicit tests and branches to implement it. That's why we used soft-wiring technology in the first place. But until now we've been very brief about the other complications this brings. In most situations, we need a caching system to avoid wasting time by generating shaders every time a render state changes (both the terms shader and render state are generalized here). The best time to generate a shader is right before it is used, because then neither the externally controlled state nor the internal state (for example, the quality of perspective correction) will change. For every state change we have to carefully register which shader needs updating. This demands one uniform interface. In swShader, the whole state machine is controlled through the Renderer class. Vertex and pixel pipelines, both fixed-function and pro-grammable, are respectively controlled through the VertexProcessor and Pixel-Processor class. All they really do is avoid that the Renderer class becomes gigantic, and they manage states independently. The renderer retrieves states like the output vertex format from the vertex processor and passes them to the pixel processor. Also the Clipper and Rasterizer classes are separate components of the renderer.

Every time a new shader is needed, we have to check if it's already in the cache. To determine this, the current state has to be compared with the states implemented by the shaders in the cache. This would be quite slow if every render state is compared individually. We solved this by creating a stamp for every complete state. It literally adds all the individual state parameters in one 32-bit variable. So they are not unique per complete render state, but when they differ, we know that they were not generated from the same state. So when a new shader is needed, the stamp for the current state is computed, and it is compared to the ones in the cache. When it differs, we know this is the wrong shader. If it matches, we still have to check the full state to make sure the stamps are not coincidentally equal for different states. The vertex processor, ras-terizer, and pixel processor all control states independently, so, for example, a state for the vertex pipeline doesn't directly influence what shader the pixel pipeline uses. This sounds very logical, but in practice it can be hard to assure this. All these classes derive from the Context class to efficiently share data like interpolants, so it is very tempting and sometimes even ambiguous to store a state in the context. One such situation is when we store the pointers to the textures that are bound to the samplers. The vertex shader might check if there is really a texture bound to a certain stage, to eliminate processing of texture coordinates that aren't used. But this is context data, and shouldn't be used as a state that determines the shader. There's a big chance that we forget to include these as the actual state related to the shaders. In this case we can end up with shaders that miss textures, or worse, shaders that attempt to sample nonexistent textures.

To avoid these serious problems as much as possible, we can get a little help from C++. The shared data in the context should only be used in runtime intrinsics. If it's used anywhere else, as a state, we want to get a compiler error. This can be achieved with the temporaries like Float4. The trick is that when they are declared static, they are associated with the same non-overlapping stack space from the start of the appli-cation. This effectively solves the problem mentioned in the section about optimiza-tions, but the drawback is obviously that it uses memory less efficiently. But context data had to be static anyway! And now we'll get an error if any of this data is used as a state. The only thing we have to assert is that all context data uses temporaries, but this is easier. We can now also ban explicit calling of register allocation functions everywhere. This can be enforced by overloading them, in the Context class!

There are typically several hundred states. Storing them all in the cache to be used as the identifying key is a bit inefficient. But luckily most states can only have a few enumerated values, so it can be compacted. In swShader, it is implemented like this:

```
const int a = 0 + BITS(COLOR_LAST);   // colorDepth
const int b = a + BITS(DEPTH_LAST);    // depthCompareMode
const int c = b + BITS(ALPHA_LAST);    // alphaCompareMode
const int d = c + 1;                   // depthWriteEnable
…

state.setPipelineState(colorDepth            << 0 |
                       depthCompareMode      << a |
                       alphaCompareMode      << b |
                       depthWriteEnable      << c |
            …);
```

The BITS macro computes how many bits are needed to store the last value of the enumeration type. There's a 32-bit pipeline state and 32-bit sampler state for every texture stage. So relatively little storage space is required but it's still useful to compare stamps first. Working with these compact 32-bit states also makes it easy to compute the stamp.

The next big difference between the CPU and the GPU is their memory hierarchy. A CPU has two (or even three) levels of cache that can be around a megabyte in size. A GPU on the other hand has no centralized big cache but a lot of bandwidth for RAM access. So obviously we can't use the same approaches. We have to take advantage of the CPU's big cache as much as possible.

The typical way for graphics hardware to draw an array of indexed triangles is to look up the three vertex indices, read the corresponding vertices from the vertex cache if they have been processed recently, or wait for them to be processed by the vertex pipeline, and then send those vertices to the rasterizer. All of this is done in parallel with little queues so nothing really has to wait and the vertex pipeline can even look ahead at what vertices will be needed next. Implementing this exactly the same way on a CPU isn't efficient. The problem is that everything would be done sequentially, so the cache is constantly used for different tasks. It would be filled with vertex pipeline data, rasterizer data, and pixel pipeline data (textures). This situation can be improved by first processing many vertices, then rasterize many triangles, and then process many pixels. Primarily, how do we keep vertex processing apart?

The most obvious answer would be to process all vertices in the whole vertex buffer first. This isn't efficient either though. Recall from the previous section that it's much easier to send "full" vertices to the rasterizer. They can be several hundred bytes long and only a few vertex components will be used so it is very wasteful with memory and inefficient with cache. Furthermore, we don't want to dynamically allocate this memory for every render call, nor do we want to attach an output buffer to every vertex buffer that is bigger than the vertex buffer itself. What we can do instead is process a batch of around 16 triangles. This only requires one buffer of output vertices of a few kilobytes. It would even fit in the L1 cache! A vertex cache of 16 or more vertices assures that nearly every vertex is processed only once. This approach is also easy to configure for processors with other cache configurations.

As we've noted before, the GPU can do many tasks in parallel. That, and the fact that it has many pipelines, results in its far superior performance compared to the CPU, even though it's clock frequency is nearly ten times lower. Luckily, CPUs are heading the same way. Intel has taken the first important step to bring parallel processing to the consumer market with its Hyper-Threading (HT) technology. It enables the core to choose between two threads for the instructions to execute. The main benefit from this is that when one thread is temporarily blocked, it can stay busy with the instructions from another thread. Such blocking can happen whenever instructions are dependent on the result of a high-latency operation, like a SIMD instruction or load/store operation. This clearly means it can help a lot for our renderer!

It also imposes some limitations though, but avoiding those we can still get great performance increases from HT technology. The first thing to note is that the same cache is shared among multiple threads. If we're not careful this means the threads disturb each other by constantly fighting for cache space. Data that is useful for one thread can be overwritten by another thread. This causes a cache miss which might take longer than the actual benefit we got from HT technology! The problem can be minimized by letting two threads work on nearly the same data sets. An easy way to do this is by letting one thread process all uneven triangle batches, and the other thread all even batches. We just need a second context for sharing data, but this can be easily achieved by making every variable an array. A second limitation of HT technology is that we have no absolute control any more of the order in which instructions arrive. So we no longer get any benefit from re-ordering instructions to spread the use of execution units and memory accesses. But there's no need to worry at all! HT technology actually helps the scheduling process, because it always looks for instructions to be sent to the execution units. So penalties and stalls are automatically minimized.

Future CPUs can further enhance HT technology by allowing more threads, and using more execution units. If every component is duplicated and separated these are also called multi-core processors. This will require a whole new way of application programming, because clock frequencies won't rise much higher, or will even lower, so using many threads as efficiently as possible will become crucial. Transistors that were previously needed for the huge cache, jump prediction and deep pipelining can then be used for extra execution units because high latency won't matter that much any more. Future GPUs can evolve the same way. The increasing programmability demands more flexible and efficient use of the available execution units. And threading assures that many tasks can run in parallel on every available execution unit. Obviously, CPUs and

GPUs will retain their own specialization, but physical and architectural limitations will eventually drive them closer together in overall performance.

Now back to today's reality: software rendering doesn't have the enormous fill rate hardware rendering offers. Not even the highly advanced techniques introduced in all the above brings us close. For now, we've always focused on using the CPU's available brute-force power by only executing the instructions that are really needed, but not how to use this still limited power wisely.

Overdraw Reduction

Most hardware relies heavily on the z-buffer alone for visibility determination. This isn't workable for software rendering, since a lot of pixels that don't end up in the final image will have wasted precious memory bandwidth and processing power. Furthermore, applications only implement rudimentary culling techniques to decide what is sent to the graphics card. This section will deal with both these problems.

Behind the renderer's interface, we are in full control. The CPU might not be the fastest number cruncher, but it can be used to implement "intelligent" algorithms that solve problems more efficiently. We can take short cuts and outsmart the GPU at several points. At a resolution of 800×600, a 3.2 GHz CPU can spend 200 clock cycles per pixel if we target a framerate of 33. And since a Pentium 4 can ideally start executing a new SSE instruction every clock cycle, which corresponds to a MAD instruction every two clock cycles, we get 100 shader instructions per pixel! We have to keep in mind that texture sampling is a complex operation, but either way this is enough processing power for per-pixel shading. But it's not enough for shading every pixel two times or more. Luckily there is a technique that ensures every (non-transparent) pixel is drawn only once: deferred rendering.

In the context of visibility determination, deferred rendering means we split the rendering of a scene into two main passes. First we render the whole scene only to the z-buffer, then we render the scene with shading enabled but with z-write disabled. When the first pass is finished, only the nearest pixel's z component is stored in the z-buffer. This means we can identify the nearest pixels, and only render those. This is done in the second pass, where the z-buffer is only read to determine what pixels need to be shaded. For software rendering, this approach only has advantages. The number of operations is nearly unchanged. All that is done is decoupling the z-buffer compare and doing it in an earlier pass. But what about vertex processing and rasterization? This is negligible. For the first pass, which we'll call the z-pass, vertices don't have to be lighted, only transformed. It's easy to add an array of transformed positions to every vertex buffer. Rasterization will have to do some setup twice, but we can now write a rasterizer and pixel pipeline that is highly specialized at doing only the z-pass.

So why is deferred rendering so little used with hardware rendering? It's mainly because it doubles the number of vertices and pixels that need to be sent though the pipelines. Classic hardware rendering generally does not have shortcuts in these pipelines that make simple tasks like only a transformation and only z-buffer operations significantly faster than full vertex and pixel processing. It can save a considerable amount of memory bandwidth though, but some arithmetic operations the pipeline makes, or can make, just go to waste. There's no such waste with a CPU. It is general-purpose and every execution unit can be used by any task. So it doesn't have any negative impact if the rendering process is split up into a z-pass and a shading pass. It also doesn't matter if there is an imbalance between vertex processing and fill rate need. This makes the CPU more efficient than the GPU. Luckily, GPUs are evolving to more general-purpose architectures as well.

All z-buffer tasks still take a considerable amount of memory bandwidth. Although the 3.2 GHz Pentium 4 has 6.4 GB/s bandwidth, this corresponds to two bytes per clock cycle. If, for example, we clear the z-buffer with 128-bit SSE instructions, it means we get a throughput of one instruction every eight clock cycles. In other words, we're wasting 87.5% of processor time. Time which could have been used to perform precious arithmetic operations. Luckily there's an elegant solution for this problem. Note that with a 32-bit floating-point z-buffer we're only using the [0.0, 1.0] range. So after one frame, one might consider to render the next frame in front of the previous, using the [−1.0, 0.0] range, then the [−2.0, −1.0] range, etc. This does not work, since the latter range has much lower precision, and the higher the exponent the worse it gets [1, 2]. The solution is to render in the [0.0, −1.0] range. Now everything is in front of the previous frame, but inverted, but we can just invert the depth compare mode as well! So it only takes one simple render state change to clear the whole z-buffer, and the process can be repeated. There's one important assumption being made here: the scene must fill the whole z-buffer. If this is not the case, artifacts will occur. There is no easy way to detect this, so it's best to enable the optimization manually per application.

Memory bandwidth and latency for the z-buffer can still be an important bottleneck, especially for scenes with very high overdraw. The real cause of the high bandwidth need is that the z-buffer is much too big to fit into the cache. To make it fit, we can use tile rendering. This is, rendering smaller rectangles of the scene at a time. With a tile size of 100 × 100, we'd use 40 kilobytes of cache memory for the z-buffer, and we'd need 48 tiles for 800 × 600 resolution. Unfortunately this means we now have 48 times more clipping operations. That's a high cost to solve the overdraw problem. But we don't really need more clipping, cache size is not a hard limit, we just want to keep memory accesses close together. An alternative is to sort the polygons so they are more or less located in tiles. To avoid sorting every polygon individually and to keep the number of state changes low, we can sort per batch. In many cases the polygons in a batch are close together anyway.

For the same reason it is useful to do culling per batch. An axis-aligned bounding box can be computed quickly in model space, and the frustum can be transformed to model space for every new model transform matrix. To avoid retransforming it for other batches in different tiles that use the same matrix, the frustum data can be stored together with the transform matrix. This frustum culling together with back-face culling can be done in the z-pass and the results can be reused in the shading pass to avoid processing too many vertices.

Further possibilities for overdraw reduction are endless. You are in control of the "architecture" and "driver" of the renderer. Although it still is no match for hardware rendering, unless maybe for extreme situations, software rendering allows for experimentation. Many, if not all, rendering techniques and optimizations were first implemented using a software renderer before they became used for hardware rendering. Note again that techniques like deferred rendering are not yet as efficient on hardware as they are in software. Some techniques could even use some explicit support from the rendering API.

DirectX library

Finally, we can bring it all together to run actual applications. And there's no better way to do this than to write our own DirectX DLL. Although it is certainly more efficient to use the renderer class directly, it would require the application programmer to learn the new interface. And even though it is very similar to DirectX, programmers generally don't want to put any effort into software rendering support. It is also hard to get enough reference material for thorough testing of the renderer since we'd have to write it ourselves. Writing a renderer and writing an application that uses it is two different things that are best kept separate. So the benefits of using an existing API far outweigh the disadvantages.

So how do we start writing a DLL? It is actually quite easy. All we have to do is configure the compiler to generate a .dll file instead of an .exe file. Then we define what functions have to be externally accessible by writing them in a .def file. The DirectX d3d9.dll only has one function, CreateDevice, all other functions are accessible through the COM interface it returns. So the .def file looks very simple:

```
LIBRARY
EXPORTS
Direct3DCreate9
```

That's it! As noted the DirectX DLLs use the COM programming model, but don't let that scare you either. It's very easy to define classes in C++ that behave just like COM interfaces. All necessary declarations are already in d3d9.h. It's a tedious task even to set up a framework though, because the DLL has several hundred functions accessible through the interfaces. IDirect3DDevice9 alone has more than one hundred functions. Well, don't worry about that, because the [framework] is freely available.

You might notice that it's not an entirely empty implementation. At every function, an exception is thrown. This makes it easy to let the debugger halt at every unimplemented function. This allows you to, for example, place the DLL next to one of the executables from the DirectX tutorials, and implement only the functions it really uses. The main advantage of this approach is that you don't have to implement the whole DLL before you're sure even simple applications can run. Many applications make use of D3DX functions, which in turn use D3D9 functions. So it's not only the functions that get called directly by the project and that you see in the source code that need to be implemented first.

Most of the implementation itself should be a relatively simple mapping between DirectX calls and `Renderer` functions. The hardest part is to write stub code for unsupported features. Returning a `D3D_OK` code is not always the best solution, especially not for functions that should return a valid pointer to certain objects. On the other hand the application might decide to exit when you don't return what it expects, or it might not check the returned code at all and use invalid data. After all, applications that expect hardware acceleration also often make assumptions about the behavior of some calls. So it's best to let most unimplemented functions return `D3DERR_INVALIDCALL` (standard in my framework) and only change it when the applications really expect another value. Also, reporting the capabilities correctly can be difficult. We don't want the application to exit (like when it expects hardware T&L), but we also would like it to choose the simplest rendering path. There's not much more to say about this. There's a lot of trial and error needed to make an application run using the software renderer, especially when we don't have the source code.

Shaders are passed to the DLL in a binary format instead of readable instructions. Although this might at first seem to complicate things, it's actually very convenient. It means we don't have to write our own parser, we just have to translate the format to our own instructions. The binary instruction format is described nearly completely in the d3d9types.h file, where they are called instruction tokens. Further information from the [Driver Development Kit] is also available. There are several main types of tokens like the version token, instruction tokens, source parameter and destination parameter tokens, and the end token. Because all these tokens are 32 bit and they are just a sequence of bit fields, it is very useful to have a C++ structure that describes them. For example, pixel shader instruction tokens have this structure:

```
struct InstructionToken
{
        unsigned long opcode : 16;

        union
        {
                unsigned long control : 8;
                unsigned long comparison : 3;

                struct
                {
                        unsigned long project : 1;
                        unsigned long bias : 1;
                };
        };
```

```
                    unsigned long size : 4;
                    unsigned long predicate : 1;
                    unsigned long reserved : 1;
                    unsigned long coissue : 1;
                    unsigned long zero : 1;
            };
```

This makes decoding them very elegant. Because all shader versions share the same instruction structure, only a few adjustments have to be made to decode all the different versions. A nice consequence of this is that Version 1.* shaders can easily be implemented using a Version 2.0 pipeline (or higher). This functional backward compatibility is obvious if we consider that multiple versions of pipelines on hardware implementations would have been very wasteful. So, in this context, we benefit from it as well to implement all shader versions quickly. But it also shows that once again software rendering is more flexible. It is more efficient to implement Version 1.* shaders using MMX for the registers.

One last thing that is worth mentioning is how to actually implement deferred rendering. All render calls have to be stored in a buffer, together with all state changes, to be able to render the scene in two passes. Storing vertex buffers and other resources is no problem since we are in full control of them. We also don't have to wait for End-Scene before we can start rendering. The z-pass is totally independent and can be done immediately.

Ideas and Closing

Where do we stand now? First the bad news. A lot of work still needs to be done! Implementing the DLL is a gigantic task that is currently only in an experimental phase. We've also only presented one successful way for overdraw reduction, because this article is just too short to discuss other interesting methods like [Hierarchical Occlusion Maps]. Some topics like rasterization and texturing couldn't be explained in much detail either. To compensate that we've provided a list of links below, that have been very useful to design and implement the other parts of the software renderer.

The good news is, soft-wiring technology allowed us to very rapidly implement processing pipelines with revolutionary performance and flexibility. All practical results to date can be found on the accompanying CD-ROM, and many new demos and code will be available via the [swShader] Website in the future. They show that on modern processors, software rendering can be an alternative for hardware rendering when performance is of secondary importance. Software rendering offers endless possibilities that can be tuned for a specific application, and wipes all compatibility problems away. In this sense it is very similar to rendering on a console.

With the advent of new CPU designs with multi-core configurations coming to the consumer market, we'll also see the parallel processing power increase. Together with their already record-breaking clock speeds, they will allow intelligent specialized software rendering to become a viable alternative to brute-force generalized hardware rendering. And after all, they are growing closer every generation and only minor differences will separate hardware rendering from software rendering. Shader programming is already software rendering. Also, a technique similar to soft-wiring is already used to dynamically generate shader code. And with every new version of DirectX and the Shader Model, the programmability will increase. Therefore it is important to target the highest possible specifications, like DirectX Next and Shader Model 4.0, once they become available.

And let's not forget that this technology is not limited to software rendering. In every application where processing pipelines are used with a lot of states, soft-wiring can help it reach maximum efficiency. One such application is video encoding, where [SoftWire] is already being used. Other examples are Digital Signal Processing (DSP), and hardware verification. SoftWire also serves very well as a JIT compiler back-end for scripting languages. Using the technology for radically different rendering technology like ray-tracing is worth exploring as well.

But most of all, soft-wiring allows fun experimentation, to try things that have never been tried before. So let's have fun and do what we like to do!

References

[AviSynth Video Post-Production Tool], *http://www.avisynth.org.*
[C++ Compiler Compiler], Alec Panovici, *http://cppcc.sourceforge.net.*
[Compilers: Principles, Techniques and Tools], A. Aho, R. Sethi, and J. Ullman.
[d3d9.dll Framework], Nicolas Capens, *http://sw-shader.sourceforge.net.*
[Direct3D Driver Shader Codes], *http://www.osr.com/ddk/graphics/d3denum_0bhj.htm.*
[Hierarchical Occlusion Maps and Occlusion Culling], Hansong Zhang, *http://www. cs.unc.edu/~zhangh/hom.html.*
[IEEE Floating-Point Format], *http://en.wikipedia.org/wiki/Floating-point.*
[Linear-scan copy propagation], Nicolas Capens, *http://compilers.iecc.com/comparch/ article/03-11-046.*
[Online Tutorial], SoftWire tutorial, *http://softwire.sourceforge.net/tutorial.html.*
[Perspective Texture Mapping], Chris Hecker, *http://www.d6.com/users/checker/ misctech.htm.*
[Real Virtuality demo], *http://softwire.sourceforge.net/extra.html.*
[Reentrant Polygon Clipping], Ivan E. Sutherland and Gary W. Hodgman.
[Sourceforge.net], SoftWire runtime assembler, *http://softwire.sourceforge.net.*
[swShader software renderer], *http://sw-shader.sourceforge.net.*
[Tommesani.com], SIMD assembly documentation, *http://www.tommesani.com/ Docs.html.*

Useful links

Google, *http://www.google.com.*
Real-Time Rendering Resources, *http://www.realtimerendering.com.*
3D Pipeline Tutorial, *http://www.extremetech.com/article2/0,1558,9722,00.asp.*
flipCode—Game Development News & Resources, *http://www.flipcode.com.*

Perspective texture mapping, Chris Hecker, *http://www.d6.com/users/checker/ misctech.htm.*

Run-Time MIP-Map Filtering, Andrew Flavell, *http://www.gamasutra.com/features/ 19981211/flavell_01.htm.*

Intel IA-32 Processor Manuals, *http://www.intel.com/design/pentium4/manuals/ index2.htm.*

NVidia Developer Relations, DirectX, *http://developer.nvidia.com/page/directx.html.*

Microsoft DirectX, MSDN Documentation, *http://msdn.microsoft.com/library/ default.asp?url=/nhp/default.asp?contentid=28000410.*

On the CD-ROM

Real virtuality demo
Per-pixel lighting demo
OpenGL wrapper demo
Stencil shadowing demo
DirectX 8 DLL demo
swShader 0.3.0 source code
SoftWire 4.4.2 source code
D3D9 DLL framework
And more…

3.3

Tactical Path-Finding Using Stochastic Maps on the GPU

Khanh Phong Ly

Introduction

Scenario

Suppose a penguin P wants to move from somewhere in a territory to one or more fishing holes in the ice. There are polar bears in the territory that P wants to avoid (Figure 3.3.1). The ice is slippery so there is a small chance that P will travel in a direction that deviates from the intended one. P wants to get to one of the holes in the quickest time and with the least danger. Which path will P aim for?

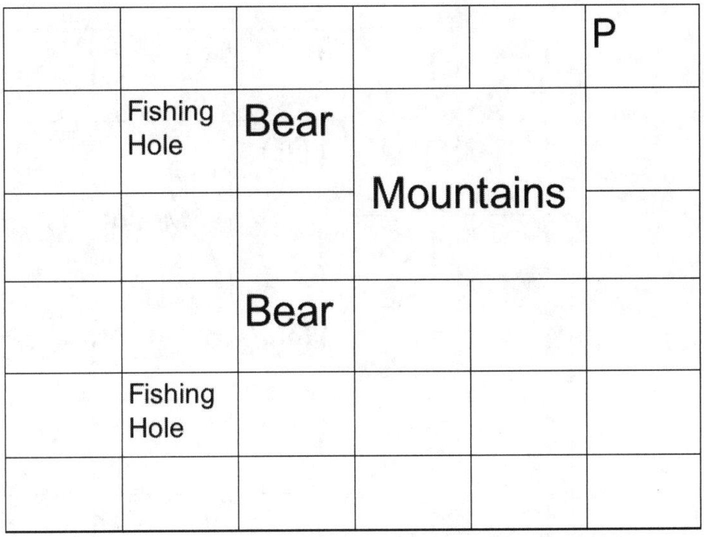

				P
	Fishing Hole	Bear		
			Mountains	
		Bear		
	Fishing Hole			

FIGURE 3.1.1 *The territory.*

We solve this problem using dynamic programming. A good introduction is given by [Pivazyan03] and [Goodman98]. For more depth and theory refer to [Bertsekas96] . Unlike the A* algorithm [Stout00] where the cost of moving from any position to an adjacent one is deterministic (the outcome is always the intended action),

313

dynamic programming tries to find the optimum path knowing that outcomes could stray from the intended actions[1].

We will not go into the theory of DP, which has many applications and is a large area of research, but will concentrate on its application to pathfinding using a stochastic map. A brief explanation of the algorithm follows.

The territory is divided into a grid of cells with costs (stochastic map.) After a certain number of iterations, these cell costs stabilize and represent the cost of reaching a goal cell from that cell. We try to find paths with minimum cost. Each cell represents a "state" of the system and we can model pathfinding as a Markov chain[2]. If neighboring cells hold the cost of reaching a goal from their locations, then by simply choosing to move to the one with the minimum cost we are guaranteed to find the minimum cost to a goal cell from our current cell.

In this article, an implementation of this algorithm on the GPU is discussed.

The Algorithm

We begin with a map of the territory, a grid of cells (`OriginalValueMap`). Each cell holds a positive value representing the cost of moving into the cell. Cells to be avoided are given high cost. Goal cells are given a value of zero (Figure 3.3.2).

1	1	1	1	1	1
1	0	100	Mountains		1
1	1	1			1
1	1	100	1	1	1
1	0	1	1	1	1
1	1	1	1	1	1

FIGURE 3.3.2   *Cells assigned values to reflect the cost of moving into them.*

---

[1]A* is used for tactical pathfinding in [Sterren02]. I recommend that the reader browse this for comparison.
[2]The Markov property is that knowledge of the state at time t is all the information about the present and past relevant to predicting the future [Goodman98]. It can be seen that local optimality translates to global optimality.

A table stores the likelihoods for outcomes for each intended action (`ActionOut-comeProbabilityTable`). For example, Figure 3.3.3 shows the action-outcome probabilities for the possible actions in Figure 3.3.4 if the likelihood of ending up in a cell to the left or right of the intended direction is 0.1.

		Outcome Probabilities							
		0	1	2	3	4	5	6	7
Actions	0	.9	.05	0	.05	0	0	0	0
	1	.05	.9	.05	0	0	0	0	0
	2	0	.05	.9	0	.05	0	0	0
	3	.05	0	0	.9	0	.05	0	0
	4	0	0	.05	0	.9	0	0	.05
	5	0	0	0	.05	0	.9	.05	0
	6	0	0	0	0	0	.05	.9	.05
	7	0	0	0	0	.05	0	.05	.9

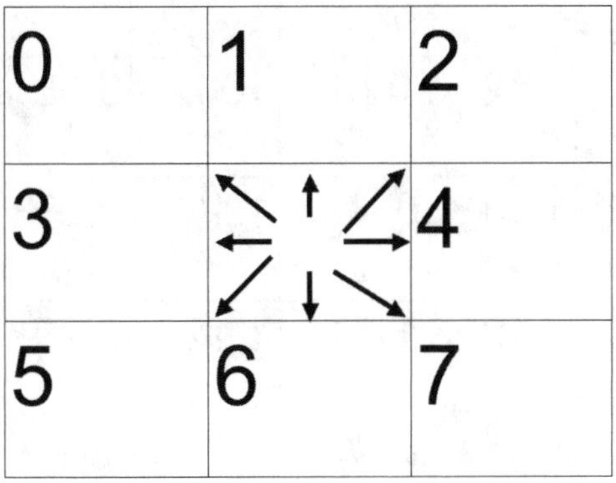

FIGURES 3.3.3 AND 3.3.4   *Action-outcome probabilities for transitions to neighboring cells.*

That's all the initial data required. The algorithm is as follows:

At each step we maintain a map of the iterated cell values (`CurrValueMap`). After a set number of iterations, the cell values will converge and will hold the lowest Expected[3] cost of reaching a goal cell from that cell (see Figure 3.3.5).

---

[3]"Expected" in the statistical sense., i.e., average.

Then by inspecting the values in CurrValueMap we create an associated decision map (ActionMap) that represents what action should be taken from each cell in the territory.

So, we calculate CurrValueMap as follows:

1. Initialize CurrValueMap with OriginalValueMap.
2. For each cell in CurrValueMap, compute the Expected action value E(U) for each possible action in the cell as follows[4]:
   - E(U) = $\Sigma_{\text{all outcomes}}$ (probability of outcome* cost of outcome).
   - Choose the action with the lowest E(U) = Emin.
   - Set the cell's value to Vcurrent = Emin + Voriginal.
3. Repeat Step 2 for the next iteration.

[ROUTINE 1.]

1.18	2.27	3.20	11.35	10.24	9.07
1.32	0	100.3			7.96
1.18	2.23	3.09	Mountains		6.85
1.12	1.16	100.1	3.68	4.67	5.95
1.16	0	1.16	2.59	3.75	4.94
1.12	1.16	1.12	2.20	3.33	4.48

FIGURE 3.3.5   *The cell values converge to these values as the number of iterations increases.*

After an arbitrary number of iterations we create the ActionMap as follows:

1. For each cell in territory, and for each possible action:
   a. compute cost of action = the cost of moving to the destination cell.
   b. Set cell action to be the action with lowest cost (see Figure 3.3.6).

---

[4]If outcome is not possible, we might try to land on a boundary cell, then we are "bounced" back into the current cell. In this case, the outcome state is taken to be the current state and the cost is the value of the current cell.

[ROUTINE 2.]

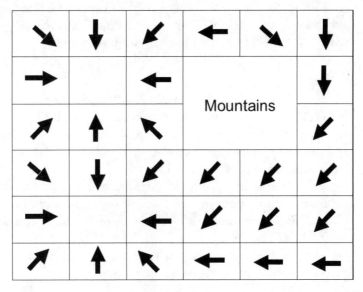

FIGURE 3.3.6 *The arrows show the best action to take at each cell.*

How many times do we iterate? We care less that the CurrValueMap values stabilize but that the action values stabilize. A general rule of thumb is that the number of iterations is at least equal to the number of moves in the best path [Pivazyan03.]

The ActionMap stabilizes for regions closest to the goal cells first. These regions "grow" outwards until the whole map is stabilized. This can be seen in the Demo on the CD-ROM if the reader chooses to display the ActionMap and then reset the process to iterate from the original values.

ON THE CD

We now move onto details of implementation on the GPU.

Implementation

Why It Makes Sense on the GPU

First, the direct neighbors of each cell are the only states that can be reached from the current cell. These are limited to a small number (whether we choose to define this as 4 or 8). This is not necessarily the case for other dynamic programming applications where states can transition to others in more general ways; maybe more complex structures like graphs may be needed for efficiency.

Second, the algorithm used to generate the cell values is intrinsically parallel, we can process more than one cell simultaneously at each iteration.

Third, floating point precision on the GPU now makes it possible. (See why floating point representation is necessary in the results section.)

Last, the current generation of graphics hardware has fast vector multiply, vector comparison, and accelerated dot product. These instructions will accelerate parts 2.a and 2.b. of ROUTINE 1 as shown in the next section.

Details

We implement the algorithm with PS2.0 shaders, one to calculate `CurrValueMap` (ROUTINE 1) and one to create the `ActionMap` (ROUTINE 2.) To pass the values to the pixel shader we store the map data as textures and render a multi-textured quad to the screen on each pass. The quad is sized to obtain a 1:1 screen pixel-to-texel ratio. Depth and stencil tests are turned off.

We choose to use textures to store precomputed intermediate values because of the limited instruction set and limiting 64 non-texture load instruction limit in PS2.0. This primarily aids computation of conditionals in the algorithm.

To the details …

The possible actions from each cell are 0, 1, 2…8. each number representing a direction of movement as shown Figure 3.3.4.

Pre-Computation

Raw data:

- A texture representing the original cell values, the `OriginalValueMap`. This has `D3DFORMAT = D3DFMT_R32F`.
- A boundary map texture. Cells marked as boundary cells cannot be traversed. This is not used directly in the shaders.
- An `ActionOutcomeProbabilityTable`.

From this we generate further data:

1. A `NeighborhoodMask` (stored in 2 textures[5]). Each cell has a mask of 8 components. Each component specifies whether the neighbor in the given direction is a boundary cell or not. `D3DFORMAT = D3DFMT_A8R8G8B8` as it's widely supported, but `_A4R4G4B4` or any other 16-bit ARGB format could be used if supported. For example, for the very top left cell in our example, the 8 components of the mask would be (0, 0, 0, 0, 1, 0, 1,1).
2. `ActionResidueProbabilities` (8 components stored in 2 textures). Essentially stores the chances of being bounced back into the current cell for each direction we try to move. `D3DFORMAT = D3DFMT_A16R16G18B16`.

---

[5]If more instruction slots were available, we might choose to pack this data into 1 texture as only a Boolean value is required.

Step 2.a.i expanded would be:

```
accumProbs= 0;
accumSum= 0;
For ( i=0;i<numoutcomes;i++)
{
        if ( outcome possible ) // i.e. check that outcome cell is not
                               // a boundary cell
        {
                accumProbs =   accumProbs + Prob(i);
                accumSum = accumSum  + Prob(i)*CellVal(i)
}
}
accumSum = accumSum + (1-accumProbs)*CellVall(currentCell);
```

Note that `(1-accumProbs)*CellVall(currentCell)` accounts for the "bouncing" back of Penguin P into the cell from a boundary cell. Now, rather than calculating `(1-accumProbs)` we precompute and store in `ActionResidueProbabilities`.

Again, for example, taking the top left cell, and the `ActionOutcomeProbability` `Table` of Figure 3.3.3, the first component of the `ActionResidueProbabilities` would be = 1. That is, if we intend to head in direction 0 we will definitely end up back in this cell. If we try to head in direction 2, there is a 95% chance of ending up back in this cell.

The whole `ActionResidueProbabilities` vector for this cell is (1, 1, .95, 1, 0, .95, 0.05, 0).

Runtime

So during runtime we load the `OriginalValueMap`, `NeighborhoodMask`, `Action-ResidueProbability`, and the `CurrentValueMap`[6] as textures.

The `ActionOutcomeProbabilityTable` is small enough to fit in the constant registers[7].

ROUTINE 1: CurrentValueMap Iteration

```
//————————————————————————————————————--

ps.2.0
/*
#define root2 1.414213562373f
#define FLT_EPSILON    1.192093e-6f
```

---

[6]A double buffer is used. The current values are read from one buffer and the resultant values are written to the other.
[7]8 actions and 8 outcomes, hence 16 4vecs are used.

```
#define FLT_MAX          3.4028e38f

    def c16, root2, 1.0f, root2, 1.0f
    def c17, 1.0f, root2, 1.0f, root2
    def c18, 1.0f, 1.0f, 1.0f, 1.0f
    def c20, FLT_MAX, FLT_MAX, FLT_MAX, FLT_MAX
    def c21, FLT_EPSILON, FLT_EPSILON, FLT_EPSILON, FLT_EPSILON
    def c22, 0,0,0,0
*/
#define AOPM    c0       // AOPM = action probability map. takes up 16
4vecs.
#define GEOMETRIC_FACTOR0   c16      // 2 4VECS
#define GEOMETRIC_FACTOR1   c17      // 2 4VECS
#define ONE                         c18

#define TEX_DX              c19.xyzw // texel increment amount.
                                    // add this to offset the sampler.
#define TEX_DY              c19.wzyx
#define MAXVAL              c20
#define MINABSVAL           c21
#define ZERO                        c22

#define CELLVAL             r0      // cell value.
#define CELLVAL0    r1.x
#define CELLVAL1    r1.y
#define CELLVAL2    r1.z
#define CELLVAL3    r1.w
#define CELLVAL4    r2.x
#define CELLVAL5    r2.y
#define CELLVAL6    r2.z
#define CELLVAL7    r2.w
#define CELLVALS_0  r1
#define CELLVALS_1  r2

#define ACTIONCOST0         r3.x
//…
#define ACTIONCOST7         r4.w
#define ACTIONCOSTS_0 r3
#define ACTIONCOSTS_1 r4

#define RESIDUEPROB0  r5.x
//…
#define RESIDUEPROB7  r6.w
#define RESIDUEPROBS_0 r5
#define RESIDUEPROBS_1 r6

#define NEIGHBRMASKS_0 r7
#define NEIGHBRMASKS_1 r8
```

```
        dcl t0.xy
        dcl_2d s0                         // current cell values
        dcl_2d s1                         // neighborhood maska
        dcl_2d s2                         // neighborhood maskb
        dcl_2d s3                         // Action Residue probabilities_a
        dcl_2d s4                         // Action Residue probabilities_b
        dcl_2d s5                         // initial cell values.
    //————————————————————————————————————————
```

TEX_DX and TEX_DY are loaded at runtime along with the other consts. They are 1/width and 1/height of the data maps.

Note the geometric factors (GEOMETRIC_FACTOR0, GEOMETRIC_FACTOR1). This accounts for the fact that moving diagonally into a cell costs more than moving in either an east-west or north-south aligned direction[8].

```
    //————————————————————————————————————————
    texld   CELLVAL, t0, s0 // load cell val
    add     r2, CELLVAL.x, -MINABSVAL
    texkill r2              // if cell value is eq or lt zero, kill
                           // rendering of pixel.

    //————————————————————————————————————————
    Boundary cells and goal cells are always zero value.
    We process neither by subtracting a small value to make them fail
    texkill.

    //————————————————————————————————————————
            // load neigbours and pack into 2 * 4vecs
            add          r3.xy, t0, -TEX_DY
            texld   r9, r3, s0
            mov          CELLVAL1, r9.x

            add          r3.xy, r3, -TEX_DX
            texld   r3, r3, s0
            mov          CELLVAL0, r3.x

            // …

            add          r7.xy, r7, TEX_DY
            texld   r7, r7, s0
            mov          CELLVAL5, r7.x


            texld   r7, t0, s1              // load neighbor mask for cell
            texld   r8, t0, s2
```

---

[8]This is a purely geometrical factor if the costs represent different terrains. However, it could also be considered a time elongation factor if the cell values represented cost rates; the longer it takes to traverse the cell, the more it costs.

```
mul     CELLVALS_0, CELLVALS_0, r7     // precalculate cost * mask
mul     CELLVALS_1, CELLVALS_1, r8

        // bake with geometric factors
mul     CELLVALS_0, CELLVALS_0, GEOMETRIC_FACTOR0
mul     CELLVALS_1, CELLVALS_1, GEOMETRIC_FACTOR1

//----------------------------------------------------------------.
```

Load neighboring cell values and pack into 2 4vecs ready for vector operations on the values. If the neighboring cell is a boundary cell then the mask would set the cost of the neighbor to zero, as it's cost will not contribute to the expected value of the action.

Multiply diagonal cell costs by root(2).

```
//----------------------------------------------------------------.
texld RESIDUEPROBS_0, t0, s3 // load residue probabilities for each
                            // action.
texld RESIDUEPROBS_1, t0, s4


// NOW CALCULATE COSTS FOR EACH ACTION
dp4         r11, c0, CELLVALS_0    // action 0
dp4         r9, c1, CELLVALS_1
add         r10, r11, r9
mad         ACTIONCOST0, RESIDUEPROB0, CELLVAL.x, r10

dp4         r11, c2, CELLVALS_0    // action 1
dp4         r9, c3, CELLVALS_1
add         r10, r11, r9
mad         ACTIONCOST1, RESIDUEPROB1, CELLVAL.x, r10

// ...

dp4         r11, c14, CELLVALS_0   // action 7
dp4         r9, c15, CELLVALS_1
add         r10, r11, r9
mad         ACTIONCOST7, RESIDUEPROB7, CELLVAL.x, r10

// for intended actions that are invalid (ie cant intend to go south
// against a wall)
// set the cost to be the max cost
cmp     ACTIONCOSTS_0, -NEIGHBRMASKS_0, MAXVAL, ACTIONCOSTS_0
cmp     ACTIONCOSTS_1, -NEIGHBRMASKS_1, MAXVAL, ACTIONCOSTS_1

//----------------------------------------------------------------.
```

Here the expected costs for each action are calculated. The code section 2.a.i. of ROUTINE 1 detailed above is done here. Note that the last two lines indirectly implement the "if (outcome possible)" part of section 2.a.i.

This is because we take the invalid action out of contention in part 2.b. where we look for the action with least cost.

```
//─────────────────────────────────────────────────────.
        // find minimum of the 8 components.
min     r11, ACTIONCOSTS_0, ACTIONCOSTS_1
mov     r9, r11.wzyx // copy last 2 components to be compared with first 2
min     r10, r11, r9
mov     r11, r10.y
min     r9, r10, r11

texld r1, t0, s5  // original cost vals.
add     r9.x, r9.x, r1
mov     oC0, r9
//─────────────────────────────────────────────────────.
```

We find the action with the minimum expected cost and add it to original cost val.

ROUTINE 2: ActionMap Generation

We generate a texture that holds the action id associated with each (non-boundary) cell in the territory. We load up the current cell values and neighborhood mask as before.

Cell and neighboring values are loaded and packed as in the implementation of ROUTINE 1. A similar use of the cmp instruction finds the action id for each cell.

Results

Performance

The software implementation and the GPU implementation were compared on an AMD athlon 1200+ , 512Meg ram with an ATI Radeon 9600 Pro.

A performance gain of 10 to 30 times over the CPU version was achieved. This was using 128*128-sized textures for the territory maps. The gain increased as the number of iterations per frame was increase from 2 to 200+. The asymptotic gain limit seems to be around 30.

The timings measured the time it took to iterate the CurrValueMap n times followed by the creation of the ActionMap. In the case of the GPU version, the timing includes loading back into main memory of both the CurrValueMap and the Action-Map.

Limitations

Could we pass large textures to this implementation? Yes, but with minor changes to the algorithm. This is because the geometrical factor used in computing the Curr-ValueMap puts a limit on the size of the shortest path and hence the size of map that can be used.

Consider neighbors of a goal cell. A move diagonally onto these neighbors would incur a cost of `squareroot(2)*minimum` cost. Diagonal moves onto these next-neighbors from other cells would incur another `squareroot(2) factor` (see Figure 3.3.7). So a path from a distant cell to a goal cell could incur potentially a 2 to the power of path-length/2, even without considering the cell cost values on the path[9].

So a path length of 256 would inherit an accumulated geometrical factor of around 2 to the power of 128 or 3.40282366e+38, i.e., the biggest number representable on most 32-bit machines. At this point things would break down and incorrect actions would be generated.

That's why in the code we scale `OrigValueMap` costs down to use as much of the dynamic range of a float as possible, which should be around 1e44. This is so theoretically but in practice, the top limit is observed to be around 1e27. This suggests a true hardware precision lower than 32 bit on the GPU. Areas with cell values greater than roughly 1e21 give incorrect action values in those regions of the `ActionMap` as calculations overflow.

If diagonal movements were not allowed (can only move in four directions) then the geometrical factor as shown in Figure 3.3.7 can be eliminated. Now, the costs of neighbors are summed along the path without scaling, and grow roughly at O(L) where L is the length of the path from the cell to a goal cell. Now there is practically no limit on the size of the territory map[10].

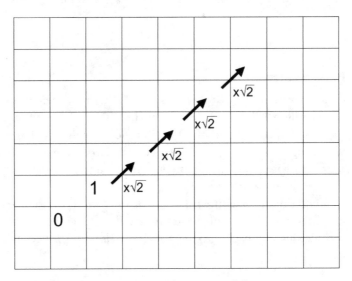

FIGURE 3.3.7 *Propagation of geometrical factor.*

[9]This is only approximate as neighboring costs are modulated by the action-outcome probability distribution.
[10]Cost of cells are summed from the neighbour, so texures of 1e22 * 1e22 could be used if all the original cell values were scaled down to 1e-6. The smallest representable 32-bit float is roughly 1e-7.

Improvements

More instruction slots and a larger instruction set, with branching in PS3.0 would allow for more flexible shader implementations. Currently around 35 instructions in the `ActionMap` generating ROUTINE 2 are duplicates of those in ROUTINE 1. If we could flag whether to generate an `ActionMap` on the same pass then ROUTINE 2 can be merged into ROUTINE 1 saving these superfluous instructions.

Summary

The parallel nature of the DP algorithm used in pathfinding makes it conducive to implementation on the GPU. With vector multiply and comparison the algorithm is speeded up greatly on Pixel Shader 2.0. Further efficiencies can be achieved with Pixel Shader 3.0.

References

[Bertsekas96] Bertsekas, Dimitri, "Neuro-dynamic Programming," Athena Scientific, 1996.

[Goodman98]   *http://www.math.nyu.edu/faculty/goodman/teaching/Comp_Fin_98/lecture_1/lecture_1.html.*

[Sterren02] van der Sterren, William, "Tactical Path-Finding with A*," *Game Programming Gems 3*, Charles River Media, 2003.

[Stout00] Stout, Bryan, "The Basics of A* for Path Planning," *Game Programming Gems*, Charles River Media, 2000.

[Pivazyan03] Pivazyan, Karen, "NPC Decision Making: Dealing with Randomness," *Game Programming Gems 4*, Charles River Media, 2004.

3.4

FX Composer 1.5—
Standardization

Chris Maughan and Daniel Horowitz

Introduction

In the article, "The Design of FX Composer" [Maughan04], we outlined the design decisions made to develop the FX Composer Shader development IDE. This tool, freely available from *http://www.nvidia.com/fxcomposer*, enables development and performance testing of DirectX shaders, based on the .fx file format specification.

Around the time the article was published, Version 1 of FX Composer shipped, and we began planning the next version of the tool. In general we were happy with the features that shipped in Version 1, but at the same time had a long list of features that didn't make the cut. We wanted to target the new version at the release of DirectX 9c, the upcoming API update from Microsoft. It was also tied into NVIDIA's chip development cycles, as we wanted to offer new features for our recently announced GeForce 6800 line of processors, in particular—shader model 3.0 support. Another key feature of DirectX 9c was the DirectX Standard Semantics and Annotations (DXSAS). With these features in mind, and given a tight schedule, we needed to focus on getting Version 1.5 into the hands of developers. With DXSAS we believed that developers would be able to achieve a much greater range of effects, to the extent that full game engines could be built on this technology; the obvious advantage being a standardized file format that all developers could use to share effects. Indeed, in Version 1 of FX Composer we shipped in excess of 120 effect files, the start of what we hope will be a large free library of effects that games developers can use "out of the box," or modify for their own needs.

At the same time, we had some longer term plans for FX Composer that we wanted to address. While the tool has a powerful runtime engine, the user interface did not effectively expose all of its features. Additionally, to ease developer integration of FX Composer into the production pipeline, we understood the need to ship an effective and easy-to-use API to gain access to the FX Composer functionality. This would enable developers to import and export their own geometry into the tool, as well as control other features such as the geometry pipeline. Among feedback from developers using the tool, the most regular request was importer plugin support, but we also had a long list of requests that we wanted to accommodate as best we could.

This article outlines the new features of FX Composer 1.5; with a focus on the standards we implemented to enable developers to share and use FX Composer in their production pipelines. We will also offer a useful introduction to the scripting extension which takes the DirectX Effects file format to a new level of sophistication.

DirectX 9c

In the summer of 2004, Microsoft shipped an update to the DirectX 9 API. The most important part of this API from NVIDIA's perspective is Shader model 3.0. This enables us to take advantage of new features in our chips, such as shader branching and vertex texturing. The DirectX 9c update is essentially an improved set of API libraries, with the underlying runtime changed only a little. In order to get these new features into FX Composer therefore, it was simply a matter of updating a few API changes, and recompiling against the current SDK. Because the SDK is statically linked in terms of the D3DX library, this step has to be done to offer the new version of FX Composer to developers. Once FX Composer is recompiled against the new SDK, all profiles supported by DirectX 9 are immediately available through the IDE. This means that FX Composer 1.5 supports shader profiles ps_1_0, ps_1_1, ps_2_0, ps_2_a, ps_2_b, ps_3_0, as well as the equivalent vertex shader profiles. In order to support multiple techniques, developers have simply to setup techniques within the .fx file to support the shader model they are targeting. At start of day, FX Composer will search the profiles and only enable those supported by the underlying hardware.

COM Support and C# Scripting

In the design article in GPU Gems [Maughan04], we talked about the general design of FX Composer, and how we implemented a COM-like solution in our engine. It soon became apparent as we started the work for 1.5, that our nearly-but-not-quite COM approach was going to hold back some of the cooler things we could do with the engine. Our ultimate goal was to offer full scripting, and plugin development as COM components. In an ideal world, we would enable programmers to write scripts in their own language, and simply hook into the FX Composer API to control the engine. As well as supporting a cleaner SDK model, converting to a true COM solution would enable much simpler interaction with .NET managed code. A clear goal we have for the future is enabling a richer user interface, with fairly advanced controls. We reasoned that this job would be much easier if we could use the productivity features of .NET to help us build our UI components, and integrating unmanaged code with managed code is much easier when your engine is based on COM.

While this decision was great from a design standpoint, it was a living nightmare in terms of bringing everything into line with COM standards. While we had a COM-like solution, we had bent the rules because we could, and many interfaces were not compliant—our worst offence being that we had passed smart pointers to interface methods. As any COM programmer knows, you need to return HRESULT codes from interface methods when marshalling them across process boundaries, and we had not implemented our interfaces this way, instead often returning 'bool.' These problems aside, the future prospects for a clean SDK with cool scripting features could not be resisted, and we began modifying some 100+ interface definitions, and several more coclass objects. The work was tedious in the extreme, and it was decided early on that this would be an on-going effort that would be partially exposed in Ver-

sion 1.5, with the full SDK being offered when we shipped Version 2.0. Our goal for
1.5 was simply to ship a geometry import SDK, which covered the majority of developer requests, while giving us more time to ship the final version which would include
many exciting plugin options, such as geometry modifiers, and dynamic scripting.

As a test of our new COM-based engine components, we added a .NET assembly
to the project. This assembly could be called from FX Composer, and it could in turn
call back into the engine. In the assembly we implemented trivial scripting support,
where FX Composer could pass it a C# or indeed a VC.NET script file and have the
.NET runtime compile it on the fly and run it. To do this, we simply exposed the
.NET assembly as a COM component, and had the FX Composer unmanaged code
call it. This feature was a fun weekend project, but we suspect that it will become a
key part of the FX Composer SDK in the future. It's now possible in FX Composer to
create a C# script file, compile it and have FX Composer highlight syntax errors, just
as it would with an .fx file. The script can then run and easily call the engine to create
scene objects, export material data, etc. The following shows a simple script which
enumerates the plugins currently running in FX Composer, and outputs them to a
messagebox. Note that it calls back into the FX Composer engine using the INVSys-
tem interface, the main FX Composer engine entry point.

```
using System;
using FXCUtil;
using interop.nv_sys;

namespace PluginList
{
public class Simple : IFXCScript
{
        // Script entry point.
        public bool Run(INVSystem Sys)
        {
                string PluginList = "";
                uint Num = Sys.GetNumPlugins();

                for (uint Current = 0; Current < Num; Current++)
                {
                        INVPlugin Plugin;
                        string Name;
                        Sys.GetPlugin(Current, out Plugin);
                        Plugin.GetPluginName(out Name);
                        PluginList += Name;
                        PluginList += "\n";
                }

                System.Windows.Forms.MessageBox.Show(PluginList,
                    "Current Plugins");
                return true;
        }
}
}
```

It is quite amazing that engine scripting support was implemented in FX Composer in a matter of hours. Although the conversion of the rest of the engine to COM will take some time, this feature is very powerful. We can imagine a scenario in FX Composer 2.0 where a developer needs to test a particle system; he can implement the particles in a C# script, load it into the scene as a geometry plugin, and write an .fx file to modify the material of the particles, all within the IDE of FX Composer. Since all .NET code is compiled on the fly into optimized assembly code using the Just In Time compiler, the script will also be optimal.

At time of writing, we note that an example of .NET scripting has been added to the DirectX 9c SDK. It will be interesting in future to see developers start to use this feature in games. The version in the SDK uses a different approach to ours, by creating an app domain inside the main binary, instead of calling an external COM interface; but the end result is the same—engine scripting with a trivial amount of code.

FX Composer IDE changes

Render Target Visualization

Version 1.0 of FX Composer used a fairly simple device model. For each window in the system, we simply allocated a new Direct3D device object. While this resulted in an easy separation between all the application's docking panels, it did cause some wasted resources. For example, when viewing a material with a render target associated, that target would be created in three different devices contexts. The texture would be used to generate the live material preview, to display it in the texture window, and to display it in the actual scene. We wanted to improve on this situation somewhat, but maintain the flexibility of the UI code. The solution we came up with was a parent device concept. Each parent device would manage a collection of windows, and each window would own an off-screen render target and z buffer. This enabled us to have a parent device for the main scene window, and a parent device for the materials window, but to have the texture panel share the resources of one or the other trivially. Not only did this save texture memory, but it enabled us to have the texture panel display render targets that the main scene was using. In FX Composer 1.0, it was only possible to view the render target associated with the preview material. While this was a very useful feature, developers asked that the main render window's targets should also be available for viewing. We achieved this with the bloom effect rendering to texture targets. The system is fully interactive, and it's possible to modify the main scene objects while watching the texture targets update. Switching between the material and the engine preview is achieved at the press of a button on the textures panel.

Improved Texture/Material Panel

The textures and materials panels give FX Composer real 3D views of objects in the system, such as materials and textures. This is a departure from typical 3D applications which have typically featured non-interactive materials. One of the successes of Version 1 was the material panel in particular, showing live previews of materials on real mesh objects.

We did want to improve the user interface of the texture panel and the material panel a great deal in Version 1.5. Due to time constraints, we implemented some obvious tweaks, but left the majority of the rework until Version 2. Additions in 1.5 include arbitrary zooming of materials/textures, and visualization of the color component channels in textures (red, green, blue, alpha). In particular alpha visualization was a common request for debugging shaders.

Properties Panel Updates

The properties panel has been one of the most complex and time consuming pieces of FX Composer to get right. As mentioned in our previous article, we used an MFC toolkit from BCG Software (*www.bcgsoft.com*). While their properties panel is powerful, it is difficult to extend, and we spent much time writing custom drawing code for UI widgets, and tracking down odd bugs—complicated by the dynamic nature of the updates in that panel. Two very common requests were satisfied by the new panel updates in 1.5, the first request being the ability to export the properties of a material to a file. The new save button on the properties panel will dump the list of properties to a standard xml format for easy parsing. This works for any object in the system with properties, not just the materials, and is a handy way to take a snapshot of current state.

The second most requested feature was for more flexible handling of property values. Developers often got frustrated when they inserted key frames accidentally and couldn't change them, or modified the default values in their .fx files but couldn't view the updates, since the material was remembering their preset property values across compiles. Two new buttons satisfy these needs. The first resets the current property values to the numbers in the .fx file, the second removes all the current key frames, leaving the value at key frame 0 alone.

In the future, we would like to provide a much more flexible user interface to control key frame values, but these quick fixes for Version 1.5 make life much easier for shader authors. This is an example of something that the engine can easily handle, but a user interface is not yet available to fully control it. We're confident moving forward that the existing engine is flexible and powerful enough to accommodate a more complete user interface in future versions.

Shader Perf Panel

A popular feature with developers on FX Composer 1.0 is the shader performance scheduler. In a nutshell, this panel gives the developer a way to see how many cycles a given shader will take to run on a given graphics architecture. The obvious addition for Version 1.5 was to build in scheduling for our NV4x architecture. This is a more complex problem than it may appear, since our scheduling information comes direct from the driver, and several libraries have to be compiled into FX Composer to make it work correctly. We added a tweak in Version 1.5 to make the cycle counts a little more accurate by trying to predict how long a texture fetch will take. The shader perf panel is a project on its own, and work continues to improve the data we give to developers.

DirectX Standard Semantics and Annotations

Background

When Microsoft created Direct3DX® Effects, it was designed to be as open and versatile as possible. They found that it served its purpose very well. In fact, they found developers using techniques and passes in ways we never anticipated. The design of Direct3DX® Effects spurred enormous creativity, but it lacked elements of structure needed to allow them to be easily shared. They saw many independent companies attempt to fill this void by creating their own incompatible system focused on their usage scenarios. The DirectX® Standard Annotations and Semantics (DXSAS) specification was designed by Microsoft, in collaboration with its partners, to inject into Direct3DX® Effects the context and instructions needed to drive a more general operating logic and data input mechanism. Furthermore, it enables custom effects to be used in digital content creation packages so that artists and developers can preview their shaders before their graphics engine is ever created.

How It Works

Application developers which write DirectX® Standard Annotations and Semantics (DXSAS) compliant software can take advantage of DXSAS enabled FX files to automatically understand how to apply an Effect. The DXSAS accomplish all of this through 3 major components: semantics, annotations, and scripts. Each of these are metadata in the shaders but are used by Direct3DX® and applications to provide instructions, data context, and comment.

Semantics

Direct3DX® Effects currently leverage semantics to tie geometry to shader inputs without requiring parameter naming conventions. Semantics can also be applied to parameters. This characteristic is leveraged by DXSAS to more clearly type data exposed external from the shader. It is even further clarified by annotations. Two examples include labelling a matrix as a world-view-projection transform and labelling a float4 a diffuse color:

```
float4x4 myTransform : WORLDVIEWPROJECTION;
float4 myColor : DIFFUSE;
```

DXSAS contains the most usable combinations of joint, world, view, projection, inverse, and transpose matrices along with standard lighting, coloring, and bounding definitions.

Annotations

Annotations are not required anywhere by the Direct3DX® Effect framework. DXSAS define annotations to expand semantics and provide additional data such as data-type characteristics, user interface, resource loading, scripting, etc. An example of an annotation might be a hint to associate a file with a texture type, which is defined as a string—"ResourceName":

```
texture myBumpMap
<
String ResourceName="bump.dds";
//…place additional annotations here…
>
```

The most important Annotations are:

```
String Object; // the object the parameter is bound too
String Frustum; // the frustum the view dependent parameter is bound
to
String Space; //define the space which the data should be represented
String Script; //define operating logic scoped by annotation place-
ment
```

Scripts

With shader sharing in mind (and without operating logic) the best a developer can do with an arbitrary Effect is to execute the first valid technique and each pass contained within. This is very limiting to an Effect developer. Scripts are something completely new to the Direct3DX® Effect framework due to DXSAS. They bring Effects to a new level of self-described operation and versatility. Scripts can not only expose standard materials, but magnificent post-processing effects such as high dynamic range, per-light shadow-buffers, and other complex connected shader networks without being tied directly to one application. The annotation script strings break down into a stream of statements where each statement is a command-value pair.

```
String Script= "command=value;";
```

Values are either strings or parameter names which provide the necessary data for that command. Values were designed to retrieve their data rather than being inline because it allows tools to generate UI interfaces so that artists may tweak the script at runtime. Some of the commands that DXSAS scripts expose are: loops, assigning render target, changing frustums, setting techniques and passes, drawing, and deferring operations to other effects in a shader network. As an example, the following script fragment is applied to a technique in an .fx file to implement a "bloom" effect, where a scene is downsampled into a render target, and an alpha channel used to apply a brightness bloom to the whole scene. The complete .fx file ships with FX Composer 1.5, and can be found at *MEDIA\HLSL\scene_bloom.fx.*

```
float std : StandardsGlobal <         //The DXSAS startup parameter
string ScriptClass = "scene";         //is it applied to the object
                                      // or scene?
string ScriptOrder = "postprocess";   //in what order?
string ScriptOutput = "color";        //What will be in the set
                                      // render targets?
string Script =                       //This is the main script!
"Technique=Glow;";                    //It sets the technique to
                                      // glow and runs it's script

> = 0.80; //version number

Technique Glow<
String Script=                        //This is the glow
                                      // technique's script!
"RenderColorTarget0=SceneMap;"        //It is hiding the default
                                      // render target
"RenderDepthStencilTarget=DepthBuffer;" //It is hiding the default
depth-stencil
"ClearSetColor=@farColor;"            //Prepare the default clear
                                      // color
"ClearSetDepth=@farDepth;"            //Prepare the default clear
                                      // depth
"Clear=Color0"                        //Clear the color
"Clear=Depth"                         //Clear the depth
"ScriptSignature0=color;"             //What do we expect in our
                                      // render targets?
"ScriptExternal=GlowDefaultRender;"   //Allow another shader to
                                      // render
"Pass=BlurGlowBuffer_Horz;"           //Set pass and jump to it's
                                      // script
"Pass=BlurGlowBuffer_Vert;"           //Set pass and jump to it's
                                      // script
"Pass=BlurGlow_Composite;";           //Set pass and jump to it's
                                      // script
float3 farColor= (0,0,0);             //this is a value being
                                      // fetched from the script
float farDepth= 1.0;>                 //this is a value being
                                      // fetched from the script
{
Pass BlurGlowBuffer_Horz<
String Script=                        //This is the pass's script!
"RenderColorTarget0=HBlurMap;"        //It will blur onto this
                                      // target
"Draw=Buffer;";>                      //Use D3D Draw call with a
                                      // full screen quad
{/*put device state here*/}
```

```
Pass BlurGlowBuffer_Vert<
String Script=                          //This is the pass's script!
"RenderColorTarget0=VBlurMap;"          //It will blur onto this
                                        // target
"Draw=Buffer;";>                        //Use D3D Draw call with a
                                        // full screen quad

{/*put device state here*/}
Pass BlurGlow_Composite<
String Script=                          //This is the pass's script!
"RenderColorTarget0=;"                  //It will blur onto the
                                        // default target
"RenderDepthStencilTarget=;"            //It will blur onto the
                                        // default depth-stencil
"Draw=Buffer;";>                        //Use D3D Draw call with a
                                        // full screen quad

{/*put device state here*/}
}
```

Standard Semantics and Annotations in FX Composer

To implement the DXSAS specification in FX Composer was a non-trivial task. Not only did we need to ensure that the engine understood all of the semantics and annotations, but we also had to worry about backwards compatibility with old effects, while ensuring that the 100+ effects we shipped all complied with the standard. On top of this, the Script support required a fundamental rethink about how the engine was implemented, in order to fully support it. With the Script extensions to .fx files, control over the order in which the rendering engine draws things is given over completely to the effect author. With our engine already in place, this change caused many headaches as we moved towards a solution that matched the specification, even as the specification itself was being refined.

We did have two advantages, which made our task a little easier:

- FX Composer 1.0 shipped based on a very early annotations and semantics specification. Although it was early, the basic layout was in place, and we modified the support right up until the end of the beta program to get as close as we could. We also implemented an XML file which contained a list of all the semantics and annotations that we supported, as well as flags to indicate if they were private to FX Composer or part of the up-coming specification. To ensure future compatibility, and to assist developers with mapping from their own standard semantics, we added an option to configuration XML called a "mapping." This enabled developers to add custom mapping from their internal semantic names to the ones that FX Composer understood.
- Seeing the need for a scripting language built into .fx files, we had already implemented a language to extend .fx file functionality. This support, dubbed "Scene

Commands," enabled users to add XML commands into the comments section of an .fx file. FX Composer would read this XML and use the material as a "scene" effect, essentially allowing it to control how the scene was drawn. This functionality took us a long way, and enabled some of our best effects. It was however a restrictive subset of what would become the DXSAS, so we still had work to do to move to this new format, while providing support for our legacy scene commands feature.

What we found as work progressed was that FX Composer's main rendering window interface became a thin wrapper around the device calls, with a little management, and the scripting engine took on more responsibility for controlling it. This enabled us to grow quite a powerful scripting engine which called a "generic" window interface. The window interface was implemented by the material and scene panel to make rendering of complex scene commands generic across the application windows. Note that "Script/DXSAS" support is not to be confused with FX Composer ".NET Scripting" support, but we have considered the possibility in future that the script execute engine could be controlled by a .NET script, enabling developers to tweak the engine support by supporting custom 'hints' within the FX Composer IDE. In DXSAS a "hint" is a command that is typically understood by a proprietary engine. In the future we may be able to let the developer design and implement their own hints using FX Composer, by giving them total control over the engine draw commands, but with the starting point of a full Script implementation in C#.

Conclusion

In FX Composer 1.5 we concentrated on building a layer of flexibility not seen in a shader development tool before. By concentrating on the emerging DXSAS standard, and working towards a very windows-friendly set of COM API's, we hope to continue to lay solid foundations for a tool that is here to stay. We hope that developers will think of FX Composer as their first stop to building .fx files that conform to a standard, and will build the necessary support into their engines so that this technology will work with no programmer interaction. In a utopian world of game development, an artist should, and we hope will, be able to download any conceivable effect for their game engine and start using it immediately in FX Composer or any other DCC tool.

Reference

[Maughan04] Maughan, Christopher, *The Design of FX Compose*, Addison-Wesley, 2004.

IMAGE SPACE

Introduction

Jason L. Mitchell

It is increasingly common for 3D games to apply 2D operations to rendered images in order to enhance or stylize their appearance. We refer to this 2D image domain as image space. In this section devoted to *image space,* we present six articles that expand on the current state of the art and illustrate the power of commercial 3D graphics accelerators to perform sophisticated image space operations.

In "A Steerable Streak Filter," Chris Oat describes the implementation of a steerable streak filter which can be used to create realistic or stylized light streak patterns. The key innovation is these filters can be steered so that they cause streaks in different directions depending upon where they appear on screen. This can be used to simulate diffraction effects such as the bent streaks that you see from an oncoming car's headlights shining through your own windshield when driving at night.

It is very common for game developers to apply some sort of simple blur filter to their scenes to increase the apparent brightness of very bright portions of the scene. This blur, however, should be a function of the actual image and hence should not remain the same size throughout the game. In "Adaptive Glare," Tiago Sousa describes an adaptive glare technique used in the game *Far Cry* which takes the unblurred contents of the scene into account when applying the image space bloom. This prevents overblurring in some scenes and to some extent simulates the human eye's accommodation to varying lighting conditions.

In the film world, individual shots are routinely post-processed in order to enhance the intended mood of the scene. This often amounts to applying an arbitrary transfer function to shift the image's colors in color space. Ronny Burkersroda describes in the article "Color Grading," a technique for performing color grading in real time using graphics hardware and also outlines a method for defining color grading functions in a way which is friendly to artists.

As we collectively move toward a more cinematic look in our real-time 3D applications, we must examine the properties of real physical cameras. One such property, which can be simulated fairly naturally with an image space approach, is depth of field. Thorsten Scheuermann and Natalya Tatarchuk present a number of improvements to previous real-time image-space depth of field implementations in "Improved Depth of Field Rendering."

Certain genres such as horror games like the *Resident Evil* series present 3D characters composited with a set of pre-rendered backdrops with a stationary camera. In such scenarios, it is possible to perform precomputation which enables an application to "relight" the scene later according the evolving game world. In "Lighting Precomputation Using the Relighting Map," Tien-Tsin Wong, Chi-Sing Leung, and Kwok-Hung Choy present an algorithm for relighting such scenes realistically.

In our final image space article "Shaderey—NPR Style Rendering," Aras Pranck-evičius presents a case study of a particular non-photorealistic renderer which performs many of its most important tasks in image space. This includes image space outlining and hatching as well as color space quantization to further provide a stylized illustrated look.

4.1

A Steerable Streak Filter

Chris Oat

Introduction

This article presents an image filtering technique for generating directional streaks across an image from light sources or bright reflections. This technique is based upon work done by Masaki Kawase for the XBox game *Double-S.T.E.A.L.* (called *Wreckless: The Yakuza Missions* outside of Japan) and described at CEDEC 2002 [Kawase02]. What makes our extension of this technique interesting is our use of a filter kernel which is *steerable* [Freeman91]. That is, the filter kernel can take on different shapes and orientations at different locations in the image in order to simulate diffraction or to further stylize the image.

Background

Anyone who has driven at night is probably familiar with how the light emitted from the headlights of oncoming traffic streaks across one's field of view, seeming to smear across the windshield itself. Imperfections in the car's windshield, frequently the result of windshield wipers scratching small grooves in the glass, scatters incoming light in a way that causes it to appear to flare out from its source [Nakamae90].

Light streaks are the result of light scattering as it passes through a lens or aperture. Cracks, scratches, grooves, dust, and lens imperfections cause light to scatter and diffract. Light has many opportunities to scatter as it travels from its source to the photoreceptors in the viewer's eye or a camera. Our eyelashes and even the eye's lens can diffract and scatter incoming light. The more intense the incoming light is relative to the surrounding ambient light level, the more perceivable the scattering will be. Because of this, light streaks are an important visual cue that help the viewer discern the relative brightness of light sources in comparison to their surroundings [Spencer95].

As shown in Figure 4.1.1, the amount of scattering and the orientation of the scattered light rays depend on the orientation and physical properties of the media through which the light is being transferred. Rather than simulate the complex light transport that results in light streaks (which would require computationally expensive ray tracing algorithms), we seek to mimic the perceivable end result using a postprocess image filter. Our method for replicating the perceivable effects of light streaking is an image space technique that relies on a steerable streak filter. This filter is intended to be applied to a rendered scene image and results in directional streaking of bright lights and reflections across the image. The results of the filter are composited back onto a rendered image before presenting the final result to the user.

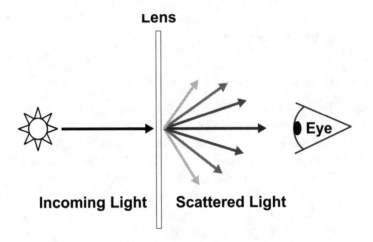

FIGURE 4.1.1   *Light scatters as it passes through glass. Surface imperfections in the glass determine in which direction light rays will scatter.*

Steerable Streak Filter

Like all image-space techniques, the streak filter uses multiple rendering passes that each draw a full screen quad to an off-screen render target using various renderable textures as input. Figure 4.1.2 illustrates the high-level algorithm for applying the streak filter to a rendered scene.

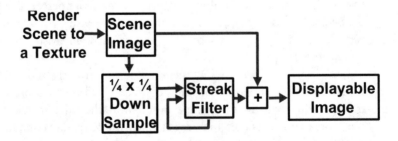

FIGURE 4.1.2   *Applying the streak filter to a rendered scene: Render scene to a texture, down sample, iterate the streak filter several times, composite streaks back onto scene image and then finally display the composite image.*

We begin by rendering the scene to an off-screen render target that we call the "scene image." Next, the scene image is downsampled using a box filter. This downsampling step reduces the number of pixels that will subsequently be processed by the streak filter, thus increasing performance. As a side effect, the streaks will be slightly more blurred, which is generally desirable. The first pass of the steerable streak filter takes the downsampled scene image as input and renders into an additional off-screen buffer. The streak filter works by "ping-ponging" between two off-screen buffers. That is, one buffer is used as input while the other is used as output. After each iteration of the filter, the roles of these off-screen ping-pong buffers switch (what was previously the input buffer becomes the new output buffer, etc.). Thus, the results of one iteration of the filter may be used as the input for the next iteration of the filter. Each pass may be thought of as a progressive refinement that increases the smoothness and length of the streaks. The filter kernel shape and sample weights change slightly for each iteration.

First Pass

As shown in Figure 4.1.3, the kernel operates on four samples from the downsampled scene image.

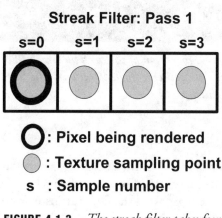

FIGURE 4.1.3 *The streak filter takes four samples, one sample at the location of the pixel being rendered and three additional samples in the direction of the streak.*

The first sample is taken at the screen location of the pixel being rendered. Three additional samples are taken from neighboring pixels. The neighboring pixel locations are determined according to the orientation of the streak. Each neighboring sample is weighted and attenuated according to its sample number, a constant attenuation and the pass number.

$$weight = a^{(b*s)}$$

$$a = attenuation = [0.9, 0.95]$$

$$b = 4^{(pass-1)}$$

$$s = sample\_number$$

The attenuation is a constant term that may be tweaked to adjust the strength of the streaks. Generally, an attenuation term in the range 0.9 to 0.95 gives reasonable results. The term b above is the screen space distance between sample points, for each pass of the filter the sample points are taken further from the pixel being rendered. Figure 4.1.4 illustrates the progression of the streak filter for multiple passes.

FIGURE 4.1.4   *Progression of the steerable streak filter. (left) The scene image. (middle) Intermediate results after a single iteration of the filter. (right) Results from two iterations of the streak filter.*

Second Pass

For each pass of the filter, the kernel is expanded in the direction of the streak. Figure 4.1.5 illustrates the shape of the streak filter's kernel during the second pass of the filter.

Each successive pass of the filter further expands the kernel in the direction of the streak. The kernel expands by sampling increasingly distant neighbors. For a given pass, the distance between neighbors is specified by the term b. As you can see, the overall size of the kernel grows for each pass. For a given pass, the distance between neighbor samples is equal to the size of the kernel from the previous pass (the squared distance from the previous pass). While each pass uses an increasingly larger kernel than the previous pass, the individual sample weights decrease as their distance from the pixel being rendered increases. Frequently, only two passes are necessary to achieve acceptable results. Of course, this is dependent on the resolution of the source image and the size of the streaks you wish to generate.

So far, our streak filter only streaks in a single direction as specified by the 2D per-pixel streak orientation vector (sampled from the streak orientation texture).

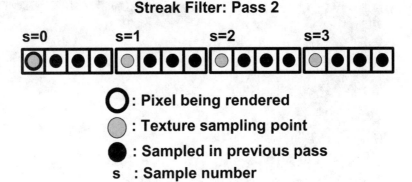

FIGURE 4.1.5 *The second pass of the streak filter expands the kernel in the direction of the streak. Four samples are taken, one at the location of the pixel being rendered and three additional samples at every fourth neighboring pixel in the direction of the streak.*

Applying this process in only a single direction results in streaks with only a single "radial arm." For a more interesting effect with several streak directions, the multi-pass streak filter must be executed several times (one execution for each per-pixel streak direction). When applying the streak filter multiple times for multiple streak directions, it is important to keep a clean version of the down-sampled scene image around. If you reuse the downsampled scene image as one of the ping-pong render targets, then you won't have the original downsampled scene image to use for the next application of the streak filter. Since each application of the streak filter requires multiple passes, the number of streak filter applications should be kept small. For most scenes, four applications of the streak filter should produce reasonable results (4 streaks × 2 passes per streak = 8 passes total).

Streak Direction

As mentioned earlier, the important property of our extension to Kawase's streak filter is steerability. Our filter kernel may be oriented on a per-pixel basis, allowing us to vary the direction in which the streaks will radiate. Streak orientation may be specified on a per-pixel basis by sampling an orientation texture. The orientation texture may correspond to the surface properties of a scratched windshield or some other scattering media. Orientation vectors are packed into a texture by placing vector components into the color channels of each texel. The streak orientation texture will be screen aligned and sampled during each pass of the streak filter. Because we are working in image space, only 2D streak directions are needed. Thus, only two channels of the streak orientation texture are needed to store orientations. The remaining channels may be used to store such things as transparency masks or per-pixel streak attenuation values. Figure 4.1.6 illustrates two possible streak orientation textures.

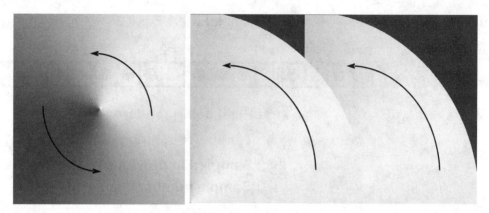

FIGURE 4.1.6   *2D streak orientations are stored in the red and green channels of a texture. (Left) A circular streak orientation texture. (Right) A streak orientation texture that mimics scratches that windshield wipers leave on a car's windshield.*

To save texture memory, it may be desirable to only store a single streak orientation texture even if you wish to apply the streak filter multiple times for multiple streaks. A single streak orientation texture may be reused for each successive application of the streak filter by rotating the streak orientation vector by some fixed amount for each application of the streak filter. For example, if four streaks per-pixel are desired, the streak filter algorithm must be applied four times, each time the per-pixel streak direction should be rotated by 90 degrees. Streak directions are 2D vectors in screen space so rotating them is simply a matter of rotating about the z axis (the axis perpendicular to the screen). Each application of the streak filter will produce streaks oriented in slightly different directions. These streaked images may then be composited back onto the scene image. Figure 4.1.7 demonstrates four applications of the streak filter, rotating the per-pixel streak direction by 90 degrees each time and blending the results of each application.

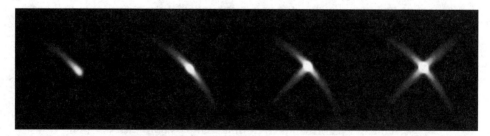

FIGURE 4.1.7   *The streak filter is applied four times to the same scene image (progressing from left to right). Each application of the streak filter rotates the streak direction by 90 degrees and the results of each application of the filter are blended to create a final composite with four streak directions.*

Pixel Shader

Implementing the streak filter is simply a matter of writing some pixel shader code to compute the sample points and weights. The streak filter is implemented here as an HLSL function and may be called from a pixel shader. It is assumed that the caller of this function has sampled the streak orientation texture and will determine the attenuation value.

```
#define NUM_SAMPLES 4
float3 SteerableStreakFilter (sampler tSource, float2 texCoord,
                              float2 pxSize, float2 dir,
                              float attenuation, int pass)
{
   float2 sampleCoord = 0;
   float3 cOut = 0;

   // sample weight = a^(b*s)
   // a = attenuation
   // b = 4^(pass-1)
   // s = sample number

   float b = pow(NUM_SAMPLES, pass);

   for (int s = 0; s < NUM_SAMPLES; s++)
   {
      float weight = pow(attenuation, b * s);

   // dir = per-pixel, 2D orientation vector
      sampleCoord = texCoord + (dir * b * float2(s,s) * pxSize);
      cOut += saturate(weight) * tex2D (tSource, sampleCoord);
   }

   return saturate (cOut);
}
```

Results

The steerable streak filter was used to produce the image shown in Figure 4.1.8. Headlight geometry was drawn into a scene image and then downsampled using a standard box filter. A two-pass streak filter was applied four times to produce four streaks radiating from the headlights. The streak orientation was specified using the streak orientation texture (from Figure 4.1.6) that mimics the scratches in a car's windshield. As you can see, the four radial arms of the streaks caused by the two headlights are oriented differently. Some of the radial arms are even bending according to the grooves in the car's windshield as encoded in the streak orientation texture.

FIGURE 4.1.8 *The steerable streak filter was used to streak the headlights of oncoming traffic in this image.*

Conclusion

This article presented a steerable streak filter that can be used to simulate the diffraction of light caused by windshields, lens apertures, and even our eyelashes. Light streaks are a popular stylistic element and can be an important visual cue for perceiving the relative brightness of a light source such as the approaching headlights of oncoming traffic as seen through a car's windshield. A major advantage of this filter is that it can be oriented on a per-pixel basis via a streak orientation texture.

References

[Freeman91] William T. Freeman and Edward H. Adelson, "The Design and Use of Steerable Filters," IEEE Trans. Pattern Analysis and Machine Intelligence, 13:891–906, 1991.

[Kawase02] Masaki Kawase. "Double-S.T.E.A.L Techniques," CEDEC 2002. *http://www.daionet.gr.jp/~masa/column/2002-09-22.html.*

[Nakamae90] Eihachiro Nakamae, Kasufumi Kaneda, Takashi Ocamotoand Tomoyuki Nishita, "A Lighting Model Aiming at Drive Simulators," SIGGRAPH 1990, pp. 395–404.

[Spencer95] Greg Spencer, Peter Shirley, Kurt Zimmerman, Donald P. Greenberg, "Physically-Based Glare Effects for Digital Images," SIGGRAPH 1995, pp. 325–334.

4.2

Adaptive Glare

Tiago Sousa

Introduction

As indicated by the number of image-space articles in this book and its predecessors, scene post-processing effects are fast becoming commonplace in games. Glare effects, also referred to as *glow* or *bloom*, are achieved through image post-processing techniques in order to produce a color bleeding effect around the brightest pixels in a scene. This is both an interesting stylistic element and a subtle but important cue to the user that conveys information about the relative brightness of different areas of an image. The technique described in this article is implemented in Crytek's CryEngine and used in the popular game *Far Cry*, as shown in Figure 4.2.1, and Color Plate 6.

FIGURE 4.2.1   *CryEngine screenshot, featuring the game Far Cry. CryENGINE © 2004 Crytek. All Rights Reserved. Far Cry © 2004 Crytek. All Rights Reserved. Published by UbiSoft Entertainment. Trademarks belong to their respective owners.*

In this article, we will discuss the implementation details of an inexpensive adaptive glare technique. The technique relies upon only 1.1 pixel shaders and hence may be performed on most mainstream gaming PCs and game consoles. Besides being inexpensive to execute, the technique is adaptive, which means that the threshold for what is considered "bright" in a given image can vary according to the brightness of the scene.

Overview

Before diving into the implementation details, it is important to understand the overall strategy of this image post-processing technique. A number of intermediate images will be generated and processed as shown in Figure 4.2.2.

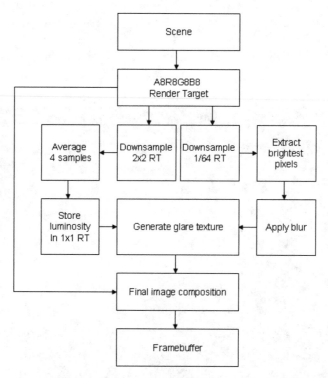

FIGURE 4.2.2   *Overview of adaptive glare implementation steps.*

The initial input to this process is our rendered scene. This can be generated by doing a StretchRect operation from the back buffer to a texture of the same size or by rendering the scene directly into a texture. In either case, this initial image is the same size as the back buffer and is stored in an RGBA texture with 8 bits per channel.

This input texture is resized into two other textures, a very small 2×2 texture and another which is 1/64 the size of the back buffer. This small 2×2 texture will be further downsampled to 1×1 in order to compute a single value for the average luminance of the scene. From the 1/64-sized texture, the brightest pixels will be blurred. This blurred texture will be composited with the initial scene image, including effects from the average luminance.

Adaptive Glare Algorithm

As mentioned above, there are two main textures required to implement this effect: the *luminance texture* and the *glare texture*.

Luminance

The luminance texture is generated by performing a `StretchRect` from the original scene image into a 2×2 texture. This 2×2 texture is further downsampled to 1×1 and converted to a single scalar luminance value as shown in Figure 4.2.3. Naturally, all of these operations are performed on the GPU in order to avoid any CPU intervention.

(a) Original scene texture

(b) Scene scaled to 2×2

(c) Scene luminance

FIGURE 4.2.3 *Luminance computation.*

This single average luminance is computed by the GPU in a pixel shader by rendering a screen-aligned quadrilateral into the 1×1 luminance texture from the intermediate 2×2 texture. The shader samples the intermediate 2×2 texture four times using pick-nearest filtering. The samples use texture coordinates which have been offset by 0.5 in the vertex program:

```
OUT.Tex0.xy = IN.TexCoord0.xy + vTexOffset01.xy;
OUT.Tex1.xy = IN.TexCoord0.xy + vTexOffset01.zw;
OUT.Tex2.xy = IN.TexCoord0.xy + vTexOffset02.xy;
OUT.Tex3.xy = IN.TexCoord0.xy + vTexOffset02.zw;
```

where:

```
vTexOffset01.xyzw = ( -0.5, -0.5 , -0.5, 0.5)
vTexOffset02.xyzw = ( 0.5, -0.5, 0.5, 0.5)
```

In the pixel shader, these four samples are averaged and converted to luminance:

```
// average color samples
float3 vAvgColor = saturate(vColor01.xyz * 0.25 +
                            vColor02.xyz * 0.25 +
                            vColor03.xyz * 0.25 +
                            vColor04.xyz * 0.25);

// only output luminance
OUT.Color.xyz = dot(float3(0.3, 0.59, 0.11), vAvgColor.xyz);

// glare amount interpolation value
OUT.Color.w = vGlareAmountLerp.w;
```

These four samples could also be automatically averaged using a single sample with bilinear filtering, saving some instructions in the pixel shader. In order to smooth out the luminance over time and avoid popping, this result is blended with the luminance of the previous frame. The blending ratio can be tuned to various values depending on the desired effect.

Glare

Now that we have computed a single luminance value for the scene and blended it with the running luminance from the previous frames, we can compute the *glare texture*. The first step in computing this texture is downsampling the original scene image to an extremely low resolution texture with 1/64 of the original resolution (1/8 in height and 1/8 in width). This can be done by using the StretchRect API or by manually rendering a screen-aligned quadrilateral and performing the filtering in a pixel shader. From this 1/64-sized texture, the brightest pixels are extracted using a simple thresholding operation.

```
// remove low-luminance colors
float3 vFinalGlare = saturate(vGlareColor.xyz - vGlareParams.xyz)
                     * vGlareParams.w;

// modulate brightest pixels by inverse luminance
OUT.Color.xyz = vFinalGlare.xyz *(1- vGlareAmount.w);
```

where:

- vGlareColor is the current glare texture
- vGlareParams.xyz is the threshold value (0.4 is usually a good value)
- vGlareParams.w is the maximum user defined amount of glare
- vGlareAmount is the luminance

After this thresholded image is computed, a simple blur operation is performed, resulting in a glare texture like the one shown in Figure 4.2.4(c).

(a) Original scene texture   (b) Thresholded image   (c) Blurred glare texture

FIGURE 4.2.4 *Glare texture creation steps.*

Final Image Composition

In our final step, we will composite the glare texture over the original scene image. A simple approach would be to just add the glare texture to the original scene image. In this case, care must be taken when generating the glare texture or the scene can end up looking extremely bright in some situations. To avoid this, the threshold could be adjusted according to the precomputed ambient lighting in the current sector/scene, but this will depend on the game engine structure. A more robust method of compositing the glare texture with the original scene image is to make the glare contribution proportional to the luminance of the pixel in the original scene image. Composing the final image this way will display a visible but subtle glare on low-luminance pixels, avoiding the extremely bright cases.

```
// Compute scene with full glare
float3 vFinalGlareColor = saturate(vGlareColor.xyz +
                                    vScreenColor.xyz);

// Compute scene luminance
float  fLum = dot(vScreenColor.xyz, float3(0.3, 0.59, 0.11));

// Interpolate between current scene and scene with full glare
OUT.Color.xyz = saturate(vScreenColor.xyz*(1-fLum) +
                        vFinalGlareColor.xyz*fLum );
```

For yet another look, it is possible to combine the glare texture with the original scene image using the following inverse multiplication operation:

```
vFinalGlareColor = saturate(vGlareColor.xyz + vScreenColor.xyz –
                        vGlareColor.xyz * vScreenColor.xyz);
```

Minimizing Artifacts

Simply using the `StretchRect` API to perform many of the downsampling operations in this algorithm is prone to artifacts on high-frequency scenes since not enough filtering is performed. This can lead to wild variations in the luminance computation and flickering as the scene changes or the user's view changes. An alternative method which minimizes this problem is to first resize the original scene image into a low-resolution texture (128 × 128 or less) and generate mipmaps all the way down to 1 × 1. This will create a more accurate and stable luminance result but is more costly than the method outlined in this article.

Further Improvements

One of the goals of any kind of glare effect is to approximate the look of high-dynamic range rendering. Once we do have access to real-time high-dynamic range rendering, it will possible to use this luminance computation technique to dynamically control the tone mapping step in the high-dynamic range rendering process.

Sample Application

A sample application is available in the companion CD-ROM. The sample application uses a very simple scene showing three brightly colored teapots inside an opened dark cube as shown in Figure 4.2.5. This is done so that you can easily see the result of the adaptive glare when moving from inside to outside of the cube. The mouse and the W and S keys can be used to move the camera. F1 enables the glare effect described in this article while F2 disables it.

FIGURE 4.2.5   *Adaptive glare demo.*

Conclusion

The article presented an empirical technique to achieve a well-behaved and natural looking glare effect. The final post-processed image contains a subtle glare which adjusts smoothly based upon the luminance of the rendered scene. This technique is currently being used in Crytek's CryEngine, which is used by the recent popular game *Far Cry*.

Acknowledgments

Special thanks to Wolfgang Engel for his great help and patience in reviewing and suggesting ways to improve this article. Thanks also to Martin Mittring and Carsten Wenzel for reviewing the article and suggesting ideas for higher quality image compositing and artifact minimization. Also, special thanks to Márcio Martins for reviewing the article and providing the model loader used in the sample application.

Additional References

[Kawase03] Masaki Kawase, "Frame Buffer Post-processing Effects in Double-S.T.E.A.L," GDC 2003.

[Kawase04] Masaki Kawase, "Practical Implementation of High-dynamic Range Rendering," GDC 2004.

[Vlachos03] Alex Vlachos, Greg James, "Special Effects with DirectX 9," GDC 2003.

4.3

Color Grading

Ronny Burkersroda

Introduction

Color grading is an image space technique which can be used to adjust the look or visual atmosphere of a rendered image by applying a function to it after it is rendered. This function can be defined in any number of ways from simple gamma curves to arbitrary functions in 3D lookup tables. Color grading is a standard part of the film-making process that allows directors to tune colors shot-by-shot in post-production to achieve a desired visual feel. In this chapter, we will present a means for performing color grading on real-time scenes so that game developers can also employ this technique to enhance the visual feel of their games.

Mapping Colors to Colors

A simple way to define a function which maps input colors to output colors is a gamma curve (one curve each for red, green, and blue). This kind of function is being used in every game running today in order to map the rendered frame buffer's colors to the proper gamut for transmission to a display such as a computer monitor. Such curves are useful, but limited in their expressiveness when performing color grading to achieve a dramatic look (see Figure 4.3.1).

Another alternative would be to use post-processing to apply color grading using a pixel shader to evaluate a more sophisticated mapping function than a simple gamma curve. Such implementations can be costly, however, since these functions can be expensive to evaluate over and over again for each pixel in the input image. Such functions are also not easily implemented on older shader hardware which has only ps.1.x support.

In this article, we will pre-calculate our color grading functions and store them in a lookup table that we will implement using a volume texture. This not only reduces the post-processing cost to a simple lookup, but also allows us to easily combine different color grading functions together if we choose to do so to obtain a particular look.

Since our goal is to map an 8-bit per channel RGB input color to a 32-bit output color, there are 256^3 possible input colors and each texel in the volume texture will contain 32 bits. This results in a 64 MB volume texture. Using a texture of this size in order to support color grading would be prohibitively expensive for most games, even on the most high-end graphics cards. Of course, since we are using texture mapping hardware to implement our lookup table, we can take advantage of filtering and compression to reduce the size of the table we need to store in memory. By using a DXT1

(a) The original scene, which has a very warm tone

(b) The scene graded a cold atmosphere using the algorithm described in this chapter

(c) A sepia-graded image

(d) An experimental grading operation

FIGURE 4.3.1 *Various color-graded images of a screenshot from a bowling-like game developed by Media Seasons in Leipzig, Germany. Note the variety of looks that are achievable. Note also that the GUI is not affected by the grading.* © *2004 Media Seasons.*

format texture instead of the 32-bit color format, we could store the 256^3 texture in just 8 MB. Alternatively, we could decrease the texture size to 64^3 and use trilinear filtering for the volume map to interpolate between the 64 steps along each dimension. This 32 bit 64^3 texture takes up only 1 MB. Of course, both compression and downsizing of the lookup table can decrease the quality of the color grading function. Because of the relative simplicity of our mapping functions, however, we find that trilinear filtering the samples from the 64^3 volume texture provides acceptable results, giving us a good balance of performance, memory usage and quality. In fact, for a cartoon effect, it is possible to use an even smaller volume texture with point sampling as shown in Figure 4.3.2.

FIGURE 4.3.2 *Using a low-resolution volume map and point sampling results in a toon effect.*
© 2004 Media Seasons.

Implementation

Now that we have introduced our strategy for mapping input colors to output colors, we will describe our color grading implementation in detail.

Color Grading Texture

Naturally, the first step in implementing color grading is filling the volume texture with a table that maps input colors to output colors. If you intend to update this table frequently, the texture should be created in the default pool with the dynamic flag. The texture can be calculated in the application or loaded from a pre-calculated dataset.

The `D3DXFillVolumeTexture()` and `D3DXFillVolumeTextureTX()` routines are useful when evaluating the functions in the application at load time, but care must be taken with the texture coordinates which are passed to the fill routine. Because the texture coordinates passed to the fill routine are located at texel centers, the input values will vary not between 0 and 1 but between *texel size / 2* and *1 − texel size / 2*, where *texel size* is *1 / texture size*.

`D3DXCreateVolumeTextureFrom[…]` functions are able to load previously stored volumes from DDS files. To store a texture to such a `DirectDraw Surface` file on disk in the first place, the convenient `D3DXSaveTextureToFile[…]` functions can be used.

Scene Texture

Like any of the post-processing techniques discussed in this book, we must start with our rendered scene in a texture map. This can be done by rendering directly into the texture or by using the `StretchRect()` API to copy the scene image from the back buffer into a texture map. While this second option requires an additional step, it is preferable because the `StretchRect()` operation is very fast and because rendering the scene into the back buffer allows the use of multisample antialiasing, which should be used by all modern 3D applications.

Now that we have both the color grading texture and the scene texture, we will perform the color grading operation by drawing a screen-aligned quadrilateral into another texture, just like any of the other image space techniques described in this book.

ps.1.1

When using a 1.1 pixel shader, the scene texture must be set to stage 0 and the volume texture must be set at least to stage three because a sampled color cannot be used directly as a texture coordinate. The shader instruction `texm3x3tex` performs a multiplication of the sampled color with a 3×3 matrix. The first two rows are multiplied by `texm3x3pad` and `texm3x3tex` multiplies the third row before sampling the graded color. Every row is a 3D dot product that results in one component of the volume texture coordinate:

$$u' = \mathbf{T_1} \cdot \mathbf{C}$$
$$v' = \mathbf{T_2} \cdot \mathbf{C}$$
$$w' = \mathbf{T_3} \cdot \mathbf{C}$$

where $\mathbf{T_x}$ is the texture coordinate at stage x

$\mathbf{C}$ is the source color with the three channels as components

u', v' and w' are components of the resulting 3D texture coordinate $\mathbf{T'}$

The resulting texture coordinate, $\mathbf{T'}$, is used to sample the graded color from our 3D lookup table. Because we want to simply use C_r as u', C_g as v' and C_b as w' we use a 3×3 identity matrix where $\mathbf{T_1}$ is (1, 0, 0), $\mathbf{T_2}$ is (0, 1, 0) and $\mathbf{T_3}$ is (0, 0, 1). The resulting pixel shader is shown in Listing 4.3.1.

Listing 4.3.1   Color Grading with Pixel Shader 1.1

```
ps_1_1                    ; declaration of required pixel shader version

tex        t0             ; load original color
texm3x3pad t1, t0         ; calculate x-component of the look-up vector
texm3x3pad t2, t0         ; calculate y-component
texm3x3tex t3, t0         ; calculate z-component and sample color

mov        r0, t3         ; output graded color value
```

After the declaration of the shader version, the original color is loaded from the screen texture into `t0`. Then this register is dotted with the three input $\mathbf{T_x}$ vectors (`t1-t3`) which contain our 3×3 identity matrix. The three resulting scalar values are used as a 3D texture coordinate to sample the graded color into `t3`. Finally, this color is copied into `r0`, which is used as output of the pixel shader.

ps.1.4

Using pixel shader version 1.4 is much easier because the original color can be directly used as texture coordinate without having to multiply by an identity matrix. In this pixel shader, the screen texture is set to stage one and the volume map to stage zero. The original color is loaded from the scene texture into a temporary register, r1, in the first phase. In the second phase, r1 is used as a 3D texture coordinate to do a dependent look up from the volume texture to obtain our final graded color.

Listing 4.3.2   Color Grading with Pixel Shader 1.4

```
ps_1_4              ; declaration of required pixel shader version

texld   r1, t1    ; load original color

phase               ; set phase to enable registers as source for texld

texld   r0, r1    ; load graded color
```

ps.2.0

A pixel shader of version 2.0 and higher needs to declare all input registers and samplers. As a result, the first three instructions of this shader declare the screen aligned texture coordinates, the 2D scene texture sampler and the volume color grading sampler. After these declarations, the original color is loaded and used as a texture coordinate to look up the final color from the volume color grading texture. Finally, this color is copied to the output color register. The partial precision modifier _pp is used for several of the instructions because it can run faster on some hardware and the full precision is not needed for most operations in this very simple shader.

Listing 4.3.3   Color Grading with Pixel Shader 2.0

```
ps_2_0                      ; declaration of required pixel shader version

dcl         t0            ; texture coordinate
dcl_2d      s0.rgb        ; sampler for original color from 2D image
dcl_volume  s1.rgb        ; sampler for graded color from volume map
texld_pp    r0, t0, s0    ; load original color

texld_pp    r1, r0, s1    ; load graded color
mov_pp      oC0, r1       ; output graded color value
```

As you can see, the ps.1.4 and ps.2.0 versions are both very simple and will map to identical operations on ps.2.0-capable hardware. As a result, you may prefer to just use the ps.1.4 version and to switch to the ps.1.1 version only for older ps.1.1 hardware.

Defining the Color Grading Function

Now that you know how to use a color grading lookup texture in your application, how might you go about defining the color grading function in the first place? More importantly, how might you allow your artists to do it in an intuitive way? For best results, it always pays to stick with tools that artists already know. We have found it is useful to have artists take an in-game screenshot rendered with the engine and manipulate the colors in their favorite image editing tool until they have achieved the desired color-graded look. Then, using both the input reference screenshot and the manipulated result, we are able to determine a function which maps from one to the other by filling in our volume texture according to the mapping from the input image to the graded image.

Partially Grading a Frame

To grade only parts of a scene, it is possible to use the stencil buffer to mask off various regions of the screen while rendering the scene. This can be used to apply different color-grading functions to different regions of the scene or to prevent color grading altogether, as was done for the GUI in Figure 4.3.1. For every group of objects that should be adjusted by a particular color grading function, we set the pixels of the stencil buffer to one unique value by setting `D3DRS_STENCILPASS` to `D3DSTEN-CILOP_REPLACE` and setting `D3DRS_STENCILREF` to the unique value when we do our initial scene rendering. In the post-processing phase, we perform one color grading pass for each different color grading function we wish to use. On each of these passes, we set `D3DRS_STENCILREF` to the appropriate value set `D3DRS_STENCILFUNC` to `D3DCMP_EQUAL`.

Sample Code

ON THE CD

The companion CD-ROM contains a library which can be included in any Direct3D 9 project, allowing you to add color grading to your projects very quickly and easily.

Conclusion

We have described a real-time color grading algorithm which will allow you to infuse your game with more visual atmosphere at a very low cost. The approach easily fits into any engine which is already doing any kind of image space post-processing and is scalable all the way down to first generation shader hardware. In addition to the algorithm itself, we have presented an intuitive method that allows artists to fine-tune color-grading functions themselves using tools they already use every day.

4.4

Improved Depth-of-Field Rendering

Thorsten Scheuermann and Natalya Tatarchuk

Introduction

Computer graphics provides the means to mimic the reality of the world on a computer screen. Certain visual cues have traditionally been particularly difficult to approximate accurately in real time due to the complexity of calculations necessary to create these effects. Good approximations of depth of field have been limited to the domain of the film industry, considered too expensive to compute correctly in real-time environments.

The physical properties of real-world camera lenses cause parts of a scene at certain depths to appear blurry, while maintaining sharpness in other areas. While this blurriness can be thought of as an imperfection or an undesirable artifact, it can also be used as a tool to provide valuable visual cues and guide a viewer's attention to important parts of a scene. In fact, it is an accepted part of the visual vocabulary of photography and cinematography that we are constantly consuming in photographs, television, and movies. Photographers and cinematographers frequently use this effect to provide emphasis or to convey a particular emotion in a scene.

Current graphics APIs do not support physical camera models directly and hence we cannot create depth-of-field effects without some additional work. Fortunately, using the latest crop of graphics chips and their powerful shaders, we can achieve convincing depth-of-field in real time. This article explains an extension of an approach to calculate depth-of-field efficiently using programmable graphics hardware. Previously, two techniques for calculating depth-of-field effects in real-time were described in detail in [Riguer03].

The first approach utilized a new DirectX 9 feature called *multiple render targets* (MRTs), which is the ability to output data to multiple render targets simultaneously. This feature was used to output color, depth information, and a blurriness factor to two render targets during scene rendering. In a subsequent image space step, the depth-of-field effect was applied by post-processing the rendered image with a Poisson disk blur filter.

The second approach rendered the scene at full resolution to an offscreen buffer, outputting depth information for each pixel into the alpha channel of that buffer. After downsampling the image, a Gaussian blur filter was applied. Finally the original scene rendering was blended with the downsampled blurred image based on the depth of each pixel from a specified focal plane.

While both methods generated reasonably convincing effects, we found that both of these approaches lacked a convenient way for artists to set the actual depth range for the depth-of-field effect in a given scene. Additionally, the first technique also tended to display aliasing artifacts for large blur kernels, and the second technique did not handle blurring of objects close to the camera. In order to make depth-of-field truly usable in a game environment, artists must have intuitive control over the effect's parameters. This article describes an improvement to the two depth-of-field approaches explained in [Riguer03], combining ideas from both techniques to create an improved depth-of-field technique. We will describe an image-space algorithm for generating a depth-of-field effect in real time by first rendering the scene's degree of focus into the destination alpha channel and subsequently performing image processing and compositing on the rendered result.

Figure 4.4.1 shows an example of the depth-of-field effect being used in ATI's demo *Ruby: The DoubleCross*.

FIGURE 4.4.1   *A screenshot of ATI's RADEON X800 launch demo* Ruby: The Double-Cross, *showcasing the depth-of-field technique.* © *ATI Technologies 2004.*

Camera Models

Pinhole Camera Model

Real-time graphics applications typically use a pinhole camera model for projecting the 3D scene on the screen. In this model, light scattered from the environment needs to pass through an infinitely small hole to hit the image plane, as shown in Figure 4.4.2. For each point in the scene, the hole will let exactly one light ray pass, which results in a projected image that is always in perfect focus.

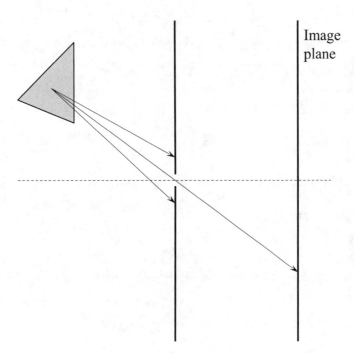

Image plane

FIGURE 4.4.2 *Pinhole camera model.*

Thin Lens Camera Model

Lenses in real-world cameras have finite dimensions so that from each point in the scene, a whole ray bundle can pass through them. The ray bundle is refracted through the camera lens which refocuses the rays at a certain distance from the lens. If the rays are refocused on the image plane, the point will be in focus. Otherwise the cone of refracted light rays will intersect the image plane in an area that is approximated by a circle called the circle of confusion (CoC). Figure 4.4.3 illustrates how the thin-lens camera model works. The parameters used in the thin-lens camera model are the focal length f, the lens aperture number (or f-stop) a, and the focal distance d_{focus}.

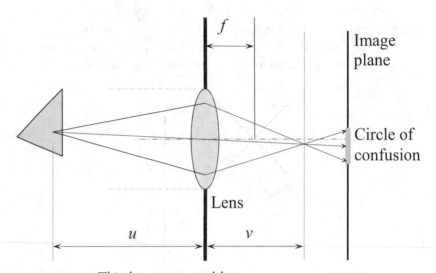

FIGURE 4.4.3   *Thin-lens camera model.*

The relationship between f, the distance u of a point from the camera lens, and the distance v behind the lens at which its image is in focus is described by the thin-lens equation:

$$\frac{1}{u} + \frac{1}{v} = \frac{1}{f} \tag{4.4.1}$$

[Potmesil81] provides a formula for computing the CoC diameter for a point at distance d from the camera:

$$coc = \left| \frac{fd}{d-f} - \frac{fd_{focus}}{d_{focus} - f} \right| \left(\frac{d-f}{ad} \right) \tag{4.4.2}$$

The solid line in Figure 4.4.4 represents the CoC diameter as computed by Equation 4.4.2 as a function of distance from the camera. We will discuss the dotted-line approximation to this curve later in the article.

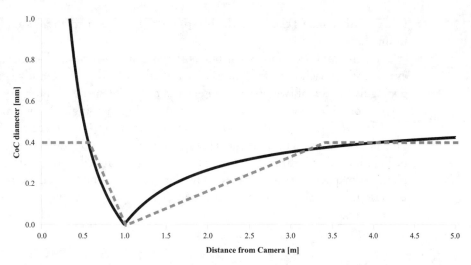

FIGURE 4.4.4 *The circle of confusion diameter plotted over camera distance (Camera parameters: f = 35mm, a = 2.4, d$_{focus}$ = 1m) is shown in comparison to our piecewise linear approximation.*

Scene Rendering

The first rendering pass of our approach renders the scene into a texture the size of the screen. In addition to rendering color data, the destination alpha channel is filled with a special value that controls the amount of blurriness for each pixel and contains information about the depth of a given pixel in the scene. This information is required in the depth-of-field post-processing pass.

The first approach described in [Riguer03] used MRTs to store depth information along with a separate blurriness factor. We designed a technique to use a single render target to output all necessary information, reducing memory consumption and eliminating the need to use MRTs.

Depth and Blurriness Representation

When looking at an image exhibiting depth-of-field, it is practically impossible to tell exactly how blurry a particular spot on the image should appear. We can take advantage of this by simplifying the representation of the blurriness over distance from the camera, as long as the main features are preserved. We parameterize our representation using the maximum blurriness coc_{max} that can be applied to the image and the distance of three planes from the camera. Objects on the focal plane (distance d_{focus}) are in perfect focus while objects in front of a near blur plane or behind a far blur plane (distances d_{near} and d_{far}) are maximally blurred. We use an additional parameter (*clamp*$_{far}$) that allows clamping the blurriness of far objects to a fraction of the maximum blur.

It is important to notice that our post-processing algorithm does not require the exact depth of each pixel for a satisfactory depth-of-field effect. Simply being able to distinguish which of two pixels is closer to camera is adequate. This observation is the key for combining depth and blurriness information in a single channel for output.

Using d_{near}, d_{focus}, and d_{far}, we can define *relative depth* as a piecewise linear mapping of camera depth into the [-1, 1] range, as illustrated in Figure 4.4.5. The distance of all points on or in front of the near blur plane are mapped to -1, points on the focal plane are mapped to 0, and points on the far blur plane and beyond are mapped to 1. Because the function is monotonous between d_{near} and d_{far}, the depth relationship between pixels is maintained.

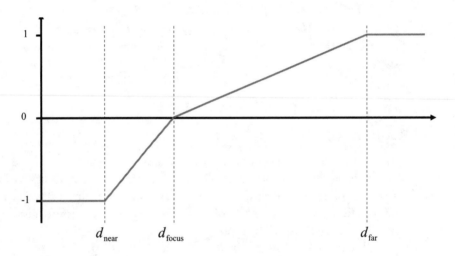

FIGURE 4.4.5   *Relative depth plotted over camera depth.*

The great advantage of this representation is that converting a pixel's relative depth into its blurriness is very simple:

$$coc = coc_{max} |depth| \qquad (4.4.3)$$

Relative depth is packed into the [0, 1] range and stored in destination alpha, so that the post-processing pixel shader can convert this value back into blurriness efficiently. In the DirectX 9 ps_2_0 shader model, the following conversion code uses three instruction slots:

```
blurriness = abs(2*maxBlur * alpha - maxBlur);
```

Figure 4.4.6 shows the alpha channel of an example scene for different focal distances.

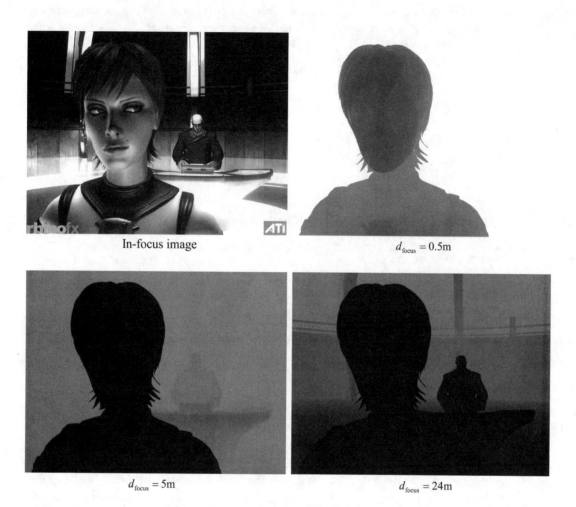

In-focus image

$d_{focus} = 0.5m$

$d_{focus} = 5m$

$d_{focus} = 24m$

FIGURE 4.4.6 *Contents of the alpha channel representing both depth and blurriness for different focal distance settings.* © *ATI Technologies 2004.*

In all of the HLSL vertex shaders used to render the scene, we use a routine we call `ComputeCameraDepth()` to compute the depth of each vertex in camera space.

```
float4x4 mViewMatrix;    // view space transformation matrix

float ComputeCameraDepth (float4 worldSpacePos)
{
   // transform position into view space
   float4 vViewPos = mul (mViewMatrix, worldSpacePos);
```

```
      return vViewPos.z;
  }
```

The camera depth is interpolated across the polygon in a texture coordinate component, which is used by the pixel shader as an input to an HLSL subroutine called ComputeDepthBlur():

```
float d_focus;      // focal plane distance
float d_near;       // near blur plane distance
float d_far;        // far blur plane distance
float clamp_far;    // far blur limit (must be between 0 and 1)

float ComputeDepthBlur(float depth)
{
    float f;

    if (depth < d_focus)
    {
        // scale depth value between near blur distance and
        // focal distance to [-1, 0] range
        f = (depth – d_focus)/(d_focus – d_near);
    }
    else
    {
        // scale depth value between focal distance and far
        // blur distance to [0, 1] range
        f = (depth – d_focus)/(d_far – d_focus);

        // clamp the far blur to a maximum blurriness
        f = clamp (f, 0, clamp_far);
    }

    // scale and bias into [0, 1] range
    return f * 0.5f + 0.5f;
}
```

All HLSL pixel shaders used to render the scene must return the result of Compute DepthBlur() in the alpha component of the final shader output. HLSL makes it easy to add this code to a set of shaders. Note that it is recommended to compute the relative depth parameter with ComputeDepthBlur() in the pixel shader rather than the vertex shader. Computing this value in the vertex shader and interpolating over large polygons crossing the focal plane would incorrectly blur the polygon regions near the focal plane.

Rendering Transparent Objects

Despite using the alpha channel to store the depth and blurriness information, we can still render transparent alpha-blended geometry. Each transparent object must be rendered in two passes. During the first pass, the object is rendered only to the R, G, and B channels with alpha blending enabled. In the second pass the output of Compute-DepthBlur() is rendered to the alpha channel of the same render target.

Post-Processing

Now that we have populated the alpha channel of our rendered scene with a value representing both depth and blurriness, we can perform a series of image-space operations to compute depth-of-field as shown in Figure 4.4.7.

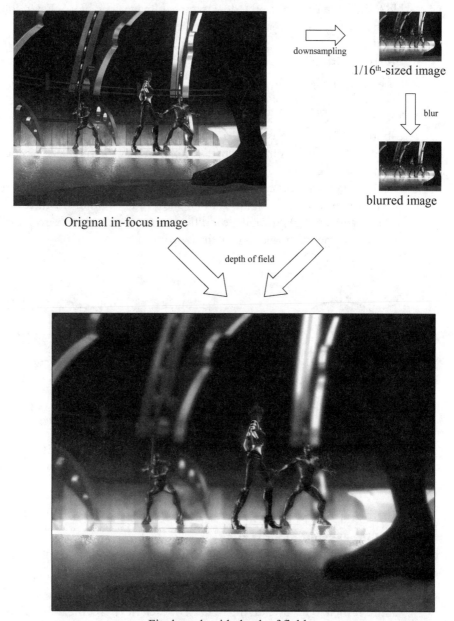

FIGURE 4.4.7 *Post-processing steps to generate the final image with depth-of-field.*

Pre-Blurring Pass

Before rendering the final image with depth-of-field, we create a blurred low-resolution version of the rendered scene image. First, we downsample it to 1/16 of its original size using a 4×4 box filter implemented with four bilinear texture lookups. For a 1024×768 buffer, this results in a 256×192 image. Next, we apply a 3×3 separable Gaussian blur filter to the downsampled image. The blurry low-resolution image will be used in out-of-focus regions of the final image.

Blurring with a Poisson Disc Filter Kernel

To blur the image according to the blurriness factor stored in the alpha channel we use a Poisson disc kernel (as described in detail in [Riguer03]), which averages a number of samples distributed in a circular area according to a stochastic Poisson disk distribution. One sample is located at the center of the disc. The sample positions are stored as 2D offsets from the center sample, so that the filter size can be adjusted by scaling the offsets.

The filter kernel is centered on each pixel being blurred and scaled to match the size of that pixel's CoC. Figure 4.4.8(a) shows a diagram of the filter kernel. Figures 4.4.8(b) and 4.4.8(c) illustrate how different kernel sizes average over smaller or larger areas of the original image to vary the blurriness.

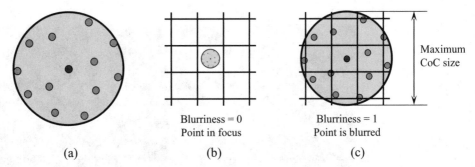

(a)   (b)   (c)

FIGURE 4.4.8   *(a) The Poisson disc filter kernel. (b) A point in focus with a small filter kernel. (c) A blurry point with a large filter kernel.*

Post-Processing Algorithm

The pixel shader used for applying the depth-of-field blur to produce the final image starts out by fetching the center sample from the full-resolution image, storing its relative depth found in the alpha value and converting it to get the pixel's filter kernel radius. It then loops over all filter taps. For each filter tap, the filter sample position is computed by scaling the normalized sample position (stored in the `poisson` array) by the kernel radius and scaling and biasing it to be centered on the current pixel position. Samples are fetched from both the full-resolution and the pre-blurred low-resolution image. Next, these samples are blended based on the blurriness encoded in the alpha value of the full-resolution sample. If the blurriness is high, the low-resolution sample contributes more to the blended result. If the blurriness is low, the low-resolution sample contributes almost nothing to the final result. For high blurriness, mixing in a contribution from the low-resolution image for blurry pixels reduces aliasing artifacts which appear in earlier methods [Riguer03].

Reducing Leaking Artifacts

One problem frequently evident with image space depth-of-field effects is an artifact known as "leaking," in which sharp foreground objects leak onto a blurry background. This artifact, which appears as a halo around sharp foreground objects, is caused by the large filter kernel of a blurry background pixel sampling from areas that belong to a sharp foreground object. As in [Riguer03], we work around this problem by lowering the weight of samples that are in focus and have a lower depth than a blurry center sample. The relative depth stored in the alpha channel is used for finding samples that match these criteria. Figure 4.4.9 illustrates the effect of our leaking reduction step.

Without leaking reduction   With leaking reduction

FIGURE 4.4.9   *The leaking reduction step removes the unwanted halo around Ruby's face.*

Post-Processing Pixel Shader

To apply the post-processing shader, we render a full-screen quadrilateral, making sure that texels and screen pixels are properly aligned.

For a rendering resolution of 1024×768 we have achieved good results with a depth-of-field shader that uses eight filter taps. Modern HLSL compile targets such as ps_2_b can execute the shader in a single pass. When using the ps_2_0 compile target, two passes are required because of the instruction limit. Here is the HLSL code of our depth-of-field post-processing algorithm:

```
// full resolution image
sampler tSource;

// downsampled and pre-blurred image
sampler tSourceLow;

// contains poisson-distributed positions on the unit circle
float2 poisson[8] = {
  float2( 0.0,      0.0),
  float2( 0.527837,-0.085868),
  float2(-0.040088, 0.536087),
  float2(-0.670445,-0.179949),
  float2(-0.419418,-0.616039),
  float2( 0.440453,-0.639399),
  float2(-0.757088, 0.349334),
  float2( 0.574619, 0.685879)
};

// pixel size (1/image resolution) of full resolution image
float2 pixelSizeHigh;

// pixel size of low resolution image
float2 pixelSizeLow;

// maximum CoC radius and diameter in pixels
float2 vMaxCoC = float2(5.0, 10.0);

// scale factor for maximum CoC size on low res. image
float radiusScale = 0.4;

float4 PoissonDOFFilter(float2 texCoord)
{
  float4 cOut;
  float discRadius;
  float discRadiusLow;
  float centerDepth;

  cOut = tex2D(tSource, texCoord);    // fetch center tap
  centerDepth = cOut.a;               // save its depth

  // convert depth into blur radius in pixels
  discRadius = abs(cOut.a * vMaxCoC.y - vMaxCoC.x);
```

```
    // compute disc radius on low-res image
    discRadiusLow = discRadius * radiusScale;

    // reuse cOut as an accumulator
    cOut = 0;

    for(int t = 0; t < NUM_TAPS; t++)
    {
        // fetch low-res tap
        float2 coordLow = texCoord + (pixelSizeLow * poisson[t] *
                          discRadiusLow);
        float4 tapLow = tex2D(tSourceLow, coordLow);

        // fetch high-res tap
        float2 coordHigh = texCoord + (pixelSizeHigh * poisson[t] *
                           discRadius);
        float4 tapHigh = tex2D(tSource, coordHigh);

        // put tap blurriness into [0, 1] range
        float tapBlur = abs(tapHigh.a * 2.0 - 1.0);

        // mix low- and hi-res taps based on tap blurriness
        float4 tap = lerp(tapHigh, tapLow, tapBlur);

        // apply leaking reduction: lower weight for taps that are
        // closer than the center tap and in focus
        tap.a = (tap.a >= centerDepth) ? 1.0 : abs(tap.a * 2.0 - 1.0);

        // accumulate
        cOut.rgb += tap.rgb * tap.a;
        cOut.a += tap.a;
    }

    // normalize and return result
    return (cOut / cOut.a);
}
```

Using Camera Lens Parameters for Depth-of-Field Calculations

Controlling the depth-of-field effect by setting the distances for the focal, near and far blur planes is intuitive and offers artistic freedom. However, there may be cases where it is desirable to use the focal length, f-stop, and focal distance parameters of a real camera to control the depth-of-field effect. [Hummel02] (as referenced by [Donald02]) provides the necessary formulas to compute the near and far blur distances from the real camera parameters:

coc = maximum circle of confusion diameter

Hyperfocal distance: $h = \dfrac{f^2}{a\,coc}$ (4.4.4)

Near blur plane distance: $d_{near} = \dfrac{h\,d_{focus}}{h + \left(d_{focus} - f\right)}$ $\hspace{2cm}$ (4.4.5)

Far blur plane distance: $d_{far} = \dfrac{h\,d_{focus}}{h - \left(d_{focus} - f\right)}$ $\hspace{2cm}$ (4.4.6)

The maximum circle of confusion diameter c used in these equations needs to be in the same distance unit used for the other parameters. To convert our maximum blur radius from pixels to a real-world distance unit, we must make an assumption about the film format used in the virtual camera. Film formats are specified by their width: 35 mm or 70 mm are common formats. Using the film format, we can compute coc as

$$coc = \frac{width_{film}\,coc_{max}}{screenRes_x}.$$ $\hspace{2cm}$ (4.4.7)

It is important to be aware of the fact that objects far away from the camera do not become arbitrarily blurry. Instead, the CoC diameter for far points approaches a limit. Using a CoC diameter above the limit when computing the far blur distance d_{far} will give an incorrect result because the denominator $h - (d_{focus} - f)$ becomes negative. To handle this case, we first need to compute the maximum CoC for points at infinity. The parameter d_{far} approaches infinity as the denominator goes to zero, so we can compute the maximum CoC by plugging Equation 4.4.4 into the equation $h - (d_{focus} - f) = 0$ and solving for coc, which yields

$$coc_\infty = \frac{f^2}{a\left(d_{focus} - f\right)}.$$ $\hspace{2cm}$ (4.4.8)

Large changes of d_{far} when crossing between the cases $coc_{max} \le coc_\infty$ and $coc_{max} > coc_\infty$ can cause a visual discontinuity in the scene's degree of focus even when the camera parameters are smoothly animated. To avoid this discontinuity, we compute d_{far} differently for each case:

Case 1: ($coc_{max} \le coc_\infty$)
An intermediate value $d_{far}^{90\%}$ is computed at 90% of coc_{max} by evaluating Equations 4.4.1 and 4.4.3 with $coc = 0.9\,coc_{max}$. To compute d_{far} we extrapolate linearly:

$$d_{far} = d_{focus} + \frac{\left(d_{far}^{90\%} - d_{focus}\right)}{0.9}$$ $\hspace{2cm}$ (4.4.9)

Case 1: ($coc_{max} > coc_\infty$)
Similarly to case 1, we compute $d_{far}^{90\%}$ at 90% of coc_∞, and extrapolate to coc_{max} to yield d_{far}:

$$d_{\mathrm{far}} = d_{\mathrm{focus}} + \left(d_{\mathrm{far}}^{90\%} - d_{\mathrm{focus}}\right) \frac{coc_{\max}}{0.9\,coc_{\infty}} \tag{4.4.10}$$

We also pass the proper far blur clamp value to the shader, so that the blurriness can be limited correctly:

$$clamp_{\mathrm{far}} = \frac{coc_{\infty}}{coc_{\max}} \tag{4.4.11}$$

Conclusion

In this article, we presented a new and improved technique for rendering depth-of-field effects in real time using image processing and compositing techniques with Poisson disc filtering. This approach has the advantage of efficient memory utilization because it uses the alpha channel of an existing render target. This is accomplished by a data representation that allows packing depth and blurriness information into a single value. The use of a pre-blurred image in the post-processing step improves image quality by reducing aliasing artifacts. The plane distance parameters for controlling the depth-of-field effect are intuitive for artists. However, we also described how to use physical lens parameters instead.

Overall, the technique provides flexibility and artistic control over the final effect, which is evident from the screenshots of ATI's RADEON™ X800 real-time demo *Ruby: The DoubleCross*, which was featured in the SIGGRAPH 2004 Computer Animation Festival.

References

[Donald02] Donald, J. "The Ultimate Depth-of-Field Skinny," available online at *http://www.dvinfo.net/articles/optics/dofskinny.php*, November 22, 2002.

[Hummel02] Hummel, R. "American Cinematographers Manual," 8th edition, *American Society of Cinematography*, 2002.

[Potmesil81] Potmesil, M., Chakravarty, I. "A Lens and Aperture Camera Model for Synthetic Image Generation," *Computer Graphics,* Vol. 15, no. 5 (SIGGRAPH 1981):pp. 297–305.

[Riguer03] Guennadi Riguer, Natalya Tatarchuk, and John Isidoro, "Real-Time Depth of Field Simulation," *ShaderX²*, Wordware 2003

4.5

Lighting Precomputation Using the Relighting Map

Tien-Tsin Wong, Chi-Sing Leung, and

Kwok-Hung Choy

Introduction

Lighting is a key component in creating dramatic atmosphere in game scenes, especially in horror games. However, it is always difficult to achieve dynamic lighting due to the scene complexity, intensive lighting computation, and the scarce computing resource during the runtime. Techniques for lighting precomputation reduce the runtime workload by shifting the major computation to an offline phase. One simple and popular example is to store the precomputed luminosity information in the lightmap (texture) and blend it with the surface texture to produce lighting effect. Unfortunately, such lighting is static.

It would be nice to have a variable lightmap that changes dynamically according to the light source. To do so, we need a way to compactly represent hundreds or even thousands of lightmaps, and a way to retrieve the desired lightmaps in real time. In this article, we propose a representation, *the relighting map*, which can be used to represent variable lightmap. It stems from the previous work [Wong97a] in image-based relighting. With such representation, dynamic lighting can be achieved as follows. In the preprocessing phase, the game developer first prepares an arbitrary number of representative lightmaps using any modeler and renderer. These precomputed reference lightmaps are then encoded into a set of highly compressed relighting maps. Each relighting map is simply a texture. During the runtime, the lightmap corresponding to the desired lighting condition can be synthesized (relit) in real time by linearly combining these relighting maps. For those games (such as *Resident Evil* and *Alone in the Dark*) that have a fixed viewpoint, their backgrounds can be represented by the relighting map as a whole.

The relighting map technique employs a locally supported *spherical radial basis function* instead of the globally supported spherical harmonics used in previous work [Wong97a][Wong03]. In other words, it is more capable in capturing high-frequency lighting features such as shadow and specular highlight. Moreover, the homogeneity and simplicity of spherical radial basis function makes the real-time rendering more efficient and practical than that of spherical harmonics.

Preparing the Relighting Maps

Input Images

The reference images (or lightmaps) are created with a directional light source as the sole illuminant. Each of them corresponds to a distinct light vector (**L**) sampled on a unit sphere, as illustrated on the left hand side of Figure 4.5.1. There can be an arbitrary number of samples scattered on the sphere. The only requirement is the light vector must be known. The massive color values are then rebinned in such a way that all values related to the same pixel window are grouped together. The right hand side of Figure 4.5.1 illustrates the rebinning. Each tile corresponds to one such group of color values. It tells us the color of that pixel when the scene is illuminated by a varying directional light. Note that the smoothness of color in a tile facilitates the compression.

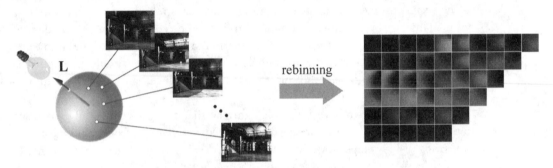

FIGURE 4.5.1 *Reference images are rebinned to maximize data correlation for compression.*

Each tile is in fact a spherical function, as every color value inside corresponds to a sample scattered on sphere. We call it the *Apparent BRDF* (ABRDF) [Wong97a]. Interestingly, it is closely related to Bidirectional Reflectance Distribution Function (BRDF). It differs from BRDF in that it may contain high-frequency shadow and other global illumination effects, such as caustics. Such high-frequency lighting effects will be over-blurred by the globally supported spherical harmonic which is commonly used for BRDF representation.

Spherical Radial Basis Function

Instead, we propose to use the spherical radial basis function [Broomhead88] [Jenison96]. Its locality nature is desirable in capturing shadows, highlights, and caustics. The basic idea is to approximate each ABRDF by a linear combination of k spherical radial basis functions R_i,

$$\sum_{i=0}^{k-1} c_i R_i(\mathbf{L})$$

(4.5.1)

Figure 4.5.2 illustrates such approximation graphically. Intuitively speaking, the ABRDF is approximated by a weighted sum of bumps (spherical radial basis functions R_i), each oriented in different direction. The input to R_i is the light vector $\mathbf{L}$ that actually looks up the value on sphere. The basis function R_i returns scalar value. The more radial basis functions are employed, the more accurate the approximation is. A useful number of basis functions k is 15 to 35. Since R_i are predefined and common for all ABRDFs, only the k coefficients c_i have to be stored for representing each ABRDF.

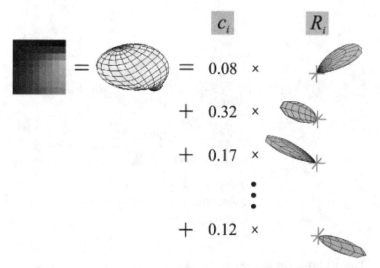

FIGURE 4.5.2 *Color values associated with the same pixel window are approximated by the linear combination of differently oriented spherical radial basis function.*

Each spherical radial basis function (Equation 4.5.2) is actually a Gaussian function of the angle between the light vector $\mathbf{L}$ and the corresponding radial basis center $\mathbf{Q}_i$ laid on sphere. Both $\mathbf{L}$ and $\mathbf{Q}_i$ must be normalized. The center $\mathbf{Q}_i$ determines the orientation of the bump. All bumps have the same spread Δ. The spread Δ is selected as the minimal geodesic distance between two neighboring centers. The centers $\mathbf{Q}_i$ and the spread Δ are pre-selected before the encoding process.

$$R_i(\mathbf{L}) = \exp\left(-\frac{\left[\cos^{-1}(\mathbf{L}\cdot\mathbf{Q}_i)\right]^2}{2\Delta^2} \right) \qquad (4.5.2)$$

To represent the radiance in different direction, centers $\mathbf{Q}_i$ are uniformly distributed on sphere. There are several methods for generating uniformly distributed points on sphere. In particular, we use a deterministic method to generate a stochastic-like pattern, known as Hammersley point set (Figure 4.5.3). The source code for generating the Hammersley point set is available on the homepage listed in [Wong97b].

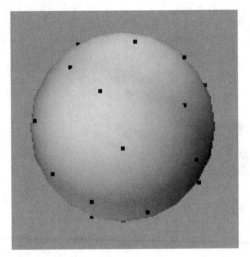

FIGURE 4.5.3   *The distribution of 30 radial basis centers generated using Hammersley point set.*

The Relighting Maps

In other words, after the approximation, the array of tiles in Figure 4.5.1 is converted to an array of k-dimensional coefficient vectors, as shown in Figure 4.5.4. Let's call these vectors the SRBF vectors from now on, where SRBF stands for Spherical Radial Basis Function. The total size of the SRBF vectors is much smaller than that of the original color values. Hence, compression is achieved.

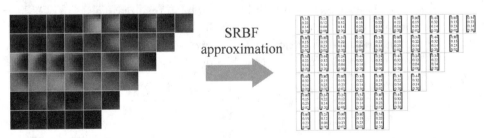

FIGURE 4.5.4   *The spherical radial basis function approximation converts the ABRDF's (tiles on the left) to SRBF vectors for storage reduction.*

Equation 4.5.1 is the key to relighting. Given a specific **L**, Equation 4.5.1 allows us to quickly look up (reconstruct) a pixel value due to that lighting direction without reconstructing the whole ABRDF. To relight the whole image, Equation 4.5.1 is performed for all pixels. Obviously, this computation is fully *parallelizable*. Hence it allows us to use SIMD-based GPU to achieve real-time rendering.

In order to parallelize the computation, we need to rebin the array of k-dimensional SRBF vectors to form k *relighting maps*, as in Figure 4.5.5. They are rebinned in the following manner. The first coefficients of all SRBF vectors are grouped to form the first relighting map. This process is repeatedly applied to form other relighting maps. Each relighting map is an image of real values (which can be positive or negative). These relighting maps represent the precomputed lighting effect in the form of textures. They are the data to be stored on disk and they will be loaded as textures for rendering. By linearly combining these maps, we can simulate different lighting effects.

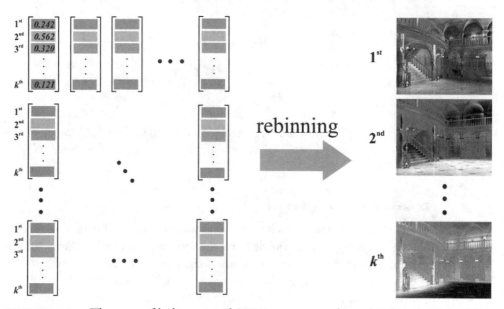

FIGURE 4.5.5   *The array of k-dimensional SRBF vectors are rebinned to form k relighting maps.*

Directional-Source Relighting

Image-Wise Linear Combination

With these relighting maps, we can synthesize complex lighting effects by image-wise or pixel-wise linear combination of them. The rendering process is actually a reconstruction process that independently computes Equation 4.5.1 for every pixel in the image/lightmap. The computation reconstructs (or "looks up") a color value from the encoded SRBF coefficients by feeding a light vector **L**. The simplest case of relighting is directional-source relighting. In this case, every pixel is fed with the same light vector L_0 and hence the same $R_i(L_0)$. Therefore, the relighting can be regarded as a linear combination of relighting maps c_i and scalars $R_i(L_0)$ in Figure 4.5.6. The evaluation of $R_i(L_0)$ can simply be done by software instead of GPU, as there are only k evaluations. Then, the relighting maps can be blended together with $R_i(L_0)$ as the scaling factors.

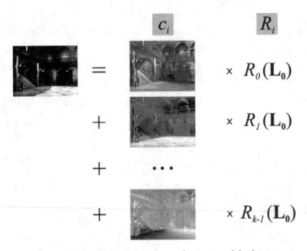

FIGURE 4.5.6   *Relighting by a directional light is a simple image-wise linear combination of relighting maps and weights $R_i(L_0)$.*

Directional-Source Shader

We use OpenGL and Cg to implement a directional-source relighting shader. First of all, the relighting maps are loaded into the texture units of GPU. Since the number of textures allowed for processing in one shader pass is usually limited, the relighting process has to be divided into multiple passes. The intermediate result should be stored in an offline pixel buffer for accumulation. The following code shows the linear combination of three relighting maps.

```
float4 DirShader(
  uniform samplerRECT c0,            // map c₀
  uniform samplerRECT c1,            // map c₁
  uniform samplerRECT c2,            // map c₂
  uniform float R0,                  // R₀(L₀)
  uniform float R1,                  // R₁(L₀)
  uniform float R2,                  // R₂(L₀)
  uniform float4 lightcolor,         // light color
  float3  texCoord : TEXCOORD0
): COLOR
{
  float4 acc;
```

```
acc    = h4texRECT(c0,texCoord.xy) * R0;    // c₀R₀
acc   += h4texRECT(c1,texCoord.xy) * R1;    // c₁R₁
acc   += h4texRECT(c2,texCoord.xy) * R2;    // c₂R₂
acc   *= lightcolor;
acc.w = 1;
return acc;
}
```

Note that R_i returns positive value while the relighting maps may contain negative values. Depending on available resource, the relighting maps can be stored as standard 8-bit integer textures or floating-point textures (16-bit half float is usually sufficient). Even with 8-bit precision, the image quality may not be reduced too much. If integer textures are used, attention must be paid on handling the numeric range of values. These relighting maps can be further compressed in memory using hardware supported texture compression such as S3TC.

Figure 4.5.7 shows the directional-source relighting of two scenes, "house" and "caustics." Scene "house" in Figures 4.5.7(a) and (b) mimics typical horror game

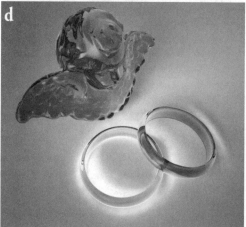

FIGURE 4.5.7 *Two scenes relit by directional light source. (a) and (b) show the "house" scene while (c) and (d) show the "caustics" scene.*

scene. The lighting effect can be easily modified in real-time to achieve the desired horror atmosphere. Twenty relighting maps are used in this example. Scene "caustics" in Figures 4.5.7(c) and (d) demonstrates the ability of spherical radial basis function in capturing rapidly changing caustics and shadow. Thanks to the locality nature of spherical radial basis function, only 25 relighting maps are used to achieve the real-time relighting. Note that it takes 40 minutes to render one frame in "caustics" data set on Pentium IV 2.8 GHz CPU using Mental Ray.

Point-Source Relighting

Per-Pixel Linear Combination

Point-source relighting is basically the same as that of directional light source. The major difference is that the light vector $\mathbf{L}$ is different for each pixel. Hence, $R_i(\mathbf{L})$ have to be evaluated for each pixel. Figure 4.5.8 illustrates such difference when compared to Figure 4.5.6. $R_i(\mathbf{L})$ are maps of scalars instead of scalars. Instead of a linear combination of images as in Figure 4.5.6, we now have a per-pixel linear combination of color values. Note that the scalar maps $R_i(\mathbf{L})$ look like "partially illuminated" depth maps.

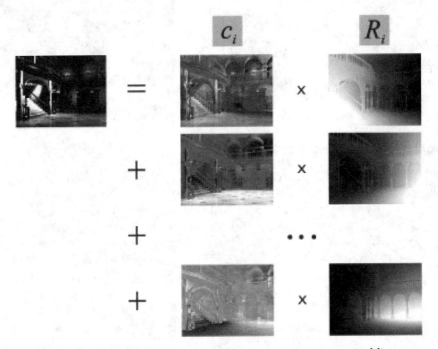

FIGURE 4.5.8   *Relighting by a point light source requires a per-pixel linear combination of color values.*

Computing the Light Vector

The major difficulty of point-source relighting is the computation of R_i. To do so, we have to first compute the light vector for each pixel. Given the depth map, the light vector is computed by Equation 4.5.3:

$$\mathbf{L} = \mathbf{S} - \left(\mathbf{E} - \frac{\mathbf{V}}{|\mathbf{V}|} d \right) \qquad (4.5.3)$$

where $\mathbf{S}$ is the position of the point light source; $\mathbf{E}$ is the viewpoint; $\mathbf{V}$ is the viewing direction associated with the interested pixel; and d is the depth value of that pixel. Since $\mathbf{E}$, $\mathbf{V}$, and d are all known and only $\mathbf{S}$ varies during the runtime, we can precompute $\mathbf{P} = \mathbf{E} - d\mathbf{V}/|\mathbf{V}|$ (the intersection points between the viewing rays $\mathbf{V}$ and the scene) and store them as a vector map. During the runtime, the equation $\mathbf{L} = \mathbf{S} - \mathbf{P}$ is computed to determine the light vector $\mathbf{L}$ in a per-pixel manner.

Evaluating the Basis Functions

One major advantage of spherical radial basis function over spherical harmonic basis functions is its *homogeneity*. In the case of spherical harmonic basis functions, different basis functions are different and higher order ones are more complex than the lower order ones. The *heterogeneity* of spherical harmonics imposes difficulty in the real-time evaluation of spherical harmonic basis functions (there can be millions of evaluations). In [Wong03], the evaluation of the spherical harmonic basis functions is achieved by looking up a series of precomputed cubemaps. However, the limited resolution of cubemaps introduces error, especially for high-order basis functions. As the number of basis functions increases, the number of cubemaps also has to be increased. Hence this approach becomes impractical when a large number of spherical harmonic basis functions are used.

On the other hand, all spherical radial basis functions have the same Guassian form except with different centers $\mathbf{Q}_i$ (Equation 4.5.2). Therefore, the computations needed in evaluating different basis functions are the same. In practice, the evaluation of R_i in Equation 4.5.2, can be easily accomplished by looking up a high-resolution *1D table* with $\hat{\mathbf{L}} \cdot \mathbf{Q}_i$ as the index, where $\hat{\mathbf{L}}$ denotes the normalized $\mathbf{L}$. This table is precomputed to store the evaluations of $R\left(\hat{\mathbf{L}} \cdot \mathbf{Q}_i \right)$. The domain of R_i is [−1, 1] while its range is [0,1]. Figure 4.5.9 plots this function. Hence, each evaluation requires only a dot product, $\hat{\mathbf{L}} \cdot \mathbf{Q}_i$, and a table lookup.

Figure 4.5.9 shows that R_i increases as the light vector $\mathbf{L}$ approaches $\mathbf{Q}_i$ and decreases rapidly as $\mathbf{L}$ leaves $\mathbf{Q}_i$. Hence it explains the bump shape of R_i in Figure 4.5.2. As the light vector $\mathbf{L}$ is derived from the depth map and the Gaussian fall-off surrounds $\mathbf{Q}_i$, it explains why the R_i maps in Figure 4.5.8 look like "partially-illuminated" depth maps. The direction $\mathbf{Q}_i$ actually determines which part of the image is "illuminated."

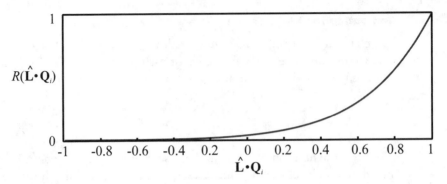

FIGURE 4.5.9   *The evaluation of R_i can be done by a dot product and a lookup of this 1D table.*

Attenuation

To model the distance fall-off effect of a point light source, we can simply multiply the linearly combined result by an attenuation factor. Figure 4.5.10 illustrates the attenuation graphically. The attenuation factor is obtained from the light vector (without normalization). The attenuation formula we use is $a_o/|\mathbf{L}|$, where a_o is a user-defined constant; and $|\mathbf{L}|$ is the magnitude of $\mathbf{L}$ or the distance from the light source to the intersection point.

linearly combined result   attenuation   final result

FIGURE 4.5.10   *The distance fall-off effect is incorporated by multiplying the linearly combined result with an attenuation factor.*

Point-Source Shader

The following point-source relighting shader is implemented in Cg. It computes the light vector $\mathbf{L}$ from the depth map, computes the dot product $\hat{\mathbf{L}} \cdot \mathbf{Q}_i$, evaluates R_i by table lookup, and applies the attenuation. For program clarity, only three relighting maps are combined in this code.

```
      float4 PtShader(
uniform samplerRECT c0,                           // map C₀
uniform samplerRECT c1,                           // map C₁
uniform samplerRECT c2,                           // map C₂
uniform float3      center0,                      // Q₀
uniform float3      center1,                      // Q₁
uniform float3      center2,                      // Q₂
uniform samplerRECT ipmap,                        // map of intersection
                                                  // points
uniform samplerRECT RBFtable,                     // R()
uniform float       htablesize,                   // half size of R table
uniform float3      lightpos,                      // S, position of light
                                                  // source
uniform float4      lightcolor,                   // light color
uniform float       a_o,                          // a₀, attenuation scaling
                                                  // factor
    float3  texCoord : TEXCOORD0
): COLOR
{
    float4  acc;                                  // accumulation variable
    float   atten;                                // attenuation
    half3   P;                                    // P, point of intersection
    float3  L;                                    // L, light vector
    float2  lookup;                               // lookup index

    P       = h3texRECT(ipmap,texCoord.xy);  // lookup P
    L       = (lightpos - P);                // L = S - P
    atten   = a_o / length(L);               // attenuation = a₀/|L|
    L       = normalize(L);                  // normalize L
    lookup.y = 0.5;

    // Evaluate and accumulate c₀R₀
    lookup.x = (dot(L,center0)+1) * htablesize; // L·Q₀
    acc      = h1texRECT(RBFtable,lookup)*h4texRECT(c0,texCoord.xy);

    // Evaluate and accumulate c₁R₁
    lookup.x = (dot(L,center1)+1) * htablesize; // L·Q₁
    acc     += h1texRECT(RBFtable,lookup)*h4texRECT(c1,texCoord.xy);

    // Evaluate and accumulate c₂R₂
    lookup.x = (dot(L,center2)+1) * htablesize; // L·Q₂
    acc     += h1texRECT(RBFtable,lookup)*h4texRECT(c2,texCoord.xy)

    acc     *= atten*lightcolor;
    acc.w    = 1;
    return acc;
}
```

Figure 4.5.11 shows the point-source relighting of two scenes, "house" and "caustics." With the relighting maps, we can approximate the complex "caustics" effect in real-time on a normal PC. Note the change of caustics near the rings and angel in Figures 4.5.11(c) and 4.5.11(d). See the companion CD-ROM for demo.

ON THE CD

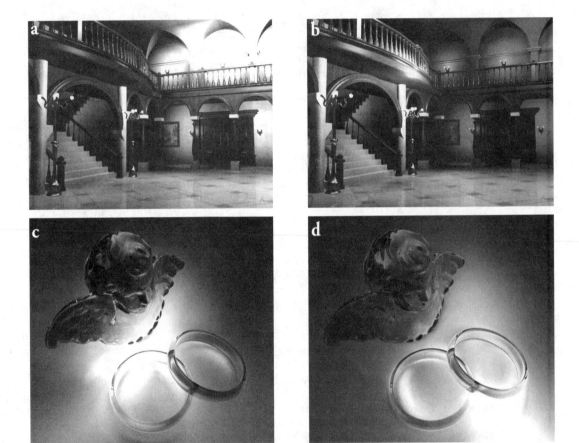

FIGURE 4.5.11 *Two scenes relit by point light sources. (a) and (b): "house" scene relit by yellow and white point sources respectively. (c) and (d): "caustics" scene relit by white and yellow point sources respectively.*

The Variable Lightmap

We now illustrate an example usage of the relighting map as a variable lightmap in representing time-consuming lighting effects, caustics and shadow. In this example, we model the caustics and shadow cast by the semi-transparent angel statue on a table.

Both the viewpoint and light source move in real time. We first model a 3D scene using a modeler (Figure 4.5.12(a)). Then, we generate a set of precomputed lightmaps (Figure 4.5.12(b)) and encode them as the relighting maps. These lightmaps are actually the photon maps on the table.

During the runtime, the rendering is divided into multiple passes. In the first pass, the current lightmap is synthesized from the relighting maps according to the current light source position. Then an image is generated from the current viewpoint with the generated lightmap mounted on the table. Note that the semi-transparent angel is not rendered at this moment. Finally, the angel is rendered with the previously generated image as background to simulate the refraction. The rendered angel is then superimposed onto the previously generated image to return the final image. With this approach, the time-consuming caustics computation can be shifted to offline, with the expense of some simple linear combination of relighting maps. Figure 4.5.12(c) shows the screenshots from the real-time demo (see the companion CD-ROM).

ON THE CD

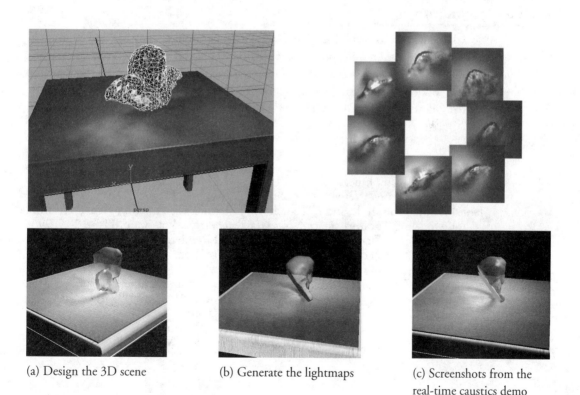

(a) Design the 3D scene   (b) Generate the lightmaps   (c) Screenshots from the
                                                          real-time caustics demo

FIGURE 4.5.12 *The variable lightmap.*

Conclusion

In this article, we have illustrated how to represent the expensive precomputed lighting effects using spherical radial basis function. The coefficients of spherical radial basis functions are organized to form the relighting maps. The synthesis of lighting effect is basically a linear combination of relighting maps either in an image-wise (directional light source) or a pixel-wise (point light source) manner. The locality nature of relighting map captures shadows, highlights, and caustics. Its homogeneity and simplicity offers a practical and simple solution to point source and spotlight rendering, which is tedious in spherical harmonic base. It also offers a scalable solution. Depending on the amount of available resource on GPU, the developer can trade for higher image quality by keeping more relighting maps, or less resource consumption by lowering the image quality. Interested readers are referred to the companion CD-ROM as well as the following web site for updated demos, toolkit, and source code: *http://www.cse.cuhk.edu.hk/~ttwong/demo/relightmap/relightmap.html.*

ON THE CD

Acknowledgments

We would also like to thank Jianqing Wang for preparing the "caustics" and "lightmap" data sets, Kin-Ting Lam for preparing the "house" data set, Ka-Ling Fok, Lai-Sze Ng, and Ping-Man Lam for preparing the demos. The work is supported by the Research Grants Council of the Hong Kong Special Administrative Region, under RGC Earmarked Grants (Project No. CUHK 4189/03E and CityU 1122/01E).

References

[Broomhead88] Broomhead, D. S. and D. Lowe, "Multivariate Functional Interpolation and Adaptive Networks," *Complex Systems*, Vol. 2, pp. 321–355, 1988.

[Jenison96] Jenison, R. L. and K. Fissell, "A Spherical Basis Function Neural Network for Modeling Auditory Space," *Neural Computation*, Vol. 8, pp. 115–128, 1996.

[Wong97a] Wong, Tien-Tsin, et al., "Image-based Rendering with Controllable Illumination," Proceedings of the 8th Eurographics Workshop on Rendering, St. Etienne, France, June 1997, pp. 13–22.

[Wong97b] Wong, Tien-Tsin, et al., "Sampling with Hammersley and Halton Points," *Journal of Graphics Tools*, Vol. 2, No. 2, 1997, pp. 9–24. *http://www.cse.cuhk.edu.hk/~ttwong/papers/udpoint/udpoints.html.*

[Wong03] Wong, Tien-Tsin, et al., "Real-Time Relighting of Compressed Panoramas," *Graphics Programming Methods*, Charles Rivers Media, 2003, pp. 375–288.

4.6

Shaderey—NPR Style Rendering

Aras Pranckevičius

Introduction

In this article, we describe a set of techniques for shading an outdoor scene using a non-photorealistic rendering (NPR) style. These techniques were used in the first place entry "Shaderey" in the Beyond3D/ATI shader competition that took place in the fall of 2003. The outdoor environment rendered by "Shaderey" consists of terrain, clouds, trees, a house, a sky sphere, and some lakes as shown in Figure 4.6.1.

FIGURE 4.6.1 *"Shaderey" scenes*

The NPR techniques used here operate strictly in image space, relying on two important images of the scene: one containing color information and the other containing normals and depth. The process consists of two parts:

Rendering: Render scene into color and normal/depth targets
Postprocessing: Apply a series of filters in image space to generate final NPR result

The post-processing filters applied are: color distortion in HSV space [Smith78], a very simple form of screen space "hatching," and edge outlining from normal/depth discontinuities [Saito90][Card01]. These filtering operations will be described in detail below. First, however, we will describe "Shaderey" scene rendering.

Scene Rendering

All scene objects such as the trees and the house are simply frustum-culled. The terrain is a 512×512 height field and is divided into fixed-sized (32×32 quadrilateral) chunks. Each chunk that passes frustum culling is simply rendered without any form of LOD. A single 1024×1024 projected shadow map is used for the whole scene. The trees and the house cast shadows while the terrain simply receives shadows. The shadow map is sampled using four jittered pick-nearest samples, which are averaged in the shader to improve the shadow boundaries. The shadow map does not cover the whole terrain but, rather, moves with the viewer in order to cover the area immediately in front of the viewer.

To simulate the simple reflective lakes, the rest of the world is rendered into a small planar reflection map, with the camera mirrored through the water plane. This texture map is projected onto the lakes while two scrolling EMBM-style bump maps are used to produce waves. To save on geometry cost, the terrain rendered into the reflection map has a lower LOD than the normal terrain. Atmospheric light scattering is computed per-vertex for all objects [Hoffman02].

In addition to rendering the simple colored scene into the back buffer, the scene's normals and depths are also rendered into an A8R8G8B8 texture that is the same size as the screen. The world-space normals of the scene are stored in RGB while an inverted depth is stored in alpha as shown in Figure 4.6.2.

FIGURE 4.6.2   *World space normals in RGB, inverted depth in alpha.*

A High Level Shading Language (HLSL) function for correctly computing the world space normals and this special inverted depth in the vertex shader is shown below:

```
// Outputs normal in RGB, sort-of-depth in A.
//   p - Final (clip space) position
//   n - World space normal
static inline float4 gNormalZ( float4 p, float3 n ) {
    float4 o;
    o.xyz = n * 0.5 + 0.5;          // into 0..1 range
```

```
        o.w = 100.0 / (p.w + 100.0);  // kind-of-depth
        return o;
}
```

Using DirectX 9's Multiple Render Target (MRT) support, the rendering of this normal and depth information can be done at the same time as the color rendering. If MRT isn't supported on the graphics device, the normal/depth image can be rendered separately without affecting the remaining steps of the algorithm. When rendering the terrain into the normal/depth texture, the pixel shader samples the shadow map and inverts the interpolated depth value for shadowed pixels as shown in [Card01]. The reason for this will become clear as we describe "Shaderey's" post-processing techniques.

Image Post-Processing

Now that we have rendered the scene to our color and normal/depth images, we can perform a series of image processing steps on these images to stylize the color using HSV space as well as draw outlines and perform a style of hatching.

Color Distortion

The first image processing step that we will perform is a color distortion to achieve a stylized look. The input to this step is the color image shown on the left side of Figure 4.6.3. The color distortion proceeds as follows:

1. Downsample color texture into a smaller (512 × 512) texture.
2. Convert from RGB to HSV color space and quantize color values. This color space conversion is done via a dependent lookup into a volume texture. The volume texture is accessed using the original RGB color values as 3D texture coordinates. The color fetched from the volume texture is in HSV space. Because a small volume texture (32 × 32 × 32) is used without any filtering, this color space conversion also quantizes the colors.
3. Sample the same image at two displaced positions; using two 2D offset textures. The texture coordinates used to access the offset textures are controlled from the application code so that they move more or less with the view (the viewer's yaw angle scrolls the offset textures horizontally while the viewer's pitch scrolls them vertically). These additional color samples are converted to HSV as well.
4. Displace colors in the image. Now we have two additional displaced image samples. First we check the absolute difference between them and do nothing if it is below some threshold (or else the result will have a distracting "shower door" effect). If the samples are different enough, we output the average of them in S and V channels, keeping hue from the original center sample. This effectively displaces image saturation and value at color boundaries.
5. Convert back from HSV to RGB using another volume texture lookup.

The result of this color distortion is shown on the right side of Figure 4.6.3.

FIGURE 4.6.3   *Normal color rendering and distorted colors.*

The HLSL pixel shader for steps 2–5 of the color distortion operation is shown below. This code must be compiled for the ps_2_0 or higher compile target:

```
struct PS_INPUT {
    float2 uv[2] : TEXCOORD0; // base UV, displace UV
};
float4 psMain( PS_INPUT i ) : COLOR
{
    // sample RGB, convert into HSV
    half3 base = tex2D( smpBase, i.uv[0] ).rgb;
    base = tex3D( smpRGB2HSV, base ).rgb;

    // get two displaced sample locations
    half2 bleedB = tex2D( smpBleedB, i.uv[1] ).rg*2-1;
    half2 bleedC = tex2D( smpBleedC, i.uv[1] ).rg*2-1;
    float2 uvB = i.uv[0] + bleedB * (8.0/512);
    float2 uvC = i.uv[0] + bleedC * (-7.0/512);

    // sample base at displaced locations, convert to HSV
    half3 baseB = tex2D( smpBase, uvB ).rgb;
    baseB = tex3D( smpRGB2HSV, baseB );
    half3 baseC = tex2D( smpBase, uvC ).rgb;
    baseC = tex3D( smpRGB2HSV, baseC );
    half3 bleed = baseB*0.5 + baseC*0.5;

    // final color is base if differences in HSV values
    // are smaller than tresholds; else average of
    // displaced values
    half3 diff = abs(baseB-baseC) - half3(1/8.0,1/3.0,1/3.0);
    half3 final = all( diff < float3(0,0,0) ) ? base : bleed;

    // leave original hue channel
    final.r = base.r;
```

```
        // convert back to RGB
        return tex3D( smpHSV2RGB, final );
    }
```

Edge Detection and Hatching

In order to give an illustrated look to our NPR scene, it is necessary to render dark outlines and hatches over the image to provide edge and shading information. In "Shaderey," edge outlining and screen-space hatching will be performed in one step. This step employs a three-tap filter to compute edges in the normal/depth image and also applies a simple hatch texture for shaded regions using the dot product of the normal and a world-space light direction from the sun. Both edges and hatching come out of this process in white, as shown in Figure 4.6.4. This color is inverted during final image composition so that the edges come out black and the hatches attenuate the colors in the shaded scene.

FIGURE 4.6.4 *Edges and hatching.*

The HLSL pixel shader for the combined outlining and hatching steps is shown below. This code must be compiled for the ps_2_0 or higher compile target:

```
half4 psMain( float2 uv[3]:TEXCOORD0 ) : COLOR
{
    // sample center and 2 neighbours
    half4 cbase = tex2D( smpBase, i.uv[0] );
    half4 cb1   = tex2D( smpBase, i.uv[1] );
    half4 cb3   = tex2D( smpBase, i.uv[2] );

    // normals into -1..1 range
    half3 nbase = cbase.xyz*2-1;
    half3 nb1   = cb1.xyz*2-1;
    half3 nb3   = cb3.xyz*2-1;
```

```
// edges from normals
half2 ndiff;
ndiff.x = dot( nbase, nb1 );
ndiff.y = dot( nbase, nb3 );
ndiff -= 0.6;
ndiff = ndiff > half2(0,0) ? half2(0,0) : half2(1,1);
half ndiff1 = ndiff.x + ndiff.y;

// edges from Z
float2 zdiff;
zdiff.x = cbase.a - cb1.a;
zdiff.y = cbase.a - cb3.a;
zdiff = abs( zdiff ) - 0.02;
zdiff = zdiff > half2(0,0) ? half2(1,1) : half2(0,0);

// sample hatch
half4 chatch = tex2D( smpHatch, i.uv[0] );
// dot normal with light
half dotNL = dot( nbase, vLightDir );
// hatch blend factor
half factor = saturate( (1.0 - 0.9 - dotNL) * 2 );
chatch *= factor;

return chatch + ndiff1 + dot(zdiff,half2(1,1));
}
```

Final Image Composition

After these two image processing operations, the distorted colors are modulated with the inverted edge/hatch image to provide the final result as shown in Figure 4.6.1.

Conclusion

This article presented the non-photorealistic rendering techniques used in the Shaderey demo. These techniques are applied in image space, making it easy to incorporate them into existing rendering frameworks.

Source Code

ON THE CD

The full "Shaderey" demo with source code is included on the companion CD-ROM.

References

[Card01] Drew Card and Jason L. Mitchell "Non-Photorealistic Rendering with Pixel and Vertex Shaders," *ShaderX*, Wordware, pp. 319–333, 2001.

[Hoffman02] Naty Hoffman and Arcot J. Preetham, "Rendering Outdoor Light Scattering in Real Time," Game Developers Conference, 2002.

[Saito90] Takafumi Saito and Tokiichiro Takahashi, "Comprehensible Rendering of 3-D Shapes." Computer Graphics (SIGGRAPH '90 Proceedings), pages 197-206, 1990.

[Smith78] Alvy Ray Smith, "Color Gamut Transform Pairs," SIGGRAPH 78, pp. 12-19.

SHADOWS

Introduction

Eric Haines

Creating shadows in interactive applications continues to be an active area of research. New methods are continually being developed to address various aspects of the problem, such as shadow realism (both physical and perceived), softness, generality, and speed of rendering. Since there is no single algorithm that performs all these aspects of shadowing well, researchers have tackled the problem from a wide variety of directions. This section consists of four articles on the subject.

In the article, "Poisson Shadow Blur," Mitchell describes how to quickly generate drop shadows that have soft penumbral edges by using an filter that gives a variable blur. The result is visually convincing, and has already been implemented in one commercial game. An advantage of the technique is that it works well as an optional addition to the traditional hard-edged drop shadow technique.

The article, "Fractional-Disk Soft Shadows," by Valient and de Boer explores performing soft-shadowing when using a shadow buffer. They consider how to perform a type of percentage-closer filtering using graphics hardware to accelerate the process. A full account of the strengths and weaknesses of the various methods is presented.

In "Fake Soft Shadows Using Precomputed Visibility Distance Functions," Pranckevičius explores the idea of using spherical harmonics to capture the effect of shadowing objects in an environment. Though spherical harmonics are typically used for slowly changing phenomena, and shadows change rapidly from light to dark, the author presents some methods that ameliorate this mismatch and give surprisingly believable results.

King and Newhall's "Efficient Omnidirectional Shadow Maps," rounds out this section. They present a number of practical methods that considerably increase the speed of generating and accessing a set of shadow maps for lights inside a scene, as well as improving the quality of the results.

5.1

Poisson Shadow Blur

Jason L. Mitchell

Introduction

This article describes a simple method for simulating a natural shadow penumbra for applications which render simple grayscale shadow textures of dynamic characters and subsequently project these textures onto scene geometry such as the ground. This idea of rendering black or gray characters onto a white background for subsequent projection onto scene geometry is quite common in games but often results in blocky hard-edged shadows. With higher resolution shadow textures, the blockiness can be eliminated, but this often results in a sharp shadow that may draw too much attention and not integrate well with the overall look of the game. This article presents a simple texture-space technique to improve the quality of this type of shadow, in particular by generating a more natural looking penumbra.

First, the shadow-casting object or character is rendered into a texture. Subsequently, a filter with a Poisson disk sampling pattern is used to blur this texture. The size of the blurring kernel is designed to be larger at the top of the texture, where the object is likely to be far from the ground. The blurred image is gradually sharper toward the bottom of the texture, where the object typically contacts the ground, giving the impression of a natural penumbra. This texture is then applied to the shadow receivers.

Rendering the Shadow Texture

The first step in this process is rendering the shadow texture. This is typically done by first clearing a renderable texture to white and rendering some shadow-casting geometry in solid black or gray. It is important to point out that we are not referring to a shadow depth map, only a regular texture map, which will be projected onto appropriate scene geometry. The term *shadow texture* is used throughout this article in order to try and avoid confusion with what most people refer to as a *shadow map* or *shadow depth map*.

The shadow casting and receiving geometry can be anything in the scene about which you have knowledge of a shadow casting/receiving relationship. The case that we'll discuss here is a shadow-casting character or group of characters moving around an environment which will receive the shadows, as this is very common in a variety of genres such as sports, fighting, role playing, and real-time strategy games.

Filtering the Shadow Texture

What we have described so far is a technique that you'll see used frequently in games. In fact, this is what makes this Poisson shadow-blurring technique attractive; games can easily turn this feature on or off in an engine based on the capabilities or performance of the graphics card in the system. Ideally, this new technique will drop right into many in-development titles and provide them with a way to improve the look of their rendering on systems with at least ps_2_0-capable graphics cards. In fact, this is exactly what happened with *Dungeon Siege® II*, developed by Gas Powered Games®. In the sample application on the CD-ROM and in *Dungeon Siege II*, characters are rendered to shadow textures as shown in Figures 5.1.1(a) and 5.1.1(c).

Because the shadow-casting light in the scene always strikes the scene at an angle in *Dungeon Siege II*, the feet of the character, which are near the ground, appear toward the bottom of the shadow texture, while the head, which is farther from the ground, appears near the top. Because of this orientation, blurring this texture in such a way that the kernel is large at the top of the texture and small at the bottom will result in a convincing penumbra as shown in Figures 5.1.1(b) and 5.1.1(d). This works very naturally for the bipedal characters typical in *Dungeon Siege II* and other games, but you could imagine some very large character like a giant ant which had some feet that appear near the top of the shadow texture. In this case, the shadows of these feet would be overly fuzzy near their contact point with the ground, ruining the illusion of a natural penumbra. For most cases, however, this simple spatially-varying blur works out quite well since the feet appear near the bottom of the shadow texture.

(a) Hard shadow texture from sample application

(b) Blurred shadow texture from sample application

(c) *Dungeon Siege II* shadow texture

(d) Blurred *Dungeon Siege II* shadow texture

FIGURE 5.1.1   *Shadow textures before and after blur.*

Poisson Disk Filter

After rendering a shadow texture, it is filtered using a spatially-varying filter kernel. We chose to use a Poisson disk filter kernel because of its spectral properties and because it is very natural to make this a spatially-varying filter using shader hardware. Specifically, the Poisson disk is a low-pass filter which we can shrink and grow at different places in our shadow texture based upon some criteria. In this case, the criterion will be simply the v texture coordinate.

Filters with Poisson disk distributions are commonly used in graphics. These filters have some number of taps which are distributed stochastically within the footprint of the filter. There are a number of stochastic filters with various properties, but the Poisson disk is popular due to its spectral properties [Cook86]. A Poisson disk distribution is a Poisson distribution with the added property that samples must be some minimum distance apart to avoid clumping. To generate a Poisson disk distribution, points are added at random but removed if they are too close to any previous points. This results in a distribution which is more even looking than a regular Poisson distribution, as shown in Figure 5.1.2.

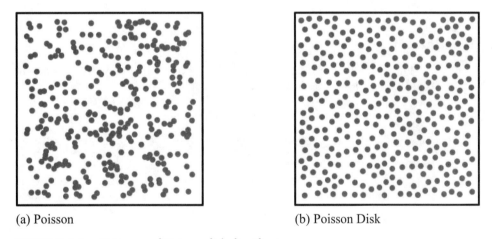

(a) Poisson   (b) Poisson Disk

FIGURE 5.1.2   *Poisson and Poisson disk distributions.*

For our application, we chose to use filter taps (texture samples) within a circular area, so we experimentally determined a distance which reasonably consistently generated a Poisson disk distribution with twelve taps inside the unit circle. One such kernel is shown in Figure 5.1.3.

The blur that we will apply to our shadow texture to generate a believable penumbra uses a Poisson disk of samples whose distance from the center filter tap is scaled with the v texture coordinate. That is, at the end of the texture where $v = 1$, there is almost no resulting blurring, while at the end of the texture where $v = 0$, the shadow texture is quite blurry, as shown in Figure 5.1.1.

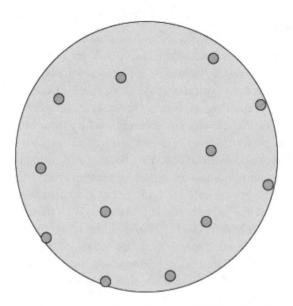

FIGURE 5.1.3   *12-tap Poisson disk filter kernel.*

The Shader

This spatially-varying Poisson disk filter is implemented with the following Direct3D HLSL shader code:

```
#define NUM_BLUR_TAPS 12

float2 filterTaps[NUM_BLUR_TAPS] = {{-0.326212f, -0.405805f},
                                    {-0.840144f, -0.07358f},
                                    {-0.695914f,  0.457137f},
                                    {-0.203345f,  0.620716f},
                                    { 0.96234f,  -0.194983f},
                                    { 0.473434f, -0.480026f},
                                    { 0.519456f,  0.767022f},
                                    { 0.185461f, -0.893124f},
                                    { 0.507431f,  0.064425f},
                                    { 0.89642f,   0.412458f},
                                    {-0.32194f,  -0.932615f},
                                    {-0.791559f, -0.597705f}};

sampler OverlaySampler;
// Routine to blur monochrome image
float4 ps_shadow_blur(float2 tc0 : TEXCOORD0) : COLOR
{
   float colorSum = 0.0f;
   float fScale = 0.02f;

// Run through all taps in the Poisson disk
for (int i = 0; i < NUM_BLUR_TAPS; i++)
{
```

```
        // Compute tap coordinates
        float2 tapCoord = tc0 + filterTaps[i] * fScale * (1.0f-tc0.y);

        // Fetch tap sample
        float tapColor = tex2D(OverlaySampler, tapCoord);

        // Accumulate color and contribution
        colorSum += tapColor;
    }

    // Divide down the accumulated color
    float finalColor = colorSum / NUM_BLUR_TAPS;

    return float4 (finalColor, finalColor, finalColor, finalColor);
    }
```

Glancing over the code, you'll first see an array of twelve two-tuples, which are the 2D offsets from the center of our filter kernel (shown graphically in Figure 5.1.3). These 2D offsets can be scaled in order to scale the size of the kernel. In fact, this is what is done on the first line inside of the for loop—the current filter tap is scaled as a function of both $1-v$ and a global scale factor fScale. The result is used as a 2D offset from the interpolated texture coordinate which would otherwise provide a 1:1 mapping of input to output pixels. This loop executes for all twelve samples, accumulating scalar data into the float colorSum (since this code is written to filter grayscale images only). Finally, the color sum is divided by the number of taps and returned.

Automatic Mipmap Generation

Another level of quality that can be added to dynamic shadow textures is per-frame generation of mipmaps. Most games have historically skipped this step due to poor API support. In recent years, both OpenGL and Direct3D have added an automatic hardware-accelerated mechanism for generating mipmaps. This feature is particularly useful for dynamic textures such as our shadow textures. Given that shadow textures are typically projected onto ground geometry that can be viewed at fairly oblique angles, it can be a significant visual quality boost to mipmap such textures and use trilinear and/or anisotropic filtering. Depending on the type of game and typical viewpoint of the camera, this may or may not be worth the additional cost.

Results

The following scene from *Dungeon Siege II* shows this technique in action. In Figures 5.1.4(a) and 5.1.4(c) we show a traditional technique that does not use Poisson shadow blurring. In Figures 5.1.4(b) and 5.1.4(d), we show the same scene with Poisson shadow blurring. Notice that the shadow of the character is sharp near the point that the character's feet make contact with the ground but blurrier as distance from this point increases.

(a) Hard Shadow (without other lighting)   (b) Poisson Blurred Shadow (without other lighting)

(c) Hard Shadow (with other lighting)   (d) Poisson Blurred Shadow (with other lighting)

FIGURE 5.1.4   *Poisson Shadow Blur in Dungeon Siege II*

Future Enhancements

Other metrics (besides the *v* texture coordinate) can be used to scale the Poisson disk of samples. In fact, as shown in the *ShaderX²* article "Real-Time Depth-of-Field Simulation," by Guennadi Riguer, Natalya Tatarchuk, and John Isidoro as well as the follow-up *ShaderX³* article "Improved Depth-of-Field Rendering," by Thorsten Scheuermann and Natalya Tatarchuk (page 363), the size of the Poisson disk can be determined per-pixel and taps can even be discarded [Riguer03] [Scheuermann04].

Keller and Heidrich showed in their paper, *Interleaved Sampling*, that it can sometimes be advantageous to sample fewer times but to vary the sampling patterns used in neighboring pixels [Keller01]. This would be straightforward to add to the Poisson shadow-blurring technique and may yield even higher quality results.

Acknowledgments

Thanks to James Loe of Gas Powered Games for the screenshots that illustrate the use of this technique in *Dungeon Siege II*.

Sample Application

The sample ShaderX3_LightShafts on the companion CD-ROM illustrates a number of different rendering techniques, including the Poisson shadow-blurring technique outlined in this article. In particular, the shader called ps_shadow_blur() in the file OverlayQuad.fx contains the code central to this article.

References

[Cook86] Robert L. Cook, "Stochastic Sampling in Computer Graphics," *ACM Transactions on Graphics* Volume 5, Issue 1, pp. 51–72, 1986.

[Keller01] Alexander Keller and Wolfgang Heidrich, "Interleaved Sampling" Eurographics Workshop on Rendering Techniques, pp. 269–276, 2001.

[Riguer03] Guennadi Riguer, Natalya Tatarchuk and John Isidoro, "Real-Time Depth of Field Simulation," *ShaderX²*, Wordware 2003.

[Scheuermann04] Thorsten Scheuermann and Natalya Tatarchuk, "Improved Depth-of-Field Rendering," *ShaderX³*, Charles River Media 2004.

5.2

Fractional-Disk Soft Shadows

Michal Valient and Willem H. de Boer

Introduction

This article describes a simple, practical, and fairly effective way to approximate soft shadows. The actual implementation is a slight modification of percentage closer filtering (PCF) [Reeves87, Bunnell04]. PCF was originally designed to address the aliasing problem inherent in shadow mapping. It also has the welcome side effect of generating soft shadow edges, which resemble simple constant-width penumbrae. In this article we will show how a slightly modified PCF algorithm can produce more realistic penumbrae. We will use stochastic sampling varied per pixel to obtain reasonable results while using fewer shadow map samples.

Previous Work

Our algorithm extends the well-known shadow-mapping algorithm published by Lance Williams in 1978 [Williams78]. This two-pass algorithm is currently popular because of its simplicity and execution speed on modern graphics hardware. Its main disadvantage is that it suffers from aliasing problems because of the finite resolution and precision of the shadow map. Reeves et al. proposed a method for anti-aliasing shadow maps called percentage closer filtering [Reeves87]. The idea is to first perform a number of depth tests in a certain region of lightspace using unfiltered samples from the shadow map, and then use this information to calculate the percentage of shadow this region receives. Performing this type of anti-aliasing can be done by the GPU [Bunnell04].

We refer the interested reader to the summary report by Hasenfratz et al. [Hasenfratz03] for more background information about various real-time soft shadow algorithms.

Soft Shadows

Our algorithm considers four types of regions: fully lit, umbra, and two types of penumbra, which are divided by the original hard shadow boundary (see Figure 5.2.1(a)). In one penumbra region (P2) the shadow increases and borders the fully shadowed umbra region; this is the inner penumbra region. In the other region (P1) the shadow intensity decreases and ends in full light; this is the outer penumbra region. The point Pe divides P1 from P2, and is where the hard shadow falls for a point light at the center of the area light (i.e., the hard shadow boundary).

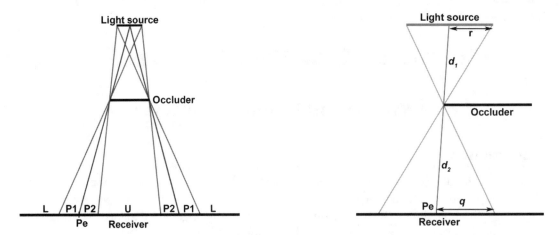

FIGURE 5.2.1   *(a) Four types of shadow regions—umbra (U), inner penumbra (P2), outer penumbra (P1), and full light (L). (b) Penumbra region radius computation components.*

Now consider Figure 5.2.1(b). The receiver is considered to be of constant z in lightspace (i.e., it is perpendicular to the light's shadow map direction). The circular lightsource casts inner and outer penumbra regions onto the receiver. We shall consider an arbitrary point P on the receiver. The key observation is that we can convert the effect of an area light on a lit point as being approximately equivalent to the effect of a point light on a lit disk. The amount of light that P receives from the lightsource is proportional to the fraction of the area of a disk D^1 with radius q and center P is being lit by a point lightsource located at the center of the area lightsource. This means that to calculate the amount of light arriving at any point P on the receiver, we simply construct a disk of radius q with center at P and facing the light, and divide the area lit by the total area of the disk. This gives us a scalar value in the range [0.0, 1.0], where 0.0 means completely shadowed and 1.0 means completely lit. Note how with this 2D construction the point Pe in Figure 5.2.1(b) will be classified as having a shadow value of 0.5.[2]

The radius q of the disk for an arbitrary point on the receiver is computed from the radius of circular light source r, the difference in light space depth between the lightsource and the occluder d_1 and the difference in depth between the receiving point and the occluder d_2. Notice the geometrical relationship between disk radius q, the difference in depth between receiver and occluder d_2, the difference in depth

---

[1]Note that if L were star-shaped, for example, this disk would instead be a star-shaped region.

[2]In 3D, points like Pe do not always have a shadow value of 0.5, e.g., at a convex silhouette vertex the value is higher than 0.5, at a concavity it is less than 0.5.

between occluder and lightsource d_1, and the radius of the lightsource r, as shown in Equation 5.2.1:

$$q = \frac{d_2}{d_1} r \qquad (5.2.1)$$

We need to stress the fact that q is the same for *every* point P on the constant z receiver in Figure 5.2.1(b); its value can be calculated by using Equation 5.2.1 as if we were calculating q for Pe. Intuitively, this means that to calculate the disk radius for any point P (even on receivers of non-constant z), we must first find the corresponding point Pe that lies in the *same imaginary plane of constant z* as P, and calculate q using that. This turns out to be difficult to do in practice, therefore our actual implementation allows only an approximation of the actual disk radius to be computed by far easier means. However, we will describe a slightly more accurate method in the subsection "Implementation without Preprocessing."

Stochastic Sampled Percentage Closer Filtering

In the previous section, we showed how to compute the amount of shadow point P receives by considering the ratio between the lit part of a disk centered at P and the total area of this disk. In the discrete case we can implement this by picking a finite number, N, of samples in the disk and finding how many of these samples are lit. This is essentially equivalent to performing percentage closer filtering in terms of the algorithm's behavior. The main change we make is that the radius q varies as *d1* and *d2* change, whereas with the standard PCF approach this radius is kept more or less fixed[3]. Increasing the radius of the penumbra region means the disk covers more shadow map texels and so we need to enlarge the filtering kernel for the PCF appropriately. However, the resulting increase in the number of samples means a slower processing speed. To compensate for this we will process only a fraction of the texels in the region.

For a given receiver point we randomly choose some texels within the disk region, and perform PCF using these. The main advantage of this method is that for the average case we get acceptable results with less computational cost. The disadvantage is that the shadows are less precise. We use less texels, so we lower the Nyquist limit of the sampled shadow data, which could result in aliasing [Cook86]. This problem is not that serious overall, since soft shadows are normally low-frequency by nature. The main objectionable drawback is that any aliasing has been replaced by noise due to stochastic sampling. This manifests itself as noisy penumbrae. However, this looks better than the banding artifacts that would otherwise occur.

One of our goals is to do as little computation as possible, so we choose the number of samples based on the disk radius q. Equation 5.2.2 shows the function that returns the number of samples depending on the disk area (with radius q).

---

[3]In the original paper, this region is not really kept fixed, but changes with the size of the particular camera space region.

$$f(q) = \left\lceil \frac{\pi}{a} q^2 \right\rceil \qquad (5.2.2)$$

The constant a specifies the ratio between the real sample count and the desired sample count. Of course, other equations are possible. Figure 5.2.2 shows PCF sampling kernels based on Equation 5.2.2.

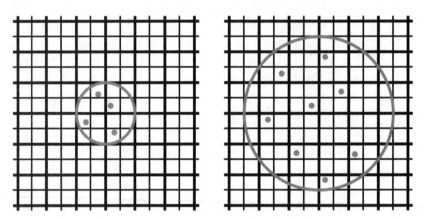

FIGURE 5.2.2   *PCF kernel based on Equation 5.2.2 for q = 2, a = 2 (left), and q = 5, a = 2 (right).*

This sampling method works only for points on receivers that are of constant z in light space (essentially, perfectly facing the light). To see an example of when the technique fails, consider the left side of Figure 5.2.2. The point P has now been chosen to lie well outside the shadowed regions. However, a problem occurs because the disk centered about P penetrates the receiver plane and is therefore partially shadowed by the receiver itself. Brabec et al. [Brabec02a] solve this problem by assigning unique IDs to objects, which allows them to discard occlusion information whenever the ID of a point on the receiver matches the ID of the point occluding it. Unfortunately, this solution has the effect that objects cannot cast soft shadows onto themselves. If instead we store the back-faces rather than the front-faces in the shadow map the problem goes away. This method is also known as second-depth shadow mapping and is described in [Wang97] and [Zioma03], where it is used to solve a similar problem.

Unfortunately, the same artifact is now relegated to disks that cross back-facing surfaces, an example of which is shown in Figure 5.2.4. Consider the right side of Figure 5.2.2, which is a cross-section of a simple scene consisting of two solid objects. The thick gray lines indicate those points on the objects that are stored in the actual shadow map (they are the nearest back-faces as seen from the lightsource). Point P_2 (which happens to lie in a penumbra region in this particular case) has its disk illustrated by the black horizontal line. Notice how this disk penetrates the receiver object; all points in the disk that are to the right of P_2 are *incorrectly* classified as being occluded by the receiver itself. We solve this by considering these points in the disk as not occluded, as follows. We will take C as an example point. The same test needs to be performed for every point in the disk. We construct a disk around C, by using Equation 5.2.1 (where d_1 is the distance between Cs and the lightsource and d_2 is I_2). If P_2 is *not* contained in this new disk (i.e., is outside the radius r_2) we know that C was *incorrectly* classified as occluded, and we therefore count it as not occluded instead. Note how with this construction, point A, which is *correctly* classified as occluded, will remain occluded by this additional test, because its disk contains P_2, i.e., P_2 is inside A's disk of radius r_1.

A similar but less disturbing artifact is illustrated in Figure 5.2.3(c). Point B (which is inside the object) in the disk centered at P is now incorrectly classified as not occluded. This results in point P being assigned a higher PCF (i.e., less in shadow) value than it should actually get.

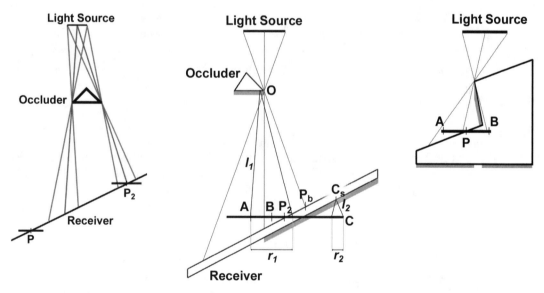

FIGURE 5.2.3   *(a) A side view of a receiving plane of non-constant z in lightspace (left). Notice how the disk (which is of constant z) with center P penetrates the plane. (b) The penetrating disk problem (right). (c) Point P is assigned a higher PCF value than it should really get (i.e., is brighter than it should be), as point B on the disk has been incorrectly classified as not occluded.*

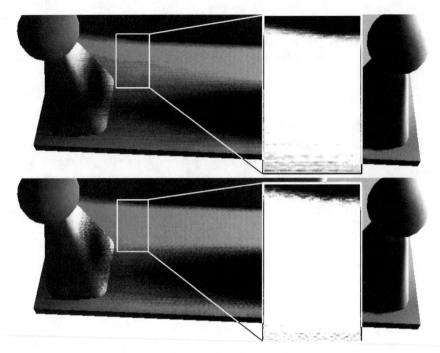

FIGURE 5.2.4   *The upper figure shows self-shadowing that occurs in the outer penumbra region, because the slab is thin and its backface shadows the sample disks. The bottom shows the (more) correct outer penumbra regions once our two-step method is applied. The brightness and contrast of the zoomed-in areas was modified so the problem is more visible.*

Implementation

ON THE CD

In this section we will describe the ps_3_0 version of our implementation, which features loops and flow control, which are the main components needed for the full version of our algorithm. We will outline the implementation steps in detail, but avoid the use of shader code listings in favor of higher-level pseudocode. On the CD-ROM you can find the fully documented source code using HLSL for ps_3_0, ps_2_a (ps_2_b), and a limited version for ps_2_0 hardware.

There are four major parts of the algorithm: noise map generation, shadow map generation, shadow map pre-processing, and final rendering.

Noise Map Generation

To obtain random coordinates during rendering we use a special noise map, which can be of arbitrary dimensions. This noise map needs to be generated only once. Each texel of this map contains random values in the range [0.0, 1.0] in each color channel. The red and green channels are used to modify the original shadow map coordinates, and they have to meet the following constraint that makes them lie in the unit disk:

$$(2texel.r - 0.5)^2 + (2texel.g - 0.5)^2 \leq 1 \qquad (5.2.3)$$

During rendering these coordinates will be scaled by the disk radius so they fit in the actual disk.

Each row of values in the red and green channels of the map is generated using a Poisson disk distribution (see Cook [Cook86] and the article "Poisson Shadow Blur," on page 403 for more on this subject). During the final rendering step we sequentially sample the rows of the map to obtain disk sample coordinates.

The blue and alpha channels contain random values without the constraint in Equation 5.2.3, and we use these only once per pixel to compute the initial random coordinates used later for the sequential reading of the red and green channels, as will be explained in the final rendering step.

Shadow Map Generation

This step is almost identical to the standard shadow mapping algorithm, but with two small changes. First, we render only polygons facing away from the light. Second, the shadow map does not contain the lightspace z coordinates. Instead we compute for each vertex the distance to the light in world space, linearly interpolate this distance across the triangle, and store this in the shadow map. Values in the light's attenuation range are mapped linearly into the range [0.0, 1.0] using Equation 5.2.4 (where d_{light} is distance from light in world space, $l_{AttenuationStart}$ is the lowest allowed distance from light, and $l_{AttenuationEnd}$ is the maximum allowed distance from the light). This is described in more detail by Valient [Valient03]. Brabec describes an even more clever computation of linear distance [Brabec02b].

$$ShadowMap.r = \frac{d_{light} - l_{AttenuationStart}}{l_{AttenuationEnd} - l_{AttenuationStart}} \qquad (5.2.4)$$

Shadow Map Preprocessing

The distance stored in the shadow map does not provide us with enough information. The problem is that points in outer penumbra region P1 have no information about the nearest occluder in the shadow map—they are considered lit as far as the shadow map algorithm is concerned. Therefore we perform a preprocessing step where we add this missing information to the shadow map. For each texel T of the shadow map that can—during final rendering—be mapped to a point in region P1 we store the depth of the occluder nearest (in the lightspace x and y dimensions) to T in the shadow map. During final rendering we use this value to estimate the approximate difference in depth between T and its occluder. This difference is then used to compute the disk radius for T.

Points that lie either in the umbra or in the completely lit region should be processed as quickly as possible; the PCF operation for these points is redundant, and should therefore be avoided. To accomplish this we store for each texel in the shadow map the distance to the nearest hard shadow boundary (the point Pe in Figure 5.2.1(b)). This information will be used to identify such points as being too far away, which allows us to skip the costly PCF operation for these points.

Preprocessing is done in multiple passes and the final shadow map will contain the original depth values in the red channel, the depth of the nearest occluder in the green channel, and the distance to the nearest shadow boundary in the blue channel (see Figure 5.2.5).

FIGURE 5.2.5   *Individual channels (RGB) of the shadow map after preprocessing—original depth in red, nearest occluders in green, inversed distance to hard shadow boundary in blue (modified to be visible).*

To implement this, we start by applying an edge detection filter to the shadow map. The resulting edges specify the hard shadow boundaries (point Pe in Figure 5.2.1(b)). If a texel is classified as belonging to such an edge we store its depth value in the green channel, otherwise we store 1.0 (the maximum depth) in the green channel. Because the edge detection filter can (and in practice will) also mark some texels near the real edge, we do not directly copy the depth value from the red channel to the green channel. Rather, we choose the minimum of the depth values from neighboring texels. For edge texels we also store a value of one distance unit into the blue channel (this is 1/256 for shadow map with resolution 256×256). In subsequent passes we will use this value to accumulate the distance from the edge. The following pseudo-code illustrates the first pass.

```
For each shadow map texel t
{
    bool bIsEdge = DetectEdge(t);
    if (bIsEdge)
    {
        float fMinDepth = GetMinimumAreaDepth(t);
        t = float4(t.x, fMinDepth, fDistanceUnit, 0);
    }
    else
        t = float4(t.x, 1.0f, 0, 0);
}
```

For each texel in subsequent passes we check for a value other than 1.0 in its green channel and that of its neighbors. We use the minimum of these depths and store it in the green channel of the texel.

We also compute the maximum of the blue channel values. If the maximum is greater than zero we add one distance unit to this value and store it in the blue channel.

By repeating this pass several times we distribute the occluder depth into the green channel and accumulate an approximate (inverse) distance to the nearest edge in the blue channel. The exact number of passes depends on the largest allowed penumbra radius.

```
For each shadow map texel t
{
    //Get average depth (ignore 1.0f)
    float fDepth = GetMinimumAreaDepth(t);
    float fMax = GetAreaMaximum(t,bluechannel);
    if (fMax > 0) fMax = t.z + fDistanceUnit;
    t = float4(t.x, fDepth, fMax, 0);
}
```

Final Rendering

The final rendering step is straightforward. First we decide to which region (see Figure 5.2.1(a)) our point belongs. We sample the shadow map to decide whether the point lies in shadow or not. We also obtain the nearest occluder depth from the green channel, as well as the distance to the nearest shadow boundary from the blue channel.

If our point is in shadow, we use the original depth value in the shadow map (red channel) to compute the disk radius. If this radius exceeds the maximum allowed radius, we clamp it.

If our point is lit, we use the depth of the nearest occluder (green channel). If this value is 1.0, we consider the point as fully lit. Otherwise, we use the nearest occluder depth to compute the disk radius and clamp it to the maximum allowed radius if necessary.

Before doing any further processing we determine the distance of the point to the nearest shadow boundary by using the blue channel of the shadow map. If this distance is greater than the disk radius, the point cannot be in a penumbra region and we consider the point as either fully lit, or fully shadowed, and so are done. For all other pixels we compute the soft shadow values using stochastic sampled PCF as shown in the pseudocode listing following. For each iteration of the while loop we sequentially sample the rows of the noise map, and scale and translate the values in the red and green channels of the noise map to fit into the disk radius. We use the resulting locations as our PCF samples. The quality of the final shadow is greatly affected by the way in which we choose the initial sampling coordinates vNoiseCoords for the current pixel. If we just use interpolated coordinates (e.g., screen coordinates or shadow map coordinates) we get vertical banding artifacts. This happens because neighboring pixels that share the same y coordinate will use very similar PCF samples, due to the sequential reading in the while loop. To avoid this problem we store pure random values into the blue and alpha channels of the noise map. We sample the noise map using the canonical screen coordinates of our current pixel to index into the noise map's blue and alpha channels. This ensures that neighboring screen space pixels will not use the same PCF samples.

The following bit of pseudocode shows the final rendering pass:

```
For each screen pixel p
{
    //Obtain projective shadow map coordinates.
    float2 vShadowMapCoord = input.xy / input.w;
    float4 cShadow = tex2D(ShadowMap, vShadowMapCoord);
    float fHardShadow = GetHardShadow(p, cShadow.r);
    float fPenumbraRadius = 1.0f;
    if (fHardShadow == 0)
        fPenumbraRadius =
            min(fMaxRadius, GetPenumbraRadius(p, cShadow.r));
    else if (cShadow.g == 1.0f)
        return fHardShadow;
    else
        fPenumbraRadius =
            min(fMaxRadius, GetPenumbraRadius(p, cShadow.g));
    if (fPenumbraRadius > cShadow.b)
        return fHardShadow;

    //Soft shadows
    float2 vNoiseCoords = tex2D(NoiseMap, p.xy).ba;
    float fSampleCount = GetSampleCount(fPenumbraRadius);
    fSampleCount = min(fMaxSampleCount, fSampleCount);
    float fCounter = fSampleCount;
    floaf fFinalShadow = fHardShadow;
    while (fCounter > 0)
    {
        float2 vNoiseCoord2 = tex2D(NoiseMap, vNoiseCoords);
        vNoiseCoord2 = vNoiseCoord2 * fPenumbraRadius;
        cShadow = tex2D(ShadowMap, vShadowMapCoord + vNoiseCoord2);
        fFinalShadow += GetPCFShadow(p, cShadow.r);
        vNoiseCoords.x = vNoiseCoords.x + fOneRow;
        fCounter−;
    }
    return fFinalShadow / fSampleCount;
}
```

Modifications to the Standard Implementation

Implementation on ps_2_0 Hardware

The pixel shader 2.0 specification imposes certain constraints to the implementation. The first one is the relatively small number of instructions that a shader is allowed to have, which forces us to break the PCF loop into several passes. Luckily there is the possibility of using a method similar to deferred shading [Thibieroz03], which enables us to completely skip the vertex processing phase. In the first pass we render the following data to each pixel of a texture: the shadow map coordinates (two channels), and the normalized distance from the light (one channel). The last channel contains the disk radius and the result of the hard shadow packed together. In subsequent passes we perform just the loop part of the algorithm and accumulate the shadow intensity in the alpha channel of the framebuffer. The final pass performs full lighting computations and uses alpha blending to modulate each result with the corresponding shadow value.

Implementation without Preprocessing

Our algorithm can be used without preprocessing the shadow map. The distance map and nearest occluder map are used solely for calculating the disk radius and doing early-out tests. Without them the disk radius calculation proceeds as follows. For pixels that are occluded, the disk radius q is approximated by considering the difference in lightspace depth between the current pixel and its occluding shadow map texel (which is equivalent to what we described in the standard implementation). If the current pixel is not occluded, we can set q to its minimum allowed value and use this. Doing so yields aesthetically pleasing results. However, a more correct way to calculate q for this case would be to find the maximum of the difference in depth between each sample in the disk to its (possible) occluder (*not* the minimum of the distances; remember we have rendered the back faces to the shadow map, not the front faces). This implies that we first use the disk (with radius set to the maximum) to find this maximum difference in depth. We then use this distance (which is *d2* in Figure 5.2.1(b)) to calculate the corrected disk radius, and then perform the actual PCF with this corrected radius.

Results

Figures 5.2.6 and 5.2.7 show shadows produced by our soft shadow algorithm. The brute-force ps_2_0 version runs at 15–20 fps with a resolution of 1024×768 on a Radeon 9800 with 17 shadow map preprocessing passes and 5 complete final rendering passes (with 10 noise texture reads and 10 shadow map reads for each pass).

Notice how the penumbra regions are noisy. In typical game situations this noise is masked by the use of high-frequency diffuse textures, or bump maps.

FIGURE 5.2.6   *Final rendered images. These are using the current ps_2_0 version where the initial randomization step is skipped, so banding is visible.*

FIGURE 5.2.7   *Final rendered images. These are from current ps_2_0 version.*

Artifacts and Limitations

Although our algorithm produces aesthetically pleasing results in most cases, it can also produce artifacts in the inner penumbra regions. These artifacts are quite common for shadow-map-based algorithms because the map stores the depth of only the nearest occluder. This means that if we try to compute the width of the penumbra region for objects that overlap in shadow map space we can get highly varying disk radii for points that are close together. Figure 5.2.8 shows this case on the right. For point *a* the disk radius is computed using the distance to occluder *occ2*. Point *b* should be deeper in shadow, but the shadow map stores *occ1* at this point and so our algorithm uses too large a disk radius for point *b*. Because of this mismatch, the shadow intensity can be vastly different from that of *a*, despite these two points being very close to each other.

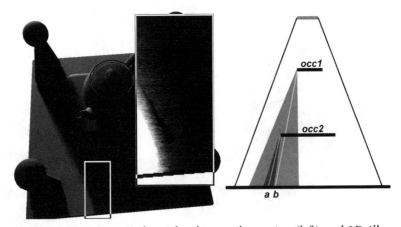

FIGURE 5.2.8   *Incorrectly rendered penumbra region (left) and 2D illustration of the cause of the error (right). The brightness and contrast of the zoomed-in area was modified so the problem is more visible.*

We also place the following limitations on the algorithm to make it behave nicely in terms of performance. The first limitation is that we define a maximum disk radius. Any greater radius is clamped to this maximum value. This allows us to limit the number of preprocessing steps. This limitation can be removed by using a different approach to preprocessing; see the Optimizations section.

The other limitation that we place on the algorithm is that we define a maximum number of PCF samples[4]. Because we can use only a finite number of samples, N, the eventual value PCF returns can ever be one of only N discrete values. This explains the banding artifacts in Figures 5.2.6 and 5.2.7, which we can mask by the use of noise (as explained in the previous section). In the limit as we take the number of samples to infinity, our method will produce smooth penumbra transitions, without any of the banding artifacts.

Optimizations

We could gain extra speed during the preprocessing phase by trying to change the preprocessing time from $O(n^2)$ to $O(n \log n)$, where n is the pixel count of the shadow map, utilizing similar techniques used for separable filtering. We refer interested readers to the GDCE presentation by Chris Oat [Oat03]. By using this method we can cover a wider area using fewer passes.

We can also gain speed by using fewer PCF samples for points that are farther away from the viewer. Therefore, we could modify Equation 5.2.2 to take into account the distance from the viewer.

We could also omit the noise map and store the Poisson disk samples in constant registers. Then we use the same set of random coordinates for each pixel (see the article "Poisson Shadow Blur" on page 403 for more on this subject).

Conclusion

We have presented a method that is capable of producing aesthetically correct soft shadows with inner and outer penumbrae. The actual implementation uses a modified version of PCF. The first modification is the variable width filtering kernel (i.e., disk). The second is the additional test performed during PCF that helps us to reject false shadow contributions. Using a Poisson disk distribution for the samples helps to hide banding artifacts caused by the limit on the number of samples. This banding is especially noticeable in large penumbra regions. The noise map can easily be replaced by a (smaller) one-dimensional texture or even by a fixed-size constant array of random coordinates for speed critical applications. With the additional power that flow control brings on ps_3_0 (or ps_2_x with caps) hardware, we are able to compute and use the minimum number of samples necessary for each pixel.

---

[4]This is a limitation of the ps_3_0 specification, which can perform loops with only a non-variable loop-count.

Acknowledgments

The first author would like to thank Andrej Ferko for his valuable comments. The second author would like to thank Steve Hill for being such a good sounding board, and we would like to thank Eric Haines for his feedback and useful suggestions.

References

[Brabec02a] Brabec, S., and Seidel, H-P., "Single Sample Soft Shadows using Depth Maps," *Graphics Interface* (2002): pp. 219–228.

[Brabec02b] Brabec, S., Annen, T., and Seidel, H-P., "Practical Shadow Mapping," *Journal of Graphics Tools* (2002): pp. 9–18.

[Bunnell04] Bunnell, M., and Pellacini, F., "Shadow Map Antialiasing," in Randima Fernando, ed., *GPU Gems*, Addison-Wesley (2004): pp.185–192.

[Cook86] Cook, R., L., "Stochastic Sampling in Computer Graphics," *ACM Transactions on Graphics*, Vol. 5, no.1 (1986): pp. 51–72.

[Hasenfratz03] Hasenfratz, J., M., Lapierre, M., Holzschuch, N., and Sillion, F., "A survey of Real-Time Soft Shadow Algorithms," *Computer Graphics Forum*, Vol 22, no.4 (December 2003).

[Oat03] Oat, Ch., "Real-Time 3D Scene Post-processing," GDCE 2003, available online at *http://www.ati.com/developer/gdce/Oat-ScenePostprocessing.pps.*

[Reeves87] Reeves, W. T., Salesin, and D. H., Cook, R. L., "Rendering antialiased Shadows with Depth Maps," *Computer Graphics,* (SIGGRAPH '87 Proceedings): pp. 283–291.

[Thibieroz03] Thibieroz, N., "Deferred Shading with Multiple Render Targets," in Engel, W.F., ed., *ShaderX²—Shader Programming Tips & Tricks with DirectX 9*, Wordware Publishing, 2003.

[Valient03] Valient, M., "Shadow Mapping with Direct3D 9", in Engel, W. F., ed., *ShaderX²—Shader Introduction & Tutorials*, Wordware Publishing., 2003.

[Wang97] Wang, Y., and Molnar, S., "Second-depth Shadow Maps," UNC-CS Technical Report TR94-019, 1994.

[Williams78] Williams L., "Casting Curved Shadows on Curved Surfaces," *Computer Graphics*, Vol 12, no. 3 (SIGGRAPH '78 Proceedings): pp. 270–274.

[Zioma03] Zioma, R., "Reverse Extruded Shadow Volumes," in Engel, W. F., ed., *ShaderX²—Shader Programming Tips & Tricks with DirectX9*, Wolfgang F. Engel, ed., Wordware Publishing, 2003.

5.3

Fake Soft Shadows Using Precomputed Visibility Distance Functions

Aras Pranckevičius

Introduction

Dynamic real-time shadowing techniques are commonly used these days. However, approaches such as shadow volumes or shadow maps model direct shadowing only, and cannot produce global illumination effects or soft shadows. In recent years, new techniques such as Precomputed Radiance Transfer are gaining momentum.

This article presents a technique that is faster to compute than PTRs and can handle some cases PRTs cannot. This algorithm renders fake soft shadows in static scenes using precomputed visibility distance functions. The technique handles dynamic local light sources and executes entirely on modern graphics hardware.

Standard Shadowing Techniques

Commonly used shadowing techniques are:

- Precalculated lighting, usually stored at vertices or in lightmaps. Unfortunately, dynamic geometry or lights are difficult to handle with this type of technique.
- Shadow volumes, usually using stencil buffers or destination alpha channel.
- Texture-based approaches, including simple projected shadows, shadow maps (depth or ID based), and various extensions to them.
- Precomputed radiance transfer (PRT) based techniques [Sloan02]. These precompute and approximate a radiance transfer *function* at many points in the scene. However, supporting local lights, especially inside concave objects, is not easy.

Our Technique

At the heart of our shadowing algorithm are precomputed visibility distances. Take a static scene and, for every point on its surface and in each possible direction, compute the distance to nearest occluder. When rendering, fetch the distance in the light's direction and compare with the distance to the light. This classifies the rendered point as being in shadow or not.

Sadly, there is no practical way to store the full visibility distance information for all points in the scene. Half of the solution is to store visibility information only at a "dense enough" resolution; the other half is to approximate and compress this visibility information.

PRT methods generally produce better results, can use real-world area light sources, and can model advanced light transport effects like interreflection and subsurface scattering [Sloan03a]. Our technique has one advantage, however—it does not require light to come from outside of the rendered object (using PRT, light must come from infinitely distant source or at least from outside of object's convex hull). Using visibility distance functions, light sources can be anywhere, much like in traditional shadowing methods. The scene depicted in this article's figures is a single closed object, and all lights are actually inside it.

The following section describes each component of the technique in detail.

Visibility Distance Functions

The visibility distance function for some point p is a (hemi)spherical function that for any given direction returns a scalar visibility distance value. The visibility distance in some direction is the distance to the nearest occluder.

The functions are precomputed and stored at many scene surface points: at vertices for finely tessellated geometry, or in texture maps with a unique parameterization. It does not matter exactly how the functions are stored and approximated. In an ideal world there would be no approximation at all, but there is no practical way to store and evaluate many thousands of spherical functions. So, visibility distance functions have to be compressed in such a way that enables efficient evaluation (perhaps on graphics hardware) and that does not take much memory to store.

In this article, low-order spherical harmonics (SH) are used to approximate and store the functions. This is not normally considered the most suitable choice, as the visibility distance function often has large discontinuities, but SH is easy to encode and efficient to evaluate, and with some care can give plausible results.

The visibility distance function for point p is precomputed using Monte Carlo integration [Green03]:

* Trace many rays from p into the scene and check for the nearest collision. In this implementation, AABB trees are used for quick collision checks [Terdiman01] and the rays are uniformly distributed on a sphere[Green03]; each point has 2500 rays cast from it.
* Project the results onto each of the SH basis functions, obtaining an SH encoded visibility distance function. For this article, 5th order SHs are used, so each function is 25 floating-point coefficients.

Other techniques for precomputation are possible, such as getting distances from a GPU-rendered cubemap depth buffer.

Rendering

Rendering is performed for each light, accumulating its contribution. Shadow calculation (which may be at the vertex or fragment level) is done for each light pass:

1. Calculate direction (x, y, z) and distance d_L to the light source.
2. Evaluate the visibility distance function in direction (x, y, z), call this d_V. Our functions are stored in SH form, so first project (x, y, z) onto SH basis functions and dot the result with visibility distance SH coefficients.
3. If $d_V < d_L$, the point is in shadow (the light is beyond the occluder). The shadow modulation factor is: `shadow = dV >= dL ? 1 : 0`.
4. Perform any local lighting calculations and modulate the results with the shadow.

However, there still are several problems. A typical image is shown in Figure 5.3.2 (compare this to Figure 5.3.1, where standard shadow maps are used). The shadows are not very correct, to say at least, and there are no signs of soft shadows at all!

FIGURE 5.3.1 *Scene rendered with standard shadow maps.*

FIGURE 5.3.2 *Scene rendered with visibility distance functions, using 5th order SH and binary shadow comparison.*

This is where some faking comes in. Low-order SH approximation essentially "blurs" our visibility distance functions, removing high-frequency details—that is why the strange shadows are in Figure 5.3.2. We can notice that global illumination solutions usually are brighter than direct illumination solutions due to multiple light bounces, so it is not very bad to slightly brighten the shadowed areas. We do this by making the comparison of rendering step 3 smooth instead of binary:

Shadow modulation factor is: `shadow = saturate( (dV/dL-1.0/3.0)*1.5 )`.

In this way, shadows start to "fade in" when $d_V < d_L$, giving some appearance of soft shadows and global illumination (Figure 5.3.3), and hiding SH approximation errors. Of course, the function chosen for smooth comparison is based on experimentation only; the only requirement of this function is that the shadow modulation factor should be 1.0 when $d_V \geq d_L$, and fade to zero when the d_V / d_L ratio decreases.

FIGURE 5.3.3 *Scene rendered with visibility distance functions, using 5th order SH and smooth shadow comparison.*

Rendering Details

For reference, the scene used in all the figures is $19 \times 19 \times 6$ meters in size and subdivided at 0.2 meters resolution, producing 57 thousand vertices and 100 thousand triangles. The whole scene is a single object. Three attenuated point lights are used, and the user is able to "fire" additional short-lived lights. Visibility distance functions are computed and stored in vertices, 25 coefficients for 5th order SH taking up 100 bytes per vertex (reduced versions are possible, using as low as 9 or 4 coefficients). Shadow maps used for comparison are 512×512 R32F format; shadowing uses one sample from the shadowmap without any filtering.

Three detail levels are implemented, one using a full 5th order SH, with evaluation happening both on vertex and pixel levels; the other two are low-quality versions using 3rd and 2nd order SHs, with all shadow calculation happening at the vertex level.

Rendering with 5th Order SH

Spherical harmonics of 5th order produce 25 coefficients. We need to evaluate such a SH-encoded function in the light's direction. Up to 3rd order SH (i.e., the first nine coefficients) can be easily and efficiently evaluated analytically in the vertex shader [Ramamoorthi01][Sloan03b]. The remaining 16 coefficients are passed to a pixel shader as four sets of 4D texture coordinates and their effect computed there.

SH basis functions for these coefficients are stored in specially made $64 \times 64 \times 6$ cubemaps (Q8W8V8U8 format). One cubemap can hold four basis function parameters so four cubemaps are needed. Cubemap texels are computed using standard D3DX functions:

```
void WINAPI gSHCubeFiller( D3DXVECTOR4 *out,
    const D3DXVECTOR3 *uvw, const D3DXVECTOR3 *texelSize,
    void* data )
{
    float coeffs[SH_COEFFS+4]; // SH_COEFFS=25
    int offset = *(int*)data;
    D3DXVECTOR3 dir;
    D3DXVec3Normalize( &dir, uvw );
    D3DXSHEvalDirection( coeffs, 5, &dir );
    const float window = 0.75f;
    *out = D3DXVECTOR4(&coeffs[offset]) * window;
}
// later create the cubemaps
int shOffset = 9; // first 9 analytically
for( int cm = 0; cm < 4; ++cm ) {
    D3DXCreateCubeTexture( device, 64, 0, 0, D3DFMT_Q8W8V8U8,
        D3DPOOL_MANAGED, &mTexSHCubes[cm] );
    D3DXFillCubeTexture( mTexSHCubes[cm], gSHCubeFiller,
        &shOffset );
    shOffset += 4;
}
```

Vertex shader for scene rendering in HLSL for vs_1_1 profile:

```
// input vertex
struct VS_INPUT {
    float4 pos : POSITION;
    float3 normal : NORMAL;
    float4 shA : BLENDWEIGHT0; // first 9 coeffs
    float4 shB : BLENDWEIGHT1;
    float  shC : BLENDWEIGHT2;
    float4 shD : BLENDWEIGHT3; // last 16 coeffs
    float4 shE : BLENDWEIGHT4;
    float4 shF : BLENDWEIGHT5;
    float4 shG : BLENDWEIGHT6;
};

// output vertex
struct VS_OUTPUT_25 {
    float4 pos   : POSITION;
    float  vdist : TEXCOORD0; // vis.distance from 9 coeffs
    float4 sh[4] : TEXCOORD1; // last 16 coefs
    // xyz — dir to light; w - dist to light
    float4 light : TEXCOORD5;
    float4 color : COLOR0;    // vertex lighting
};

// Evaluate SH function in direction v (9 coeffs)
float evalSH9( VS_INPUT i, float3 v ) {
    const float PI = 3.14159265;
    const float SPI = sqrt(PI);
    const float N0 = 1.0/2.0/SPI;
```

```
const float N1 = sqrt(3)/2.0/SPI;
const float N2 = sqrt(15)/2.0/SPI;
const float N3 = sqrt(5)/4.0/SPI;
const float N4 = sqrt(15)/4.0/SPI;
float res;
// first 4 components
res = dot( i.shA.wyzx,
    float4( float3(-N1,-N1,N1)*v, N0 ) );
// next 4 components
float4 comb = v.xyzx * v.yzzz; // xy, yz, zz, xz
float4 tmp2 = float4(N2, -N2, N3*3, -N2) * comb;
tmp2.z -= N3;
res += dot( tmp2, i.shB );
// 9th component
res += N4 * (v.x*v.x-v.y*v.y) * i.shC;
return res;
}

// Vertex shader
VS_OUTPUT_25 vsMain25( VS_INPUT i ) {
    VS_OUTPUT_25 o;
    // transform
    o.pos = mul( i.pos, mViewProj );
    // to light, distance
    o.light = tolight( i.pos, vLightPos );
    // vertex lighting
    o.color = lighting( i.normal, o.light, vLightColor );
    // evaluate first 9 coeffs
    o.vdist = evalSH9( i, o.light.xyz );
    // pass last 16 to ps
    o.sh[0] = i.shD; o.sh[1] = i.shE;
    o.sh[2] = i.shF; o.sh[3] = i.shG;
    return o;
}
```

The pixel shader continues evaluating the visibility distance for the remaining 16 coefficients. It uses four premade SH basis cubemaps (smpSH0 to smpSH3), source in HLSL for ps_2_0 profile:

```
float4 psMain25( VS_OUTPUT_25 i ) : COLOR
{
    float3 l = i.light.xyz;
    float dl = i.light.w, dv = i.vdist;
    dv += dot( texCUBE( smpSH0, l ), i.sh[0] );
    dv += dot( texCUBE( smpSH1, l ), i.sh[1] );
    dv += dot( texCUBE( smpSH2, l ), i.sh[2] );
    dv += dot( texCUBE( smpSH3, l ), i.sh[3] );
    // smooth comparison
    float shadowFactor = saturate( (dv/dl-0.3333)*1.5 );
    // binary comparison
    //float shadowFactor = dv >= dl ? 1 : 0;
    return i.color * shadowFactor;
}
```

Rendering with Lower-Order SH

Lower-order SH for visibility distance approximation may be used, sacrificing some quality for lower computing and memory requirements. Interpolating a full four texture coordinate sets and sampling four cubemaps per rendered pixel is not very fast, and keeping 25 coefficients for each vertex is not a small amount of memory.

The first natural approximation is to drop the last 16 coefficients, thus keeping the 3rd order SH coefficients. This can be evaluated nicely in a vertex shader, and even the final shadow factor calculation can be done at vertex level, reducing our pixel shader to simple color output. Both now can be done on DX8 level or even older hardware:

```
struct VS_OUTPUT_LO {
    float4 pos   : POSITION;
    float4 color : COLOR0; // vertex lighting
};
// Vertex shader
VS_OUTPUT_LO vsMain9( VS_INPUT i )
{
    VS_OUTPUT_LO o;
    o.pos = mul( i.pos, mViewProj );
    float4 light = tolight( i.pos, vLightPos );
    o.color = lighting( i.normal, light, vLightColor );
    // shadowing
    float dv = evalSH9( i, light.xyz );
    float dl = light.w;
    float shadowFactor = saturate( (dv/dl-0.3333)*1.5 );
    o.color *= shadowFactor;
    return o;
}
// Pixel shader
float4 psMainLo( VS_OUTPUT_LO i ) : COLOR
{
    return i.color;
}
```

It is possible to go even further and use 2nd order SH approximation, reducing the per vertex storage to four coefficients and distance evaluation to just a couple of instructions.

Results

Figure 5.3.4 compares standard shadow mapping with various levels of visibility distance SH approximation (5th, 3rd, and 2nd SH order). Surprisingly, rendering performance with our method is acceptable at low SH levels.

FIGURE 5.3.4   *Comparison of shadow maps (1st column) and shadows using visibility distance functions (2nd–4th columns, using 5th, 3rd, and 2nd SH order respectively). Shadows lose their form when using low-order SH, but in most cases still look plausible. Top row renders at 79, 54, 139, and 159 FPS on Radeon 9800Pro at 1024 × 768 screen resolution.*

Using SH for visibility distance functions is a gross approximation, however, the resulting images somehow manage to look acceptable. There are some cases where all these approximations and fakes do fail, especially when the light is very near occluders in several directions and far from occluders in other directions, as shown in Figure 5.3.5.

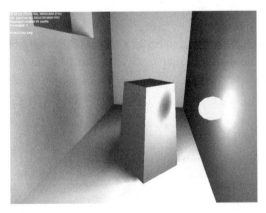

FIGURE 5.3.5   *Shadowing failures (the ball is the light source). The most obvious failure is false shadow on the front of the box like object.*

There still are some interesting ideas to try, such as storing visibility distance functions in textures or using other approximation and compression techniques [Sloan03a].

Conclusion

This article presents a technique to render fake soft shadows in static scenes using precomputed visibility distance functions. The technique handles dynamic local light sources and executes at acceptable speeds on modern graphics hardware, with faster lower-quality fallbacks possible on low-end hardware.

References

[Green03] Green R., "Spherical Harmonic Lighting: the Gritty Details," Game Developers Conference, 2003.

[Ramamoorthi01] Ramamoorthi R., Hanrahan P., "An Efficient Representation for Irradiance Environment Maps," ACM Transactions on Graphics (SIGGRAPH 2001), 2001: pp. 497–500.

[Sloan02] Sloan P.P. et al., "Precomputed Radiance Transfer for Real-time Rendering in Dynamic, Low-frequency Lighting Environments," ACM Transactions on Graphics (SIGGRAPH 2002), 2002: pp. 527–536.

[Sloan03a] Sloan P.P. et al., "Clustered Principal Components for Precomputed Radiance Transfer", ACM Transactions on Graphics (SIGGRAPH 2003), 2003

[Sloan03b] Sloan P.P. "Efficient Evaluation of Irradiance Environment Maps" from *ShaderX²*, Wordware, 2003: pp. 226–232.

[Terdiman01] Terdiman P., "Memory Optimized Bounding Volume Hierarchies', available online at *http://www.codercorner.com/Opcod.pdf*, 2001.

5.4

Efficient Omnidirectional Shadow Maps

Gary King and William Newhall

Introduction

Shadows are an important visual cue in 3D scenes; they are the primary mechanism for giving users information about the relative positions of objects. Unfortunately, integrating shadows into real-time applications is difficult and substantially increases performance requirements. Due to their cost, it is critical that any shadow implementation be as efficient as possible. This means that only the minimum amount of geometry (and pixels) required to add shadows to a scene be rendered, and rendering these objects as efficiently as possible. This article focuses on algorithms that will improve the performance and quality of omnidirectional shadow depth maps. For clarity, we will limit the scope of this article to implementations using cube maps [Greene86], although most of these techniques are directly applicable to other environment map types, such as dual-paraboloid and tetrahedral.

Review of Omnidirectional Shadow Mapping

ON THE CD

In order to implement the optimizations that will be discussed later in this article, we need a basic cube map shadow map implementation as a starting point. For an excellent step-by-step description of cube map shadow maps (including fallbacks for older hardware and drivers), see Philip Gerasimov's article in *GPU Gems* [Gerasimov04], or see the source code for the demo accompanying this article (contained in R32FCubemap.[cpp/h/fx]).

For our quick and dirty shadow cube map implementation, we will use single-component 32-bit floating-point cube maps (D3DFMT_R32F in DirectX 9-speak). At the time of writing, this format was supported on Radeon 9500+, GeForce FX-series[1], and GeForce 6-series GPUs. Floating point cube maps naturally lend themselves for use as shadow maps: at each texel, store the radial distance (or squared radial distance) of the occluder from the light source, in light-space. To transform a vertex into light-space, simply subtract the light's position from the vertex's position, where both positions are defined in a common space (e.g., world-space).

---

[1]D3DFMT_R32F exposed in Forceware 60-series and later drivers for GeForce FX GPUs.

To render the shadow map, iterate through the scene six times (one for each face), and transform the light-space vertex by the face's view-projection matrix (remember to clear the Z-buffer for each face).

Finally, to use the shadow map when rendering the final scene, first transform the rasterized fragments into light-space. Since this transform is a linear operation, it can be computed per-vertex and interpolated per-pixel. Compare the distance of each pixel to the values stored in the shadow map (plus a small bias, to avoid precision problems that can lead to self-shadowing). If a pixel's distance from the light is farther than the distance stored in the shadow map, it is in shadow.

The last thing we will add to this basic shadow cube map implementation is shadow filtering. As you can see in Figure 5.4.1, point-sampling leads to noticeable stair-stepping artifacts dividing shadowed and unshadowed regions. These artifacts are known as shadow aliasing, and can be hidden by super-sampling the depth comparison in the final pixel shader. Simple implementations perform depth comparisons with multiple shadow texels and average the results (percentage closer filtering); more advanced implementations perform a true reconstruction filter on the results to get a smoother shadow edge (e.g., bilinear PCF). Because true bilinear filtering on cube maps is an extremely expensive process, we will use an approximation described by Arkadiusz Waliszewski that uses eight shadow comparisons and three vectorized LERPs [Waliszewski03].

FIGURE 5.4.1 *Point-sampling the depth comparison yields a harsh transition at shadow boundaries.*

Optimizing Shadow Texture Computation

Looking at this example, the first thing you should notice is that omnidirectional shadowing is extremely expensive. Even with per-object view frustum culling implemented for all rendering passes, the sample application increases from 18 milliseconds per frame without shadows to 125 ms with filtered shadows on a Quadro FX Go1000—rendering the shadows is more than four times as expensive as rendering the rest of the scene! If a game is going to include fully dynamic shadowing, this has to be improved if real-time frame rates are going to be achieved.

Culling Cube Map Faces—
Intersection of Two Frusta

The most effective optimization we can perform is not rendering faces of the shadow map, which saves both shadow map fill and vertex processing. The question then is how to cull portions of the shadow map without introducing differences in the resulting image. In order to do this, we are going to extend the simple axis-aligned bounding box frustum culling in the sample application to also cull against other frusta.

Figure 5.4.2 illustrates how the six shadow map frusta are located relative to the view frustum for a variety of light positions. In all cases, if the light source is outside of the view frustum, then we can skip rendering at least one face of the shadow map.

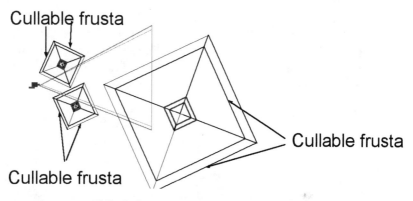

FIGURE 5.4.2 *If the light source is outside of the view frustum, at least one face is cullable.*

Frustum culling an arbitrary frustum, *F*, against a view frustum, *V*, is only slightly more complicated that frustum culling an axis-aligned bounding box. First, we need to determine if the two frusta intersect. We only need to handle four cases in order to determine this, and these cases can be divided into two symmetric tests: a boundary point of one frustum is inside the other frustum, or a boundary edge of one frustum intersects one or more clip planes of the other frustum. A frustum has 8 boundary points and 12 boundary edges. A boundary point is the intersection of any three clip planes, and a boundary edge is the intersection of two neighboring clip planes. In pseudocode, this looks like:

```
HalfIntersection( Frustum A, Frustum B )
P = points(A)
    For all p in {P}
            If inside(p, B)
                    Return intersection
    E = edges(P)
    For all e in {E}
            If intersect(e, B)
                    Return intersection
    return !intersection
```

```
Intersection( Frustum F, Frustum V )
return HalfIntersection(F,V) ||
       HalfIntersection(V,F)
```

Applying this to shadow frusta is straightforward: for each face of the shadow map, compute if the view frustum intersects the shadow face frustum (or vice-versa). If the two frusta do not intersect, we know that the shadow face doesn't affect the final image and we can skip all additional processing of it.

Improved Frustum Culling for Shadow Passes

We can apply this improved frustum-frustum culling code for shadow-casting objects, too. In most scenes, it is reasonable to assume that a small percentage of objects are casting visible shadows. However, simply performing bounding-box culling between shadow casters and the view frustum will not behave correctly—the shadows will "pop" into view. Similarly, simply culling shadow caster bounding boxes against the shadow frustum may result in invisible shadows being drawn, spending GPU cycles unnecessarily. To understand why this happens, look at Figures 5.4.3 and 5.4.4.

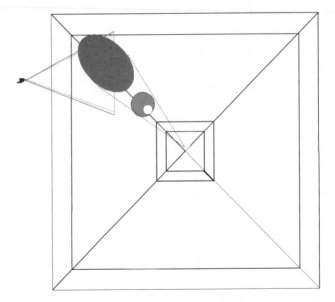

FIGURE 5.4.3   *An off-screen object casts a shadow into the visible scene.*

In order to properly cull a projected shadow against the view frustum, we need a representation of the projected shadow. Since we are casting shadows from point lights, we know that all shadow rays emanate from the same point. This is analogous to all rays converging to the same point, as is the case with perspective projections.

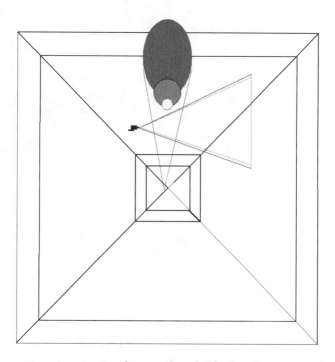

FIGURE 5.4.4 *An object within the shadow frustum casts an invisible shadow.*

Therefore, if shadow casting objects are represented as bounding boxes, a frustum can be used to represent the projected shadows, and we can reuse the frustum-frustum culling test developed above.

To build this frustum, the demo computes a tight bounding cone surrounding the light position and each shadow caster's world-space bounding box. This cone is trivially converted into a centered frustum. Note that better algorithms for building frusta from bounding boxes exist [Schmalstieg99], but for our purposes, this algorithm works fine.

There is one special case that needs to be handled for robust shadow-caster culling: when the light is inside a shadow caster's bounding box. In this case, one frustum is insufficient for representing the projected shadow (see Figure 5.4.4). However, if the light is attenuated, a bounding box bounding the entire light range[2] can be used instead, and simple bounding box culling can then be used.

At this point, our improved omnidirectional shadow-mapping algorithm is:

---

[2]Although the actual light range is infinite, a good approximation is to define the light range as the distance were the light intensity falls below a minimum (visible) threshold.

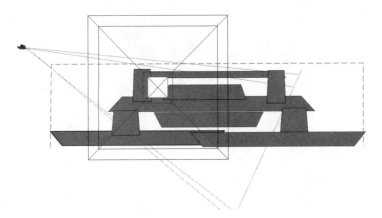

FIGURE 5.4.5   *Light source inside a shadow caster's bounding box casts a shadow on multiple cube faces.*

```
for all I in { cubemap faces }
        if intersect(view_frustum, frustum(I))
                set render target (I)
                for all O in { scene objects }
        if intersect(frustum(O), view_frustum)
        draw(O)
```

Optimizing Rendering With Shadow Textures

Scissoring

So far, the optimizations we've implemented have primarily helped cases where the light source is outside of the view frustum, and focused on reducing the cost of generating the shadow maps. However, lights are frequently inside the view frustum. Applying a shadow map in a pixel shader is costly, too, especially if filtering is applied.

In many cases, when a light source is inside the view frustum, it affects only a small number of pixels on the screen; Figure 5.4.5 demonstrates such a case. Using a brute-force algorithm, we might spend millions of GPU cycles computing per-pixel lighting with filtered shadows for every pixel in the frame, even though the light affects only a small percentage of those pixels! We can take advantage of a feature recently added to Direct3D called the scissor test to quickly cull away most of these pixels.

To use the scissor test, we need to define a *scissor rectangle* representing the region of the screen affected by the light source. Any pixels inside this rectangle will pass the scissor test and get fully shaded, other pixels are quickly rejected. To compute this rectangle, build an axis-aligned bounding box around the light source with side length equal to double the light's radius of effect. Transform this bounding box into post-projective view space, and find its bounding rectangle. The scissor rectangle is this bounding rectangle, clipped to the screen extents (see Figure 5.4.6). To avoid problems with negative w coordinates, when the viewer is inside the light's bounding box, set the scissor rectangle to the full screen size.

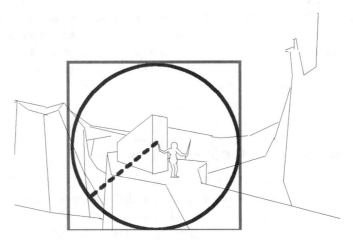

FIGURE 5.4.6 *Circle represents light range from torch, scissored to rectangle.*

Optimizing Shadow Texture Resolution

The last algorithmic optimization we will add builds upon some of the code developed for the scissoring optimization, and addresses a related observation: given a cube map edge length of 512, rendering all 1.2 M texels in the cube map when the light affects only 20,000 pixels in the final image is overkill. In addition to costing more pixel fill to render the shadow map, using an unnecessarily high resolution shadow map will reduce the texture cache hit rate when performing shadow comparisons, which also hurts performance on the shading pass.

In order to perform this optimization, we will need multiple cube maps with different resolutions. GPUs already have a mechanism for supporting this, mipmaps [Williams81]. In the demo, we exploit mipmaps to reduce the number of unique textures we need to create and manage; we do not use mipmap filtering. Because we will only render 1 mip-level per shadow map, we need to force the GPU to texture from a specific LOD. This can be accomplished trivially using the texCUBElod intrinsic in 3.0 pixel shaders. However, for non-shader model 3.0 hardware, something else is required. We achieve this "something else" by some rather unintuitive use of the LOD bias and max mip-level sampler states (D3DSAMP_MIPMAPLODBIAS and D3DSAMP_MAXMIPLEVEL)[3]. Isotropic texture LOD is computed as:

```
lod' = max( MAXMIPLEVEL, log₂(rho) + MIPMAPLODBIAS )
```

---

[3]In OpenGL, setting both GL_TEXTURE_MIN_LOD and GL_TEXTURE_MAX_LOD to the desired LOD will have the same effect.

This will force the hardware to texture from MAXMIPLEVEL level if we can guarantee that MAXMIPLEVEL is always greater than the computed LOD. This will be the case if MIPMAPLODBIAS is set to a large negative number, equal to at least the number of levels in the mipmap pyramid.

Now that we can texture from and render to specific mipmap levels, how do we decide which level is appropriate for the frame? A straightforward approach is to loosely apply the Nyquist theory to shadow map resolution: if N faces of the cube map are visible, covering S pixels on screen, choose the coarsest mipmap level with edge length M such that $N*M2 >= c*S$, with c equal to 2.0. This is not correct, since shadow maps aren't sampled uniformly with respect to the viewer, but it is a reasonable approximation (if your application demonstrates aliasing problems, try increasing c).

Virtual Shadow Depth Cube Texture Mapping

We can further improve the performance of our shadow cube texture maps if we can reduce the cost of supersampling and filtering when texturing from a shadow cube texture. The problem with our existing FP32 approach is that each filter tap requires a separate texture instruction, and each shadow compare requires arithmetic instructions and bilinear filtering in the fragment program is just too expensive in terms of instructions and register utilization.

An ideal approach would be to use the D16 and D24 shadow depth texture formats (as supported by Geforce3, Xbox, GeForce4, GeForceFX, and GeForce6) to perform four-tap bilinear percentage closer filtering for each texture fetch. These formats support shadow compare and bilinear percentage closer filtering for each texture instruction.

As an added benefit, shadow textures rendered using the D16 and D24 shadow texture formats take considerably less time to create for a variety of reasons:

- Less memory bandwidth required (especially in the case of D16)
- Fewer transactions, giving better bandwidth efficiency (no color buffer writes)
- Modern GPUs have accelerated depth-only rendering and compressed depth buffers

There is only one problem with D16 and D24 shadow depth texture formats: They don't work with cube maps. Neither DirectX 9 nor OpenGL support depth texture cube maps.

The solution is to render the six faces of the cube map as six subrectangles within a single 2D depth texture which we call the *virtual shadow depth cube texture,* or VSDCT. The fragment program then performs the necessary calculations to map the 3D light vector to the 2D VSDCT texture coordinates, computing the shadow depth used for the shadow map compare. There are three phases to these calculations:

- Cube map transformation (mapping a 3D vector to a 2D vector and a cube face)
- Texture coordinate remapping, scaling, and cube face address offset
- Shadow depth projection, perspective, and viewport transformations

While there are many calculations going on here, the actual implementation of these calculations can be substantially optimized by using an *indirection cube map* to accomplish the first two phases and all of the transformations in the final phase can be combined with a scalar reciprocal and a scalar multiply-add (see Figure 5.4.7).

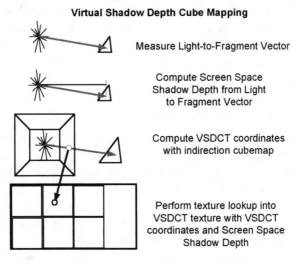

FIGURE 5.4.7 *Conceptual diagram of Virtual Shadow Depth Cube Texturing.*

Because we are using an indirection cube map to map cube texture coordinates to arbitrary points on a 2D texture we now have the freedom to size our shadow textures to arbitrary resolutions. In terms of pixel shader instruction efficiency it is best to use a VSDCT in which all the virtual cube map faces have the same resolution.

Cube Map and Depth Calculations for Rendering with VSDCTs

To combine elements of conventional cube mapping and shadow depth texturing to achieve omnidirectional shadow depth texturing the fragment program computes must now perform a number of calculations that are ordinarily performed by fixed-function hardware.

Cube Mapping Calculations

To correctly map the unnormalized 3D light vector to 2D texture coordinates on the VSDCT we need to accomplish the same sort of calculations that are performed by the texture unit in applying fixed-function cube mapping. Many hardware cube map implementations are conceptually arrays of six 2D textures. The process of mapping 3D vectors to texture coordinates is divided into three steps: face selection, coordinate transformation, and coordinate scaling.

Cube map face selection determines which of the six faces the 3D vector intersects. This can be determined by analyzing the relative magnitude and signs of the three components. After selecting the appropriate face, the texture coordinates are projected onto the unit cube (by dividing by the absolute value of the largest component), and rotated into the face's normalized device coordinates by conditionally swizzling and negating the other two texture coordinates. Finally, these coordinates are remapped to texel locations by applying a simple scale and offset. The indirection cube map mentioned above is used to implement these fixed function operations for VSDCTs, since performing the actual math inside a fragment program requires over 30 instructions.

Depth Coordinate Calculations

We need to apply the same projection, perspective, and viewport transformations to the R coordinate shadow depth that were applied to the depth values by the hardware when the shadow map was created. This is performed in two steps: *shadow depth ordinate selection*, and *projection transformation*.

To properly compare the shadow depth texture, the fragment program needs to compute an eye-space shadow depth from the 3D light vector components. This is known as shadow depth ordinate selection. Because each cube map face projection is exactly 90°, it can be shown that the eye-space depth coordinate is equal to the absolute value of the largest magnitude light vector component. We will call this *MA*. Because the VSDCT texture is storing screen Z, rather than eye-space Z, the same projection transform used for rendering the VSDCT faces needs to be applied to the shadow ordinate. In Direct3D, the canonical perspective projection matrix is:

$$
P = \begin{bmatrix}
\dfrac{1}{\tan(fovx * 0.5)} & 0 & 0 & 0 \\[2ex]
0 & \dfrac{1}{\tan(fovy * 0.5)} & 0 & 0 \\[2ex]
0 & 0 & \dfrac{Z_{far}}{Z_{far} - Z_{near}} & 1 \\[2ex]
0 & 0 & \dfrac{-Z_{far}Z_{near}}{Z_{far} - Z_{near}} & 0
\end{bmatrix}
\tag{5.4.1}
$$

But for the shadow comparison, we only care about how the projection transform affects the Z component, Z_p.

$$
Z_p = Z_{eye} \times \frac{Z_{far}}{Z_{far} - Z_{near}} - \frac{Z_{far}Z_{near}}{Z_{far} - Z_{near}}
\tag{5.4.2}
$$

and the value of the homogenous term W_p:

$$W_p = Z_{eye} \qquad (5.4.3)$$

It is vital that we use a projection matrix with a value of 1 in element (3, 4) because we need W_p to equal eye space Z, which equals the MA value we measured from our light-to-fragment vector.

Dividing Z_p by W_p produces screen space Z_s (Z_p normalized to a range of [0–1.0]):

$$Z_s = \frac{Z_p}{W_p} \qquad (5.4.4)$$

This value will be used for the shadow map compare within the texture pipeline. Since $W_p = Z_{eye}$ we can find Z_s by dividing both terms of Z_p by Z_{eye}:

$$Z_s = \frac{\dfrac{Z_{eye}Z_{far}}{Z_{far}-Z_{near}} - \dfrac{Z_{far}Z_{near}}{Z_{far}-Z_{near}}}{Z_{eye}} = \frac{Z_{far}}{Z_{far}-Z_{near}} - \frac{Z_{far}Z_{near}}{Z_{eye}\times\left(Z_{far}-Z_{near}\right)} \qquad (5.4.5)$$

reordering and substituting MA for Z_{eye}:

$$Z_s = \frac{-1}{MA}\times\frac{Z_{far}Z_{near}}{Z_{far}-Z_{near}} + \frac{Z_{far}}{Z_{far}-Z_{near}} \qquad (5.4.6)$$

Thus, our fragment program can compute shadow depth by computing the reciprocal of MA and applying a constant scale and a constant bias using a Multiply-Add instruction. This can be seen in VSDCT.fx.

Constructing Virtual Shadow Depth Cube Map Textures

Allocate the VSDCT Depth Buffer Render Target

When initializing your application (or at level load time) allocate the VSDCT surface with a power-of-two resolution that is large enough to accommodate six virtual cube faces at a reasonable resolution. The indirection cube maps will constrain our sampling to prevent cube seam crossings, so there really is no requirement to arrange the virtual cube face subrects contiguously.

In Direct3D, VSDCT surfaces can be created by allocated using `CreateTexture()` with a depth format (e.g., `D3DFMT_D24X8`) with `D3DUSAGE_DEPTHSTENCIL` specified. This is exactly like creating a 2D shadow map surface; for more details, see the comments in the accompanying source code (`VSDCT.cpp`).

Render the Virtual Cube Faces

Projection Matrices
To simplify the depth calculations required by the fragment program when applying the VSDCT we will use the same projection matrix for all of the cube faces. To maximize precision the near and far depth plane values should be selected by checking the bounding boxes of objects within the effective range of the light. The near depth plane should be as large as possible and the far depth plane should be as small as possible.

For maximum precision and efficiency, this matrix must have a 90° field of view in X and Y and must have a 1 in element (3, 4) so that the W value computed by the projection matrix will equal eye-space Z. If element (3, 4) is not equal to 1.0 then elements (1, 1), (2, 2), (3, 3,), and (4, 3) must be divided by the reciprocal of element (3, 4) and element (3, 4) must be replaced with 1.0.

Readying the Render Target and the Viewport
Set the render target write mask to disable color and stencil reads and writes. Clear the depth buffer. For each virtual cube face set the viewport to the rectangular region of the VSDCT that has been allocated for the virtual cube face.

Indirection Cube Map
The complete chain of cube face selection, coordinate rotation, side divide, (S, T) remap, (U, V) scaling, and cube face offset can all be accomplished with a single texture lookup into an *indirection cube map*. This cube map is created offline and can be used with multiple VSDCT textures provided that all faces of the virtual shadow cube map have the same resolution and that every virtual shadow cube map that employs this indirection cube map will use the same subrect configuration on every frame.

The format of an indirection cube map is G16R16 and its resolution should be selected based on the resolution of the virtual shadow cube map and the desired dynamic range of the shadow. We can trade dynamic range to reduce indirection cube map memory bandwidth consumption by selecting a lower number of grey levels than the bilinear filtering hardware supports. This is accomplished by computing the resolution of the indirection cube map this way:

$$N_i = 2^{\lceil \log_2(N_s)\rceil + \min(\lceil \log_2(G)\rceil, D) - D} \tag{5.4.7}$$

where N_s is the resolution of the shadow map cube face, G is the number of desired grey levels from a bilinearly filtered shadow map comparison, and D is the number of bits of precision that the underlying hardware uses for texture derivatives (on GeForce FX and GeForce 6-series GPUs, $D = 8$). So, as an example, for a shadow cube map with 256×256 texel faces, and 16 desired grey levels from the final shadow comparison, $N_i = 16$.

Issues and Potential Enhancements

Shadow Texture Aliasing Artifacts

No depth shadow-texture mapping paper would be complete without acknowledging the great unsolved problem of shadow-texture mapping. Because shadow-texture mapping involves a threshold test between two entirely different sets of point samples, the aliasing artifacts are significantly more pronounced in the form of self-shadowing and light leaks. Taking more samples, using larger filtering kernels, and applying depth bias or slope-scale depth bias can reduce the visibility of these defects. However, the root cause of the problem is that we are attempting to compare measurements taken with two entirely different sample sets and reconcile them with a filter.

Sampling across Cube Map Seams

An unavoidable sampling artifact occurs when sampling quads that straddle multiple cube map faces. Ideally, the hardware filtering would walk across the boundary, sampling all the right texels along the way. Unfortunately, there is no way to arrange the virtual cube faces within the VSDCT such that all seam crossings are correct (see Figure 5.4.8). Our workaround for this issue is to build the indirection and uvScaleBias textures to avoid sampling across seams. This has the side effect of reducing texture lookups on seams to point sampling. Thankfully, this artifact is rarely noticeable, especially when multiple VSDCT samples are used to perform higher-order PCF.

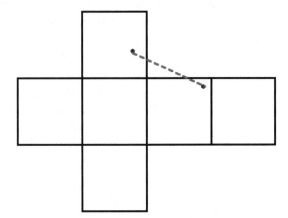

FIGURE 5.4.8 *Incorrect sampling across cube seams. The blue dots are adjacent texture samples, separated by unused VSDCT texels.*

Additional Sampling and Filtering

Many applications perform multiple, offset shadow map lookups to mask objectionable shadow map aliasing. For the same reasons that cube seam lookups need to be constrained to individual VSDCT faces, performing simple 2D offsets is insufficient. The correct way to perform higher-order PCF on VSDCTs is to offset the original 3D vector, perform the indirection lookup using this vector, and use the result to fetch from the VSDCT.

Nonuniform Cube Map Sampling

Texels on a cube map (or VSDCT) are not distributed uniformly across the sphere— the sample resolution at the center of each cube map face is more than 5× the resolution at the corners. A potential way to reduce visible shadow map aliasing without increasing the resolution is rotating the cube map to provide maximal texel density near the focal point. This is left as an exercise to the reader.

Conclusion

Despite its visual impact, real-time dynamic shadowing has been avoided in most games due to its huge performance cost. However, most of this performance cost can be avoided—we have provided a number of techniques that dramatically improve the performance (and quality) of omnidirectional shadow maps. By applying all of these techniques to our demo, it ran nearly three times faster on GeForce FX products, and over one and a half times faster on GeForce 6-series products. In our demo, VSDCTs provided the largest individual benefit for lights filling the full screen, but were also the most complicated to implement. For smaller lights, scissoring and reducing shadow texture resolution provided performance gains comparable to VSDCTs, with significantly less implementation complexity. Due to this performance increase, using these optimizations in games will allow users without the highest-spec PCs to enjoy dynamic shadowing.

References

[Gerasimov04] Gerasimov, Philipp, "Omnidirectional Shadow Mapping," in Randima Fernando, ed., *GPU Gems*, Addison-Wesley, pp. 193–203, 2004.

[Greene86] Greene, Ned, "Environment Mapping and Other Applications of World Projections," *IEEE Computer Graphics and Applications*, 6(11), pp. 21–29, Nov. 1986.

[Schmalstieg99] Schmalstieg, Dieter and Robert F. Tobler, "Fast Projected Area Computation for Three-Dimensional Bounding Boxes," *Journal of Graphics Tools*, 4(2), pp. 37–43, 1999.

[Waliszewski03] Waliszewski, Arkadiusz, "Floating Point Cube Maps," in Wolfgang Engel, ed., *ShaderX²*, pp. 319–324, 2003.

[Williams78] Williams, Lance, "Casting Curved Shadows on Curved Surfaces," *Computer Graphics (Proc. Siggraph '78)*, 12(3), pp. 270–274, August 1978.

[Williams81] Williams, Lance, "Pyramidal Parametrics," *Computer Graphics (Proc. of SIGGRAPH 83)*, 17(3), pp. 1–11, 1983.

3D ENGINE DESIGN

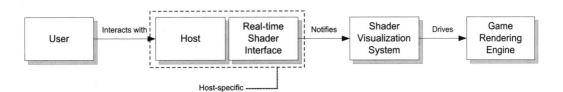

Introduction

Tom Forsyth

This book presents many wonderful shaders and algorithms. But very often the trickiest aspect of shaders is not writing the things themselves, but writing the code to support and debug them. Graphics engines have had to change a lot recently to cope with the enhanced flexibility that shaders present, and it can be daunting knowing how to tackle the extra complexity.

The tools pipeline has also had to change, but there progress is slower—in part because shaders present such a rapidly-moving target. To that end, this section includes some helpful hints, some useful libraries, some interesting artist tools, and some case studies.

"An Extensible Direct3D Resource Management System," by Bahnassi makes keeping track of assets such as textures, vertex buffers, and shaders simple, and elegantly deals with all the nasty edge cases when users change resolution, switch to other programs, or move the application to a different display.

"Integrating Shaders into the Vision Rendering Engine," by Frommhold and Born is a discussion with examples of taking an existing rendering engine and upgrading it to use shader systems; striking a balance between flexibility, ease of use and speed.

"Effect Parameters Manipulation Framework" is another useful drop-in article by Bahnassi, and gives some handy macros and functions to make management and debugging of complex shader systems a little easier on the eyes and brain.

Bahnassi and Bahnassi return with the article "Shader Visualization Systems for the Art Pipeline" showing how to integrate shader authoring into existing content-creation pipelines using plug-ins for the major tool vendors.

And finally, Gosselin, Sander, and Mitchell's "Drawing a Crowd" illustrates that shaders are not just about pretty effects. Sometimes they can radically change the design of an engine and allow scenes that were previously unattainable.

6.1

An Extensible Direct3D Resource Management System

Wessam Bahnassi

But Why?

DirectX should allow developers to create Windows applications that exist together on the desktop and leverage existing Windows components. This way a user can be playing a game, minimize the window, work on another application, and then come back to where they left off in their game [Bargen/Donnelly98a].

And look what this has brought upon us! Direct3D developers are destined to handle the ever occurring case of another application barging right into the game's solitude, stealing away its resources at any time. This might be a mail notification message, a scheduled task, or even a virus alert! When such an event occurs, all video memory resources owned by the game can be lost, and need to be restored before they can be used again.

No, the solution is not to get away from handling these cases by trying to disable application switching and its relevant key combos (Alt-Tab, Ctrl-Alt-Delete, Windows-D, and the rest of them). This is very bad behavior because it gives a negative feeling to end-users that their systems have become a slave to that game. On the developer's side, this actually makes for more trouble rather than solving problems. Avoiding the issue not only means that once the game is gone, it will never come back, but it takes away many abilities that are important during development. Suppose that you have a buggy pixel shader that appears deep in the game. Running the whole game on the Reference Rasterizer is not an option here, as your frame rate counter drops from 60 FPS to 60 SPF! Now you think, if only you could play the game using the Hardware rasterizer and just switch to the Reference Rasterizer when the buggy shader comes in, you would save yourself a great deal of time. However, switching to the Reference Rasterizer mid-game is not easy, because it is not just that your 3D device becomes lost, but it must be completely destroyed then recreated, taking away every resource you allocated through it! You need some way that can make your resources persist such cases, or you will have to scramble the whole game code so you can jump right into that buggy effect—not a good idea.

As you might have noticed, this implies that you will have to keep track of each and every Direct3D resource you created in your application, so you can restore its data correctly when the time comes. There are several methods available to solve the issue. One of them is the method used in the Sample Framework [DXSDK1]. In short, it exposes to the application a set of "notifications" that should be overridden to deal with all Direct3D resources the application uses throughout its life. The biggest problem with such a system is that it works on a per-instance basis, which means that more and more annoying restoration code has to be added as soon as any new Direct3D resource instance is declared. This might be suitable for small samples that aim to show how to use the API itself rather than hiding it. But for larger applications, this is not very good in terms of software engineering, not to mention the pain of successfully managing such a thing in a real-world game, which implies a large number of different Direct3D resources that come and go as the game progresses.

In the following pages, a much more natural system is described that works very well with larger applications, while requiring minimum coding effort. The system can handle simple device loss cases, plus the heavy device change ones—releasing then recreating the Direct3D device right from scratch. In addition, by the end of this article we cover a couple of different usage schemes with this system that solve other problems common to Direct3D applications in an automated and easy way using the same system.

But When?

If a DirectX application is minimized, or the user has switched to another application using Alt-Tab, the surfaces that are located in display could be lost when a new application takes over. Display memory surfaces will also be lost when changing display modes (note that surfaces in system memory can never be lost) [Bargen/Donnelly98b].

But let us leave that generalization aside and dig a little bit into technical details. When your `IDirect3DDevice9` object goes into a lost state, the data you have put on the device's video memory (both local and non-local) is all gone, so you have to put it back before you can use it again. So the chore breaks down into these two tasks:

- Detecting that the device has been lost
- Restoring data back to its original state prior to device loss

The device can be brought into a lost state in response to several scenarios. The following list covers most of the situations, though *not all of them*; some of which are taken directly from [DXSDK2] and [Bargen/Donnelly98b]:

- Device running in full-screen display mode that is different from the current desktop mode or format. Then the device window gets minimized for some reason, requiring the desktop to restore its mode/format.
- A power management event (e.g., sleep or standby).
- Device running in windowed mode. Some process causes desktop display mode to change (might be your application's process!).
- Failure of the `IDirect3DDevice9::Reset()` method.
- A mysterious internal driver error due to an obscure device state setup. This is rare (on the driver side at least) but happens.

The last case in the previous list is a bit special, as a simple `IDirect3DDevice9::Reset()` call usually won't be able to recover the device back from its unconsciousness. Rather, a hard device release and recreate is mostly needed. Device recreation is also required in several other cases, mostly user related, such as changing device type (e.g., hardware to Reference Rasterizer) or choosing a different adapter on the system.

Prior to calling `IDirect3DDevice9::Reset()`, the Direct3D API requires that you must release all resources allocated in `D3DPOOL_DEFAULT`, or the function will not succeed. This is not much of a problem actually, as a variety of Direct3D resources can survive a reset (including shaders). The bad news is with a device recreate. Here, any Direct3D object that was ultimately created by `IDirect3DDevice9` cannot be kept, no matter on what pool it is placed in (again, including shaders). All must be released, or Direct3D objects will be leaking all around.

Now that we have covered the cases where resource restoration is required (almost at any time!), and we have a rough idea of the things needed to handle the situation successfully, we can design a solution.

But How?

"You are encouraged to develop applications with a single code path to respond to device loss. This code path is likely to be similar, if not identical, to the code path taken to initialize the device at startup." Microsoft, "DirectX 9.0 Programmers Reference," 2002 [DXSDK2].

In practice, things are trickier, but we want the solution to be as easy, quick, simple, short, efficient, extensible, robust, fully-featured, non-limiting, and self-contained as possible (if such a solution really exists).

As we saw in the previous sections, we have to know if the device is lost before we can handle it correctly. This means that we need access to the application's active `IDirect3DDevice9`. We also need to keep a list of all Direct3D resources currently allocated using that device. A natural solution to the problem comes by introducing two new related classes, called `SXProbe` and `SXResource`.

As the name implies, `SXProbe` will be responsible for "probing" the device to know whether it is lost or not. `SXResource` is a base class that will be used to wrap Direct3D resources needed to persist device loss and recreation.

Below is a code snippet that shows the `SXProbe` class declaration:

```
class SXProbe
{
public:
  // Device Management
  HRESULT AttachToDevice(PDIRECT3DDEVICE9 pDevice,
    D3DPRESENT_PARAMETERS *pPresentParams);
  HRESULT DetachFromCurrentDevice(void);
  HRESULT ProbeDevice(void);
  HRESULT ResetDevice(D3DPRESENT_PARAMETERS *pPresentParams);
```

```
  // Resource Management
  HRESULT AddResource(SXResource *pResource);
  HRESULT RemoveResource(SXResource *pResource);

private:
  // Notification Functions
  HRESULT NotifyLoss(void);
  HRESULT NotifyRelease(void);
  HRESULT NotifyRestore(void);

  // Internal Members
  SXResourcesList m_lstResources; // Registered Resources List
  D3DPRESENT_PARAMETERS m_paramsPresent;
  // For restoration purposes
};
```

ON THE CD

A couple of internal member variables which are not important for our current discussion have been omitted. The complete declaration can be found on the companion CD-ROM.

Note that the SXResourcesList is a new type defined as:

```
typedef std::list<SXResource*> SXResourcesList;
```

Following is the declaration of the SXResource base class:

```
class SXResource
{
public:
  SXResource();
  virtual ~SXResource();

protected:
  friend class SXProbe;  // Open access for the probe

  // Overrides
  virtual HRESULT OnDeviceLoss(void);
  virtual HRESULT OnDeviceRelease(void);
  virtual HRESULT OnDeviceRestore(void);

  // Internal Members
  SXProbe *m_pOwnerProbe;
};
```

SXResource is merely a simple base class that the Direct3D wrapper classes will derive from, overriding only the required functions.

Tables 6.1.1 and 6.1.2 list the functions of the SXProbe and SXResource class respectively, along with a description of each function's purposes:

Table 6.1.1 Description of the SXProbe Class Member Functions

Function Name	Description
AttachToDevice	Bind this probe to an existing `IDirect3DDevice9`. Once bound, the probe can be used to detect the device's state. The probe can be attached to a single device only.
DetachFromCurrentDevice	This function must be called prior to releasing the current device to inform registered resource about this event.
ProbeDevice	Using `IDirect3DDevice9::TestCooperativeLevel()`, this function checks if the device is lost or not, and automatically restores it if necessary.
ResetDevice	Applies new presentation parameters to the currently attached device. It is important to use this function in place of `IDirect3DDevice9::Reset()` so the class can correctly notify registered resources about the reset.
AddResource	Register a new `SXResource` with the probe/device. Registration can occur once per resource. Subsequent calls on the same resource are all redundant. Note that the function will fail if the resource is already registered with a different `SXProbe`. Resources cannot be shared across probes/devices. Only registered resources will be informed of the various device events that might occur.
RemoveResource	Only unregisters the resource. No deletion/memory free operations are done of any kind on the original object.
NotifyLoss	An internal function that iterates all the registered resources, calling their overriden `SXResource::OnDeviceLoss()` member function.
NotifyRelease	Same as above, but calls `SXResource::OnDeviceRelease()` instead.
NotifyRestore	Same as above again, however, this calls `SXResource::OnDeviceRestore()` to tell the resources that the device is now up and running.

Table 6.1.2 Description of the SXResource Class Member Functions

Function Name	Description
OnDeviceLoss	Called when the resource is required to release all of its internal Direct3D objects that are residing in video memory (i.e., `D3DPOOL_DEFAULT`). The resource must keep backup data required to restore its Direct3D objects upon the next request to `OnDeviceRestore()`.
OnDeviceRelease	Called when the resource is required to release all of its internal Direct3D objects that were ultimately allocated through `IDirect3DDevice9`. Backup data must be available for restoration through an upcoming call to `OnDeviceRestore()`.
OnDeviceRestore	Called when the resource must restore its Direct3D objects back to their operational state, either from simple loss, or hard release cases.

Speaking of SXResource, it is worth noting that across all calls of OnDeviceSome-thing(), the IDirect3DDevice9 object is valid. The word "valid" here has several meanings. For OnDeviceLoss() and OnDeviceRelease(), it means that the IDirect3DDevice9 object is just a valid COM object, but is not valid for display purposes. This allows calling non-device-relevant functions (e.g., IDirect3DDevice9::GetDirect3D()) on the object prior to releasing it. However, for OnDeviceRestore(), the object is totally valid and ready for display. It can be used to create new objects (shaders, render targets, vertex buffers, etc.) or query certain hardware capabilities.

Usually, a loss notification is followed by a restore at some point later. However, in some circumstances, a loss notification might be followed by a release notification (this happens with internal driver errors). Thus, the resource must be ready to handle such a case by acting safely with object pointers. The DirectX SDK Sample Framework comes with a nifty macro called SAFE_RELEASE() which is very handy to use for such cases.

But Where?

"A lost device must recreate resources (including video memory resources) after it has been reset. If a device is lost, the application queries the device to see if it can be restored to the operational state. If not, the application waits until the device can be restored" [DXSDK02].

Now that the probe is ready, it must be placed in its correct place in the code. First, the application must have a unique SXProbe instance corresponding to each IDirect3DDevice9 object it intends to have. So, an application that uses two IDirect3DDevice9s simultaneously must have two SXProbes running. For simplicity, a single device is assumed here. The code can be duplicated for other devices too. The code snippets listed next are taken from the sample code in the companion CD-ROM, which is based on the DirectX SDK's Sample Framework. Listing 6.1.1 shows how the framework creates the device, and how it attaches the probe:

ON THE CD

Listing 6.1.1 Device Creation Code in the Sample Framework

```
// Create the device
hr = m_pD3D->CreateDevice(m_d3dSettings.AdapterOrdinal(),
    pDeviceInfo->DevType,m_hWndFocus, behaviorFlags,
    &m_d3dpp,&m_pd3dDevice);

if( SUCCEEDED(hr) )
{
  // Attach the probe
  hr = m_Probe.AttachToDevice(m_pd3dDevice,&m_d3dpp);
  if (FAILED(hr))
    return hr;
  .
  .
  .
}
```

The application starts by successful creation of an `IDirect3DDevice9` object. Right after that, the probe is bound directly to the device. Note that the address of the `D3DPRESENT_PARAMS` structure that was used in `m_pD3D->CreateDevice()` has been passed also to the `AttachToDevice()` function. This is required so the probe can use the same settings when calling `IDirect3DDevice9::Reset()` after loss. All that is left now is to place a couple of calls to `SXProbe::ProbeDevice()` in the relevant code areas.

There are two suitable positions that we can place our probe at. These are:

- Prior to rendering a scene. For example, just before `IDirect3DDevice9::Begin-Scene()`.
- Just after calling `IDirect3DDevice9::Present()`. This works by intercepting the call's return value, and resetting the device upon failure.

The first option is usually better, simply because this way the application can avoid rendering at all if the device is lost and cannot be restored at the moment. This is also much safer if the rendering code contains locks and direct access to Direct3D resource memory (even though Direct3D tries to fake such locks when the device is lost). The sample code probes at both places just for complete illustration:

```
HRESULT CD3DApplication::Render3DEnvironment()
{
  HRESULT hr;

  // Make sure device is good and running
  hr = m_Probe.ProbeDevice();
  if( D3DERR_DEVICELOST == hr )
  {
      // The framework blindly intercepts this
      // return value and tests it for failure.
      // When that is the case, it quits the
      // application directly. Here, we just
      // return success, but raise the m_bDeviceLost
      // flag, which tells the framework to stop
      // rendering, but keep probing the device at
      // constant low-frequency intervals.
    m_bDeviceLost = true;
    return S_OK;
  }
  if (FAILED(hr))
    return hr;

  if (m_bDeviceLost)
  {
    if( FAILED( hr = Reset3DEnvironment() ) )
      return hr;
    m_bDeviceLost = false;
  }

  .
  .
  .
```

```
// Render the scene as normal
if( FAILED( hr = Render() ) )
  return hr;
UpdateStats();

// Show the frame on the primary surface.
hr = m_pd3dDevice->Present( NULL, NULL, NULL, NULL );

// Make sure device is good and running
hr = m_Probe.ProbeDevice();
if( D3DERR_DEVICELOST == hr )
{
  m_bDeviceLost = true;

  // Raise device loss flag, and return
  // success to suppress the framework from
  // exiting the whole application
  return S_OK;
}
if (FAILED(hr))
  return hr;
return S_OK;
}
```

In the code above, SXProbe::ProbeDevice() gets called once at the beginning of the function and once near its end. This will check if the device is lost, and restores it automatically if it can. If the device cannot be restored yet, the usual D3DERR_ DEVICELOST value will be returned, and the application can respond to this in the way it finds suitable (the sample framework just halts rendering). Note the call to Reset3DEnvironment() from the sample framework. This function was previously used much the same way as SXResource::OnDeviceReset(), however, now it is almost empty, as it just restores some common render states. Still, it can be removed, but it was preferred not to do so to avoid big changes to the framework's code.

Since the framework allows the user to change the output device at any time, that must be taken into account too. Changing the device requires detaching the probe from the old device then attaching it to the new one. This is very easy:

```
void CD3DApplication::Cleanup3DEnvironment()
{
  // Detach from the device
  m_Probe.DetachFromCurrentDevice();
  if( m_pd3dDevice != NULL )
  {
    if( m_pd3dDevice->Release() > 0 )
        DisplayErrorMsg( D3DAPPERR_NONZEROREFCOUNT, MSGERR_APPMUS-
TEXIT );
    m_pd3dDevice = NULL;
  }
}
```

The framework then calls the device creation code in Listing 6.1.1, bringing the new device to life.

Now that the probe has been placed correctly, resources can be registered with it. This is as simple as:

```
m_Probe.AddResource(&m_Font);
m_Probe.AddResource(&m_Teapot);
m_Probe.AddResource(&m_Meshes[0]);
m_Probe.AddResource(&m_Texture);
m_Probe.AddResource(&m_ShaderTween);
```

Given that the resources added above are inherited from SXResource and override the relevant functions, this is all that is needed to make these resources survive the loss/recreation scenarios mentioned earlier. Some code design patterns might find it better to move the call of SXResource::AddResource() into SXResource's constructor and take the address of an existing probe as a parameter. The calls in the code above can be placed in some application initialization function (OneTimeSceneInit() in the sample).

But What?

"All video memory must be released before a device can be reset from a lost state to an operational state. This means that the application should release any swap chains created with IDirect3DDevice9::CreateAdditionalSwapChain and any resources placed in the D3DPOOL_DEFAULT memory class. The application need not release resources in the D3DPOOL_MANAGED or D3DPOOL_SYSTEMMEM memory classes. Other state data is automatically destroyed by the transition to an operational state" [DXSDK02].

But that only covers those resource required to override SXResource::OnDeviceLoss(). For device recreate, every Direct3D resource must be released. In the sample application, we provide simple implementations for some of the most relevant resources used:

- Static vertex and index buffers
- Vertex and pixel shaders
- 2D textures

Each of these resource classes handles the subject in a different manner. Static vertex and index buffers rely on having a system-memory copy always ready for backup. In this implementation, the vertex and index buffers are placed in D3DPOOL_DEFAULT, and thus they get released in both OnDeviceLoss() and OnDeviceRelease(), then they get recreated from scratch at OnDeviceReset(). Dynamic vertex and index buffers are a similar case. As they are always placed in D3DPOOL_DEFAULT, they do not differ in any thing from other D3DPOOL_DEFAULT resources with regard to restoration code. Actually, such dynamic resources almost always have a backing system memory copy that the application writes to prior to uploading that data to the vertex or index buffer. This is also required in order to make use of fast AGP writes, which are required to be sequential and DWORD aligned.

Vertex and pixel shaders do not lose their data on device loss, so there is no need to override `OnDeviceLoss()`. However, they are released when `OnDeviceRelease()` is called. Shaders restore themselves from a backup copy of the binary shader function (expressed through an array of DWORDs) which is obtained from compiling an assembly shader using D3DX.

Textures are similar to shaders since they are placed in `D3DPOOL_MANAGED`, so it is only about handling their `OnDeviceRelease()` and `OnDeviceRestore()` functions. In the sample application, textures restore themselves by simply loading art from the original file on disk, thus they just need the file name string to restore!

As we have seen, it is up to the engine to decide how to handle the different loss/restore cases, and how to provide backup memory upon restoration. Sometimes, the system memory backup is already there for other purposes (e.g., geometry data for collision detection might be the same used to fill the vertex/index buffer). In other cases it may not be ideal to keep such a copy, as in the case with textures. However, this must be balanced with the additional load time required when restoring the resource, which might become large and annoying, requiring a separate loading screen for the restoration operation itself! Also, if the media is not guaranteed to be available at all times, then that resource is pretty much limited to the first solution.

Another thing to watch for is shader scalability and changing device settings. For example, suppose that we have created the device with Software Vertex Processing turned on. This allows the creation and use of v3.0 shaders (which are not supported by current hardware). Suddenly, the application is forced to switch to Hardware Vertex Processing, which only supports v1.1. What to do with the shader? Again it is up to the engine to decide how to respond to this issue. Mostly, it will have to degrade the shader's target platform by trying to compile it back to v1.1. This means that a backup copy of the shader's source should be kept rather than the binary function (as in the sample application). The same question arises from changing the settings to higher ones. Should the shader be recompiled to a higher version? This depends on the circumstances. For game release, it might be desirable to recompile for the new platform (thus making use of its new capabilities), or just leave the shader on its current version. However, this will not work for the debugging stage, as when the application is requested to switch to the Reference Rasterizer (which supports all shader versions exposed by the runtime) one might end up debugging a shader version that is different than the one being worked on. The same story repeats for textures, and it gets more complicated when the texture is bound to a specific shader version (this includes other shader-dependant resources too, such as shader-specific vertex streams). Such decisions are usually taken at a higher level than shaders and textures.

In addition to the conventional Direct3D resources covered in the previous discussion, there are some additional benefits that result from this system. Here is a brief summary of them:

Persistent States: Often, a game has some global states set once at start of day. These states never change, or change very infrequently (e.g., projection matrix, static lights, etc). In order to guarantee that they are always correctly applied to the device no matter if it gets lost/recreated, a class can inherit from SXResource and just override OnDeviceRestore() to apply these states once the device has been restored, thus guaranteeing that they will always have effect.

Memory Approximation: If the D3DPOOL_DEFAULT resources have a raw Direct3D-ready backup copy, the probe can be used to make some rough estimations of video memory used by the application. This is done by summing the size of all the memory allocated by the backup copies. Note that this *is* a rough estimation, as graphics drivers can mangle and compress the data internally. Still, such information can be very useful. For example, an engine can use this estimate to make better level-of-detail decisions for resources that are to exist in its world.

Event-based Device State Information: An application can inject an "information resource" object that tells the application that its 3D device has been lost, released or restored. This might be useful, for example, when an application wants to suspend its operation upon device loss, then continue when it comes back again. Note that while this is true, some part of the application must keep probing the device at specific intervals to try reacquiring the device.

Device Memory Management: The Direct3D API recommends creating all D3DPOOL_DEFAULT resources first, then following them by D3DPOOL_MANAGED ones [DXSDK03]. This can be easily achieved using this system. Since SXProbe has a complete list of the associated resources, it can separate those managed ones from unmanaged into distinct lists, then create D3DPOOL_DEFAULT first, followed by the rest of D3DPOOL_MANAGED resources by calling their OnDeviceRestore().

Words on the Sample Application

ON THE CD

The sample application provided on the companion CD-ROM shows the usage of the discussed system through a simple vertex shader that deforms a textured ball. The sample is based on the DirectX SDK Sample Framework. This framework already comes with its own resource management system. The sample provided here is a modified version of the same framework. This can show the difference between the two approaches. The modification is done by carefully injecting SXProbe into the framework's CD3DApplication base class. The sample also provides wrapper SXResource classes for Direct3D vertex and index buffers, vertex and pixel shaders and 2D textures (plus a wrapper for that CD3DFont object used to output text).

The system is declared in SXDevice.h and implemented in SXDevice.cpp. Sample wrappers are written in SXSampleResources.h and SXSampleResources.cpp.

Conclusion

Throughout this article, the different IDirect3DDevice9 loss, release, and restore scenarios are illustrated. The article also exposes a resource management system that makes handling this stuff very easy. This is done by placing a device probe (class SXProbe) around rendering code hotspots. The probe notifies all SXResource instances registered with it about the various device events that occur. Resources in turn can handle these notifications in a suitable way by overriding the provided notification functions from the base SXResource class.

After integrating this system into the engine, resources can be added easily by a single line of code, which can be the same line that declares the resource, thus freeing the programmer from having to manually keep track of resources used. Management code becomes centralized and this removes the need to add code at different places in the application. Direct3D resource leaks caused by bad management are also eliminated.

In addition, the article shows some small tricks that can be achieved using this system; these include device state persistence, memory usage approximation and device memory management.

References

[Bargen/Donnelly98a] Bargen B. and Donelly P. "Shaping DirectX," *Inside DirectX*, Microsoft Press1998, pp. 4–5.

[Bargen/Donnelly98b] Bargen B. and Donelly P. "Lost Surfaces," *Inside DirectX*, Microsoft Press, 1998, pp. 80–81.

[DXSDK1] Microsoft Corporation, "Sample Framework," DirectX 9.0 Programmer's Reference.

[DXSDK2] Microsoft Corporation, "Lost Devices," DirectX 9.0 Programmer's Reference.

[DXSDK3] Microsoft Corporation, "Application-Managed Resources and Allocation Strategies," DirectX 9.0 Programmer's Reference.

6.2

Integrating Shaders into the Vision Rendering Engine

Dag Frommhold and Florian Born

Shaders in the Early Days

It all began in the year 2000, when we—back then still working under the company name "Vulpine GmbH"—concluded that our engine licensees would benefit from more flexibility in defining their own material and effects properties. At about the same time, we had been asked by nVidia about contributing a demo to the NV20 launch, and since the Geforce 3 (as it was later called) provided a limited amount of programmability in addition to the OpenGL fixed function pipeline, revising our fixed-function renderer was a good idea. The obvious way to achieve the goals of providing more flexibility and quickly exposing new hardware features was a shaders and effects system.

The version of our shader-based rendering pipeline was added to the Vision engine fairly quickly. It mostly involved defining data structures for storing the state setup including pixel and vertex shaders, creating new rendering methods to provide the shaders with the vertex and texture data they needed, and exposing all the new functionality in the engine API. However, that did not really mean that we were already finished—in fact, we had to spend quite a lot of time on making the shader system general enough to support all (or at least most) of the complex effects we and other people conjured up while actually working with the new engine version.

Within the scope of this article, we want to share some of the ideas and solutions that we came up with during the last few years, most of which actually found their way into the Vision shader system. In general, the concepts presented here are independent of each other, and it should be rather easy to integrate them with the engine of your choice.

Shaders in the Vision Engine

The Vision engine is a commercial multi-platform game engine that forms the basis for a number of game projects currently in development. The development studios working with it have quite different focus areas (e.g., realistic rendering versus cel shading), target platforms (PC versus consoles) and game genres (ranging from the traditional FPS to strategy titles). Thus, flexibility and ease of use were important aspects in the development of the Vision engine in general and the shader system in particular. Even though the pixel or vertex shader implementations may differ depending on the platform, the general concept is platform-independent, and most of the concepts presented in this text are useful on both PC and consoles.

A "shader" in the Vision engine refers to a specific state setup—including, but not limited to, texture states, vertex and pixel shaders—that is used for rendering a set of geometry. On top of this, there are so-called "effects," which include an arbitrary number of shaders and also store fallback information for lower-end graphics cards. Fallbacks are alternative, usually simpler, versions of a complex shader that are used whenever the hardware requirements for a shader version higher up in the hierarchy are not met. (See Figure 6.2.1.)

While shaders and effects are usually defined by programmers in our proprietary shader tool (few artists want to burden themselves with pixel or vertex shader programming, even in HLSL or GLslang), they can expose arbitrary parameters for each shader. These parameters—for example, the hair length in a fur shader—can then be set by the artists in the tools they are working with. Effect libraries created with our shader tool can be loaded in Vision's scene editor and content integration tool vEdit, where effects can be assigned to arbitrary batches of geometry.

The engine creates shader instances from the effect hierarchy at runtime. Separate shader instances are created from the same effect when different parameters are used.

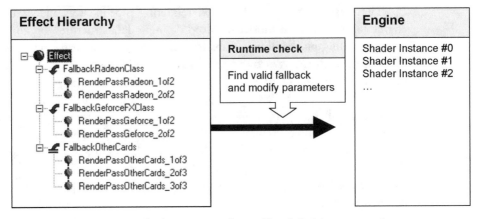

FIGURE 6.2.1   *Creating shader instances from effect definitions at runtime.*

Assigning Shaders to Geometry

Shaders can be used for a wide variety of purposes. For example, they may define a specific rendering style (e.g., cel shading) or material properties (e.g., reflectivity) of some geometric objects in a scene. Such shaders are usually statically assigned by the artists in their favorite production tools, and in most cases do not need to be updated, removed, or replaced in runtime.

However, shaders can also be used for dynamic effects, such as volumetric fog or dynamic lighting, which require a totally different approach. For example, imagine a simple shader that simulates a point light source by rendering an additively blended pass over all the geometry in a certain spherical volume around the light position. If this point light is supposed to move, the geometry it affects will also change, so there is no way to *statically* assign the shader to some of the geometry in the scene. For performance reasons, you obviously do not want to assign the shader to *all* the objects in a scene either, but rather only the objects that are actually within the light's sphere of influence (see Figure 6.2.2). In other words, a dynamic, volume-based approach for assigning shaders is required.

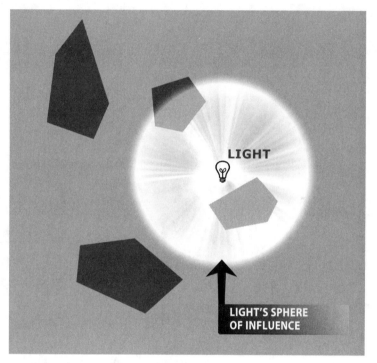

FIGURE 6.2.2 *A light's sphere of influence.*

In general, we found it helpful to differentiate between the following types of shaders, based on the way they are assigned:

- Shaders that are statically assigned by artists in the production tools: material properties, rendering styles.
- Shaders that are dynamically assigned in the game code—for example, when highlighting selected objects.
- Volume-based shader assignments—useful for dynamic lights, volumetric effects, and the like.

If the approach to shaders is a fairly general one, having all three ways of assigning shaders to the geometry in the scene is important. While the first two assignment types are pretty self-explanatory, it makes sense to take a closer look at the third one, since the case already mentioned—a simple point light source, and thus a spherical volume of influence—is only one of a number of shapes that can prove helpful. For example, simple axis-aligned bounding boxes are sometimes more useful than spheres, since overlap tests with boxes are very fast and often more accurate than spherical volumes. On the other end of the spectrum, spotlights or projectors require cones or frustums instead of spheres or boxes, and the same goes for volumetric effects that are simply rendered as overlays on top of the actual geometry (see Figure 6.2.3).

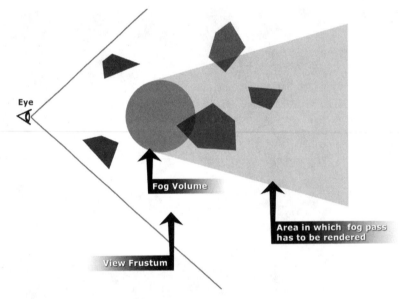

FIGURE 6.2.3   *Fog volume.*

It is likely that there are more useful shapes that have not yet been considered—there are many interesting future applications for volume-based shader assignment.

Rendering Order

Many engines use some sort of simple "base texture*static lighting" pass (which we will simply call "base pass" for the sake of brevity) on most of the geometry *before* applying any shaders. On some of the geometry, this may already be sufficient—for example, if there are no dynamic lights affecting it, or there are simply no complex materials applied. On other parts of the scene, it saves pixel processing power by setting the depth buffer with a simple shader before more complex pixel shaders are applied.

As long as rendering is limited to simple single-pass cases, it is rather obvious in which order the primitives have to be drawn: first, render all the opaque objects roughly front-to-back in order to improve early Z rejection, then render all the translucent objects, sorted back-to-front, to minimize visual artifacts. However, as soon as additional rendering passes are added, the problem of finding the right rendering order gets a little more complex. Here are a few examples of what has to be considered:

- There are shaders which have to be drawn *before* the usual base*lighting pass is rendered—for example, a cartoon outline shader that uses a vertex program to extrude the rendered geometry along the normal vectors in order to draw black outlines.
- Other shaders, such as additional rendering passes for dynamic lights, are usually drawn as an additive blend pass *after* the base*lighting pass.
- Yet other shaders—fog effects, for example, which can be rendered as an additional pass over the geometry—should be rendered after almost everything else, since the effects they represent are in fact not properties of the rendered surface itself, but rather properties of the space between the rendered surface and the camera.

Additionally, the order in which various rendering passes have to be performed is not only a function of the respective shader, but also of the earlier rendering passes over the same geometry. Assuming that translucent geometry is rendered without writing to the depth buffer, it can generally be considered a bad idea to do something like this:

```
void RenderLoop1 ( )
{
  RenderBasePass(OPAQUE_PRIMITIVES);
  RenderBasePass(TRANSLUCENT_PRIMITIVES);
  RenderEffects(ALL_PRIMITIVES);
}
```

The problem with this pseudocode is that the separate effects rendering pass over all the geometry will most likely result in the effects pass over static geometry being drawn on top of the already rendered translucent geometry. This will happen even if the respective static geometry is actually *behind* the translucent primitives. In order to solve this problem completely, all effects on translucent primitives would have to be rendered right after rendering the primitive itself. But this is not very feasible due to performance concerns—there would simply be too many state changes. Instead of this, it is more acceptable to render the effects passes separately for opaque and translucent primitives. As long as the artists know how to handle translucent geometry and are aware of the fact that there are limitations to be considered, a loop like the following one will be sufficient:

```
void RenderLoop2 ( )
{
  RenderBasePass(OPAQUE_PRIMITIVES);
  RenderEffects(OPAQUE_PRIMITIVES);
  RenderBasePass(TRANSLUCENT_PRIMITIVES);
  RenderEffects(TRANSLUCENT_PRIMITIVES);
}
```

The problem that still has to be solved is the rendering order between the base pass and the (potentially multiple) shaders applied to the same geometry. In the Vision engine, we introduced a property that specifies whether a shader is supposed to be rendered before or after the base pass. This way, it is possible to render the cartoon outlines mentioned above before the base pass is drawn, and if the geometry is illuminated by a light source, a lighting shader can be rendered on top of the base pass. Additionally, it is important that individual shaders within the same category (pre versus post base pass) can be sorted against each other, for example, by simply specifying a sorting key. This helps when there is, for example, a lighting shader and a volumetric fog shader, both of which are rendered after the base pass—using a sorting key ensures that the fog is always rendered last.

With these modifications, the rendering loop pseudocode looks something like this:

```
void RenderLoop3 ( )
{
  RenderEffects(OPAQUE_PRIMITIVES, PRE_BASEPASS);
  RenderBasePass(OPAQUE_PRIMITIVES);
  RenderEffects(OPAQUE_PRIMITIVES, POST_BASEPASS);
  RenderEffects(TRANSLUCENT_PRIMITIVES, PRE_BASEPASS);
  RenderBasePass(TRANSLUCENT_PRIMITIVES);
  RenderEffects(TRANSLUCENT_PRIMITIVES, POST_BASEPASS);
}
```

Naturally, these issues are only relevant if the engine uses multi-pass rendering. In very basic rendering systems where only the base pass is required, the drawing order is usually not as critical, and the same goes for very advanced engines which use some sort of deferred shading or automatically collapse everything into a single rendering pass. However, since most engines used for production rather than experimental purposes perform multiple rendering passes on some of the geometry, drawing order considerations will almost always be an issue.

Shader Callback Functions

In addition to the state setup information, some callback mechanisms are provided for shaders. In an object-oriented approach these callbacks are just virtual member functions of the shader class. There are two different types of callback functions:

1. A per-frame callback function. This callback gets executed once per frame for each shader instance. The code in the shader callback allows the programmer to modify the shader variables each rendering tick (i.e., each time the engine's main rendering loop is called). This is used extensively for animated shaders, e.g., pulsating colours, scrolling texture coordinates, and the like.

2. A per-primitive callback function. In this case, "primitive" refers to a group of triangles using the same shader. This gets called just before a batch of triangles is rendered with the shader. Furthermore, the return value of the callback determines whether the geometry in question should not be rendered at all, rendered once, or if it should loop and enter the callback function again after rendering. The following code shows an example of how to use per-primitive callbacks to iterate through all light sources that influence a primitive and render this geometry with a specific shader. Thus, by resubmitting the same geometry for rendering with a slightly different shader setup, this callback represents an additive multi-pass lighting algorithm. With the most recent shader models, this loop could be performed in vertex and even pixel shaders in a single pass, so this sample could be the fallback for an older shader model.

```
int ShaderCallbackIterateLights(Shader_t *pShader, int iGeomType,
        int iPrimitiveIndex)
{
  static int iLightList[256];
  static int iIteration = 0;
  static int iLightCount;
  if (iIteration==0)
  {
    // get a list with relevant light indices from the engine
    iLightCount = GetRelevantLights(iLightList, iPrimitiveIndex);
  }

  if (iIteration==iLightCount)
  {
    // all lights done - abort the loop
    iIteration=0;
    return CALLBACK_ABORT;
  }

  // do setup for light #iLightList[iIteration]
  pShader->iTrackLightIndex = iLightList[iIteration];
  pShader->iModifiedMask |= MODIFIED_TRACKED_LIGHT;

  iIteration++;

  // render geometry and call this function again
  return CALLBACK_LOOP;
}
```

Note that the callback is not called for each single triangle—this would be far too expensive—but rather on batches of triangles meeting a defined set of criteria such as material properties and the light sources illuminating them.

Another example of using a per-primitive callback function is rendering the shells of a fur shader. Using the callback function, the shader loops through each single shell and increases the normal extrusion distance in each iteration. In addition, the callback function can determine the on-screen projected size of the fur layer distance and thus reduce the number of shells based on the mesh's distance (see Figure 6.2.4). This results in a quite effective level of detail mechanism for fur rendering.

28,000 Polygons   5,500 Polygons

FIGURE 6.2.4   *Fur: reducing fur shells according to distance.*

However, this loop cannot be performed inside current vertex or pixel shaders since the shells define a "real" volumetric effect with different geometry for each pass, and the number of rendered triangles depends on the effect's input parameters. Today's graphics hardware does not support generating triangles on the fly, and even when it does there is always older hardware to consider.

```
int ShaderCallbackFurShells(Shader_t *pShader, int iGeomType,
    int iPrimitiveIndex)
{
  static int iFurShellCount = 16;
  static int fFurLength = 5.f;
  static int iIteration = 0;
  if (iIteration==0)
  {
```

```
   // modify iFurShellCount according to distance
   […]
}

   if (iIteration==iFurShellCount)
{
   // abort the loop
   iIteration=0;
   return CALLBACK_ABORT;
}

   // this value will be tracked to the vertex program parameters
   pShader->fVertexShaderConstReg[0].x =
      fFurLength*(float)(iIteration+1)/(float)iFurShellCount;
   pShader->iModifiedMask |= MODIFIED_VERTEXSHADER_CONST;

   iIteration++;

   // render geometry and call this function again
   return CALLBACK_LOOP;
}
```

Both types of shader callback functions can be implemented by the game programmer and have to be registered through the engine API in order to be available to the shader system.

These two types of callbacks are a powerful construct for game programming, because the programmer gains low-level control over the shader setup in an optimized rendering pipeline. Animating, triggering, or individually highlighting single objects becomes a matter of a few lines of custom code.

Reducing Overhead for State Setup

Two of the most important goals of a shader-based rendering pipeline are batching triangles with the same shader setup and reducing state setup changes.

Batching triangles of static geometry with identical material properties is not only a question of efficient rendering, but also of optimized content. For example, the content creation tools or exporter plug-ins can already sort primitives by material. On the other hand, when performing hierarchical visibility checks, the order of primitives will change due to recursively traversing through visibility trees. In this case, it is more efficient to sort the lists of batches again before rendering them in order to avoid excess state changes.

Things get a bit more complicated when transparencies are involved. For instance, for a forest with hundreds of tree instances sharing the same model it would be very efficient to render all trees as a single batch. But in this case artifacts such as glowing branch textures or view dependent popping will occur because of the problems when alpha-blended textures write (or do not write) to the Z buffer. Thus, objects have to be sorted back-to-front in order to minimize artifacts. Still, objects at about the same distance can be sorted by render state again. In order to give programmers control over the sorting behavior of object instances, a sorting key is defined for each object that is a combination of render state, distance, and user definable key. These criteria can be encoded into a single 64-bit value. The more significant criteria are assigned to higher bit ranges to guarantee priority when sorting. The following pseudocode shows how the significance of each of the criteria can be defined.

```
int64 iKey = (iUserKey<<48) | (iDistance<<16) | iStateSetupID;
```

The distance value can be divided by a constant factor to reduce the significance of the distance on sorting, and deliberately discards the fractional remainder. This groups objects of similar distance for efficient sorting by render state rather than exact distance:

```
int iDistance = ((int)pObject->GetCameraDistance()) / 100;
```

Some effort should be put into reducing the state setup overhead when performing the state setup for individual shaders when rendering a list of geometry batches. The batches might differ in their individual diffuse base texture, light map texture, normal map texture, etc., which are defined in the content creation tools. Since shaders can reference these individual textures, the engine needs to perform different texture setups for each geometry batch in this case. In other cases, this is unnecessary, since the shader uses the same textures wherever it is used. A straightforward way to optimize this is to analyze the shader structure at creation time and store a hint in the shader that no batch-specific textures are used, in which case no texture setup has to be performed between batches.

Thus, the function RenderBatchListWithShaderDumb can be optimized as shown by the pseudocode in function RenderBatchListWithShaderSmart.

```
RenderBatchListWithShaderDumb(Shader_t *pShader, ...)
{
  SetupShaderState(pShader);
  for (i=0;i<iNumBatches;i++)
  {
    BindBatchSpecificTextures(pBatch[i]);
    RenderBatch(pBatch[i]);
  }
}

RenderBatchListWithShaderSmart(Shader_t *pShader, ...)
{
  SetupShaderState(pShader);
  for (i=0;i<iNumBatches;i++)
  {
    if (pShader->bHasBatchSpecificTextures)
      BindBatchSpecificTextures(pBatch[i]);
    RenderBatch(pBatch[i]);
  }
}
```

When dynamically updating a shader in a callback function, the shader state must be set up for each pass. The setup overhead can be reduced to a minimum if the shader structure provides a bit mask for flags that specify the parts of a shader that actually have been changed in the callback. As in the callback examples earlier in this article (the MODIFIED_TRACKED_LIGHT and MODIFIED_VERTEXSHADER_CONST flags), a callback function usually updates only very specific parts of a shader, such as vertex program constant registers, color values, etc.

A general and also very common way to reduce setup overhead is to use inlined wrapper functions for the graphics API.

```
inline XEnableAlphaTest()
{
  // comparing against "true" is important—see below
  if (g_bAlphaTestEnabled==true)
    return;
  glEnable(GL_ALPHA_TEST);
  g_bAlphaTestEnabled = true;
}
```

The branch prediction of the CPU is usually rather effective here and saves function calls even if the driver has similar checks.

Please note that the global state variable g_bAlphaTestEnabled needs to be set per render context. When switching a context, e.g., when rendering to a p-buffer or texture, the value of g_bAlphaTestEnabled must be set to an undefined value, e.g., 0xff, thus forcing the function to set the state. This is why the code checks equality with true, rather than just checking truth.

These wrapper functions not only save CPU performance, but also help when porting the engine to other graphics APIs.

Textures

Textures are crucial for shaders. In addition to the standard diffuse base textures or light maps, shaders often require textures of special formats such as normalisation cubemaps or special case lookup tables. Some of these custom textures can easily be created procedurally by program code instead of having artists define them manually. For instance, if a special logarithmic falloff or an exponential gradient is required in a lookup texture, this would clearly be a matter of just a few lines of code (instead of having a discussion on the aesthetic qualities of lookup tables with your lead artist). A common example of using lookup textures with a characteristic function encoded is a specular lighting shader that maps the dot product of normal vector and light direction to a texture coordinate.

To integrate both traditional and procedurally generated textures into the shader system of the Vision engine, we implemented something we called modifier callback functions. A modifier function is called with raw texel data, modifies the data and uploads the texture with a new required internal format. A good example for a modifier function would be a function that converts a grey-scale bump map into a normal map.

```
Stage0.texture = base_texture;
Stage1.texture = ConvertToRGBNormalmap("bumpmap.tga", 100.f);
```

This pseudocode shows the texture setup for two stages in a shader definition. The texture of stage 1 is created by modifying the input data of the bumpmap.tga texture. The float parameter 100.f is passed to the modifier function and is interpreted as a bumpiness scale (100%) for this specific modifier function.

The implementation of the modifier function itself takes the raw source data of the texture as input and returns a pointer to the modified raw data:

```
void *ConvertToRGBNormalmap(void *pSrcData, int iWidth,
      int iHeight, int iColorDepth, int iMipLevel,
      int &iNewTexFormat, float fBumpiness)
{
   […]
}
```

In our engine implementation, custom modifier functions have to be implemented and registered and can finally be accessed in the shader definition as shown in the pseudocode above.

Once a modifier function is implemented, the custom parameters can be tweaked while playing around with the shader in the shader editor. For instance, the specular exponent encoded in a lookup-table texture can be increased or decreased.

This system turns out to be very flexible and covers a lot of the texture types that would be cumbersome for artists to create manually. Some examples for using texture modifiers are:

- Converting height maps to vector maps (though for fine details, using dedicated art tool plugins is recommended)
- Normalization cubemaps
- All kinds of gradients and characteristic functions for texture lookups
- Cel shading lookups with dedicated mipmap levels
- Creating texture alpha channels for texture "color key" emulation

The Future

Modern high-level shading languages support a much higher degree of flexibility than the first pixel and vertex shader implementations introduced with DirectX 8. The introduction of dynamic loops and branches in vertex and even pixel shaders allows for a much more general approach to defining shaders. For example, iterating through lists of light sources or the bones of a skinned mesh is now easily possible in a vertex shader, whereas earlier shader models required separate shaders for each number of iterations. Similarly, combinations of multiple effects do not require separate shaders any more, since the permutations can be handled by conditionals in the shader itself. Of course, the concept of generality has its caveats as well, especially regarding performance concerns, so it will still be necessary to find a suitable balance here. However, it is expected that having lots of special-case rendering code in modern 3D engines will be replaced by fewer, but more general approaches.

Another important concern for modern shader systems is the fact that the features exposed in high-level shading languages—such as inlined function calls, long shader programs, and loops and branches—make it possible to perform pass collapses. Instead of rendering all the geometry in a scene multiple times with different shaders, it is now feasible to reduce the number of rendering passes automatically (i.e., without specifically involving coders or artists). Artists simply assign individual sets of effects to the objects in a scene, with each effect defining its specific input and output parameters. The engine could then assemble shaders depending on the set of effects assigned to the individual batches of geometry. The concept of functions calls in shaders should make such an implementation significantly easier.

Today, shaders are still often used for "eye candy" in scenes that largely rely on the fixed function pipeline to draw most of the geometry. It is more than likely that with graphics chips getting more and more powerful, and support for DX7/DX8 graphics hardware being phased out, this is going to change. In many cases, this has already happened for vertex shaders. The transition to a rather general shader model makes it possible to use and combine shaders more freely, thus improving the workflow for programmers and artists alike.

6.3

Effect Parameters Manipulation Framework

Wessam Bahnassi

Low-Level Business

With the release of Microsoft DirectX 7 SDK, Direct3D developers had their first sight on what is called *D3DX*, or the *Direct3D Extension Library*. As the name implies, D3DX provides additional services and helper functions for common 3D tasks. Since then, the D3DX library evolved from being a simple library into a complex one that is used daily to accomplish common 3D graphics operations in Direct3D applications. However, the latest couple of major versions of D3DX exhibited the introduction of the D3DX *effects system* [DXSDK1]. The D3DX effects system is represented by its main COM interface ID3DXEffect, which can be used to work with *effect files*.

Effect files provide an elegant approach to control device states, in addition to their ability to house HLSL shaders, which might be the most important feature. Because of this, effect files began to spread widely. Many of the samples in this book are written in HLSL. The HLSL language itself has been covered thoroughly in many places like [DXSDK2] and [PEEPER1]. However, the other side of the story gets mostly ignored, which is the access API, or ID3DXEffect to be specific.

Below is a simple effect file that performs alpha-testing with a specific threshold:

```
DWORD dwAlphaThreshold = 0;

technique tecTransparency
{
  pass passTransparency
  {
    AlphaTestEnable = True;
    AlphaRef = <dwAlphaThreshold>;
    AlphaFunc = Greater;
  }
}
```

When correctly compiled and applied through ID3DXEffect, rendered objects will pass the alpha test only if they output alpha values greater than 0. Let us assume that the application needs to raise the alpha test reference value for some specific objects (for example, tree leaves), this can be done by the following piece of code:

```
// Assuming that 'pEffect' is initialized
// correctly with the effect above
D3DXHANDLE hParam = pEffect-> GetParameterByName
    (NULL,"dwAlphaThreshold");
pEffect->SetInt(hParam,0x00000024);
```

Yes, that D3DXHANDLE must be obtained for any parameter to be accessed. This might be acceptable for a while, but with rapid development and shader prototyping, things become more mundane and very annoying. It even gets worse when the effect involves nested structures and array variables. D3DXHANDLEs splatter everywhere in the code just to access a simple annotation associated with a small parameter.

Up, Up, and Away!

A high-level solution would be more than welcome to hide D3DXHANDLEs and ID3DXEf-fect::Get*ByName() calls from the application's source code, which allows for more productivity and much cleaner code. The method exposed here adds a thin layer over ID3DXEffect to make the process of parameter retrieval and manipulation more natural. This overlaid framework features easy access (read and write) to:

- All scalar effect parameters of any type
- 2D, 3D, and 4D floating-point vectors, which are very common types
- N-by-n matrices, with 4×4 matrices as a special case
- Arrays of any type
- Structure members of any depth
- Strings
- Annotations on all parameters, techniques, and passes
- Vertex and pixel shaders
- Textures (of any class, e.g., cube or volume)

In addition, the framework can:

- Quickly animate floating-point scalar and vector parameters, integers, and colors (encoded in D3DCOLOR form)
- Type-cast between different value types
- Attach to an existing effect object

The framework is made of four tightly-bound classes. These are SXEffect, SXEff-Param, SXEffVariant, and SXEffAnimation.

Below is a sample effect file—SomeEffect.fx—that will showcase how values can be accessed by the framework:

```
float fSomeFactor <
string strObject="Beam";
int iObjectID=1;
> = 1.24f;
float3 vec3Light = {0,-1,0};
float4 vec4Diffuse;
```

```
matrix matWorld = {1,0,0,0, 0,1,0,0, 0,0,1,0, 0,0,0,1};
float aSomeTable[] = {1.1,2.5,3.5,4.5,4.5,4.5};
Texture texDecal;

struct SINCOS
{
  float fSin;
  float fCos;
};

SINCOS AngleTrig = {0.5f,0.5f};

technique tecSquish <int iTecID = 24;>
{
  pass passSquish <int iPassID = 44;>
  {
    .
    .
    .
  }
}
```

and this is the code that loads and evaluates the effect's parameters:

```
// Create effect
SXEffect m_Effect;
m_Effect.CreateFromFile(m_pd3dDevice,"SomeEffect.fx");

// Get float value
float fSomeFactor = m_Effect("fSomeFactor");

// Get string annotation
PCSTR pszObject = m_Effect("fSomeFactor").Annotation("strObject");

// Set integer annotation
m_Effect("fSomeFactor").Annotation("iObjectID") = 12;

// Get light vector
D3DXVECTOR3 vec3Light = m_Effect("vec3Light");

// Get matrix translation x
float fX = m_Effect("matWorld").mat(3,0);

// Set array element to float value
m_Effect("aSomeTable")[0] = m_Effect("fSomeFactor");

// Access struct member
m_Effect("AngleTrig")("fSin") = sinf(D3DX_PI/3.0f);

// Get technique's annotation
int iTecID = m_Effect.GetTechnique("tecSquish").
Annotation("iTecID");

// Get pass's annotation
int iPassID = m_Effect.GetTechnique("tecSquish").
GetPassAnnotation("passSquish","iPassID");
```

```
// Animate a parameter [-12,24]
m_Effect("fSomeFactor").Animate(-12.0f,24.0f);

// Select a texture into the device
m_pd3ddevice->SetTexture(0,m_Effect("texDecal"));
```

Who said life is not beautiful? After using the framework, accessing the parameters in C++ becomes as easy as in VBScript!

Down, Down to the Design of the Framework

The framework starts its life through the SXEffect class. The SXEffect class is responsible for loading an effect or attaching to an existing one. When that gets successfully accomplished, the class can provide access to all top-level parameters and techniques declared in the file. The code snippet below shows the declaration of the SXEffect class:

```
class SXEffect
{
public:
  // Construction/Destruction
  SXEffect();
  ~SXEffect();

  // Initialization
  HRESULT CreateFromFile(PDIRECT3DDEVICE9 pDevice,
      PCTSTR pszFileName);
  HRESULT AttachToExisting(LPD3DXEFFECT pEffect);
  void Clear(void);

  // Operations
  SXEffParam& operator() (PCSTR pszParamName,
      D3DXHANDLE hParent = NULL);
  SXEffParam& GetTechnique(PCSTR pszTechniqueName);
  void SetAnimWeight(float fTime);

  // Notifications
  HRESULT OnDeviceLoss();
  HRESULT OnDeviceRestore();

  // Access
  LPD3DXEFFECT GetD3DXEffect(void) const;

protected:
  // Internal Properties
  LPD3DXEFFECT m_pEffect;
  SXEffParamsHash m_hashParams;
  SXEffParam m_paramInvalid;      // Error Code
};
```

Table 6.3.1 explains the purpose of some of the class's member functions:

Table 6.3.1 Main Member Functions of the SXEffect Class

Member Function	Purpose
CreateFromFile	Initialize this instance from an effect file (.fx) on disk.
AttachToExisting	Initialize this instance from an effect successfully created before.
operator ()	Get the top-level parameter with the specified name. Note that the second hParent parameter defaults to 'NULL' and must not be passed by the user.
GetTechnique	Get the technique with the specified name. Annotations are the only sort of information that can be obtained from techniques.
SetAnimWeight	Update animated parameters based on the specified interpolation weight.
OnDeviceLoss	Call this function when the device is lost.
OnDeviceRestore	Call this function after the device is restored successfully.

Both SXEffect::operator() and SXEffect::GetTechnique() return a reference to an SXEffParam object. In the latter case, the returned SXEffParam can be only queried for its annotations. Requests for value will fail.

One more thing to note is the presence of the two resource management functions OnDeviceLoss() and OnDeviceRestore(). These need to be handled correctly so the internal ID3DXEffect can restore its internal Direct3D objects after device loss. See [BAHNASSI1] for more information on handling such cases.

Another key class in our framework is the SXEffVariant. This class is the one responsible for providing access to the actual parameter's value. Below is a listing of the class's declaration:

```
class SXEffVariant
{
public:
  // Type Checking
  bool IsValid(void) const;
  bool IsA(D3DXPARAMETER_TYPE eParamType) const;
  bool IsA(D3DXPARAMETER_CLASS eParamClass) const;
  D3DXPARAMETER_TYPE GetType(void) const;
  D3DXPARAMETER_CLASS GetClass(void) const;

  // Matrix/Array Accessors
  float mat(int iCol,int iRow);
  SXEffVariant& operator[](int iIndex);  // Arrays only
  UINT GetElemsCount(void) const; // Arrays only
  UINT GetVectorSize(void) const; // Vectors only

  // Value Get
  operator bool(void);
  operator int(void);
  operator float(void);
```

```
        operator D3DXVECTOR2(void);
        operator D3DXVECTOR3(void);
        operator D3DXVECTOR4(void);
        operator D3DXMATRIX(void);
        operator PCSTR(void);

        operator PDIRECT3DVERTEXSHADER9 (void);
        operator PDIRECT3DPIXELSHADER9 (void);
        operator PDIRECT3DBASETEXTURE9 (void);

        // Value Set
        SXEffVariant& operator= (const SXEffVariant& varVal);
        SXEffVariant& operator= (bool bVal);
        SXEffVariant& operator= (int iVal);
        SXEffVariant& operator= (float fVal);
        SXEffVariant& operator= (const D3DXVECTOR2& vec2Val);
        SXEffVariant& operator= (const D3DXVECTOR3& vec3Val);
        SXEffVariant& operator= (const D3DXVECTOR4& vec4Val);
        SXEffVariant& operator= (const D3DXMATRIX& vec4Val);
        SXEffVariant& operator= (PCSTR pszVal);
        SXEffVariant& operator= (PDIRECT3DVERTEXSHADER9 pVal);
        SXEffVariant& operator= (PDIRECT3DPIXELSHADER9 pVal);
        SXEffVariant& operator= (PDIRECT3DBASETEXTURE9 pVal);

      // Animation
      void CancelAnimation(void);
      void Animate(float fKey1,float fKey2);
      void Animate(const D3DXVECTOR2& vec2Key1,const
          D3DXVECTOR2& vec2Key2);
      void Animate(const D3DXVECTOR3& vec3Key1,const
          D3DXVECTOR3& vec3Key2);
      void Animate(const D3DXVECTOR4& vec4Key1,const
          D3DXVECTOR4& vec4Key2);
      void Animate(int iKey1,int iKey2);
      void AnimateAsColor(D3DCOLOR clrKey1,D3DCOLOR clrKey2);

    protected:
      // Construction/Destruction
      SXEffVariant(SXEffect *pOwnerEffect,D3DXHANDLE hParam);
      ~SXEffVariant();

      // Internal Properties
      SXEffect *m_pOwnerEffect;
      D3DXHANDLE m_hParam;
      SXEffVariantElemHash m_hashElems;        // Array elements
      SXEffAnimation *m_pAnim;
    };
```

The class makes heavy use of operator overloading. Besides these functions, Table 6.3.2 describes the purpose of other functions in the class:

Table 6.3.2 Main Member Functions of the SXEffVariant Class

Member Function	Purpose
IsValid	If calling this function returned 'false', then this SXEffVariant object does not represent a valid parameter value in the relevant effect.
IsA	Provides type information by confirming whether this variant is of the specified type/class or not.
mat	Get the value of a matrix element at the specified column and row.
operator []	Valid for array parameters only. Get an element of the array at the specified index.
GetElemsCount	Returns the number of elements in this array (assuming that this is an array parameter).
GetVectorSize	Returns the number of columns (dimension) of this vector parameter.
Animate	Start a simple LERP (linear interpolation) between two key values.
AnimateAsColor	Same as above. However, this function LERPs between two integers assuming that they represent D3DCOLOR values (i.e., A8R8G8B8).
CancelAnimation	Stop animation on this parameter and freeze its current value.

The presence of SXEffVariant::IsValid() was necessary because the framework must always return a valid SXEffVariant object even if it was asked about a non-existing parameter. This sort of friendly behavior does not mean that the framework hides invalid parameter requests, as any value requests on such variants will show error messages in the debugger's output window.

When the parameter is declared in the effect, it gets declared with some type. Asking SXEffVariant to retrieve the same value in a different type will result in a type cast.

The third class in the framework, SXEffParam, actually inherits from SXEffVariant and adds a little functionality over its base class. This functionality provides access to the parameter's annotations, and if the SXEffParam represents a technique returned from SXEffect::GetTechnique(), then the SXEffParam::GetPassAnnotation() member function becomes valid and provides access to an annotation associated with a specific pass within the parent technique.

It's worth noting that the framework avoids allocating unnecessary objects. Rather, it allocates parameters and variants on demand. In addition, later requests to the same parameter go through a hash table, skipping ID3DXEffect::Get*ByName() calls. The hash table look up should be fast. Still, this can be totally avoided by saving the address of that continuously used parameter aside and using it to directly access the parameter later.

In production code, it appeared to be expensive to have the framework lookup the parameter in each rendered frame, especially with effects that contain many accessed[1] parameters with long variable names, as the culprit showed to be in the hash map string compare. With an effect containing about 8 parameters (including an array), performance was not much affected until the application exceeded more than 50 para-

---

[1]Since the framework only hashes parameters that have been explicitly queried by the user, then unreferenced parameters have no entry in the hash map. Unreferenced parameters do not affect performance.

meter accesses per frame. Note that parameter value manipulation does not have any overhead because the framework implements that as inline functions that call directly into D3DX. It is advised to obtain frequently changing parameters at start of day, and keep references to them that can be directly used to manipulate the value. This way, framework overhead will be totally eliminated in high-frequency rendering calls.

Words on the Sample Application

ON THE CD

The sample application provided on the companion CD-ROM illustrates the usage of the framework discussed here. The application loads a simple effect from a .fx file, then manipulates its parameters to indirectly control the device's states and shader constants values.

The framework is declared in SXEffect.h and implements its functions in SXEffect.cpp and SXEffect.inl.

Conclusion

The latest version of the D3DX library provides great facilities for effects development and shader programming through its ID3DXEffect interface. However, it imposes a certain usage method that relies on the user keeping D3DXHANDLEs all over the code, which decreases simplicity and productivity. The SXEffect framework is a thin and friendly layer that removes these limitations by providing fast and convenient access operators to almost all parameters that can be declared in an effect file. The result is code that is clear and easy to understand and maintain. In addition, it provides facilities for quickly animating parameter values for fast visualization of effect changes over time. With this framework, programming effects through the ID3DXEffect interface becomes as easy as a scripting language while still maintaining high-speed and low-memory usage.

Acknowledgments

Thanks to Abdul-lateef Haji Ali for helping profile the framework as well as other things throughout the article.

References

[BAHNASSI1] Bahnassi, Wessam, "An Extensible Direct3D Resource Management System" *Shader X³: Advanced Rendering with DirectX and OpenGL, http://www.shaderx3.com.*

[DXSDK1] Microsoft Corporation, "Effects" DirectX 9.0 Programmer's Reference.

[DXSDK2] Microsoft Corporation, "High-Level Shader Language" DirectX 9.0 Programmer's Reference.

[PEEPER1] Peeper, Craig and Jason L. Mitchell, "Introduction to the DirectX High-Level Shading Language," *ShaderX²: Introductions & Tutorials with DirectX 9,* pp. 1–61, *http://www.shaderx2.com.*

6.4

Shader Visualization Systems for the Art Pipeline

Homam Bahnassi and Wessam Bahnassi

What Is the Story?

As we are all experiencing, real-time shaders are quickly growing in complexity to achieve advanced results that approach the quality gained from non-real-time renderers. This is coupled with the speedy evolution of shader-capable hardware.

To get the most from this technology, these shaders should be exposed to artists, and under their control. However, shaders are mostly code, and code is the last thing an artist likes to see. Shaders need to be exposed in a more logical manner that allows fine tuning to get good results. Otherwise, one might write a shader implementing some realistic effect, but the lack of artistic control will make it look dull. Thus, we need a system that allows artists to see these shaders in action as they tweak their parameters.

In this article, the terminology *shader visualization system* not only means a system that shows the results of shaders, but allows for prototyping them too, without the need for round trips through compiled code for each change in the shader's functionality. This is very important because it reduces the number of "model-export-view" iterations to a minimum in the art pipeline, and prevents 3D objects from bouncing back and fourth between art and programming departments. Also, the word "shader" here does not necessarily resolve to shader code, rather it resembles a complete effect that may be composed of vertex and pixel shaders, in addition to device states and related resources (i.e., textures).

This article provides the guidelines that lead to a shader visualization system correctly integrated into the art pipeline; and to a very powerful integration with the 3D engine, allowing realization of the full power of shaders inside real-world applications.

Our Audience

Developing effective shaders requires a blend of an artistic touch and a technical knowledge of shader hardware and systems. Typically, no one person can provide both, and it is unreasonable to require most artists to write shader code for every simple effect. At the same time, it must allow as much control over complex shaders as is feasible, and also to prototype the look of complex shaders, even if they are then hand-optimized later. Therefore, the system must be aware that it has multiple audiences, both technical and artistic.

From these principles, we see that the system should be targeted at both artists and programmers. It may implement different interfaces for each of them (as in the case of ATI's RenderMonkey), or keep them tied together while governing interfaces that are simple enough to be used by artists (as in the case of DSK|ShaderBass).

. . . And Our Host

The last couple of years have seen the release of several shader prototyping IDEs, mainly from major 3D hardware vendors. This is one way of implementing shader visualization systems. The other way introduced here is the integration method. Rather than having an independent application used for shader prototyping, some sort of "advanced plug-in" is integrated inside the art pipeline's 3D art package, giving artists immediate feedback. The plug-in provides a new view that displays the results exactly as will be viewed in the final rendering engine. This method is new and is just maturing in industry-standard 3D art packages that are commonly used by today's game 3D art pipelines. The system becomes an integrated part of the host application, and leverages the host's interfaces to communicate with users. This method, as opposed to the previous independent solution, has the following advantages:

- The system is implemented using the actual game engine as the renderer. This prevents unhappy surprises caused by different rendering engines outputting different results. WYSIWYG! The actual power of the game's effects rendering engine gets exposed to its full potential.
- Artists keep working in the same environment they are used to work in, improving productivity and speed.
- Shaders operate on existing geometry. Integration allows artists to directly experience the results of their work. They get real-time feedback as they work on modelling the shape, texturing it with UV sets, and modifying its normals. Shapes can be animated and moved around freely to show their behavior in response to user input. Invalid shader output caused by bad geometry can be instantly detected and handled. The shader's results can be previewed on the different levels-of-detail of the same mesh, allowing artists to make tweaks that give the best results on all these levels.
- By integrating the system into the host 3D package's environment, the system inherits all the powerful controls and user-interface elements provided by the host. This leverages the many years of effort in bringing the best user experience for manipulating scene properties in a comfortable manner. 3D art packages contain great controls for specifying colors, light properties, camera properties, and directional values, all of which can be animated and specified through natural methods. Additionally, almost all art packages include some sort of scripting engine. This allows shader programmers to easily prototype their algorithms' calculations in scripts, before passing the results as uniform constants accessed inside the shaders. Scripts have access to almost all aspects of their host, allowing calculations to use important values as their inputs (e.g., time).

- Prevents the art pipeline creating unnecessary details. A common example is determining the size of the image file used to texture an object. The game camera can be simulated, and the size of the texture can be determined quickly to guarantee good details at the expected distances, saving 2D artists from authoring high-detail texture maps that will not be used.
- Exchanging shaders among teammates is easy and automatic. The host's scene description file contains the full shader along with its associated resources in the scene file's database. Managing shaders becomes easier and more professional.
- Integrated systems are capable of viewing multiple objects in the same scene, each rendered with a different shader. This way, shaders can be tested to see how they interact with each other. Independent systems usually provide view for only one effect operating on one 3D mesh at a time.

Of course, nothing is ever free. System integration does not come without a price. Below are the disadvantages resulting from such systems:

- The system is only usable under the specific host it was developed for. It cannot be reused under another package. It requires writing code for each 3D package it is supposed to work under, which might be very time-consuming, because (as we will see later) each 3D package provides its own way of exposing real-time shaders through the SDK. Independent systems do not exhibit this problem.
- Integrated systems depend on the capabilities of their host. If the host is not ready or does not provide easy methods to support integration, then the system's implementation will suffer from bad integration, or it might fail to integrate at all! Also, the host 3D package might impose limitations of some kind on the rendering engine, preventing it from exposing all of its capabilities.
- Performance might be severely hurt by the complex calculations that the host performs before submitting scene content to the rendering system.

Thinking about these disadvantages, we find that two of them do not cause much trouble in practice. The fact that integrated systems are not portable across different hosts is of minimal concern. Companies tend to concentrate on a single 3D package for game content and shader visualization. Other packages might exist in the same pipeline, but these are mostly not used for in-game content (only for tasks such as game movies and cutscenes). So, a company usually needs to implement its shader visualization system only once.

The second issue is performance. Again, this is not a big concern as long as the system provides real-time interaction with the user, which is easy to achieve. In practice, the shader visualization system does not usually render continuously. It only needs to render upon scene changes. Thus, it does not even have a frame-rate.

This leaves only one disadvantage. The fact that not all 3D packages support real-time shaders is fortunately solving itself. Major 3D software companies already understand the importance of the presence of real-time shader display facilities in their solutions, and they are increasingly supporting the subject with each new version of their software.

With this discussion, it becomes clear that the advantages of such a system easily outweigh its disadvantages. The next section will show how to design such systems so that they can be successfully used in the production pipeline, including a discussion of how the host can provide such capabilities.

The Words

Before a system can be designed, it should have its expected features specified. This is very important in shader visualization systems because new features frequently require certain design requirements that might be hard to introduce late in the project. Following is a list of the needed features, as viewed from the perspective of the users. The list also provides reasons why each feature is important, plus an example or two from systems implementing such a feature:

- Operates on a per-material basis. That is, each material can specify its own real-time shader. This material can be assigned to one or more objects. Thus, different objects in the scene with different materials can have different shaders or different shader parameters applied. The real-time shader option can appear either as a standalone material, or as an additional option that gives real-time rendering properties, plus the conventional material's options.

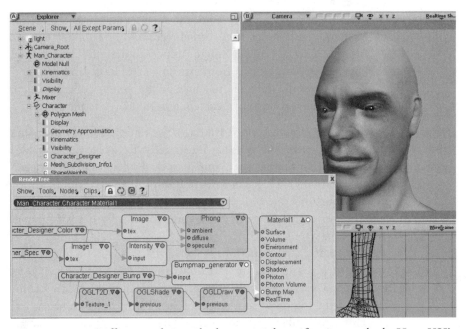

FIGURE 6.4.1 *Different real-time shader material specification methods. Here, XSI's render tree exposes a real-time rendering port among other ports that are used for mentalRay rendering in the same time. The real-time port accepts OpenGL, DirectX, and Cg shaders.*

- Exposes shader inputs and effect parameters relevant to artists. Parameter names and types should be read from the provided shader code, and exposed using the host application's user interface, or allow the user to connect 'controllers' to these exposed parameters. These parameters should be exposed in a user interface-friendly method. That is, they should make full use of available controls (e.g., color pickers) provided by the host.

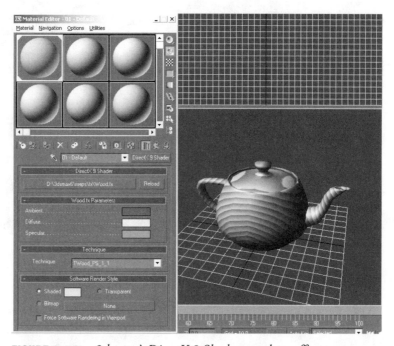

FIGURE 6.4.2   *3ds max's DirectX 9 Shader populates effect parameters in the specified .fx file and exposes them to the user. Artist-relevant parameters are specified by adding a specific annotation in the effect's code.*

- Supplies easy ways to express common shaders and effects. There should be a uniform set of components that at least allow users to specify common effect properties, such as material properties, texture sampling options, and similar. Relying on code to specify such inputs stands against user-friendliness. Soon, the user finds that performing even the simplest effects becomes a very mundane task. For example, a system might provide a component that allows the user to set fixed-function material information directly rather than requiring custom shader code.
- Responds instantly to most parameter value changes. This provides easy and quick experimentation with the ways different shader input values affect the final results. This is not a recommendation on all inputs. For example, shader compilation can be too expensive to update continuously. Such expensive changes can

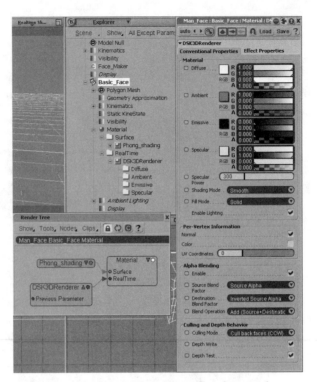

FIGURE 6.4.3   *Part of the DSK3DRenderer node in DSK\ShaderBass. This part allows users to control material values, alpha-blending options and many other commonly used aspects.*

be triggered by the user explicitly, or by tracking changes such as a texture file's modification time stamp.

- Displays results in a special window that is integrated into the host's workspace. For example, rendering can take place in one of the host's views, or can happen in a separate window that can be moved and resized freely to be placed in the place the user finds suitable, which might be on a second monitor (very common in artist workstations). In addition, it is useful to have the output window resize to the resolution that the game will run at.

- Has direct methods to alter all the device states, not just the shader properties. The system should expose render states, texture-stage states, sampler states, alpha-blend states, bump properties, and so on. These should be exposed in a logical manner. Available states values shown in the interface should be concise but descriptive. The settings may be grouped logically in separate components.

- Loads and maps textures into samplers or binds them to shader inputs. The maximum number of file formats should be supported, especially those formats used by the host. This is important to avoid crippling the art pipeline during production.

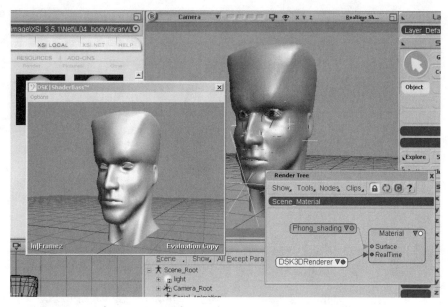

FIGURE 6.4.4 *The output window is the most important part of the system. It should be placed in a well-considered area of the host's workspace. Here, DSK|ShaderBass (Direct3D-based) outputs its results in Softimage|XSI's OpenGL environment by providing a separate hovering window, which can be set to cover one of the workspace's view sets.*

The system should handle almost all types of textures (1D, 2D, 3D (volumes), and cube maps). Each type has its uses in shaders and so cannot be ignored. Also, it is useful to allow the user to override the original image file dimensions and hardware format during file load.

In addition to standard textures, there is the growing need for render-target textures in today's shaders. So, these should be exposed also. This allows the user to specify the current render target for each instance of a material.

- Supports multi-pass rendering. Note that material properties may change completely between passes. One pass uses one shader, the second uses another, or none at all! Each pass has its own device states and render target. Additionally, the user must be able to specify whether to clear the target's frame-buffer color or z stencil buffers to user-defined values.
- Performs object-level and polygon-level z-sorting for alpha-blended effects or those that require some specific rendering order.
- Includes 2D blitting capabilities. This very important feature is overlooked by many systems. Many shaders rely on rendering full-screen quads to achieve post-process effects and filtering. Quads usually cover the whole rendering window, and should be rendered with vertex and pixel shaders acting on them.

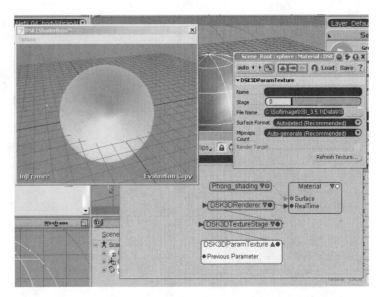

FIGURE 6.4.5   *The DSK3DParamTexture node in DSK\Shader-Bass handles loading textures in several formats, plus it provides users with the option to mark this texture as a render target. Note the 'Refresh Texture...' button which forces the system to rerender the texture from its sources.*

- Can pass multiple arbitrary per-vertex user data down to the rendering engine, which can be mapped into vertex shader input registers.
- Automatically generates per-vertex tangent and binormal information from object normals and UV coordinate sets. This is imperative to implement per-pixel lighting shaders. The method used to generate this information must be consistent with that used in the final rendering engine to guarantee consistent output results. Alternatively, such information can be exported along with the rest of the geometry data so it can be directly used by the game engine.
- Immediately propagates changes on the scene's current camera properties (eye position, target position, field-of-view, etc.) and light properties (type, color, range, etc.) to the shader rendering window.
- Logs error and status messages about the system's current state. These messages should be logged to a place that is easily noticed by the user. The host's default log area is common.
- Exports the effect's description to the game engine with the minimum hassle.
- Does not crash! Unlike scripted plug-ins, shaders usually have deep access to the host's data structures, meaning that any shader crashes can lose artist work. Execution speed should be sacrificed for robustness wherever necessary.

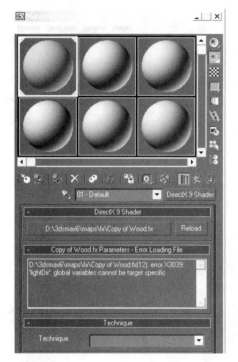

FIGURE 6.4.6 *On the left, 3dsMAX DirectX 9 Shader logs effect compilation errors inside the Material Library. This sometimes hides important errors away from the user. On the right, XSI's script log is utilized by DSK\ShaderBass to show the current state of the rendering engine.*

The number of requirements is large indeed. However, they are important and should be taken into consideration right from the start to avoid having to reengineer the whole system when a new feature is required.

. . . And the Deeds

During the discussion of implementation details, the following terms are used:

Shader: A collection of device states and vertex/pixel shader code that define a complete effect.

System: The shader visualization plug-in that will render content using a 3D engine (usually the same engine used in the game).

Host: The 3D software that the *System* will plug into. This is the tool that artists use to produce in-game 3D content.

User: Someone (or something) who uses the *Host* to access the *System* to implement *Shaders.* Generally, the user is a 3D programmer or an artist.

Where should the system be plugged into the host? Figure 6.4.7 shows a high-level view of the full "real-time rendering pipeline" architecture:

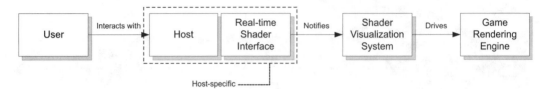

FIGURE 6.4.7   *The relations between different components in a real-time rendering pipeline that can exist in a 3D package.*

In a very abstract definition, the system is just a translator that translates the host's scene properties into the game's rendering engine. It is of course more than that, because it is assumed that exposed shader parameters are part of the system rather than being part of the host's scene description (actually they are both).

The host's internal scene database should generally not be accessed directly by any plug-in. So in this case, the host provides an interface that allows access to this data in a manner that avoids compromising the scene database's integrity. This is the real-time shader interface shown in the pipeline diagram above. This interface hides the internal scene database format, and provides the system with a more friendly interface to the same database that can be used (maybe directly) in real-time rendering. This interface can hide away version differences from the system so it is not affected by each change in the 3D software's internal structure. The system's code needs to be updated only when the real-time rendering interface changes.

Looking at the first of the requirements listed above, it directs us to a specific rendering method. For each material, render all objects using that material, then jump to the second material, and so on. The affected geometry is sent once for each pass in that material (many effects have multiple passes).

The UML Sequence diagram in Figure 6.4.8 shows how all these concepts work together.

Although the diagram shows the flow for rendering one object only, it is intended for several objects. The `BeginMaterial` and `EndMaterial` notifications are to be executed for each active material in the scene. For each of these, there is one or more passes that get executed. Within each pass, all affected objects are "sent" (we will discuss this shortly) to the system. The system sets per-object states, then sends the geometry down to the low-level rendering pipeline.

One important aspect to be aware of is how geometry is to be sent to the system. The diagram shows how the *Real-time Shader Interface* "pulls" geometry information from the host. This is not directly relevant to the system. What is relevant is whether the system pulls geometry from the real-time shader interface or the interface pushes

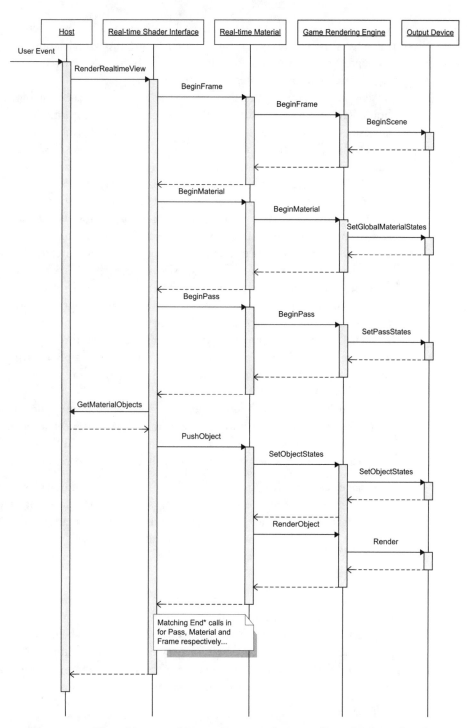

FIGURE 6.4.8 *This abbreviated UML Sequence diagram illustrates the order of operations done in the full real-time rendering pipeline. Some operations are actually done in loops (e.g.,* PushObject*).*

geometry into the system. Each method has its pros and cons. Generally, having the real-time shader interface push geometry into the visualization system is better, although it can waste some resources for effects that do not rely on scene geometry (e.g., particles generated internally by the engine).

For any operation between the `BeginFrame` and `EndFrame` block, the system should have quick access to general non-geometric scene information, such as the current camera properties, and the currently active lighting properties.

The last entity that appears in the diagram is the *Output Device*. This is the object that provides low-level rendering methods (e.g., an `IDirect3DDevice` or an `HGLRC`). Usually, it is the responsibility of the visualization system to create and manage this object. This gives the freedom of choosing the appropriate output device to the system (e.g., `IDirect3DDevice8` or `IDirect3DDevice9`). However, today's 3D software tends to provide this object and expect the plug-in to use this object for output. This restricts the system to a great level (for example, it cannot switch to the Direct3D Reference Rasterizer), and for some engines it is incompatible. For example, if the provided object is `IDirect3DDevice8` and the engine is based on Direct3D 9 then the system cannot output anything unless the 3D package upgrades its Direct3D interface. Besides, providing an output device object to the system assumes that the underlying engine has some sort of an `AttachToExisting()` method, which is not the case for all engines. Such an issue can be worked around by simply ignoring the provided output device and creating a suitable one independently, and perhaps attaching it to a new window.

In order to realize the concepts discussed, we skim over a quick review of implementations of shader visualization systems in some major 3D packages, coupled with a set of code snippets that are taken from each application's SDK. These illustrate each 3D package's model for exposing real-time shaders to third-party developers:

Softimage|XSI 3.5: XSI 3.5 provides what they call real-time shader plug-ins. Real-time shaders are dealt with in much the same way XSI deals with mentalRay shaders (with some additional restrictions). That is, a material has several input ports that can have render nodes attached to them, resulting in treelike nodal connections. A material has two outputs, a mentalRay output and probably a real-time output.

Figure 6.4.1 shows how render trees can be expressed inside XSI, the tree shown has mentalRay output and a real-time OpenGL output.

Each real-time node in XSI is a distinct object that can be managed by a compiled plug-in library. Multiple nodes can be provided by a single library. Nodes define how their interface looks like and what controls should they expose (using SPDL[1] files). At code level, the plug-in developer is responsible for writing several functions that

---

[1]Softimage Plug-in description Language. A SPDL file defines the plug-in's user-interface and contains the specifications of the parameters, inpt and output ports, and any extra logic for the plug-in.

receive notifications about the specific node. These functions should be exported with a specific signature. For example, the following functions are the notification functions for the DSK3DRenderer node:

```
RTSHADER_API void DSK3DRenderer_GetRequirement(
LPVOID pPpgParams,LPVOID pSystemParams,
LONG lRequirement,LONG *pOutResult)
{
    // We need z-sorted triangles
    if (lRequirement == RTS_REQUIRE_ZSORT)
        *pOutResult = 1;
}


RTSHADER_API void DSK3DRenderer_Init(LPVOID pSysParams)
{
    SystemParams *pSystemParams =
        (SystemParams*)pSysParams;
    new DSKSBRenderer(pSystemParams->Instance);
}

RTShADER_API void DSK3DRenderer_Exit(LPVOID pSysParams)
{
    SystemParams *pSystemParams =
        (SystemParams*)pSysParams;
    DSKSBRenderer *pRenderer =
        DSKSBNode::GetRendererByXSIPhenomenon(
            pSystemParams->Instance);
    DSKSAFE_DELETE(pRenderer);
}

RTSHADER_API void DSK3DRenderer_Eval(
    LONG lStripesCount,BYTE *pStripeData,
    LPVOID pPPGParams,LPVOID pSysParams)
{
    RenderToOpenGL(lStripesCount,pStripeData,
        (DSKSBRENDERER_PPG*)pPPGParams);

    SystemParams *pSystemParams =
        (SystemParams*)pSysParams;
    DSKSBRenderer *pRenderer =
        DSKSBNode::GetRendererByXSIPhenomenon(
            pSystemParams->Instance);

    // Get the parameters
    pRenderer->UpdateParamsFromPPG(
        (DSKSBRENDERER_PPG*)pPPGParams);

    // Output
    pRenderer->Render(lStripesCount,pStripeData);
}
```

All the functions receive a SystemParams structure that contains important information (e.g., time, shader handle, geometry handle).

The DSK3DRenderer_Eval() function also receives the node's user-interface data (the pPPGParams argument) and—most importantly—the geometry it should render (made of triangle strips and triangle lists). In XSI 3.5, Begin and End notifications for frame, material, and pass are not well defined. DSK|ShaderBass adds an additional layer that emulates these notifications and passes them to the rest of the system. The geometry passed is composed of non-indexed triangle lists or triangle strips. Vertices come in a static structure that contains all information common to real-time shaders. Per-vertex user information can be obtained by other indirect methods.

Softimage|XSI 4: The new version of XSI comes with a revamped system. The real-time shader interface has been split into two parts: the *Graphics Sequencer* and the Real-time Shader. The Graphics Sequencer is responsible for preparing the rendering context (window and device, or the *Output Device* in our terminology) and receives frame notifications (e.g. BeginFrame, BeginPass...etc.), while the Real-time Shader serves the same functionality as in XSI 3.5 discussed before. The addition of the Graphics Sequencer provides an elegant method of allowing systems to use the rendering context they require. The sequencer registers with XSI the notification functions that will be called upon the occurrence of common events relevant to real-time shaders (those displayed in the UML diagram shown before).

3dsMAX 5: Hardware Shaders in 3dsMAX use an object-oriented approach to allow 3rd party developers write plug-ins that can render geometry using specific shaders and effects. 3dsMAX provides a readily-built 'DirectX 9 Shader' material that can be useful to some limit, but it may not fit for shader prototyping. 3dsMAX's architecture allows developers to write "boxed" shaders that provide an already-written effect that exposes artist controls for tweaking. Thus, to implement a useful shader visualization system, a separate independent interface might be required to provide a workspace for composing shader pieces together, as in the case of the Cg plug-in for 3dsMAX.

Maya 6: Maya also uses the object-oriented approach to expose its real-time rendering abilities. *Hardware Shader* nodes can be plugged in a material to provide specialized rendering techniques. The SDK provides a base class MPxHwShaderNode that can be inherited from to provide user-defined hardware shaders. Maya assumes that shaders will display their results in its workspace's OpenGL viewports. It exposes the M3dView class, which provides information about camera and lights, as well as an MDrawRequest that provides per-object information like its transformation as well as a set of other nifty data. Below is a code snippet of the MPxHwShaderNode class declaration:

```
class OPENMAYAUI_EXPORT MPxHwShaderNode : public MPxNode
{
public:
    enum Writeable {
            kWriteNone          = 0x0000,
```

```
                kWriteVertexArray              = 0x0001,
                kWriteNormalArray              = 0x0002,
                kWriteColorArrays              = 0x0004,
                kWriteTexCoordArrays           = 0x0008,
                kWriteAll                      = 0x000f
};

   // Override this method to set up the OpenGL state
   virtual MStatus bind(const MDrawRequest& request,
                                            M3dView& view);

// Override this method to return OpenGL
// to a sane state
virtual MStatus unbind(const MDrawRequest& request,
                                           M3dView& view );

// Override this method to actually draw
// primitives on the display
virtual MStatus geometry(
               const MDrawRequest& request,
               M3dView& view,
               int prim,
               unsigned int writable,
               int indexCount,
               const unsigned int * indexArray,
               int vertexCount,
               const int * vertexIDs,
               const float * vertexArray,
               int normalCount,
               const float ** normalArrays,
               int colorCount,
               const float ** colorArrays,
               int texCoordCount,
               const float ** texCoordArrays) = 0;

// Override this method to specify how
// many "normals" per vertex
// the hardware shader would like.
// Maya can provide from 0 to 3
// normals per vertex.  The second and third
// "normal" will be tangents.  If you do
// not override this method, Maya will
// provide 1 normal per vertex.
virtual int normalsPerVertex();

// Override this method to specify how many texture
// coordinates per vertex the hardware shader would
// like Maya to provide.
// Maya may not provide this many if they are not
// available.  If you do not override this
// method, Maya will provide 0 texture
// coordinates per vertex.
virtual int texCoordsPerVertex();
```

```
                    // Specifies whether or not the hw shader uses
                    // transparency.  If so, the objects that use this
                    // shader must be drawn after all
                // the opaque objects.
                    virtual bool hasTransparency();
        };
```

Through this elegant interface, Maya communicates geometry information by passing independent streams of per-vertex data, which is only supplied upon the system's request. The node's code also specifies the user-interface elements that should appear to allow control of the node's parameters.

Systems based on Direct3D can create their own viewport outside the host's workspace and render to it independently.

This model is great for boxed effects. Systems can also implement connected node systems (as in XSI) in Maya, which helps users to prototype shaders in an easy manner. This is done by using shading network (through HyperShade or MultiLister), which invokes each connected node until the end of the tree. The overall model still ignores some important aspects (such as clear notification functions and passes), which require additional work from the plug-in to compensate, but it is not impossible.

Implementation Blurbs . . .

The previous section showed how hosts expose their real-time rendering interfaces. Each host imposes certain techniques to be used in response to the interface it provides.

Some hosts require the plug-in system to manage its own output device. In that case, the system should be careful how it creates this device and how it affects the host. For example, XSI calls its real-time shaders in a multi-threaded way. The thread that initializes the shader is different to the one that calls its evaluation function. In Direct3D world, this requires the IDirect3DDevice object to be created with the D3DCREATE_MULTITHREADED flag.

Another creation flag that might affect the host's operation is the D3DCREATE_FPU_PRESERVE flag. 3D applications usually change the FPU state during their calculations. If Direct3D is allowed to modify the FPU state without restoring it, then the host will start acting strangely and provide inconsistent results.

Another point to be considered is the vertex format. The samples displayed before show how different hosts provide geometry information in different formats. One provides vertex information as a single stream of a fat structure that can accommodate all information. Another provides separate streams for each available piece of information found in the geometry. The system must ensure that this representation is compatible with the underlying rendering engine. If not, it should reorganize the information into a compatible format that can be consumed directly by the rendering engine. The final format of the vertex also affects how vertex shaders expect information to be mapped into its input registers. The mapping should be documented so that shader developers take this information into account while writing shader code. Special considerations should be taken while doing the reformatting. Some effects use the fixed-function pipeline instead of using shaders. This adds some restrictions on the final vertex format. Also, the system should define rules on how to map per-vertex user data into vertex shader input registers, or at least allow the user to do so.

Many of today's shaders require tangent and binormal information to be accessible in the vertex shader. Some hosts provide this information automatically, and some do not. In this case, the system should calculate the information itself prior to passing it to the rendering engine.

The system uses the same rendering device to output different objects using different materials. Each material alters certain states on the device. The rendering engine must be aware not to propagate these states to other materials. For example, if a material turns on alpha-testing, and another material does not return this state to its default value, then the second material will render with alpha-testing intact, which would produce unexpected results.

Vertex and pixel shader code can be allowed to be input from external files rather than restricting users to type code in simple edit boxes. This way, users are free to use whatever application they like to do the job. For example, some might use a full IDE like Microsoft Visual Studio that provides syntax coloring and allows shader debugging, which can be very useful.

And Still Pushing Further . . .

The subject of real-time shaders inside 3D authoring software is quickly growing. For example, some systems implement the prototyping functionality through a different approach. This approach hides shader code totally from the user. Instead, it provides a set of connectable nodes that contain shader fragments that, when composited together, achieve a specific effect. A good example of such a system is the new Cg real-time shader implementation found inside XSI 4's mentalRay render nodes (grouped in Metashaders). These nodes mimic the functionality of their mentalRay counterpart, but in real-time. The nodes together assemble a complete shader program that gets compiled and executed on geometry seen in XSI's viewports. This visual method of shader authoring is very user-friendly and eases the requirement of having to learn a specific shader language.

Another feature that is currently evolving is inter-shader connections. That is, one shader passes its output to the input of another shader and so on. This feature can be achieved with the new capabilities of the new shader platforms (DirectX version 2.0 and 3.0 of vertex and pixel shaders).

Conclusion

The evolution of shader visualization systems allows more complex effects and shaders to be defined, and helps get the best results out of a specific shader. These systems should provide a set of minimum needs required by today's advanced shaders. A system is implemented as a plug-in that is integrated into a 3D package that provides various facilities. Such facilities are exposed through a real-time rendering interface. For a system, it is this interface that is important. Implementation details specific to each 3D package can be found in the package's SDK, which usually comes with samples and case studies for implementing such systems.

In the next couple of years, we expect this experience to grow much further to the degree that it allows the actual game engine to run completely inside the 3D package with all of its visual controls displayed (e.g., HUD). We are already starting to see such implementations taking place, such as XSI 4's Custom View Host which allows complete applications to run inside XSI while interacting with its scene database.

The subject can take books to fully cover all the implementation details, which might still be incomplete because of low-level engine details.

These are exciting days we are living in the world of shaders and game development. Who knows what might come next? Maybe the game ends being completely implemented inside a 3D package, which gets published instead of publishing the stand-alone game!

Acknowledgments

Special thanks go to Maggie Kathwaroon of Softimage for her great help in exposing the new features of real-time shaders, which are shown in this article.

6.5

Drawing a Crowd

David R. Gosselin, Pedro V. Sander, and
Jason L. Mitchell

Introduction

In this article, we present a technique for efficiently rendering a large crowd of characters while taking steps to avoid a repetitious appearance. There are many typical scenes in games, such as large battles or stadium crowds, which require the rendering of large numbers of characters. We will describe techniques used to draw such crowd scenes, including methods for rendering multiple characters per draw call, each with their own unique animation. We will also outline tradeoffs which can be made between vertex and pixel processing in order to increase vertex throughput (the typical bottleneck in a crowd scene). Next, we will discuss a set of pixel shading tricks to allow the individual characters to have a unique look, despite being drawn from the same instanced geometry as the other characters in the scene. We will conclude with a discussion of instancing of shadow geometry.

Instancing

In order to achieve our goal of drawing over a thousand characters on screen simultaneously, we must first reduce the number of API calls needed to draw the geometry. If we were to try to make a thousand or more draw calls through the API, we would quickly get swamped by API overhead and setup costs. Clearly, this means that we need to draw several characters per draw call. In order to accomplish this, we pack a number of instances of character vertex data into a single vertex buffer. We do all of the skinning on the graphics hardware, so we pack multiple character transforms into the constant store for each draw call. This allows us to draw several unique instances of the character each with its own unique animation in a single draw call.

Since we plan to do all character skinning in the vertex shader, the main factor which limits the number of characters we can draw per API call is the number of vertex shader constants available to store the characters' skeletal animation data. To keep the number of constants used by each character to a reasonable level, we limited the skeleton of each character to only twenty bones. While this number is quite low for a generic character, for a crowd scene this can be enough to create a good character animation. At first glance, this gives us three characters per draw call (20 bones * 4 vectors * 3 characters = 240 constants). Due to the fact that animation data typically contains no shears, it is possible to shave off one of the columns of each matrix. This brought our total up to 4 characters per draw call (20 bones * 3 vectors * 4 characters = 240 constants). We investigated using a quaternion plus a translation to store each bone transform, which would have further compressed the transforms and allowed us to draw even more characters per draw call. However, the associated vertex shader cost (to effectively turn the quaternion into a transformation matrix) was a bit too high for our purposes and offset the gains made by being able to draw more instanced characters per call. By drawing groups of four characters, we can reduce the number of draw calls to between 250 and 300 for a crowd of a thousand plus characters, which is reasonable for today's hardware. The downside of this tight constant store packing is that there is not a lot of room left over for additional constants. This is not too bad since all of the lighting will be performed in the pixel shader. The few constants needed in the vertex shader are the view/projection matrix and the camera position.

It is also important to reduce the cost of the actual vertex shader processing in order to draw a large crowd, since vertex shading is generally the bottleneck for such scenarios. To save vertex shader operations, we can store our character's normal map in object space rather than tangent space and avoid having to skin the tangent and binormal vector, thereby saving two matrix multiplies. Using this method, we skin the normal vector in the pixel shader once it has been read from the normal map. This technique requires that we pass the blended skinning matrix down to the pixel shader. This blended matrix is computed before skinning the position in the vertex shader. The HLSL shader code for assembling and blending the matrices in the vertex shader is given below:

```
float4 rowA[80];
float4 rowB[80];
float4 rowC[80];
float4x4 SiComputeSkinningMatrix3Rows (float4 aWeights,
                                       int4 aIndices)
{
    float4x4 mat = 0;
    mat._m33 = 1.0f;
    for (int bone = 0; bone < 4; bone++)
    {
        mat._m00 += (rowA[aIndices[bone]].x * aWeights[bone]);
        mat._m10 += (rowA[aIndices[bone]].y * aWeights[bone]);
        mat._m20 += (rowA[aIndices[bone]].z * aWeights[bone]);
        mat._m30 += (rowA[aIndices[bone]].w * aWeights[bone]);

        mat._m01 += (rowB[aIndices[bone]].x * aWeights[bone]);
        mat._m11 += (rowB[aIndices[bone]].y * aWeights[bone]);
        mat._m21 += (rowB[aIndices[bone]].z * aWeights[bone]);
        mat._m31 += (rowB[aIndices[bone]].w * aWeights[bone]);

        mat._m02 += (rowC[aIndices[bone]].x * aWeights[bone]);
        mat._m12 += (rowC[aIndices[bone]].y * aWeights[bone]);
        mat._m22 += (rowC[aIndices[bone]].z * aWeights[bone]);
        mat._m32 += (rowC[aIndices[bone]].w * aWeights[bone]);
    }
    return mat;
}
```

Once this matrix has been computed, there is still a bit of work left for the vertex shader. It needs to compute the skinned position and then multiply that by the view and projection matrix as shown in the following code.

```
float4x4 mSkinning = SiComputeSkinningMatrix3Rows
  (i.weights,
   i.indices);
 float4 pos = mul (i.pos, mSkinning);
 o.worldPos = pos;
 o.pos = mul (pos, mVP);
```

additionally, the vertex shader needs to compute the view vector.

```
o.viewVec = normalize(worldCamPos - pos);
```

The rest of the vertex shader is dedicated to passing along all of this information to the pixel shader. With these optimizations, the resulting vertex shader code weighs in at around sixty instructions. By combining all of these techniques, we are able to reduce the cost of vertex processing, which is generally the bottleneck when drawing large crowds of characters.

Character Shading

Even though the characters in our example are relatively low polygon models (1100 triangles), we can still make them look quite detailed using per-pixel lighting. In our example, we use one directional light to simulate the lighting coming from the sun and up to three local diffuse lights. All of these lights use a normal map generated from a high-resolution model as shown in Figure 6.5.1(c). Since these normals are in object space, we need to skin them by the matrix computed in the vertex shader. The vertex shader passes down a 3×3 matrix and the pixel shader can simply multiply the fetched normal by this interpolated matrix. For diffuse lighting we just use the Lambertian model.

In our application, specular lighting is only computed for the directional "sun" light. This is computed based on the view vector computed in the vertex shader. The HLSL code fragment below shows this computation.

```
float3 view = normalize (i.viewVector);
float3 reflectionVec = reflect (view, normal);
float RL = saturate (dot (reflectionVec,
                     (float3)(vLightDirection)));
float3 specular = vLightColor * pow (RL, vLightDirection.w) *
                  (gloss+.1);
```

As you can see from the code, a gloss map such as the one shown in Figure 6.5.1(b) is used to attenuate the specular term. This allows for regions of differing shininess. Also note that the specular exponent is packed in with the interpolated light direction to avoid using up an additional constant vector.

(a) Base Map

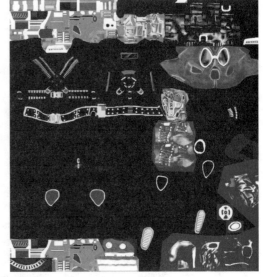

(b) Gloss Map

(c) Object Space Normal Map

FIGURE 6.5.1   *Character textures.*

In order to give the characters an even more realistic look, an ambient occlusion map is used [Landis02]. This map is also generated from a high-resolution model and roughly represents the amount of light that could possibly reach each texel on the model from the external lighting environment. The ambient occlusion map is shown in Figure 6.5.2(a). This term is multiplied by the final lighting value (both diffuse and

(a) Ambient Occlusion

(b) Ground Occlusion Texture

FIGURE 6.5.2 *Occlusion maps.*

specular) and provides a realistic soft look to the character illumination. Since this map is pre-computed it is not technically correct for every frame of animation, however, the results are still quite compelling.

The final term in our basic character lighting is a ground occlusion texture. This is a projected texture that represents an occlusion term based on a given character's position on the terrain. It is similar to the technique described in [Hargreaves03]. In this technique we use our character's position to access a ground-based occlusion texture as shown in Figure 6.5.2(b). This texture represents roughly the amount of illumination on the character from the "sun" based upon his position on the terrain. By using this texture, we can create the illusion that the characters are being softly shadowed by the terrain as they move around it.

In order to implement this technique, the character's position on the terrain needs to be turned into a texture coordinate. The computation of the texture coordinates for this texture is a simple scale and bias on the world space position, which is computed in the vertex shader and passed down to the pixel shader via a texture coordinate interpolator.

```
float2 floorCoord = vFloorCoordScale.xy * i.worldPos.xz +
                    vFloorCoordBias.xy;
float floorAttenuation = tex2D (tFloor, floorCoord);
```

The product of just these two occlusion terms is shown in Figure 6.5.3. The ambient occlusion and terrain occlusion terms are both multiplied by the final lighting (both diffuse and specular).

FIGURE 6.5.3   *Occlusion terms. © ATI Technologies 2004.*

Random Coloring

Up to this point, each of the characters has been shaded identically. Though the animations are distinct and characters are individually shadowed with the terrain occlusion term, they still have a very uniform coloring. While this can look reasonably good—and the sheer number of characters drawn gives an incredible impression—ideally each character could be distinctive in some way. In order to accomplish this task, the shaders need some way to figure out which of the four characters in a given draw call is currently being processed. If the constant store for the vertex shader is packed in such a way that all of the bones for the characters are contiguous within the constant store and the number of bones per character is known, the vertex shader can compute which character is being drawn. The code fragment for this is shown below.

```
float id = int((i.indices.x+.5)/nBones);
```

In our example, we just want the characters to look different, so a vector of four random numbers is generated for each draw group. For a given set of four characters, this set of four random numbers is the same every frame. Given the character ID computed in the above code fragment, the vertex shader can then select one of these four random numbers and send the result down to the pixel shader using the following code snippet.

```
float4 pick = float4(id==0,id==1,id==2,id==3);
float fRand = dot(pick, vRandomVec);
o.texCoord = float3(i.texCoord, fRand);
```

A picture of the crowd drawn using just this random number can be seen in Figure 6.5.4.

FIGURE 6.5.4 *Character ID as color.* © *2004. ATI Technologies, Inc.*

In the pixel shader, this random number is used to change the tinting on the different characters in the scene. To do this, a small 2D texture, shown in Figure 6.5.5(a), was created. Note that this texture is 16×2. That is, the texture contains 16 pairs of colors. Each pair of colors in this texture represents the darkest and lightest tinting of a given character. In addition to these colors, a mask texture, shown in Figure 6.5.5(b), was generated to specify which portions of the characters should be tinted. The tinting then occurs by sampling both the dark and bright tint colors from the small 2D texture. The luminance of the base texture is then used to interpolate between these two tint colors. Finally, the mask texture is used to linearly interpolate between the tinted color and the untinted base color. The code fragment for this can be found below.

```
float4 cColorLow  = tex2D(tColor, float2(0, i.texCoord.z));
float4 cColorHigh = tex2D(tColor, float2(1, i.texCoord.z));
base = lerp(base, lerp(cColorLow, cColorHigh,

dot(float3(0.2125,0.7154,0.0721),base.xyz)),
                tex2D(tColorAlpha, i.texCoord.xy).r);
```

Using this technique allows us to give each of the characters a slightly different color, increasing the variability of our crowd of instanced characters without increasing the size of our dataset or the number of draw calls made.

(a) Color lookup texture

(b) Lerp texture

FIGURE 6.5.5   *Character color modification textures.*

Random Decals

In order to add further uniqueness to the characters, we also use the random number described in the previous section to selectively add decals to the characters' uniforms. To accomplish this, we need two textures: A decal alpha texture, which stores a different shade of gray as an ID for each decal region (Figure 6.5.6(a)); and a decal color texture, which stores the decal images (Figure 6.5.6(b)). Both of these texture maps use the same texture coordinates as the base map.

In order to selectively add the decals based on the random number, the pixel shader first fetches the decal ID of the current sample from the decal alpha texture. If the value is non-zero, the pixel shader then has to determine whether to add the decal or not. The following piece of code determines whether to add the decal based on the random number passed down to the pixel shader and the decal ID:

```
float temax = tex2D(tDecalAlpha, i.texCoord.xy).r;
float fDecalAlpha = step(0.2,
    (temax*i.texCoord.z*1000.) % 1.) > 0;
```

If fDecalAlpha is 1, then a decal sample is used for that pixel. Note that, because the computation fDecalAlpha uses the decal ID, some of the decals might be turned on while others might be turned off for a given character.

Figure 6.5.7 shows some examples of characters with different decals on the same location. By looking at the decal color texture (Figure 6.5.6(b)), one will notice that there are two color images stored for each decal, thus allowing us to randomly pick between the two different decals for a given decal region. One of the images is shifted a little bit to the right from the original decal region identified by the decal alpha texture (Figure 6.5.6(a)). This was possible because our decals were placed in such a way that we could create a shifted copy without overlapping the original. We would expect it to be possible to create a shifted copy in some direction in most cases, unless the character has decals covering a very large portion of the base map. Below is the code to randomly determine whether to use the shifted decal, and to set the base color to be either the value of the base map, or the value of the decal map, depending on fDecalAlpha.

```
float2 decalBias = float2(0.068359, 0.0);
//determines whether to bias or not on the decal lookup
decalBias *= int(i.texCoord.z * 4322. % 2.);

base = lerp(base, tex2D(tDecal, i.texCoord.xy+decalBias),
        fDecalAlpha);
```

An important observation is that the decal alpha texture must be sampled using "nearest" as the filter. That is because, if bilinear or trilinear interpolation is used, the border of the decals could assume different shades of gray, thus having different decal IDs, causing it to possibly be selected when it should not, or vice versa. Even if "nearest" is used, we get some aliasing artifacts at the decal boundaries. In order to remove

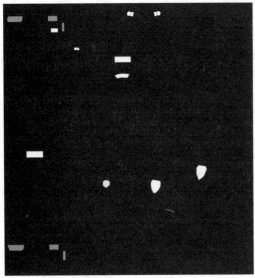 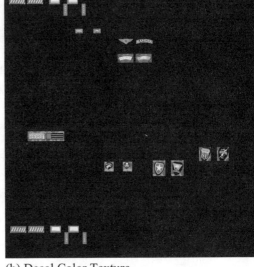

(a) Decal Alpha Texture   (b) Decal Color Texture

FIGURE 6.5.6   *Character decal textures.*

these artifacts, we make the colors of the decal and the base map match closely near the boundary.

FIGURE 6.5.7   *Decals applied.* © *ATI Technologies 2004.*

Shadows

Shadows are an important visual cue for placing characters on the terrain. Given the number of characters we are drawing, it would be impractical to use a sophisticated shadow volume or shadow depth map approach to generate shadows. In our example, we have a fixed directional light and the characters' only animation is to run. These conditions allowed for a sequence of shadow maps to be pre-generated (see Figure 6.5.8). These shadow maps are stored as a 2D texture and, with a bit of math in the vertex shader, we can figure out the texture coordinates for each frame of animation. The trick then becomes how to position quads with these textures on the terrain in a convincing way as well as how to draw them efficiently.

FIGURE 6.5.8 *Character shadow texture.*

Similar to the way we draw the actual characters, the shadow quads are drawn in large instanced batches. A vertex buffer is populated with two hundred quads onto which we will texture map our characters' shadows. We then draw several of these batches per frame to draw the shadows for all of the characters in just a few draw calls. As with the characters themselves, the shadow quads' transformations are handled by the vertex shader hardware.

Like the character animation, vertex shader constant store is the limiting factor which determines how many shadows we can draw in a single call. In order to draw the shadow quads efficiently, we pack the constant store with a very specific transformation that is compressed significantly. A single 4D constant vector is used to represent the transform for each shadow quad, allowing us to draw many shadow quads in one API call. The first three components of each shadow quad transformation vector represent the translation of the quad (i.e., its position in 3-space). The last component is divided into two parts. The integer portion is the frame number for the shadow map animation. This is later used to index into the precomputed shadow texture. The fractional part of the last component represents the slope of the running character. This slope is used to angle the quad to match the terrain. Each quad vertex contains a single "bone" index which is used by the vertex shader to reach into the constant store and get the proper transform. The vertex shader code to unpack and transform the vertices is shown below:

```
float4 vPosFrameSlope = vTransFS[i.indices.x];
float slope = frac (vPosFrameSlope.w);
float frame = vPosFrameSlope.w - slope;
slope = 2.0*slope - 1.0;
```

```
float4 pos = float4 (vPosFrameSlope.xyz, 0.0) + i.pos;
pos.y += slope * i.pos.z;
o.worldPos = pos;
```

By using this efficient packing, the shadow quads can be drawn in blocks of two hundred, making them very hardware and API friendly. In order to avoid incorrect Z occlusions, the vertex shader performs a pseudo Z-bias. The vertex shader code for this is shown below:

```
o.pos = mul (pos, mVP);
float invCamDistance = 1.0/sqrt (dot (pos - worldCamPos,
                                      pos - worldCamPos));
o.pos.z -= 2000.0 * invCamDistance;
```

The pixel shader then looks up the proper frame from the shadow map texture. In order to keep the shadows consistent with the character lighting, the shadow quad pixel shader also needs to perform the same dimming based on the ground occlusion texture. The results of all these steps can be seen in Figure 6.5.9, which shows a screen shot from the final demo.

FIGURE 6.5.9   *Final result. © ATI Technologies 2004.*

Conclusion

We have presented a technique for efficiently rendering large crowds of characters in real time using standard APIs. We have demonstrated processing tradeoffs that can be made to reduce vertex shader load in order to increase the number of characters that can be drawn in a given scene. We have also discussed a number of pixel shader techniques which allow us to reduce the appearance of repetition in the crowds of instanced characters. Finally, we concluded with a discussion of instancing of shadow geometry to further integrate our animated crowd of characters into our scene.

While we have employed some clever tricks to implement instancing, we have done it in a robust manner on existing APIs. In fact, there is no reason that many of these techniques cannot be ported all the way down to 1.1 shader hardware. Microsoft has also recognized the importance of instancing for scenarios like large crowd scenes and has retrofitted an instancing API into DirectX 9 for use on hardware which supports 3.0 shaders. As of the release of the DirectX 9.0c runtime update, devices which support the 3.0 shader model must also support an instancing API to allow a single `DrawIndexedPrimitive()` call to draw multiple instances of the same object with unique per-instance data such as transforms. This only works with indexed primitives. We refer you to the latest DirectX SDK for documentation and sample code which illustrates proper usage of this new instancing API.

References

[Hargreaves03] Hargreaves, Shawn, "Hemisphere Lighting with Radiosity Maps," *ShaderX2*, Wordware Publishing Inc, 2003 pp. 113–122.

[Landis02] Landis, Hayden, "Production-Ready Global Illumination," RenderMan in Production (SIGGRAPH 2002): Course 16.

TOOLS

Texture Operations on a 256x256 Texture ATI R9800XT (linear filtering)

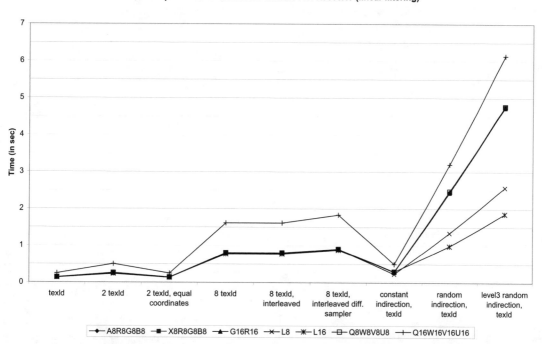

Introduction

Willem H. de Boer

Tools are the most important part of any development pipeline. A good set of tools can speed up development and therefore reduce project development time and costs.

The growing programmability of modern graphics cards is both a blessing and a curse: on the one hand, new possibilities and freedoms are being opened up to developers, but at the same time the added hardware complexity is making performance tuning more difficult. To help tune your application, Joachim Diepstraten and Mike Eißele analyze the performance of recent graphics cards in their article "In-Depth Performance Analyses of DirectX 9 Shading Hardware Concerning Pixel Shader and Texture Performance."

To alleviate the need to write the same basic stub code to set parameters, load textures, and create vertex declarations over and over again, Magnus Österlind uses a wraparound *.fx files, that is described in "Shaderbreaker."

To reduce the number of shaders, Shawn Hargreaves describes in his article, "Generating Shaders from HLSL Fragments," how to automatically generate large numbers of shader permutations from a smaller set of handwritten input fragments.

7.1

In-Depth Performance Analyses of DirectX 9 Shading Hardware Concerning Pixel Shader and Texture Performance

Joachim Diepstraten and Mike Eißele

Introduction

The growing programmability of modern graphics cards is both a blessing and a curse: on the one hand, new possibilities and freedoms are being opened up to developers, but at the same time the added hardware complexity is making performance tuning more difficult.

With a fixed function pipeline, graphic performance problems were restricted to a limited number of standard issues, for example, batching of calls, sorting, blending, and texture usage. With the introduction of DirectX 9 and its new shading languages for pixel and vertex processing, modern graphics cards have finally transcended from simple programmability to real programmability.

This has brought new optimizing challenges, in particular for cases that deal with large data input streams. This especially applies to fragment processing. Let us assume a typical view-port having at least 800×600 pixels, which means 480,000 pixels have to be processed in the best case and this does not even take overdraw into account, which often happens. Therefore, many of today's real graphical applications are either CPU bound or fragment bound. It is likely that the number of fragment bound applications will increase even further, as a common trend can be seen in shifting more tasks from the CPU to the GPU. This means optimized shaders will probably have a significant impact on the performance of current and future graphical programs, and in an interactive application every millisecond counts.

The problem is that optimizing shaders for maximum performance is a very difficult task, especially when you consider the spectrum of hardware platforms a PC application typically has to run on. Although shader functionality on current graphics cards is compatible with a certain version number, execution speed may still differ largely between GPUs of different vendors. Without this particular knowledge, achieving good performance on a broad range of graphic cards is nearly impossible. Unfortunately, until now a detailed performance analysis has, at least to our knowledge, not yet been available.

The use of high-level shading languages does not necessarily improve this situation. Compilers are not required to be designed to optimize performance, or they simply are not allowed to because they have to stick to the provided syntax. Also, often, shader code needs optimization on such a high level that it is impossible for a high-level shading language compiler to execute without having the necessary application semantics, for example, shifting computations from pure shader arithmetic instructions to a texture used as look-up table.

In the following pages we will examine these issues by providing a detailed look at the performance of arithmetic instructions on different graphic architectures, investigating different texture formats, sizes, and filtering, and providing a recommendation on their usage. Additionally we took several performance optimization tips, found on various Web pages of GPU vendors and pages concerning graphics programming and analyzed the truth behind them. The investigation in this article concentrates on hardware that is at least capable of executing pixel shader Version 2.0.

Measurement Methods

ON THE CD

Although there are many different benchmarking tools available for testing graphics hardware or a complete system [FutureMark03, ShaderMark04, MachTest02] we wrote a special benchmarking program (which is available on the CD-ROM accompanying this book) to test the performance of different shader instructions, combinations of shader instructions, and different texture formats. The reason why we did not simply use a standard benchmarking tool is that these general tools have one major problem: they are suitable for an end-user to test his system performance, but they do not really provide detailed information to a developer (except maybe to the developer of the benchmarking tool itself). Another issue one faces when using these tools, is that, in general, they test only certain aspects of the entire graphics pipeline—e.g., fill rate tests—or even the entire system's performance and not just certain aspects, as we will try to do.

When designing a benchmarking tool for testing the fragment processing performance of a GPU, extra care has to be taken that the measured timings only reflect the rasterization parts of the pipeline. This can be ensured by using a bunch of pre-transformed vertices that go through the vertex processing stage without requiring any additional processing. They are directly pushed to the triangle setup engine and afterwards send to the rasterization unit. Care has to be taken that the number of fragment operations is large enough, otherwise the error in time measurements—which is the result of common drifts in the CPU timer or other small hiccups in the system—will become too large.

Unfortunately, when a program is fragment bound, certain problems can occur that not everyone might be aware of. In newer versions of the Windows Operating system like Windows 2000 / XP a so-called Watch-Dog timer has been introduced to allow the operating system's kernel to shut down malfunctioning device drivers that do not return after a certain period of time. This can be thought of as an I-am-still-alive-signal. Now the problem is that this Watch-Dog timer can not distinguish between a device which truly is not responding and an execution within the device that takes longer than the timer setting allows. When running beyond the fragment capabilities of the graphics card the execution time of a legal draw call can easily exceed the timeframe allowed by the timer. This problem would not be dramatic if the timer setting were consistent between every configuration. Unfortunately, this is not the case and it seems that the device driver is able to influence it. It is even possible for a device driver to send an I-am-still-alive-signal to the operating system at arbitrary times that are out-of-synch with receiving API calls. Regrettably, we did not find a satisfying solution to this problem; therefore we were forced to leave out the more time-consuming test shaders.

Another interesting behavior of Direct3D can be observed when one tries to measure the exact time a single draw operation requires in the render loop. By simply taking the time before the draw call and again after the buffer swap call, the elapsed time can vary dramatically between frames and, therefore, no real conclusion can be drawn. The reason for this behavior is that Direct3D allows the GPU to batch up to three complete frames, which allows a driver to immediately release control back to the CPU without introducing major stalls to the overall system. This behavior is desirable for applications that require both a significant amount of CPU and GPU processing time. However, this is a nightmare for a benchmarking tool trying to reliably measure atomic operations. It would not be accurate to use the average of the elapsed time across a few rendered frames since this would include a significant period of time spent performing other operations that do not belong to the actual fragment processing. Additionally, we noticed that on some cards the first two or three frames are rendered slightly slower than subsequent ones, especially after switching between shader programs. Luckily, this problem can be solved by dispatching an asynchronous query to the GPU. The following lines of code show how this can be achieved:

```
            .
            .
            .
LPDIRECT3DDEVICE->DrawPrimitive(….);
IDirect3DQuery9* l_query;
LPDIRECT3DDEVICE->CreateQuery(D3DQUERYTYPE_EVENT,&l_query);
l_query->Issue(D3DISSUE_END);
LPDIRECT3DDEVICE->EndScene();
LPDIRECT3DDEVICE->Present(NULL,NULL,NULL,NULL);
HRESULT result = l_query->GetData(DataType,l_query->GetDataSize(),
                                  D3DGETDATA_FLUSH);
while (result != S_OK)
  result = l_query->GetData(DataType,l_query->GetDataSize(),
                            D3DGETDATA_FLUSH);
            .
            .
            .
```

With the help of the above query it is possible to stall the CPU until the frame has been processed by the GPU.

The outline of our test is as follows: we draw 1500 quads—all vertices of which are pre-transformed as stated above and each of these quads has a size of 512×512 pixels. By disabling depth tests and depth writes we get a massive amount of overdraw, which is required to reach the rasterization bound of a card. The 1500 quads are rendered 15 times with the same pixel shader, textures, and the necessary shader constants. Before each `DrawCall` and after each backbuffer swap, if the query that follows the backbuffer swap returns OK, the timer values of the high-precision multimedia timer are stored. The difference between both timings is computed and written to a protocol file. Afterwards, the worst three timings are removed and from the remaining the average value is taken in order to negate effect of initial slowdown when switching render states.

Arithmetic Instruction Performance

The pixel shader 2.0 profile provides a rich set of arithmetic instructions and allows an adequate number of instruction slots that many shaders are likely to take full use of.

These different arithmetic instructions can be divided into three main groups. The first one is the group of very common ones like: *add, mad, mul, dp3,* and *dp4.* In general, these are used very frequently. The second group can be classified as sparsely used and these are: *cmp, rsq, rcp,* and *frc.* The last group consists of a collection of macros or instructions that according to the DirectX 9 specification can take up more than one instruction slot. These are in particular: all the matrix multiplication macros, *nrm, pow, lrp, crs,* and *sincos.*

1. "Common" Instructions

Figure 7.1.1 shows the performance of the *add* instruction. The *mul, dp3,* and *mad* instruction show nearly the same performance characteristics as that of the *add* instruction. As can be seen for ATI architectures a doubling in the number of instructions simply implies a doubling in the execution time of the shader. The older Geforce FX line has a slightly better ratio that even seems to improve with an increasing number of instructions. Only the overall execution time for full 32-bit processing is larger. The newer Geforce FX 5950 shows an even better ratio between increasing the number of instructions and their execution time. It clearly shows that the card is able to process two or more instructions in one cycle. It also indicates that long pixel shaders are likely to perform better on Nvidia's FX architecture. Mixing registers, which means not always using the same register as target register, has no impact on the overall shader performance on both architectures. But surprisingly, there is a difference between using *add* instructions that use only temporary registers as source and destination and using a mixture of temporary register and constant registers. Using constants is slightly better on the ATI architecture and, surprisingly enough, using constants on the newer Geforce FX results in a significant speed penalty while on the older FX version it behaves similar to ATI. No difference in the performance characteristics between the two ATI revisions can be observed, apart from the fact that the overall performance of the newer version is better. For the low-end market we also included tests for an FX5650Go that can be found in portable computers. It was only possible to include figures for the first three tests because the others were too time-consuming and the Watch-dog timer killed the application before the tests were able to finish. Nevertheless, for the remaining tests no difference in behavior could be observed for the 5650 compared to its larger desktop version (FX5800). It is worth noticing that the overall rasterization performance is approximately only a fourth of the desktop cards.

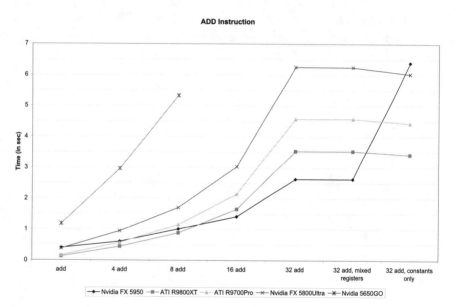

FIGURE 7.1.1 *Performance of the pixel shader 2.0 add instruction on different DirectX 9 compliable graphic cards.*

2. "Sparsely Used" Instructions

A typical shader only uses a small number of these instructions, therefore, we have classified them as sparsely used. This is, of course, a matter of opinion and may depend largely on the actual shader code, but we think you will only find a small number of these instruction calls in a real pixel shader. Therefore, we did not conduct the same extensive testing as we did with the previous group.

Figure 7.1.2 shows the timing figures for the *rcp, rsq, cmp,* and *frc* instructions. On the ATI cards, nearly all of these instructions behave similarly to the other more common arithmetic instructions. Equivalently to the previous group, a doubling in instruction count implies a doubling in shader execution time. A little exception to this rule seems to be the compare operation. It appears to scale slightly better than the other instructions. One can only wonder why, but it is certainly nice to know. When we look at the figures for the FX architecture we soon notice that the FX does not like compare instructions at all. It even turns out to be the most costly operation of all single-slot instructions. Therefore, we recommend not to use it if you can prevent it. Surprisingly, there is also a difference in performance between reciprocal and reciprocal square root. One gets the feeling that a reciprocal square root instruction is not handled as a single instruction, but rather appears to be a combination of two more simple ones (like a square root and a reciprocal). The timings show at least a nearly twice as long execution time compared to *rcp*. This is another proof that the Nvidia FX architecture is very different from ATI's. The mobile version of the FX chip shows the same characteristics as the desktop version.

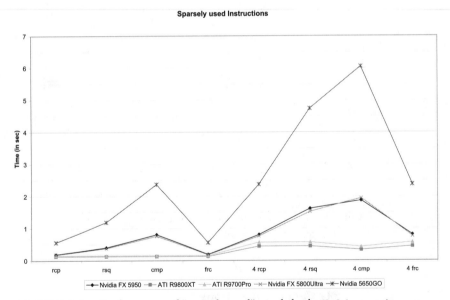

FIGURE 7.1.2   *Performance of "sparsely used" pixel shader 2.0 instructions on different DirectX 9 capable graphic cards.*

3. Complex Instructions and Macros

Complex instructions are instructions that, according to the DirectX 9 shader specification, can take up more than one instruction slot. This, however, does not prevent a

GPU manufacturer to implement a more efficient version that takes up fewer slots. Instruction macros like *m3 × 3, m4 × 3, m4 × 4*, etc., can be added to this list although they are not atomic instructions but placeholders for the corresponding multiple single instructions.

Figure 7.1.3 shows the measurement results for complex instructions and macros. We also tested a corresponding simulation routine made up of the atomic instruction equivalents for some macros and other complex operations to see if the GPU uses a special code path for instructions that belong to this group. However, our measurements did not show any signs that this is actually being done. It seems that macros really only are compile-time placeholders for their corresponding atomic instructions on both architectures.

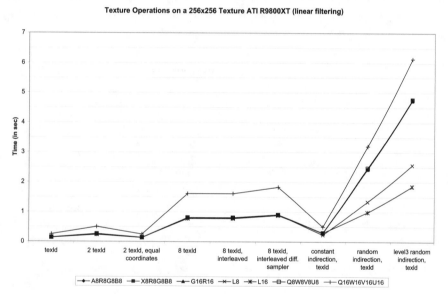

FIGURE 7.1.3   *Performance of pixel shader 2.0 complex instructions and macros on different DirectX 9 capable graphic cards.*

For complex instructions on the ATI R3xx architecture the maximum number of instruction slots needed corresponds quite well to the execution time required. For example, a *pow* which is specified as taking up three slots requires approximately three times the execution time compared to an atomic *add* instruction. The same holds true for *nrm* and it seems that *sincos* is the only one which is faster than the specified eight instructions found in the DirectX 9 SDK documentation. On Nvidia's FX architecture things are a bit different, for example, *sincos* does behave like an atomic instruction and represents one of the highlights of the FX series. However, *pow* needs less than 1.5 times the amount of time than *add,* and *nrm* requires less than two times the processing time. Even when we consider that the Nvidia FX can actually execute two arithmetic instructions per cycle, this would only explain the required time for *pow* but not for *nrm*. Also, these do not scale as well as the other arithmetic instructions.

4. Other Things

We also measured the performance of a random combination of frequently and less frequently used arithmetic instructions. The total number of instructions ranged from 4 to 16 (see Figure 7.1.4). For most cases the ATI cards showed significant better performance. When comparing the results from the previous sections this is not very surprising as all instructions—excluding macros and complex operations—require the same amount of time. On the FX architecture this is a different story, as some of the "slower" instructions seem to bring down the overall performance. The best candidates for these instructions are rsq and cmp.

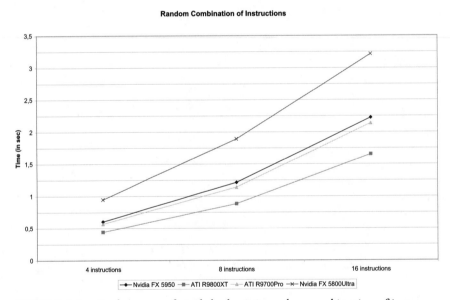

FIGURE 7.1.4   *Performance of pixel shader 2.0 random combination of instructions on different DirectX 9 capable graphic cards.*

In the next step, the partial precision modifier was used to check if using it has any impact on performance. As expected, it had no influence on the ATI cards as they do not allow 16-bit operations in the fragment pipeline. On the Nvidia cards, several different results were observed. Very surprisingly, and in contrast to many rumors, the influence of the partial precision modifier is very hard to predict on the old FX line. It seems that its performance depends on many factors which are unclear to us; nearly all of our test shaders failed to show any significant performance improvement. In contrast, on the newer Nvidia cards like the FX 5950 we observed for nearly all arithmetic instructions a doubling in performance when using _pp. Exceptions are *rsq, rcp, pow,* and *sincos.* It seems that for these no 16-bit versions are available.

We would like to add another final remark about partial precision: extra care should be taken when mixing non-partial precision with partial precision instructions on the FX architecture, as we found several cases in which this is will be rewarded with an extra speed penalty. The full precision version will even end up being faster than the version with instructions using mixed precision. Therefore, we recommend to either use partial precision for the whole shader code, or to take extensive measurements while mixing partial precision instructions with full precision instructions.

Also, measurements for a combination of swizzles and writing masks were conducted and even these showed quite unexpected results. All the allowed swizzle operations in the pixel shader 2.0 profile (*.x, .y, .z, .w, .xyzw, .wzxy, ,yzxw, .zxyw*) have no influence on the ATI R3xx architecture. It does not matter if you use a swizzle or not. Things are different for the FX line, even between chip revisions. The FX 5800 for example shows the same behavior as the ATI cards. On the FX 5950, however, a difference between swizzle types can be observed. The single swizzles *(.x, .y, .z, .w)* and the simple swizzles (*.xyzw, .wzyx*) show no speed penalty. For the other two swizzle types we observed a performance decrease of roughly 60% compared to using no swizzles.

For write masking every possible combination of write masks was tested for their effect on shader performance. One might think write masks do not have any influence on performance; unfortunately this is absolutely not the case. We see a 14% performance hit for every write mask on the FX 5800, a 33% performance hit for three component write masks (like .xyz) on the FX 5950 and a 27% performance hit for any type of masking except for three component masks on the ATI R3xx-based cards. This means that if write masking is not really required it is wise to avoid it.

Texture Performance

A lot of pixel shaders use textures as data input. A shader often combines these textures into a final pixel color. Examples for input textures are: shadow maps, lighting maps, surface color maps, normal maps, bump maps, or lookup tables for arithmetic functions that are too complex to be performed by the shader itself. Thus, the performance of texture operations can be crucial to the overall performance of the shader. Therefore, several tests were conducted to measure the performance of different common texture formats and texture sizes along with different texture filtering modes.

The section is divided into three categories: power-of-two textures, representing sizes of, for example 256 × 256, non-power-of-two textures, and finally cube texture maps.

Power-of-Two Textures

We used several different texture sizes ranging from 4×4 to 512×512 texels. The textures consisted of random patterns stored in different common texture formats. Figure 7.1.5 represents the measured times for a simple texture load for different formats and sizes on the ATI R9800XT. Filtering was set to D3DTEXF_LINEAR. Figure 7.1.7 illustrates different texture operations using a 256×256 size texture again on the ATI R9800XT. Equal texcoords mean the same texture coordinates were used to look up the value in a texture. Otherwise, a different coordinate set was used for each look-up. Interleaved means an alternation between arithmetic and texture instructions is done rather than first doing all the texture operations and then the arithmetic instructions. Finally, different sampler means the texture slot was changed for each texture look-up; otherwise, the look-up was done using the same texture sampler. Figures 7.1.6 and 7.1.8 represent the results for the same tests on the Geforce FX 5950. The results show that both systems have similar performance in texture loading. The ATI has a slightly lower starting point and can keep the performance up to a texture size of 256×256, while the FX card is able to catch up and overtake the ATI card at a 512×512 texture size. Performance starts to depend on the bitdepth (except for the 64-bit wide texture format Q16W16V16U16 which is not supported by the FX) from a texture size of 256×256. From that point on it starts to have an impact on the actual performance.

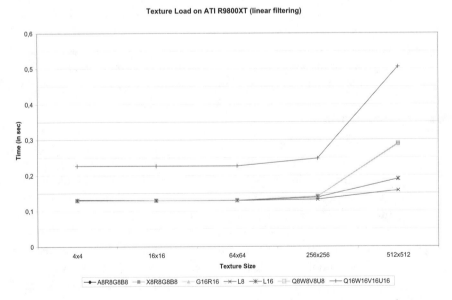

FIGURE 7.1.5   *Power-of-two texture load on ATI R9800XT series using linear filtering, different texture formats, and sizes.*

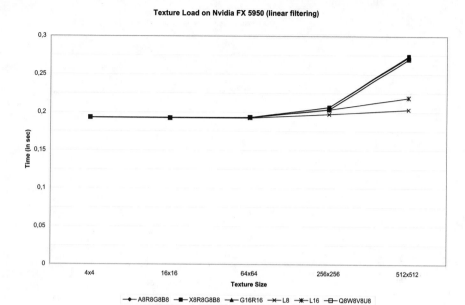

FIGURE 7.1.6   *Power-of-two texture load on Nvidia FX 5950 series using linear filtering, different texture formats, and sizes.*

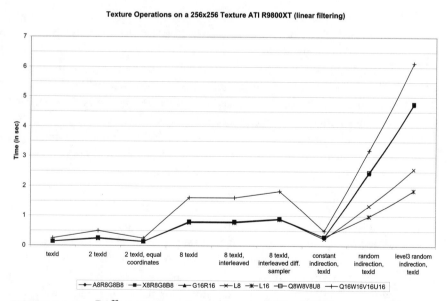

FIGURE 7.1.7   *Different texture instructions on 256×256 size power-of-two texture using ATI R9800XT series with linear filtering.*

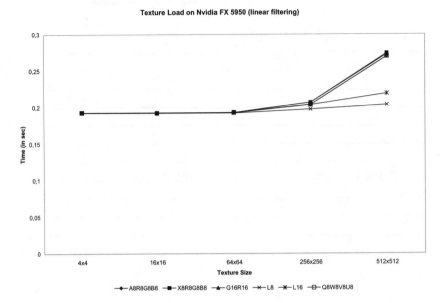

FIGURE 7.1.8 *Different texture instructions on 256 × 256 size power-of-two texture using Nvidia FX 5950 series with linear filtering.*

Using twice as many texture loads with different texture coordinates, but with the same texture sampler, approximately doubles the times on both architectures. The ATI scales slightly better than the NV. Interleaving texture operations with arithmetic instructions does not have any influence on the effort spent by the shader. On the other hand, switching the sampler has an influence at least on the ATI architecture and inexplicably, for luminance 16-bit textures on the Nvidia FX 5950 as well. Also, we can see that the FX architecture does not like constants in the indirection measurements. The speed penalty can mostly be related to the use of constants. On the ATI a constant texture indirection is nearly as fast as a normal texture look-up. The ATI also seems to cope better with texture indirection in general at least for the 32-bit wide texture formats. Lower bit texture formats like 8 bit and 16 bit seem to be handled better on the FX architecture. Why the luminance 8-bit format is slower with indirection than its 16-bit counterpart on the ATI is a mystery to us. We think it is related to the swizzle pattern. Interesting to note is that the ATI architecture seems to be able to detect when a shader tries to load from the same texture with the same texture coordinate but to a different register. In this case the load will not be executed, and the result will simply be copied to the register. This behavior could (and probably should) be attributed to the driver optimizing away the load. On the older FX revision 5800 things do not look that different except for luminance 16 bit, which falls completely out of line. It is already remarkably slower just doing a simple texture load. In contrast, the 8-bit wide texture formats already start to become marginally faster at a size of 64×64 texels. The overall performance is approximately in the same range. On the ATI 9700 series we do not see a difference to its successor (9800) only its overall performance (as we have already seen with the arithmetic instructions) is slightly lower.

When using point sampling, the speed improvement on the ATI R3xx for general texture look-ups is about 12%, but indirections are improved dramatically by an impressive 400% gain. This shows clearly that when using indirections one should switch to point sampling whenever possible. On the NV FX 5950, the speed gained by using point sampling with indirections is even more dramatic: it is approximately 500% and in some cases even more, coming very close to the speed of R3xx texture indirection. Apart from that, switching to point sampling does not result in any significant performance increase on the FX 5950. On the older FX architecture, no difference in texture performance can be seen switching from linear to point sampling— not even for indirections.

Non-Power-of-Two Textures

For non-power-of-two textures we used texture sizes that are close in total size to their power-of-two counterparts. We also included tests that use the same total size but swapped the width and the height dimension, to see if this might have an effect on the memory layout used by the card. Additionally, pseudo one-dimensional textures were used. We use the term pseudo because these are 2D textures but with one dimension set to one texel. (Direct3D has no native support for 1D textures). Figures 7.1.9 and 7.1.10 show the corresponding times for linear filtering and non-power-of-two textures on the ATI R9800XT and Nvidia FX 5950. The measured times show that, contrary to older DirectX 7 and 8 compatible hardware, non-power-of-two textures no longer have to be slower than their power-of-two versions and it is fairly save to use them instead of having to waste memory by enlarging textures to match a power-of-two size.

Interestingly when looking at the ATI R3xx figures one might have noticed that the times are little bit better when the texture is wider than it is tall, even if it is only roughly a 1% gain. When using more than one texture look-up from the same texture, or different ones using different texture coordinates, this relationship changes to the opposite and a 2–3% performance increase can be seen for textures having a larger y dimension. This might be an effect of the caching strategies the GPU uses. Even more interesting are the results obtained by using pseudo 1D textures. In this particular case, textures using the y dimension for storing the 1D values are 5–16% faster depending on their size. This means that when you have large 1D look-up tables it might be better to arrange them in vertical order instead of horizontal on the ATI R3xx-based cards. The Nvidia FX 5950 line does not cope as well with non-power-of-two textures since a performance decline between 13-37% depending on the texture size can be expected for textures that have a nearly equal total number of texels to a corresponding power-of-two version. Things start to get dramatic when we consider indirections, for example, the largest tested texture size (604×409) had to be

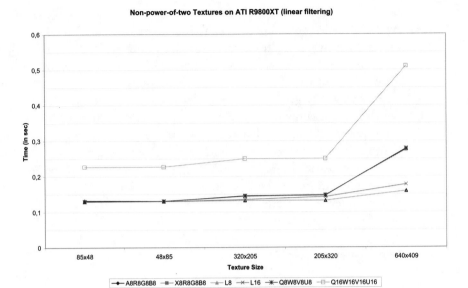

FIGURE 7.1.9 *Non-power-of-two texture load on ATI R9800XT series using linear filtering, different texture formats, and sizes.*

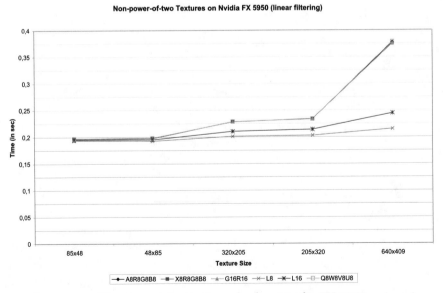

FIGURE 7.1.10 *Non-power-of-two texture load on Nvidia FX 5950 series using linear filtering, different texture formats, and sizes.*

excluded from the tests because it simply took too long and therefore triggered the watchdog timer. For smaller texture sizes an approximate 200% performance decrease has been noticed. Additionally, in the case of indirections the FX 5950 seems to prefer texture formats that are wider than they are tall. Opposite to the ATI architecture a marginally better performance can be expected for pseudo 1D textures when the data in the texture is arranged in the horizontal dimension and not in the vertical dimension. Non-power-of-two textures are slower than power-of-two textures on the FX 5800 as well, the factor is similar to what we saw for the FX 5950. This, of course, contradicts the fact mentioned at the beginning of this section, which states that the performance decrease of non-power-of-two textures is non-existent on DirectX 9 hardware. But at least one can say it is no longer that dramatic when not extensively using texture indirections. One reason for the poor indirection performance on the FX series seems to be (according to Nvidia) that extra instructions have to be added to the pixel shader when using non-power-of-two textures; these instructions map the [0, 1] coordinate range to image coordinates.

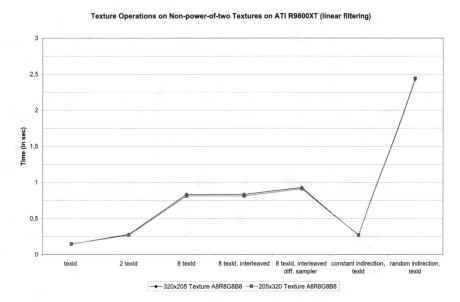

FIGURE 7.1.11   *Different texture operation on a non-power-of-two texture on ATI R9800XT series using linear filtering, using A8R8G8B8 texture format.*

Cube Maps

Cube texture maps were originally invented to fake reflection and refraction effects and were already part of the DirectX 7 specification. Although probably not used as frequently as normal 2D textures, they are still utilized nowadays for many different things besides faking reflections, like renormalization maps, shadow calculation, local

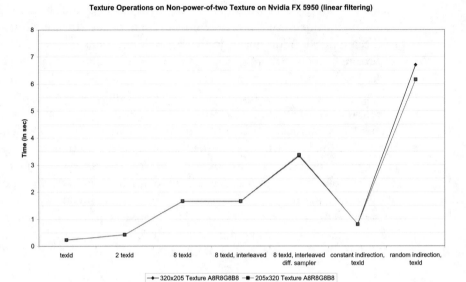

FIGURE 7.1.12 *Different texture operation on a non-power-of-two texture on Nvidia FX 5950 series using linear filtering, using A8R8G8B8 texture format.*

reflection shading, etc. Therefore, their influence on rasterization performance might be interesting to investigate. Until now, cube maps have mostly been allowed only to have square power-of-two dimensions. Therefore, we tested three standard sizes, 16×16, 64×64, and 256×256 texels. To get an adequate coverage of the cube map texture space, the texture coordinates were chosen so that each vertex of the rendered quads mapped to the opposite side of a cube's longer diagonal.

The cube texture map performance on the ATI is not that different from that of standard 2D textures, it is at an equal level and depends on the bit width, and it scales with the same factor as standard 2D textures. The only thing that stands out is that the A8R8G8B8 format appears to be a little bit slower than other 32-bit wide formats. Even for indirections, the penalty is similar to what we see for 2D textures (see Figure 7.1.13). For the new revision of the Nvidia FX architecture, performance also does not vary too much between cube texture maps and 2D textures (see Figure 7.1.14). For indirections, signed texture formats in particular suffer from a small performance drop (app. 8–9%) compared to 2D texture maps. The 8-bit and 16-bit luminance textures show a significant performance improvement of nearly 100% when using random indirection inside the cube map. This might be related to the random pattern since all offsets are going in a specific direction. When using point sampling together with cube texture maps on the ATI R3xx GPU cards, only a small improvement is experienced. Exceptions to this are indirections, as these approximately have the same speedup factor when using point filtering as 2D textures have. Exactly the same behavior can be observed for the Nvidia FX 5950 as well: nearly the same performance for normal texture operations and a dramatic performance increase for indirections. All cube map operations are around 20% slower on the FX 5800 compared to the newer FX 5950 when using linear filtering, otherwise no difference can be observed.

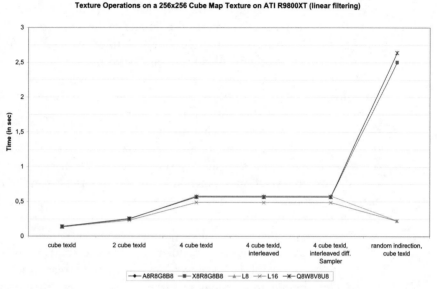

FIGURE 7.1.13   *Different texture operation on a 256 × 256 cube texture map on ATI R9800XT series using linear filtering and different texture formats.*

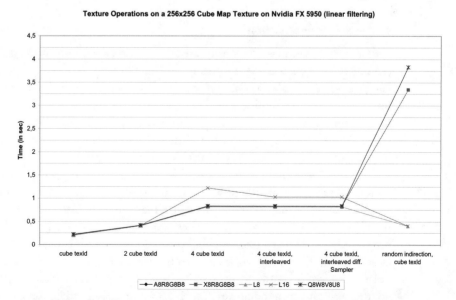

FIGURE 7.1.14   *Different texture operation on a 256 × 256 cube texture map on Nvidia FX 5950 series using linear filtering and different texture formats.*

Arithmetic versus Texture

The task of developing pixel shader code can also be seen as the task to evaluate a fixed number of mathematical functions, each based on several input parameters. The challenge is to perform the calculations with just enough precision as to make sure that no visual artifacts occur and, thereby, minimize processing time and memory usage of the GPU. There are several options that influence these quantities. First, functions or parts of functions can be calculated offline and stored in textures. The shader program can then skip the costly calculations by just performing a simple texture look-up. As modern GPUs provide 1D, 2D, cube, and 3D textures, it is possible to store functions that depend on up to three parameters. These are the dimensions of the look-up texture. The drawback of using this approach is that the texture memory and the memory bandwidth requirements strongly depend on the precision, resolution, and domain required for the function to be evaluated. The second approach for optimizing a function evaluation within a shader, is to use a less accurate approximation of the function. In several cases, polynomials or Taylor series expansion can be used, but also other approximations, e.g., the Newton-Raphson method for root finding are possible. Nvidia's FX GPUs offer a third way to speed up the execution of your shader code by supporting the so-called partial precision modifier _pp. However, as already stated above, one must use this modifier carefully and compare the resulting performance to that of the full precision version. The question that remains is: when do we use which technique to get the optimal pixel shader code? The previous sections give very useful hints to ease this decision. For some common functions this decision has to be considered very often and, therefore, we will provide an in-depth analysis of these.

1. Vector Normalization

Vector normalization is frequently used in pixel shaders. Four general techniques are examined to normalize a vector: using the built-in *nrm* instruction, manually normalizing the vector via a *dp3, rsq, mul* command sequence, approximating the normalization via the Newton-Raphson method, and using cube texture look-ups. The manually normalizing command sequence performs equally to the *nrm* instruction as already stated before. For the Newton-Raphson technique, only the first iteration step was implemented as otherwise the performance would have been much slower than an *nrm* instruction. Therefore, the results of this technique are only valid when normalizing vectors that are only slightly denormalized. However, the measurements prove that the Newton-Raphson method performs worse than the *nrm* instruction on the R3xx and the FX series, although only the first iteration step is evaluated. The final alternative for normalizing a vector is to use a cube texture look-up with a 128×128 or 256×256 cube texture. To achieve adequate precision each component of the pre-computed, normalized vector is stored in 16-bit fixed point precision. On ATI GPUs a cube texture with four components each with 16-bit precision can be used. On contrast, the setup for Nvidia GPUs uses two textures because three or four component cube textures with more than 8-bit precision per component are not supported by the FX series in DirectX. Both versions performed better than the *nrm* instruction. Nevertheless, since the performance gain is moderate one has to consider if the additional texture look-up and memory requirement is worth the speedup.

2. Exponential Function

Per-pixel lighting is getting more and more popular especially since the availability of efficient real-time bump mapping techniques. The equations used to evaluate the lighting equation greatly differs from application to application. But nearly all of them, at least those lighting models that have a specular component, have to raise a function value to a given specular power. The simplest solution to evaluate an exponential function is to use the native *pow* pixel shader instruction. If the specular exponent is a fixed, small integer number the exponentiation can be rolled out manually via a succession of *mul* operations. The fallback implementation is to use texture look-ups. If the specular exponent is fixed, a 1D texture is sufficient, and for a varying exponent a 2D texture can be used. Typical specular exponents lie in the range of 5 to 200. Measuring the performance of the *pow* instruction versus manually rolling out the exponent evaluation indicates that on Nvidia cards exponents of four and up should not be implemented via successive multiplications. On ATI cards this threshold is at roughly an exponent of eight. Using a 2D texture look-up to evaluate the power function is even faster on both architectures and, therefore, this technique is the first choice when implementing a production pixel shader code. The only drawback when using textures is that the range of the values that are used for look-ups should be minimized since they directly influence the texture size and, therefore, the texture memory consumed by the look-up texture.

3. Calculating the Sine or Cosine

Evaluating the sine or cosine of an angle can become a very costly operation. As stated in the DirectX documentation the *sincos* command is by far the most advanced instruction, consuming up to eight instruction slots. One might expect that this command is the performance killer for every pixel shader code. Alternatives to evaluating the sine or cosine are either a polynomial approximation by orthogonal polynomials, a Taylor series expansion, or a 1D texture look-up with pre-calculated sine/cosine values. As already shown, the Nvidia hardware performs much better on the *sincos* command than any ATI hardware based on the R3xx architecture. Therefore, on Nvidia hardware one should always use the native instruction, which is faster than a polynomial approximation or the texture look-up variant. Even a partial precision shader that evaluates only four elements of, for example, the Taylor series performs worse. On ATI GPUs the *sincos* command performs at exactly the same speed as an evaluation of a polynomial approximation with five elements in a pixel shader program. Therefore, it seems that the *sincos* is internally rolled out to an evaluation of a polynomial approximation. The fastest solution to evaluate the sine/cosine on R3xx class GPUs is to use a texture look-up. Therefore, this variant should be used whenever your shader code allows for an additional, possibly dependent, texture look-up. Another benefit of this method is that it takes up less instruction slots than the *sincos* command.

4. Evaluating the Fresnel Term

In its simplest form, the Fresnel term describes the ratio of reflection and refraction of transmissive surfaces. The ratio depends on the refractive index of the material and the angle-of-incidence. A straightforward implementation of this function uses about 20 arithmetic instructions. To speedup the evaluation of the function it could be pre-calculated and stored in a 2D texture. But since in most cases the refraction index of the material does not change across a surface, the refraction index can be assumed to be constant and the pre-calculated texture can be reduced to a 1D texture. The implementation via arithmetic instructions also benefit from this assumption and the number of used instructions decreases slightly. For further optimizations a function approximation can be used. Since the Fresnel term is often used to render water surfaces that have a refractive index of 1.33, several functions to approximate the Fresnel term exist. We examined two of them: a simple approximation that can be implemented with three arithmetic instructions and a more sophisticated one that uses five arithmetic instructions. While the simple approach produces visible differences compared to a correct evaluation of the Fresnel term it already exceeds the execution time of the texture look-up method. This result can be seen on all ATI and Nvidia cards that we tested, and thus it is clear that the best technique to implement the Fresnel term is to use a simple texture look-up.

Common Pitfalls and Rumors

In this section we briefly discuss some advice and pitfalls from talks of Nvidia and ATI concerning shader performance [Cebenoyan03, Rege04, Riguer02, Spitzer03] or other common beliefs and compare them to our findings:

1. **Use ps_2_a Profile for Nvidia FX series when using DirectX 9**
   Our opinion: In general we could not notice any performance gain by using this profile, we tried most of our test shaders and we did not see any performance improvement.
2. **Use a mixture of texture and math instruction**
   Our opinion: We think this rescheduling is already done in the graphics card driver as we did not notice any difference between using texture loads first and then math or interleaving both.
3. **Enable co-issue of scalar and vector instructions**
   Our opinion: We tried to find the co-issue even with an example which is provided by ATI, but we were unable to reproduce the effect and on the

Nvidia FX architecture. This attempt was even rewarded with an approximate 13% performance loss. We recommend therefore to be careful when trying out co-issues. It is better to rely on the driver to do a rescheduling.

4. **Group non-dependent texture instructions together**
Our opinion: Similar to case 3 we think the driver already does this.

5. **Use *mad* instructions where possible**
Our opinion: We noticed that individual *mul* instructions followed by an *add* in struction using the same target register is detected by Nvidia and ATI and is automatically replaced by a *mad* instruction.

6. **Instruction modifiers are for free, aren't they?**
Our opinion: No, unfortunately on some hardware they are not! Be careful on the FX 5950 it can cost you up to 66% in performance.

7. **Do not use *texkill* if it really is not necessary**
Our opinion: True, *texkill* should not be used to try to gain performance as rather the opposite will happen: it introduces stalls in the pipeline and performance will be lost. Again this can be seen on both architectures. The only difference one can see between the two architecures is that a late *texkill* in the pixel program is slower than an early *texkill* on the Nvidia FX architecture.

8. **_pp modifier on texture loads?**
Our opinion: Possible, but it is quite unpredictable what will happen. Only use _pp on texture loads if you switch all your arithmetic instructions to _pp as well, otherwise this may result in a performance drain.

Conclusion

Our measurements show that in most situations the performance of a shader can be predicted by simply counting instructions. However, there are still several cases in which the execution time cannot easily be explained. Therefore, we have provided our benchmark tool to measure the performance of production-level pixel shader code variants. This becomes even more important when you have to consider the different GPU architectures that your shader code has to run on, since it is nearly impossible to write shader code that runs at an optimal performance on all the current architectures. An adequate solution to this misery is to shift as many function evaluations from arithmetic slots to pre-calculated look-up tables—stored in 1D, 2D, or cube texture maps—whenever possible. This assumption can easily be verified by the fact that a texture look-up is executed at the same speed as a single atomic arithmetic instruction. However, we expect that this ratio will change in favor of arithmetic instructions with the upcoming GPU generations.

References

[Cebenoyan03] Cebenoyan, Wloka "Optimizing the Graphics Pipeline," *Game Developer Conference,* 2003.

[FutureMark03] FutureMark Corporation, "3DMark2003," available at *http://www. futuremark.com.*

[MachTest02] Hopf, M., "MachTest," available at *http://www.vis.uni-stuttgart.de/ machtest/.*

[Rege04] Rege, Brewer, "Practical Performance Analysis and Tuning," *Game Developer Conference,* 2004.

[Riguer02] Riguer G., "Performance Optimization Techniques for ATI Graphics Hardware with DirectX 9.0," ATI Whitepaper 2002.

[ShaderMark04] Bruckschlegel, T. "ShaderMark V2.0," available at *http://www. shadermark.de.*

[Spitzer03] Spitzer J., "OpenGL Performance Tuning," *Game Developer Conference,* 2003.

7.2

Shaderbreaker

Magnus Österlind

Introduction

While experimenting with different shaders and .FX files, we found that we were writing the same basic stub code to set parameters, load textures, and create vertex declarations over and over again.

To alleviate this, the shaderbreaker was born; a wrapper around .FX files that tries to automate as much of the repetitive work as possible.

Overview

There are a few steps involved in getting the shaderbreaker system working. These are briefly discussed here, and in more detail in the next section.

Offline: We make use of annotations in the .FX files to mark parameters, textures, and vertex streams. We also output a text file when we export a scene from our DCC tool, which contains information about which shader an object uses along with each object's material and texture properties.

Init Time: The engine initializes a number of "parameter sources," which are basically pairs consisting of a name and a function pointer. The parameter sources are responsible for generating the value of the parameter, which is then subsequently set in the .FX file.

We parse all the .FX files that are located in the common effects directory. For each .FX file, we create a shaderbreaker. Each shaderbreaker collects information on parameters, vertex declarations, and the type of texture it needs. Connections between the parameters to be set and the parameter sources that generate the values are also created.

Object Load Time: For each object we load, we connect it to a shaderbreaker. We use the texture information in the shaderbreaker to load textures of the required type.

The Details

The Parameter System

A parameter is defined as a value that comes from somewhere inside the engine (the parameter source), and that wants to be associated with a parameter in the .FX file (via a parameter sink).

The parameter system is a "source" and "sink" system. A parameter source is a function that, when called, will return a value of a certain type. A parameter sink is a void (or HRESULT if errors are to be propagated) function, that takes a parameter source as input, and sets the value in the .FX file.

Adding Parameter Sources

The bookkeeping of all the parameter sources is handled by a component called the connection manager. The connection manager contains a list of connections. A connection is a mapping between names and function calls. We can add parameter sources, and retrieve a particular parameter source by its name.

```
class CConnectionManager
{
public:

    typedef CConnection<float>          FLOAT_CONNECTIONS;
    typedef CConnection<D3DXVECTOR3>    VECTOR3_CONNECTIONS;
    typedef CConnection<D3DXVECTOR4>    VECTOR4_CONNECTIONS;
    typedef CConnection<D3DXMATRIX>     MATRIX_CONNECTIONS;

    FLOAT_CONNECTIONS&          FloatConnection();
    VECTOR3_CONNECTIONS&        Vector3Connection();
    VECTOR4_CONNECTIONS&        Vector4Connection();
    MATRIX_CONNECTIONS&         MatrixConnection();

private:
    FLOAT_CONNECTIONS           m_FloatConnections;
    VECTOR3_CONNECTIONS         m_Vector3Connections;
    VECTOR4_CONNECTIONS         m_Vector4Connections;
    MATRIX_CONNECTIONS          m_MatrixConnections;
};

    template< class T >
    class CConnection
    {
    public:

        typedef boost::function< T() > PER_SHADER;
        typedef boost::function< T (NGeomObject::CBase*) >
                PER_OBJECT;
```

```
            // per shader connections
            void        AddPerShaderConnection( const std::string&
                            rstrConnectionName, PER_SHADER pfn );
            bool        FindPerShaderConnection( PER_SHADER* ppfn,
                            const std::string& rstrConnectionName );

            // per object connections
            void        AddPerObjectConnection( const std::string&
                            rstrConnectionName, PER_OBJECT pfn );
            bool        FindPerObjectConnection( PER_OBJECT* ppfn,
                            const std::string& rstrConnectionName );

        private:

            typedef std::map< std::string, PER_SHADER >
                            PER_SHADER_PARAMETER_MAP;
            typedef std::map< std::string, PER_OBJECT >
                            PER_OBJECT_PARAMETER_MAP;

            PER_SHADER_PARAMETER_MAP    m_PerShaderParameterMap;
            PER_OBJECT_PARAMETER_MAP    m_PerObjectParameterMap;

        };
```

By using `boost::function`, and `boost::bind`, we are able to easily store both class member functions and free functions as parameter sources.

Parameters can be one of two types: per shader, and per object. Per-shader parameters are shared by all the objects that are to be rendered by a specific shaderbreaker; for example, view and projection matrices. Per-object parameters are specific to each object, and thus have to be set before each object is rendered. Examples of per-object parameters are object-to-world matrices, material properties, etc.

There are two main tasks that have to be performed when the engine is first initialized: adding parameter sources to the connection manager, and parsing the .FX files.

Creating Parameter Sources

When the engine initializes, we add a number of parameter sources that will be used in the .FX files.

In the example shown here, we add light positions, light directions, view, projection and world matrices; however, just about anything could be added as a parameter source.

```
HRESULT CWorld::AddParameterSources()
{
```

```
              // add light connections..
              m_pConnectionManager->Vector3Connection()
               .AddPerShaderConnection( "LightPos",
                  boost::bind( CLightManager::GetDefaultLightPos,
                  m_pLightManager ) );

              m_pConnectionManager->Vector3Connection()
               .AddPerShaderConnection( "LightDir",
                  boost::bind( CLightManager::GetDefaultLightDir,
                  m_pLightManager ) );

              // "world" connection..
              m_pConnectionManager->MatrixConnection()
               .AddPerObjectConnection( "World", ObjectToWorld );

              // camera connections..
              m_pConnectionManager->MatrixConnection().AddPerObjectConnection
               ( "WorldViewProjection", WorldViewProj);
              m_pConnectionManager->MatrixConnection().AddPerShaderConnection
               ( "View",
                  boost::bind( NCamera::CFreeFlyCamera::GetViewMatrix,
                        &m_FreeFlyCamera) );

              m_pConnectionManager-
     >Vector3Connection().AddPerShaderConnection("EyePos",
                  boost::bind( NCamera::CFreeFlyCamera::GetPos,
                        &m_FreeFlyCamera) );

          return S_OK;
     }

     D3DXMATRIX ObjectToWorld( NGeomObject::CBase* pObject )
     {
          return pObject->GetObjectToWorldMtx();
     }

     D3DXMATRIX WorldViewProj( NGeomObject::CBase* pObject )
     {
          const D3DXMATRIX& mtxView = l_pWorld->GetFreeFlyCamera()
              ->GetViewMatrix();
          const D3DXMATRIX& mtxProj = l_pWorld->GetFreeFlyCamera()
              ->GetProjectionMatrix();

          D3DXMATRIX mtxTmp;
          D3DXMatrixMultiply( &mtxTmp, &pObject
              ->GetObjectToWorldMtx(), &mtxView );
          D3DXMatrixMultiply( &mtxTmp, &mtxTmp, &mtxProj );

          return mtxTmp;
     }
```

Parsing .FX Files

There are three things that we are interested in when parsing an .FX file: techniques, parameters, and textures. To be able to extract the information, annotations are added to the .FX files. An example of annotations is shown below:

```
float3 LightPos            <      string Type = "PerShader"; > ;
float3 LightDir            <      string Type = "PerShader"; > ;
float3 EyePos              <      string Type = "PerShader"; > ;

float4x4 View        : VIEW    <    string Type = "PerShader"; > ;
float4x4 World       : WORLD   <    string Type = "PerObject"; > ;
float4x4 WorldViewProjection   <    string Type = "PerObject"; > ;

texture Tex0               <      string Type = "Diffuse"; > ;

technique TPS20
{
    pass P0
    <
        string stream0_0      = "Pos";
        string stream0_12     = "Normal";
        string stream2_0      = "Texture0";
    >
}
```

Techniques

We iterate through the techniques found in the .FX file, and for every pass of each technique, we create a vertex declaration using the tags in the .FX file.

The first number after the `stream` tag is the stream index, and the second number is the stream offset. The stream names ("Pos," "Normal," "Texture0," etc.) correspond to matching stream names which are stored in our exported geometry.

The techniques are named according to the lowest pixel shader version that is needed to run them; an appropriate default technique can be selected by examining the D3DCAPS.

Parsing the Parameters

We iterate through all the parameters in the .FX file, and depending on the parameter type, we do a number of different things

```
D3DXEFFECT_DESC effectDesc;
m_pEffect->GetDesc( &effectDesc );

for( UINT iParam = 0; iParam < effectDesc.Parameters; iParam++ )
{
```

```
D3DXHANDLE hParam = m_pEffect->GetParameter( NULL, iParam );
D3DXPARAMETER_DESC desc;
m_pEffect->GetParameterDesc( hParam, &desc);

// check if the parameter is per shader or per object..
const bool bPerShader = FindNamedAnnotation( m_pEffect,
                          hParam, "Type", "PerShader" );
const bool bPerObject = FindNamedAnnotation( m_pEffect,
                          hParam, "Type", "PerObject" );

switch( desc.Class )
{
case D3DXPC_SCALAR:
// see below..
break;
```

Scalars, Vectors, and Matrices

When we find a scalar, vector, or matrix parameter, we want to create an automatic binding between the source that is responsible for creating the value, and a parameter sink, which is responsible for actually setting the parameter using the appropriate ID3DXEffect method (e.g., SetFloat(), SetVector(), SetMatrix(), etc.).

We do this by creating "sink wrappers," which are member functions of the shaderbreaker that take a parameter source and a name as input. There are two wrappers for each supported type: one for the per-shader parameters, and one for the per-object parameters. When called, the sinks will invoke the parameter source, and bind its return value by name to the correct parameter in the shader.

```
HRESULT CShaderBreaker::SShaderBreakerImpl::Vector4Sink(
    const std::string& rstrName,
    CConnectionManager::VECTOR4_CONNECTIONS::PER_SHADER callBack
)
{
    return m_pEffect->SetVector( rstrName.c_str(), &callBack() );
}

HRESULT CShaderBreaker::SShaderBreakerImpl::MatrixSink(
    const std::string& rstrName,
    CConnectionManager::MATRIX_CONNECTIONS:: PER_SHADER callBack
)
{
    return m_pEffect->SetMatrix( rstrName.c_str(), &callBack() );
}

HRESULT CShaderBreaker::SShaderBreakerImpl::MatrixPerObjectSink(
    const std::string& rstrName,
    CConnectionManager::MATRIX_CONNECTIONS::PER_OBJECT callBack,
    NFaceBlock::CBase* pFaceBlock )
{
    return m_pEffect->SetMatrix( rstrName.c_str(),
                            &callBack(pFaceBlock) );
}
```

When a parameter is found, we check if it is per shader, or per object, and query the corresponding parameter source from the connection manager. If found, we use `boost::bind` to bind the source to the sink, and add the parameter to either the per-shader or per-object parameter list. Using `boost::bind` for this is pretty nifty; we are able to store parameter connections of any type in a single list, which greatly reduces the amount of code that needs to be written.

One thing to note is that we use `bind`'s _1 notation in the per object side of the if-statement. This is used as a placeholder, saying that we will fill in the missing parameter later. This makes sense, because we are binding a function that needs a pointer to an object to be executed, but we have not loaded any objects yet.

```
if( bPerShader )
{
    ConnectionManager::MATRIX_CONNECTIONS::PER_SHADER pfn;
    if( !pConMan->MatrixConnection().FindPerShaderConnection
      (&pfn,desc.Name) )
    {
        LOG_WARNING( "Unable to find connection for: " << desc.Name
                     << std::endl );
    }
    else
    {
        m_PerShaderConnections.push_back(
            boost::bind(&CShaderBreaker::SShaderBreakerImpl::
                 MatrixSink, this, std::string(desc.Name), pfn )
        );
    }
}
else
{
    ConnectionManager::MATRIX_CONNECTIONS::PER_OBJECT pfn;
    if( !pConMan->MatrixConnection().FindPerObjectConnection
      (&pfn,desc.Name) )
    {
        LOG_WARNING( "Unable to find connection for: " <<
                     desc.Name << std::endl );
    }
    else
    {
        m_PerFaceBlockConnections.push_back(
                         boost::bind(

&CShaderBreaker::SShaderBreakerImpl::MatrixPerObjectSink,
             this, std::string(desc.Name), pfn, _1 ) );

    }

}
```

Textures

To be able to automatically load and bind the textures that we need, we tag textures in the .FX file with annotations describing their type; for example, diffuse, gloss map, or normal map. Each shaderbreaker uses these tags to build a list of textures that it requires. This list will be used (i) at load time, to get the texture name from the objects, and to load the correct textures; and (ii) at run time, to set the correct textures before rendering.

```
texture Tex0    <    string Type = "Diffuse"; > ;
```

Load Time

Each scene that is to be loaded by the engine has an associated text file that contains information about the objects in the scene. We store the shader that each object uses, along with material and texture properties.

```
[01 - Default]
Ambient = 0.588235 0.588235 0.588235
Diffuse = 0.588235 0.588235 0.588235
Diffuse_Amount = 1.000000
Diffuse_Filename = tex08.jpg
ShineStrength = 0.810000
Shininess = 0.390000
Specular = 0.900000 0.900000 0.900000
Transparency = 0.000000

[GeoSphere01]
Material = 01 - Default
Shader = Texture
```

When we load an object, we look for the shader that it uses; and if found, we load the textures required by the shader. The object is then added to the shaderbreaker's list of objects that must be rendered.

Render Time

Rendering with the shaderbreaker system is very straightforward. For each shaderbreaker, the following steps are performed:

- Set the current technique
- Set the "per shader" parameters
- For each pass of the effect: Set the vertex declaration
- For each (visible) object: Set the "per object" parameters
- Set the textures
- Set the vertex buffers
- Do the render call

Objects are naturally grouped by shader, which is beneficial to execution speed on modern graphics hardware.

Error Handling

Error handling is added at a number of different stages in the system. When we parse the .FX files, and connect parameters to parameter sources, we can report if any parameters are left unconnected. We also report if any textures are left unbound, or if the vertex streams do not match.

Conclusion

In this article we have presented a flexible and robust system for experimenting with shaders, which can also be used in a production engine. A few additions that we will be exploring in the near future are adding more tags (for creating and binding to render targets), and implementing a LOD/shader fallback system were objects either belong to multiple shaderbreakers, or the shaderbreakers themselves have LOD fallback techniques.

References

- Boost (*www.boost.org*).

Generating Shaders from HLSL Fragments

Shawn Hargreaves

Introduction

You can do all sorts of interesting things with shaders: this and previous ShaderX books are full of examples. Alongside their power, however, programmable shaders can lead to an explosion of permutations: my last Xbox game contained 89 different pixel shaders, and my current project already has far more. Many of these shaders are variations on a few basic themes, for instance, level-of-detail approximations of a material, or the same lighting model both with and without animation skinning. The total number of combinations is huge and is increasing all the time. Typing everything out by hand would be time consuming, error prone, and a maintenance nightmare.

This article will describe how to automatically generate large numbers of shader permutations from a smaller set of handwritten input fragments.

Common Solutions

Uber Shaders

A common solution to the permutation problem is to write a single shader that implements a superset of all desired behaviors, and to let the application disable whatever elements are not currently required. This can be achieved in various ways.

It could be as simple as setting shader constants so as to ignore the effects of any unwanted calculations. However, this wastes GPU horsepower, as the data is still actually being calculated before it is thrown away.

Static flow control instructions in vs 2.0 and ps 2.x are ideal for this task, and take no time to execute at least on some hardware. Complicated control flows will inevitably limit the ability of the optimizer to understand what is going on, however, and if you try to cram too many features into a single shader, instruction count limits can be a problem.

It can be done entirely as a preprocess, using `#ifndef` blocks to enable and disable various parts of the code, and compiling the same source multiple times with different preprocessor settings to generate all the different permutations.

The problem with these approaches is that they require all your shader techniques to be merged into a single monolithic program. The core lighting model, one-off special effects, debugging visualisation aids, and things you experimented with six months ago and then discarded, all get tangled up to the point where you dare not change anything for fear of breaking the entire edifice. Not exactly what is generally accepted as good coding practice!

Microshaders

An alternative approach is to write many small fragments of shader code, and then concatenate these into various combinations. This could be as simple as performing a strcat() call to combine bits of shader source code. Alternatively, you can use tools like NVLink or the D3DX fragment linker to merge fragments of already-assembled shader microcode.

Back in the days of shader 1.x, at Climax we used the C preprocessor to #include source fragments in a suitable order. For instance, here is the highest quality version of the character vertex shader from *MotoGP*:

```
#define WANT_NORMAL

#include "animate.vsi"
#include "transform.vsi"
#include "light.vsi"
#include "fog.vsi"
#include "radiosity.vsi"
#include "envmap.vsi"

mov oT0.xy, iTex0
```

This approach worked reasonably well for simple shaders, but it was hard to keep track of which input values and registers were used by which fragment. To make things more scalable and robust, some kind of automated register allocation was needed. Fortunately, this is exactly what HLSL does for us!

High-level shader languages are the greatest boon imaginable to anyone trying to generate shader code programmatically. When two fragments want to share a piece of data, they just need to refer to it by the same variable name, and then the compiler figures out what register to put it in. When each fragment wants their own private piece of data, a trivial string substitution is enough to mangle the variable names so the compiler sees two different symbols, and will hence allocate two different registers. Perhaps most important of all is that the HLSL compiler does an extremely good job at removing dead or redundant code.

It is common for one shader fragment to calculate several intermediate values, only for a later fragment to overwrite all but one of these with different data. Likewise, several fragments may independently perform the same calculation, such as transforming the input normal to view space. It would be a hassle to manually detect and remove this kind of redundancy, but fortunately there is no need for this. The fragment combiner only has to say what it means, ignoring any duplicate or unused calculations that may result, as the compiler can be trusted to make the details efficient.

In the next section we will describe the main concepts behind our approach to generating shader permutations from HLSL fragments.

HLSL Fragments

We store each shader fragment as a text file, which contains pieces of shader code along with an interface block defining the required usage context.

The following example shows one of the simplest possible fragments, which is a single 2D colormap texture[1]:

```
interface()
{
    $name = base_texture
    $textures = color_map
    $vertex = uv
    $interpolators = uv
    $uv = 2
}

ps 1_1

void main(INPUT input, inout OUTPUT output)
{
    output.color = tex2D(color_map, input.uv);
}
```

Pixel and vertex processing is linked together, so each fragment contains both pixel and vertex shader code in a single file. When multiple fragments are concatenated, the final pixel and vertex shaders are generated in parallel. This linkage presents a convenient interface to the outside world, which also removes the potential error of selecting a mismatched shader pair. It also makes it easy to optimize code by moving calculations back and forth between the vertex and pixel units. However, it does sometimes produce redundant outputs, because many different pixel shaders often share the same vertex shader. This problem can be handled externally to the generation system by merging duplicate compiled shaders if these have identical token streams.

The above fragment does not include any vertex shader code. In this case our framework will generate a standard pass-through vertex function, which simply copies each input straight across to the output. This is an increasingly common case as more and more processing tends to be done on a per-pixel basis.

Code Generation

During development, shaders are generated and compiled the first time each combination is requested by the engine, but the results can be saved to disk in order to avoid

---

[1] We reused an in-house Climax script parser to read the interface block. However, this format could just as easily be XML or something as simple as a "var = value" type of file.

this runtime overhead in the final product. The generation process tries to compile to the lowest possible shader version first, and then tries higher versions if that fails to compile. An example of this is a concatenation of many small ps 1.1 fragments, which could produce a shader too long to work in the 1.1 model. Individual fragments can also label themselves as requiring a specific minimum version; if fragments use features specific to ps 2.0 or 3.0, we do not have to waste time trying to compile for earlier models.

In the interface block, shader fragments report what resources they require:

- The params statement lists any constant registers used by the fragment.
- The textures entry declares what texture samplers it will use.
- The vertex statement describes the format of the vertex shader input data.
- The interpolators line declares what data needs to be output from the vertex shader and input to the pixel shader.

Any of these declarations can be annotated with type information, metadata-allowing editing tools to handle materials in a sensible way, and conditional tests, in case the fragment wants to adapt itself depending on the context in which it is being used. As a very simple example, the fragment shown above declares that the uv vertex input and interpolator channel is a 2-component vector.

Given a list of fragments, we generate a complete shader by performing a number of textual search and replace operations. There is no need to actually parse the syntax of the HLSL code, because our goal is to combine the fragments, rather than to compile them directly ourselves!

We will show how our framework works by considering a simple example. Let's say we want to concatenate the base_texture fragment shown earlier with an equally simple detail_tex fragment:

```
interface()
{
    $name = detail_tex
    $textures = detail_map
    $vertex = uv
    $interpolators = uv
    $uv = 2
}

ps 1_1

void main(INPUT input, inout OUTPUT output)
{
    output.color.rgb *= tex2D(detail_map, input.uv) * 2;
}
```

The first step is to output all the constants and samplers required by each fragment. For the pixel shader, neither fragment has requested any constant inputs, but they both want one texture sampler. Names must be mangled to avoid conflicts, which can be done by appending the particular fragment index. However, the generated code is more readable if it also includes the shader name. The resulting code is:

```
// base_texture0 textures
sampler base_texture0_color_map;

// detail_tex1 textures
sampler detail_tex1_detail_map;
```

Next, the input structure is declared. This is built by concatenating the data requested by each fragment, and allocating usage indices to avoid conflicts. Each fragment gets a nested structure declaration, again with mangled names:

```
// —— input structures ——
struct base_texture0_INPUT
{
    float2 uv : TEXCOORD0;
};

struct detail_tex1_INPUT
{
    float2 uv : TEXCOORD1;
};

struct INPUT
{
    base_texture0_INPUT base_texture0;
    detail_tex1_INPUT detail_tex1;
};

INPUT gInput;
```

Due to an inconsistency in shader versions prior to 3.0, color and texture interpolators are not interchangeable: the two color interpolators have a limited range and precision. In other words, fragments should prefer to use color interpolators whenever possible, and leave the more powerful texture interpolators to fragments that really require the extra precision. This becomes a problem when the concatenation of fragments require more color interpolators than are available. Therefore, the allocator needs to be somewhat flexible. It can never assign a texture interpolator request to a color channel because of the limited range, but if the color channels run out, it can use texture interpolators to satisfy any further color requests.

The vertex shader output structure is a duplicate of the pixel shader input, while the pixel shader output (in the absence of any fragments that use multiple rendertargets or oDepth) is very simple:

```
// —— output type ——
struct OUTPUT
{
    float4 color : COLOR0;
};
```

The core of the shader program is a block copy of the HLSL code for each fragment, with mangled function, structure, and variable names:

```
// ─── shader base_texture0 ───
void base_texture0_main(base_texture0_INPUT input, inout OUTPUT
                        output)
{
    output.color = tex2D(base_texture0_color_map, input.uv);
}

// ─── shader detail_tex1 ───
void detail_tex1_main(detail_tex1_INPUT input, inout OUTPUT
                      output)
{
    output.color.rgb *= tex2D(detail_tex1_detail_map,
                              input.uv) * 2;
}
```

Finally, the main body of the shader is generated, which simply calls each of the
fragments in turn:

```
// ─── entrypoint ───
OUTPUT main(const INPUT i)
{
    gInput = i;

    OUTPUT output = (OUTPUT)0;

    base_texture0_main(gInput.base_texture0, output);
    detail_tex1_main(gInput.detail_tex1, output);

    return output;
}
```

The global gInput structure is unimportant in this example, but it can be useful
in a few unusual situations where one fragment wants to access the inputs of another.

This entire process may seem like a ridiculous amount of work, with an excessive
amount of code generated, especially when you consider that it compiles down to
something as small as:

```
    ps_1_1
    tex t0
    tex t1
    mul_x2 r0.xyz, t1, t0
+ mov r0.w, t0.w
```

But that would be missing the point: the size of the intermediate code is unimportant as long as the input fragments are easy to write, and as long as the eventual
compiled code is efficient.

The real advantage of our system is that with no extra effort, we can now generate shaders that apply for example two, three, or more detail textures on top of each

other, using the same shader fragment for each layer. We can also combine detail textures with whatever other fragments we might write in the future, without ever having to reimplement that particular shader behavior.

Shade Trees

Offline rendering systems, such as Maya's Hypershade material editor, often describe their shaders as a tree or graph of pluggable components, and allow the user to connect the inputs and outputs in whatever way they desire. Our framework is very basic in comparison, being just a linear chain of operations, which is in many ways reminiscent of the old DX7 texture cascade.

We justify this simple design based on the type of scenarios in which shaders are most commonly employed. There are three typical patterns:

- Some shaders are requested purely by code, for drawing a specific graphical effect such as a particle system or explosion.
- Some shaders are created by artists, combining different material fragments in an editing tool.
- Perhaps most often, the core of a shader is created by artists, but the runtime code may then want to modify this, for instance, by adding some lighting, fogging, or animation fragments to the end of the chain.

In the first case, where shader descriptions are constructed by code, linear structures are significantly easier to work with. C++ has powerful grammatical features for declaring lists and arrays, but lacks any direct way of embedding trees into source code. Statements like:

```
setShader(ShaderList(ST::base_texture,
                     ST::detail_texture,
                     ST::normalmap,
                     ST::fresnel_envmap,
                     ST::light_specular,
                     ST::fog,
                     ST::depth_of_field));
```

are easy to write, easy to read, and efficient to execute in a way that would be impossible with a more flexible shade tree.

In the second case, where shaders are built by artists, tree structures are complicated to explain, difficult to visualise, and prone to error. In contrast, a linear layering can be instantly understood by even the least technical of artists, because this mental model is already familiar not only from Photoshop, but also from the most basic processes of working with physical paint. The more we can translate the power of programmable hardware into familiar artistic terms, the better the results we will get out of our existing artists, without having to turn them into programmers first!

Yet, most of the really interesting things just cannot be done using a linear model. Take for example an environment map, where the amount of reflection is controlled by the alpha channel of an earlier texture layer. Or a specular lighting shader, which takes the specular power from a constant register which belongs to the base texture material, except for those pixels where an alpha blended decal fragment has overwritten this with a locally varying material property.

To allow for such things, fragments must have the ability to import and export named control values. The actual plumbing happens automatically: whenever a fragment tries to import a value, this value gets hooked up to any previous exports of that same name, or to the default value if no such export is available. This behavior resembles the flexibility of a full shade tree, while maintaining the simplicity of linear shader descriptions. It also provides a valuable guarantee that the results will always work. Any fragment can be used (and will function correctly) in isolation, but when several fragments are combined they will automatically communicate to develop more sophisticated abilities.

This level of robustness is particularly desirable when we want to programmatically add new fragments to the end of an artist-constructed material. In our current pipeline, artists do not work directly with lighting shaders, however, they do have access to fragments that export control values such as the gloss amount, specular power, Fresnel factor, and the amount of subsurface scattering. The editing tool takes whatever material the artist has constructed, and concatenates a fragment which implements a single directional preview light. This fragment imports the various material parameters to make the preview as accurate as possible.

A game engine, on the other hand, is likely to use more sophisticated lighting techniques. In our case this happens to be deferred shading. We take the exact same materials as used in the art tool, and concatenate a deferred shading fragment, which imports the material attributes, then writes them out to the various channels of multiple render targets, with the actual lighting being evaluated later. Existing material fragments work unchanged despite the rendering being done in such a fundamentally different way, the only requirement being that everyone agree on a standard name for each import/export value.

HLSL Metafunctions

In order to communicate material parameters between fragments, we require two new HLSL keywords: "import" and "export". These are done purely by string manipulation, replacing each call with suitable generated code.

The "export" keyword is very simple, as shown by the following fragment which implements a simple 2D base texture and exports its alpha channel as a `specular_amount` control value:

```
ps 1_1

void main(INPUT input, inout OUTPUT output)
{
    float4 t = tex2D(color_map, input.uv);

    output.color.rgb = t.rgb;

    export(float, specular_amount, t.a);
}
```

The preprocessor recognizes the export call, and replaces it with a global variable assignment:

```
// —— shader base_texture0 ——
float base_texture0_export_specular_amount;

void base_texture0_main(base_texture0_INPUT input, inout OUTPUT
                        output)
{
    float4 t = tex2D(base_texture0_color_map, input.uv);

    output.color.rgb = t.rgb;

    // metafunction: export(float, specular_amount, t.a);
    base_texture0_export_specular_amount = t.a;
}
```

Later on, another fragment might try to import the specular amount value:

```
float spec = 0;

import(specular_amount, spec += specular_amount);
```

which the preprocessor turns into:

```
float spec = 0;

// metafunction: import(specular_amount,spec += specular_amount);
spec += base_texture0_export_specular_amount;
```

The content of the import call is expanded once for each matching export. If no other fragment has exported such a value, no such expansion will be available, and the default spec = 0 is used instead. If more than one fragment has exported the value, multiple lines of code are generated (one for each fragment that has exported the value). In the example above this will have the effect of spec being a sum of all the different values. It is up to the caller to decide how the values should be combined: adding is often appropriate, or multiplying, or performing a function call, or perhaps just an assignment that discards all but the most recent value.

The code that is generated by this construction is often full of redundancies, such as the line that adds to zero in the above example, or a global variable generated by export that will never actually be imported by later fragments. Fortunately, the compiler is smart and will fix such things for us.

Adaptive Fragments

It is often useful for a shader fragment to be able to change its behavior based on the context in which it is being used. For instance:

- A fragment that uses one texture, a set of UV coordinates, and a scalar fade value. This works fine in the ps 1.1 model, but needs two interpolator channels because ps 1.1 does not allow a single interpolator to be used both as a texture lookup and as a direct input. If we were compiling for ps 2.0, however, it would be more efficient to pack our data into a single xyz interpolator. It would be nice if we could still support ps 1.1 whenever possible, and in those cases where another fragment requires us to compile for ps 2.0, switch to a different implementation that takes better advantage of this more powerful hardware model.
- A lighting shader. Should we do our lighting per vertex, or per pixel? It depends on the context. Per-vertex lighting can make sense for distant or highly tessellated objects. But when using a normal map, it would not make sense to evaluate the lighting anything other than on a per-pixel basis. It would be nice if a single fragment could adapt to both situations.

All fragments provide a list of defines in their interface block. Some of these are used to send requests to the code generator; for instance, asking for input normals to be made available, or declaring the intention to use multiple render target outputs. Another use of defines is for communication with other fragments, declaring facts like "I provide a perturbed normal for each pixel," which can modify the behavior of any later fragments in the chain.

When generating shader code, the defines set by each input fragment are merged into a single list, along with the target shader version. Any aspect of the shader can be tagged with conditionals that test this list of defines, so that it can select different input constants, interpolators, or blocks of shader code depending on the context in which it is being used. In addition, the combined list is #define'd at the start of the generated HLSL program, so it can be tested using preprocessor conditionals within the code itself.

The following is an example of a context sensitive hemisphere lighting fragment that can work either per vertex or per pixel. To decide if the input constants should be made available to either the vertex shader or the pixel shader, we test the ppl (which stands for per pixel lighting) define. The fragment requests a color interpolator channel if it is doing per-vertex lighting, and provides alternative blocks of shader code for each possible situation:

```
interface()
{
    $name = light_hemisphere

    $params = [ ambient, sky, diffuse ]

    $ambient = [ color, vs="!ppl", ps="ppl" ]
    $sky     = [ color, vs="!ppl", ps="ppl" ]
    $diffuse = [ color, vs="!ppl", ps="ppl" ]

    $interpolators = color

    $color = [ color, enable="!ppl" ]
}

// the core lighting function might be wanted in the vertex
// or pixel shader
vs (!ppl),
ps (ppl)

float3 $light(float3 normal)
{
    float upness = 0.5 + normal.y * 0.5;
    float3 hemisphere = lerp(ambient, sky, upness);
    float d = 0.5 - dot(normal, WorldLightDir) * 0.5;
    return saturate((hemisphere + d * diffuse) * 0.5);
}

// per vertex lighting shader
vs (!ppl)

void main(out OUTPUT output)
{
    output.color.rgb = $light(gInput.normal);
    output.color.a = 1;
}

// when doing vertex lighting, just modulate each pixel by the
// vertex color
ps (!ppl)

void main(INPUT input, inout OUTPUT output)
{
    output.color.rgb = saturate(output.color.rgb *
                                input.color * 2);
}

// per pixel lighting shader
ps (ppl)

void main(inout OUTPUT output)
{
    output.color.rgb = saturate(output.color.rgb *
                       $light(gInput.normal) * 2);
}
```

If we compile this fragment on its own, ppl has not been defined anywhere, so the core light function is used to generate a simple hemisphere lighting vertex shader:

```
vs_1_1
def c8, 0.5, -0.5, 0, 1
dcl_position v0
dcl_normal v1
mad r0.w, v1.y, c8.x, c8.x
mov r0.xyz, c6
add r0.xyz, r0, -c5
dp3 r1.x, v1, c4
mad r0.xyz, r0.w, r0, c5
mad r0.w, r1.x, c8.y, c8.x
mad r0.xyz, r0.w, c7, r0
mul r0.xyz, r0, c8.x
max r0.xyz, r0, c8.z
min oD0.xyz, r0, c8.w
dp4 oPos.x, v0, c0
dp4 oPos.y, v0, c1
dp4 oPos.z, v0, c2
dp4 oPos.w, v0, c3
mov oD0.w, c8.w
```

But now, let's introduce a tangent space normal mapping fragment:

```
interface()
{
    $name = normalmap
    $defines = ppl
    $textures = normalmap
    $vertex = uv
    $interpolators = [ uv, tangent, binormal ]
    $uv = [ 2, want_tangentspace=true ]
}

vs 1_1

void main(INPUT input, out OUTPUT output)
{
    output.uv = input.uv;

    output.tangent  = mul(input.uv_tangent,  NormalTrans);
    output.binormal = mul(input.uv_binormal, NormalTrans);
}

ps 2_0

void main(INPUT input, inout OUTPUT output)
{
    float3 n = tex2D(normalmap, input.uv);

    gInput.normal = normalize(n.x * input.tangent  +
                              n.y * input.binormal +
                              n.z * gInputNormal);
}
```

Note the annotation on the uv parameter in the interface block, which requests that tangent and binormal vectors be provided along with the texture coordinates. This fragment does not actually do anything on its own, other than modifying the value of gInput.normal, which can be used as input by subsequent fragments.

If we now ask our framework to generate a shader that combines normalmap and light_hemisphere, the adaptive mechanism swings into action. Because the normalmap fragment has defined ppl, different parts of the lighting code are included, resulting in a normal mapped hemisphere lighting pixel shader:

```
ps_2_0
def c4, 0.5, -0.5, 1, 0
dcl t0.xyz
dcl t1.xy
dcl t2.xyz
dcl t3.xyz
dcl_2d s0
texld r0, t1, s0
mul r1.xyz, r0.y, t3
mad r1.xyz, r0.x, t2, r1
mad r1.xyz, r0.z, t0, r1
nrm r0.xyz, r1
dp3 r1.x, r0, c0
mad r0.w, r0.y, c4.x, c4.x
mov r0.xyz, c2
add r0.xyz, r0, -c1
mad r0.xyz, r0.w, r0, c1
mad r0.w, r1.x, c4.y, c4.x
mad r0.xyz, r0.w, c3, r0
mul_sat r0.xyz, r0, c4.x
mov r0.w, c4.z
mov oC0, r0
```

Conclusion

Our approach has proven to be successful at encapsulating a wide range of shader behaviors, allowing fragments to be combined in a multitude of ways, entirely automatically.

It is remarkably robust: when we first implemented deferred shading, our existing texture blending, normal mapping, and animation fragments continued to work without a single modification!

It is efficient, too: we've yet to find a single shader that could be manually optimized in ways that were impossible within the fragment combining system.

One disadvantage is the need to describe a precise interface to each fragment, which makes it hard to plug in third-party shader code. In practice it rarely takes more than a few minutes to add the required annotations, but this is still an irritation. Such things could be streamlined if the system was built on top of the D3DX effects framework, but that was not an important goal in this article.

Debugging can be awkward, because compiler error messages refer to the generated shader rather than to your input fragments. Decent tool support for viewing the intermediate code is crucial. Ultimately it all comes down to the numbers. If you have five, ten, or even fifty shaders, this system is probably not for you. If you have thousands, however, automation is your friend.

ENVIRONMENTAL EFFECTS

Introduction

Willem H. de Boer

On the most abstract level, this section encompasses the interaction of photons with air molecules; a very complex phenomenon, which is usually modeled in physics using particle transport theory. At the base of this theory lies the equation of transfer, which has many different guises. This is a very mighty equation, in that, from it, all the equations that are central to global illumination and volume visualization (e.g., Kajiya's rendering equation, the radiosity equation, and the volume rendering integral used in medical imaging) can be derived.

Jason L. Mitchell's article, "Light Shaft Rendering," discusses a technique for rendering volumetric light shafts, which is an improvement over methods used by most games today. This technique applies slice-based volume rendering methods to the task of visualizing volumetric light shafts.

Rainbows increase the realism and the mood of a game scene. The article, "Rendering Rainbows," by Clint S. Brewer describes how to render photo-realistic rainbows in real-time 3D applications.

A plausible rendered sky and physically correct attenuation of distant objects are both vital for portraying realistic outdoor environments. In "A Practical Analytic Model for Daylight with Shaders," Marco Spörl describes the implementation of a system running on DirectX 9 level hardware, which renders real-time physically-based skylight and aerial perspective for clear day skies.

Flight simulators, space simulators, and first person shooters all need realistic looking clouds in order to appear convincing. With many applications allowing the user to roam the sky, the traditional method of simply rendering a sky-sphere or box might no longer be sufficient. In "Volumetric Clouds," Jesse Laeuchli describes how to render clouds with a simple slice-based method.

8.1

Light Shaft Rendering

Jason L. Mitchell

Introduction

This article discusses a technique for rendering volumetric light shafts, which is an improvement over methods used by most games today. This technique applies slice-based volume rendering methods to the task of visualizing volumetric light shafts. Previously, Dobashi and Nishita have published a series of papers on applying slice-based volume rendering to this task [Dobashi02]. Here, we will present several improvements to Dobashi and Nishita's techniques, which are made possible by current graphics hardware with at least ps_2_0 shader support.

Light Shafts in a Scene

Typically, in real-time 3D graphics, we use simple fog models and particle systems to simulate the effect of light scattering back to our eye from particulate matter suspended in the air. These effects are important in giving us a sense of scale and otherwise enhancing the realism in our scenes, but we can do better on hardware with sophisticated shaders and high fill-rate. The effect that we will achieve in this chapter is the visualization of lit particulate matter or "participating media" in our scene. The particulate matter can be non-uniform in density and will be correctly shadowed by the scene as shown in Figure 8.1.1.

FIGURE 8.1.1 *Real-time volumetric light shafts.*

Previous Approaches

Most games render light shafts by drawing polygons representing the bounding region of the desired light shafts as shown in Figure 8.1.2(a). The polygons are blended with the scene and, when used well, are reasonably good at giving the sense of illuminated particulate matter in the air. The polygons are usually textured with a noise texture which may have slowly animating texture coordinates to give the sense of dust wafting gently through the space.

Some games further dice up this pyramidal light volume with additional polygons as shown in Figure 8.1.2(b) [Lepage04]. This gives an additional sense of parallax as the camera moves relative to the light shaft, since points *within* the volume are shaded. While drawing the bounding volume of the desired light shafts is usually cost effective, it is not always convincing. The illusion tends to break down as the user moves relative to the volume, particularly if the volume ever gets clipped by the camera's front clip plane.

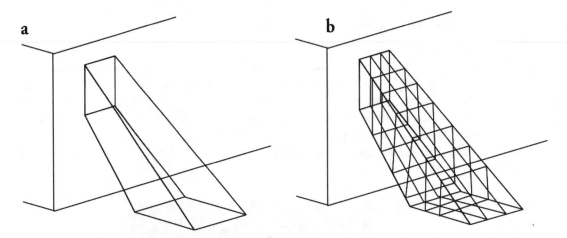

FIGURE 8.1.2   *Light-space sampling planes. (a) extruded window, (b) diced extruded window.*

Another class of approaches has been explored by [Mech01] and [James03]. These two articles discuss approaches in which the lengths of rays through a given volume are computed by adding and subtracting depths of front and back facing polygons which represent the bounding volume of the particulate matter. These are clever techniques which can integrate naturally with the geometry of 3D scenes, but they do not allow for light color variation, non-uniform density, or complex shadowing.

Volume Rendering Approach

The approach discussed in this chapter is based upon techniques used in the scientific visualization community, specifically *slice-based volume rendering*. Instead of rendering geometry which is fixed in world space or the space of the light casting the light shafts, we render geometry which is consistently oriented in view space in order to integrate along rays through light volume.

After the rest of the scene has been drawn, a series of planes are drawn perpendicular to the viewing direction, as shown in Figure 8.1.3. These planes are additively blended with the frame buffer in order to accumulate the light that the particulate matter in the scene scatters back along the rays to the viewpoint through each pixel.

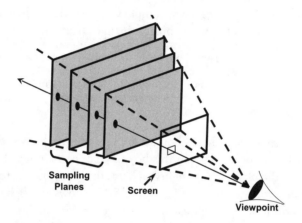

FIGURE 8.1.3 *Integration using sampling planes.*

Whenever you are shading in general, you are computing the amount of light scattered back to the eye through a given pixel, but you can get away with rendering just the simple polygonal surface of objects, which are opaque. In the case of semi-transparent volumetric data such as light shafts, you sample along rays *through* the volume in order to sum up all of the scattered light. This is the reason that we draw a set of sampling planes aligned in view space, to allow you to sample along all of the rays through the volumetric light shafts.

These sampling planes are shaded by projecting a number of textures onto them from the position of the light source. The intention is to approximate the integral along a ray from the eye through each pixel on the screen and, in turn, through each sampling plane. The end result should approximate the amount of light scattered back to the eye by the simulated particulate matter in the air (i.e., the light shaft).

Positioning the Sampling Planes

For our purposes, we model lights as projective (think of a flashlight or slide projector). As a result, each light has a position, direction, up vector, horizontal and vertical fields of view, as well as near and far planes. In short, each light has a frustum just like any usual viewer of a 3D scene. A given light source only casts light within its frustum. This is important, because it means that the only region in space that we need to sample is the region inside the frustum.

The vertex data representing the sampling planes must be transformed to the proper position in eye space each frame. This is done with a simple trilinear interpolation trick performed in the vertex shader. The sampling plane vertex buffer contains some number of quads (100 in the example application on the CD-ROM) evenly distributed in z and fully filling the unit cube. The data is layed out this way in the vertex buffer so that the following simple vertex shader code will transform it to fill the view-space-aligned bounding box of the light frustum.

```
// Trilerp position within view-space-axis-aligned bounding
// volume of light's frustum
float4 pos = vMinBounds * vPosition +
            (vStretchedMaxBounds * (1.0f - vPosition));
pos.w = 1.0f;
```

The view-space-aligned bounds are loaded into the constant store and the shader trilinearly interpolates within this box to place each vertex. This means that the positioning of the planes is very lightweight, as the shader is able to correctly compute their positions with the above code. Figure 8.1.4 shows the light frustum with sampling planes positioned perpendicular to the view direction (from the viewer at left). The sampling planes fully fill the view-space-aligned bounding box of the light frustum.

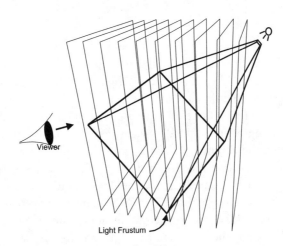

FIGURE 8.1.4   *Sampling planes.*

Shading the Sampling Planes

Now that we have positioned the sampling planes in order to allow us to uniformly sample along the rays from our eye through the light frustum, how exactly should we shade them? There are a number of terms in our lighting equation, each of which adds an additional level of realism and control:

- Light scattering
- Cookie / Gobo
- Shadow
- Noise / Nonuniformity

The first term is the most complex and is used to describe how much light would reach our eye if the particulate matter were of uniform density, while the remaining three terms essentially mask off the scattered light in different ways.

Light Scattering

A lot of work has gone into studying how light scatters in volumes of particles and how this affects what we see. It is well known that applying some sort of fog model to expansive outdoor scenes is fundamental to evoking a proper sense of scale. This is done in all flight simulators and in other 3D applications which have to render large outdoor scenes. Recently, these algorithms have been advanced even further, as many forms of scattering have been incorporated into usable models [Preetham99] [Dobashi02]. Various terms such as the density of the particles, the distances of the light and eye from a given particle, and angular falloff all contribute to the amount of light scattered to the viewer. Since some of these (such as angular falloff) can be baked into the cookie (see next section) and because we plan to render non-uniformly dense particles anyway, we ignore all of these terms except for the $1/distance^2$ light intensity falloff, which is the most important aspect of light scattering. You can think of the amount of light scattered to our eye from a given particle as simply a scalar multiplied by $1/distance^2$, with all of the other terms of our lighting equation potentially masking this off. To illustrate the effect of the $1/distance^2$ term, Figure 8.1.5 shows a spotlight emitting a cone of light with different kinds of falloff terms. Figure 8.1.5(a) shows a conic volume of light with no falloff at all. Figure 8.1.5(b) shows a falloff which is proportional to one over the distance from the light source. Figure 8.1.5(c) shows a fall off which is proportional to $1/distance^2$, which gives an effect that is reasonably close to what one observes in the real world. In our example application, we chose to add a small ambient term to the $1/distance^2$ term as shown in Figure 8.1.5(d).

Throughout the rest of this article, we will be masking off the intensity of this scattered light with three more terms: a light cookie, shadows, and noise.

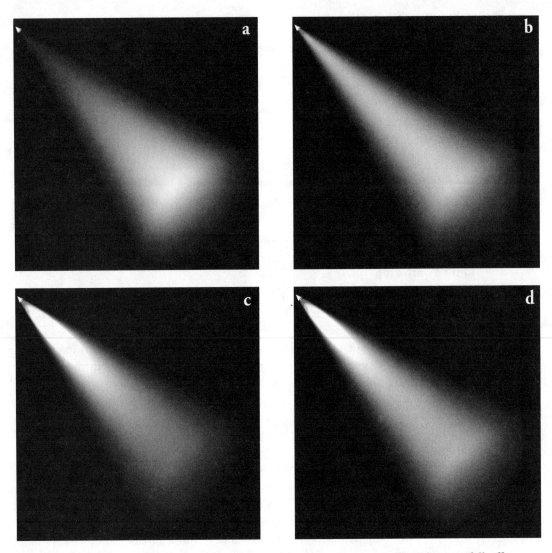

FIGURE 8.1.5   *Various options for light intensity. (a) constant intensity, (b) 1/distance fall-off, (c) 1/distance² fall-off, (d) 1/distance² + ambient fall-off.*

The Light Cookie

The second term in our lighting equation is commonly referred to as a *cookie* or a *gobo* in stage lighting. It is a simple cut-out, which is used to shape the light cast onto a scene including, in our case, particulate matter in the air. Different cookies can be used to shape the resulting light shafts in interesting ways, as is commonly done in theater and film. Examples of cookies are shown in Figure 8.1.6.

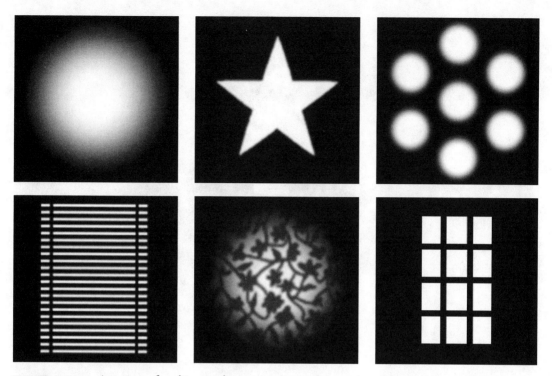

FIGURE 8.1.6 *A variety of cookie or gobo textures.*

Shadows

The next term used to mask off scattered light is the shadow term of our lighting equation. For any 3D point in the light frustum, we must be able to determine whether or not the point is shadowed by the rest of the scene. The most natural tool to use for this task is a *shadow map* [Williams78]. To create the shadow map, we must render the depths of our scene from the point of view of our projective light source into a separate texture, which we may update every frame. Figure 8.1.7 shows a typical shadow map for our test scene. Distance from the light source is stored as a scalar, hence black is near and white is far.

When rendering the light shafts, the shadow map is projected onto the sampling planes with projective texture mapping. The light-space depth is interpolated across the sampling planes and can be tested against the value from the shadow depth map at each pixel of each sampling plane. If the interpolated depth is greater than the value from the shadow map then the point must be shadowed by objects in the scene and the scattered light is multiplied by zero to mask it out. Figure 8.1.8 shows the result of including shadows in the lighting equation. The streaks through the light volume caused by the shadows give a very dramatic look, particularly when the light or the viewer (or both) are in motion.

FIGURE 8.1.7   *Shadow depth map.*

FIGURE 8.1.8   *Applying shadows using a shadow map. (a) no shadows, (b) with shadows.*

Noise

An easy way to make the light shafts appear even more interesting and volumetric is to project noise onto the sampling planes. This gives the impression of non-uniformity of the particulate matter in the air and just generally adds visual interest. In our example application, two repeating (tileable) 2D grayscale noise maps, shown in Figure 8.1.9, are projected onto the sampling planes and are scrolled slowly in different directions.

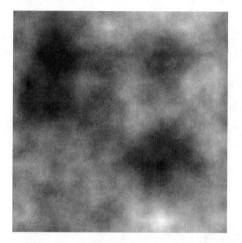
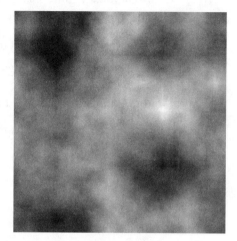

FIGURE 8.1.9 *Projective tiling noise textures.*

Compositing these two noise maps together gives a realistic dynamic appearance to the light shafts. Figure 8.1.10 shows the scene with and without the use of noise. Of course, the true impact of the noise is best perceived in motion.

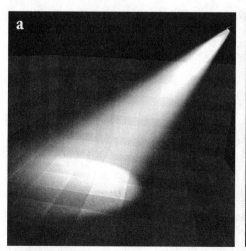
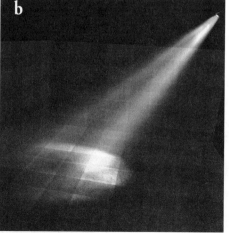

FIGURE 8.1.10 *Projecting noise into the light volume. (a) no noise, (b) with noise.*

Light Shaft Pixel Shader

Now that we have described the various terms in our lighting equation, we can have a look at the pixel shader which computes the final scattered light intensity for each sample in our light volume. The following DirectX® High Level Shading Language (HLSL) shader is used by our example application to do this math.

As you can see from the function prototype, there are three sets of projective texture coordinates interpolated across the sampling planes. These are used to sample the shadow map and the two noise maps. In addition to these projective texture coordinates, the light space position and the light space depth are interpolated in another texture coordinate. These will be used in the shader to compute distance attenuation and in the shadow mapping computation. The final interpolated parameter acts as a mask which is used to route our final intensity into the proper channel of our output buffer. This will be discussed in more detail later in the section on quality.

```
float4 ps_main(float4 tcProj : TEXCOORD0,
            float4 tcProjScroll1 : TEXCOORD1,
            float4 tcProjScroll2 : TEXCOORD2,
            float4 lsPos_depth : TEXCOORD3,
            float4 ChannelMask : COLOR0,

            // Uniforms to generate shader permutations
            uniform bool bScrollingNoise,
            uniform bool bShadowMapping,
            uniform bool  bCookie) : COLOR
{
    float compositeNoise = 0.015f;
    float shadow = 1.0f;
    float4 cookie = {1.0f, 1.0f, 1.0f, 1.0f};

    float shadowMapDepth;
    float4 output;

    if (bCookie)
    {
        // Sample the cookie
        cookie = tex2Dproj(CookieSampler, tcProj);
    }

    if (bScrollingNoise)
    {
        float4 noise1 = tex2Dproj(ScrollingNoiseSampler,
                                    tcProjScroll1);
        float4 noise2 = tex2Dproj(ScrollingNoiseSampler,
                                    tcProjScroll2);
        compositeNoise = noise1.r * noise2.g * 0.05f;
    }

    shadowMapDepth = tex2Dproj(ShadowMapSampler, tcProj);

    if (bShadowMapping)
    {
```

```
                    if (lsPos_depth.w < shadowMapDepth)
                        shadow = 1.0f; // The pixel is in light
                    else
                        shadow = 0.0f; // The pixel is occluded
                }

                // Compute attenuation 1/(s^2)
                float atten = 0.35f + 20000.0f /
                                dot(lsPos_depth.xyz, lsPos_depth.xyz);

                float scale = 9.0f / fFractionOfMaxShells;

                float intensity = compositeNoise * luminance(cookie.rgb) *
                                    scale * atten * shadow;

                // Route intensity to correct channel
                return intensity * ChannelMask;
            }
```

After the interpolated parameters, you see three parameters of type uniform bool, which are used for code specialization. These inputs are known at compile time (because they are uniform) and are used by the compiler to optimize out dead code. Since this pixel shader is used in the D3DX Effects framework, a given technique generates a specialized version of this pixel shader by passing Booleans to the shader as shown below.

```
        technique clip_nonoise_shadow_cookie_technique
        {
            pass P0
            {
                VertexShader = compile vs_1_1
                                vs_project_scrolling_noise_1();
                PixelShader  = compile ps_2_0 ps_main(false,   // noise
                                                      true,    // shadow
                                                      true);   // cookie
            ...
```

This technique uses the shadow map and the cookie, but no noise. A specialized version of the shader, which doesn't do any of the noise sampling or compositing, is generated by the compiler and used by the application at runtime if noise is not needed.

Looking back to the pixel shader itself, you can see the various blocks of the shader which are bracketed by if tests of these three uniform Boolean variables. What this means is that it is only necessary to maintain this one HLSL main function despite the fact that many different shaders are generated for use at runtime.

The first block of the shader, which is bracketed by a uniform Boolean, is the cookie sampling. By default, the cookie color is white, but this default color will be overridden if bCookie is true.

Subsequently the noise texture may be sampled. You'll note that the same texture is sampled twice with two different sets of projective texture coordinates. This is because we have chosen to store our two different repeating grayscale noise maps in the red and green channels of the same actual texture map for convenience. These two samples are then composited together, extracting out the two different scalar channels we are looking for.

After the noise is sampled and composited together, we optionally sample our shadow depth map and compare against the interpolated depth. If the shadow depth map sample is nearer the light, then our sample is in shadow and our shadow term is zero. If the shadow depth map sample is farther from the light, then our sample is in light and our shadow term is one.

Since we always compute distance attenuation, we compute the value of the variable `atten` in code, which is not bracketed by a uniform Boolean variable. Since we are drawing our sampling planes as large quads that are not tessellated, we cannot compute distance from the light in the vertex shader and interpolate it. Instead, we interpolate the 3D light space position and compute the 1/distance² attenuation term in the shader by taking the reciprocal of the light space position dotted with itself. This is further tweaked with a few magic constants which are a function of the scale of the world used in the example application. The variable `scale` is used to scale the contribution of each sampling plane in the event that less than the maximum number of planes is drawn. As an optimization, the example application will scale down the number of sampling planes used if the user moves far away from the light volume, hence, this scale factor must be dynamic. Finally, the terms are all multiplied together, giving our three masking terms (cookie, shadow, and noise) an opportunity to mask out the light scattering term. The very last operation in the pixel shader multiplies the scalar intensity computed above with a 4D vector called `ChannelMask`. This effectively routes the scalar intensity to one of the four channels of our render target. The motivation for this will become clear as we discuss ways to improve the quality of this effect.

Quality

As discussed earlier, this technique relies upon sampling along rays through a volume which contains lighting information. In graphics, we are constantly sampling a variety of different signals and any time that we perform sampling, we must consider antialiasing. This is true when rasterizing polygons, which have hard edges, and sampling from texture maps, which may have high spatial frequency components. When rasterizing, we apply multisample full-scene anti-aliasing and when sampling from textures, we antialias the textures by performing some sort of filtering such as trilinear filtering of mipmaps.

Likewise, when we are reconstructing volume data, we must be careful not to take too few samples along each ray and miss high-frequency components in the signal, such as the shadow map edges. This means that we want to use as many sampling planes as possible in order to increase our sampling frequency. We could also try and filter the components of our lighting equation, particularly the shadow map in order to possibly get away with fewer sampling planes [Reeves87]. In our example application, however, we have chosen to use inexpensive pick-nearest filtering of the projective shadow texture. If we use too few sampling planes, we will not reconstruct the shadow edges well enough and will get stair step artifacts as shown in Figures 8.1.11(a) and 8.1.11(b). These two images show our scene with 25 and 50 sampling planes respectively, in order to illustrate the perils of undersampling the volume. In Figure 8.1.11(c), which was drawn with 100 sampling planes, the stair step artifacts are essentially gone.

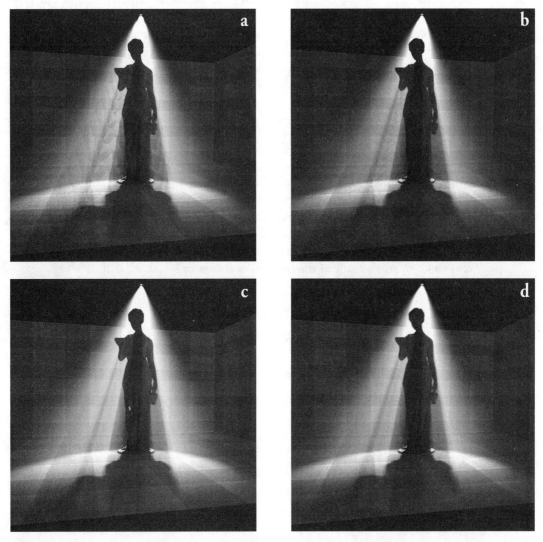

FIGURE 8.1.11   *Varying numbers of sampling planes. (a) 25 planes, (b) 50 planes, (c) 100 planes, (d) 100 planes with blurring.*

As mentioned above, in order to antialias the sampling of the shadows, we want to draw as many sampling planes as possible. On current graphics architectures, we can only perform alpha blending to surfaces which have at most 8 bits of precision per channel. So, if we are drawing a lot of sampling planes, each plane can only add a bit or two of data to the frame buffer. This can lead to quantization or *banding* in the resulting image.

If you can live with a monochrome light color, there is a simple trick that can be employed to dramatically increase precision. In our example application, we have chosen to render into an offscreen RGBA image rather than render directly to the back buffer. We perform additive blending and render each sampling plane into only one of red, green, blue, or alpha by using the `ChannelMask` parameter in our pixel shader shown above. This allows us to accumulate the light from one quarter of the planes in each of our four 8-bit channels, dramatically increasing the number of bits that can be contributed by each sampling plane. When compositing this offscreen RGBA buffer to the final image in the back buffer, we sample it multiple times to provide a small amount of blurring as shown in Figure 8.1.11(d). This softens the look of the light shafts and further reduces aliasing. Of course, this is less needed on hardware which supports blending to surfaces of more than 8 bits per channel.

Efficiency

Since this technique is so fill-rate bound, we want to reduce the number of pixels filled in order to increase performance. As a result, the most important optimization one can make to this rendering technique is the aggressive use of user clip planes to cut down on fill rate. As mentioned earlier, we model each light as a projective light which has its own frustum. While the sampling planes bound this frustum, they also cover a lot of area outside of the frustum as shown in Figure 8.1.12(a).

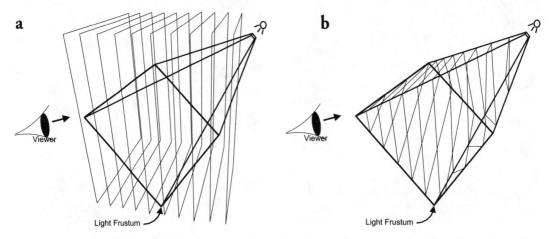

FIGURE 8.1.12   *Clipping to light frustum. (a) unclipped sampling planes, (b) clipped sampling planes.*

Since only regions inside of the light frustum will receive any light, we can safely clip away the parts of our sampling planes which lie outside of the light frustum as shown in Figure 8.1.12(b). For typical viewer and light configurations, this results in a massive performance boost which is essentially the difference between this technique being considered real-time and not real-time on current hardware. In fact, hardware implementations which support user clip planes through raster rather than proper geometric techniques suffer such a massive performance loss as to be non real-time.

In certain scenarios, it may be desirable to further restrict the light volume. For a light shining in a window as in Figure 8.1.2, it may make more sense to use the plane of the window instead of the light's front plane to further clip the sampling planes. Likewise, the floor plane of the room in Figure 8.1.2 may be a better choice than the light's far plane. In short, it is desirable to aggressively minimize the number of pixels filled by whatever means necessary.

Future Enhancements

What we have described thus far is a robust means for rendering volumetric light shafts at interactive rates. One obvious area for improvement is better shadow map filtering [Reeves87]. While this will result in a more expensive pixel shader, it may allow you to get away with using fewer sampling planes. Another area to be explored is a technique called *interleaved sampling*, which employs screen-space dithering techniques to hide aliasing and banding [Keller01]. Interleaved sampling should be reasonably straightforward to integrate into the existing technique. It may also prove useful to move to a ray-casting approach, where different proxy geometry is drawn and where simpler *stopping criterion* shaders can be used to skip over the computation of pixels that are known to be in empty or shadowed regions of the light volume [Krüger03].

Example Application

ON THE CD

The sample `ShaderX3_LightShafts` on the companion CD-ROM illustrates the process of drawing volumetric light shafts with the technique outlined in this article.

References

[Dobashi02] Yoshinori Dobashi, Tsuyoshi Yamamoto and Tomoyuki Nishita, "Interactive Rendering of Atmospheric Scattering Effects Using Graphics Hardware," *Graphics Hardware* 2002.

[James03] Greg James, "Rendering Objects as Thick Volumes," *ShaderX²*, Wordware 2003.

[Keller01] Alexander Keller and Wolfgang Heidrich, "Interleaved Sampling," Eurographics Workshop on Rendering Techniques 2001.

[Krüger03] Jens Krüger and Rüdiger Westermann, "Acceleration Techniques for GPU-based Volume Rendering," *IEEE Visualization 2003*.

[Lepage04] Dany Lepage, Personal Communication, 2004.

[Mech01] Radomír Mech, "Hardware-accelerated Real-time Rendering of Gaseous Phenomena," *Journal of Graphics Tools*, 6(3):1–16, 2001.

[Nishita01] Tomoyuki Nishita and Yoshinori Dobashi, "Modeling and Rendering of Various Natural Phenomena Consisting of Particles," Proc.Computer Graphics International 2001.

[Preetham99] Arcot Preetham, Peter Shirley and Brian Smits, "A Practical Analytic Model for Daylight," SIGGRAPH 1999, pp. 91–99, 1999.

[Reeves87] William T.Reeves, David H.Salesin, and Robert L.Cook, "Rendering Antialiased Shadows with Depth Maps," *Computer Graphics* (SIGGRAPH '87 Proceedings), 21(4):283–291, July 1987.

[Williams78] Lance Williams, "Casting Curved Shadows on Curved Surfaces," pp.270–274 SIGGRAPH 1978.

8.2

Rendering Rainbows

Clint S. Brewer

Introduction

This article describes how to render photo-realistic rainbows in real-time 3D applications. The rainbow is yet another tool available to us that increases the realism of our scenes. Whenever the sun is in the right position and we look towards rain, mist, clouds, waterfalls, or foggy valleys, we see strange colors hovering before us. These colors are arranged in the typical arc shape we have come to recognize as a rainbow. We can use these rainbows to enhance the realism of our outdoor scenes, in spell effects, and to create a mystical mood.

The goal of this article is to give you an understanding of the basic theory behind the formation of rainbows, and to give a clear idea of how to add them to your game engine.

Theory

The Elements of a Rainbow

Figure 8.2.1 shows the features of the typical rainbow we would like to simulate. You can see the bright primary rainbow and the lighter secondary rainbow in the mist of the waterfall. Inside the arc of the primary rainbow, the light is a bit brighter. As you can see there is no rainbow in the shadowed regions.

Causes of a Rainbow's Elements

Rainbows are caused by the interaction of small spherical drops of water and rays of sunlight. The water drops refract the different wavelengths of sunlight by different amounts, splitting the final light we see into various colors, just like a prism does. As shown for the primary rainbow in Figure 8.2.2, the light rays are refracted when they enter the water droplet, reflect internally, and are refracted again when they leave the water droplet.

Figure 8.2.3 shows that for the secondary rainbow the light rays undergo two internal reflections before travelling back to our eye. As the light rays interact more with the water droplet, some of the light's intensity is lost. This explains why the secondary rainbow is much fainter in appearance than the primary rainbow. Also note that the colors of the secondary rainbow are in the reverse order of those of the pri-

FIGURE 8.2.1   *Photograph of primary and secondary rainbows.*

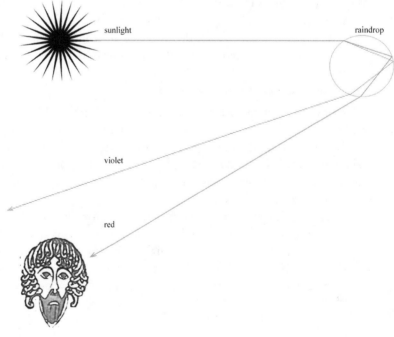

FIGURE 8.2.2   *Single internal reflection of the primary rainbow.*

mary rainbow. You can see in Figure 8.2.3 that the second internal reflection causes this change of order.

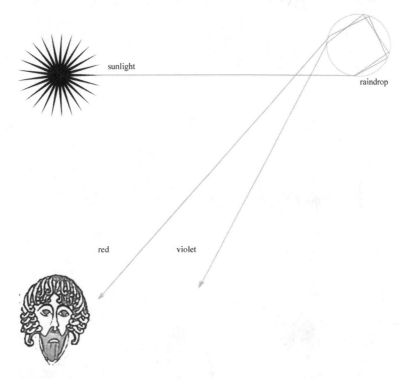

FIGURE 8.2.3   *Two internal reflections causing the secondary rainbow.*

As shown in Figure 8.2.3, the final color of the rainbow depends on which wavelength of light is bent back towards us just enough to reach our eye. This depends on the position and angle of the ray of sunlight, the size and position of the water droplet, and the position of the viewer. Due to the distance of the sun, we can consider all sunrays to be parallel to each other as they reach the earth's surface (i.e., a directional light) so there is only one possible direction any sunray can have. We can therefore simplify the problem to be a function of the radius of the water drops in the air, and the angle-of-deviation. Figure 8.2.4 shows that the angle-of-deviation is the angle between the view vector and the light vector.

Because the color of the rainbow depends on the angle between the view vector and the sun light rays, we can see that the rainbow is a circle of light that has the shadow of the viewer's head as its central point. This point shown in Figure 8.2.5 is called the anti-solar point because it is directly opposite the sun from the viewer's perspective.

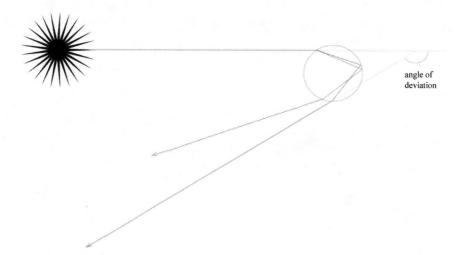

FIGURE 8.2.4   *The angle-of-deviation.*

FIGURE 8.2.5   *The anti-solar point.*

Mathematical Models

Various theories that explain the effects of diffraction and interference of light have been used to model a rainbow. Mie scattering theory and the Debeye series model all of the scattering of light by tiny spheres [Laven04]. The Airy Integral can be used to model the primary and secondary rainbows and requires less computation [Lee98]. The intricacies of these models are beyond the scope of this article but we encourage you to investigate the references listed for details.

Algorithm

Now that we have a better understanding of what causes the various elements of a rainbow, we can explore our technique for rendering it in a game. Here is a high-level overview of the technique:

- Render the water vapor in the scene to a moisture texture
- Render the scene normally to the back buffer
- Render a full-screen quad to the back buffer in eye space

For each pixel of the full-screen quad

- Calculate the angle-of-deviation
- Use the angle-of-deviation to index into a rainbow look-up texture
- Multiply the rainbow color by the moisture texture
- Add the final color back into the scene

Implementation Details

Look-Up Texture

Instead of calculating the mathematical model of scattering at runtime, we choose to use a pre-generated look-up texture that will be indexed by the angle-of-deviation. Mr. Philip Laven has written a wonderful program for exploring the various mathematical models called MiePlot and kindly allowed us to use it for our simulation [Laven04B].

ON THE CD

Using MiePlot we are able to generate a 1D look-up texture that stores the color of scattered light for each angle-of-deviation between 90° and 180°. We have included several look-up textures for different radii of water droplets on the CD-ROM.

Calculating the Angle-of-Deviation

The full-screen quad is rendered in homogeneous clip space with a vertex and pixel shader. Since we know that the eye position is located at the origin in camera space, it is easy to get the view direction for each vertex. For each vertex of the quad we transform the vertex position by the inverse projection matrix and subtract it from the eye position. Once we have the eye vector in eye-space, we will also need to transform the world-space sunlight vector into eye-space.

```
float4 tempPos     = float4(IN.Position, 1.0);
tempPos            = mul(tempPos, ProjInv);
OUT.vEyeVec        = float3(0.0, 0.0, 0.0) - tempPos;

float4 tempLightDir = float4(-LightVec, 0.0);
OUT.vLightVec       = normalize(mul(tempLightDir, View).xyz);
```

Both the eye and light vectors are passed through to our pixel shader as texture coordinates and interpolated across our quad. The light vector is constant across the quad and ready to be used at each pixel. However, the eye vector must be renormalized at each pixel. After normalization, we have two unit length vectors and can take their dot product to get the cosine of the angle-of-deviation.

```
float cosTheta = dot(IN.vLightVec, normalize(IN.vEyeVec));
```

This gives us a value in the range [–1, 1], which corresponds to an angle-of-deviation between 0° and 180°. We then use this value to index into the one-dimensional rainbow look-up texture to find the color of the rainbow. We set the texture sampler AddressU and AddressV modes to CLAMP so that cosTheta will always lie in the range [0, 1], which corresponds to an angle-of-deviation between 90° and 180° as we have stored them in our look-up texture.

Combining with the Rest of the Scene

To combine the rainbow with the rest of the scene, we created a moisture texture, which is simply an encoding of how much water vapor is in the scene at each pixel. Water in our scene is represented by a cloudy skybox, an animated rain skybox, and standard distance-based fog. All of this is rendered into the moisture texture as a grayscale value where white means maximum moisture and black means no moisture at all.

Next we render the scene as normal. Then we multiply the rainbow color by the moisture texture so that in areas of little moisture there will also be very little of the rainbow visible. Finally we use additive alpha blending to combine the final rainbow with the normal scene. Figure 8.2.6 shows these steps in action.

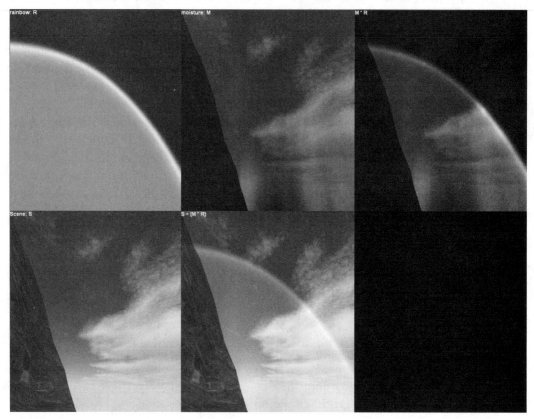

FIGURE 8.2.6 *The steps of rendering the rainbow in a 3D scene.*

Discussion

We were able to quickly get the effect working by making use of MiePlot's data to generate lookup textures. These textures saved a lot of time we would otherwise have spent translating the various mathematical models into shader code. It also allowed us to experiment with different models easily. This also meant we did not have to write and execute an expensive shader that calculates the light scattering equations at every pixel. However, we do make use of dependent texture reads at each pixel, which can be costly. Pixel shader model 3.0's dynamic branching support will allow us to avoid the dependent texture read for those values of the angle-of-deviation of which we know will make too small a contribution to the final image. We would like to use the Airy Mathematical Model to see if it requires less execution time than the dependent texture read.

One drawback of our technique is that the scene is required to be rendered once for the moisture texture, and again into the backbuffer. Depending on the complexity of the scene geometry contributing to the moisture texture, this may be a very costly operation. If the destination alpha channel is not being used, then it might be possible to render the moisture to the destination alpha channel while at the same time rendering it to the color buffer. If Multiple Render Targets (MRT) are available then those could be used instead of the alpha channel.

Improvements and Other Uses

Instead of executing a pixel shader for every pixel on the screen, we could render a dome with the single one-dimensional look-up texture mapped along its sides. The tip of this dome is always centered on the anti-solar point (Figure 8.2.5). You simply blend this dome into the scene based on the moisture texture to achieve approximately the same effect as our pixel shader, but using the fixed-function pipeline.

We can use the Rainbow Shader to reproduce other atmospheric phenomena by changing the lookup texture and the way we index it. Fogbows, Halos, and Corona can all be simulated with the technique presented here. We have also experimented with using the look-up texture to simulate abalone shell to some success.

In practice we found that one of the most visually important parts of the technique was the moisture texture. Anything that improves your rendering of sunlight and moisture in the atmosphere will also greatly improve this technique. The other environmental effects presented in this section should be combined with this shader to produce a very realistic rainbow.

Conclusion

We have covered the theory behind rainbows, and have shown a way to add them to your game engine. While not a perfect implementation, our technique is easy to use and creates visually pleasing rainbows. The next time we gaze over that beautiful misty terrain, waterfall, or foggy valley, and the sun is just right, we hope we get to see a rainbow.

References

[Cowley04] Cowley, Less, "Atmospheric Optics," available online at *http://www.sundog.clara.co.uk/atoptics/phenom.htm*, May 02, 2004.

[Hoffman02] Hoffman, Nathaniel, and Preetham, Arcot J., "Photorealistic Real-Time Outdoor Light Scattering," in *Game Developer Magazine* (August 2002): pp. 32–38.

[Laven04] Laven, Philip, "The Optics of a Water Drop," available online at *http://www.philiplaven.com/*, May 02, 2004.

[Laven04B] Laven, Philip, "MiePlot," available online at *http://www.philiplaven.com/mieplot.htm*, May 02, 2004.

[Lee01] Lee, Raymond L. and Frasier, Alistair B., *The Rainbow Bridge: Rainbows in Art, Myth, and Science*, The Pennsylvania State University Press, 2001.

[Lee98] Lee, Raymond L., "Mie Theory Airy Theory and the Natural Rainbow," *Applied Optics*, Vol. 37, No. 9, 1998.

8.3

A Practical Analytic Model for Daylight with Shaders

Marco Spörl

Introduction

A plausible rendered sky and physically correct attenuation of distant objects are both vital for portraying realistic outdoor environments. This article describes and evaluates the implementation of a system running on DirectX 9 level hardware, which renders real-time physically-based skylight and aerial perspective for clear day skies based on [Preetham99A]. The results are compared to Naty Hoffman's work on real-time outdoor light scattering, which evolved from [Hoffman02A] to [Hoffman02B], and its latest revision [Hoffman03].

ON THE CD

The full source code for our implementation along with our version of Hoffman's model for comparison purposes—both using OpenGL and Cg for rendering—is available on the companion CD-ROM.

A Light Scattering Crash Course—
Part 1: The Basics

Without the earth's atmosphere, the sky would appear as black as at night even in the daytime, because we would be able to stare directly into outer space. That thin layer surrounding our planet scatters the incoming sunlight, resulting in a sky colored with every shade imaginable. Before hitting the atmosphere, sunlight is made up of light of every wavelength and is therefore almost pure white. On its way to a viewer's eye, the light is attenuated due to absorption and scattering. We will not deal with absorption, as it converts incoming radiation to heat and does not contribute to the visible color of the sky. Instead, we will concentrate on scattering.

Two types of atmospheric particles responsible for the clear sky scattering model will be described here. *Rayleigh* scattering [Rayleigh71] covers scattering by air molecules smaller than the light's wavelength. Put simply, Lord Rayleigh's theory states that the shorter the wavelength of the light hitting a particle, the greater the probability that it will be scattered. Ever wondered why the sky is blue? As blue light has a shorter wavelength than red light, it is most probably a blue photon that hits our eye when we look at the sky on a clear day. In contrast, *Mie* scattering deals with light scattering from haze particles that are much bigger than molecules (e.g., water vapor, smoke, and dust). This effect does not add to the actual color but to the "opacity" of the atmosphere. In other words, Mie scattering does not describe *what* we see but *how much* of it is visible or how murky it is. See [Lynch95] for more on scattering and other outdoor phenomena.

A parameter that is used to describe the "state" of the atmosphere is *turbidity*. As [Preetham99A] states, "turbidity T is the ratio of the optical thickness of the haze atmosphere (haze particles and molecules) to the optical thickness of the atmosphere with molecules alone," and is defined as:

$$T = \frac{t_m + t_h}{t_m} \qquad (8.3.1)$$

where t_m is the optical thickness of the molecular atmosphere and t_h is the vertical optical thickness of the haze atmosphere. This equation states that the higher the presence of air molecules (and therefore, the more Rayleigh scattering), the clearer the day. On the other hand, the higher the turbidity (and therefore, the more Mie scattering contributing to the scene) the hazier the atmosphere. For example, a turbidity of 2 describes a clear day whereas a turbidity of 20 represents thick haze.

Before moving on to the explanation of the formulas needed to compute skylight and aerial perspective, please note the following: Preetham's model is not a full-blown sky simulation (which should include overcast skies, clouds, weather phenomena, day/night changes, etc.) but an analytic model based on empirical data. There are several general methods that are able to fully simulate a daylit sky under all conditions, but they are not suited for real-time rendering. Therefore Preetham's group chose the work of Nishita et al. [Nishita96] to simulate the U.S. Standard Atmosphere and they used the results to derive the data needed for the distribution coefficients, the sky luminance, and the sky chromaticity values described later (this explains where those arbitrary looking values come from in the succeeding sections).

A Light Scattering Crash Course—
Part 2: Sky Color

Let us move on to describing the skylight model, which is fairly straightforward. All that has to be done is to compute the sky's chromaticity and luminance for a given sun position, view direction (i.e., normalized vertex position, since we are rendering a sky dome), and turbidity. These values are computed using Perez' five parameter model describing the sky luminance distribution:

$$F(\theta, \gamma) = \left(1 + Ae^{B/\cos\theta}\right)\left(1 + Ce^{D\gamma} + E\cos^2\gamma\right) \qquad (8.3.2)$$

where A is the distribution coefficient for darkening or brightening of the horizon, B the distribution coefficient for the luminance gradient near the horizon, C the distribution coefficient for the relative intensity of the circumsolar region, D the distribution coefficient for the width of the circumsolar region, and E the distribution coefficient for relative backscattered light. The angle θ between sun direction and view direction and the angle θ between zenith and view direction are specified as shown in Figure 8.3.1.

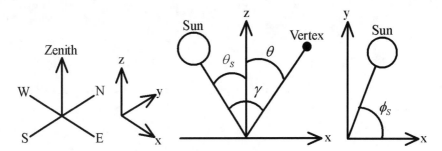

FIGURE 8.3.1   *The variables used for the sky dome.*

Given the current turbidity, the distribution coefficients for luminance Y and chromaticity values x and y are defined as follows:

$$
\begin{bmatrix} A_Y \\ B_Y \\ C_Y \\ D_Y \\ E_Y \end{bmatrix} = \begin{bmatrix} 0.1787 & -1.4630 \\ -0.3554 & 0.4275 \\ -0.227 & 5.3251 \\ 0.1206 & -2.5771 \\ -0.0670 & 0.3703 \end{bmatrix} \begin{bmatrix} T \\ 1 \end{bmatrix}
$$

(8.3.3)

$$
\begin{bmatrix} A_x \\ B_x \\ C_x \\ D_x \\ E \end{bmatrix} = \begin{bmatrix} -0.0193 & -0.2592 \\ -0.0665 & 0.0008 \\ -0.0004 & 0.2125 \\ -0.0641 & -0.8989 \\ -0.0033 & 0.0452 \end{bmatrix} \begin{bmatrix} T \\ 1 \end{bmatrix}
$$

(8.3.4)

$$
\begin{bmatrix} A_y \\ B_y \\ C_y \\ D_y \\ E_y \end{bmatrix} = \begin{bmatrix} -0.0167 & -0.2608 \\ -0.0950 & 0.0092 \\ -0.0079 & 0.2102 \\ -0.0441 & -1.6537 \\ -0.0109 & 0.0529 \end{bmatrix} \begin{bmatrix} T \\ 1 \end{bmatrix}
$$

(8.3.5)

See [Poynton00] if you are not familiar with the CIE xyY and CIE XYZ representations of color.

Using Equation 8.3.2, the sky's luminance in the view direction is given by:

$$Y = Y_z \frac{F(\theta,\gamma)}{F(0,\theta_S)} \tag{8.3.6}$$

where θ_S is the sun's angle from zenith, and Y_z is the zenith luminance defined as:

$$Y_z = (4.0453T - 4.9710)\tan\chi - 0.2155T + 2.4192 \tag{8.3.7}$$

and

$$\chi = \left(\frac{4}{9} - \frac{T}{120}\right)(\pi - 2\theta_s) \tag{8.3.8}$$

Zenith chromaticity values x and y are defined similarly to luminance:

$$x = x_z \frac{F(\theta,\gamma)}{F(0,\theta_S)} \tag{8.3.9}$$

$$y = y_z \frac{F(\theta,\gamma)}{F(0,\theta_S)} \tag{8.3.10}$$

where x_z and y_z are the zenith chromaticity values given by:

$$x_z = \begin{bmatrix} T^2 & T & 1 \end{bmatrix} \begin{bmatrix} 0.00166 & -0.00375 & 0.00209 & 0 \\ -0.02903 & 0.06377 & -0.03202 & 0.00394 \\ 0.11693 & -0.21196 & 0.06052 & 0.25886 \end{bmatrix} \begin{bmatrix} \theta_s^3 \\ \theta_s^2 \\ \theta_s \\ 1 \end{bmatrix} \tag{8.3.11}$$

$$y_z = \begin{bmatrix} T^2 & T & 1 \end{bmatrix} \begin{bmatrix} 0.00275 & -0.00610 & 0.00317 & 0 \\ -0.04214 & 0.08970 & -0.04153 & 0.00516 \\ 0.15346 & -0.26756 & 0.06670 & 0.26688 \end{bmatrix} \begin{bmatrix} \theta_s^3 \\ \theta_s^2 \\ \theta_s \\ 1 \end{bmatrix} \tag{8.3.12}$$

A Light Scattering Crash Course—
Part 3: Aerial Perspective

When we look at distant objects in the outdoors they appear bluer and also brighter the farther they are removed from us. This effect is called airlight [Lynch95] or *aerial perspective* and is specified as:

$$L(s) = L_0 F_{ex} + L_{in} \qquad (8.3.13)$$

where s is the distance traveled by the object's source color L_0 ray to reach the viewer, F_{ex} is the extinction factor, and L_{in} is the light scattered into the viewing ray direction. Both the extinction factor and the inscattered light depend on a total and an angular scattering coefficient. The total scattering coefficient is given by:

$$\beta(h(x)) = \beta^0 u(x) \qquad (8.3.14)$$

where β^0 is the value of the coefficient at the earth's surface,

$$u(x) = \exp\left(-\alpha\left(h_0 + x\cos\theta\right)\right) \qquad (8.3.15)$$

is the ratio of density at point x to the density at the earth's surface, and θ is the exponential decay constant. The angular scattering coefficient is defined as:

$$\beta(\omega,\theta,\phi,h(x)) = \beta^0(\omega,\theta,\phi)\, u(x) \qquad (8.3.16)$$

See Figure 8.3.2 for the specification of the angles used.

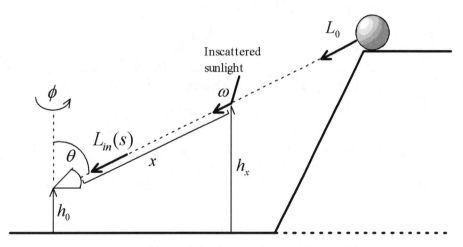

FIGURE 8.3.2   *The variables used for the aerial perspective model.*

The angular and total scattering coefficients for air molecule scattering (i.e., Rayleigh scattering) are specified as:

$$\beta_{Ray}(\theta) = \frac{\pi^2\left(n^2-1\right)^2}{2N\lambda^4}\left(\frac{6+3p_n}{6-7p_n}\right)\left(1+\cos^2\theta\right) \qquad (8.3.17)$$

$$\beta_{Ray} = \frac{8\pi^3 \left(n^2 - 1\right)^2}{3N\lambda^4} \left(\frac{6 + 3p_n}{6 - 7p_n}\right) \tag{8.3.18}$$

where n is the refractive index of air, N the number of molecules per unit volume, and p_n is the depolarization factor. The corresponding coefficients for haze scattering (i.e., Mie scattering) are given as:

$$\beta_{Mie}(\theta) = 0.434c \left(\frac{2\pi}{\lambda}\right)^{v-2} \frac{1}{2} \eta(\theta) \tag{8.3.19}$$

$$\beta_{Mie} = 0.434c\pi \left(\frac{2\pi}{\lambda}\right)^{v-2} K \tag{8.3.20}$$

where c is a concentration factor relative to the turbidity. Junge's exponent v, $\eta(\theta)$ (a scattering term) and K (a spectrum) are given in [Preetham99A].

Extinction Factor

The extinction factor used in Equation 8.3.13 describes the attenuation of light over a certain distance and is specified as:

$$F_{ex} = \exp\left(-\int_0^s \beta dx\right) \tag{8.3.21}$$

Plugging in the total scattering coefficient from Equation 8.3.14 and integrating, we get the extinction factor for a single type of particle:

$$F_{ex} = \exp\left(-K\left(H - u(s)\right)\right) \tag{8.3.22}$$

where

$$K = -\frac{\beta^0}{\alpha\cos\theta} \tag{8.3.23}$$

and

$$H = \exp\left(-\alpha h_0\right) \tag{8.3.24}$$

As we are dealing with both air molecule scattering and haze scattering, the final extinction factor is defined as:

$$F_{ex} = \exp\left(-K_{Mie}\left(H_{Mie} - u_{Mie}(s)\right)\right)\exp\left(-K_{Ray}\left(H_{Ray} - u_{Ray}(s)\right)\right) \tag{8.3.25}$$

Inscattered Light

Using the angular scattering coefficient from Equation 8.3.16, the light scattered into the viewing direction (θ, ϕ) at a point x is described as:

$$S(\theta,\phi,x) = \int L(\omega)\beta(\omega,\theta,\phi,h)\,d\omega$$
$$= \int L(\omega)\beta^0(\omega,\theta,\phi)\,u(x)\,d\omega$$
$$= S^0(\theta,\phi)\,u(x) \tag{8.3.26}$$

where $L(\omega)$ is the sun spectral's radiance in direction θ and S^0 is the light scattered into the viewing direction at the earth's surface. To obtain the total amount of light scattered in, we have to take into account the extinction factor over a distance from the viewer's position to a point x. The result is the inscattered light for a single type of particle:

$$L_{in} = \int_0^s S^0(\theta,\phi)\,u(x)\,F_{ex}(0..x)\,dx \tag{8.3.27}$$

As we still need to address both air molecule scattering and haze scattering, the final term for inscattered light is given by:

$$L_{in} = S_{Mie}^0(\theta,\phi)\,I_{Mie} + S_{Ray}^0(\theta,\phi)\,I_{Ray} \tag{8.3.28}$$

One major problem remains: what about the integral part of Equation 8.3.28? The expanded version of the specific section is:

$$I_{Mie} = \int_0^s u_{Mie}(x)\exp\left(-K_{Mie}\left(H_{Mie} - u_{Mie}(x)\right)\right)\exp\left(-K_{Ray}\left(H_{Ray} - u_{Ray}(x)\right)\right)dx \tag{8.3.29}$$

One method described in [Preetham99A] assumes that in case of $|s\cos\theta| <<$ the following approximation applies:

$$\exp\left(-K\left(H - u(x)\right)\right) = \exp\left(-\beta H\frac{1 - \exp(-\alpha x \cos\theta)}{\alpha\cos\theta}\right) \approx \exp(-\beta Hx) \tag{8.3.30}$$

thus, Equation 8.13.29 can be rewritten as:

$$I_{Mie} = \int_0^s \exp(-H_{Mie})\exp(-\alpha_{Mie}x\cos\theta)\exp(-\beta_{Mie}H_{Mie}x)\exp(-\beta_{Ray}H_{Ray}x)dx$$
$$= \exp(-H_{Mie})\frac{1 - \exp\left(-\left(\alpha_{Mie}\cos\theta + \beta_{Mie}H_{Mie} + \beta_{Ray}H_{Ray}\right)s\right)}{\alpha_{Mie}\cos\theta + \beta_{Mie}H_{Mie} + \beta_{Ray}H_{Ray}} \tag{8.3.31}$$

I_{Ray} is solved for in a similar fashion.

Although the assumption for Equation 8.3.30 only holds when either the distance s is very small or the view direction is close to the horizon, we will apply it to all computations made for inscattered light in the vertex program. The reasons for this are discussed later.

Implementing Sky Color

As we can see from Equations 8.3.3 through 8.3.12, there are only two parameters that have a major influence on the sky's appearance in the presented model: sun direction and turbidity. Furthermore, only the Perez (Equation 8.3.2) uses varying data that needs to be taken care of in the vertex program. Whenever the turbidity changes, our implementation recalculates the pre-computed values for the sky luminance and sky chromaticity distribution coefficients according to Equations 8.3.3, 8.3.4, and 8.3.5. Similarly, when the sun changes its position, the zenith luminance, Equation 8.3.7, and zenith chromaticity values specified by Equations 8.3.11 and 8.3.12 are calculated and stored for use in the vertex program.

The first things to compute in the vertex program are the various angles for Equation 8.3.2:

```
        float3 direction= normalize( mul( a_world, IN.Position ).xyz
);

        float theta     = dot( a_zenithDirection, direction );
        float gamma     = dot( a_sunDirection, direction );
        float cos2gamma = gamma * gamma;
              gamma     = acos( gamma );
```

The world matrix and the directions of both zenith and sun are passed to the shader as constants.

Next up is the Perez function itself. Note how Equations 8.3.6, 8.3.9, and 8.3.10 all make use of Equation 8.3.2 separately. But as we will be running our program on a GPU, we can make good use of its vector computation capabilities to reduce the number of instructions needed:

```
        float3 num = (1.0 + a_A * exp( a_B / theta )) *
                     (1.0 + a_C * exp( a_D * gamma ) +
                      a_E * cos2gamma);
        float3 den = (1.0 + a_A * exp( a_B )) *
                     (1.0 + a_C * exp( a_D * a_thetaSun.x ) +
                      a_E * a_thetaSun.y);
        float3 xyY = num / den * a_zenithColor;
```

The distribution coefficients as well as the zenith chromaticity values and the zenith luminance are pre-computed as described above. They are passed in as CIE xyY 3-component vectors. While the resulting chromaticity values do not need further manipulation, the luminance range is too high to be directly displayed on a standard computer monitor; if used directly, the resulting image will be completely white. Therefore, a simple exposure function [Elias] is applied first:

```
        xyY.z = 1.0 - exp( -a_exposure * xyY.z );
```

As the final operation of the sky color vertex program, the CIE xyY representation is converted to CIE XYZ:

```
float3 XYZ;

XYZ.x = (xyY.x / xyY.y) * xyY.z;
XYZ.y = xyY.z;
XYZ.z = ((1.0 - xyY.x - xyY.y) / xyY.y) * xyY.z;
```

and finally the result is converted to RGB values using the Rec. 709 color conversion matrix [Poynton00]:

```
OUT.Color = mul( a_colorConvMat, XYZ );
```

Implementing Aerial Perspective

Before entering the vertex program, a massive amount of pre-computation based on the source code accompanying the paper [Preetham99B] is needed for the aerial perspective. The methods used for the sky color explained above are modified to take care of changes to the turbidity and sun position. Each time the turbidity changes, the total and angular scattering coefficients for both air molecule (Rayleigh) and haze (Mie) scattering are calculated using Equations 8.3.17 through 8.3.20. Each change to the sun position requires a recalculation of the light scattered into the viewing ray direction, as defined in Equation 8.3.26 as $S^0(\theta,\phi)$. This is done for all angles θ in the range $[0, \pi]$ and for all angles ϕ in the range $[0, 2\pi]$. In our implementation these ranges are divided into five sections, resulting in a $(5 + 1)x(5 + 1) = 36$-element table for each of the two particle types used later as the shader constants a_S01 and a_S02. To make use of this table inside the vertex shader we have to determine the view direction first of all:

```
float3 eyeVert   = mul( a_worldView, IN.Position ).xyz;
float3 direction = normalize( eyeVert );
```

Using this, we can a apply a rough linear approximation to the acos function (to save the instructions and constant registers needed for the Cg library version) to determine the angle θ in the range $[0, \textit{\#Bins}]$:

```
float thetav = ((-direction.z + 1.0) / 2.0) * a_bins.x -
                   epsilon;
        thetav = max( thetav, 0.0 );
```

The constant component a_bins.x holds the number of bins used—five in our case as mentioned above. Likewise a linear approximation to the atan2 function is used to get the angle ϕ in the same range:

```
float2 dirTemp = normalize( float2(direction.x, direction.y )
);

if( dirTemp.y < 0.0 )
    dirTemp.x = -(dirTemp.x + 2.0);
```

```
float phiv = ((-dirTemp.x + 1.0) / 4.0) * a_bins.x - epsilon;
       phiv = max( phiv, 0.0 );
```

Taking these "angles," we can retrieve the corresponding $S_{Mie}^{0}(\theta,\phi)$ and $S_{Ray}^{0}(\theta,\phi)$:

```
int   i = thetav;
float u = thetav - i;
int   j = phiv;
float v = phiv - j;

int4 indices;
indices.x = i * a_bins.y + j;
indices.y = (i + 1) * a_bins.y + j;
indices.z = i * a_bins.y + j + 1;
indices.w = (i + 1) * a_bins.y + j + 1;

float4 factors;
factors.x = (1.0 - u) * (1.0 - v);
factors.y = u * (1.0 - v);
factors.z = (1.0 - u) * v;
factors.w = u * v;

float3 SOMie = factors.x * a_SOMie[ indices.x ]
             + factors.y * a_SOMie[ indices.y ]
             + factors.z * a_SOMie[ indices.z ]
             + factors.w * a_SOMie[ indices.w ];

float3 SORay = factors.x * a_SORay[ indices.x ]
             + factors.y * a_SORay[ indices.y ]
             + factors.z * a_SORay[ indices.z ]
             + factors.w * a_SORay[ indices.w ];
```

Note that a_bins.y holds the number of bins plus one.

We continue to compute the inscattered light L_{in} by calculating the distance from the eye point to the current vertex:

```
float s = length( eyeVert );
```

and the denominator from Equation 8.3.23 for both particle types:

```
float B1 = a_alpha.x * direction.z;
float B2 = a_alpha.y * direction.z;
```

Now we have everything ready to implement Equation 8.3.31 for air molecule and haze scattering:

```
float3 IMie = ((1.0 - exp( -(B1 + a_C1plusC2) * s) ) ) /
              (B1 + a_C1plusC2)) * a_constants.x;
float3 IRay = ((1.0 - exp( -(B2 + a_C1plusC2) * s) ) ) /
              (B2 + a_C1plusC2)) * a_constants.y;
```

Constant registers `a_constants.x` and `a_constants.y` contain the result of Equation 8.3.24. `a_C1plusC2` holds the constant $\beta_{Mie}H_{Mie} + \beta_{Ray}H_{R_t}$. Finally, we implement Equation 8.3.28:

```
float3 Lin = SOMie * IMie + SORay * IRay;
```

and convert the resulting CIE XYZ vector to RGB using the same Rec. 709 color conversion matrix as used for the sky color:

```
OUT.Inscatter = mul( a_colorConvMat, Lin );
```

Converting the extinction factor Equation 8.3.25 to code is straightforward:

```
float3 Fex = exp( -a_betaMie * a_constants.x * evalFunc( B1, s ) ) *
             exp( -a_betaRay * a_constants.y * evalFunc( B2, s ) );
```

`a_betaMie` and `a_betaRay` are the Mie and Rayleigh total scattering coefficients passed in as constants. The method `evalFunc` handles errors that would occur for vertices at the same height as the camera and is defined as:

```
float evalFunc( float a_B, float a_s )
{
    float result;

    if( abs( a_B * a_s ) < 0.01 )
        result = a_s;
    else
        result = (1.0 - exp( -a_B * a_s )) / a_B;

    return result;
}
```

As with the inscattered light, the extinction factor has to be converted to RGB:

```
OUT.Extinction = mul( a_colorConvMat, Fex );
```

To get the final pixel color, the fragment shader must implement Equation 8.3.13. In our sample implementation it is solved as:

```
float3 PreethamTerrainShader( vert2frag          IN
                            , uniform float3    a_lightVec
                            , uniform sampler2D a_terrainMap
                            , uniform sampler2D a_normalMap
                            ) : COLOR
{
    float3 normal = 2.0 *
            (tex2D( a_normalMap, IN.NormalCoord ).xyz - 0.5);
```

```
        float3 light  = saturate( dot( normal, a_lightVec ) );
        float3 albedo = tex2D( a_terrainMap, IN.TerrainCoord ).xyz;

        return light * albedo * IN.Extinction + IN.Inscatter;
    }
```

Discussion

For comparison purposes we have implemented an OpenGL/Cg version of [Hoffman03]. This section compares the two methods in terms of appearance of the sky color and the aerial perspective (i.e., the terrain) as well as the size and, therefore, the performance of the shader.

Appearance of the Sky

Generating a believable clear day sky is the strength of Preetham's method. At noon, it shows a rich blue color which brightens near the horizon. Although there is no explicitly rendered sun, a solar aureole is clearly visible. But after all, the model is a clear sky model, which means it does not hold for high turbidities and therefore is not capable of producing convincing results for a hazy atmosphere. To simulate the latter, the CIE overcast sky model [CIE03] had to be implemented and the results mixed as proposed by the CIE.

In contrast, the sky is the weakness of Hoffman's algorithm. It produces an unnaturally bright area opposite the sun direction and therefore exhibits a dark band across the sky. The sun itself is very apparent. To be more exact: it is huge. No matter which direction the user is facing, he cannot escape the enormous white sun. But as Hoffman's method uses the same shader for both sky color and aerial perspective, a hazy sky can be simulated using the right combination of parameters.

Appearance of the Terrain

For a clear day, both methods are equal from a visual point-of-view. But in general, Hoffman's method performs much better due to performance issues described shortly. This is in contrast to the lack of support for a hazy atmosphere of Preetham's model as described above.

Instruction Count

We compare the number of instructions for both models when compiled for the Cg profile CG_PROFILE_ARBVP1. Hoffman's method uses the same shader and precomputed constants for both sky color and aerial perspective. Pre-computation is relatively cheap and the vertex program uses only about 50 instructions.

As for pre-computation, Preetham's model for the sky color is not very demanding. The sky shader uses a bit more than 100 instructions. Replacing the exp standard library function with exp2 would have saved about 30 instructions but reduces the overall visual quality of the sky.

The aerial perspective code is the real bottleneck. While we try to stay in CIE XYZ color space for as long as possible, the pre-computation step requires a lot of time whenever one of the major parameters (i.e., turbidity or sun position) change. It gets even worse when we look at the vertex program. Most of the constant registers are filled with the tables for S^0 leaving no room for other data-demanding algorithms like character skinning. Even after preliminary optimizations, the program currently compiles to more than 200 instructions, which is definitely too many for a wide range of graphics cards as the targeted OpenGL extension only guarantees a maximum of 128 instructions.

Conclusion

For the first time, we presented an implementation of [Preetham99A] for both sky color and aerial perspective at interactive frame rates. The comparison to another model showed no clear overall winner. While the method presented here excels at rendering a clear day sky, it lacks the ability to produce hazy atmospheres or to render airlight efficiently. Two interesting research topics for the future would be to shift the aerial perspective code from per-vertex to per-pixel computations, and to combine Preetham's sky model (with the addition of the CIE overcast sky model as described above) with Hoffman's aerial perspective model.

References

[CIE03] Commission Internationale de l'Eclairage, "Spatial Distribution of Daylight—CIE Standard General Sky," Joint ISO/CIE Standard, ISO 15469:2004 (E) / CIE S 011/E:2003.

[Elias] Elias, Hugo, "Exposure," available online at *http://freespace.virgin.net/hugo.elias/graphics/x_posure.htm*.

[Hoffman02A] Hoffman, Nathaniel and Arcot J. Preetham, "Rendering Outdoor Light Scattering in Real Time," *Proceedings of Game Developer Conference* 2002 (CD-ROM).

[Hoffman02B] Hoffman, Nathaniel and Arcot J. Preetham, "Photorealistic Real-Time Outdoor Light Scattering," *Game Developer Magazine* (August 2002): pp. 32–38.

[Hoffman03] Hoffman, Nathaniel and Arcot J. Preetham, "Real-Time Light Atmosphere Interaction for Outdoor Scenes," *Graphics Programming Methods*

[Lynch95] Lynch, David K. and William Livingston, *Color and Light in Nature*, Cambridge University Press, 1995.

[Nishita96] Nishita, Tomoyuki, Yoshinori Dobashi, Kazufumi Kaneda, and Hideo Yamashita, "Display Method of the Sky Color Taking into Account Multiple Scattering," *Pacific Graphics '96* (1996): pp. 117–132.

[Poynton00] Poynton, Charles, "Frequently Asked Questions about Color," available online at http://www.poynton.com/ColorFAQ.html, April 2, 2000.

[Preetham99a] Preetham, Arcot J., Peter Shirley, and Brian Smits, "A Practical Analytic Model for Daylight," *Computer Graphics, Annual Conference Series,* 1999: pp. 91–100.

[Preetham99b] Preetham, Arcot J., Peter Shirley, and Brian Smits, "Example Code (v 0.2) from A Practical Analytic Model for Daylight," available online at http://www.cs.utah.edu/vissim/papers/sunsky/code/, August 17, 1999.

[Rayleigh71] Rayleigh, L. "On the scattering of light by small particles," *Philosophical Magazine* 41 (1871): pp. 447–454.

8.4

Volumetric Clouds

Jesse Laeuchli

Introduction

Many of today's applications require the rendering of clouds: flight simulators, space simulators, and first person shooters all need realistic looking clouds in order to appear convincing. With many applications allowing the user to roam the sky, the traditional method of simply rendering a sky-sphere or box might no longer be sufficient. This article will demonstrate how realistic and convincing looking clouds can be rendered using HLSL pixel shaders.

The Algorithm

Theory

The cloud rendering technique described in this article involves representing a cloud as a *modified* implicit equation and visualizing it using volumetric rendering.[1] A good model for cloud rendering was proposed by David Ebert [Ebert98]. It involves the following three-dimensional implicit equation:

$$F(x,y,z) = (x - C_x)^2 + (y - C_y)^2 + (z - C_z)^2 = c \qquad (8.4.1)$$

The evaluation of this equation with a volumetric rendering system produces a sphere with center (C_x, C_y, C_z) and radius c. This function can be interpreted as the density of the cloud. An fBm (ie., fractional Brownian motion) fractal [Ebert98] is used to modify the parameters of the density function, and the result is rendered volumetrically to produce an image that closely resembles a cloud. The overall structure of the cloud can be altered by creating several implicit equations of different radii, and blending the results together. The cloud can be further tweaked by performing a weighted blending of the modified implicit function with a turbulence function. There is no constraint on the type of implicit function used. While this article uses spheres, other functions like ellipses work just as well.

---

[1] An implicit equation is a function that is defined in terms of algebraic relations, and cannot in general be solved for in terms of one variable. For example, the equation:

$$X = xy + x^{2y}$$

cannot be solved explicitly.

Implementation Preliminaries

Before we can implement the shader, a volumetric rendering system must be written. We employ a simple slice-based method as described in [Mitchell04]. First, several quads are drawn one after the other, perpendicular to the view direction. The more quads used the better the resulting image. An alpha texture is applied to each quad. Three-dimensional textures are extremely useful for this task [Kraus03]. Below is the code used to implement this in DirectX:

```
float depth=1;
float dinc=.02;
for(int i=0;i<50*6;i+=6)
{
    // Front triangle
    // Quad depth
    pVertices[i].position = D3DXVECTOR3( -2.f, -2.f,  depth );
    pVertices[i].rgba = D3DXCOLOR( 255, 255, 255, 255 );
    pVertices[i].u=0;
    pVertices[i].v=0;
    pVertices[i].s=depth;//Index into 3D texture

    ....//Setup other vertices of the quad here

    depth-=dinc;
}
```

One other issue remains before the shader can be implemented: A noise function is required, which will modify the input parameters of the implicit function. Generating noise—especially per-pixel noise—can be too costly to perform in a pixel shader. A straightforward solution to this is to pre-calculate noise and store it in a three-dimensional texture. A limitation of this method is that we can only store a finite amount of noise, due to memory constraints. Unless the noise function stored in the texture is tileable, there will be visual errors in the clouds being rendered. This will manifest itself as visual discontinuities along the boundaries of the noise texture. Creating a tiled version of the noise function only needs to be done once, however. Included in the CD-ROM is the code for generating tiled noise in a three dimensional texture. It works by taking the average of the noise function along all the noise function's parameters.

ON THE CD

Shader Implementation

Now that the noise texture is ready for use, the actual HLSL shader that generates the cloud can be implemented. The first step is to create the fBm fractal:

```
//Several octaves of tiled Perlin noise added together to
//generate an fBm fractal.
float4 perturb=tex3D(BaseTexture, In.tex.xyz)+
                (.5*tex3D(BaseTexture, 2*In.tex.xyz))+
                (.25*tex3D(BaseTexture, 4*In.tex.xyz))+
                (.125*tex3D(BaseTexture, 8*In.tex.xyz));
```

After the fBm function is generated, it is scaled to provide more control over the cloud structure. The fBm function is then added to the input parameters of the implicit function as follows:

```
//scale the noise based on the input parameters
point.xyz+=(perturb.xyz/NoiseScale1);
```

Next, the implicit function is generated. In the example below, an implicit spherical equation with centre at (0.5, 0.5, 0.5) is evaluated:

```
float d=sqrt((point.z - .5)*(point.z - .5)+
             (point.y - .5)*(point.y - .5)+
             (point.x - .5)*(point.x - .5));
```

The result d is blended with the turbulence function. Higher values of blend will make the cloud appear more turbulent, while lower values will make it appear more structured.

```
float4 turbperturb=2*(tex3D(BaseTexture, In.tex.xyz)-.5);
float d=lerp(1-d*2,turbperturb.x,Blend);
```

Note that 1-d rather than d is used as the first parameter. This inversion is required, as the desired output of the alpha-blended quads should be 1 where the density is highest. Also note that the variable d is multiplied by 2 to scale the cloud's size.

Finally, the result is scaled slightly for better visual quality and to enhance the cloudlike appearance of the image. This is done by multiplying d by any number larger than 1.0. After this is done, the value of d is examined. If it is less than .01, we simply use d as the alpha component. If the result is larger than .01, we raise d to the 1.45th power. Because the highest value d can have is 1.0 at the centre of the implicit function, this has the effect of increasing the cloud's transparency exponentially as opposed to linearly.

```
Out.dif.x=d*5;
Out.dif.y=d*5;
Out.dif.z=d*5;
if(d<.01)
{
    Out.dif.w=d;//Output to the alpha component
}
else
{
    Out.dif.w=pow(d,1.45);//Output to the alpha component
}
```

As mentioned before, it is possible to change the overall structure of the cloud by generating more than one implicit surface, and blending the results together. Simply generate two implicit surfaces using the steps above, and interpolate between them using a user defined blending value (see Figure 8.4.1):

```
float cloud=lerp(d,d2,ImplictBlend);//blend between two clouds
```

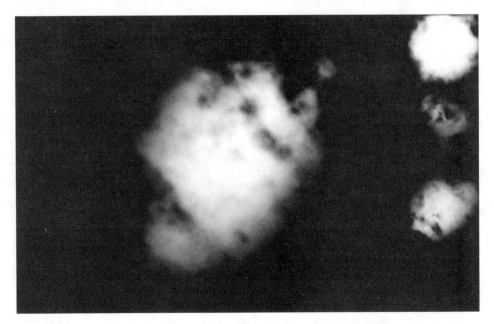

FIGURE 8.4.1   *Clouds generated using implicit surfaces.*

Shading and Lighting

The cloud's appearance can be improved by lighting (i.e., shading). This is done by noting that the normal of an implicit function is defined by :

$$F(x,y,z) = 0$$
$$N = \nabla F(x,y,z)$$

To implement this, we calculate the gradient of the noise function before hand, and store it in the other parts of the RGB components of the texture. This normal is then accumulated in successive octaves to form a normal vector for the cloud, which is subsequently normalized and used for DOT3 per pixel lighting. While this does not take into account any of the physical aspects of real cloud lighting, it does provide a much more convincing image of the cloud (see Figure 8.4.2).

The modifications to the shader are quite minor. First the combined normals must be normalized as below:

```
float3 normal=perturb.xyz/sqrt(dot(perturb.xyz,perturb.xyz));
```

Once this is done the lighting calculations can be preformed:

```
Out.dif.xyz=1-dot(2*(normal.xyz-.5),lightpos.xyz);
```

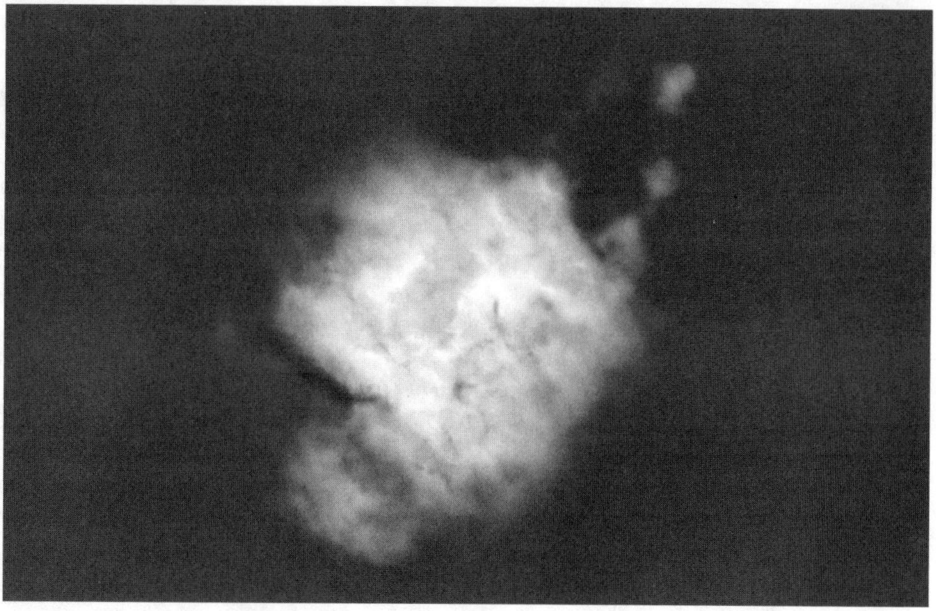

FIGURE 8.4.2 *Cloud with shading.*

Further Improvements

There are several ways to extend and optimize the basic method. As mentioned previously, there are other implicit functions, which will produce different types of clouds. Also, if four-dimensional textures are used, the fourth dimension can be interpreted as time to animate the clouds. Unfortunately, at the time of writing, hardware that supports four-dimensional textures is fairly rare. A final optimization is to render the clouds using impostors. As the shape and appearance of the cloud does not vary dramatically with user position and time, it is a good candidate for rendering using impostors.

Conclusion

In general, this method of cloud rendering provides a good way to render clouds, while utilizing the capabilities of the current generation of programmable graphics hardware. Our method offers a flexible model which provides much control over the overall shape and structure of the generated clouds.

References

[Ebert98] Ebert, David S., et al., *Texturing and Modeling: A Procedural Approach* (Second Edition), San Diego: Academic Press, 1998.

[Kraus03] Kraus, M., "Truly Volumetric Effects," in W. F. Engel, ed., *ShaderX²: Shader Programming Tips and Tricks with DirectX9*, Wordware Publishing, 2003.

[Mitchell04] Mitchell, J. M., "Light Shaft Rendering," in W. F. Engel, ed., *ShaderX³: Advanced Rendering with DirectX9 and OpenGL*, Charles River Media, Hingham, MA, 2004.

APPENDIX

About the CD-ROM

The CD-ROM contains the example programs with source accompanying the chapters. Also included are the latest Microsoft® DirectX 9 System Development Kit (SDK), and other useful demos. The directory structure closely follows the book structure by using the chapter number as the name of the subdirectory; the DirectX SDK is in the DirectX SDK folder.

General System Requirements

To use all of the files on the CD-ROM, you will need:

- The DirectX 9 summer update 2004 SDK
- OpenGL 1.5-compatible graphics card
- A DirectX 8, 8.1, or 9.0-compatible graphics card
- Windows XP with the latest service pack
- Visual C++ .NET 2003
- Some require Visual Studio C/C++ 6.0
- 512 MB RAM
- 500 MB of free space on your hard drive
- Pentium IV/ATHLON with more than 1.5 GHz
- The latest graphics card drivers

Updates

Updates of the example programs will be available on *www.wolfgang-engel.info* and on *www.charlesriver.com*.

Comments, Suggestions

Please send any comments or suggestions to *wolf@shaderx.com*.

Have fun!

—Wolfgang Engel

INDEX